CRIES OF THE SEA
World Inequality, Sustainable Development and the Common Heritage of Humanity

Publications on Ocean Development
Volume 33

*A Series of Studies on
the International, Legal, Institutional and Policy Aspects
of Ocean Development*

General Editor: Shigeru Oda

Cries of the Sea

World Inequality, Sustainable Development and the Common Heritage of Humanity

PETER BAUTISTA PAYOYO

MARTINUS NIJHOFF PUBLISHERS
THE HAGUE / LONDON / BOSTON

A C.I.P. Catalogue record for this book is available from the Library of Congress

ISBN 90-411-0504-2

Published by Kluwer Law International,
P.O. Box 85889, 2508 CN The Hague, The Netherlands.

Sold and distributed in the U.S.A. and Canada
by Kluwer Law International,
675 Massachusetts Avenue, Cambridge, MA 02139, U.S.A.

In all other countries, sold and distributed
by Kluwer Law International, Distribution Centre,
P.O. Box 322, 3300 AH Dordrecht, The Netherlands.

Layout and camera-ready copy:
Anne-Marie Krens, Oegstgeest, The Netherlands

Printed on acid-free paper

All Rights Reserved
© 1997 Kluwer Law International
Kluwer Law International incorporates the publishing programmes of
Graham & Trotman Ltd, Kluwer Law and Taxation Publishers,
and Martinus Nijhoff Publishers.

No part of the material protected by this copyright notice may be reproduced or
utilized in any form or by any means, electronic or mechanical,
including photocopying, recording, or by any information storage and
retrieval system, without written permission from the copyright owner.

Printed in the Netherlands

To my wife, Au

TABLE OF CONTENTS

ACKNOWLEDGEMENTS	xiii
ABBREVIATIONS	xv
INTRODUCTION	1
PART 1 – INTERNATIONAL LAW IN AN UNEQUAL WORLD	13

I INEQUALITY IN THE INTERNATIONAL COMMUNITY — 15

A. Widening Global Disparities on the Large	16
B. Wither Global Inequality?	22
C. International Law	28
D. Inequality	31
E. Growing Disparities	36
F. The International Law of Global Disparities	41
Conclusion	45

II WORLD INEQUALITY AND THE 1982 UN CONVENTION ON THE LAW OF THE SEA — 49

A. Domains of Disparity in the Law of the Sea – Old and New	49
B. Disparity and the 1982 Convention: Preambular Aspects	53
C. UNCLOS III: The North-South Agenda in the Traditional Domains	58
1. Institutional Context	60
2. Substantive Law Context	67

D. The North-South Dialogue in the Second Committee of UNCLOS III: Global Wealth Redistribution Through Extended Coastal State Jurisdiction — 71
  1. The Significance of the EEZ in Global Wealth Redistribution — 73
  2. The Nature of the General Preference Given to Developing States Concerning Fisheries Access to the EEZ — 75
  3. The Needs and Interests of Developing Land-Locked and Geographically Disadvantaged States — 77
E. The North-South Dialogue in the Third Committee of UNCLOS III: Legal Aspects of International Cooperation for Development and Global Sharing in the Oceans — 82
  1. Protection and Preservation of the Marine Environment — 83
  2. Marine Scientific Research — 89
  3. Development and Transfer of Marine Technology — 95
  4. International Cooperation and Extended Coastal State Jurisdiction as Complementary Principles of the New Ocean Order — 102
F. UNCED and Equality of Capacity for Rights and Obligations: The Customary Law of Capacity-Building in the Oceans — 108
  1. Revitalizing the Unrealized Promise of the EEZ — 109
  2. From UNCLOS to UNCED: Transforming the Legal Framework of Global Inequality — 113
  3. The Legal Basis of Capacity-Building for Sustainable Development in the Oceans — 119
  4. The International Law of Global Disparities versus The International Law of Sustainable Development — 140

Conclusion — 150

PART 2: – THE COMMON HERITAGE OF HUMANITY AND
WORLD INEQUALITY 157

III THE COMMON HERITAGE OF HUMANITY: A LEGAL
PRE-HISTORY 159

   A. The Common Heritage of Humanity as an Invoked Principle
in the 1982 UN Convention on the Law of the Sea 165
   B. A Question of Frontiers: The Area and its Resources 167
      1. Towards Internationalizing the Deep Seabed 170
      2. The Stakes Behind Internationalization 177
      3. International Law on the Margins of the Deep Seabed 180
      4. The Omnipresence of the Continental Shelf 205

Conclusion 219

IV BEYOND *MARE LIBERUM* AND *MARE CLAUSUM*: THE COMMON
HERITAGE OF HUMANITY AS A FUNDAMENTAL PRINCIPLE OF
INTERNATIONAL LAW 227

   A. The Common Heritage of Humanity Principle and Part XI of
the 1982 Convention 232
      1. Textual Overview 232
      2. The Severability of the Common Heritage of Humanity
Principle from the Seabed Mining Regime 237
      3. The Special Legal Status of the Area and the Principles
Governing the Area 239
   B. The Common Heritage of Humanity Principle as Plea for
Development and Peace 247
      1. New Deep Sea Resources and The Development
Imperative 248
      2. Developing Countries and the "Race to Grab" the Deep
Seabed 251
      3. Global Distributive Justice and the Question of Continental
Shelf Outer Limits 256
      4. The Question of Limits (Again) and the Common Heritage
of Humanity Principle 264

5. The Programmatory Law of the Common Heritage of Humanity	295
6. The Reservation of the Common Heritage for Peaceful Purposes	313
C. The Common Heritage of Humanity and the Principle of Benefit-Sharing	320
1. Benefit of Humanity as a Rule of Decision	323
2. Benefit of Humanity and the Special Needs and Interests of the Developing Countries	326
3. The Interests and Needs of Developing Countries under Part XI of the 1982 Convention	329
D. The Common Heritage as Environment	332
1. Overcoming a Sectoral Approach to Marine Environmental Protection	334
2. Existing Environmental Law for the Area and its Resources	337
3. International Responsibility under the Environmental Law of the Area and its Resources	340
4. Scientific Research and the Environmental Protection Regime for the Area	342
5. Institutional Aspects of Sustainable Development of the Area and its Resources	347
Conclusion	349

V THE INSTITUTIONAL ELEMENT OF THE COMMON HERITAGE PRINCIPLE: TOWARDS AN INTERNATIONAL ORGANIZATION FOR SUSTAINABLE DEVELOPMENT?   359

A. The Institutional Significance of the Common Heritage of Humanity Principle	363
1. Pre-1970 Developments: The Basic Issue in International Organization Defined	363
2. The Issue of International Machinery in the Seabed Committee	370
3. The Developing Countries: The Common Heritage of Humanity Principle as a New Modality of International Organization	372

4. The Industrialized Countries: An International Agency to Promote and Guarantee Assured Access to Seabed Mineral Resources 376
5. The Impact of the Declaration of Principles Resolution on the Original Positions on International Machinery 380

B. Institutional Development and Innovation for the Area in UNCLOS III: Eroding the Moral Force of the Common Heritage of Humanity Principle 389
1. Activities Contemplated by the Regime 389
2. Assured Access to Nodules Under the Parallel System 395
3. Decision-Making in the Execution of a Design 407

C. The 1994 Implementation Agreement: Universality and Sacrifice in the Law of the Sea 421
1. Towards a Universal Interest in the Universality of the Convention 426
2. Stability and Change in the Deep Seabed Regime 429
3. The 1994 Implementation Agreement as Process 438
4. A Renegotiated Part XI and the Old Politics of Assured Access 444

Conclusion 452

VI GENERAL CONCLUSIONS:
The International Law of Sustainable Development and the Future of the Common Heritage Principle in a World of Growing Disparity 461

APPENDIX
United Nations General Assembly Res. 2749 (17 Dec 1970): *Declaration of Principles Governing the Sea-bed and the Ocean Floor and the Subsoil Thereof Beyond the Limits of National Jurisdiction* 475

REFERENCES 481

INDEX 535

ACKNOWLEDGEMENTS

This research project would not have been possible without the caring support and the considerable encouragement that I have received from several institutions as well as mumerous individuals throughout the period of my graduate studies.

I express my deepest gratitude, first, to the institutions: to the University of the Philippines College of Law and the Dalhousie Law School – for having afforded me the time and space to carry out this project; to the Killam Trust for awarding me a three-year fellowship to pursue a doctoral degree; and to the International Ocean Institute for the most meaningful exposure to the *problématique* of my research.

To the extent that these institutions are also the special people with whom I shall with all affection associate this work, I should mention the following individuals. In the UP College of Law, I owe a profound debt of gratitude to Dean Merlin Magallona, former Dean Pacifico Agabin, my colleague Professor Popo Lotilla, Professor Hydee Yorak, and Justice Florentino Feliciano. In the Dalhousie Law School, I thank Dean Dawn Russell, former Dean Joe Ghiz, Professor Bruce Archibald, Dr. Edgar Gold, Dr. Aldo Chircop, Professor Donat Pharand, and the great mentors whose friendship will always be warmly cherished: Professor Douglas Johnston and Judge Ronald St.J. Macdonald. Christian Wiktor and his very able library staff smothered me with the books that became my cozy shelter especially during the winter months in Halifax. I must also acknowledge my cheerful neighbourhood team: "mother" Sheila Wile and fellow-travellers Nahid (and Family), David, and Stuart.

The International Ocean Institute is, certainly, no other than God-sent Elisabeth Mann-Borgese herself. She has assured me of her sustained guidance and love which no sailor in the rough but exciting seas of ocean law and policy can really do without. My adventures with her, in *Pacem In Maribus* or elsewhere, have rewarded me and my wife more lasting memories and frienships than we could ever have imagined. Thus, I also thank those in the big (and still growing) IOI family who have, in one way or another, prodded me to search for new vistas – in the depths of the ocean or in the depths of the soul: Jan van Ettinger, Christopher Pinto, Abdul Koroma, Alexander Yankov, Hasjim Djalal, Joseph Warioba, Anton Vratusa, Don Mills, Frank Njenga, Tom Fuse, Norton Ginsberg, and the two giants from the tiny Maltese isles: Fr. Peter S. Inglot, and Ambassador Arvid Pardo.

Writing this work away from home would have been unbearable were it not for my surrogate family in Halifax. I was indeed fortunate to have been welcomed in the hearths and hearts of Yolly & Max, Lita & Tante, Norma & Ralph, and Ninong & Ninang – to them all I say *Mabuhay* and *Salamat Po*. Friends in the Netherlands have likewise kept me company there, in their own memorable ways – especially cheering up my wife when I had to tarry a little while longer in Halifax. Thank you Jan & Peet; Chris & Linda; Jan & Anna Marie; Morita & Johan, Orchid & Eddie; Maritza, Baby, Anna, Bea, Tina and Marlie. Finally, my family in the Philippines, by affinity or consanguinity, have given their spiritual comfort and loving assurances without fail. Without the simple joys and peace on the home front which they continuously shared to me, defending the case for harmony and humanity – as I do in this book – would have been quite impossible.

Lastly, I kiss and embrace my wife for having endured those solitary seasons when I had to write up my piece in some far and lonely corner. Now that the living-apart is over, we shall be marching on again, close together.

ABBREVIATIONS

AFRICAN J INT & COMP L	African Journal of International and Comparative Law
AJIL	American Journal of International Law
ASIL Proc	American Society of International Law Proceedings, Annual Meeting
AUSTRALIAN YBIL	Australian Yearbook of International Law
BOSTON COLL INT & COMP L R	Boston College International and Comparative Law Review
BYIL	British Yearbook of International Law
CAL L REV	California Law Review
CASEWESTERN RES J INT L	Casewestern Reserve Journal of International Law
CLOS	United Nations Convention on the Law of the Sea With Index and Final Act, UN Sales No. E.83.V.5
COLUMBIA J TRANS L	Columbia Journal of Transnational Law
I COMMENTARY	M. Nordquist (Ed.-in-chief), *United Nations Convention on the Law of*

	the Sea 1982: A Commentary Vol. 1 (1985)
II COMMENTARY	S. Nandan, S. Rosenne & N. Grandy (Eds.); M. Nordquist (Ed.-in-chief), *United Nations Convention on the Law of the Sea: A Commentary* Vol. 2 (1993)
IV COMMENTARY	S. Rosenne, A. Yankov & N. Grandy (Eds.); M. Nordquist (Ed.-in-chief), *United Nations Convention on the Law of the Sea: A Commentary* Vol. 4 (1991)
Dept of State BULL	US Department of State Bulletin
ECOLOGY L QTLY	Ecology Law Quarterly
ECOSOC Off Rec	Official Records of the UN Economic and Social Council
EJIL	European Journal of International Law
EPL	Environmental Policy and Law
GEORGETOWN INT ENV L REV	Georgetown International Environmental Law Review
HARV INT L J	Harvard International Law Journal
HDR	Human Development Report (UNDP)
House Interim Report	US Congress, House. Interim Report on the United Nations and the Issue of Deep Ocean Resources, together with hearings by the Subcommittee on International Organizations and Movements of the Committee on Foreign Affairs

	(US Government Printing Office, 1967)
HUMAN RIGHTS QTLY	Human Rights Quarterly
ICJ Rep	International Court of Justice Reports
ICLQ	International and Comparative Law Quarterly
IJMCL	International Journal of Marine and Coastal Law
ILC YRBK	Yearbook of the International Law Commission
ILM	International Legal Materials
INDIAN J INT L	Indian Journal of International Law
JOHN MARSHALL L R	John Marshall Law Review
JWTL	Journal of World Trade Law
LOUISIANA L REV	Louisiana Law Review
LoS BULLETIN	Law of the Sea Bulletin (published by the Division of Ocean Affairs and the Law of the Sea, UN Secretariat)
LSI	Law of the Sea Institute
MICHIGAN L REV	Michigan Law Review
NAT RES L	Natural Resources Lawyer
NETH INT L REV	Netherlands International Law Review
NETH YRBK INT L	Netherlands Yearbook of International Law

NILOS DOCUMENTARY YRBK	International Organizations and the Law of the Sea Documentary Yearbook (Netherlands Institute for the Law of the Sea)
NORTHWESTERN J INTL L & BUS	Northwestern Journal of International Law and Business
NYU J INT L & POL	New York University Journal of International Law and Politics
OCEAN & COASTAL MGMT	Ocean and Coastal Management
OCEAN YRBK	Ocean Yearbook
ODIL	Ocean Development and International Law
PV #	United Nations General Assembly Official Records, First Committee (Provisional Verbatim Records); number and date of First Committee meeting indicated
SAN DIEGO L REV	San Diego Law Review
SBC Rep	Report of the United Nations Seabed Committee 1969- 1973 (Ad Hoc SBC Rep, the 1968 Report of the Ad Hoc Committee)
UNCLOS III Off Rec	Official Records of the Third United Nations Conference on the Law of the Sea
UNCLOS I Off Rec	Official Records of the First United Nations Conference on the Law of the Sea
UN GAOR	United Nations General Assembly Official Records

UNTS	United Nations Treaty Series
VA ENV L J	Virginia Environmental Law Journal
VA J INT L	Virginia Journal of International Law
YALE L J	Yale Law Journal
YRBK INTL ENV L	Yearbook of International Environmental Law
ZaöRV	Zeitschrift Für Ausländisches Offentliches Recht und Vokerrecht

INTRODUCTION

When lawyers speak of "the 1982 United Nations Convention on the Law of the Sea", it can be assumed that they are referring to international law, or a special branch of international law. The key terms in the entire phrase are "Convention" and "Law", rendering the object called to our attention the guarded lore of a profession. As a lawyer myself, I could not agree more to the fact that a "thing" called law is involved here.

But "the 1982 United Nations Convention on the Law of the Sea" is certainly more than just arcane specialist knowledge. The other terms in the description, as I will attempt to show in this book, are equally, if not more, critical in the understanding of text: "1982", "United Nations", and most assuredly "the Sea." These are the terms, taken together with "Law", that make the entire subject a unified whole. They impart a real context to the lawyer's law. They also define basically what that law is and is not, imputing a vitality and passion to a subject that are frequently absent when the Convention is simply dealt with as a disciplinary preserve. This is not to say that history, international relations and the global environment are "things" that are alien to international lawyers when they refer to the Law of the Sea. The relevance of these considerations is more or less a given in many disquisitions about the legal order of the oceans. But the issue perhaps is whether these factors should remain in the immediate background of legal discourse rather than considered as an essential part of it. What does not often appear evident is the manner in which the forces of law, history, international politics, and marine ecosystems directly contrast and combine to change our modes of thinking – including lawyers' thinking – about the Law of the Sea, in particular, and about the business of being and living in international society, in general. This is the reason, I would argue, why "the 1982 United Nations Convention on the Law of the Sea" is such an outstanding piece of law. For me, the Convention represents a fundamental departure in the way the world is conceived and, more importantly, changed. The ambition of this book is to convince the international lawyer that "the 1982 United Nations Convention on the Law of the Sea" justifies this claim.

The core of a new and fundamental departure in the 1982 Treaty is embodied in its Part XI, cryptically entitled "The Area." There is, it must be noted, nothing quite extraordinary about the "Area", which is defined in a rather dry manner by the Convention as "the sea-bed and ocean floor and subsoil thereof, beyond the limits of national jurisdiction."[1] The spectacular feat of Part XI, however, lies in its pronouncement – by way of a new legal principle that should not be taken for granted – that "The Area and its resources are the common heritage of mankind."[2] It is submitted that this is a pronouncement that marks a genuine confluence of law, politics, history and nature which will detain the thoughts of jurists, scientists, and theologians alike in decades to come. Why the Common Heritage of Humanity, which I shall elaborate on as "fundamental legal principle", presents such a great challenge for new understanding or "new thinking" – to employ an expression that has facilitated a monumental transition in recent world history[3] – is explained, in the first instance, by a gut-feel for the term. A fully reasoned-out explanation will no doubt support this first uncontrived impression. But apart from the technical justifications, the principle goes beyond its narrow legal content. Again, the terms "common", "heritage" and "humanity" – whether read separately or jointly, literally or figuratively – invite a larger perspective on the underlying law. It is in the spirit of sharing the prospects of a deeper and wider realization about "the 1982 United Nations Convention on the Law of the Sea" that I undertake the task of clarifying the Principle of the Common Heritage of Humanity.

A brief note on terminology should immediately be made at this point. While it would seem proper to substitute the apparently gender-biased term "Common Heritage of Mankind" with the expression "Common Heritage of Humanity", the former will nonetheless still be employed in this book to refer to a legally-precise technical concept. A more general reference to the equivalent formulation "Common Heritage of Humanity" is, however, warranted –

---

1 Art. 1(1)(1), *United Nations Convention on the Law of the Sea* (UN Sales No. E.83.V.5)[hereafter, CLOS].
2 Art. 136, *id.*
3 *See* M. Gorbachev, *Perestroika: New Thinking For Our Country and the World* (1987).

as it will be shown in Chapter III – in the context of its significance as a fundamental principle of international law.

There are four main reasons why a study of the Common Heritage of Humanity principle in international law is called for in the mid-1990s. The first is the entry into force of the 1982 United Nations Convention on the Law of the Sea on 16 November 1994. The Convention is a unique document in international law and international relations not only because it is the very first comprehensive and legally binding instrument on "sustainable development" that has been brought into effect to govern a vast portion of the earth's surface environment, the oceans.[4] It is also, more importantly, the legal setting where the novel concept of the "common heritage of humanity" finds its most detailed and most advanced expression. Because the Convention has cradled, in a special sense, the evolution and institutionalization of this concept – a concept that, in more ways than one, introduced the international community to unexplored and unorthodox possibilities in international law – its entry into force marks a turning point when a politico-legal concept is irrevocably transformed into an operational legal principle. Those who are familiar with the long-drawn controversy surrounding the Common Heritage regime of the Convention will agree that its much-awaited entry into force puts to rest many of the controversies that were, are, or will be associated with the simple but dense proposition that "The Area and its resources are the common heritage of humanity." The inauguration on a new stage of a hard-won consensus in the law of the sea expressed by the Common Heritage of Humanity principle deserves a moment of stock-taking on an achievement that may not likely be repeated in the history of international law-making. It took over a decade since the adoption of the 1982 Convention, and over a quarter of a century since the concept was broached in the United Nations, to consolidate the Common Heritage principle to the normative position where it stands today.

The second, closely related reason, is the need to spell out the relationship of the Common Heritage of Humanity with the concept or principle of "sustainable development" itself. While there seems to be a fairly unanimous conviction that the 1982 Convention as a whole is a veritable document of sustainable

---

4   In the language of Chapter 17 of Agenda 21, the 1982 UN Convention on the Law of the Sea "sets forth rights and obligations of States and provides the international basis upon which to pursue the protection and sustainable development of the marine and coastal environment and its resources." Para. 17.1, Agenda 21. *UNCED Report*, UN Doc. A/CONF.151/26 (Vol. II).

development, there is less sympathy around for the view that Common Heritage of Humanity principle fosters or is supportive of sustainable development. The resistance against such a reassuring conception of the Common Heritage of Humanity principle is inexplicable from a logical standpoint, because the Common Heritage of Humanity principle and its detailed elaboration are very much a part of the Convention. It must be recognized though that there had been, as there still are, vested political interests that would not like to see a largely vague "feel good" notion of sustainable development corrupted by the normative specifics of the Common Heritage of Humanity principle. The link between the "new" and fashionable sustainable development thinking and the "new thinking" embodied in the Common Heritage of Humanity principle remains to be identified. It is also submitted that this link needs to be politically nurtured.

A third, somewhat urgent, reason why the Common Heritage of Humanity principle deserves investigation is the coming into operation, simultaneously with the entry into force of the 1982 Convention, of the July 1994 "Agreement relating to the implementation of Part XI of the United Nations Convention on the Law of the Sea of 10 December 1982."[5] In appearance, never in the past had there been such an intense and sustained interest in establishing the mechanisms to "implement" international law in a remote environment like the deep seabed, notwithstanding the acknowledged fact that actual deep sea-bed mining – the primary activity governed by the common heritage of humanity principle under the Convention – is not foreseeable in generations to come. One is tempted to say that if the same commitment and energy devoted to conceiving and realizing the "implementation" of the Common Heritage regime were to be replicated in other areas of international law, and there is reason to believe that the Agreement is precedent-setting in every respect,[6] many global problems on the enforcement of substantive rules of international law in fields like environmental protection, trade, and human rights can certainly be overcome in no time at all. But in reality, however, the Agreement was actu-

---

5 *See* UN Doc. A/RES/48/263 (17 August 1994).
6 One year after this "implementation agreement" was adopted, a United Nations Conference adopted on 3 August 1995 the *Agreement for the Implementation of the United Nations Convention on the Law of the Sea of 10 December 1982, relating to the Conservation and Management of Straddling and Highly Migratory Fish Stocks*. Text in 34 ILM 1542-1580 (1995).

ally meant to introduce substantial amendments or major adjustments to the Common Heritage regime of the Convention.

What is amazing for the purposes of this study is the radical manner by which such "Implementation Agreement" displaced normative and institutional elements of the Common Heritage of Humanity under the 1982 Convention. Whether in the municipal or international law setting, it is an unusual practice to deliberately annul substantive law in its major aspects in order to "implement" it, or stated differently, to modify a law before it comes into effect. The transition undergone by a legal principle from its recognition in fact to its execution as law, akin to that wondrous period between the moment of conception and the actual birth of a human being, is itself an important subject of inquiry on the nature of the legal process. Investigating the impact of the recent Agreement on the Common Heritage principle in particular, and on international law in general, is necessarily part of exploring the intricacies of a new mode of legal consciousness offered by the Common Heritage of Humanity principle.

The agenda of the recently concluded fiftieth anniversary year of the United Nations in 1995 is a last, but not the least significant, reason why an engagement with the Common Heritage of Humanity principle is imperative. For good cause, the golden anniversary year of the United Nations occasioned a well-deserved review of the record of the Organization, as well as the principles and purposes on which it is based as an international organization. In the normative field, such a review had surely provided singular opportunity to reflect upon a "United Nations legal order" as an indispensable component of post-war international life.[7] A crucial dimension of this meditation was certainly a closer examination of the facilitative role of the United Nations Organization in the evolution, production, and strengthening of international law as a fundamental institution of the post-war, and post-cold war, international community.[8] This focus must be reinforced. At a time when so much pressure

---

7   A spate of literature has come out of the anniversary year. For a thorough exposition of the role of the United Nations in the definition and maintenance of an international legal order *see* O. Schachter & C. Joyner (Eds.), *United Nations Legal Order* (2 Vols.) (1995). *See also* C. Tomuschat (Ed.), *The United Nations at Age Fifty* (1995).
8   The linkage between the heightened importance of international law in the world community and the celebration of the fiftieth anniversary of the United Nations is made in the UN General Assembly Resolution proclaiming the UN Decade of International Law (1990-1999). *See* UN Doc. A/RES/44/23 (17 Nov. 1989).

is being brought to bear on the United Nations System to meet the growing and multifarious demands of global governance, international law – or its creation, consolidation, or application – is manifestly an invaluable resource, an indispensable policy instrument, at the disposal of the United Nations and world leadership. Recall how many law-making diplomatic conferences have so far been held under the auspices of the United Nations. Recall too how many programmes, agencies, and international organizations, not to mention specific regimes and legal principles, have sprung from these law-making initiatives. The significance of international law in any approach to global governance cannot be over-emphasized.[9]

In the arena of the oceans, the staggering output of the United Nations in terms of international law and institutions is definitely impressive, and it is likely that the UN will remain at the forefront in promoting and safeguarding all manner of ocean law and institutions, at global, regional, national and even sub-national levels. A universally accepted United Nations Convention on the Law of the Sea, and as matter of consequence the Common Heritage of Humanity principle, are undoubtedly a new addition in the legal arsenal of the United Nations in building a durable framework of global governance.[10] The "revolutionary" role of the Common Heritage of Humanity principle, in this regard, is at once made apparent as evidenced in the previous attempts and by current proposals to extend the principle to other realms of global governance.[11] If

---

9   *See* Report of the Commission on Global Governance. *Our Global Neighborhood* (1995).

10 The point is emphasized in Secretary-General Boutros Boutros-Ghali's *An Agenda for Development*, para. 177, UN Doc. A/48/935 (6 May 1994):
    The United Nations Convention on the Law of the Sea ... now provides a mechanism for addressing development questions related to all aspects of the use of the sea and its resources. As new technologies and the hunger for new resources increase the capacity of nations to exploit the ocean's resources, the Convention provides a universal legal framework for rationally managing marine resources and an agreed set of principles to guide consideration of the numerous issues and challenges that will continue to arise. From navigation and overflights to resource exploration and exploitation, conservation and pollution and fishing and shipping, the Convention provides a focal point for international deliberation and action.
    See also B. Boutros-Ghali, "Foreword" in the *Symposium on The United Nations: Challenges of Law and Development*, 36 HARV INT L J 267-271 (1995).

11 *See* for e.g. most recently, E.M. Borgese, *Ocean Governance and the United Nations* 236 (1995) proposing a reconstitution of the UN Trusteeship Council mandate as follows: The Trusteeship Council shall hold in sacred trust the Prin-

the deep seabed can be proclaimed the common heritage of all humankind, why indeed is it not possible to apply the same legal principle – the same technique of governance, with all the necessary accompanying norms and institutions – to other spheres of concern like world food resources, outer space, energy, the atmosphere, tropical forests, the polar regions, high seas fisheries, biodiversity and biotechnology resources, culture, etc.? The implications of the Common Heritage of Humanity principle to the purposes of the United Nations and their achievement are considerable and need to be carefully considered in light of the pressing relevance and necessity of creative international norms and legal institutions in the preservation and/or advancement of a viable global order. In the principle might lie the potential of plotting new directions and new operational frameworks for the United Nations through international law.

The above-stated reasons for an up-dated and more strategic investigation of the Common Heritage of Humanity principle should also suggest the reasons why international law on the whole is itself in need of some kind of major synthesis. In the 1990s and beyond, international law is increasingly looked upon to make more meaningful, if not directly contribute to the full realization of, an ambitious global programme of "sustainable development" – a new and promising concept already referred to.[12] Lately, the 1995 World Summit for

---

    ciple of the Common Heritage of Mankind. It shall monitor compliance with this principle in accordance with international law, in Ocean Space, Outer Space, the atmosphere as well as Antarctica and report any infringement thereof to the General Assembly and/or the CCSSD [*i.e.,* the UN Commission for Comprehensive Security and Sustainable Development which replaces the UN Security Council]. It shall deliberate on its wider application to matters of common concern affecting comprehensive security and sustainable development and the dignity of human life, and make its recommendations to the authorities and institutions concerned. The Trusteeship Council shall act as the conscience of the United Nations and the guardian of future generations.

12 The Report of the World Commission on Environment and Development, *Our Common Future* (1987), advanced and popularized "sustainable development" which is a concept that transcends differences in political and economic ideologies as well as national, social, and cultural systems. The 1992 United Nations Conference on Environment and Development (UNCED), which was convened to consider, *inter alia*, the recommendations of this Report, adopted as its most significant output Agenda 21, a comprehensive action plan for "a global partnership for sustainable development." *See* Preamble, Agenda 21, UN Doc. A/CONF.151/26 (12 August 1992) (Vol. I).

Social Development added that sustainable development should be "people-centred",[13] all the more placing on international law expectations for wider inclusiveness, relevance, and urgency which it is only beginning to come to grips with. It is because of this novel and expanded agenda of international law that more and more international lawyers are seeking ways and means of effectively generating and enforcing international law. The old, all too familiar paralysis of international law on account of the bewailed absence of a world government, or a semblance of it, to administer and enforce international law is giving way to the growing realization that international law could be made tangible and effective through decentralized functional mechanisms of global governance. The point is well-emphasized by the Commission on Global Governance, which endorsed the notion of global governance, rather than world government.[14] In this context, new horizons in international law-making are being opened up precisely because new techniques and methods are being uncovered in the application, execution, or enforcement of universal international law.[15] This leads back to the question of workability and effectiveness, through international law, of omnipresent international organizations and institutions, such as the United Nations System. If it can be imagined that the status of international law today lies somewhere between an outmoded but addictive "international law of co-existence" and the ideal but elusive "international law of cooperation", to use Professor Wolfgang Friedmann's classic categories,[16] the long-term prospects of international law, including the law of the sea, deserve fresh re-examination. This is the underlying rationale for the conviction that the Common Heritage of Humanity principle demands nothing less than a new sensibility in international law.

It is on the basis of the need to re-conceptualize the operational relevance of international law in the 1990s that this book on the Common Heritage of Humanity principle is written. At the outset, it must be made clear that the purpose is neither to inflate the self-importance of international law in contemporary international society nor to applaud the merits of the exciting principle of the Common Heritage of Humanity. Although my biases as a lawyer from the "Third World" whose partisanship for celebrating solidarity-based ap-

---

13 *Declaration of the World Summit for Social Development*, para. 24, UN Doc. A/CONF.166/L.3/Add.1 (10 March 1995).
14 *Our Global Neighbourhood, supra* note 9 at xvi-xvii, 2-7.
15 On this concept, *see* J. Charney, *Universal International Law* 87 AJIL 529 (1993).
16 W. Friedmann, *The Changing Structure of International Law* (1964).

proaches to pressing international law problems cannot be concealed, I have determined to analyze the Common Heritage of Humanity principle from an outlook that takes a skeptical view of *both* international law and the Common Heritage of Humanity concept. This is perhaps the more suitable attitude. For the value of any conceptual study of this kind should lie in the critical attitude it maintains towards its subject matter and itself. An unconventional attitude is also called for if only to amplify the observation that the Common Heritage of Humanity principle makes imperative efforts to develop a new synthesis in contemporary international law. This is the only way it seems how the study can draw attention to what can be distilled as truly essential and enduring about the Common Heritage experience in the 1982 United Nations Convention on the Law of the Sea.

METHODOLOGICAL NOTE

This study will focus on the problem of disparity in international society – what it is, how it is perpetuated, and how it could be addressed from the standpoint of international law. The Common Heritage of Humanity principle, as evolved in the context of the law of the sea, will serve as the main fulcrum in the analysis. Necessarily, the detailed historical treatment of the principle, especially its origins in the arena of diplomacy and international politics, will be given. The underlying purpose is to demonstrate the role of the Common Heritage of Humanity principle in a world of growing disparity.

From the perspective of a story-teller, the history of any particular subject – like the Third UN Conference on the Law of the Sea, "sustainable development", or the "Common Heritage of Humanity" – is never free from the bias, or the fact, of personal interpretation. Notwithstanding the massive documentary material on the matter or the direct verbal testimonies made available to the author – sources of narrative accounts which are reflected in the study – there is an evident partiality or inadequacy in the mainstream historical record which this book seeks to confront by way of its interpretation, re-interpretation or revision. For this reason, and to avoid accusations of unwarranted subjectivity and arbitrariness, the historical method which will be used to illuminate the Common Heritage principle in a more objective manner is the story-telling technique afforded by the concept of "paradigm" or "paradigm shift", as this is called in the literature on the philosophy of science.

Plan of the Study

The book will proceed in two Parts. The First Part, divided into two Chapters, offers a general perspective on the phenomenon of worsening North-South inequality as a problem of international law. More specifically, it examines the prospects of North-South disparities in the context of the new international law of the sea and the emerging norms of sustainable development. The Second Part, with three major Chapters, dwells on the Common Heritage of Humanity and its significance in a grossly unequal world.

Chapter I introduces and examines the notion of "the international law of global disparities." The methodological, doctrinal and historical aspects of this framework-setting idea will be explored as a basic explanation for the phenomenon of growing disparities in the post-war international community. A clarification of the Positivist doctrine of sovereign equality in international law is given in the context of what I call the "old" and "new domains" of inter-State inequality, particularly between developed States and developing States. The problematic of North-South inequality is more specifically reflected in the historical movement to establish norms and institutions for development and global sharing in the contemporary law of the sea which is recounted in Chapter II.

Chapter II thus begins with the presentation of the hypothesis on the "international law of global disparities" in the normative setting of oceans, where the "old" and "new" domains of inequality are clearly defined. It then proceeds to analyze the provisions of the 1982 Convention on the Law of the Sea dealing with the old or "traditional" areas of inequality between developed and developing countries. This domain of inequality was considered in the various subjects for negotiations in the Second and Third Committees of UNCLOS III. The interaction of and the linkages between the positive law output of UNCLOS III and the normative outcome of the 1992 UN Conference on Environment and Development (UNCED) in this domain will be considered in the last section of the Chapter. It is here in this Chapter where the idea of "the international law of sustainable development" will be broached as an alternative ethos or paradigm of international law.

Chapters III, IV and V of the book (or Part 2) are fully devoted to the elaboration of the Common Heritage of Humanity. These three Chapters investigate the scope of the Common Heritage of Humanity principle *ratione loci*, *ratione materiae* and *ratione temporis*, respectively, as a fundamental principle of international law. A somewhat detailed historical treatment, accorded to each of these facets of the principle, will be given in order to set the record straight, if I may use that expression, on the issues involved. For such purpose the underlying methodological device which will be used to throw light on the problematic of the Common Heritage of Humanity principle is the "paradigm" – a concept whose progeny in the scientific literature will be briefly described in Chapter III.

Chapter III will, hence, inquire into the history and normative significance of "the Area." The discussion of the proposition that the Area is a legal frontier, or a potential new domain of disparity between North and South, is set against the background of developments related to the "exploitability clause" of the 1958 Geneva Convention on the Continental Shelf. The clash of nationally-driven interests and cosmopolitan projections of international control with respect to a space that is actually entirely fictive or notional will set the tone for this discussion. The conclusion reached is that the historical and political rationale for the Common Heritage of Humanity principle is closely associated with the question of the legal existence of the Area.

Chapter IV further deliberates on the historical origins of "the Area" in relation to the emergence of specific normative elements of the Common Heritage of Humanity principle. The main argument advanced in this Chapter is that the Common Heritage of Humanity principle is a new fundamental principle of international law, neither derived from nor harnessed by the *mare clausum* and *mare liberum* doctrines in the classical law of the sea. It is this feature that makes the Common Heritage of Humanity principle a potentially preeminent rebuttal to the "international law of global disparities", providing a regime where the ideal equality of rights and obligations of States could obtain. The Common Heritage of Humanity principle is a fundamental norm that is by and large programmatory in intent and multi-functional/territorial in orientation, as seen in the historical and doctrinal definition of its normative elements. The four general elements of the Common Heritage of Humanity principle will be identified as (1) reservation for peaceful purposes, (2) benefit-sharing, (3) environmental protection of the marine environment, and (4) institutional development for the Area and its resources. The fourth-mentioned "institutional" element is described more fully in Chapter V.

The concluding substantive Chapter of the book, Chapter V, addresses the most critical element of the Common Heritage of Humanity principle – its institutionalization through the International Seabed Authority. This Chapter will begin by positing "two competing visions" of institutionalization for the deep seabed, which are aligned, respectively, to the competing paradigms of governance: "sustainable development" and "global disparities." On the one hand is the vision of international control that proceeds from the ameliorative principle of the Common Heritage of Humanity, and on the other lies the aggressive vision of "assured access" as a guiding framework for the establishment of an international machinery for the deep seabed. The interplay and "reconciliation" of these mutually exclusive visions in the negotiation environment of UNCLOS III will then be described at length. How these contradictory visions were disposed of later in the 1994 Agreement Relating to the Implementation of Part XI will, likewise, be considered. The hope is expressed that the implications of the 1994 Agreement on the institutional element of the Common Heritage of Humanity principle, or its scope *ratione temporis*, will provoke critical questions about the relevance and significance of the Agreement *vis-à-vis* the pursuit and establishment of an "international law of sustainable development."

Chapter VI sets forth a summary and the general conclusions of this study.

PART 1

INTERNATIONAL LAW IN AN UNEQUAL WORLD

I

INEQUALITY IN THE INTERNATIONAL COMMUNITY

It is not a secret that the world community has become a grossly inegalitarian society. Half a century after the United Nations proclaimed sovereign equality and equal rights of nations large and small,[1] over 180 of its member-States today are separated by wide – and widening – disparities in political power, economic and technical resources, and opportunities for development, security and survival. Although certain material inequalities have, by definition, always existed between States, the nature of the present, ever-growing disparities dividing the countries of the world is such as to call into question the very character and ends of international society itself.[2] If the multiplication of disparities among States is a necessary consequence and a permanent feature of membership in this society, it is fitting to ask whether the United Nations should still aspire for an egalitarian world order, or whether it should be founded on different aims and principles altogether.[3] A widely accepted recognition that *growing inequality* – not merely considerable inequality – is normal and the

---

1 *See* invocations of "equal rights" in the Preamble, Art. 1(2), and Art. 55, *Charter of the United Nations and the Statute of the International Court of Justice* (UN: 1974).

2 For an early study investigating this question in a polemological context, *see* WD Verwey, *Economic Development, Peace and International Law* (1972).

3 A. Magarasević, "The Sovereign Equality of States" in M. Sahović (Ed.) *Principles of International Law Concerning Friendly Relations and Cooperation* at 187-189 (1972), states that the principle of sovereign equality in the UN Charter was innovatively linked to the achievement of the goals of the UN. These goals include those spelled out in Art. 1(3) and Art. 55 of the Charter, on international cooperation for economic and social progress and development. *See also* V. Pechota, "Equality: Political Justice in an Unequal World" in R.St.J. Macdonald & D.M. Johnston (Eds.), *The Structure and Process of International Law: Essays in Legal Philosophy, Doctrine, and Theory* at 454-455 (1986).

inevitable fate of nation-States in the twenty-first century would at least help redirect the focus of statecraft and global governance to the other pressing demands of planetary survival. It could also remove many sources of friction and conflict which have been, and continue to be, founded on the hope that global equality, as a paramount article of faith of the United Nations, is worthwhile and meaningful.

While the intensification of both globalization and localization trends seems to reduce the profile of the State as well as inter-State differentials in international relations, the nation-State is still the fundamental point of reference in international life and remains the key fact in comprehending the scale of a blatantly unequal world. The information and communications era which fashioned the reality of today's global village makes the contrasts and inequalities among States all the more conspicuous, and perhaps even tragic. Just when standards and definitions of material well-being have begun to converge, or perhaps because of these convergent perceptions of globalized "standards of living", it has become all too apparent that actual well-being throughout the world is not quite uniformly shared. While some have a surfeit of well-being, others have too little. So many people in so many places are discovering the engulfing proportions of that gap in material prosperity which exists between the most developed State and the most deprived. And so many of them realize that an overwhelming number of States – most probably including the one to which they belong – lie close to the 'most deprived'.

A. Widening Global Disparities on the Large

It is significant to note that the issue of post-war global disparities is often portrayed in terms of the historical North-South divide in international society, whereby a few rich countries are distinguished in their level of standards of living, prosperity, or development from the majority of States who are poor and remain "less developed" – *i.e.*, the Third World. With the collapse of the Communist empire and the disappearance of "East-West" confrontation, distinctions on the basis of privilege and class in the international community of States have risen to more prominence. The consensus is that the magnitude of the divide – the "glaring contradiction", to use the words of the 1995 World

Summit for Social Development⁴ – has in fact swelled, revealing new qualitative dimensions of world inequality. From the perspective of the recent Report of the Commission on Global Governance, there are now "different Souths and different Norths."[5] A handful of "haves" are separated from the multitude of "have-nots" by a widening "development gap", visualized through the familiar socio-economic indicators.

In 1993, for instance, about 1.3 billion people, a bit over the total population of developed countries combined, lived in the abject conditions of absolute poverty.[6] This constitutes one-fifth of the world population, a figure which only inadequately conveys a magnitude that grows by the day.[7] This fifth of humanity also generates 1.4% of the global GNP and shares 0.9% of overall world trade.[8] In contrast, the twenty percent richest Northern minority enjoys 84.7% of world GNP, 84.2% of world trade,[9] 94.6% of all commercial lending, 80.6% of all domestic savings, 80.5% of all domestic investments, and 94% of all research and development.[10] Of the 1.3 billion poorest people, two-thirds live in ten countries which together receive less than one-third of Official

---

4 *Declaration of the World Summit for Social Development*, para. 13. UN Doc. A/CONF.166/L.3/Add.1 (10 March 1995).
5 *Our Global Neighbourhood, op. cit.* 140.
6 *Id.* at 21; 1994 HDR 135, 174-175. *The Programme of Action of the [Cairo] International Conference on Population and Development* estimates that the number of people living in poverty is approximately 1 billion and continues to mount. Para. 3.11. *See* UN Doc. A/CONF.171/13 (18 October 1994).
7 Almost 80% of the world's 5.63 billion people are in the least developed regions of the world, with population growth concentrated in the poorest countries: every day 377,000 new human beings are born, every year the world population is increased by 90 million, three-fourths of which is accounted for by developing countries, sharing only 15% of the total world income. *See* Opening Speeches of UN Secretary-General Boutros Boutros-Ghali and Egyptian President M.H. Mubarak at the Cairo Conference, UN Doc. A/CONF.171/13/Add.1 (18 October 1994).
8 From 1960-1970, the equivalent figures were, respectively, 2.3% (for world GNP) and 1.3% (for world trade). 1993 HDR 27.
9 *Ibid.*
10 E. Childers & B. Urquhart, *Renewing the United Nations System*, 1994 DEVELOPMENT DIALOGUE no. 1 (special issue) at 53. Furthermore, 95% of all patents are owned by proprietors located in the developed countries. *See* E.-U. Petersmann, *The Transformation of the World Trading System through the 1994 Agreement Establishing the World Trade Organization*, 6 EJIL at 206 (1995).

Development Assistance (ODA), with the relatively richer developing countries and such countries with high military spending receiving the bulk of this ODA.[11] When it is considered that this ODA accounts for only a little over 0.3% of the rich countries' GNP,[12] a far cry from the 0.7% "best efforts" international target agreed upon way back in 1970,[13] it is not surprising to see widespread resentment or cynicism in the way the wealth and welfare of the world are presently distributed.

The "widening gap in global opportunities", as the UNDP puts it,[14] is further reflected in resource flow imbalances occurring between the rich North and the poor South. In 1970, the debt service ratio (defined as a percentage of exports of goods and services) for all developing countries was 13.3%; in 1991, this rose to 21.3%.[15] In the 1980's, considered the "lost decade" for many developing countries,[16] indebted developing countries transferred an average of 2.5%, and for some 6% or more, of their GDP abroad,[17] thus "sharing" their much needed financial resources to the developed world.[18] This contradiction reiterates what has all along been an obvious discrepancy: the underrepresentation of the poor countries in global decision-making and economic governance.[19] To add paradox to irony, the UN Secretary General recently noted that, notwithstanding aggregate declines in global military expenditures, 86% of all arms supplies now flowing world-wide is accounted for as exported by the five permanent members of the UN Security Council.[20] On the other hand, little of the estimated US $425 billion peace dividend realized in the industrialized

---

11 1994 HDR 72.
12 ODA as a percentage of OECD GNP in 1970 was 0.31; in 1980 it was 0.35 and in 1992 it was 0.33. 1994 HDR 197; 1991 HDR 53.
13 *See* UNGA Res. 2626 (XXV), para. 43; *Declaration on International Economic Cooperation*, UN Doc. A/RES/S-18/3 (1 May 1990), para. 27; *Declaration of the World Summit for Social Development, supra* note 4, Commitment 9(1).
14 1992 HDR Ch. 3.
15 1994 HDR 168-169. For the least developed and sub-Saharan countries, the debt service ratio in 1971 was about 4.5% and around 25.2% in 1991.
16 *Declaration on International Economic Cooperation, supra* note 13, para. 7.
17 *An Agenda for Development, op. cit.* para. 61.
18 *See also* 1991 HDR 22; 1990 HDR 79.
19 *Our Global Neighbourhood, op. cit.* 187.
20 *An Agenda for Development, op. cit.* para. 32. For the increasing trends in military expenditures in the Third World, *see* 1990 HDR 76-78.

countries between 1987 and 1992 appears to have been channelled into development.[21]

The disparities in resource consumption are no less unsettling. In 1965 the per capita commercial energy consumption in all developing countries was 200 KOE (*i.e.*, kilograms of oil equivalent) while in the industrialized countries, it was 3,360 KOE; in 1991, the per capita energy consumption in the developing world was 550 KOE, and 4,840 KOE for the developed countries.[22] As a consequence, about six billion metric tons of greenhouse gases are emitted each year in the industrialized North[23] and about 68% of the world's industrial waste are generated by them.[24] In the poor South, on the other hand, the "consumption" of tropical forests runs at a rate of one soccer field per second[25] and at least 14 million people have become environmental refugees as a result of growing ecological degradation.[26] The spill-over of human displacements as well as of social exclusion in the South to the North, caused not only by environmental distress but also by a host of social, economic, ethnic and political factors, has become a very serious problem which is only starting to be addressed by the international community through an amorphous global programme for social integration.[27] In the meantime, draconian policies are being adopted in the rich countries to arrest mass migration from low-income ones – a situation that sometimes suggests, in the candid words of the Commission on Global Governance, the inconsistency if not hypocrisy of some governments in the way they treat labour migration.[28] It is certainly not far-fetched to observe that material disparities between North and South increasingly dictate differences in the individual availment as well as mass enjoyment of self-worth and dignity.

---

21 *An Agenda for Development, id.*, para. 31.
22 1994 HDR 178-179.
23 1991 HDR 29. Seventy-one percent of the world's carbon monoxide emissions are accounted for by the developed countries. 1993 HDR 13.
24 1993 HDR 13.
25 1993 HDR 12.
26 *See* 1991 HDR 29.
27 *See Declaration and Programme of Action of the World Summit for Social Development*, *supra* note 4, Commitment no. 4, and Ch. 4, esp. under item E; *An Agenda for Development, op. cit.* para. 101.
28 "They claim a belief in free markets (including labour markets), but use draconian and highly bureaucratic regulations to control cross-border labour migration." *Our Global Neighbourhood, op. cit.* 206.

The North-South divide is a historical phenomenon which is not unacknowledged in realm of international law. Various developments in post-war international law-making in fact directly arise from the assumption that there is a North and there is a South. Many minds have grappled with the issues posed by the problems of global disparity, and those who believe that international law can rectify the wrongs of a highly inegalitarian international society have not hesitated to marshall every available international legal resource to support their cause.[29] Some crucial doctrinal aspects, as well as the features of the diplomatic setting, of the post-war movement to instrumentalize international law for the achievement of egalitarian goals will be considered in this book. On the other hand, there are also those who view international law as unavailing in this respect, and would prefer to judge the status of the North and the South

---

29 The enormous literature on what was known as the "New International Economic Order" or, now labelled the "international law of development", or still more recently, the "law on the right to development" is proof of the intense attention given to the rethinking of the role of international law in reducing global disparities. In regard to the "Right to Development", which is the concept that marks a recent turn in the reconceptualization of North-South legal relations, some notable works that came after the adoption by the UN General Assembly of the 1986 *Declaration on the Right to Development*, Res. 41/128 are: the contributions of M. Flory, "Adapting International Law to the Development of the Third World", P. Alston, "The Right to Development at the International Level", & W.D. Verwey, "The New International Economic Order and the Realization of the Right to Development and Welfare" all three in F. Snyder & S. Sathirathai (Eds.), *Third World Attitudes Towards International Law* at 799-851 (1987); F. Snyder & P. Slinn (Eds.), *International Law of Development: Comparative Perspectives* (1987); P. de Waart, P. Peters & E. Denters (Eds.), *International Law and Development* (1988); F.V. Garcia-Amador, *The Emerging International Law of Development* (1990); contributions of Judge Bedjaoui in M. Bedjaoui (Ed.), *International Law: Achievements and Prospects* (1991); R.L. Barsch, *The Right to Development as a Human Right: Results of the Global Consultation* 13 HUMAN RIGHTS QRTLY 322 (1991) and literature cited therein; S.R. Chowdhury, E. Denters & P. de Waart (Eds.), *The Right to Development in International Law* (1992); J. Paul, *The Human Right to Development: Its Meaning and Importance* 25 JOHN MARSHALL L REV 235 (1992); H. Charlesworth, *The Public-Private Distinction and the Right to Development in International Law* 13 AUSTRALIAN YBIL 190 (1992); O. Okafor, *The Status and Effect of the Right to Development in International Law* 7 AFRICAN J INT & COMP L 865 (1995); and J. Paul, *The United Nations and the Creation of an International Law of Development* 36 HARV INTL L J (1995). *Cf.* the "right to sustainable development" in *infra* 117 *et seq.*

according to pre-decolonization standards of sovereign equality and statehood.[30] And those who consider themselves as taking a neutral view would focus instead on the established, universally accepted formal procedures of international law-making as the crucial basis for policy action to achieve any community goal, like world egalitarianism.[31]

The Common Heritage of Humanity principle is one pivotal concept which was introduced and developed according to the shifting logic of North-South politics. It is informed by the common perception of States that international disparities run along North-South lines, and thus seeks to respond to the requirements, normatively and institutionally, of addressing these disparities. From the vantage point of this book, the Common Heritage of Humanity principle is a development in international law that calls for a reappraisal and reimagination of the North-South divide which, if current trends continue, will likely become a more critical sour point in the law of nations in the years to come. The Common Heritage of Humanity principle, whose progressive development especially in the Law of the Sea took place alongside the evolutionary transformations of the North-South divide, is a *locus classicus* of international law articulating a position on the outstanding world-wide human predicament of global disparities.

Before a more detailed discussion is given on the linkage between the Common Heritage of Humanity principle and global disparities, together with the prior explanation on how and why international law is implicated in global disparities, it is important to bring into view the debate on global disparities on the broad front of international studies. This necessary diversion will show the larger horizon on which the international legal aspects of the North-South divide can be appreciated. The question to be asked, which does not readily admit of an obvious answer, is: why should we bother at all with global equality?

---

30   *See* R. Jackson, *Quasi-States: Sovereignty, International Relations, and the Third World* (1990), generalizing on the character and future of the entire South according to what he calls the "negative sovereignty game" in the decolonized world.
31   *See* G.M. Danilenko, *Law-Making in the International Community* (1993); P. Slinn, "Differing Approaches to the Relationship Between International Law and the Law of Development," in Snyder & Slinn, *supra* note 29 at 35-36.

B. Wither Global Inequality?

It is recognized that anyone, including governments and States, can have reasoned preferences about the desirability or undesirability of deepening global disparities. The widely-shared hope or conviction, perhaps deriving from an attachment to the fundamental objectives of the UN Charter,[32] is that global disparities are odious.[33] A recent restatement of this position, outside the walls of the United Nations, is the Report of the Commission on Global Governance, which couched the inequality issue in terms of the "global neighbourhood value" of "justice and equity":

> A concern for equity is not tantamount to an insistence on equality, but it does call for deliberate efforts to reduce gross inequalities, to deal with factors that cause or perpetuate them, and to promote fairer sharing of resources. A broader commitment to equity and justice is basic to more purposeful action to reduce disparities and bring about a more balanced distribution of opportunities around the world. A commitment to equity everywhere is the only secure foundation for a more humane world order in which multilateral action, by blunting current disparities, improves global well-being as well as stability.[34]

---

32 Art. 1(3) of the UN Charter, *supra* note 1, speaks of international cooperation in solving economic, social, cultural, humanitarian problems and respect for human rights. Art. 55, more specifically states:
With a view to the creation of conditions of stability and well-being which are necessary for peaceful and friendly relations among nations based on respect for the principles of equal rights and self-determination of peoples, the United Nations shall promote:
   a. higher standards of living, full employment, and conditions of economic and social progress and development;
   b. solutions of international economic, social, health, and related problems; and international cultural and educational co-operation; and
   c. universal respect for, and observance of, human rights and fundamental freedoms for all without distinction as to race, sex, language, or religion.
33 In relation to the re-structuring of the UN for global equity and sustainable development, *see* Childers & Urquhart, *op. cit.* Chaps. IV – VIII. The authors speak of the "potentially catastrophic North-South divide." *See also* 1996 HDR 4: "Development that perpetuates today's inequality is neither sustainable nor worth sustaining."
34 *Our Global Neighbourhood, op. cit.* 51. *See also* M. Lachs, "Some Thoughts on Equality" in R.St.J. Macdonald (Ed.), *Essays in Honor of Wang Tieya* 483-488 (1994).

There are, however, certain totalizing views which argue to the contrary, asserting that global disparities are basically acceptable on either practical or ethical grounds. Two such views are particularly fashionable, and should be mentioned. First, there are those who, believing that global disparities are either inevitable or perfectly natural, will base their contention on the perenniality, universality or even necessity of rich-poor chasms. "They that have odds of power exact as much as they can, and the weak yield to such condition as they can get."[35] The supporters of this view will hence be skeptical of, if not be cynical about, any "utopian" enterprise to question this hard wall of reality. Such is the "realist" position that has its many shades of expression in international studies.[36] Moreover, a second line of opinion goes, inter-State equality does not really produce utopia but dysphoria. On the basis of the reasoning that people and States project culturally diverse assessments of a global order based on material disparities, it is concluded that ethical choices presented by radically different perceptions of global inequality may prove incommensurable. The only effect of a movement towards levelling equality, or the spurious goal of global development, is homogenization and cultural domination of a nasty

---

35 Thucydides, *The Peloponnesian War* The Thomas Hobbes Translation, Vol. II, Bk. V, Sec. 89, at 365 (1959).

36 Global inequalities may be seen as inevitable from the workings of zero-sum power-maximization and power-balancing contests among States. This is the conclusion that is suggested in the classic text of post-war realism: H.J. Morgenthau, *Politics Among Nations: The Struggle for Power and Peace* (6th ed., 1985). A recent re-statement of liberal internationalism also corroborates the conclusion that global disparities are unavoidable. See F. Fukuyama, *The End of History and The Last Man* (1992), who conceives of the division of nation-States into a "post-historical world" (*i.e.*, most developed countries) and a "historical world" (*i.e.*, most of the Third World), the latter being restrained by various irrationalities and handicaps, often cultural, towards the realization of a plentiful liberal democratic order. This classification of nation-States arises from the effects of an assumed world-wide *thymos*, manifested in the global "struggle for recognition." See especially Parts IV and V. Curiously, even thinkers from the left who suggest the resilience of the world capitalist order, are by implication arguing for a similar conclusion. See I. Wallerstein (Ed.), *World Inequality* 9-28 (1975) who maintains, from a "world-system perspective", that the world capitalist economy, which is by definition unequal, is here to stay. All these views, even if their respective purveyors would surely refuse to be lumped together, will be considered "realist" because they accept as beyond refutation the reality of privilege and inequality at the international level.

kind, which everybody is better off without.[37] It is therefore futile, in this view, to search for a policy to produce sameness and rectify disparities, if at all they need to be rectified.

Both these positions in "realism" and "relativism", if we may call them these, are strong arguments that would dispel the practical and heuristic significance of the idea of global disparities as a threshold problem in the critique and construction of the international order. Surely, there are elements of truth and conviction in each of the narratives that they proffer, just as there are equally valid claims that can be asserted on behalf of the equally absolute countervailing arguments in humanism,[38] universalism,[39] or ecologism.[40]

---

37 *See* C. Douglas Lummis, "Equality" in W. Sachs (Ed.), *The Development Dictionary: A Guide to Knowledge as Power* 38-52 (1992) advocating the possibility of "the effective equality of incommensurables" for a just global order.

38 *See* for e.g. F. Fanon, *The Wretched of the Earth* (1963) for a dispassionate plea to the decolonizing Third World not to follow the European model but to lead the rest of the world in an new world humanistic campaign. *See also* B. Ward, *Rich Nations, Poor Nations* (1961) for a cogent argument for liberty based on the revolution of equality between rich and poor States. The argument that there is a distinct and innocent constitution of human nature that should strive for the ideal of equality is given in the penetrating classic J. Rousseau, *Discourse on the Origin and Foundations of Inequality among Men* (Second Discourse) in *Collected Writings of Rousseau*, Vol. 3 (1992).

39 The extension of the welfare State concept to the scale of international society is a universalist argument for reducing global disparities. *See* R.St.J. Macdonald, D.M. Johnston, & G.L. Morris, "The International Law of Human Welfare: Concepts, Experience, and Priorities" in R.St.J. Macdonald, D.M. Johnston, & G.L. Morris (Eds.), *The International Law and Policy of Human Welfare* 3-79 (1978). The human rights movement may similarly be considered in this light. Specifically, the so-called "right to development" for both individuals and States, set in an inegalitarian international community, aims at significant international equalization in material standards. *See supra*, note 28. "Development", as a levelling idea, has been conceptualized and implemented according to the "modernization" and "dependency" theories in Third World studies. *See* B. Hettne, *Development Theory and the Three Worlds* (1990). In international relations, notions of distributive justice or equality as a universal desideratum may be conceived under "Cosmopolitan" (*i.e.*, Kantian) and "Communitarian" (*i.e.*, Hegelian) approaches to international relations. *See* C. Brown, *International Relations: New Normative Approaches* (1992).

The ivory tower debate involving all these theoretical positions on world inequality, or the usefulness of the idea of international equality, is certainly not settled and will likely intensify with the growing proportions of global disparity. On this philosophical plane, the "correct" position among competing views or intellectual traditions cannot be known, or may simply be dictated by taste or preferred practices.[41] However, each one of these ideas on world equality may further be assessed according to their status in explanatory knowledge. This clarification should enable international lawyers to locate more intelligibly the elaboration of the Common Heritage of Humanity principle in the broad setting of international studies on world inequality.

It should be noted that the inevitably sweeping observations and judgements made in all the above interpretive versions of global inequality, the assured style of their rationality or epistemology, contain varying degrees of generalization or oversimplification. Caution is required in the instrumental deployment of any of these grand outlooks not only because their respective conclusions are immediately controvertible by the opposing outlooks. Also, the explanatory macrocosm in which these outlooks construct and justify their specific arguments for or against global inequality (e.g., Fukuyama's evolutionist account of liberal democracy, or Fanon's progressive march of humanism) partake of intellectually suspect "grand narratives." If it is accepted that the entire world is fast heading towards a post-industrial society, then such "grand narratives", we are told by a philosopher, have really lost their appeal and credibility.[42] This evaluative outlook may be put in the form of a challenge: Who, in the complex and contradictory world of the twenty-first century, can speak for "the others" and confidently declare "I know whereof I speak"? If it is assumed that the expressions of opinion that truly count are "voices", rather than

---

40 See D. Meadows, et al., *The Limits to Growth* (1974) for a defense of a positive linkage between global equality in the distribution of resources and an idealized "equilibrium state"; *see also* the commentary of the Executive Committee of the Club of Rome, annexed in *id.*, at 185-197.
41 See A. MacIntyre, *Whose Justice? Which Rationality?* (1988), on the incommensurability of "traditions"; and T. Kuhn, *The Structure of Scientific Revolutions* (1970) on the incommensurability of competing "paradigms."
42 In J.F. Lyotard, *The Post-Modern Condition: A Report on Knowledge* (1984), "postmodern" is defined "incredulity toward meta-narrative." Lyotard, using the concept of language games to explain knowledge, discerns the crisis of legitimation of two grand narratives: the belief in humanity as hero and the belief in the speculative unity of knowledge.

"vocabularies", particular explanatory accounts of global (in)equality need not, therefore, be based on or justified according to some grand unimpeachable episteme concerning all human nature and the universal human condition. If a meaningful answer is to be given to the question of whether global disparities are good or bad, it would seem to be more appropriate to resort to the device of a simple, "local" narrative. Perhaps what is required is a specific case illustrative of global inequality, or a commitment to global equality – a story which will reveal important microscopic details about the workings of power, prejudice and passion in the creation of global disparities. The story of the Common Heritage of Humanity principle, it is submitted, will provide such an opportunity.

At this juncture, therefore, one can simply plead for suspended judgement among theoretical partisans in the global (in)equality debate. From the standpoint of an international lawyer, the debate conducted on this level could make sense only if the notion of equality is explored more concretely as a specific operation of international law. The well-known pragmatism of lawyers is best captured in the following insight, which is worth quoting in full:

> In assessing the significance of equality in actual life, we must be on guard against two equally harmful extremes. One might be called the zealotry of absolute claim, a tendency to view any departure from the ideal, however justified, as a wrong that overshadows anything else, and ready to wreak society to vindicate its claim. This tendency is oblivious of the complex sociological, political and legal problems that arise in the application of equality in contemporary society and rejects the notion that any principle takes its content and colouring from the surroundings in which it operates. The other danger is the worship of the order of things which accepts inequality and resultant injustice as something that is normal because it cannot be avoided, given the laws of nature operating in the ungovernable world. It rejects equality among states as a fiction and dismisses the claims based on it as artificial and implying assumptions which cannot be tested but by the actual exercise of physical force.

Neither of the two positions can provide a ground for meaningful discussion. The former is unrealistic in that it precludes the consideration of objective differences among states and in the circumstances in which equality takes its shape. The latter forecloses any positive inquiry because of its assertion that the conception is erroneous in theory and non-realizable in practice. The truth, as is often the case in matters concerning society, lies in a middle course: the equality of states is neither a categorical imperative nor is it a misconception. It is the sum of conditions under which one state's sovereignty can be combined with the sovereignty of other states according to universal principles of justice and law. The verification of the postulate involves evaluation of the meaning of equality of states, of its mode of operation, and also of its place among other legal rules. An appraisal along these lines will bring forth the realistic measurement of the concept as an implement substituting fairness for arbitrariness, promoting common goals and facilitating progress.[43]

In this book, the Common Heritage of Humanity principle is a specific illustration of, or a "local narrative" on, the contentious issue of equality among States in contemporary international society. Its evolution partakes of an international social experiment that will have to be tested against the "grand narratives" of equality in international relations *and* international law, which it will in turn interrogate. If this "middle ground" (*i.e.*, between extremes of "grand narratives") experiment proves that international society can be meaningfully conceived in terms of the idea of equality of States, the realists and relativists would of course have something to think about. To be sure this experiment, as will be shown in subsequent Chapters, although already concluded in some of its significant phases, is still very much work-in-progress – a continuing story – and its end-result may well simply confirm what a realist or a relativist had known all along. And so the question could be posed: Has the Common Heritage of Humanity principle been established as a norm of international law on the recognition that global disparities are not inherent, and that international equality could certainly be a worthy quest in global justice? Realist and relativists alike should benefit from an investigation of an extant approach in the realm of international law to understanding the phenomenon, and indeed the problem, of equally sovereign yet unequally empowered sovereign States.

This brief detour on the equality debate in international studies brings the course of inquiry back to the subject of the role and function of international law, and for that matter the Common Heritage of Humanity principle, in the existence of global disparities. The exploration of North-South inequality in the context of the Common Heritage of Humanity principle will be done in

---

43 Pechota, *supra*, note 3 at 458. *See also* O. Schachter, *Sharing the World's Resources* 7 (1977) on his point that "general egalitarianism must become specific egalitarianism", and D.M. Johnston, "The Foundations of Justice in International Law" in MacDonald, Johnston & Morris, *supra* note 39 at 134, for the view that "[c]ommon views on what constitutes the good international society will only come, however, gradually, from the convergence of views on what constitutes the good national society."

Part II of the book. For the remainder of this Chapter we will consider the relationship between global disparities and international law in general, and spell out the arguments in support of the proposition that international law, in its practical operations, contributes to the creation of world inequality. More particularly, it will be explained how and why international law works to create *widening* global disparities, as described above. There are several analytic steps to be taken in the argument, which involve defining the relevant terms: "international law", "inequality", and "widening disparities." The result of the analysis is the tentative conclusion that the structure of international law in force not only reinforces existing disparities but strategically facilitates the addition of new ones. This is the "international law of global disparities" which underlies the legal relations between the North and the South in general. It is this same ethos of the prevailing normative order which pervaded the negotiations in the Third United Nations Conference on the Law of the Sea (UNCLOS III).

C. INTERNATIONAL LAW

Three broad and exhaustive interpretations of, or theoretical approaches to, international law *vis-a-vis* the existence of gaping global disparities may be noted briefly. First, as a consent-based structure of norms and rules, international law reflects the dominant and entrenched national interests that perpetuate the system of political, economic and social inequality at the international level. The exercise of rights and obligations, as well as the interactions of reciprocity, consensus, and compromise among the subjects of international law produce what is in reality an inegalitarian outcome. Without the common will or consent of the established powerful States no change in the distribution or redistribution of values, which is determined by the substance and execution of prevailing norms, can be foreseen. Factual disparities among States in a rule-based system are nothing less than a direct result of the structural operation of norms.

Secondly, viewed as a comprehensive process of decision-making, international law narrates the metamorphosis of international society, or lack of it, upon which derives the authority of the *status quo*. Thus, disparate claims and expectations of relevant actors do not converge in a policy that would otherwise lead to more equal relations, or to an equality-generating dispensation, within the international community. The international law-making exercise is precluded from moving towards the goal of an egalitarian community order.

If human dignity means equal opportunities in world decision-making participants must constantly demand reforms in this policy process to achieve global equality.

Thirdly, as a discourse or distinctive mode of argument, international law collapses as a framework for intersubjective understanding between those who prefer the *status quo* and those who are aggrieved by it and desire to see changes in the direction of establishing world equality. There are no commonly accepted values or "rules of the game" around which a consensus on the issue of global disparity may be formed and communicated. International social life as it is thus presently constituted goes on unperturbed in the production and reproduction of global disparities.

On all these three simplified accounts of the international legal order,[44] it could be readily seen that the human institution called international law generally acts as a conservative force in international society. Notwithstanding the underlying potential and potency of international law in the transformation of inter-State relations, it would seem that it is totally unable to overcome disparities in international society.[45] While international law provides some

---

44 These three interpretations of international law follow, respectively, the Positivist, the Natural Law, and (more recently) the Discursive theories of international law. Illustrative of their contemporary formulations, on which these summaries are based, are the following leading perspectives. For the first, *see* R. Jennings & A. Watts, I *Oppenheim's International Law*, Ch. 1 "Foundation of International Law" 1-115 (9th ed. 1992). For the second, *see* M.S. McDougal & W.M. Reisman, "International Law in Policy-Oriented Perspective" in Macdonald & Johnston, *supra*, note 2 at 103-129. And for the third, *see* F. Kratochwil, *Rules, Norms, and Decisions: On the Conditions of Practical and Legal Reasoning in International Relations and Domestic Affairs* (1989).

The openly political approach to international law and its problems, typified in M. Koskenniemi, *The Politics of International Law* 1 EJIL 4 (1990), may be seen as closely allied in methodological argument with the Discursive School. For an overview of this line of thought 'critical' of liberal (*i.e.*, rule-based positivism and process-based natural law) modes of interpreting international law, *see* A. Carty, *Critical International Law: Recent Trends in the Theory of International Law* 2 EJIL 66 (1991), and N. Purvis, *Critical Legal Studies in Public International Law* 32 HARV INT L J 81 (1991).

45 A similar process has already been observed at the national level in regard to the inequality-perpetuating mechanisms in the domestic legal order of liberal-democratic States. *See* J.H. Schaar, "Some Ways of Thinking About Equality" and "Equality of Opportunity, and Beyond", both in J.H. Schaar, *Legitimacy in*

kind of a forum where competing interests or contradictory tendencies bearing on the issues of distributive justice, marginalization, inequity, or imbalance in the international community struggle for acceptance and normative recognition, the outcome of any competition or exchange in this forum – which is manifested in the aggravated North-South gap described earlier – could be anticipated: the perpetuation of an inegalitarian world order. To this extent, international law participates in the definition or legitimation of inequality between States. It is the invisible force behind every concrete manifestation of global disparity, making growing inequality among nations an unmoving and unmoved reality. Contemporary international law is not just simply rules, or process, or discourse. It is a body of positive rules which command global disparities; it is a process of authoritative decision that produces global disparities; and it is the dominant if not the dominating discourse on the justification of global disparities.

The unequal position of States in the international community, and the growing material-cum-legal differences among them, could be more clearly described through the dominant and firmly established Positivist interpretation of international legal relations. This book will employ the Positive approach in the overall analysis of global disparity and focus on the consequences of this approach as a method of reasoning, without necessarily subscribing to Positivism's ultimate worth or validity. It will be noted that, generally, the Natural Law and the Discursive approaches to international law explain global inequality in political and moral terms. Accordingly, these latter schools of thought impute the cause of growing North-South disparities to the realm of politics and morality.[46] This should perhaps be the case as there seems to be

---

the Modern State 167-209 (1981).

46 Natural Law exponents would just have to insist on "equality" as a universal value in human reason to be able to realize it on the international plane. In the words of the exponents of Natural Law: "it will not be possible to solve the present and acute problems of the international community, especially the problems of maintaining world peace and bringing about the necessary development of the Third World, without having due regard to the principles and norms of natural law [*e.g.*, equality] to which the long tradition of universal reason and authority refers us." A. Verdross & H.F. Koeck, "Natural Law: The Tradition of Universal Reason and Authority" in MacDonald & Johnston, *supra* note 3, 17-42 at 42. On the other hand, advocates of the Discursive or Post-modern School would not have any logical difficulties in positing the value of "equality" as a basic postulate in global human communication to achieve consensus and eventually transform the world.

no reason why morals, or indeed the wider considerations of power and politics, should be excluded from legal analysis. At least, the resulting arguments will make lawyers aware that there are more fundamental values in the legal ordering of international life than just self-contained rules.

But Positivism claims scientific status because of its pretensions for objectivity and value-neutrality. International law, the advocates of Positivism assert, exists independently of policy or morality, and its identity is the outcome of a specific, homogenous and highly self-conscious method in legal reasoning.[47] In this sense, and in contrast to the Natural law or Discursive outlooks, international law is an indifferent technical instrument that could be adapted to accomplish any policy purpose.[48] As such, it could be a direct causative agent in producing social effects such as equality, or, conversely, disparities. On these assumptions, Positivism should initially be preferred as the analytic framework for explaining global disparities. Since it tenets imply a direct connection between an autonomous sphere of international law and the social reality of global disparities, the relationship between international law and growing global disparities can be more fully explored using Positivist presuppositions.

D. INEQUALITY

In the Positivist framework, the existence of an "international community" is not denied.[49] But what happens within this community is largely determined

---

See Kratochwil, *supra* note 44, concluding Ch.; Koskenniemi, *supra* note 44, upholding the validity of unpretentious political choice; and Carty, *supra* note 44, on "legal translation."

47 *See e.g.*, M. Bos, "Will and Order in the Nation-State System: Observations on Positivism and International Law" in MacDonald & Johnston, *supra* note 3 at 51-78.

48 *See* P. Weil, *Towards Relative Normativity in International Law?* 77 AJIL 413-442 (1983).

49 *See Barcelona Traction Case*, 1970 ICJ Rep at 32, referring to "obligations of a State towards the international community as a whole." Art. 53 (on *Jus Cogens*) of the Vienna Convention on the Law of Treaties also makes reference to "the international community of States as a whole." Text in 8 ILM 679 (1969). *See also* Danilenko, *supra* note 31 at 11-13.

by the processes of consensual interaction among equally sovereign States;[50] there is no authority superior to that of the State.[51] Over time, certain fundamental principles develop in this community, which underpin its stability and the certainty of legal relations.[52] One such fundamental legal principle is the principle of "sovereign equality." It is the foundational doctrine or principle of sovereign equality – a cornerstone of the international community order[53] – that secures in *lex lata* the rule of law in international society.[54]

---

50 *See* Jennings & Watts, *supra* note 44 at 339.
51 G. Schwarzenberger, *The Fundamental Principles of International Law*, RECUEIL DES COURS 195-383, at 223 (1955-I).
52 Schwarzenberger, *ibid.*, identifies seven pillars of classical international law: sovereignty, recognition, consent, good faith, self-defense, international responsibility, and freedom of the seas. In this schematization, the principle of equality is merged with sovereignty.
53 Professor I. Brownlie, in his *Principles of International Law* at 287 (4th ed. 1990), remarks that "the sovereignty and equality of states represent the basic constitutional doctrine of the law of nations, which governs a community consisting primarily of states having a uniform personality." The most specific and widely-quoted formulation of the principle of sovereign equality is found in the 1970 *Declaration on Principles of International Law Concerning Friendly Relations and Co-operation among States in Accordance with the Charter of the United Nations*, Res. 2625 (XXV) (24 October 1970): *The Principle of Sovereign Equality of States*: All States enjoy sovereign equality. They have equal rights and duties and are equal members of the international community, notwithstanding differences of an economic, social, political or other nature.
In particular, sovereign equality includes the following elements:
(a) States are juridically equal;
(b) Each State enjoys the rights inherent in full sovereignty;
(c) Each State has the duty to respect the personality of other States;
(d) The territorial integrity and political independence of the State are inviolable;
(e) Each State has the right to freely choose and develop its political, social, economic and cultural systems;
(f) Each State has the duty to comply fully and in good faith with its international obligations and to live in peace with other States.
54 On the subject of sovereign equality of States, *see* A.D. McNair, *Equality in International Law*, 26 MICHIGAN L REV 131-149 (1927); P.J. Baker, *The Doctrine of Legal Equality of States*, 4 BYIL 1-20 (1923/24); H. Kelsen, *The Principle of Sovereign Equality of States as a Basis for International Organization*, 53 YALE L J 207-220 (1944); H. Weinschel, *The Doctrine of Equality of States and its Recent Modification*, 45 AJIL 417-442 (1951); P.H. Kooijimans, *The Doctrine of the Legal Equality of States* (1964); A. Magarasevic, *supra* note 2; G. Evans, *All*

The paradox is that it is precisely through the exercise of the right of States to be "equal" under international law that leads to their material inequalities. This effect follows from the finding that "it is the exercise of [States'] equal sovereignties which has resulted in their unequal rights and duties."[55] Equality is here understood as equality of capacity for rights and obligations. This is the meaning of equality that will be adopted in this book. Equality before the law only assumes that States have equal capacity for acquiring rights and assuming duties, which does not imply that States must have actually identical rights and duties.[56] Under classical international law, which Professor W. Friedmann described in its proper context as the "international law of co-existence",[57] equal capacity is defined as autonomy, capability, and freedom to engage or not engage in such myriad activities as trade, foreign aid, diplomacy, defense and weapons testing, navigation and communication, high seas fishing, outer space exploration, recognition, participation in international organization, and in all other matters falling within the "sovereign prerogative" of a State not otherwise controlled by general international law. But the fact is that States, individually or collectively, execute through this prerogative, foreign policies that inevitably affect the other States' capacity to exercise their rights and

---

States are Equal, But..., 7 REVIEW OF INTERNATIONAL STUDIES 59-66 (1981); V. Pechota, *supra* note 2; R. Anand, *Sovereign Equality of States in International Law*, 197 RECUEIL DES COURS 99-228 (1986-II); P. Slinn, "Implementation of International Obligations Towards Developing States: Equality or Preferential Treatment" in W. Butler (Ed.), *Control Over Compliance With International Law* 165-174 (1991); B. Broms, "States" in M. Bedjaoui (Ed.), *International Law Achievements and Prospects* 60-61 (1991); H. Suganami, "Grotius and International Equality" in H. Bull, B. Kingsbury & A. Roberts (Eds.), *Hugo Grotius and International Relations* 221-240 (1992); C. Warbrick, "The Principle of Sovereign Equality" in V. Lowe and C. Warbrick (Eds.), *The United Nations and the Principles of International Law: Essays in Memory of Michael Akehurst* 204-229 (1994); Lachs, *supra* note 34.

55 Warbrick, *id.*, at 206.
56 Pechota, *supra* note 3 at 464, outlines 4 elements of equality under the law: equal protection, equality *fori*, sovereign immunity, and equal capacity. It is the "equal capacity" meaning of sovereign equality that accounts for the non-identical rights of States. Equality as "equality of capacity for rights and duties" is a principle that was first critically analyzed in E. DeWitt Dickenson, *The Equality of States in International Law* (1920). See McNair, *supra* note 54 at 136-139. *Cf.* Broms, *supra* note 54.
57 Friedmann, *op. cit.*

obligations. This suggests that the resulting inequalities are very much a function of the existing international order founded on the *laissez-faire* operations of consent and consensus.

How then are inequalities – or the disparities in actual State capabilities and in nations' standards of living – produced and maintained by the principle of equality? Equal freedom among States, it must be noted, rests on a strong presumption of non-interference.[58] It is qualified only by a weak rule of non-discrimination in international law and is not tethered by any general norm of positive-discrimination (or affirmative action).[59] As a consequence, the international community where the principle of sovereign equality prevails will consist of States whose parity in power, disposable resources, or material well-being is largely dictated by the overall relationships of exchange and interaction, operating through the practices of consent and reciprocity, among members pursuing their own interests. In this context, self-interest is not inconsistent with the pursuit of "beggar-thy-neighbor" policies:

> The result is, in general international law, that states are able to take advantage of their material advantages to influence the content of international law, and furthermore strong states are better equipped to secure compliance with duties owed to them and to resist attempts to make them perform their own obligations. Whatever the formal equality of states, the substantive law is influenced by the material differences between them, even if it does not mirror them exactly.[60]

The international legal order is, therefore, governed by a fundamental principle, or a primordial legal standard, of "equality" which is observed more in the breach than in the compliance. Conventional law-making between States that have in reality unequal capacities for rights and obligations had historically taken the form of "unequal treaties" – treaties concluded through duress, undue influence, or improper coercion. These "unequal treaties" had on many occasions permanently impaired some States' capacity for further acquiring and exercising rights.[61] Decolonization is as much a process of the new States'

---

58 *See* Weil, *supra* note 48.
59 Warbrick, *supra* note 54, at 207-208.
60 *Id.*, at 210.
61 McNair, *supra* note 54, at 151-152; Pechota, *supra* note 3, at 464.

overcoming the effects of unequal treaties[62] as their acquisition of actual capacity for rights through formal independence. Still, as Lord McNair once asserted, although equality in the sense of "equality in capacity for rights and obligations" does not embody contemporary reality, it is a standard that "much remains of good for application in order to achieve it."[63]

Indeed, international relations analyst would characterize the international community under the regime of co-existence as "anarchical and oligarchical."[64] There is inequality *par excellence* in the international system not because of original and natural inequalities in population, resources, or geographic position when States come into existence. There is inequality because of the unevenness of their subsequent development in industrial civilization and progress[65] as sanctioned by international law. The North-South disparity is immediately comprehensible in this light because the new States which emerged from decolonization found themselves in a position where, notwithstanding their acquired sovereign status, their capacities for rights and obligations were certainly much less consolidated than the corresponding capacities of the established former colonizing States.[66] When these States were admitted to the international community, they had no choice but accept the "loaded dice" of "sovereign equality." Naturally, the powers which have already established themselves much earlier proved themselves with better "equal capacity" to exercise their rights and obligations.[67] All this should make it abundantly clear why the "realist" position in the world (in)equality debate, adverted to earlier, is vindicated by a

---

62 Arts. 48-52 of *The Vienna Convention on the Law of Treaties, supra* note 49, now provides as grounds for the invalidity of treaties "error", "fraud", "corruption", and "coercion."
63 McNair, *supra* note 54, at 152.
64 R. Tucker, *The Inequality of Nations* 3 (1977). *See also* H. Bull, *The Anarchical Society: A Study of Order in World Politics* (1977).
65 Tucker, *ibid*.
66 Bedjaoui, *supra* note 29, at 2 & 6, describes this classical pre-decolonization international "law of co-ordination" (rather than a "law of subordination" of subjects to the community) as an (a) oligarchic law governing relationships between civilized States belonging to an exclusive club; (b) plutocratic law enabling those States to exploit weaker peoples; (c) a non-interventionist law as far as possible, in other words a law just sufficiently detailed on the one hand to allow a wide measure of easy-going *laissez-faire* to the Dominant States in the club and, on the other, to reconcile the freedom to do anything to which each one of these States was entitled.
67 *See* Anand, *supra* note 54, at Chs. III-IV.

Positivist appreciation of "equality" in international law. "Justice is agreed when the necessity is equal; otherwise, the strong do what they must and the weak suffer what they can."[68]

E. GROWING DISPARITIES

There is no question that the "international law of co-existence" does not require States to redress disparities in the international community.[69] Although the Charter of the United Nations introduced the principle of equality as a necessary precondition for the attainment of egalitarian universal aims, like peace, cooperation for progress, and development,[70] the doctrines of equality and autonomy of States have by and large prevailed over the ability of international institutions like the United Nations to create regimes redressing unequal capacities.[71] Thus, the "sovereign equality" principle in international law, in a quite significant way, is responsible for or causative of actual gaps in inter-State socio-economic conditions. The situation has given rise to the following remark:

> [The] enormous inequities among 'all peoples' [in Art. 1(3) of the UN Charter] amount to a comprehensive failure to achieve the Charter's objectives. They are also an escalating threat to world stability and peace. Even with the most effective international machinery such disparities could not have been fully overcome in only fifty years. But the United Nations has not been able to play its Charter role as 'a centre for harmonizing the actions of nations' in this most fundamental and dangerous of problems. It may well be that history will judge this to have been the greatest failure of the world organization in its first fifty years.[72]

This lament should not occasion any surprise, considering that the United Nations, if it were to effectively discharge its "harmonizing" tasks, must solicit the will of each member-State that will have to be brought to bear on the

---

68 *See* Thucydides, *supra* note 35.
69 *See* Warbrick, *supra* note 52, at 208.
70 Magarasevic, *supra* note 2, at 188-189; Pechota, *supra* note 2, at 454-455, 466.
71 Schwarzenberger, *supra* at 49, asserts that the "change in emphasis of the United Nations [from "equality"] to "sovereign equality" does not change the environment of international customary law" based on sovereignty. He would consider the United Nations as a "quasi-order" in international law.
72 Childers & Urquhart, *op. cit.* 54.

challenge of global amelioration. To the extent that all affected States must consent to any programme or regime of positive discrimination,[73] and the historical evidence is clear that this has not generally transpired, disparity will persist. There seems to be no other way of looking at the North-South gap which had widened over time. In a *laissez-faire* setting where conventional or customary international law is generated, the failure or indifference of the more powerful Northern States in establishing conditions[74] that would genuinely create "equality of capacity for rights," especially with respect to the South, would preclude the emergence of universal rules promotive of equality.[75]

The specific effect of *widening* inequalities between the North and the South could be conceived, more significantly, from the viewpoint of *two spheres or domains* where the "equality of capacity for rights" principle may be applied. The first is the domain already regulated by traditional rules or regimes of international law. In this domain, inequalities have existed even before decolonization. This is the enormous field where the doctrine of sovereign equality had been and is being played out within the framework of the international law of co-existence. Activities with international dimensions like trade, navigation, transnational resource extraction, the protection of foreign investments, scientific research, migration, and arms control easily come to mind as illustrative of the international rules and norms which perpetuate if not reproduce disparities among States. Principles like non-discrimination and reciprocity, *pacta sunt servanda*, freedom of the seas, non-interference, and the international standard of compensation operate within this sphere. In this

---

73 Warbrick, *supra* note 54, at 216; Pechota, *supra* note 3, at 475.
74 This indictment against the North is made by Childers & Urquhart, *op. cit.* 55, as follows:
At a time of ever more urgent need for coherent macro-economic strategy and policy for the *whole* world, no such strategy or policy exists or is even under discussion, either in the United Nations or outside it. There is much talk in meetings of the industrial countries about 'the global economy', but on close examination this turns out to be overwhelmingly concerned with their North-North economy.
75 McNair, *supra* note 54, at 152 takes the view that insofar as the principle of equality is taken to mean "equality for law-making purposes", as distinguished from "equality of capacity for rights", the unanimity requirement is a "clog" in legislating universal international law. This is the "orthodox mechanisms of international law-making" referred to by Warbrick, *supra* note 54, at 216, on which depend the implementation of structures and standards to mitigate material differences between States.

traditional domain, "equality of capacity" among States serves as an ideal standard against which the prevailing rules and norms could be assessed. For example, the "generalized system of preferences"/"enabling clause" in the General Agreement on Tariffs and Trade regime is a rule of compensation productive of equality of capacities between rich and poor States. It was intended to counter the rigorous application of the inegalitarian rule of reciprocity in international trade relations. Considering that the consent of the States benefiting from the established rules in the specific domain of trade is required in order to abandon or completely revise rules such as reciprocity, it is to be expected that there has not been much success in realizing "equality of capacity" in this domain. At best, States adversely affected by the established rules can plead for exceptions, as in the GATT regime.[76] From this perspective, it could be maintained that the "under-development"[77] of the South had taken place in these traditional domains of inequality.

The second sphere or domain where the "equality of capacity" principle could find application in a North-South context would be, logically, that which lies outside the regulatory regimes of the classical "international law of coexistence."[78] Historically, the need for international legal regimes in this domain was only felt during or after decolonization. In this *new domain*, no conventional rules have yet been developed and the broadest customary norms or general principles only can be invoked as being applicable. It is because no *specific* rules exist in these domains, that it is proper to consider them as "unregulated" by international law. The domains of extra-territorial spaces are exemplary. Deep seabed mining activities; the exploitation of outer-space, the

---

76 A radical critique of the 'international law of development' asserts that norms concerned with development "can only be exceptions to the legal and economic order of industrial power, and a fragile exception at that." M. Chemillier-Gendreau, "Relations Between the Ideology of Development and the Development of Law" in Snyder & Slinn, *supra* note 29, at 63.
77 The "international law of underdevelopment" was put forward by Professor M. Benchikh. *See* M. Flory, "A North-South Legal Dialogue: The International Law of Development", in Snyder & Slinn, *supra*, note 29 at 14-15. For a description of the relevance of the theory of dependency and under-development in law, *see* S. Adelman & A. Paliwala, "Law and Development in Crisis" in S. Adelman & A. Paliwala (Eds.), *Law and Crisis in the Third World* 1-26 (1993).
78 Pechota, *supra* note 3 at 466, sees this as the domain where equality is applied "outside the limits of international law." The identification of this domain does not necessarily imply that there is *lacunae* involved.

celestial bodies, and other extra-planetary resources; the management of global biodiversity; and the regulation of global atmospheric environments are some domains that fall within this sphere.

In the new domain of inequality the possibility is ever-present of invoking or applying overly-broad and highly general, autonomy-based, rules or principles that would likely lead to more North-South inequalities of capacity (and, therefore, very likely to lead to further disparities in standards of living). One such rule, arising from the doctrine of sovereign equality, is exemplified by the principle laid down in the *SS Lotus* case: that there can be no presumption of restrictions or limitations upon the sovereignty or independence of States.[79] This rule assumes that States should be considered under the law as theoretically equal in initial capacities, even if in fact they are not. Inasmuch as there is a posited equal freedom of all States in all matters not regulated by international law.[80] the practical effect of applying this doctrine of equality in the new domain would be a higher degree of factual inequality of capacity for rights among States in favor of the States which are initially stronger or more powerful in a material sense.

As in the traditional domain of inequality among States, the only way of avoiding the emergence of disparity through the operation of general customary law in the new domain is through the consensual process of regime-creation through international convention. This strategy to uphold equality of capacity in the new domain may be coupled with *ad interim* arrangements to prevent the pre-emption of the law by the more powerful States, as suggested by some authorities:

> Given the competitive nature of international relations, the freedom of action in these spheres [*i.e.,* in the "new domain"] is a relative quality fluctuating with the circumstances and possessed by different states in a different degree, but in no case absolutely and finally as it is by the major powers. Applied to such operations as harnessing the resources of the deep sea-bed – activities yet unregulated by positive international law – the doctrine conduces in the final analysis to the perpetuation of factual inequality and prejudices future international regulation. The only way in which the international community can avert such developments is

---

79 *SS Lotus Case (France v. Turkey)* 1927 PCIJ Rep. Series A. No. 10, at 19. *See also* Jennings and Watts, *supra* note 44, at 390-391.
80 *See Asylum Case (Columbia v. Peru)* 1950 ICJ Rep at 275, on equal rights to qualify offenses for the purpose of diplomatic asylum.

to fill the legal vacuums and pending the emergence of new international rules to arrange for moratoria on the prejudicial activities.[81]

In sum, disparities among States in a North-South context, *i.e.,* the unequal capacities for rights and obligations between rich and poor States, are growing because of the impact and on account of the effects of the principle of sovereign equality in two domains: first, in the "traditional domain" where the rich States have always enjoyed their freedom or the exercise of their superior positions in sovereign equality; and secondly, in the "new domain" where they can potentially extend or establish such freedom or assert the right to autonomy, non-interference and/or sovereign equality. The validity of these two domains is a corollary and a reasonable reinterpretation of two paramount processes in the Positivist conception of international law-making, described as follows:

> As a system of legally binding principles and norms governing relations of the members of the international community, international law, too, has to reflect the changing conditions within this community. Continuous law-making becomes a natural political-legal response of a developing legal system to new community problems and needs. Broadly speaking, there are two basic ways in which the international legal system can accommodate the changing needs and demands for normative regulations. The first involves law-making in new areas thus far ungoverned by international law; the second reflects the need for a constant upgrading and refinement of already existing law.[82]

International law founded on the fundamental principle of "sovereign equality" leads to widening disparities in the capacity of States for rights and obligations – in both old and new domains of law – because there had been more emphasis on the "sovereignty" or autonomy/non-interference element of the principle than on the other element of "equality", *i.e.,* "equality of capacity for rights and obligations." This, in brief, is the basis for the "international law of global disparities."

---

81 Pechota, *supra* note 3, at 466. Note that Professor Pechota assumes that there are "legal vacuums" (*lacunae*) involved, notwithstanding his admission that the principle of freedom, or the *SS Lotus* principle, can have possible application. Anent this concept of *lacunae*, see H. Lauterpacht, *The Function of Law in the International Community* 70 *et seq.* (1966).
82 Danilenko, *supra* note 31, at 1.

F. THE INTERNATIONAL LAW OF GLOBAL DISPARITIES

It is thus apparent that Positivist international law, which provides the regulative framework for defining the relations and interactions of States based on the rule of sovereign equality, has a pivotal role to play in an inegalitarian international community. Whether the world community of States is viewed as a basically well-ordered system or a predominantly anarchic society, the international legal order of equally sovereign but unequally empowered States is an essential fact of the global social landscape and its organization. As it was examined, a Positivist application of international law is the normative backbone of this social order and definitely assumes a crucial position in the perception, production, and regulation of global disparities and, consequently, the prevailing international social hierarchy.

The relationship of the content and overall structure of international law to actual world conditions of disparity is admittedly more complex than what the preceding doctrinal analysis of sovereign equality reveals. Although it cannot be asserted too hastily that there is a direct causal relationship between all the fundamental strictures of international law, on the one hand, and reality of world disparities, on the other, neither can it be maintained that whatever connection there exists between them is merely accidental or contingent. There is little doubt that post-war international law had always been central to the real-life drama of deepening global disparities. The "international law of disparities" is a reasonable inference from the stubborn persistence of these disparities in the old and new domains. Thus, if a tree is known by its fruit, as an aphorism puts it, the character or ethos of international law, or the post-war international legal framework, admits of definitive characterization. On this metaphor, is difficult to deny that an international law which produces, or sustains, or is largely indifferent to conditions of world inequality is simply and plainly an inegalitarian international law.[83] That much is clear. One need not look into the vast details of the substance and process of international law to prove that the contemporary law of nations has indeed the effect of spawning greater inter-State disparities. The treatment of States as formally equal under the postulates of international law should not conceal the fact that the conduct

---

83 This echoes a parallel sentiment that if international law "maintains underdevelopment, it will be an international law of underdevelopment". M. Benchikh, *Droit international du sous-développement, Nouvel ordre dans la dépendance* quoted in Flory, *supra* note 77, at 15.

of juridical relations by States through the operations of doctrinal rules in international law, directly or indirectly, leads to more global inequality and more unequal capacities. The conclusion is unavoidable that international law, understood from a Positivist perspective, is constitutive of the current system of global inequality.

This study may initially be described as an exploration into the "international law of global disparities." The parody is deliberate, as the term does not lend itself to an investigation of the problem of formal "sources" of international law,[84] and if only to highlight the obvious fact that international law in the past half-century has greatly succeeded in maintaining the appropriate conditions for an increasingly inegalitarian world. The irony behind the label is realistic, inasmuch as the description "international law of global disparities" tests the idealized image of a legally-ordered world consisting of States with basically unlimited, unhindered sovereign powers pursuing the business of international life in accordance with the dictates of their full independence and formal equality. Rather than make us believe in the lofty egalitarian inspiration and goals of contemporary international law – already a myth insofar as its general record of "underdevelopment" in the past fifty years would show[85] – the "international law of global disparities" asks for a more truthful and sober appreciation of international law, its functions, and its consequences. As a hypothetical construct, or an analytic frame or reference for the investigation of global inequality, the tree "international law of global disparities" provides a reasonable framework for a critical analysis of the major "branches" or specific regulatory regimes of international law, like the law of the sea explored in this book. Consistent with the observed facts and trends on inter-State inequalities, the "international law of global disparities" imputes a specific function to the principle of sovereign equality and inquires into the prospects of fulfilling or attaining the legal standard of "equality of capacity for rights and obligations."

Positing the threshold concept of "international law of global disparities" would also raise, from a methodological point of view, the paramount question of its falsifiability. This is the more essential point in advancing such a notion using a Positivist perspective. At a time of growing suspicion and despair in the ability of international law to cope with the concrete problems dramatized by the issue of global inequality, it is necessary to offer proof, if proof there

---

84 *See* Art. 38, Statute of the International Court of Justice, *supra*, note 1.
85 *See* Urquhart & Childers, *op. cit.*

is, that the prevalent international law of "co-ordination" or "co-existence" – in other words, the Positivist understanding and application of international law – can serve as a legitimate technical instrument to achieve world equality.[86] Otherwise put, the challenge is to determine whether international law is still a useful political instrument and a feasible resource available to those who advocate *less* global disparities. Since it is conceivable that the future of a viable rule of law in global society will increasingly rely on the volatile political-economy of world inequality,[87] falsifying the "international law of global disparities" is of great importance to all States, not least to the actors in international civil society who look up to the State as a key institution in global reform and transformation. Had the tree of international law bore a different fruit, which could make us believe that the pursuit of an egalitarian global order could be part of the *authentic* business of international law conceived in its Positivist moment? The inquiry is thus directed to the question of whether or not international law has had its exceptional or defining moments, when it was able to contribute in significant measure to the lessening of global disparities. If so, it should be asked, "why?" and "how?".

The "international law of global disparities" should serve as a useful backdrop to the analysis of specific norms and novel concepts in international law, like the Common Heritage of Humanity. Is the Common Heritage of Humanity principle, or the specific regime where it is expressed and embodied, a valid rule of law which can be cited as an instance that falsifies the thesis of an "international law of global disparities?" Or, assuming the existence of the "international law of global disparities," is the Common Heritage of Humanity principle an expression or a manifestation of an opposing event in this "system" of law? If so, how does it impact on this framework of international law? If not, what is its significance within the "international law of global disparities?" Why is the Common Heritage of Humanity principle a crucial test in the emergence or submergence of the "international law of global disparities?" How can the lessons learned in the evolution of this principle be utilized by those

---

86 This point could be addressed to a positivist like Professor P. Weil who was quoted as saying "I am convinced that in order to carry out a good policy [*e.g.,* less global disparities], States need good law; I mean by that an instrument which is technically adapted to the ends which they want to achieve." *See* Flory, *supra* note 77, at 19.

87 Childers & Urquhart, *op. cit.* 53, warns of "expanding violence unless global equity and sustainable development are urgently addressed."

who aspire for a less inegalitarian world? Could the Common Heritage of Humanity principle be further developed and generalized as a technique against the rising tide of the "international law of global disparities?"[88] These questions unavoidably lead us to a detailed discussion of global disparity in the context of the international law of the sea.

---

88 The methodology that I propose here for the investigation of the Common Heritage of Humanity, using a hypothetical "international law of global disparities" as conceptual backdrop, refers to a critical suggestion of Professor Schwarzenberger, positivist *par excellence*, who once pointed out – with some touch of exasperated irritation – the need to assess the so-called "international law of development" in terms of its possible opposites:
It may be salutary to reflect on the helpfulness in assessing the claims in favour of an International Development Law (or International Economic Development Law) in light of
(a) a possible complementary branch of International Law on the *International Law* (or International Economic Law) *of Retrogression*, with special reference to the impact of the revival of autarkism and protectionism, chronic state insolvency and changing functions of international economic and financial institutions; *and*
(b) a hypothetical *International Law* (or International Economic Law) *of Non-Development* for the re-establishment and protection of more static communities that, in Benthamite terms of the greatest happiness for the greatest number, had not done too badly across millennia before their unasked "development." (Italics in the original)
This remark was one of his "parting thoughts" after he expressed serious misgivings about the utility of the "international law of development."
See G. Schwarzenberger, "Meaning and Functions of International Development Law" in F. Snyder & P. Slinn, *supra* note 28, at 55.
A consistently positivist methodological approach to the study of the Common Heritage of Humanity would, furthermore, find support in another statement made by Professor Schwarzenberger, that the "[c]ombined application of the framework- and perspective-concepts [like the 'international law of global disparities' and 'global inequality'] makes it possible to deal on a rationally verifiable or falsifiable footing with complex and controversial issues of an interdisciplinary character."
See G. Schwarzenberger, "The Conceptual Apparatus of International Law" in Macdonald & Johnston, *supra* note 3, at 685-712.

Conclusion

The reality of global disparity invites a unique reflection on the nature and character of the international community as it stands today. If the legal order that governs this community plays a significant role in the creation and perpetuation of inequalities among States by exacerbating the already serious North-South gap, it is fitting to ask whether such kind of community is worth preserving, and at what price. At the same time, it should be asked whether the structure of the international legal order has elements within it that can contribute in a sustained way to a more egalitarian community. Are there reasons to believe that international law, in positive doctrine and in practical application, can soon be made to work significantly in the service of less, and lessening, international disparity?

The equalization of all States' capacities for rights and obligations is an ideal towards which international law may legitimately be directed. It is an ideal that is founded on the principle of "sovereign equality" – a principle, however, whose exact opposite has been realized in practice. Inequality among States is reproduced and reinforced by the principle of equality in the setting of an international community that is wholly constituted by autonomous co-existing States. In this setting, individual States are free to choose the extent to which other States' capacities for rights and obligations should equal their own. It is a society where, unless its more powerful members would agree otherwise, the strong do what they must and the weak suffer what they can. Consent, as the key aspect of law-making among States, defines the quantity and the quality of "sovereign equality" that obtains in the international community. This conception of the international community provides justification for the hypothesis of an "international law of global disparities": those who have more get more and those who have less get less, if at all.

If the emphasis of international law is, therefore, shifted away from familiar fictive assumption that sovereign States are always equal, and towards the assumption made under the international law of global disparities that the concrete practices of "sovereign equality" create and sustain conditions for the emergence of more factual inequalities among States, the entire business of statecraft and international law-making – which had hitherto been conducted on the grand, grinding pillar of State autonomy and sovereignty – is exposed to wide critical scrutiny. In the first place, the international law of global disparities challenges the prospects of a meaningful North-South "dialogue" in the sphere of international law-making. In the absence of a significant amelioration of the North-South divide in the post-war and post-cold war international community, a total rejuvenation or even reconceptualization of the North-South dialogue seems to be imperative. The North-South dialogue, it would appear, requires a new normative basis if it is to genuinely move forward. Secondly, the role of universal international organizations, like the United Nations, in confronting the international law of global disparities will need to be examined afresh. The much bewailed "development crisis"[89] is very much a function of the failure of the United Nations as a collective will for global sharing and the pursuit of North-South equity. But the intensification of demands for development[90] means more – not less – multilateralism in the global arena. Last but not the least, to the extent that the reality of the international law of global disparities emanates from a Positivist appreciation of international legal relations, its persistence can be explained by the deep and perhaps unquestioning attachment that States and individuals alike have to a policy/conceptual apparatus that prophesies nothing else but growing inequality and the untethered freedom of States to be grossly unequal from one another in their capacity for rights and obligations. The abandonment of a positivist interpetation of the international community may offer States, and for that matter the international community itself, with some other possibilities about how international society can be re-constituted at the normative plane.

It is submitted that the history of the Common Heritage of Humanity principle in the context of the new law of the sea illuminates most distinctly the practices or methods of the international law of global disparities. More specifically, the evolution of the principle throws light on the normative process involved in the generation of new inequalities, or new differentials in legal capacity, among States. But it is the dynamic relationship between new inequalities and the inequalities perpetuated by the traditional norms of international law (or the relationship between the new and old domains of disparity)

---

89 *See* An Agenda for Development, *op. cit.*; Adelman & Paliwala, *op. cit.*

90 *See* Report of the South Commission, *Challenge to the South* (1990); *Declaration on International Economic Cooperation*, *supra*, note 13; *An Agenda for Peace*, UN Doc. A/47/277; S/24111 (17 June 1992), pars. 3, 75-76; B. Boutros-Ghali, *Agenda for Peace – One Year Later* 37 ORBIS 323 (1993); *Declaration of the World Summit for Social Development*, *supra*, note 4, para. 10 & 11. *See also Our Global Neighbourhood*, *op. cit.* In his *An Agenda for Development*, *op. cit.* para. 1 & 235, UN Secretary-General Boutros-Ghali conceives of "Development" as a fundamental human right linking five major dimensions of peace, economy, environment, society, and democracy.

that captures the staying power of the international law of global disparities. This relationship is best illustrated in the normative development of the law of the sea.

II

WORLD INEQUALITY AND THE 1982 UNITED NATIONS CONVENTION ON THE LAW OF THE SEA

A. Domains of Disparity in the Law of the Sea – Old and New

The 1982 United Nations Convention Law of the Sea is a comprehensive document that seeks to address the complex diversity of ocean-related needs and requirements of the international community. Negotiations on the Convention did not only take into account issues around the North-South divide but encompassed a whole range of concerns constituted along geographical, regional, and politico-ideological lines. Developed and developing countries alike banded and disbanded into alignments to form interest group categories like coastal States, land-locked and geographically disadvantaged States, archipelagic States, broad-margin States, or even "Good Samaritan" States.[1] The significance of these and all other interest categories in the making of a comprehensive law of the sea regime need not be overemphasized. Although the Third United Nations Conference on the Law of the Sea (UNCLOS III) which produced the new regime may be criticized as an overly long-drawn exercise (it took over ten tears for UNCLOS III to conclude its business), the protracted negotiations was precisely the price to be paid for the accommodation of all interest claims in the new legal order of the oceans. The product, as is well known, is a constitutional deal[2] which is perhaps the most gigantic redistributive undertaking in modern history. UNCLOS III was an outstanding success not basically because it was able to resolve every issue on its agenda – this proved quite impossible

---

1   *Cf.*, the categories of States employed in the text of the Convention as identified and listed in IV COMMENTARY 756-757.
2   Tommy Koh, the President of UNCLOS III who presided over its conclusion, describes the 1982 Convention as "A Constitution for the Oceans." *See* CLOS at xxxiii-xxxvii. The term "Constitution for the Oceans" as a reference to the work of UNCLOS III appears to have been first used in E.M. Borgese, "A Constitution for the Oceans" in E.M. Borgese & D. Krieger (Eds.), *Tides of Change* 340 (1975).

to accomplish under the circumstances. It was a success because the Conference brought together all States representing the widest range of ocean-related interests so that they could agree to settle *all* issues on the law of the sea.[3] The basis of this ambitious project was the recognition that "the problems of ocean space are closely interrelated and need to be considered as a whole."[4] For the first time in the history of international law-making, the ambit of political negotiations comprehended all manner of State interests impinging on every conceivable use of ocean space. Universality with respect to both issues raised and participation engendered at UNCLOS III is surely the enduring legacy of the 1982 Convention on the Law of the Sea.

The well-known split between the industrialized States and the States in the Group of 77 dramatized at UNCLOS III concerning one particular element on its agenda – namely, "the Area", or the regime of deep seabed mining[5] – should properly be viewed against the backdrop of the universality of ocean problems dealt with in the Conference. This appreciation arises from the constitutional character of the Convention, being one complex matrix of authoritative decisions concerning all ocean problems of which the deep seabed issue – an issue that finds no precedent in international law making – is only one aspect. But how important and crucial is the deep seabed issue in relation to the other issues resolved in Convention?

How one views the relationship between the deep seabed provisions of the Convention, on the one hand, and its non-deep seabed provisions, on the other, depends on a prior assessment of North-South relations as reflected in the Convention as a whole. Two competing schools of thought are readily identifiable in this regard. First, under the so-called "package deal" interpretation of the 1982 Convention,[6] the novel deep seabed regime is blended integrally with the other regimes under the Convention as a unified package of North-South bargains constitutive of the new ocean order. The deep seabed regime established by the Convention is thus as important, as indispensable, and as compelling as the other regimes thereunder.

---

3   *See* P. Allot, *Power Sharing in the Law of the Sea* 77 AJIL 1 (1983).
4   *See* first and third preambular paragraphs of 1982 Convention on the Law of the Sea.
5   *I.e.*, Part XI of the 1982 Convention.
6   *See e.g.,* T. Koh, *supra* note 2, at xxxiv; J. Evensen, "The Effect of the Law of the Sea Convention Upon the Process of International Law: Rapprochement Between Competing Points of View" in R. Krueger & S. Riesenfeld (Eds.), *The Developing Order of the Oceans 23-40* (LSI, 1985).

The other school of thought regards the original deep seabed regime spelled out under Part XI of the 1982 Convention as the outcome of an increasingly outmoded ideological strife, a contest over symbols,[7] between the North and the South. It should, therefore, be recast completely,[8] if not totally severed from the Convention,[9] in order to make it more relevant and responsive to practical community needs.[10] Consequently, the North-South controversy surrounding the deep seabed regime under the Convention – while certainly an interesting facet of the new order of the oceans – should not come in the way of making all the other more practical and weighty provisions of the 1982 Convention fully operative – such as the rules governing navigation, marine scientific research, military uses of the seas, or fisheries.[11]

It is important at this point to underline a very important qualitative difference between the seabed and the non-seabed provisions in the 1982 Convention on the Law of the Sea. This decisive difference lies in the fact that Part XI defines a new resource or a new ocean space in the legal order of the oceans,

---

7   See E. Miles, "An Interpretation of the Negotiation Process of UNCLOS III" in R.St. J. Macdonald (Ed.), *supra* note 34 Chap. I, at 551-565.
8   This advocacy comes from those who had all along objected to Part XI on grounds of "principle" and "precedent." See J. Sebenius, *Negotiating the Law of the Sea* 17, 82, 103-104 (1984).
9   The argument was, therefore, put forward to "split off Part XI from the rest of the Convention" in keeping with "new thinking." See J.N. Moore "Renegotiating Part XI: Ensuring an Effective Seabed Mining Regime" in Nordquist, *infra* note 11 at 239-246, and *infra* Chap. V note 293.
10 See for *e.g.*, E.D. Brown, *The International Law of the Sea*, Vol. 1 at 445 (1994), on the view that Part XI of the Convention is "of least practical importance in the short-to-medium term." The argument, it must be noted, rests on the assumption that the disputed deep seabed provisions of the Convention are solely and exclusively concerned with deep seabed mining. See for *e.g.*, J. Barkenbus, *Deep Seabed Resources: Politics and Technology* (1979); A. Hollick, *United States Foreign Policy and the Law of the Sea* (1981). The 1994 Implementation Agreement generally adopts this attitude with respect to Part XI of the Convention. *Infra* Chapter V. Because the prospects of deep seabed mining have receded far into the next century, the entire deep seabed issue has become moot, if not altogether retrograde, *vis-à-vis* the Convention as a whole.
11 The familiar variant of this argument is to consider the non-seabed regimes of the Convention as established in customary law. See for *e.g.*, W. Schachte, "The Value of the Non-Deep Seabed Provisions: Preserving our Freedoms and Balancing Our Interests" M.H. Nordquist (Ed.), *15th Annual Seminar of the Center for Ocean Law and Policy: Issues in Amending Part XI of the Convention* 29-42 (1991).

a previously unchartedy frontier in international law making. The element of novelty is crucial, because if we follow the logic of the hypothesized "international law of global disparities" outlined in the previous Chapter, the deep seabed regime would then stipulate a new use of the ocean that could potentially generate a "new domain" of North-South disparity. Here is a new subject matter in international law where a new allocation of capacities for rights and obligations among States had been made. From the point of view of the "international law of global disparities", it is irrelevant whether the deep seabed regime is already irrevocable international law or whether it is considered as having the least practical importance to the international community. The main issue is whether existing global inequalities in States' capacities for rights and obligations can be potentially extended and amplified in this legal frontier. What needs to be ascertained in a definitive manner is whether the deep seabed regime laid down in Part XI of the Convention contradicts or participates in the international law of global disparities.

But the hypothesis of the international law of global disparities also invites equal attention to the non-deep seabed provisions of the Convention, concerned with the regimes of territorial waters, fishing zones, the continental shelf, the high seas, scientific research, marine pollution, etc. These regimes could very well be evaluated against the background of the "traditional" domain of disparity in the international law of the sea.[12] If the redistribution of capacities for rights and obligations effected under the 1982 Convention with respect to the traditional regimes in the law of the sea had resulted in more equality among States, the North-South controversy over the deep seabed regime may indeed prove academic. For we now have in any case a Convention that overthrows the thesis that the structure and contemporary processes of international law facilitate the intesification of inequality within the international community. This repudiation, however, needs investigation. The task of the present Chapter is to look into the non-seabed regimes established by the 1982 Convention to

---

12 UNCLOS I was convened in 1958 and saw the adoption of four Conventions dealing with: the Territorial Sea and Contiguous Zone; the High Seas; Fishing and Conservation of Living Resources on the High Seas, and; the Continental Shelf. UNCLOS II, which followed in 1960, failed to resolve the unsettled question in UNCLOS I concerning of the extent of the Territorial Sea and the limits of fisheries jurisdiction. In relation to the agenda of UNCLOS III convened in 1973, the agenda covered by UNCLOS I & II would be "traditional."

determine whether there was at all any alleviation in the traditional domain of North-South disparity in the law of the sea.

B. DISPARITY AND THE 1982 CONVENTION: PREAMBULAR ASPECTS

An initial impression of the relationship between the "international law of global disparities", as postulated in the previous Chapter, and the 1982 UN Convention on the Law of the Sea may be gleaned from a reading of the Convention's Preamble. Here, in addition to the foremost reference on the "historic significance of the Convention as an important contribution to the maintenance of peace, justice and progress for all peoples of the world," there is an unambiguous declaration of intent that the Convention as a whole aims to redress the problem of North-South imbalances in a significant way:[13]

---

13 *See* first, fourth, fifth, and seventh Preambular paragraphs, CLOS. In any sociological and legal analysis of the 1982 Convention, I would emphasize the usefulness, and even necessity, of giving due attention to its preamble – the most solemn part of the document that sets out its broad goals and inspirations. For an authoritative interpretation of the Preamble, *see President's Report on the work of the Informal Plenary on the Preamble,* UN Docs. A/CONF.62/L.49 and Adds. 1-2 (27/29 March 1980), XIII UNCLOS III Off Rec 78-80. A positivist outlook on the Convention does not disregard these goals and inspirations in the exegesis of text, but must take them into account if a dynamic and instrumental conception of the Convention as international law is to brought about, *i.e.,* a law that can be interpreted as responsive and can be meaningfully adjusted to changing social conditions. *See* Vienna Convention on the Law of Treaties, Art. 31. Text in 8 ILM 679 (1969). Resort to the preamble is important to clarify broad legislative policies, *see* I COMMENTARY at 450-467, and to specify more concretely the function of the Convention in promoting common aims. *See also,* Weil, *supra* Chap. I note 48, at 419-420. Even if it is assumed that the negotiators at UNCLOS III had originally different political motivations and purposes in coming together to reform the law of the sea, the Preamble at least provides a formulation of a fundamental consensus on retrospective, prospective and introspective aspects of the entire UNCLOS III exercise. *See e.g.,* M. Bennouna, "The Multidimensional Character of the New Law of the Sea" in R.-J. Dupuy & D. Vignes (Eds.) I *A Handbook on the New Law of the Sea* 3-28, at 19 (1991) [the package deal in the new law of the sea was designed to serve the "right to development" and "strengthen the international community's efforts to reduce existing economic inequalities"].

Recognizing the desirability of establishing through this Convention, with due regard for the sovereignty of all States, a legal order for the seas and oceans which will facilitate international communication, and will promote peaceful uses of the seas and oceans, the equitable and efficient utilization of their resources, the conservation of their living resources, and the study, protection and preservation of the marine environment,

Bearing in mind that *the achievement of these goals will contribute to the realization of a just and equitable international economic order which takes into account the interests and needs of mankind as a whole and, in particular, the special interests and needs of developing countries, whether coastal or land-locked,*

Desiring by this Convention to develop the principles embodied in resolution 2749 (XXV) of 17 December 1970 in which the General Assembly of the United Nations solemnly declared *inter alia* that the area of the sea-bed and ocean floor and the subsoil thereof, beyond the limits of national jurisdiction, as well as its resources, are *the common heritage of mankind, the exploration and exploitation of which shall be carried out for the benefit of mankind as a whole, irrespective of the geographical location of States,*

Believing that the codification and progressive development of the law of the sea achieved in this Convention *will contribute to the strengthening of peace, security, cooperation and friendly relations among all nations in conformity with the principles of justice and equal rights and will promote the economic and social advancement of all peoples of the world, in accordance with the Purposes and Principles of the United Nations as set forth in the Charter*[.] (Emphasis mine)

What can logically be inferred from these clauses invoking "progress for all peoples", "equitable and efficient utilization" of ocean resources, "a just international economic order", "benefit of humanity as a whole", "justice and equal rights" for the "advancement of all peoples", and above all the "special interests and needs of developing countries"[14] is the conclusion that the Convention

---

14 The Convention does not define the term "developing States" even if it uses the term repeatedly in the text of the Convention. The United Nations has, however, established criteria for determining whether a State is developing or not. *See* IV COMMENTARY at 104. For the contribution of UNCLOS III in imparting legal significance to the term, *see* A. Fatouros, "Developing States" in R. Bernhardt (Ed.), 9 *Encyclopedia of International Law* 71-77 at 76-77 (1986).

addresses in a central way the problem of North-South disparity.[15] Historically, this is obviously demonstrated by the negotiations that took place before and during the UNCLOS III, where various "framework" issues along North-South lines were identified.[16] The Convention and its various regimes may hence be regarded as the outcome (or the integral set of results) of the North-South dialogue carried out in the UNCLOS III.[17] It is the Preamble, as the capping statement of the Convention, which captures the political, historical, and even ideological context[18] of such an outcome. The detailed provisions of the Convention acquire basic intelligibility through the interpretive frame of reference supplied by its Preamble. Thus, the legal aspects of the Preamble to the Convention should not be ignored by those called upon to interpret or apply this instrument,[19] inasmuch as the Preamble gives the broad normative outlook, or the comprehensive policy backdrop, against which specific rights and obligations in the Convention can be assessed in their proper context. It is indeed a partial study that simply investigates the particulars of the operational regimes in the Convention without any allusion to the basic North-South agenda of development and global sharing – inescapably derived from a reading of the Convention's Preamble. The North-South dialogue did provide much of the impetus behind the formation of norms, rules and institutions in the contemporary Law of the Sea.

While there is no question that the Convention, by its own terms, attempts to play a critical role in redressing the issues and concerns of the South in the important sphere of ocean law, it is probably premature to evaluate the exact impact of the Convention on existing global disparities, *i.e.,* to assess how it had successfully realized its acknowledged vision of narrowing the development

---

15   *Cf.* Preamble of the "Agreement relating to the Implementation of Part XI of the United Nations Convention on the Law of the Sea of 10 December 1982", highlighting "universal participation" as an objective of the Convention. *See* UN Doc. A/RES/48/263, Annex (17 August 1994).

16   *See* Bennouna, *supra* note 13; R. Friedheim, *Negotiating the New Ocean Regime* (1993).

17   *See* CA Jones, *The North-South Dialogue: A Brief History* at 67-71, 125-127 (1983).

18   "Context" in treaty interpretation is defined in Art. 31 (2) of the Vienna Convention on the Law of Treaties. *See also* I COMMENTARY at 466.

19   I COMMENTARY at 455.

gap between North and South. As the Convention has just entered into force,[20] and since the most serious "obstacle" to its universal acceptance, relating to Part XI of the Convention, is believed to have been only recently removed,[21] a definitive account of its overall effect in alleviating the deepening global disparities may have to wait for some time. What should probably be elaborated at the present juncture are the likely consequences of the specific regimes of global wealth distribution embodied in the Convention on the evolution of the capacities for rights and obligations of States under the new legal order of the oceans.

Moreover, it should be emphasised that the entry into force of the Convention, together with the movement towards universality in its participation, renders the Convention a most authoritative instrument in the pursuit and realization of the goals and aspirations of the international community which are amply described in the preambular clauses of the Convention.[22] If it is true that the efficacy of a normative instrument with respect to the achievement of specific goals is directly related to its unambiguous positivity[23] the Convention as a whole is a consummate tool, offering a solid normative basis, in bringing about the fulfillment of legitimate community expectations. Paramount among these expectations is "a just and equitable international economic order which takes into account the interests and needs of mankind as a whole and, in particular, the special interests and needs of developing countries, whether coastal or land-locked."[24] The acknowledgement of this expectation or legislative objective in the Preamble of the Convention is an indicator that the Convention is undoubtedly a path-breaking accomplishment in the harmonious ordering of international relations. From the perspective of the developing countries, notwithstanding the disappointments in consolidating egalitarian international rules *lex lata* concerning the land-based agenda of the New Inter-

---

20 Of the 60 required ratifications that allowed the Convention to enter into force, all but one (Iceland) were by developing States.
21 *See infra* Chap. V, Sec. C, on the 1994 Implementation Agreement.
22 *See* Art. 31, Vienna Convention on the Law of Treaties.
23 Weil, *op. cit.*
24 The specific *function* of the law of the sea, as a particular normative order, is not only to strengthen co-existence but also to foster co-operation among States party to the Convention. *See id.*, at 418-419. The reference to "a just and equitable international economic order" in the Preamble is broader than, and transcends, the "new international economic order" (NIEO) of the mid-1970s. *See* I COMMENTARY at 462 and its footnote no. 23.

national Economic Order (NIEO),[25] the principle of equality in capacity for rights and obligations among States in the ocean sphere had apparently been advanced successfully in the normative *terra firma* of the 1982 Convention on the Law of the Sea.

The purpose of this Chapter is to identify the specific regimes in the 1982 Convention which bear directly on the question of traditional North-South disparities in the law of the sea. In contrast to current exegetical representations of the international law governing these traditional domains, which assume that the newly established regimes involved can be analyzed independently of the interpretive context supplied by the Preamble to the Convention,[26] the discussion in this Chapter will attempt to bond the specific rules governing traditional regulatory areas in the law of the sea with the central aim, function, or purpose of the new ocean regime agreed upon in UNCLOS III – that of narrowing the disparity between the North and the South.

The section that follows will consider how the North-South agenda emerged in UNCLOS III, as seen in the debates that culminated in the decision to convene

---

25 See e.g. G. White, "The New International Economic Order: Principles and Trends" in H. Fox (Ed.), *International Economic Law and Developing States* 27-57 (1992) for an examination of NIEO principles against the backdrop of predominantly land-based issues like debt relief, foreign direct investment in relation to permanent sovereignty over natural resources, development assistance, and human rights. For contrasting evaluations of the NIEO as a normative project, *see* M. Bedjaoui, *Towards a New International Economic Order* (1979) and R. Olson, *United States Foreign Policy and the New International Economic Order: Negotiating Global Problems: 1974-1981* (1981). For the discussion of the legal issues involved, *see* e.g., Symposium on the New International Economic Order 16 VA J INT L No. 2 (1975-76); K. Hossain (Ed.), *Legal Aspects of the New International Economic Order* (1980); N. Horn, *Normative Problems of a New International Economic Order* 16 JWTL 338-351 (1982); JK Gamble, Jr. & M. Fraukoska, *International Law's Response to the New International Economic Order: An Overview* 9 BOSTON COLL INT & COMP L R 257-291 (1986); E.-U. Petersmann, "The New International Economic Order: Principles, Politics and International Law" in McDonald & Johnston, *supra* Chap. I note 3, at 449-461; J. Makarczyk, *Principles of a New International Economic Order: A Study of International Law in the Making* (1988); G. Marceau, *Some Evidence of a New International Economic Order in Place* 22 REVUE GENERALE DE DROIT 397-410 (1991); and NIEO discussion in ASIL Proc 459-487 (1993).
26 *See e.g.,* R.R. Churchill & A.V. Lowe, *The Law of the Sea* (2nd ed., 1988); ED Brown, *The International Law of the Sea*, 2 Vols. (1994); and T. Clingan, *The Law of the Sea: Ocean Law and Policy* (1994).

UNCLOS III. It will briefly review the material arguments behind the Third World claims for less disparity in the traditional domains of inequality in the Law of the Sea. The next two sections will then go into the assessment of specific regimes that were negotiated in UNCLOS III to meet the requirements of this North-South agenda. In the last section, the revitalization of these regimes in the context of significant international policy developments in 1990s will be described. These policy developments relate to the ocean-related deliberations and outputs of the 1992 United Nations Conference on Environment and Development (UNCED). UNCED, it will be argued, transformed the underpinnings of North-South legal relations as defined in the 1982 Law of the Sea Convention (UNCLOS). On the basis of the normative interconnections between the "UNCLOS process" and "UNCED process", which will be examined in detail, the concluding section of the Chapter will summarize the prospects of an emerging "international law of sustainable development." It will be argued that the "international law of sustainable development" fulfills the requirements of North-South cooperation in the post-UNCED era of ocean governance; it is also the alternative to the "international law of global disparities" in the law of the sea.

C. UNCLOS III:
The North-South Agenda in the Traditional Domains

The organization of work in UNCLOS III reveals the different dimensions and intensities of the North-South rift that attended this historic law-making exercise for the oceans. The three main Committees tasked to deliberate on the substantive agenda of UNCLOS III were allocated issues that more or less addressed the areas of perceived inequality in the law of the sea:

First Committee – Sea-Bed and Ocean Floor, and Subsoil Thereof, Beyond the Limits of National Jurisdiction;
Second Committee – General Law of the Sea, including in Particular the Territorial Sea, Straits, Economic Zone, Continental Shelf, High Seas, Land-Locked States' Access, Archipelagoes, Regime of Islands, Enclosed or Semi-Enclosed Seas;
Third Committee – Marine Environment, Marine Scientific Research and Transfer of Technology.[27]

---

27 For the allocation of agenda items to the three Committees, *see* UN Doc. A/Conf.62/28 (1974), III UNCLOS III Off Rec 57.

The mission of the Second and Third Committees was clearly to undertake an all-out review of the pre-existing, "traditional", "classical" law of the sea.[28] The classical law of the sea coincides with and defines the "traditional domains" of North-South inequality in the Law of the Sea. This classical, or traditional, law of the sea had defied many previous attempts at satisfactory codification, the last three having left unresolved the major question of the breadth of the territorial sea, including fisheries limits.[29] But UNCLOS III was not basically intended as a gap-filling exercise to codify or develop more completely the classical law of the sea. It was convened, more importantly, "to make new law which will, in many essential respects, be absolutely novel."[30] The reasons for this high ambition are generally known. As Professor Louis Henkin observed, the traditional law of the sea reflected the law of powerful nations, and the proliferation of new, poorer States introduced a formidable political force principally aimed at challenging, and transforming, this old law.[31] The mandates of the Second and Third Committees of UNCLOS III must, therefore, be viewed against the background of this broad effort to fundamentally re-examine, and possibly recast drastically the classical law of the sea. Perceptions of radically altered conditions in the international community in the 1960s compelled the participants at UNCLOS III to go beyond the challenge of codification

---

28 The matters assigned to the Second Committee were strictly part of what is often referred to as the "general", "traditional" or "classical" law of the sea. II COMMENTARY at 9. A special aspect of the "classical" Continental Shelf regime relating to the "new" implications of the "exploitability clause" will be discussed in the context of Committee One negotiations. *Infra* Chap. IV. The agenda of the Third Committee shares both "new" and "traditional" aspects of the law of the sea. The Third Committee agenda will be considered predominantly "classical" or "traditional" insofar as the subjects it covered were matters dealt with in UNCLOS I. *Infra* Section E below. The Third Committee's contributions in *lex lata* to the "new" problems of the law of the sea, *e.g.*, transfer of technology, have been pursued most rigorously in the context of the work of the First Committee. These "new" aspects will be treated in subsequent Chapters.
29 These were the Hague Conference in 1930, UNCLOS I in 1958, and UNCLOS II in 1960. *See* Churchill & Lowe, *supra* note 26, at 11-13.
30 R.Y. Jennings, "The Santiago Conference and the Future" in R. Churchill, K.R. Simmonds & J. Welch (Eds.), III *New Directions in the Law of the Sea* 12 (1973).
31 L. Henkin, "Old Politics and New Directions" in Churchill, Simonds, and Welch, *id.* at 3-11. *See also* UNGA Res. 2750 C (XXV) of 17 December 1970, 25 UN GAOR Supp no. 28, at 26, which called for the convening of UNCLOS III.

and progressive development of the "traditional" law of the sea,[32] as was then the case in UNCLOS I and II. UNCLOS III was more than just a conference dealing with the unfinished business of UNCLOS I and UNCLOS II.[33]

To understand the truly novel task of law-reform faced by the Second and Third Committees of UNCLOS III, it is useful to recount briefly the events that led to the calling of the UNCLOS III from the perspective of the North-South dialogue in the arena of ocean diplomacy and law. These events were triggered by a quintessential North-South disagreement in the United Nations concerning the deep seabed – the subject matter assigned to Committee One as described above. The entire effort to review and reconstruct the traditional law of the sea was in fact provoked by prior developments relating to the emergence and vindication of the unique mandate assigned to Committee One of UNCLOS III.

1. Institutional Context

When the Committee to Study the Peaceful Uses of the Sea-Bed and the Ocean Floor Beyond the Limits of National Jurisdiction[34] was set up, there was a strong expectation that this Committee will not just be another deliberative gathering in the United Nations that would deal with one more esoteric question brought to the attention of the General Assembly.[35] The Committee was established in the aftermath of the historic speech of Maltese Ambassador Arvid

---

32 "Codification and Progressive Development" in the context of the meaning of these terms in the mandate of the UN International Law Commission (ILC). Art. 1(1) and Art. 15, Statute of the International Law Commission. Text in *The Work of the International Law Commission* (UN Sales E.88.V.1, 1988). UNCLOS III did not rely on the ILC for preparatory texts, as was done in UNCLOS I.

33 T. Koh & S. Jayakumar, *The Negotiating Process of the Third United Nations Conference on the Law of the Sea* I COMMENTARY 29-134, at 36-39, 42.

34 This was the *Ad Hoc* committee created by UNGA Resolution 2340 (XXII), UN Doc. A/RES/2340 (18 December 1967), but re-constituted one year later as the permanent "Committee to Study the Peaceful Uses of the Sea-Bed and the Ocean Floor beyond the Limits of National Jurisdiction" pursuant to UN Resolution 2467 (XXIII), UN Doc. A/RES/2467 (21 December 1968).

35 Prior to the establishment of the Committee, there were several disparate initiatives in the UN dealing with international ocean policy. All these initiatives were consolidated in the mandate of the Seabed Committee. *See* UNGA Res. 2340 (XXII).

Pardo in November 1967, who then called on the international community to consider a new "common heritage" regime for the deep seabed.[36] It started as an *ad hoc* study group[37] assigned the job of looking into a very narrow but somewhat open-ended subject: "examination of the question of the reservation exclusively for peaceful purposes of the sea-bed and the ocean floor, and the subsoil thereof, underlying the high seas beyond the limits of present national jurisdiction, and the use of their resources in the interest of mankind."[38] The last phrase "in the interest of mankind" no doubt foreshadowed the controversies that were to follow. In the newly identified domain of the deep seabed, humanity was not one but two, divided into the rich nations and the poor nations.

Disagreements between developed and developing countries surfaced as soon as discussions started in the *Ad Hoc* Committee. The former favored a general statement of general principles and norms governing the deep seabed while the latter supported moves for a more detailed set of principles that could be more readily operationalized.[39] The developing countries were also inclined to give legal significance to the term "common heritage of mankind", which the developed countries were not quite prepared to do.[40] Such disagreements on fundamental matters prevented the Committee from developing an agreed set of legal principles and norms for the deep seabed.[41] This stalemate continued well up to December 1970, when the General Assembly finally adopted the landmark "Declaration of Principles Governing the Sea-bed and the Ocean

---

36 *See* Statement of Arvid Pardo, 1 November 1967, First Committee, UNGA, 22 UN GAOR, 1515th & 1516th Meeting.
37 The *ad hoc* nature of the Committee was a compromise solution; its temporary character was supposedly a guarantee against undue haste. *See* A. de Marffy, "The Pardo Declaration and the Six Years of the Sea-Bed Committee" in I Dupuy & Vignes, *op. cit.* 141-162, at 144.
38 UNGA Res. 2467 A (XXIII) (21 December 1967), UN GAOR Supp. no. 18 at 15. Ambassador Pardo, in his *Note Verbale* of 17 August 1967, had a much broader ambition for a "Declaration and Treaty", but this was re-worded to "Examination of the question" because of doubts and concerns that the original formulation "unduly emphasizes the legal objectives." *Malta: request for inclusion of a supplementary item in the agenda of the twenty-second session*, UN Doc. A/6695 (18 August 1967), UNGA Plenary, 22nd Session, 1583rd Meeting at 18-19.
39 J. Morell, *The Law of the Sea: An Historical Analysis of the 1982 Treaty and its Rejection by the United States* 25 (1992).
40 *Id.*, at 26.
41 *See infra*, Chaps. III & IV.

Floor and the Subsoil Thereof Beyond the Limits of National Jurisdiction."[42] This Resolution, it must be noted, did not really bring to an end the North-South controversy on the "common heritage" that began in the Seabed Committee. It only opened up a new chapter in the North-South split, for the difficult issues concerning the deep seabed regime were still to be threshed out in UNCLOS III.

All along, it was apparent that the Seabed Committee could not satisfactorily carry out its main task of elaborating legal principles and norms on the narrow subject of the seabed beyond national jurisdiction without delving into the complex question of the limits of coastal State jurisdiction over the adjacent seabed. This meant that a clarification of the unsettled question in UNCLOS I and UNCLOS II concerning the scope and extent of national/coastal State jurisdiction was inextricably bound up with the consideration of the new question concerning "the Area", as the international deep seabed came to be known.[43] New and traditional concerns in the Law of the Sea were unavoidably interlaced, immediately revealing the inadequacy the Seabed Committee as a forum for expanded substantive deliberations.

From a broader perspective, the need to consider all other aspects of the law of the sea in conjunction with the "common heritage question" was forced by several developments outside the Seabed Committee. First the coastal States of Latin America, in alliance with coastal States from other regions, asserted their right to extend their marine resource jurisdiction or off-shore sovereignty as far as they thought necessary.[44] This was not at all acceptable to the

---

42 UNGA Res. 2749 (17 December 1970), 25 UN GAOR, Supplement no. 28 at 24. Adopted 108 votes to 0, with 14 abstentions. [Hereafter also referred to as the *Declaration of Principles Resolution*]

43 Two relevant preambular paragraphs in UNGA Resolution 2574 A (XXIV), UN GAOR, 1833rd Plenary Meeting (15 December 1969), reads:
Having regard for the fact that the problems relating to the high seas, territorial waters, contiguous zones, the continental shelf, the superjacent waters, and the seabed and ocean floor beyond the limits of national jurisdiction, are closely linked together, *Considering* that the definition of the continental shelf contained in the Convention on the Continental Shelf of 29 April 1958 does not define with sufficient precision the limits of the area over which a coastal State exercises sovereign rights for the purpose of exploration and exploitation of natural resources, and that customary international law on the subject is inconclusive[.]

44 *See e.g., The Lima Declaration*, reproduced in L. Alexander (Ed.), *The Law of the Sea: A New Geneva Conference* 223-226 (LSI, 1971). *See also* Morell, *op. cit.* 30; Koh & Jayakumar, *op. cit.* 36-37.

maritime powers. Secondly, since 1965, the two superpowers were quietly campaigning for a maximum breadth of 12 miles for the Territorial Sea in exchange for liberal navigation rights, but wanted outstanding law of the sea issues to be discretely negotiated by the international community into "manageable packages."[45] It should also be mentioned that the UN Secretary General conducted a poll to canvass the views of the UN General Assembly membership on the desirability of a major conference to discuss all law of the sea issues;[46] an overwhelming number of countries were in favor of a comprehensive reappraisal of the law of the sea through the convening of an international conference for that purpose.[47] Last but not the least, the rising tide of decolonization led to an intense and pervasive critical questioning of the entire gamut of existing sea law on the part of the newly independent States.[48] This last item deserves further comment.

The impact of decolonization on the need to reappraise the entire corpus of ocean law cannot be over-stressed.[49] There was no doubt that the newly emerged States harbored a deep resentment against the existing "classical" international law of the sea. For was it not this European-centred classical law of the sea which was responsible for the colonial exploitation of the Third

---

45 Koh & Jayakumar, *id.* at 37; Hollick, *op. cit.* 225. The United States later changed its position in favour of a comprehensive conference. B. Buzan, *Seabed Politics* 113 (1976).
46 *See* UNGA Res. 2574 (15 December 1969).
47 UN Doc. A/7925 and Add. 1-3 (1970). UN Res. 2750 B (17 December 1970), second preambular para., UN GAOR 1933rd Plenary Meeting.
48 The Group of 77 was quick to recognize in the common heritage proposal of Ambassador Pardo an opportunity to further its aim of reducing North-South disparities. For a general assessment of the role of the "Group of 77" as an interest group in the Seabed Committee, *see* Buzan, *op. cit.* 128-130. *Cf.* E. Miles, "The Dynamics of Global Ocean Politics" in D.M. Johnston (Ed.), *Marine Policy and the Coastal Community The Impact of the Law of the Sea* 147-181, at 154 (1976) pointing out that the Group of 77 only emerged as a cohesive group when its members reached a compromise on the idea of patrimonial sea or exclusive economic zone between 1968 and 1972. *Cf.* Koh & Jayakumar, *op. cit.* at 81, clarifying that the Group of 77 in UNCLOS III was distinct from the Group of 77 of the UN General Assembly, in that the former had its own officials and working methods.
49 *See* Henkin, *supra* note 31.

World?[50] Since the new States felt that they did not participate in the making of the classical law of the sea they were, therefore, bent on reforming this major branch of international law so that it may serve their needs and interests.[51] In their view all issues in the law of the sea covering traditional and new concerns should be addressed in an omnibus fashion in order to establish a totally new regime for the oceans.

The turning point in the work of the Seabed Committee occurred during the 25th (1970) anniversary session of the United Nations General Assembly. This was the adoption by the General Assembly of a "package" of Resolutions with direct bearing the work of the Seabed Committee. One of these Resolutions, already mentioned, was the crucial Declaration of Principles Resolution, which embodied a North-South *modus vivendi* regarding the problem of "the Area."[52] The other Resolution of note enlarged the Seabed Committee and gave it a mandate as the preparatory body for an international conference on the law of the sea. The subjects to be considered in this Conference, the UNCLOS III, included the entire range of ocean law concerns.[53]

It must be noted that the specific elements of the North-South controversy that had emerged at this juncture were not only those associated with the potentially "new" domain of inequality in the law of the sea as indicated by the Declaration of Principles Resolution. In a direct way, the North-South debate on the classical or traditional law of the sea was also articulated in the above-quoted Resolution calling for an international conference on the law of the sea.

---

50 RP Anand, *Origin and Development of the Law of the Sea* (1983); RP Anand, *International Law and Developing Countries* 53-71 (1987). *See also* N. Rembe, *Africa and the Law of the Sea* (1980).

51 Koh & Jayakumar, *op. cit.* 38. *See also* R.P. Anand, "Winds of Change in the Law of the Sea" in R.P. Anand (Ed.), *Law of the Sea: Caracas and Beyond* 36-61, at 43-46 (1980); M.C.W. Pinto, "Problems of Developing States and their Effects on Decisions on the Law of the Sea" in L. Alexander (Ed.), *Needs and Interests of the Developing Countries* 4 (LSI, 1973).

52 *See also* Res. 2750 A & B, dealing, respectively, with the impact of seabed mining on the market of raw materials exports and the role of land-locked countries in the regime for the Area, specifically, and under the law of the sea, generally.

53 *See* para. 2, UNGA Res. 2750 C. The Resolution was adopted by 109 votes, with 7 votes against (all from Eastern Europe) and 6 abstentions (all developing countries). All western countries voted in favor of the Resolution. UN GAOR, Plenary Meetings, Vol. 3, 1933rd meeting.

In its preambular paragraphs three considerations presaged competing North-South approaches to law-making for the oceans.

The first was expressed in a forward-looking observation which eventually became one of the cornerstone principles of the new ocean regime negotiated in UNCLOS III: "the problems of ocean space are closely interrelated and need to be considered as a whole."[54] This statement recapitulates the experience of the Seabed Committee which found it impossible to confine the consideration of ocean issues on a sectoral basis.[55] It also repudiates the general approach taken in UNCLOS I which negotiated four separate conventions covering discrete areas of the law of the sea. More significantly, the statement prefigures the "package deal" approach and the closely-related procedural principle of decision-making by consensus later adopted by UNCLOS III.

Secondly, the Resolution calling for an UNCLOS III suggested that a comprehensive re-examination of ocean issues in their close inter-relationship should involve the widest possible participation of States.[56] This premise endorsed the idea of democratization in UNCLOS III as an inevitable consequence of the larger process of decolonization.

The contemplated inclusiveness of UNCLOS III with respect to both issues covered and the level of participation encouraged suggests a third argument on the essential North-South character of UNCLOS III. UNCLOS III was launched with the conscious commitment to give special consideration to the needs and requirements of newly independent States in the new ocean regime to be evolved.[57] Two possible methods of fulfilling the "special needs and interests" directive of UNCLOS III are conceivable. First, as a legal formula, the principle

---

54 Preambular para. 4, Res. 2750 C. See also Preambular para. 4, CLOS.
55 This is reiterated in the 7th preambular paragraph of Res. 2750 C, which reads: "Convinced that the elaboration of an equitable international regime for the sea-bed and the ocean floor, and the subsoil thereof, beyond the limits of national jurisdiction would facilitate agreement on the questions to be examined at such a conference[.]"
56 The 6th Preambular para. of Res. 2750 C reads: "Having regard to the fact that many of the present States Members of the United Nations did not take part in the previous United Nations conferences on the law of the sea[.]"
57 The 8th preambular para. of Res. 2750 C reads: "Affirming that such agreements on those questions [to be considered by the conference] should seek to accommodate the interests and needs of all States, whether land-locked or coastal, taking into account the special interests and needs of the developing countries, whether land-locked or coastal[.]"

"special interests and needs of developing countries" could be made to refer to rights and obligations in favor of developing States by way of transient or exceptional regimes deviating from rules and standards normally in force for the rest of the international community. These rights and obligations confirm a dual normative system that seeks to expand asymmetrical and non-reciprocal legal relations between developed and developing States, justified under a theory of "compensatory inequality" or "positive discrimination." This method of imparting legal content on the standard "special needs and interests of developing states" had been used in context of UNCTAD and formalized in the GATT via the "general system of preferences."[58] A second, more significant, possible deployment of the formula, which the participants in UNCLOS III were in a unique position to negotiate, is the emplacement of "special interests and needs of developing countries" as the very *raison d'etre* of any norm or regime under the new law of the sea. This means that the standard of giving special consideration to the interests and needs of developing countries will become a more or less permanent norm of international law itself – a fundamental principle of international law governing post-decolonization international society. Being generative of further principles and rules in its own right, this general standard could support the claim to the "right to development" on the part of the Third World.[59] Whatever orientation will be given to the "special case" of developing states in the new law of the sea, the essential point was accepted by all: the democratic and holistic consideration of all ocean issues in UNCLOS III necessitates giving special attention to the needs and interests of the South.

This brief review of institutional developments on the eve of UNCLOS III should explain the link between the expectation of a unified consideration of all ocean issues in UNCLOS III and the search for a solution to the broad range of North-South disagreements as these emerged in the Seabed Committee. UNCLOS III was, therefore, as much a North-South event as it was a technical conference on the Law of the Sea. Indeed, the bedrock of substantive bargains and trade-offs defined in the package that was to become the 1982 Convention on the Law of the Sea was by and large the outcome of a political process that sought to reconcile the divergent interests and perceptions of the developed

---

58 *See* P. Berthoud, "UNCTAD and the Emergence of International Development Law" in M. Zammit-Cutajar, *op. cit.* 71-98.
59 *Cf.* M. Chemillier-Gendreau, "Relations between the Ideology of Development and the Development of Law" in Snyder & Slinn, *op. cit.*

countries, on the one hand, and developing countries, on the other, on the central issues of ocean governance.

2. *Substantive Law Context*

The need for a comprehensive re-evaluation of the traditional law of the sea, which was inseparable from the search for a solution to the deep seabed predicament, is more clearly seen in the debates on substantive issues that accompanied the institutional evolution of the Seabed Committee. At the heart of these debates lay the Grotian doctrine of "freedom of the seas."

When the General Assembly decided to call for a comprehensive conference on the law of the sea, there was a pervasive awareness that the core pillar of the traditional law of the sea, the doctrine of freedom,[60] was going to be roundly challenged to its core foundations.[61] To be sure, this doctrine was already up for serious questioning immediately after the Second World War, which saw the phenomenon of widespread extensions of coastal State jurisdiction – the so-called "creeping" jurisdiction initiated by the Truman Proclamation on the Continental Shelf of 1945.[62] So widespread and profound was the cynicism against the Grotian *mare liberum* that by the time the Declaration of Principles Resolution was adopted in 1970, the consensus was well formed that only an international conference with a comprehensive mandate could remedy the much-eroded stability of, or the chaos in, the existing legal order of the oceans, founded as it was on the classical freedom of the seas principle.

Although developed and developing States alike joined in the campaign to discredit the "freedom of the seas" principle in its various manifestations,[63]

---

60 *See* Schwarzenberger, *supra* Chap. I note 51, at 195. ["freedom of the seas" as one of seven fundamental pillars of classical international law]
61 *See* Friedheim, *supra* note 16, at 19 & 272.
62 Presidential Proclamation No. 2667 (28 September 1945). Text in 1 J.N. Moore (Ed.), *International and United States Documents on Oceans Law and Policy* (1986).
63 Canada and Iceland are illustrative of the trend in the developed world that questioned the principle of freedom of the seas. Canada in 1970 established a 100-mile anti-pollution zone in the Arctic. The literature on the subject is extensive. For an overview, *see* L. Legault, *The Freedom of the Seas: A License to Pollute?* 21 U TORONTO L J 211 (1971) and L. Henkin, *Arctic Anti-Pollution: Does Canada Make – or Break – International Law?* 65 AJIL 131 (1971). Iceland, on the other

it is important to isolate the views held by the developing countries on this principle on the eve of UNCLOS III. The intention is to ascertain whether these States were able to translate their collective dissatisfaction with the regime of freedom into alternative "development-promoting", "equality-generating" regimes in the traditional law of the sea. It is submitted that the key concept or theory which portrays the alternative policy outlook of the developing countries is embedded in the concept of the "coastal State." They put forward a particular view of the "coastal State" to impart concrete meaning to the expression "special interests and needs of the developing countries."

The "coastal State" – a special sub-category of the generic term "State" with which it shares the essence of sovereignty – derives from the doctrine of the territorial sea or territorial waters.[64] It was this concept of a "coastal State" that provided the vehicle for the developing countries to conceive of normative strategies to pursue the goal of less inequality between the rich and the poor States in the classical law of the sea, *i.e.*, an approach to address the traditional domains of disparity in the law of the sea. The instrumentalization of the concept of "coastal State" jurisdiction, as a device to allocate legal competences among States, was intended to modify or reverse the classical regime of freedom. However, as it will be shown shortly, the stress on coastal State jurisdiction as a response to freedom of the seas resulted in a factual redistribution of ocean resources that did not exactly match the overall aim of development and global sharing along North-South lines. Before this and other ramifications of the "coastal State" advocacy are explored, it is useful to recall the overall argument advanced by the developing States against the freedom of the seas principle. This argument, it must be noted, was the essential justification for their invocation of the coastal State principle as a fundamental basis for reform in traditional domains of the law of the sea.

Among the consequences of decolonization in the 1960s was the realization by the majority of newly emerged States that the traditional law of the sea was completely outmoded and was, therefore, in need of revision so that it can better

---

hand, unilaterally extended its fisheries jurisdiction out to 50 miles from its shores in 1972, giving rise to the *Fisheries Jurisdiction Cases* (*UK & Federal Republic of Germany* v. *Iceland*) beginning 1972. *See* 1972 ICJ Rep at 11 and 181; 29 and 188; 1973 ICJ Rep at 3, 93, and 302; 49, 96 and 313; 1974 ICJ Rep at 3 and 175.

64 The coastal State concept in classical law is elaborated in the exposition of "territorial waters" or the "territorial State." *See e.g.,* J. Colombos, *The International Law of the Sea* at Chap. III (6th ed., 1967); P. Jessup, *The Law of Territorial Waters and Maritime Jurisdiction* at Chap. 3 (1927).

reflect their needs and aspirations. Historically, the *laissez-faire* order of the seas, founded on the doctrine of freedom, "has been designed specifically to favour the strong countries over the weak countries, the industrialized countries over the poor, and the developed over the developing."[65] This rule of freedom made it possible to accentuate inequalities among States, directly affecting the newly-acquired sovereignty and statehood of developing States.[66] The freedom of the seas, which benefitted only those States that possessed the means to utilize such freedom effectively,[67] was seen as anathema to equality of capacity for rights and obligations among sovereign States with respect to the uses of the sea.[68] If the freedom of the seas principle was to be really acceptable, then there must exist real equality of opportunity to make use of it. But this was, obviously, not the case.[69]

From the arsenal of legal concepts which evolved in the history of the law of the sea, the only principle that purported to counter freedom was sovereignty, captured in the classical doctrine of *mare clausum*. To correct existing inequalities in the traditional law of the sea, the developing countries were, therefore, predisposed to counter the doctrine of freedom with the familiar and equally well-established doctrine of coastal State sovereignty. Since the new States had to accept the whole corpus of "Eurocentric" international law as they found it when they attained independence, there was not much else available to them by way of countervailing doctrinal concepts to dethrone the doctrine of freedom. An obvious predicament, however, suggested itself: how can the logic behind the coastal State principle promote the Third World vision of development and global sharing? More specifically, how can the concept of coastal State sover-

---

65 F.X. Njenga (Kenya), UN Doc. A/AC.138/SC.II/SR.29, 31 March 1972. *See also* B.V.A. Roling, "Are Grotius Ideas Obsolete in an Expanded World?" in H. Bull, B. Kingsbury & A. Roberts (Eds.), *Hugo Grotius and International Relations* 281 (1992).
66 *See* Bedjaoui, *supra*, Chap. I note 113, at 61.
67 M.A. Ajomo, "Third World Expectations" in III Churchill, Simonds & Welch, *supra* note 30, 302-309 at 309. "Who benefits from the freedom of the Sea, if it is not those who possess the essential means to use and to exploit it, that is the powerful or capitalist forces?," J. Salmon, *Le Procede de la Fiction en Droit International* I REVUE BELGE DE DROIT INTERNATIONAL 35 (1974), quoted in Bedjaoui, *supra*, Chap. I note 113, at 61.
68 Anand, *supra* note 51, at 47.
69 *See* Statement of F.X. Njenga, *Asian-African Legal Consultative Committee Report of the Thirteenth Session* at 373 (Lagos, January 1972).

eignty accommodate the legal standard "special needs and interests of developing States"?

The evolution of the overall negotiating position of the developing countries before and during the UNCLOS III reveals the normative approach taken by the Group of 77 to resolve this question. The theory that underlies the approach taken by the developing countries may be summarized as follows: a more equitable distribution of the wealth of the sea along North-South lines could be realized not only by limiting the geographic and functional scope of freedom but also, and which is not exactly the same thing, by extending the geographic and functional reach of sovereignty.[70]

However, the geographic extension of sovereignty could not be a sufficient condition for equality in the law of the sea. Ideally, it had to be accompanied by a regime that will secure to the developing States the necessary wherewithal to exercise this extended sovereignty in the most effective and meaningful manner.[71] For the developing countries, the principle of coastal State sovereignty meant not only extended legal competence off-shore but also, more importantly, actual enjoyment of resources covered by this extended jurisdictional competence. The new regime should, therefore, be able to reallocate rights and responsibilities in favor of the developing States while ensuring the effective exercise of these rights and duties. Neither objective was forthcoming under the regime of freedom of the seas.

The developing countries established their negotiating positions in the Second and Third Committees of UNCLOS III on the basis of this core concept of coastal State jurisdiction. It supplied the governing perspective for their agenda of development and global sharing in the traditional areas of ocean law and policy. The two major elements of the negotiating outlook should be re-

---

70 The interest of coastal developing States in extending sovereignty over wider areas of maritime territory is supported by the claim to "permanent sovereignty over natural resources." *See* N. Schrijver, "Permanent Sovereignty Over Natural Resources Versus the Common Heritage of Mankind: Complementary or Contradictory Principles of International Economic Law?" in P. de Waart, P. Peters & E. Denters, *supra* Chap. I note 29, 87-101. *Cf.* Schachter, *supra* Chap. I note 43, at 124-126. [The main thrust of principle of permanent sovereignty is the nationalization of foreign firms, but that it is a manifestation of aspirations for self-rule and greater equality.]
71 The Group of 77 sought to strengthen developing States' capabilities or capacities to exercise extended national jurisdiction through the negotiations which took place in the Third Committee. *Infra*, Section E below.

71

iterated: first, a bigger share of ocean wealth, both living and non-living, in terms of the affirmation of the legal competence of developing countries over marine areas where these resources are found; and secondly, closely related to first, effective exercise of this competence or jurisdiction that will directly promote their economic development. The "special consideration of the interests and needs of developing countries" was hoped to be realized through a regime of strengthened coastal State sovereignty in both extensive-territorial terms, *e.g.* wider belt of off-shore jurisdiction, and intensive-functional terms, *e.g.,* the effective and efficacious competence over marine resources. How this conception of *mare clausum* or ocean enclosure was elaborated into rules of *lex lata* by the UNCLOS III, and how these rules in turn impacted on the existing allocation of capacities for rights and obligations between developed and developing States in the new ocean order will now be explored in some detail.

D. THE NORTH-SOUTH DIALOGUE IN THE SECOND COMMITTEE: GLOBAL WEALTH REDISTRIBUTION THROUGH EXTENDED COASTAL STATE JURISDICTION

Although the list of subjects and issues allocated to the Second Committee[72] at the start of UNCLOS III covered more than the total work of UNCLOS I,[73] the Committee did not have the benefit of prepared draft articles to guide its deliberations. It had to work virtually from scratch.[74] Nevertheless, the Committee succeeded in putting together a comprehensive package of negotiated solutions[75] to very complex issues touching on the general or classical law

---

72 *See supra* note 27 and accompanying text.
73 II COMMENTARY at 8.
74 *Id.,* at 9.
75 According to one analyst of the UNCLOS III negotiations, the "linchpins" of the entire new law of the sea, *viz.,* a 200-mile Exclusive Economic Zone, a 12-mile territorial sea, and "transit passage rights", were negotiated in the Second Committee. *See* Friedheim, *op. cit.* 77 in relation to 333. *See also* M.G. Schmidt, *Common Heritage or Common Burden?* 264-274 (1989). For the view that the UNCLOS III negotiated package included the overall compromise adopted in the First Committee, *see* for *e.g.,* Sebenius, *op. cit.* 80-81; Morell, *op. cit.* at 190-191; R. Ogley, *Internationalizing the Seabed* at 246 (1984); J. Broadus, "Introduction" in Hong, Miles & Park (Eds.), *The Role of the Ocean in the 21st Century* 329 (LSI, 1995).

of the sea. The Committee Two package had the following key elements now embodied in the 1982 Convention:

> ... (i) a territorial sea with a maximum breadth of twelve nautical miles measured from the baselines, together with a clarification of the rules governing the innocent passage of foreign ships through the territorial sea; (ii) a regime for transit passage through and over straits used for international navigation; (iii) a regime for archipelagic States and for navigation through and over archipelagic waters; (iv) access to and from the sea for land-locked States; (v) an exclusive economic zone with a maximum breadth of 200 nautical miles from the baselines, in which the coastal state has sovereign rights over the natural resources and duties regarding their management; and (vi) extension of the sovereign rights of the coastal State over the natural resources of the continental shelf to the outer edge of the continental margin, subject to the revenue sharing obligations with respect to the exploitation of the continental shelf beyond 200 nautical miles.[76]

While it is true that the general pattern of negotiations in the Second Committee that led to the adoption of these regimes did not follow a North-South orientation,[77] it must be pointed out that the Group of 77 were united round the proposition that developing States which are coastal States should have a bigger share of the resources off their coasts *vis-a-vis* third States. Against the backdrop of decolonization, this assertion of coastal State authority was *protective* in its motivation. The immediate purpose was to curb the intrusions of the strong maritime States which, using the cover of the open-access principle of freedom the seas, had hitherto exploited other States' coastal resources, conferring upon themselves undue advantages simply because they were financially and technologically more advanced.[78]

The idea that beyond the narrow confines of the territorial sea, the coastal State would retain jurisdiction and control over adjacent resources, living and non-living, as well as over all economic activities conducted therein, was realized through the *sui generis* regime of the "Exclusive Economic Zone" (EEZ).[79] The EEZ concept was one of the major contributions of the developing

---

76 II COMMENTARY at 22-23.
77 Koh and Jayakumar, *op. cit.* 70 and 81; Friedheim, *op. cit.* at 337.
78 Pinto, *supra* note 51, at 10; Njenga, *supra* note 65, at 373. *See also* E. Gold, "The Rise of the Coastal State in the Law of the Sea" in Johnston, *supra* note 48, at 13-33.
79 For a comprehensive elaboration of the EEZ, including its legislative background, *see* II COMMENTARY at 491-821.

countries in UNCLOS III, supplying the juridical cornerstone for their "theory" of coastal State sovereignty described above. It was a concept that directly arose from their needs and experiences as coastal developing States.[80] The EEZ, as an institution in positive law and as an evolving concept in ocean governance, is the Third World's response to North-South disparity engendered by the traditional law of the sea.

1. The Significance of the EEZ in Global Wealth Redistribution

Through the EEZ[81] a coastal State assumes, *inter alia*, ownership and management responsibility over all living and non-living resources situated up to 200 nautical miles from its shores – the most biologically-productive and petroleum-rich area off shore. Foreign intrusion into this area or any resource exploitation within this zone without coastal State sanction had thus been virtually abolished by the Convention. The affirmation of coastal State authority over the EEZ fulfills the goal of the developing States for extensive sovereignty.

---

80 S. Nandan, "The Exclusive Economic Zone: A Historical Perspective" in *The Law and the Sea: Essays in Memory of Jean Carroz* 171-188, at 181 (1987). The concept of the EEZ was praised by commentators from the industrialized countries when it was first introduced. *See e.g.,* E.D. Brown, "Maritime Zones: A Survey of Claims" in Churchill, Simmonds & Welch, *op. cit.* 157-192, at 167:
[The EEZ proposal] is one of the most promising developments in the international law of the sea for many years. Originating in the developing world and catering for the interests of developing coastal States, it is nevertheless formulated with moderation and based on a realistic appreciation of political feasibility.

81 B. Kwiatkowska, *The 200 Mile Exclusive Economic Zone in the New Law of the Sea* at 4 (1989), defines the EEZ, a multifunctional resource zone, as follows:
The exclusive economic zone is an area beyond and adjacent to the territorial sea that extends up to 200 miles from the [territorial sea] baselines, in which the coastal State has sovereign rights with regard to all natural resources and other activities for economic exploitation and exploration, as well as jurisdiction with regard to artificial islands, scientific research and marine environmental protection, and other rights and duties provided for in the [Law of the Sea] Convention. All States enjoy in the EEZ navigational and other communications freedoms, and the land-locked and geographically disadvantaged States – specific rights of participation in fisheries and marine scientific research.

There is, however, a trick behind the EEZ that has not escaped notice: the protective principle behind the EEZ regime, as articulated in Part V of the 1982 Convention, is available to coastal States which are developed countries as well. The EEZ, as a concept of ocean enclosure, benefits all coastal States alike, to a greater or lesser degree, irrespective of their level of development.[82] The most serious implication of the EEZ as a legal mechanism for global wealth redistribution cannot be more manifest, for the EEZ does not vindicate a North-South re-allocation of either marine wealth or legal capacities. Instead, it distinguishes its States-beneficiaries on the basis of what Professor Edward Miles called their "biogeophysical marine attributes."[83]

The EEZ, although conceived originally to secure and foster the economic development of many developing States (by putting jurisdictional barriers to the predatory exercise of the freedom of the high seas by developed States) was only indirectly and imperfectly suited to meet the "special interests and needs of developing countries."[84] The EEZ *prima facie* defines equality among States not basically as equality of capacity for rights and obligations between rich nations and poor nations, but equality among coastal States *inter se*. Naturally, those States which did not consider themselves "coastal States" – during UNCLOS III, these were grouped together as the "Land-locked and Geographically-disadvantaged States"[85] – could not benefit from this wealth distribution institution that was, by definition, only available to States with the appropriate bio-geophysical characteristics. If the impact of the EEZ is measured in terms of actual development gains realized by those States entitled to it, it

---

82 The 14 "lucky countries" with the largest EEZs are: United States (4.82 million square nautical miles [msm]), France (2.86 msm), Australia (2.41 msm), Indonesia (1.57 msm), New Zealand (1.41 msm), Britain (1.34 msm), Canada (1.29 msm), USSR (1.26 msm), Japan (1.13 msm), Brazil (0.92 msm), Denmark with Greenland (0.71 msm), Papua New Guinea (0.69 msm), and Chile (0.66 msm). C. Sanger, *Ordering the Oceans: The Making of the Law of the Sea* 64-67 (1987). *Cf.* Churchill & Lowe, *op. cit.* at 148, for a different set of rankings and figures.
83 Miles, *supra* note 48, at 149.
84 *See*, however, *infra* Sec. E, on the significance of the EEZ in the context of the work of the Third Committee.
85 Koh & Jayakumar, *op. cit.* 72-75.

is all too evident that the establishment of the EEZ has not necessarily led to the narrowing of disparities between North and South.[86]

However, it must be noted that the EEZ regime contains two instances where the juridical standard of "special interests and needs of developing States" is recognized and applied. The first is the consideration given to the interests of developing countries as one factor in the determination of the maximum sustainable yield (MSY) and/or the total allowable catch in coastal fisheries. The second is the participation of developing land-locked and geographically disadvantaged States in the living resources of the EEZ. But what is rather conspicuous is that these particular invocations of "the special interests and needs of developing States" are only weak applications of the principle of sovereign equality between rich and poor States in terms of providing the beneficiary developing States concerned with specific enforceable rights. The normative value of these equalization provisions are minuscule. In that sense, it could be maintained that they are merely of token significance.

2. The Nature of the General Preference given to Developing States concerning Fisheries Access to the EEZ

The first instance under the conventional regime of the EEZ when a developing State is given an apparent advantage over a developed State is found in the rules governing conservation and optimum utilization of living resources in the EEZ.[87] In the determination of the total allowable catch of living resources in its EEZ, a coastal State is allowed to take into consideration the "special requirements of developing States" as one qualifying factor in the determination

---

[86] For example, the impact of the EEZ on the allocation of world fisheries was described by F. Christy, *Marine Fisheries and the Law of the Sea* Special (Revised) Chapter of the State of Food and Agriculture 1992, FAO FISHERIES CIRCULAR No. 853 (1993) at 1: "In general, the redistribution of the seas' wealth has proceeded as anticipated, with a few coastal states gaining large benefits and a few distant-water fishing states incurring large losses." *See also* L. Juda, *World Maritime Fish Catch in the Age of Exclusive Economic Zones and Exclusive Fishing Zones* 22 ODIL 1, 17 (1991), concluding that in terms of actual catch of fish, the creation of the EEZs/Exclusive Fishing Zones has been of particular benefit to a relatively small number of developing States and that the traditional domination of a small club of fishing States has not been altered.

[87] *See* Arts. 61 (3) and 62 (3), CLOS.

of the MSY for fisheries.⁸⁸ Conservation measures adopted by a coastal State must produce a MSY that is determined on the basis of "relevant environmental and economic factors", which include not only addressing the requirements of developing States but also the needs of coastal communities, fishing patterns, interdependence of stocks, and recommended international standards.⁸⁹ Clearly, the "heavily qualified MSY formula"⁹⁰ is, above all, meant to affirm the wide discretion of the coastal State in matters relating to the sharing of fisheries resources in its EEZ, rather than intended to establish a positive right for any developing State as such with an interest in participating in the exploitation of these resources.⁹¹ The developing States which are entitled to have access to the surplus of the allowable catch declared by a coastal State are furthermore limited to the developing countries situated in the same sub-region or region.⁹² The fact that "developing States" is mentioned as a category of States for special consideration in access agreements with coastal States does not preclude the latter from giving priority to any other category of States.⁹³ Considering that any decision taken by the coastal State in this regard is exempt from the provisions of the Convention dealing with compulsory settlement of disputes,⁹⁴ there is, in reality, a feeble, almost non-existent, normative force⁹⁵ behind this regime of positive discrimination in support of the "requirements of developing States."

---

88 For description of living resources regime of the EEZ, see e.g., I Brown, *supra* note 10, at 221 *et seq.*; Churchill & Lowe, *op. cit.* Chap. 14; Kwiatkowska, *supra* note 81, at Chap. 2.

89 The "special requirements of developing States" in this context first appears in the text submitted by the (Evensen) Group of Experts to the Second Committee during the third session (1975) of UNCLOS III. See II COMMENTARY at 604 and 628.

90 Brown, *supra* note 10, at 223.

91 Kwiatkowska, *supra* note 81, at 48, denies any norm-creating potential in Art. 61. The "measures" referred to in that article, it is asserted, simply provide guidelines or standards for the rational management of EEZ fisheries. *Cf.* II COMMENTARY at 610, which speaks of a "duty" of a coastal State to take "measures" that have "legislative and normative implications, at whatever level."

92 Art. 62 (3), CLOS.

93 II COMMENTARY at 637: "The variety of considerations which the coastal State may entertain in giving other States the right of access to the surplus of the living resources of its [EEZ] confirms that this right of access is a relative right."

94 Art. 297 (3)(a), CLOS.

95 Brown, *supra* note 10, at 222-223; Churchill & Lowe, *op. cit.* 232-233.

3. The Needs and Interests of Developing Land-Locked and Geographically-Disadvantaged States

The second invocation of needs and interests of developing countries in the juridical arena of the EEZ pertains to the sub-regime on the participation of "land-locked and geographically-disadvantaged States" (LLGDS) in the living resources of the EEZ.[96] The category of developing LLGDS is of paramount significance in this book because it is in this group where we find the "very poorest of developing countries."[97] That said, the reality is that the situation of these countries with respect to their access to the living resources of the EEZ is no better than the generic situation of developing countries already described above. But the peculiar predicament of developing LLGDS in UNCLOS III deserves more extensive consideration, if only to highlight the manner by which the new ocean regime responds to the needs and interests of those countries with the greatest stake in the principle of sovereign equality of States in the oceans.

The main reason why the developing countries were not able to sustain a united front in the Second Committee was because the negotiations on the details of the EEZ concept eventually became a matter of bargaining between the "advantaged" coastal States, on the one hand, and "land-locked and geographically-disadvantaged States", on the other.[98] More particularly, the LLGDS – which included in its ranks both developed and developing States – felt that their views and interests on the equitable sharing of resources in the EEZ, specially fisheries, were being ignored or prejudiced by States actively or tacitly

---

96 *See* especially Arts. 69 and 70, CLOS.
97 *See Specific Action Related to the Particular Needs and Problems of Land-locked Developing Countries*, UNGA Res. 44/214 (28 February 1990). This Resolution States that of the 21 land-locked developing countries, 15 are also classified by the United Nations as least developed countries. In UNCLOS III, there was a total of 29 land-locked States identified with the LLGDS group; out of 26 "geographically disadvantaged States" in this group, 16 were developing States. *See* Koh & Jayakumar, *op. cit.* 72-73.
98 Apparently, the only time the G-77 had a consensus on the EEZ that accommodated the interests of developing LLGDS was when it submitted a working paper to the Second Committee at the third session of UNCLOS III – arguing for a stronger coastal State orientation of the EEZ concept. Koh & Jayakumar, *op. cit.* at 81; Nandan, *supra* note 81, at 185; II COMMENTARY at 531-535.

supporting the EEZ concept, *i.e.*, the favourably positioned coastal States.[99] Later, a subgroup of "developing LLGDS" was formed within the LLGDS, because some developing LLGDS felt that the developed LLGDS were unsympathetic to their concerns.[100] The long and difficult controversy surrounding the issue of participation of LLGDS in the living resources of the EEZ led to the establishment of a dedicated but unofficial negotiating group[101] to resolve the following questions:

> ... whether reference should be made to a "right to participate"; whether access should be in respect of the surplus [of the allowable catch of the coastal State in the EEZ]; whether access should be on preferential bases; whether developing and developed countries should be treated on an equal footing and finally the question of defining the category of States which could participate in exploitation according [to the article on rights of access for LLGDS].[102]

The final agreed text on the terms and conditions of participation of LLGDS in the context of the regime of the EEZ justifies the conclusion that access of LLGDS to the living resources of the EEZ of other States is really more in the nature of a "privilege", subject to all manner of coastal State discretion already alluded to,[103] rather than a "right", which is the chosen term that is employed in the Convention.[104] It should be mentioned, parenthetically, that in the course of UNCLOS III, the LLGDS group sought to establish rules for their access to the

---

99 For a description of the politics involved during the crucial stages of negotiation on the EEZ, *see* Miles, *supra* note 48, at 167-169.
100 Koh & Jayakumar, *op. cit.* 75.
101 The so-called "Nandan Group", Koh & Jayakumar, *op. cit.* at 109-110; II COMMENTARY at 690-767.
102 Statement of the Chairman of the Second Committee at the 105th informal meeting (1977) of the Second Committee. *See* II COMMENTARY at 715, 752.
103 *See* generally, S.C. Vasciannie, *Land-Locked and Geographically-Disadvantaged States in the International Law of the Sea* (1990).
104 Arts. 69 and 70 speak of the "Right" of LLGDS. II COMMENTARY at 695-696 and 737. This "right" is described as "fairly tenuous and largely depend on how much a coastal State is prepared to concede in negotiating an [access] agreement." Churchill & Lowe, *op. cit.* 321. *Cf.* Kwiatkowska, *supra* note 81, at 60, who takes the view that these articles are merely "guidelines" and do "not involve any legal right of access on the part of third states." *Cf.* Brown, *supra* note 10, at 221 and 245, is inclined to consider a "duty" to grant access, or the "obligations to share resources with other States in certain circumstances."

non-living resources of coastal States' EEZs as well. This proposal was rebuffed because it would have deprived the coastal States of their perceived vested rights in the continental shelf.[105]

Some contingent form of positive discrimination in favour of developing LLGDS was, however, established under the Convention. Developing LLGDS could potentially benefit from a regime of cooperation which is effectuated in the following circumstances:

> When the harvesting capacity of a coastal State approaches a point which would enable it to harvest the entire allowable catch of the living resources in its [EEZ], the coastal State and other States concerned shall co-operate in the establishment of equitable arrangements on a bilateral, sub-regional or regional basis to allow for participation of developing [LLGDS] of the same subregion or region in the exploitation of the living resources of the [EEZ] of the coastal States of the subregion or region, as may be appropriate in the circumstances and on terms satisfactory to all parties...[106]

The significance of this rule is emasculated by the general provision concerning the complete discretion of a coastal State over questions of access by third States in its EEZ,[107] which may lawfully disregard the category of "developing LLGDS" in the allocation of a surplus.[108] Moreover, the rule does not characterize the participation of the developing LLGDS as a right, as it merely obligates States to "cooperate" to establish arrangements.[109] Hence, there is really no category of States that is given preferential treatment in the access provisions of the EEZ.[110]

---

105 Churchill & Lowe, *op. cit.* 320.
106 *See* Arts. 69 (3) and 70 (4), CLOS.
107 Arts. 61 and 62, CLOS.
108 II COMMENTARY at 637.
109 Kwiatkowska, *supra* note 82, at 71.
110 The distribution rule in Arts. 69 and 70, CLOS, are subordinated to the general norm of distribution in Art. 62, CLOS. C.A. Fleischer, "Fisheries and Biological Resources" in Dupuy & Vignes, *op. cit.* 989-1126, at 1088-1089. Thus, it could be logically inferred that a coastal State can validly allocate its surplus to a developed LLGDS, rather than to a developing LLGDS located in the same region, notwithstanding the rule in Art. 69 (4) and Art. 70 (5), CLOS, that a developed LLGDS shall be entitled to participate in the exploitation of living resources only in the EEZs of developed coastal States of the same subregion or region. *See also* II COMMENTARY at 637.

The wide scope of coastal State discretion defined under the Convention in relation to access by third States to EEZ resources[111] proves that the EEZ - as a method of enclosure immune from judicial review[112] – is at odds with the concept of "equality" between coastal States, on the one hand, and LLGDS, on the other.[113] Clearly, the possibility of promoting the agenda of development and global sharing for the developing LLGDS through their participation in EEZ resources was never firmly secured in the language of *lex lata* under the new law of the sea.

However, outside of the resources regime of the EEZ, the Convention does provide for situations conferring a specific normative benefit to the category of LLGDS. Once again, it must be emphasized that this benefit does not proceed from the criterion of whether a State is developing or not, but simply whether it is coastal or land-locked/geographically disadvantaged. The "biogeophysical", rather than the North-South, criterion in the definition of a favorable regime for LLGDS is illustrated in two cases. First the *de facto* inequality suffered by "land-locked States" specifically prior to UNCLOS III in regard to their access to the sea in general was rectified *de jure* by the Convention, with the recognition of their unconditional "right of access to and from the sea and freedom of transit."[114] This very substantial right is, however, to be implemented through agreements on "terms and modalities for exercising freedom of transit."[115] It is also qualified by a potentially countervailing right on the part

---

111 *Id. See also* W. Burke, *1982 Convention on the Law of the Sea provisions on conditions of access to fisheries subject to national jurisdiction*, UN Doc. FAO Fisheries Report No. 293, Annex I (1983).

112 *Cf.* R.-J. Dupuy, "The Sea Under National Competence" in Dupuy and Vignes, *op. cit.* 247-307, at 307.

113 The principle of "Equality", meaning equality of capacity for rights and obligations, was frequently invoked by the LLGDS in their proposals in the Seabed Committee and the Second Committee of UNCLOS III. II COMMENTARY at 697 *et seq*. Participation of LLGDS in EEZ fisheries under the Convention is consistently iterated on an "equitable", rather than "equal", basis. Kwiatkowska, *supra* note 81 at 70. "Equal or preferential rights" is accepted as long as all the relevant States agree. *See* Arts. 69 (5) and 70 (6), CLOS. *Cf.* A. M. Sinjela, *Land-Locked States and the UNCLOS Regime* 316-317 (1983). Illustrative of the claim for equality of developing LLGDS, *see* Kampala Declaration, esp. para. 9. UN Doc. A/CONF.62/23, III UNCLOS III Off Rec at 3.

114 Part X, CLOS. *See also* J. Monnier, "Right of Access to the Sea and Freedom of Transit" in Dupuy & Vignes, *op. cit.* 501-523.

115 Art. 125 (2), CLOS.

of the transit State to protect its legitimate interests.[116] Secondly, neighboring LLGDS are given rights in respect of marine scientific research (MSR) conducted by a researching State in the EEZ of a coastal State. LLGDS are entitled to be notified of proposed MSR projects by third States intending to carry out MSR in a coastal State's EEZ. They can request for relevant information and they can even participate in such MSR projects.[117] But these rights are, expectedly, not without limitation or qualification, especially in so far as they are affected by the exercise of discretionary sovereign rights by the coastal State itself.[118]

Overall, developing LLGDS were accorded very tenuous rights under the EEZ regime of the 1982 Convention. That they could be considered a distinct category of States for special legal consideration was not at all denied in UNCLOS III. But the Convention did not lay down any unconditional obligation on the part of any State or other category of States which the developing LLGDS could cite as their corresponding right or as the basis for their preferential treatment as a subset of developing States. The image of a "typical" developing State supported by the institution of the EEZ is a developing coastal State; the LLGDS aspect of this image was either suppressed or marginalized.

In any case, it must remembered that the essential basis and the dominant ethos of the EEZ as a new juridical concept in global wealth redistribution is none other than the old doctrine of coastal State sovereignty, or *mare clausum* – a fundamental doctrine whose long history and established denotations were never basically rooted in nor inspired by the cause of decolonization or development. There is no question that the fundamental legal concepts at the disposal of the developing States in the Second Committee of UNCLOS III allowed them only modest manoeuvering room in their effort to transform the concept of "special interests and needs of developing countries" into specific rules of law. The reason for such tethered condition, it bears repeating, is the presumed acceptance by the newly emerged States of the entirety of international law as they found it when they became politically independent States. There was no "pick and choose" option regarding international norms and rules available to them upon joining the international community. Within the corpus of classical international law, however, was the principle of *mare clausum*, which, by virtue of its emphasis on coastal State control of near-shore resources, was deployed by the developing countries in their campaign against the freedom of the seas

---

116 Art. 125 (3), CLOS. *See* Churchill & Lowe, *op. cit.* at 326.
117 Art. 254, CLOS.
118 Churchill & Lowe, *op. cit.* 322; Kwiatkowska, *supra* note 81, at 144-145.

principle.[119] The coastal State principle yielded a creative approach elaborated through the developing countries' EEZ proposal, which legitimized not only legal ownership over resources but also the actualization of economic/development gains from this ownership regime. The effective utilization and practical evolution of the EEZ in support of the cause for development and global sharing was the main interest of the developing States in the Third Committee of UNCLOS III, whose work on this matter will now be considered.

E. THE NORTH-SOUTH DIALOGUE IN THE THIRD COMMITTEE: LEGAL ASPECTS OF INTERNATIONAL COOPERATION FOR DEVELOPMENT AND GLOBAL SHARING IN THE OCEANS

If the lines of a North-South dialogue were too hazily drawn in the Second Committee, the North-South cleavage figured more prominently in the Third Committee.[120] Committee Three, it will be recalled, was responsible for putting together Part XII (Protection and Preservation of the Marine Environment), Part XIII (Marine Scientific Research), and Part XIV (Development and Transfer of Marine technology) of the 1982 Convention. In considering how the negotiations leading to these regimes were influenced by the North-South agenda of development and global sharing, reference should again be made to the broad debate taking place in the background of UNCLOS III which, on the whole, pitted the "coastal State" theory of the Group of 77 against the prevalent "freedom the seas" doctrine. The Group of 77 espoused the cause of strong coastal State sovereignty in its negotiating posture with respect to the traditional domains or the classical law of the sea.[121] The aim of the Group of 77 in the Second Committee was to widen the physical-functional reach of this sovereignty beyond the confines of the territorial sea. This they succeeded in doing through the creative institution of the EEZ, which established extensive resource jurisdic-

---

119 Friedheim, *op. cit.* at 301-302 and 305, estimates that 72% of the consolidated interest of the G-77 was on coastal ocean issues. On the other hand, LLGDS on the whole, had a significant 56% interests on these same issues. Friedheim's model did not "role play" the interests of developing LLGDS as a group.

120 I agree with the view of Friedheim, *op. cit.* at Chap. 6 and 337, that there was a strong North-South line-up of issues in the Third Committee. *Cf.* Koh & Jayakumar, *op. cit.* 81, observes that the G-77 was "only moderately effective" in taking a united stand in Third Committee and dispute settlement matters.

121 Friedheim, *op. cit.* 301.

tion off-shore. In the Third Committee, the dominant interest of the G-77 was clearly to establish effective or intensive enclosure. That is, to strengthen the capacities of the developing coastal States over the EEZ and transform legal entitlement into tangible equality-enhancing development. This challenge raises the issue of the extent to which the developing countries succeeded in consolidating the normative foundations of their Third Committee goals. Making reference to the Preamble of the 1982 Convention, the question for consideration is the degree to which the output of the Third Committee took into account "the special interests and needs of the developing countries" by way of negotiated rules in *lex lata*.

Insofar as the three problem areas considered by the Third Committee – *viz.*, the marine environment, marine scientific research, and transfer of technology – can be brought to bear on the traditional domains of disparity among nations in the oceans, the unavoidable conclusion is that not much by way of rigorously defined enforceable regimes came out from the efforts of the Group of 77 to establish a "development"-inducing coastal State jurisdiction in the EEZ. However, the most significant and potentially most radical contribution in positive law made by the Third Committee with respect to promoting the "special interest and needs of developing countries" consists of the seemingly innocuous but interlocking provisions relating to the "duty to cooperate." These provisions are scattered throughout the text of the Convention especially in it Parts XII, XIII and XIV. An analysis of Parts XII, XIII and XIV of the Convention will corroborate these observations.

1. *Protection and Preservation of the Marine Environment*

UNCLOS III discussions on the subject of the marine environment greatly benefitted from the 1972 United Nations Conference on the Human Environment.[122] The overall impact of this Conference on the attitudes of the Southern leaders who were about to negotiate a comprehensive law of the sea was quite significant. For them, environmental considerations were, in general, regarded as complementary rather than anathema to the main agenda of the developing

---

122 IV COMMENTARY at 8-9.

States that focussed on decolonization and development.[123] In UNCLOS III, the incipient global environmental movement ushered in by the Stockholm Conference had the effect of introducing more sophistication to the Group of 77 core argument on extended coastal State jurisdiction. Because the "environment" was perceived as a Northern issue, the developing States saw the environmental dimension of a comprehensive ocean regime as an additional justification to argue the case for development in the scheme of coastal State sovereignty. The bargaining outlook is summarized by Ambassador Christopher Pinto, a leading figure in the Group of 77, in a statement made on the eve of UNCLOS III, which must be quoted *in extenso*:

> The preservation of the human environment (including the marine environment) from further degradation is a problem that has been brought before the international community by the highly industrialized developed countries. The developing countries regard it as a problem for which those very countries, through commercial expediency and industrial neglect, are largely responsible, and which affects the highly industrialized areas far more than those of most developing countries. While the developed countries are striving to secure international acceptance of rules and standards to combat the menace of pollution, the developing countries may be expected to be more concerned to prevent any unwarranted increase they may cause in their industrial investment and which may even impede their programs of industrialization. In general, the developing countries' position on these issues might be based on the following:
>
> (1) Degradation of the human environment is a "social cost" for which the industrialized developed countries are mainly responsible and the burden of which must be borne principally by them. The developing countries may not be able to prevent this expense being added to the cost of a finished product which they would have to buy from the developed country. The developing countries may contribute to global environmental protection measures to the extent permitted or required by their own economic development plans.

---

123 The earliest authoritative exposition of the relationship between environmental concerns and economic development from the viewpoint of the developing countries is the famous *Founex Report*. *"Development and Environment" Report of the panel of experts convened by the Secretary-General of the United Nations Conference on the Human Environment*, Founex Switzerland, 4-12 June 1971. Text in Annex I, Doc. A/CONF.48/10 (22 December 1971).

(2) An environment relatively free of pollution is a natural resource which a developing country may exploit, e.g., through offering conditions for industrial investment that impose relatively liberal environmental protection rules and standards and, therefore, offer the investor substantial financial advantages.

(3) Problems of pollution of the environment, including the marine environment, are inter-related. Piecemeal measures for pollution control (e.g., the regulation of ocean dumping on a regional basis) should be approached with caution unless satisfactory international controls that safeguard the interests of coastal states, and especially developing coastal states, can be worked out.[124]

The marine environment item was thus tactically incorporated into the broader framework of "coastal State sovereignty" negotiations being pressed by the developing countries. For them, the sectoral environmental agenda of the developed countries in UNCLOS III[125] had to be reconceived under the overall "theory" of coastal State sovereignty which the Group of 77 was propounding in the Second Committee. The concern for the protection and preservation of the marine environment supplied the developing States with a cogent argument why they should be materially assisted in strengthening their actual capabilities to discharge their environmental obligations.[126]

---

124 Pinto, *supra* note 51, at 12. This statement is consistent with and seems to be a more specific formulation of the view articulated on behalf of the developing countries in the *Founex Report, ibid.*

125 This sectoral approach which prevailed, as explained below, led to an imbalance in the normative development of rules on two levels: (1) with respect to sources of pollution in the marine environment, vessel-source pollution being accorded the greatest prominence, and (2) with respect to the isolated consideration of the marine environmental regime, the regime of MSR, and the regime for technology transfer and development. The sectoral approach, which was evident in the Stockholm Declaration, treated environmental concerns independently of other sectoral concerns like trade, security, and finance. This "sector by sector" approach in the development of environmental norms will be found inadequate for the 1990s, in view of the need for an "integrated" approach to marine environmental protection. *See* generally, *Conclusions of the Sienna Forum on International Law of the Environment*, (April, 1990) text in UN Doc. A/45/666/Annex (24 October 1990). DOALOS, 1990 UN Annual Review of Ocean Affairs.

126 In an effort to emphasize the priority of development needs over environmental concerns, some developing countries at first argued for a "double standard" concerning the obligations to protect and preserve the marine environment, higher standards for developed countries and lower, more lenient standards for developing

The logic behind the environment *cum* development argument was already put forward by the Group of 77 in the days of the Seabed Committee. With the support of some developed coastal States, like Canada and Australia, who saw a reasonable connection between marine environmental protection and stronger coastal State authority,[127] the developing countries lobbied particularly for the *obligation* of developed States to extend scientific and technical assistance to needy countries to enable them to effectively prevent or control marine pollution.[128] The developing countries also insisted that preferential treatment be given them in the allocation or utilization of funds and services of international organizations so that they could effectively carry out their obligation to protect and preserve the marine environment.[129] For the developing States the link between economic development and marine environmental protection made perfect sense, because it was only through the provision of relevant financial, technical and other assistance from the developed world that they could thereby be enabled to properly implement what was never disputed by anyone as their basic obligation to protect and preserve the marine environment.

The "special interests and needs of developing countries", meaning their well-known limited means of executing their duties respecting the marine environment, is recognized by the Convention in Article 194. This provision refers to the use by States of "the best practicable means at their disposal and in accordance with their capabilities" in carrying out their duties towards the marine environment.[130] However, what was sought as a counterpart duty of

---

countries. Friedheim, *op. cit.* at 182; IV COMMENTARY at 12. This position was later abandoned in favor of a compromise approach that emphasized harmonization of national laws and regulations with generally accepted rules, standards, procedures, and practices established through competent international organizations or general diplomatic conferences. IV COMMENTARY at 13-14. Furthermore, compliance with the obligation to prevent, reduce of control pollution would depend on the means available to developing States in discharging this obligation. J. Charney, *The Marine Environment and the 1982 United Nations Convention on the Law of the Sea* 28 INTERNATIONAL LAWYER 879, 886 (1994).

127 IV COMMENTARY at 100.
128 *See* Doc. A/AC.138/SC.III/L.41 (1973) (Kenya); IV COMMENTARY at 99-101.
129 IV COMMENTARY at 106.
130 IV COMMENTARY at 99. This provision of the Convention anticipates the concept of "common but differentiated responsibilities" embodied in Principle 7 of the 1992 Rio Declaration on Environment and Development. L. Kimball "The United Nations Convention on the Law of the Sea: A Framework for Marine Conser-

the developed States to extend the required assistance to developing countries was never firmly secured in the positive language of *lex lata*.[131] If there was at all an undertaking for them to give assistance, this Northern commitment can only be derived from the implicit trade-off underlying Article 194.[132] As it stands, however, the Convention arguably gives unfettered freedom of action on the part of those States expected to extend such assistance – whether acting through bilateral means or as members of international organizations.[133] The weak obligation of endowed developed States to assist developing States is also complemented by the *pacta de contrahendo* provisions on global and regional cooperation in Part XII.[134]

The absence of any positive Northern obligation to assist the South protect and preserve the marine environment is indicative of the Convention's failure to create new substantive obligations of a specific kind in Part XII.[135] The new obligations are procedural in nature. Furthermore, in contrast to the negotiated "umbrella" provisions on marine pollution that are broadly formulated,[136] Part XII of the Convention stipulates quite detailed rules on the

---

vation" in *The Law of the Sea: Priorities and Responsibilities in Implementing the Convention* 26 (IUCN, 1995). On the principle of "common but differentiated responsibilities", *see infra* Sec. F.3.

131 *See* Art. 202, CLOS, on "Scientific and technical assistance to developing States."

132 The claim that Art. 194 allows for a "double standard" for States – one for the South and one for the North – in discharging their basic obligation to protect and preserve the marine environment misconceives the agreement on common commitments which were already articulated in the 1972 Stockholm Conference on the Environment. Without external assistance, the developing countries would accomplish little by way of protecting the environment; the developed countries should therefore live up to their part of the bargain by providing this assistance. Kimball, *supra* note 131, at 21 and note 8 thereof. A complementary argument is given in Charney, *supra* note 127, at 886-887: The obligation of developing countries is qualified with respect to means of protecting and preserving the marine environment; these qualification is eliminated by obliging States with the necessary means at their disposal to assist and cooperate with others to make capabilities available.

133 IV COMMENTARY at 103.

134 Generally, Arts. 197, 200 & 201, CLOS.

135 Friedheim, *op. cit.* 183, dismisses the anti-pollution language of the Convention as hortatory.

136 Brown, *supra* note 10, at 336; M. McConnel & E. Gold, *The Modern Law of the Sea: Framework for the Protection and Preservation of the Marine Environment?* 23 CASEWESTERN RES J INT L 83 (1991).

enforcement of vessel-source pollution standards *ratione loci*.[137] Clearly, these highly detailed rules were never intended to address the Southern demands for stronger coastal State sovereignty by way of an assisted or expanded capacity to discharge environmental obligations.

There is thus a normative "imbalance" in the scheme of marine environmental protection laid down in Part XII of the Convention. On the one hand, there are the general and largely hortatory framework provisions on the duty to cooperate between the North and South. This means that the parties will have to meet again at a later time in order to negotiate the specific terms of their cooperation,[138] but without any obligation to enter into such specific agreements. This was all that could be secured by consensus in support of the "development" dimension of marine environmental protection under Part XII. On the other hand, Part XII secures an elaborate enforcement regime on the narrow and somewhat over-emphasized subject of vessel-source pollution. It is this lack of prominence in positive law of the North-South aspects of marine environmental protection under the Convention which accounts for the observed disjuncture between environment and development concerns in Part XII.[139] In the absence of the political conditions that could push the North and the South to cooperate under the mandatory but general terms of Part XII in relation to their common primary obligation to protect and preserve the marine environment, Part XII is simply a "half-hearted" framework agreement on Third World development through marine environmental protection. As will be explained below, however, these political conditions will soon congeal under the more

---

137 There is extensive literature on the enforcement regime concerning vessel-source pollution. *See* D. Bodansky, *Protecting the Marine Environment from Vessel-Source Pollution* 18 ECOLOGY L QTLY 719 (1991); A. Boyle, *Marine Pollution under the Law of the Sea* 79 AJIL 347 (1985); P. Dempsey, *Compliance and Enforcement in International Law – Oil Pollution of the Marine Environment by Ocean Vessels* 6 NORTHWESTERN J INTL L & BUS 459 (1984); J. Bernhart, *A Schematic Analysis of Vessel-Source Pollution: Prescriptive and Enforcement Regimes in the Law of the Sea Conference* 20 VA J INT L 265 (1980); Churchill & Lowe, *op. cit.* at 248-260; P. Payoyo, *Port State Control in the Asia-Pacific: An International Legal Study of Port State Jurisdiction* (1993).

138 M.C.W. Pinto, "The Duty to Cooperate and the United Nations Convention on the Law of the Sea" in A. Bos & H. Siblesz (Eds.), *Realism in Law Making* 153 (1986).

139 *See* Sanger, *op. cit.* 105.

sobering circumstances of the 1992 UN Conference on Environment and Development.

2. *Marine Scientific Research*

If knowledge is power, the principal manifestation of the enormous gap between the developed and the developing countries is the glaring disparity in stock of available knowledge at the disposal of these States, collectively as groups and individually as governments. Indeed, the research gap between developed and developing countries, as Professor Elisabeth Mann-Borgese points out, is the worst of all development gaps.[140] The generation of knowledge, particularly scientific knowledge and its control, as well as the practical application of knowledge (technology), therefore, became intensely debated issues at UNCLOS III. The assumption was that knowledge of (or the knowledge gap on) the oceans was determinative of the welfare and power positions of States in the international community.[141]

The overall stance of developing countries on the subject of marine scientific research (MSR) in UNCLOS III was once more reflective of their adverse attitude towards the Grotian doctrine of freedom of the seas. Freedom of research, basically advanced by the developed researching countries,[142] was opposed by the developing countries. Essentially, the latter wanted more controls over the conduct of MSR.[143] Against the background of a heightened profile for marine science and technology in the 1960s in the fields of security, marine resource development, and the protection and preservation of the marine environment,[144] the strategic importance of a control regime over MSR loomed quite large not least in the political agenda of the developing countries.

---

140 E.M. Borgese, *Ocean Governance and the United Nations* 129 (1995). *See also* Report of the South Commission, *Challenge to the South* 81 (1990).
141 As Professor E. Miles intimated, any set of strategies aimed at addressing the issue of North-South wealth distribution should include most crucially those relating to the acquisition of knowledge and capabilities. E. Miles, "Remarks" in Alexander, *supra* note 51, at 19.
142 *See* Pinto, *supra* note 51, at 12; Friedheim, *op. cit.* 211.
143 Pinto, *id.*, at 12-13; Churchill & Lowe, *op. cit.* 291.
144 IV COMMENTARY at 429-433; *Marine Scientific Research: Legislative History of Article 246 of the United Nations Convention on the Law of the Sea* iii (UN, 1994).

The motivation behind the insistence by the developing States on controls over MSR is often characterized in a negative way by some commentators. In view of the scientific and technological gap between North and South, the frequent representation made is that it must be in the interest of developing countries to curtail scientific research activities conducted by technologically advanced researching States, if only to narrow the gap in scientific and technological capabilities, or else stop it from further deteriorating.[145] Under this representation, equalization of capacities means increasing not the "haves" of the "have-nots" but the "have-nots" of the "haves." The dominant picture conjured up is thus one of a besieged Northern scientist valiantly struggling to liberate marine scientific knowledge from its politicization and bureaucratic shackling by governments in the South.[146]

---

145 Thus, a leading commentator on the subject states said that some developing countries may simply not be interested in MSR "because they do not understand it"; or that they are not interested in and should not tolerate fundamental research by foreigners because "they see no immediate benefits (in terms of economic gains) from the results of such research" and only scientifically and technologically advanced nations will benefit from its results; and that "by refusing consent for this kind of research in their offshore areas developing coastal States might prevent the gap from widening further." See A. Soons, *Marine Scientific Research and the Law of the Sea* 37-39 (1982). Friedheim, *op. cit.* 209 & 210 adds that the "large element of emotion" behind the developing countries' campaign to regulate MSR proceeds from the sense of humiliation and insult that follows from negotiating with parties more knowledgeable than they are concerning their offshore resources; it was, therefore, in their rational short-term self-interest not to allow the other party from knowing anything through MSR. It is also claimed that according to the developing countries "the marginal value of scientific inquiry increases directly with the degree of industrialization of a state. Therefore, in the short run, the essence of science [or MSR] is to increase the disparity between rich and poor, and in these circumstances science must be 'controlled' to emphasize particular local needs." G. Pontecorvo and M. Wilkerson, *From Cornucopia to Scarcity: The Current Status of Ocean Use* 5 ODIL at 395, note no. 7 (1978).

146 *See e.g.*, D. Shapely, *Oceanography: Albatross of Diplomacy Haunts Seafaring Scientist* 180 SCIENCE 1036 (1973); P. Fye, "Scientific Research in the Oceans" in Borgese & Krieger, *supra* note 2, at 306; W. Wooster, *Ocean Research Under Foreign Jurisdiction* 212 SCIENCE 754 (1981); CB Raleigh, *The Internationalism of Ocean Science vs. International Politics* 23 MARINE TECHNOLOGY SOCIETY JOURNAL 44 (1989). W. Burke, "Commentary" in A. Soons (Ed.), *Implementation of the Law of the Sea Convention Through International Institutions* 539-541 (LSI,

A more positive understanding of the attitude taken by the developing countries with respect to the issue of MSR must consider the fundamentally protective thrust of their claim to regulate MSR in their territorial waters. The perception of the erstwhile intrusiveness and potentially predatory role of MSR under a liberal regime was definitely well-founded[147] and provided a legitimate basis for the developing countries to raise critical questions concerning the ethical and political consequences of Northern scientists' pretensions at objectivity in the conduct of MSR.[148] Especially in regard to resource-oriented MSR, developing countries responded to the threats posed by the notion of unrestricted freedom in scientific research off their coasts with the assertion of sovereignty, or permanent sovereignty over natural resources.[149] This explains their specific advocacy for an absolute consent regime over MSR conducted in coastal waters, as well as for the obliteration of what was suspected as the spurious distinction between pure and applied MSR then being put forward by some developed States.[150] The historical motivation behind this preferred regulatory regime for MSR is the juridical establishment of a coastal State in full control of its resources.

The consolidation of the concept of extended coastal State jurisdiction via the institution of the EEZ in the course of UNCLOS III negotiations opened the way for agreement on a consent regime in MSR.[151] The resulting compromise, now embodied in the 1982 Convention, provided for a qualified consent regime concerning MSR in the EEZ, with considerable powers vested on the coastal

---

1993); Friedheim, *op. cit.* at 218, and in his Chap. 6 makes reference to "making the EEZ work and scientists pay."

147 *See* R. Khan, "Marine Science Research: Some Thoughts on the Implications of a Free and Consent-Based Regime" in Anand, *supra* note 51, at 293, 305.

148 *See* the insightful points raised in H.R. Bernard, "Restrictions on Oceanic Research: An Anthropologist's View" and R. Munier, "The Politics of Marine Science: Crisis and Compromise" both in Alexander, *supra* note 51, at 206 & 219.

149 *MSR: Legislative History of Art. 246, supra* note 144, at iii.

150 *See* Docs. A/Conf.62/C.3/L.13 (22 August 1974) (Columbia, on behalf of the G-77), III UNCLOS III Off Rec 254; and A/Conf.62/C.3/L.13/Rev.2 (1975) (Iraq, on behalf of the G-77), IV UNCLOS III Off Rec 199.

151 For an account of the controversial consent regime, *see* IV COMMENTARY at 433-435, 496-519; *MSR: Legislative History of Art. 246, supra* note 144; Soons, *supra* note 146, 154-218.

State.[152] However, the Convention apparently gives some indication that the traditional distinction between "pure" and "applied" research for MSR in the EEZ exists, although these terms as such are not used in the text of the Convention.[153] Moreover, the Convention does not respond to a crucial jurisdictional point raised by the G-77 concerning the use of aircraft, satellites or ocean data acquisition systems (ODAS) in the conduct of MSR.[154] This silence or deliberate omission had indeed rendered some aspects of the consent regime established in the Convention already inadequate if not obsolete in the face of the increasing the use of these instruments/techniques for MSR today.[155] On the whole, while the developing countries may have prevailed in their contention for a strong coastal State profile over MSR conducted in the EEZ,[156] this outcome was simply a projection of negotiations between "coastal States" and "researching States" as interest groups, and not a consequence of bargaining along strictly North-South lines.[157]

---

152 IV COMMENTARY at 517-519, 643-656; Kwiatkowska, *supra* note 81, 139-142, 145-146; Brown, *supra* note 10, 426-429, 433; A. de Marffy, "Marine Scientific Research" in II Dupuy & Vignes, *op. cit.* 1125-1140.

153 "Pure" or fundamental research, to which the coastal State is obliged to grant its consent under "normal circumstances", is described in the Convention as research carried out in accordance with the Convention exclusively for peaceful purposes and in order to increase scientific knowledge of the marine environment for the benefit of mankind. "Applied" or industrial research invokes the absolute consent regime in favor of the coastal State as described in Art. 246 (5). IV COMMENTARY at 518; Kwiatkowska, *supra* note 81, at 140-141; Churchill & Lowe, *op. cit.* at 293-294; Soons, *supra* note 146, at 164-179; E.D. Brown, *supra* note 10, at 419. *Cf.* E.P. Andryev, *et al.*, *The International Law of the Sea* at 174 (1988), claiming that no such distinction between pure and applied MSR is drawn by the Convention.

154 *See* item 2(b) 2(ii), of draft articles on MSR submitted by Columbia and Iraq on behalf of the Group of 77, *supra* note 150.

155 *See* Soons, *supra* note 145, at 177; Churchill & Lowe, *op. cit.* 297-299; Kwiatkowska, *supra* note 81, at 135 and literature cited therein; Brown, *supra* note 10, at 434-437; Borgese, *supra* note 140, at 26, 127.

156 MSR in the high seas is, however, still governed by the principle of freedom. Art. 87, CLOS. For MSR in the Area, *see infra* Chaps. 5 & 6.

157 The Soviet block shifted its position in support of a consent regime in 1975, thus reinforcing the claim for greater coastal State control over MSR. Soons, *supra* note 145, 160-161; Kwiatkowska, *supra* note 81, at 136. Some developing countries also noted the fact that the G-77 position on MSR did not sufficiently take into account the interests of LLGDS. *See e.g.* Statements of Singapore, Lesotho and Liberia

Nevertheless, it must be emphasized that the consent regime for MSR in the EEZ indirectly provided developing coastal States with an entry point in order to advance the cause of increasing their scientific capabilities for economic development.[158] Under the Convention, this was made possible through the provision for express coastal State rights to participate in MSR projects as well as rights to be assisted in the assessment and interpretation of research results. Surely, these are not insignificant entitlements.[159] However, the language of the Convention on this point is nothing more but an invocation of the general duty to cooperate already applied quite liberally under Part XII of the Convention in conjunction with the protection and preservation of the marine environment.

The most significant aspect of the regime under Part XIII of the Convention from the standpoint of the theme of equality, development and global sharing involves the provisions on international cooperation on MSR.[160] These provisions are singularly noteworthy because the consent regime, in practice, can be implemented only through the specific cooperative endeavors that are contemplated by these provisions. Cooperation is thus "forced" upon States as soon as coastal State consent to MSR is exercised. To illustrate, participation in research cruises or provision for assistance in the interpretation of oceanographic research results, as mandated rights made available to coastal States, are in themselves cooperative undertakings for socio-economic development. Furthermore, States are urged to cooperate in promoting the flow of scientific data and information, and the transfer of knowledge resulting from MSR, especially to developing States, and to promote the strengthening of the autonomous MSR capabilities of these States through, *inter alia*, programmes to provide adequate

---

during the Second Session in the Third Committee, II UNCLOS III Off Rec 383.
158 Kwiatkowska, *supra* note 81, at 150.
159 Art. 249, CLOS. The burden of implementing these rights, cost-wise, is imputable to the research States and Organizations.
160 For MSR in the areas under national jurisdiction, these provisions on cooperation are not only limited to Arts. 242-244 & 251 under Part XIII of the CLOS. The cooperation regime for MSR is also present in Art. 123 (Co-operation of States bordering enclosed and semi-enclosed seas); Arts. 61, 63, 65, 66, 67 and 119 (on marine living resources); Arts. 200 and 202 (Protection and preservation of the marine environment); and Arts. 266, 270, 275, and 276 (Marine Technology), CLOS.

education and training of their technical and scientific personnel.[161] Parenthetically, the origin of this specific provision is traceable to the working paper submitted by Canada to the Seabed Committee in 1972,[162] which quite interestingly put forward as its foundational argument the concept that knowledge resulting from MSR is part of the "common heritage of mankind."[163] Although not couched in the rigorous language of positive law, the restrictively-formulated duty[164] to cooperate for a North-South cause is in fact the indispensable modality that puts into operation the consent regime laid down in the Convention.[165] It can potentially be invoked by developing coastal States in any framework of international cooperation for MSR. It constitutes a necessary underpinning for a climate of trust[166] through which the rights and obligations of both coastal States and research States under the consent regime of the Convention are ultimately guaranteed.[167] All this shows that the MSR regime in the Convention was precisely designed to foster if not necessitate international cooperation.[168]

With the awareness that it is only through international cooperation on the widest possible terms and at all levels – subregional, regional, global, North-South, and South-South – that a meaningful MSR regime can be assured for the developing countries, the Group of 77 moved for the adoption of what is now Annex VI of the Final Act of UNCLOS III.[169] Capturing as it does the full consensus of developing countries on the question of marine science and technology, this Resolution outlines the programmatic elements of international cooperation on MSR aimed at reducing the North-South scientific and tech-

---

161 *See* Art. 244 (2), CLOS.
162 Doc. A/AC/138/SC.III/L.18 (25 July 1972); *See* IV COMMENTARY at 480-487.
163 Principle 1, Canadian Working Paper, *ibid.*
164 On the possibility of a narrow interpretation of Art. 244 (2) as a result of drafting changes therein, *see* IV COMMENTARY at 486.
165 *See* Kwiatkowska, *supra* note 81, at 151-152, quoting Soons, *supra* note 145, at 269.
166 Brown, *supra* note 10, at 439-440.
167 Kwiatkowska, *supra* note 81, at 151.
168 A. Yankov, *A General Review of the New Convention on the Law of the Sea: Marine Science and its Application* 4 OCEAN YRBK 150 at 164 (1983). *See also, Report of the Secretary General on the Law of the Sea: Marine Scientific Research*, para. 1-16, UN Doc. A/45/563 (11 October 1990).
169 Entitled *Resolution on Development of National Marine Science, Technology and Ocean Service Infrastructures*. For the background and legal status of this Resolution, *see* IV COMMENTARY at 741-747.

nological gap.¹⁷⁰ Among the many points it raises, the Resolution calls on developing countries to integrate MSR in their development plans and to establish MSR cooperation programmes among themselves; it urges the North to assist developing countries prepare and implement their MSR development programmes; and it pleads for a revitalized and coordinated response on the part of relevant international organizations to the MSR needs and programmes of developing countries.¹⁷¹ The Resolution, in short, expressed the expectations of the developing countries on the role of MSR under a new ocean regime as an activity governed by the traditional law of the sea.¹⁷² Although this Resolution is not directly related to the Convention,¹⁷³ it can be argued that it strengthens and enriches the overall framework of cooperation for MSR in the Convention to the extent that its substantive agenda is accommodated in the coordinated implementation of the consent regime.¹⁷⁴

3. Development and Transfer of Marine Technology

It is maintained by some commentators that Part XIV of the Convention, on the development and transfer of marine technology, does not contain rules of law but partake mostly of policy-declaring statements in the nature of *pacta*

---

170 *See* Statement of representative from Sri Lanka, introducing this Resolution at the 9th session of the Conference, 1980, XIV UNCLOS III Off Rec 43, 84; IV COMMENTARY at 747.
171 Renewed interests in the prescient Annex VI is warranted because it foreshadowed recent developments in international environmental agreements and Agenda 21. Kimball, *supra* note 131, at 19 & 109.
172 Cooperation for new initiatives in familiar areas such as fisheries and the development of off-shore resources was emphasized by the representative of Sri Lanka. *Supra* note 170.
173 IV COMMENTARY at 746-747.
174 As a result and in the spirit of this Resolution, the Intergovernmental Oceanographic Commission has, since 1985, pursued a "Comprehensive Plan for a Major Assistance Programme to Enhance the Marine Science Capabilities of Developing Countries." *See* IV COMMENTARY at 486-487, 747. *See also Note by the Secretary-General: Long-Term and Expanded Programme of Oceanographic Research*, Doc. E/1989/111 (1 June 1989).

de contrahendo.[175] This, of course, does not negate the fact that the Convention as a whole, in which Part XIII is embodied, is still a formal source of law that absolutely confers *lex lata* status to the contents of Part XIV, whose provisions admittedly are mostly formulated in vague and general language.[176] Those few provisions that are detailed enough to be more compelling in character[177] are related to the obligations of States in the process of marine technology transfer specifically associated with the functions of the International Seabed Authority.[178] These and other binding rules associated with the issue of transfer of technology will be discussed later in the context of Part XI of the Convention and the work of the First Committee.

From a contemporary perspective, the *pacta de contrahendo* language of Part XIV may be read and interpreted in two contradictory or mutually exclusive ways. First, Part XIV could be seen as one strand of the bigger debate on the issue of technology transfer that took place in the confrontational setting of the Third World move to establish a New International Economic Order (NIEO) in the mid-1970s. Indeed, it is said that the political and philosophical background of the provisions of Part XIV is supplied by two General Assembly Resolutions on the NIEO adopted in 1974:[179] Resolution 3202 (S-IV) the Programme of Action on the Establishment of a New International Economic Order; and Resolution 3281 (XXIX) The Charter of Economic Rights and Duties of States.[180] Whatever policy guidelines are enunciated in Part XIV, these are, therefore, a mere reflection of, and inseparable from, the overall directive

---

175 IV COMMENTARY at 668; Churchill & Lowe, *op. cit.* 303. *Pactum de contrahendo* means an understanding to negotiate or conclude a contract. 2 JOWITT'S DICTIONARY OF ENGLISH LAW 1304 (1972).

176 *See* BA Boczek, *The Transfer of Marine Technology to Developing Nations in International Law* 26 (LSI Paper no. 23, 1982): Part XIV is legally binding and not a "voluntary guidelines" document, although it has many watered down obligations using hortatory language.

177 J. Fons Buhl, "Development and Transfer of Marine Technology" in II Dupuy & Vignes, *op. cit.* 1146, 1148.

178 *See* Arts. 273, 274, and 275 (2), CLOS. Art. 278 on "cooperation among international organizations" could be cross-referenced with these mandatory provisions.

179 IV COMMENTARY at 666.

180 Specifically, Section IV of Resolution 3202 and Article 13 of Resolution 3281. One of the principles stated in the Declaration on the Establishment of a New International Economic Order, UNGA Res. 3201 (S-VI), par. 4(p), is the promotion of transfer of technology and the creation of indigenous technology for the benefit of developing countries.

on technology transfer of the NIEO presented by the developing States in the UNCTAD or the UN General Assembly and caustically debated in these fora.[181]

The consequence of treating Part XIV as nothing more than a specific reintroduction of the historically controversial proposals arising from the NIEO resolutions in the UN General Assembly is obviously destructive of Part XIV itself. This finding is based on a reasoning that may be outlined as follows. Generally, in the post-Cancun diplomatic era,[182] the dissipation of interest in the NIEO and its concepts, as defined both by the above-mentioned General Assembly resolutions and by the divisive circumstances surrounding their adoption, doomed the fate of Part XIV. Since the NIEO is already *passé*, Part XIV is virtually an empty framework for policy and follow-up action, long abandoned or forgotten by the international community. Specifically, to the extent that Part XIV of the Convention may have substantiated the original NIEO proposals which asserted a highly critical stance against the restrictive technological transactions of transnational corporations (TNCs), the policy shift in many countries away from this position of controlling TNCs and towards a more liberal attitude on foreign investments since the 1980s,[183] justifies the perception that even the policy preferences adopted in Part XIV have lost their ideological appeal. If the *raison d'être* of Part XIV had in fact vanished, it then logically follows that Part XIV is largely obsolete as a statement of general principles and policies, and can no longer be of service in the formation of particular regimes on the development and transfer of marine technology. If this is so, Part XIV is significant only as a historical artifact.[184]

---

181 IV COMMENTARY at 668; Churchill & Lowe, *op. cit.* 301-303.
182 *See* Jones *supra* note 17, on global negotiations and the NIEO.
183 For a description of these trends, *see* Yuwen Li, *Transfer of Technology for Deep Seabed Mining: The 1982 Law of the Sea Convention and Beyond* 134-140 (1994).
184 This, apparently, is the discernible justification for some authors' non-treatment of Part XIV. Churchill & Lowe, *op. cit.* devote 3 pages of discussion on the subject, while the Chapter on "Development and Transfer of Marine technology" in the 2-volume Handbook of Dupuy & Vignes, *op. cit.* consists of 4 pages. Brown, *supra* note 10, does not give any attention to Part XIV, as do Russian authors, Anreyev, *et al.*, *supra* note 153. D.P. O'Connell, *The International Law of the Sea* 2 vols. (1982), likewise abstained from treating the subject matter of Part XIV. T. Clingan's textbook, *supra* note 26, consideration of the subject is about half a page long, in the form of posed questions that betray his skepticism towards Part XIV. Even before the Convention was adopted, it was observed that the subject of Part XIV has been largely ignored by commentators. Boczek, *supra* note 176, at 22.

A second, more reassuring, way to read Part XIV is to consider it as an autonomous input in the process of establishing *a* NIEO, rather than as an emanation of *the* NIEO proposals then being debated in the forum of the General Assembly. UNCLOS III, in this view, was an independent forum where the possibilities of a new international economic order in the arena of the oceans have been autonomously explored[185] not basically by the developing countries only but by the entire international community as a whole.[186] Part XIV of the Convention – however abstract and general it may appear – is, therefore, nothing less than a successfully formulated NIEO concept in positive law[187] which should then be celebrated through more specific follow-up initiatives. It is

---

185 Long before the "NIEO" discourse was began in the UN General Assembly, the Seabed Committee was already considering a proposal from the developing countries for a "NIEO" in the matter of "training, sharing of knowledge and transfer of technology." *See* Doc. A/AC.138/58, reproduced in 1971 SBC Report at 202. Canada, in March 1972, also suggested a programme of work on the transfer of technology to developing countries. Doc. A/AC.138/SC.III/Rev.1. These were the precedents supporting the inclusion of an item "development and transfer of technology" in the list of subjects and issues for consideration in UNCLOS III and allocated to the Third Committee. IV COMMENTARY at 665. International programmes and practices on transfer of marine technology were already in existence even before the emotionally-charged NIEO arguments for technology transfer were raised in the General Assembly. *See* D. Kay *International Transfer of Marine Technology: The Transfer Process and International Organizations* 2 ODIL 351-377 (1974).

186 This is the argument put forward by Prof. Borgese to resolve the problematic relationship between the UNCLOS and the NIEO concepts/processes. A NIEO on land will fail without a NIEO for the sea, and each must potentiate each other. As she maintains, the issue is a conceptual problem of direction, goal and purpose. E.M. Borgese, *The New International Economic Order and the Law of the Sea* 14 SAN DIEGO L REV 584-596 (1975). *See* also Boczek, *supra* note 176, at 46, for the view that Part XIV is the result of developing countries' attempts to institutionalize the idea of the NIEO in one sectoral but vital area of technology transfer – the transfer of marine technology. *See also* A. Vratusa, "The Convention on the Law of the Sea in the Light of the Struggle for the New International Economic Order" in B. Vukas (Ed.), *Essays on the New Law of the Sea* 17-30, at 21 (Zagreb, 1985).

187 The Conventional embodiment of this concept of technology transfer is said to be potentially generative of customary law on the transfer of technology, specifically, and the duty to cooperate to aid developing countries, generally. Boczek, *supra* note 176, at 47.

submitted that the international community cannot afford to treat Part XIV as an object of continuing cynicism or indifference.

This second mode of interpretation as the preferred approach to Part XIV is countenanced by the decision-making methods of UNCLOS III. The policy-declaring provisions of Part XIV were actually adopted on the basis of consensus procedures meant to forge new – and therefore, NIEO – principles and policies on such a complex subject as the development and transfer of marine technology. The direct association of Part XIV with the confrontational strategies characteristic of the NIEO diplomacy in the UN General Assembly which was then fueled by the bitter oil politics in the 1970s is, therefore, not at all warranted.[188] This reading Part XIV is also supported by the rule of treaty construction which provides that an instrument should be interpreted in good faith in the light of its object and purpose and so as not to lead to a result that is manifestly absurd and unreasonable.[189] Lastly, this approach to understanding Part XIV is upheld by the substance of Part XIV itself, which, in its foundations, highlights the foremost importance of international cooperation in every aspect of the policy on development and transfer of marine technology[190] – far removed from the politics of indifference and beggar-thy-neighbor attitudes that had emerged in the NIEO debates in other fora.

The regime of cooperation or cooperative action in Part XIV of the Convention is indeed a unique and most significant hallmark of the Convention in the realization of a NIEO for the oceans.[191] The subject on which cooperation is enjoined most comprehensively in the Convention is the development and transfer of technology.[192] It is this framework of cooperation established in

---

188 *Cf.* M.A. Morris, "The New International Economic Order and the New Law of the Sea" in K.P. Sauvant & H. Hasenpflug (Eds.), *The New International Economic Order: Confrontation or Cooperation between North and South?* 175-189 (1977).

189 The interpretive context supplied by the Preamble of the Convention is highly significant in giving effect to Part XIV. *See* Art. 31 (2), and generally Arts. 31 & 32, Vienna Convention on the Law of Treaties.

190 Boczek, *supra* note 176, at 47.

191 For the developing countries, this NIEO for the oceans will be established on the basis of regimes that modify or supplant the principle of freedom of the seas. *See* generally B.A. Boczek, *Ideology and the New Law of the Sea: The Challenge of the New International Economic Order* 7 BOSTON COLLEGE INT & COMP L REV 1 (1984).

192 Pinto, *supra* 138 at 130, 143, also 145-154.

Part XIV which connects directly with the "mandatory" cooperative regime set forth in Part XIII[193] and, by logical extension, Part XII of the Convention. Thus, all three Parts of the Convention – on marine technology, marine environment, and MSR – are closely interwoven and should be read together for all practical purposes.[194] One could even go much further and argue that transfer of technology, dealt with in Part XIV, goes beyond the ambit of Third Committee deliberations and extends to the whole sphere of marine activities.[195]

In review, the *pacta de contrahendo* character of the provisions under Part XIV of the Convention does not diminish the norm of international cooperation which underlies them. Nor on this account does it not negate their potential to embody positive rights and obligations. If the cooperative enterprise mandated under the consent regime in Part XIII is to be fully appreciated, this must be understood as incorporating in an integral way the framework of cooperative action expressed in Part XIV, no less than the cooperative obligations stated in Part XII of the Convention on marine environmental protection. As a consequence, international cooperation on MSR in the EEZ, or in any other area under coastal State jurisdiction, has a great potential in bringing about an increase in the scientific and technological capabilities of developing coastal States, and thus contribute to the general aim of bridging the scientific knowledge and/or technological gap between the North and the South. If the regime that governs the conduct of MSR is to be workable, its infrastructure of supportive cooperative arrangements cannot be fragmented into isolated, sectoral standards of international cooperation – one for MSR *per se*, another for pollution prevention, another for technology transfer, another for fisheries management, etc. As long as it is accepted that the requirements of an effective MSR regime make imperative a strong, unified and pervasive climate of trust and international co-

---

[193] Boczek, *supra* note 176, at 31-32.
[194] Part XII, XIII and XIV of the Convention, together with Annex IV of the Final Act, are, therefore, complementary and mutually reinforcing invocations of international cooperation. *Report of the Secretary General on the Law of the Sea: Marine Scientific Research*, esp. Para. 9, *supra* note 168; Kimball, *supra* note 130, at 108. The 1972 Canadian proposal in the Seabed Committee, *supra* note 162, already recognized the inter-relationship among transfer of technology to developing countries, protection and preservation of the marine environment, and scientific research. *See also* IV COMMENTARY at 668. It is, therefore, difficult to understand the remark that there was an absence of reciprocal interests between North and South on the issue of transfer of technology. *Cf.* IV COMMENTARY at 669.
[195] IV COMMENTARY at 669; Borgese, *supra* note 140, at 26.

operation, such climate of trust and cooperation must perforce be extended to the activity of development and transfer of technology. Happily, this is what Part XIV achieves, notwithstanding the inchoate rights and obligations it defines nor the reduction of its provisions into limited non-binding statements of policy.[196] On this perspective, the North-South debate on the issue of development and transfer of technology which had proven unnecessarily pugnacious and unproductive in other fora have found a promising resolution in the new international ocean order established by the 1982 Convention.

Cooperation for marine science and technology in the traditional domains of ocean law – like fishing, shipping, environmental protection, and non-living resource exploitation – under the regime of extended coastal State jurisdiction established in the Convention is certainly a new approach to the overall problem of development and global sharing.[197] For the developing countries, whose two-fold aim was to reduce the North-South scientific and technological gap and to limit the rapacious deployment of the principle of freedom of research in their waters,[198] this approach is realistic, given the bargaining constraints

---

[196] In the Third Committee, some developed countries introduced modifications to G-77 proposals that were meant to narrow the scope of or water-down obligations on North-South cooperation, *e.g.,* the term "marine" to qualify "technology" in Art. 266 and elsewhere; dropping *"inter alia"* in Art. 268 and making reference to "States" rather than "All States" in the same article; insertion of "endeavor" to weaken the element of obligation in Arts. 269; qualifying "developing states" by "States which may need and request technical assistance in this field" in Art. 274 and proposals to delete Arts. 273 and 274. *See* IV COMMENTARY at 675, 686, 693, 694, 704, 708, 715. The Drafting Committee may also have unwittingly narrowed the scope of Articles 273 and 274 by recommending for use therein the phrase "activities in the area" (a technical term in the Convention that is confined only to "resources" in the Area, *see* Art. 1(3), CLOS in relation to Art. 133, CLOS). *Cf.* IV COMMENTARY at 709 and 717. *See infra,* Chap. V, on transfer of technology in relation to the functions of the ISA.

[197] International cooperation for marine science and technology in marine areas beyond national jurisdiction is based on different principles: essentially, "freedom" for the high seas, and the "common heritage of humanity" for the Area. *Infra* Chap. IV.

[198] From the standpoint of the advocacy for extended and strengthened coastal State sovereignty adopted by the Group of 77 in UNCLOS III, these are complementary, mutually supporting goals. *Cf.* M.I. Glassner, *Neptune's Domain* at 81 (1990). [The G-77 strove to accomplish two contradictory objectives at once: to control MSR within marine areas under national jurisdiction and to participate more actively in such MSR and share in its benefits.]

in UNCLOS III. It is also the most sustainable from the point of view of its implementation. The paradox is that even if the prevailing emphasis is on general cooperation rather than specific formal obligation,[199] the bare framework of rights and duties upon which this approach is established makes resort to the envisioned cooperative action ineluctable,[200] but always on the given assumption that the political climate for cooperation is present. Under these conditions, what is reinforced is the ideal of equality of capacity for rights and obligations between coastal developing States, on the one hand, and researching, technologically advanced States, on the other, in accordance with the principle of cooperation in international law.[201]

4. *International Cooperation and Extended Coastal State Jurisdiction as Complementary Principles of the New Ocean Order*

As described earlier, the developing countries were joined in the cause of challenging the principle of *mare liberum* which, in all its manifestations, pervaded the traditional law of the sea. Rightly or wrongly, they perceived this freedom – a pillar *par excellence* of pre-decolonization international law – as inconsistent with a new ocean order founded on more egalitarian relations between North and South. They, therefore, proposed an alternative which would advance their agenda of development and global sharing that rested on the doctrine of sovereignty, or permanent sovereignty over natural resources. This advocacy, superimposed on the concept of the coastal State, entailed both extensive physical enclosure and intensive resource competence off-shore. For the developing countries especially, such enclosure could only be meaningfully effected if it was accompanied by a regime that would directly contribute to their development.

The highly innovative institution of the EEZ was the negotiated solution to the tensions between the claims for freedom, on the one hand, and the claims for sovereignty, on the other. The concept of the EEZ, whose received status

---

199 IV COMMENTARY at 694.
200 The legal framework of such cooperation *ratione loci* is the EEZ as a multifunctional resource-oriented zone. Kwiatkowska, *supra* note 81, at 24-27. *See also* Pinto, *supra* note 138, at 153-154.
201 *See* Pinto, *id.*; B. Babović, "The Duty of States to Cooperate in Accordance with the Charter" in Sahović, *supra* Chap. I note 3, 277-322.

in customary international law is now beyond cavil,[202] will undoubtedly go down in the history of the law of the sea as the most significant contribution of the developing countries in their quest to ameliorate traditional North-South disparities in the use and enjoyment of the world's oceans.[203] In UNCLOS III, the classical law domains that were left unaffected by the introduction of the EEZ regime basically continued to be governed by the doctrine of *mare liberum*. These included navigation and communication as a traditional use, and the high seas as a traditional *res communis*.

If the position of the developing countries on the legal regime of the EEZ is examined more closely, it is evident that there was something more to their claim for extensive and intensive resource jurisdiction than just the standard argument of *mare clausum*. Contrary to the image of a self-interested territorial grab, which is projected now and then as the essential motivation behind the EEZ proposal,[204] the EEZ was advanced by the South not only as a *zone of sovereign rights* but also, and what is perhaps much more important, as a *zone of international cooperation*.[205] This conception of the EEZ as intrinsically an institution of cooperation was necessarily connected to the desire of the developing countries to transform the matrix of EEZ juridical rights and obli-

---

202 *Continental Shelf Case (Tunisia v. Libya)*, 1982 ICJ Rep 18, 74; *Continental Shelf Case (Libya v. Malta)*, 1985 ICJ Rep 13, 33.

203 *See* E.M. Borgese, *Future of the Oceans: A Report to the Club of Rome* 76-80 (1986). Kwiatkowska, *supra* note 81, at xx, believes that the concepts of the EEZ and the Common Heritage of Mankind are the major innovations in the Convention and evidence the unprecedented revolution in international law relating to ocean resources.

204 *See e.g.* 1 D.P. O'Connell, *The International Law of the Sea* 552 (1982), lamenting that the EEZ marks the triumph of individualism over collectivism in international relations; A. Casese, *International Law in a Divided World* 378 (1986), stating that developing countries acted out of sheer self-interest, not solidarity, in adopting the EEZ. *See also* A. Danzig, *A Funny Thing Happened to the Common Heritage on the Way to the Sea* 12 SAN DIEGO L REV 655-664 (1975), and Brown, *supra* note 10, at 10.

205 This element of international cooperation in the general conception of the EEZ should distinguish it from earlier maritime claims in *mare clausum* – like the Truman Proclamation on the Continental shelf of 1945, or the Latin American extensions of their territorial seas out to 200 miles – which were somehow self-aggrandizing or individualistic in their motivation. In contrast, the EEZ as a form of extended coastal State jurisdiction embodies sub-regimes that invariably advance the norm of cooperation, or the duty to cooperate, in international law.

gations into tangible benefits for economic development. Given the acknowledged lack of capabilities of developing coastal States to discover, exploit and utilize, as well as conserve the resources of their EEZ, it was important for them to consider the strategy or requisite legal mechanism to transform rights, duties and entitlement to actual improved standards of living. In fact, without this transformation secured in the legal regime of the EEZ, the whole principle of extended coastal State jurisdiction was bound to be self-defeating, and the entire project of a more equitable ocean order a sure failure.[206]

The legal mechanism that fills the gap is expressed in the concept of international cooperation, or the obligation to cooperate,[207] which was fully explored in the Third Committee of UNCLOS III. It was, therefore, a most imaginative move to anchor the consent regime of MSR to the essential requirements of international cooperation for development and global sharing. Cooperation in this instance pre-supposed reciprocity and mutual benefit, a sustainable relationship of give-and-take, thus emphasizing the fundamental equality of capacity for rights and obligations on the part of the parties involved. Notwithstanding the generality of many provisions in the Convention on the obligation to cooperate, their invocation by a developing coastal State within the overall juristic framework of the EEZ, should invariably lead to the conclusion of supplementary agreements which can then convert sovereign rights into concrete material progress.[208] The pattern of the new "international law of co-

---

206 Methodologically, the historical investigation the Law of the Sea includes inquiry on the vindication of new rules by reference to the doctrine of effectiveness. I D.P. O'Connell, *supra* note 184, at 37.
207 Few, if any, of the Conventions' provisions creating obligations of cooperation were the subject of controversies preventing their adoption by consensus. Pinto, *supra* note 138, at 153.
208 As Ambassador Pinto observes, *id.* at 153-154:
The point of departure of such [supplementary] agreements would be the basic duty of cooperation already undertaken through the Convention. It would not be the purpose of the supplementary agreement merely to re-state that duty, but rather to translate it into detailed provisions governing the prescribed actions, so that implementation can take place and be monitored by the parties. Such agreements may be expected to be as specific as possible on such matters as the timing of the prescribed actions, financial obligations, national entities responsible for tasks assigned, the establishment of joint supervisory organs and the scope of their responsibilities, safeguards as to any special risks foreseen by any of the parties, and possibly duration and modes of settling disputes, all with a view to making the agreement self-contained and co-operative activity self-sustaining, without

operation for development and global sharing" under the regime of the EEZ emerges: a developing coastal State increases its sovereign capabilities for economic development through negotiated deals with the developed community for assistance – financial, managerial, technical, or general economic – given in exchange for resource-related access to the EEZ. This resource-related, and *pro tanto* environmental-related, access to the EEZ may be for MSR, fisheries, environmental protection, and regional or global marine management initiatives.

The limitations of the cooperative framework founded on the principles of reciprocity and respect for coastal State sovereignty/jurisdiction are apparent. First, as already adverted to, developing countries that are not coastal States or that do not possess significant EEZs, *viz.*, the developing LLGDS, are by and large excluded from the benefits of this form of "international law of cooperation." The property rights that are necessarily situated in the EEZ upon which any long-term cooperative endeavor may be based and upon which continuing reciprocal interests may be defined are insignificant if not non-existent with respect to these category of States.[209] Whatever the provisions on international cooperation drawn by the Convention on behalf of these developing LLGDS, these are not, to use the language of the International Court of Justice, "of a fundamentally norm-creating character such as could be regarded as forming the basis of a general rule of law."[210] Their participation in fisheries or MSR in neighboring States' EEZs, for example, is necessarily constrained by what they can offer to the coastal State in terms of reciprocal benefit. Clearly, a different concept of international cooperation based on different regimes of inclusiveness, *e.g.* the common heritage of humanity or freedom of transit, is needed if the developing LLGDS are to partake in the equitable enjoyment of ocean wealth and resources. This was indeed what was done in UNCLOS III.

The second limitation of the regime of the EEZ as a positive law concept of international cooperation for development and global sharing inheres in the scope and rigour of coastal State sovereign rights and obligations on which is hinged the duty of States, especially States accessing the EEZ, to cooperate.

---

the need for frequent recourse to contracting parties or third-party mechanisms for interpretation.

209 R. Axelrod, *The Evolution of Cooperation* (1984) conceives of a stable relationship of sustainable cooperation between the parties, in this case between coastal States and research States, on account of their continuing interaction based on the "tit-for-tat" rule of reciprocity.

210 *See North Sea Continental Shelf Cases (Denmark and The Netherlands* v. *Federal Republic of Germany)* 1969 ICJ Rep 3, para. 72.

As long as the justification for access to the EEZ can be identified as pertaining to coastal State sovereign rights or jurisdiction in the EEZ, there is a "bankable" duty to cooperate on the part of the accessing State in regard to the development efforts of the developing coastal State.[211] For example, it was already mentioned that the consent regime in the Convention is silent as to the use of satellite remote sensing and the deployment of ODAS for MSR in coastal State territorial waters.[212] Coastal State sovereign rights in the EEZ are also qualified not only by the enjoyment of *jus communicationis* freedoms by all other States in the EEZ[213] but also by the disposition of "residual rights" therein.[214] To the extent that these "residual rights" are attributable to the coastal State, the resulting expansion of the scope of coastal State rights in the EEZ – effected through State practice or judicial interpretation – in order to widen the positive law anchor, or the "forced" basis, of international cooperation for development, should certainly be welcomed.

A last, but not the least, limitation of the doctrine of international cooperation for development in the EEZ proceeds from the empirical reality that it was mostly the developed countries and only a handful of developing countries which gained most, in territorial terms, from the institution of the EEZ.[215]

---

211 Otherwise, this duty to cooperate for development will not be "of a fundamentally norm-creating character such as could be regarded as forming the basis of a general rule of law." *See ibid.*
212 *Supra* note 154 and accompanying text.
213 These rights cover navigation and overflight, the laying of submarine cables and pipelines, and other internationally lawful uses of the sea. Art. 58, CLOS.
214 Art. 59, CLOS. On the problem of "residual rights" in the EEZ, *see* Kwiatkowska, *supra* note 81, at 227-230; C. Extavour, *The Exclusive Economic Zone* 266-272 (1979). Some "residual" or "unattributed rights", *i.e.,* which the Convention does not specify as either covered under coastal State jurisdiction or the regime of freedom, are: conduct of military exercises, manoeuvers, war games and weapons testing; emplacement of underwater listening devises for submarines, and construction and use of military installations and structures; recovery of historic wrecks and other archeological and historical objects beyond the contiguous zone; jurisdiction over buoys or other ODAS for pure scientific research; and designation of traffic separation schemes. *See* Brown, *supra* note 10, at 239-244; Churchill & Lowe, *op. cit.* 144.
215 *Supra* notes 82-86 and accompanying text. Statistics on national fisheries catches are indicative of the skewed effect of the EEZ on developing countries: for example, the top 10 developing countries that acquired the biggest EEZs account for approximately 83% of the marine catch of all developing countries, and the

This has two consequences. First, the enclosure the ocean resources effected by the developed States through their EEZs logically decreases if not eliminates the possibilities of North-South cooperation in these EEZs, for the simple reason that the access of a developing country to a developed country's EEZ is rarely if ever the case. Second, only a few developing countries can really take advantage of an expansive EEZ as a compelling arena for reciprocal bargaining in negotiations for mutually-beneficial cooperative arrangements. These considerations at once prove the very confined circumstances where international cooperation in the EEZ can lead to the actual implementation of the principle of equality of capacity for rights and obligations between developing States, on the one hand, and developed States, on the other.

Still, for developing coastal States as a whole, there is no question that the legal institution of the EEZ is a significant policy instrument which can be honed to achieve development objectives. With this purpose in mind, it can be asserted that the *coastal State* or zonal dimension of the matrix of EEZ rights and obligations is a necessary but not a sufficient condition for the instrumentalization of the EEZ regime in realizing the goals of development and global sharing. To be truly effective, this dimension must be complemented by a *cooperative* dimension if the EEZ vision of ameliorating the North-South gap is to be meaningfully pursued.[216] In UNCLOS III, this cooperative dimension was somewhat submerged in the global atmosphere of distrust and confrontation between North and South occasioned by the NIEO proposals in the UN General Assem-

---

top 15 and 20 for 91% and 96% respectively. *Law of the Sea: Report of the Secretary-General*, para. 93, UN Doc. A/46/724 (5 December 1991).

216 The interlocking existence of the "coastal State dimension" and "cooperative dimension" in the regime of the EEZ may be seen as the answer to the question "What's new about the 1982 Convention's ocean law regime?" According to Kimball, *supra* note 130, at 16, the Convention recognizes:
- that the expansion of coastal States' right to develop and manage offshore resources must be linked to the duties to conserve living resources and protect the marine environment;
- that advancing scientific knowledge and the pace of political, economic, and technological change require radical new approaches to the progressive development and implementation of a rule of law for the oceans; and
- that cooperation to strengthen all nations' scientific, technical, and management capabilities is essential if the Convention is to be meaningfully implemented.

bly.[217] There was no doubt in UNCLOS III, nonetheless, that regimes of cooperation were indispensable in the new ocean order being negotiated. The 1982 Convention, as a progressive development of the classical law of the sea, acknowledged this need in more ways than one and responded to it by putting forward the general norm of cooperation as a foundational basis for the new order of the oceans.

It did not take long for the "cooperative dimension" of the EEZ to resurface, this time under the more foreboding circumstances of global environmental decay. The cooperative element of the EEZ regime ascended to prominence with the onset of the "sustainable development" creed in the late 1980s. Thus, international cooperation for development and global sharing in the traditional domains of the law of the sea was given its historic boost "on the road to Rio and from Rio." By the late 1980s the focus had shifted to the problem of sustainable development in and for the world's oceans as a whole, and once again, the North-South dimensions of the traditional law of the sea came under review. This opens up for discussion the significance of the UN Conference on Environment and Development (UNCED), held in Rio de Janeiro in June 1992, to the overall problem of North-South inequality in the Law of the Sea.

F. UNCED AND EQUALITY OF CAPACITY FOR RIGHTS AND OBLIGATIONS: THE CUSTOMARY LAW OF CAPACITY-BUILDING IN THE OCEANS

Although it is admittedly too early to tell whether the overall implementation of the 1982 Convention has facilitated the fulfillment of its preambular policies on development and global sharing, the specific legal regime of the EEZ (which became customary law even before the adoption of the Convention[218]) is perhaps already ripe for this kind of evaluation. A generation of State practice on the EEZ had certainly occasioned prolific insights on the "coastal State dimension" of the EEZ regime.[219] What has not been sufficiently elaborated,

---

217 This explains why the particulars of the G-77 position on international cooperation for "marine science, technology and ocean service infrastructures" found its expression in Annex VI of the Final Act "as part of the progressive development of the law of the sea in a framework of close international cooperation," and not in the text of the Convention. *Cf.* IV COMMENTARY 669, 741-747.
218 *Supra* note 202.
219 *See e.g.,* Churchill & Lowe, *op. cit.*; Kwiatkowska, *supra* note 81; E.D. Brown, *supra* note 10.

however, is the extent to which this State practice, on the whole, had allowed the institution of the EEZ to participate in, or refute, the "international law of global disparities" hypothesized in the first Chapter. The EEZ, as a method of enclosure, without doubt benefitted only those few States which acquired extensive off-shore resources, generally reinforcing the traditional domain of North-South inequality.[220] But as an institution of international cooperation, there is much that remains to be said about the EEZ. Any conclusion about the affirmative role of the EEZ in the international law of global disparities unmistakably refers to the trends associated with the "cooperative dimension" of the EEZ regime. The relevant query is whether the developing coastal States had availed themselves of the egalitarian/international cooperation aspect of the regime. A review of the overall Third World experience on international cooperation in the EEZ presents a picture that is highly ambiguous.

1. Revitalizing the Unrealized Promise of the EEZ

Without going into the details of the practices and experiences of developing coastal States on international cooperation for development in their EEZs,[221] a general pattern of relevant State conduct can be charted. This will support the tentative conclusion that the EEZ cooperation regime had been relatively ineffective at least during the decade of 1980s and early 1990s.

Consider that as late as 1990, the UN General Assembly was requesting the UN Secretary-General

> ... to suggest methods and mechanisms for maximizing opportunities for the early realization for all States, during the decade beginning in 1990, of the benefits of the comprehensive legal regime established by the Convention.[222]

The Resolution that placed this request expressed the urgent concern "that developing countries are as yet unable to take effective measures for the full

---

220 *See supra* note 82.
221 A case of international cooperation that is often cited as a success in this regard is the experience of the island States in the South Pacific where the EEZ access provisions have been exploited for their national and regional development. *See e.g.*, R. Herr, *The Forum Fisheries Agency: Achievements, Challenges and Prospects* (1990).
222 *See* UN Doc. A/RES/44/26 (19 January 1990).

realization of these benefits owing to the lack of resources and of the necessary scientific and technological capabilities."[223] This concern was already somehow anticipated by the Secretary-General who had observed earlier that there was an increased awareness worldwide of the importance of the ocean sector, as well as a growing interest and need in the formulation of more comprehensive, integrated policies for marine development and management.[224]

In his Report replying to the request,[225] the Secretary General affirmed the "rich promise" offered by the Convention for all countries, especially developing countries, but lamented the fact that although the Convention confers rights under which States may explore and exploit resources, these rights have not in actual fact been translated into tangible or substantial benefits for most.[226] Many developing States were, however, slowly discovering the important contribution their extended coastal resources can make in their socio-economic development. But then these countries just did not seem to have moved forward. After surveying the situation of many countries, the Secretary-General concluded that the predominant and unfulfilled need of most developing

---

223 Preambular para. no. 13, *ibid*. This paragraph alludes to the preceding one which notes "the increasing needs of countries, especially developing countries, for information, advise and assistance in the implementation of the Convention and in their developmental process for the full realization of these benefits of the comprehensive legal regime established by the Convention." The immediately following paragraph in turn acknowledges "the need to enhance and supplement the efforts of States and competent international organizations to enable developing countries to acquire such [scientific and technical] capabilities."

224 *Law of the Sea: Report of the Secretary General*, Doc. A/44/650 (1 November 1989), para. 3 & 18. The Secretary-General has issued Reports on the Law of the Sea annually since 1983. These Reports are authorized under Art. 319, CLOS.

225 The Secretary-General submitted the requested report in two parts, as UN Doc. A/45/712 (16 November 1990) and UN Doc. A/46/722 (4 December 1991): *Law of the Sea – Realization of benefits under the United Nations Convention on the Law of the Sea: Needs of States in regard to development and management of ocean resources, and approaches for further action*. These documents should be read together with other complementing reports of the Secretary-General on matters related to the Law of the Sea during these two sessions. *See* UN Doc. A/45/721 and Corr.1 (19 November 1990), para. 1, and UN Doc. A/46/724 (5 December 1991), para. 1.

226 Doc. A/45/712, para. 11 & 12; Doc. A/46/722, para. 8.

countries remains to be that of developing a national integrated ocean policy.[227] What prevented the developing coastal States from coming up with their respective integrated ocean policies was not merely the lack of rudimentary ocean policy and management expertise and infrastructures. Their predicament also arose from the dearth of financial resources necessary to exploit their new resource base.[228] The options for a way out of the quagmire were thus outlined. But the essential precondition for a comprehensive solution, the Report argued, lies in building internal national capacities as well as in expanding and intensifying programmes of assistance to developing countries and in strengthening international cooperation in the provision for such assistance.[229]

In the meantime, as the General Assembly was welcoming the Report of the Secretary-General, massive preparations were already underway for the 1992 UN Conference on Environment and Development (UNCED).[230] As will be shown shortly, this historic Conference transformed the entire political context of interpreting and implementing the 1982 Convention on the Law of the Sea. With the rapid ascendancy of "sustainable development", coinage-turned-creed since the publication of the 1987 Report of the World Commission on Environment and Development (WCED),[231] a fresh look at the 1982 Convention was not long in coming.[232] The resurgence of interest in the oceans

---

227 Doc. A/45/712, para. 22; Doc. A/46/722, para. 18, *et seq.*
228 Doc. A/46/722, para. 26, 185-189.
229 Doc. A/45/712, para. 127; Doc. A/46/722, para. 192.
230 The convening of the UNCED was directed by UNGA Res. 44/228 (22 December 1989), a complex and highly detailed document that set the tone and direction for a comprehensive global project on sustainable development.
231 *Our Common Future, supra* Introduction note 12, otherwise known as the Bruntland Report. "Sustainable development" is defined by the WCED as "development that meets the needs of the present without compromising the ability of future generations to meet their own needs." The important contribution of the Bruntland Report to the convening of UNCED is acknowledged in UNGA Res. 44/228. *See also* the UNEP's *Environmental Perspective to the Year 2000 and Beyond*, text in UN Doc. A/42/25 (1987), UN GAOR, 42nd Session, Supp. 25, Annex 2. For a review of the various approaches to and definitions of "sustainable development" contemporaneous with UNCED, *see* D. Mitlin, *Sustainable Development: A Guide to the Literature* 4 ENVIRONMENT AND URBANIZATION 111 (1992).
232 The Bruntland Report, *id.* identified three imperatives at the heart of oceans management:
- The underlying unity of the oceans requires effective global management regimes.

as a global environmental resource in its own right was provoking a renewed appreciation of the 1982 Convention not only because of its unique normative role in the entire complex of international environmental management[233] but also, and more importantly, in light of its contribution to the deeper understanding, practical refinement, programmatic pursuit, and institutional elaboration of "sustainable development."[234] It was inevitable in this context that the

---

- The shared resource characteristics of many regional seas make forms of regional management mandatory.
- The major land-based threats to the oceans require effective national actions based on international cooperation.

The South Commission took the position that the 1982 Convention "is a legal instrument which integrates development, the environment, and the issues of disarmament and peace in the overall goal of sustainable development." *The Challenge to the South, op. cit.* 262.

233 See e.g., *Protection and Preservation of the Marine Environment: Report of the Secretary-General*, Doc. A/44/461 (18 September 1989). Among the many points raised regarding the significance of the 1982 Convention to PPME, it is asserted that the 1982 Convention is "a system for sustainable development", para. 10-13; and in para. 15-20, the belief is expressed that the Convention is a model for the evolution of international environmental law. *See also Report of the Secretary General to the UN General Assembly on the Item Law of the Sea*, Doc. A/45/721 and Corr.1 (19 November 1990), para. 5, where the confident declaration is made that

[t]he United Nations Convention on the Law of the Sea is the primary instrument for the sustainable use and development of the oceans and their resources, particularly for the facilitation of international communication, the equitable and efficient utilization of ocean resources, the conservation of marine living resources, and the study, protection and preservation of the marine environment.

Although never invoking the term "sustainable development", a post-Bruntland study that investigated the role played by the 1982 Convention in environmental management was L. Kimball, *International Law and Institutions: The Oceans and Beyond*, 20 ODIL 147-165 (1989). A similar orientation was adopted, in a more specialized way, in the 1990 international conference *Pacem in Maribus XVIII*, proceedings in A. Dolman & J. van Ettinger, (Eds.) *Ports as Nodal Points in a Global Transport System* (1992).

234 Two international conferences in 1991 dealt with the relationship between sustainable development and the law of the sea: the International Ocean Institute's *Pacem In Maribus XIX* and the Law of the Sea Institute's 25th Annual Conference. Proceedings in P.B. Payoyo (Ed.), *Ocean Governance: Sustainable Development of the Seas* (UNU, 1994) and A. Couper & E. Gold, *The Marine Environment and Sustainable Development: Law, Policy, and Science* (LSI, 1993).

nexus between the urgent need of developing countries to benefit from their expanded marine resource base and the fulfillment of the concrete requirements of sustainable development was once more reconsidered.[235] In the official process leading up to UNCED the linkage was identified, debated, and finally elaborated into a comprehensive programme of sustainable development – for the oceans, and beyond.

2. From UNCLOS III to UNCED 1992: Transforming the Legal Framework of Global Inequality

The UNCED process,[236] as much as its outputs,[237] was very much a North-South event of major historic importance[238] as UNCLOS III itself. Although UNCLOS III and UNCED differed in their starting premises, as in their contemporaneous exploration of North-South issues, both conferences addressed the same central post-war/post-decolonization problem of global sharing between

---

235 The Bruntland Commission, *op. cit.*, proposed that in order to improve regimes for ocean management, the capacity of developing countries for national action should be strengthened. This would require assistance for them to boost their legal and institutional frameworks for integrated management of coastal resources.

236 For a description of the UNCED as a "multitracked preparatory process", *see* B. Cicin-Sain & R. Knecht, *Implications of the Earth Summit for Ocean and Coastal Governance* 24 ODIL 323, 326-328 (1993). The "UNCED process" should, of course, be understood as including the "follow-up" process, or the "road from Rio", towards its implementation. L. Kimball, *UNCED and the Oceans Agenda, The Process Forward* 17 MARINE POLICY 491 (1993).

237 UNCED's substantive outputs consisted of: (1) The Rio Declaration on Environment and Development [hereafter, Rio Declaration], (2) the UN Framework Convention on Climate Change [hereafter, UNFCCC], (3) UN Convention on Biological Diversity [hereafter, UNCBD], (4) A Non-legally Binding Authoritative Statement of Principles for a Global Consensus on the Management, Conservation and Sustainable Development of All Types of Forests, and (5) Agenda 21. A handy reference for the texts of these outputs is S.P. Johnson, *The Earth Summit* (1993). For an assessment of the process and the outputs of UNCED, *see* D.M. Johnston, "UNCED: The Coastal and Ocean Challenge" in K.L. Koh, R.C. Beckman & Chia Lin Sien (Eds.) *Sustainable Development of Coastal and Ocean Areas in Southeast Asia: Post-Rio Perspectives* 1-52 (1995).

238 *See* S.P. Johnson, *ibid.*; Cicin-Sain & Knecht, *supra* note 236, and literature cited in notes 20 and 21 therein.

developed and developing countries. The historical continuity of these two mega-conferences should be emphasized. It is the subtle interweaving of North-South deliberations in both UNCLOS and UNCED legal processes which makes the UNCED radically different from the 1972 Stockholm Conference on the Human Environment.[239] This continuity is shown by the normative linkages established between the 1982 Convention and the relevant outputs of UNCED, proving beyond doubt an historic and irreversible transmutation of North-South legal relations.

In general, it can be maintained that UNCLOS and UNCED, at least from the viewpoint of the developing countries, were major attempts at the fundamental reconfiguration of North-South legal relations.[240] A broad-brush description of agendas of these conferences as seen by the South corroborates this proposition. The business of UNCLOS III for the Third World was decolonization, and UNCED was all about "sustainable development", or economic development that can sustain the local and planetary environment. In both these international conferences, the developing countries were committed to advance the cause of sovereign equality, which they believed was of key importance if the countries of the South were to be sovereign masters of their own resources, in the case of UNCLOS, and sovereign States equally responsible for the management and development of their natural environment as well as the global environment, in the case of UNCED. Although the conceptual and motivational underpinnings of each of these agendas were different, they converged in their practical aim, namely, to project the cause of strengthened national capacities on the part of developing States for the exercise of rights and the assumption of obligations. This Southern aim in UNCLOS III was described earlier in the context of their move as coastal States to reform the traditional law of the sea that was founded on the principle of freedom or open access. In UNCED, on the other hand the

---

239 Some observers, heedless of the evolving normative framework of international relations, believe that the North-South "dialogue" in the 1972 Stockholm Conference was basically no different from one carried out in the 1992 Rio Conference; the underlying assumption is the existence of an unchanged North-South bargaining setting. *See e.g.,* A. Najam, *An Environmental Negotiation Strategy for the South* 7 INTERNATIONAL ENVIRONMENTAL AFFAIRS 249 (1995).

240 For an assessment of the strategic importance of UNCED in this context, *see* M.D. Griffith, *The South and the United Nations Conference on Environment and Development: The Dawn of a Probable Turning Point in International Relations Between States* 18 OCEAN & COASTAL MANAGEMENT 55-57 (1992).

relevant position of the South, formulated during the height of UNCED negotiations, is recapitulated in the following statement:

> UNCED is of historic importance and provides the occasion at the highest levels of government to address environment and development in an integrated, comprehensive and balanced manner for the benefit of both present and future generations. We call for a new global partnership based on respect for sovereignty and the principles of equity and equality among States for the achievement of sustainable development, taking into account the main responsibility of developed countries for the deterioration of the environment, and the need for sustained economic growth and development of developing countries.[241]

The protective but proactive thrust of the Southern agenda in both the UNCLOS and the UNCED must be highlighted. The main objective was to "undo" what the developing States perceived as having been accomplished *fait accompli* by the Northern States to the prejudice of the South. In UNCLOS, they wanted to undo the perverse effects of colonization and post-colonial domination; while in UNCED, they were seeking to undo the notorious effects of global environmental degradation for which the North was largely responsible.[242] What they regarded as the injustice to be overcome in these parallel movements involved the imposition of illegitimate legal, structural and historical burdens on the developing States simply because they were late-comers in the international/global community scene, in a double sense.[243] In UNCLOS III, they were late-comers in the Euro-centric business of statehood and the enterprise of large-scale resource extraction, and were thus forced into an highly unequal or

---

241 *Kuala Lumpur Declaration on Environment and Development, Issued at the end of the Second Ministerial Conference of Developing Countries on Environment and Development*, 29 April 1992, para. 3. Text in S.P. Johnson, *supra* note 237, at 35-39.

242 In the context of the UNCED, the main responsibility for the deterioration of the planetary environment was expressly imputed on the North. *See* Preambular para. 12 & Part I, para. 9, UNGA Res. 44/228; 3rd preambular para., UNFCCC; Principle 7, Rio Declaration; and Para. 4.3, Agenda 21. It may be noted that this imputation of Northern responsibility echoes the original position of the developing countries in UNCLOS III. *See* Pinto, *supra* note 51.

243 *Cf.* H. Shue "The Unavoidability of Justice" in A. Hurell and B. Kingsbury (Eds.), *The International Politics of the Environment* 373-397 (1992), for an illuminating discussion of the two kinds of "compound injustice" suffered by the poor nations in environmental negotiations with the North.

inequitable relationship with the developed countries on this account. In UNCED, they were again the late-comers in partaking of scarce global environmental amenities, or the limited ecological capital, offered by a fragile ailing planet. The Third World response in both fora was consistent and uniform: respect for and enhancement of equality.

The "new global partnership for sustainable development"[244] between North and South as called for by UNCED was indeed a serious proposition for the developing countries. The new challenge of "integrating environment and development"[245] provided a remarkable opportunity for them not only to resurrect the enfeebled North-South dialogue that had all but collapsed in the 1980s[246] but also to come back to the theme of "development and environment" first put forward during the heady days of Stockholm.[247] If the logic of economic interdependence as a basis for global dialogue and reform under the NIEO has never been persuasive enough to the North,[248] the necessities of global ecological interdependence had finally "forced" the North to realize

---

244 See Preambular para. 3 and Principle 7, *Rio Declaration*; Preambular para. 1, *Agenda 21*.
245 See *Introductory Statement of the UNCED Secretary General at the First Session of the Preparatory Committee*. Text in Johnson *supra* note 237, at 20.
246 Griffith, *supra* note 240, at 56.
247 *Founex Report, supra* note 123. This Report sets forth, *inter alia*, that the developing countries wished to avoid, as far as feasible, the mistakes and distortions that have characterized the patterns of development of the industrialized societies; that for the poor countries development becomes essentially a cure for their major environmental problems; and that to resolve the environmental aspects of poverty, measures to be taken include use of natural over synthetic materials, relocation of industry, conservation through commodity agreements, training and education, and additional funds from developed countries. The focus of the Report though was clearly on the relationship between environmental concerns and development priorities at the national level. In contrast, UNCED explored the environment-development nexus in light of *global* environmental threats. On the necessity of global solutions to global environmental problems *see e.g.,* L. Susskind, *Environmental Diplomacy* (1994).
248 For a reflection on the meaning of economic interdependence in the context of the NIEO, see Bedjaoui, *supra* note 25 at 243 *et seq.* It should be mentioned that environmental protection provisos were included in the UNGA declarations on the NIEO. A Southern call for the management of global interdependence taking into account environmental considerations is also made in *The Challenge to the South*, *op. cit.* 283 *et seq.*

the need for a new partnership with the South, based on equality and Third World empowerment.[249] As Professor Handl explained:

> Environmental interdependence as reflected in the need to enlist the co-operation of key developing countries in order to ensure the success of international regimes for the protection of globally sensitive natural resources thus may be a turning point in North-South relations. Unlike the postulation of a "new economic order" in the 1970s, presently proposed strategies to counter the threat to global environmental security may lead to the empowerment of developing countries. By forcing developed countries squarely to face the effects of underdevelopment on global environmental protection objectives, developing countries might succeed in shedding their traditional marginal roles as international actors. In any event, the new dialogue and evolving patterns of North-South co-operation can only work to the benefit of the community of states as a whole.[250]

In juridical terms, the proposed new partnership promised the developing countries not only the right to development,[251] an unfulfilled desiderata since the First UN Development decade was launched, but also the right to cooperate and be assisted as equal stewards of the global planetary environment.[252] This latter point was already conceded in the 1972 Stockholm Conference but never seriously taken up again in subsequent North-South negotiations.[253] In practical terms, the new partnership meant that their claims for financial, technical

---

249 See Shue, *supra* note 243, who explores the bankruptcy of a "two track" negotiation strategy between North and South, one proceeding on a purely "environmental/climate track" and the other based on a "justice track."

250 G. Handl, "Environmental Security and Global Change: The Challenge to International Law" in W. Lang, H. Neuhold & K. Zemanek (Eds.), *Environmental Protection and International Law* 85 (1991). Note, however, that Professor Handl's notion of the new interdependence is qualified so as to relate only to "key developing countries" and "globally sensitive natural resources."

251 The "right to development" is acknowledged in Principle 3 of the *Rio Declaration*. It is now accorded an inter-generational meaning. *Cf.* the 1986 UNGA Res. 41/128 "Declaration on the Right to Development." Only the United States registered its opposition to the "right to development" in Rio, as it did in the General Assembly with respect to the 1986 Declaration on the Right to Development.

252 The concept of environmental stewardship by States through international cooperation in the context of respect for the principle of sovereignty is suggested in Principles 2, 3 & 7, *Rio Declaration*; Para. 1.1, *Agenda 21*; Preambular para. 6, 8, 9 and the last one, UNFCCC; Preambular para. 4, 14, and the last one, UNCBD.

253 See Principles 11 and 24, Stockholm Declaration on the Human Environment.

or compensatory assistance and other incentives for development and environmental security were now legitimate demands under the overriding norm of sustainable development[254] and were fully justified in the context of the UNCED bargaining process.[255] This also meant that the requisite Northern cooperation for Southern sustainable development, that elusive ingredient in Third World efforts for sustained economic growth, will no longer be founded on the degrading concept of foreign aid and international charity, but on the notion of equitable burden sharing for planetary development.[256] The full recognition of these postulates and claims in international law would undoubtedly accelerate the emergence of an international law of cooperation, or at least the irreversible decline of the politics of coexistence.[257]

What then, it should be asked, is the legal status of new North-South partnership based on the principle of sustainable development? Could it be maintained that there was forged in UNCED adequate elements of a new legal framework for North-South relations? If so, how does this framework influence the evolving North-South agenda of the 1982 Convention on the Law of the Sea? Finally, how does this framework tackle the central issue of equality of capacity for rights and obligations between North and South?

If one were to measure the performance of UNCED as a law-making exercise against the political expectations built into the process as set forth in UNGA resolution no. 44/227, the results generally disappoint.[258] However, an appreciation of the legal aspects of UNCED's response to the problem of sustainable

---

254 Handl, *supra* note 250, at 79-85.
255 *See* Griffith, *supra* note 240.
256 Prof. Handl refers to this change as an "entitlement reinterpretation." Handl, *supra* note 250, at 83. *See also* G. Handl, *Environmental Protection and Development in Third World Countries: Common Destiny – Common Responsibility* 20 NYU J INT L & POL 603 (1988). Even before the onset of sustainable development discourse, a moral turn in North-South legal and political relations had often been thought of as necessary in the efficient dispensation of international aid. *See* H. Singer, "The Ethics of Foreign Aid" and "Introduction" in M. Wright (Ed.), *Rights and Obligations in North-South Relations* 1-7, 84-100 (1986). The ethics of "planetary development" was a theme expounded by UN Secretary-General Boutros-Ghali in his message at the opening of UNCED on 3 June 1992. Text in Johnson, *op. cit.* at 42-48.
257 Friedmann, *op. cit.*
258 Kimball, *supra* note 236, at 491.

development in the sphere of the oceans reveals a wholly different picture of the "global bargain" struck at UNCED.

3. The Legal Basis of Capacity-Building for Sustainable Development in the Oceans

Chapter 17 of Agenda 21[259] is a comprehensive set of political commitments, a veritable global programme of action, for sustainable development in the world's oceans and coasts.[260] It has been described as the "link-pin" between the UNCLOS and UNCED processes,[261] the Chapter acknowledging up-front that the 1982 Convention on the Law of the Sea "provides the international basis upon which to pursue the protection and sustainable development of the marine and coastal environment and its resources."[262] Seven major "programme areas" are identified in this Chapter[263] under which detailed action plans outline specific prescriptions to implement a "new approach to marine

---

259 Entitled "Protection of the oceans, all kinds of seas, including enclosed and semi-enclosed seas, and coastal areas and the protection, rational use and development of their living resources." The subject of this chapter was listed as one major issue in UNGA Res. 44/228, *supra* note 231.
260 Chapter 17 is the longest and one of the most complex Chapters of Agenda 21. Johnson, *op. cit.* 307. Its initial textual organization into categories consisting of "basis for action", "objectives", "management-related activities", "data and information", "financing and cost of evaluation", "international and regional cooperation and coordination", "means of implementation", "financing and cost evaluation", "scientific and technological means", "human resources development", and "capacity building" was used as the basis of organization for all Agenda 21 Chapters. Cicin-Sain & Knecht, *supra* note 236, at 338.
261 Borgese, *supra* note 140, at 49.
262 Para. 17.1, *Agenda 21*.
263 *Viz.*, (a) Integrated management and sustainable development of coastal areas, including exclusive economic zones; (b) Marine environmental protection; (c) Sustainable use and conservation of marine living resources of the high seas; (d) Sustainable use and conservation of marine living resources under national jurisdiction; (e) Addressing critical uncertainties for the management of the marine environment and climate change; (f) Strengthening international, including regional cooperation and coordination; (g) Sustainable development of small islands.

and coastal area management and development."[264] Reiterating the principle in the Rio Declaration,[265] which is also found in the 1982 Law of the Sea Convention,[266] on "common but differentiated responsibilities" of the North and the South, Chapter 17 stipulates that

> [t]he implementation by the developing countries of the activities set forth [in the seven programme areas] shall be commensurate with their individual technological and financial capacities and priorities in allocating resources for development needs and ultimately depends on the technology transfer and financial resources required and made available to them.[267]

It is notable that within the category "means of implementation" under each of the seven programme areas of Chapter 17,[268] the interconnected measures to be taken for sustainable development are identified: on financing, scientific and technological means, human resources development, and general "capacity-building" measures. These implementation strategies outline not only the expectations of developing countries concerning the realization of their "right to development" under Chapter 17, but also the level of effort that can properly be attributed to those States and international institutions that are in a position

---

264 These new approaches, furthermore, are to be "integrated in content and precautionary and anticipatory in ambit." Para. 17.1. *Agenda 21*.
265 Principle 7, *Rio Declaration*.
266 Art. 194 (1), CLOS.
267 Para. 17.2, *Agenda 21*. In normative terms, the "new approach" entails a more subtle balance between the benefits of sustainable development, and the prescriptive functions of international instruments in affecting national development patterns. Kimball, *supra* note 236, at 492. The positive law outputs of UNCED unmistakably endorse this core principle of "common but differentiated responsibilities." See Preambular para. 6, UNFCCC and Art. 6, UNCBD. The parallel provision in these treaties reads:
The extent to which developing country Parties will effectively implement their commitments under this Convention will depend on the effective implementation by developed country Parties of their commitments under this Convention related to financial resources and transfer of technology and will take fully into account that economic and social development and eradication of poverty are the first and overriding priorities of the developing country Parties.
See Art. 4(7), UNFCCC and Art. 20(4), UNCBD.
268 Para. 17.12-17; 17.36-43; 17.64-69; 17.92-96; 17.109-115; 17.122-123; 17.133-137, *Agenda 21*.

to assist developing countries build their national capacities for sustainable development in the ocean sector.[269]

It bears emphasizing that the complex of "capacity-building" measures to implement Chapter 17, or Agenda 21 for that matter,[270] are premised on the concept of global cooperation and coordinated international action flowing from the principle of sustainable development.[271] The measures and political commitments to cooperate for capacity-building with respect to the ocean environment in turn may be regarded as more specific re-statements of the binding commitments to cooperate found in the treaties and other international agreements that are referred to in Chapter 17, like the 1982 Convention on the Law of the Sea. But – and this is the critical element of the "global bargain" achieved in Chapter 17 – these commitments spell out the "new approaches" to ocean governance because they are and ought to be "integrated in content and anticipatory in ambit."[272] Taken together, the treaty commitments alluded to in Chapter 17 and the political commitments spelled out therein define the concept and the programme of sustainable development for the oceans.

Chapter 17 of Agenda 21, as a thematic exposition of sustainable development policy for the oceans in the 1990s and beyond, prescribes a new approach to the problem of building actual capacities for developing countries, or what

---

269 Para. 37.1, of *Agenda 21*, entitled "National Mechanisms and International Cooperation for Capacity-building in Developing Countries", states that "a fundamental goal of capacity-building is to enhance the ability to evaluate and address the crucial questions related to policy choices and modes of implementation among development options, based on an understanding of environmental potentials and limits and of needs as perceived by the people of the country concerned. As a result, the need to strengthen national capacities is shared by all countries."

270 In one of its resolutions welcoming the Report of UNCED, the General Assembly endorsed the crucial importance of capacity-building for sustainable development. Res. 47/194 (22 December 1992).

271 In Agenda 21, capacity-building on the part of developing countries to implement environmental obligations are clearly inseparable from the kind of capacity-building which they require for economic and social development. Specifically, the reference in Chapter 37 to "technical cooperation" as a critical aspect of endogenous capacity-building is nothing more but international cooperation for development re-conceived in a contemporary sustainable development setting. For a defense of a comprehensive concept of capacity-building, *see* L. Guntling, *Compliance Assistance in International Environmental Law: Capacity-Building Through Financial and Technology Transfer* 56 ZaöRV 796-809 (1996).

272 Para. 17.1, *Agenda 21*; Kimball, *supra* note 236 at 491.

amounts to the same thing, of equalizing legal capacities among States. It thus goes beyond the 1982 Convention in its environmental programme of action. Moreover, Chapter 17 pinpoints new aspects of global inequality in the oceans that UNCLOS III was not in a position to address, and proposes steps to rectify these imbalances in the overall effort to enhance developing States' capacities for rights and obligations. These newly-identified areas of inequality once more derive from the basic reality of a North-South divide, with further implications on the application of the legal standard "special interests and needs of developing countries" embodied in the Law of the Sea Convention. Three such areas of new global inequality may be noted.

There is above all the problem of "small island developing States" (SIDS) as a sub-group of developing States with special interests and needs.[273] Not unlike the "developing land-locked States" or "archipelagic States" in UNCLOS III, the SIDS at the UNCED sought for a recognition by the international community of their status as vulnerable States in a precarious relationship with the marine environment. They argued that their unique social and ecological situation, increasingly threatened by global environmental degradation specifically as a result of global warming and sea-level rise, justified a special capacity-building regime on their behalf – if their opportunities for sustainable development, indeed their very survival, were to be assured.[274] The predicament of the SIDS parallels the problematic status of "micro-States" in international law which, once upon a time, had detained the attention of the United Nations in the context of the issue of their participation in international organizations in the aftermath of decolonization.[275] This "mini-state" discussion was eventually dropped from the UN agenda without a clear resolution.[276] In UNCED, the prob-

---

273 Programme Area G, Chapter 17, *Agenda 21*.
274 In relation to international and regional cooperation and coordination for SIDS in Para. 17.131-17.132 of Chapter 17, *Agenda 21* a Global Conference on the Sustainable Development of SIDS was held in Barbados from 25 April – 6 May 1993. The "special situation" of SIDS in meeting the challenge of sustainable development is described particularly in Part One of the *Declaration of Barbados*. See UN Doc. A/Conf.167/L.4/Rev.1 (5 May 1994).
275 *See e.g., Participation of Mini-States in International Affairs* 1968 ASIL Proc 155-188; S. Schwebel, *Mini-States and a More Effective United Nations* 67 AJIL (1973); and R.P. Anand, *Sovereign Equality of States, supra* Chap. I note 54, at Chap. 5.
276 M. Gunter, *What Happened to the United Nations Mini-State Problem?* 71 AJIL 110-111 (1977).

lem of "micro island States" revives the issue of the status of "lilliputian States" in international law, but now with a new twist – to test the limits of the alleged partnership for sustainable development in the oceans based on their meaningful participation in decision-making, reciprocity, integrated approaches and precautionary principles.[277] The category of SIDS, it is important to note, is given recognition in the positive law output of UNCED.[278]

A second aspect of world inequality highlighted in Chapter 17 is the participation of developing countries in sustainable high seas fisheries.[279] The 1982 Convention only vaguely refers to the special requirements of developing States in high seas fishing, without definitively according these States preferential treatment in the utilization of or access to these fisheries.[280] With the intensification and overcaptalization of high seas fishing activities, and considering the crisis involving straddling fish stocks (SFS) and highly migratory fish stocks (HMFS),[281] discussions on conservation and allocation issues concerning high seas fisheries have not avoided grappling with the North-South dimensions of the high seas fisheries problem.[282] These were addressed in the United Nations Conference on Straddling and Highly Migratory Fish Stocks, held from 1993-1995. In an important way, the results of this Conference on SFS and HMFS gave premium to the rights and responsibilities of developing

---

277 *See Statement of the Representative of Vanuatu* (on behalf of all the member States and observers that are members of the Alliance of Small Island States), 30 August 1993. Text in 1993 NILOS DOCUMENTARY YRBK 341.
278 The UNFCCC specifies that needs and concerns of SIDS are deserving of full consideration in the implementation of this Convention. *See* Art. 8 (a), UNFCCC. The UNCBD also mentions the special situation of SIDS as a factor in the disposition of financial resources for developing countries. Art. 20 (6), UNCBD. The taxonomy of States used by these Conventions are based on geographic-environmental criteria. The UNCBD, in addition, includes the category of "least developed countries" – a category that is already much in use in the United Nations.
279 Para. 17.48 & 17.69, *Agenda 21*.
280 *See* Art. 119 (1)(a), CLOS. The freedom of fishing in the high seas as provided in Art. 87 (1)(e), CLOS is qualified by a conservation and management regime generally spelled out in Arts. 116-120, CLOS.
281 *See Report of the Technical Consultation on High Seas Fishing and the Papers Presented at the Technical Consultation on High Seas Fishing*, UN Conference on Straddling Fish Stocks (SFS) and Highly-Migratory Fish Stocks (HMFS), Doc. A/CONF.164/INF/2 (14 May 1993).
282 *See Participation of Developing Countries in High Seas Fishing*, FAO Doc. FI/HSF/ TC/92/7 (June 1992).

124

countries regarding high seas fishing.[283] In this agreement, the cooperative framework within which these rights and obligations are exercised assumes the abandonment of the doctrine of freedom in regard to these fisheries[284] and validates commitments on the availability of a wide range of assistance measures for developing States,[285] consistent with the capacity-building directive in Chapter 17, Agenda 21.[286]

Lastly, Chapter 17 draws out a new field of burden sharing between North and South – the complex programme area on "addressing critical uncertainties for the management of the marine environment and climate change."[287] While this concern may be subsumed under the familiar MSR regime of the 1982 Convention[288] the issues identified are pronouncedly global in scope, making its programmatic elaboration a distinct contribution of UNCED to the analysis of the problems of ocean governance. Thus, the MSR activity involved is global in scope, makes irrelevant the distinction between pure and applied research, and precludes any incompatibility between the interests of the research State or researching international organization, on the one hand, and the coastal State, on the other. As in the UNFCCC, which embodies in binding law the climate change aspects of this programme area under Chapter 17, cooperation with

---

283 *See* Agreement for the Implementation of the Provisions of the United Nations Convention on the Law of the Sea of 10 December 1982 Relating to the Conservation and Management of Straddling Fish Stocks and Highly Migratory Fish Stocks. Text in 34 ILM 1542-1580 (1995), [hereafter, S&HMFS Agreement] esp. Part VII on "Requirements of Developing States."

284 The agreement marks the end of the regime of high seas freedom with respect to fishing SFS and HMFS. *See* J. Van Dyke, *Modifying the 1982 Law of the Sea Convention: New Initiatives on Governance of the High Seas Fisheries Resources in the Straddling Stocks Negotiation* 10 IJMCL 219 (1995). Also for an overview of the Agreeement, *see* D.A. Balton, *Strengthening the Law of the Sea: The New Agreement on Straddling Fish Stocks and Highly Migratory Fish Stocks* 27 ODIL 125-152 (1996).

285 *See* esp. Arts. 25 and 26., S&HMFS Agreement.

286 Para. 17.69, *Agenda 21*.

287 Programme Area E, Chapter 17, *Agenda 21*.

288 The objective of Programme Area E is for States to commit themselves to improved understanding of the marine environment and its role in global processes. *See* Para. 17.100, *Agenda 21*. *See also* P. Birnie, *Law of the Sea and Ocean Resources: Implications for Marine Scientific Research* 10 IJMCL 229 (1995), proposing that the scientific input needed for this improved understanding requires a liberal interpretation of the MSR regime in the 1982 Convention.

the developing countries, including assistance for building their capacities in research, is deemed indispensable.[289]

Chapter 17, like the whole of Agenda 21 or the Rio Declaration, is a non-binding instrument whose authority cannot be immediately anchored in any of the traditional formal sources of international law. Nevertheless, a certain degree of authoritativeness seems to underlie Chapter 17, setting it apart from the other Chapters of Agenda 21 in terms of normative value. Although Agenda 21 is no more than "soft law",[290] it is thus *apropos* to inquire into the normative content of the provisions of Chapter 17 – in particular, the specific commitments in this Chapter calling for cooperation among States to implement the principle of sustainable development in the oceans. These commitments to cooperate do certainly clarify their indispensable linkage with the framework of international cooperation under the 1982 Convention Law of the Sea.

From the standpoint of North-South relations, the cornerstone of the "new approach" to ocean governance advanced at UNCED is international cooperation *writ large*. Qualitatively, this cooperation is no different from the regime of cooperation already constituted by the inter-related provisions of Parts XII, XIII and XIV of the 1982 Convention. However, the cooperative undertakings for ocean sustainable development in the Conventional outputs of UNCED, or Agenda 21 for that matter, are more specific in their content, thereby assuming,

---

[289] *See* Para. 17.103 (b)(f), 17.104 (a), 17.111, 17.113, and 17.115, *Agenda 21*.

[290] Johnson, *op. cit.* at 6, claims that Agenda 21 is the "softest of soft law" which does not require truly bankable commitments to be made by any party. *See also* Cicin-Sain and Knecht, *supra* note 236, at 332, agreeing that Agenda 21 is a nonbinding document, but favourably quotes a metaphor that Agenda 21 "is a sort of softball. But it is harder softball than many hardballs I've seen in treaties." "Soft law" as thus used is understood as being equivalent to "lex ferenda" for those who wish to drawn a fine dividing line between law and pre-law, or legal and sub-legal phenomena. Handl, *supra* note 250, at 63. *Cf.* Weil, *op. cit.* at 414-415, esp. note 7, examining the concept of "soft law" against the pathology of the international legal structure, and reserves its use to rules that are imprecise and not really compelling. Further on "soft law", *see* discussion on "A Hard Look at Soft Law" 1988 ASIL Proc. 371-393, and C. Chinkin, *The Challenge of Soft Law: Development and Change in International Law* 38 ICLQ 850-866 (1989). "Soft law" had become a term-of-art especially in "international environmental law." *See e.g.,* P. Sand, *UNCED and the Development of International Environmental Law* 3 YRBK INTL ENV L 3-17 (1992); G. Palmer, *New Ways to Make International Environmental Law* 86 AJIL 259-283 (1992); and P. Birnie and A. Boyle, *International Law and the Environment* 26-30 (1992).

for all intents and purposes, the role of supplementary or follow-up arrangements, commitments, or agreements necessary to implement the *pacta de contrahendo* provisions of the Convention.[291] For example, cooperation for marine environmental protection and scientific research under the 1982 Convention is practically indistinguishable from cooperation to improve the technological and scientific capabilities of developing coastal States through international, regional or bilateral programmes in marine education and training. In their formulation, the latter is a more specific undertaking than, and is intended as a move in the direction of implementing, the broadly-stated commands in the former. The legal mandate to cooperate under the Convention is thus harmonized with and institutionalized through the details of the sustainable development imperative in the oceans as defined in a programmatic way by Chapter 17 of Agenda 21. But the details of international cooperation in Agenda 21 are more than aspirational or "programmatory" in normative value, because they incorporate in an integral way the regimes of international cooperation laid down in the positive law outputs at UNCED (*e.g.*, UNFCCC) and after UNCED (*e.g.*, S&HMFS Agreement) concerning ocean sustainable development. This en-

---

291 *Cf.* Kimball, *supra* note 236, at 491. *See* Pinto, *supra* note 138, at 154. What Ambassador Pinto said concerning the problem of cooperation under the Law of the Sea Convention is directly addressed by the cooperative undertakings under the UNCED's oceans "regime":

Cooperation is action, and the undertaking to cooperate is an undertaking to act. Where there is no action there is no cooperation. Where the co-operative obligation lacks clarity, the first step in fulfillment of the obligation to act would be to define the scope and frequency of future action regarded by the parties as being effective compliance with the undertaking to cooperate. Agreements on such future co-operative action would be the most practical means of recording the detailed rights and duties of the parties, and a State requesting the opening of negotiations on such an agreement has the right to a positive response. Co-operation would seem to reach its most developed expression in the establishment by the parties of institutions through which regular contact could be maintained, co-operative action can be monitored and supervised and, perhaps, new co-operative initiatives proposed, adopted and implemented.

It is a time for renewed and frequent contacts among those who favoured the creation of a new regime for the oceans, not with a view to traversing old ground, but moving forward to a new era of co-operative action to implement the [Law of the Sea] Convention, and demonstrate that its terms can and will be given effect through supplementary arrangements or agreements on the basis of mutual benefit, arrived at through such action.

sures an holistic or integrated approach not only to the normative definition of international cooperation but also to the institutional questions associated with the implementation of the principle of sustainable development.[292]

Cooperation under the UNCED ocean regime is also different in a quantitative sense from the cooperative regime laid out in the Convention on the Law of the Sea. This follows from UNCED's more expansive definition, or comprehension, of the "marine environment." Under Agenda 21, the "marine environment" which is subject to North-South cooperation is not only the juridically subdivided marine environment under the Law of the Sea – territorial sea, EEZ, high seas, seabed, etc. – but also includes coastal areas, SIDS, and the entire ocean environment as a single greenhouse gas global sink or as a continuous site of biodiversity.[293] In addition to reinforcing the holistic approach to sustainable development in the oceans, such expanded understanding of the "marine environment" by UNCED broadens the basis of cooperation between North and South, producing a wider scope for reciprocal interests which the cooperants can identify with. To illustrate, climate change-related MSR roughly puts a developing coastal State and a developing geographically disadvantaged State in the same "advantage" position with respect to bargaining possibilities on capacity-building *vis-à-vis* a research State or researching international organization.[294] Reciprocity, as an indispensable element of cooperative action which was given a narrow scope for North-South application in UNCLOS III, was thus broadened through Chapter 17, Agenda 21. The forthright message of UNCED is that it is only through international cooperation premised on the notion of reciprocity that the highly abstract process of integrating environmental protection and developmental goals can be converted into practical, operational decisions for sustainable development which can be taken seriously

---

292 Para. 17.1, Agenda 21. *See* also M.C.W. Pinto, "The United Nations Convention on the Law of the Sea: Sustainable Development and Institutional Implications" in Payoyo, *supra* note 234, 3-27.

293 Although the 1982 Convention defines "pollution of the marine environment", Art. 1 (4), CLOS, it does not define "marine environment" *per se* which, under Art. 192, CLOS, all States have the obligation to protect and preserve.

294 The huge investment required for this expanded reciprocity in the field of coastal zone management is described in B. Crawford, J.S. Cobb, & A. Freidman, *Building Capacity for Integrated Coastal Zone Management in Developing Countries* 21 OCEAN AND COASTAL MGMT 311 (1993).

by all sides.²⁹⁵ This justifies the conclusion, further explained below, that in the overall framework of sustainable development in the oceans through capacity-building for the developing States, the legal mandate to cooperate is founded on the essential notions of reciprocity²⁹⁶ and enlightened self-interest for global solidarity.²⁹⁷

Chapter 17 in this regard is a bankable "road map" for international co-operation,²⁹⁸ and one that has already proven its worth in two important ways. First, it succeeded in spurring a host of follow-up activities and institutional initiatives in pursuit of the Chapter's stated goal of sustainable development in the world's coasts and oceans.²⁹⁹ The relevant practice of States, on the

---

295 In the context of the failures of North-South Cooperation for development and global sharing since the 1960s, largely on account of asymmetrical relations based on "foreign aid", it is of course unrealistic to assume that North-South cooperation for sustainable development in the 1990s will all of a sudden be realized without the anchoring device of reciprocity in North-South relations. *Cf.* A. Kiss and D. Shelton, *International Environmental Law* 14-18 (1991), proposing to construct international environmental law on a basis other than reciprocity.
296 *See* Axelrod, *supra* note 209.
297 Handl, *supra* note 297, at 627. For an illuminating exposition on "solidarity", *see* R.St.J. Macdonald, "The Principle of Solidarity in Public International Law" *Etudes De Droit International En L'Honneur de Pierre Lalive* 275-307 (Geneva, 1993).
298 D.M. Johnston, *supra* note 237, at 21; Cicin-Sain & Knecht, *supra* note 237, at 350.
299 The international conferences called under Chapter 17 have all been concluded: The World Coast Conference, November 1993 (para. 17.11); Intergovernmental meeting on protection of the marine environment from land-based activities, November 1995 (para. 17.26); UN Conference on Straddling Fish Stocks and Highly Migratory Fish Stocks, concluded August 1995 (para. 17.50); and the UN Global Conference on the Sustainable Development of Small Island Developing States, April-May 1993 (para. 17.131). For a description of the impressive follow-up and implementation activities in the UN to UNCED's ocean agenda, *see* B. Kwiatkowksa, *Ocean-Related Impact of Agenda 21 on International Organizations of the United Nations System in Follow-up to the Rio Summit* 1992 NILOS DOCUMENTARY YEARBOOK xiii-lvii. According to the Multi-Year Thematic Programme of the Commission on Sustainable Development, the cluster of sectoral issues which includes ocean issues was reviewed in 1996. *See Report of Commission for Sustainable Development*, UN Docs. E/1993/25/Add.1-E/CN.17/1993/Add.1 (30 June 1993). For a more recent assessment of UNCED, *see* B. Cicin-Sain, *Earth Summit Implementation: Progress Since Rio* 20 MARINE POLICY 123 (1996), and the special

whole, is increasingly and consistently gravitating towards the expectations prescribed and policies underwritten by Chapter 17, Agenda 21. Secondly, Chapter 17 asserts, as it systematizes, the commitments to cooperate that are also covered by current "hard law" regulatory regimes giving concrete recognition to the "special interests and needs of developing countries." Taken as a whole, these *lex specialis* commitments are already ripe for normative consolidation under the general rubric *obligation to cooperate on the basis of common but differentiated responsibilities between North and South*. Thus, for the developed and developing countries alike, cooperation means capacity-building for the developing countries implemented through the principle of "common but differentiated responsibilities."

Examples of the policy areas highlighted by these binding commitments to cooperate, which illustrate the progress of North-South legal relations in the ocean sphere, include sustainable development of living resources in the EEZ (through the fisheries provisions in the 1982 Convention); conservation and management of SFS and HMFS (through the 1982 Convention and the S&HMFS Agreement); high seas reflagging of vessels (through the 1982 Convention, the 1993 Agreement to Promote Compliance with International Conservation and Management Measures by Fishing Vessels on the High Seas, and the S&HMFS Agreement); conservation of biodiversity in marine areas under national jurisdiction and biotechnology transfer (through the UNCBD and the 1982 Convention); land-based pollution (through the 1982 Convention and, as an arguable reflection of emerging customary law, the 1995 Washington Declaration on Protection of the Marine Environment from land-based activities); ship-source pollution (through the 1982 Convention and international agreements like MARPOL, the London Dumping Convention, and IMO Regulations); MSR (through the 1982 Convention and the UNFCCC); and technical assistance to SIDS (through the UNFCCC).

It must be noted that in all of these cooperative endeavors towards the implementation of the general principle of sustainable development in the oceans, the principle of sovereignty – and by definition, extended coastal State sovereignty – *in favor of developing States* is consistently upheld.[300] This

---

issue on *Earth Summit Implementation* 29 OCEAN & COASTAL MGMT nos. 1 & 2 (1996).

300 *See* for *e.g.,* 8th Preambular para., UNFCCC; 3rd Preambular para. and Art. 3, UNCBD. One of the conclusions of the Sienna Forum in regard to international cooperation advocated assistance to developing countries upon their request and

affirms the notion of equality among States and throws a skeptical light on the view which says that effective international cooperation for sustainable development requires the Southern States, more than the North, to be less strident in their advocacy for sovereignty.[301] The projection of sovereignty claims in these cooperative regimes reflected in Chapter 17 in fact supports the outlook that the rights emanating from sovereignty under the 1982 Convention on the Law of the Sea, specifically the sovereign rights in the EEZ, are

---

in full respect of their sovereignty in the collection of data and information on the state of the environment. *See Conclusions of the Sienna Forum on International Law of the Environment*, para. 15. Text UN Doc. A/45/666/Annex (24 October 1990), *supra* note 125. Principle 24 of the Stockholm Declaration, 11 ILM 1416 (1972), already foreshadowed this conclusion:

International matters concerning the protection and the improvement of the environment should be handled in a cooperative spirit by all countries, big and small, on an equal footing. Cooperation through multilateral and bilateral arrangements or other appropriate means is essential to effectively control, prevent, reduce and eliminate adverse environmental effects resulting from activities conducted in all spheres, in such a way that due account is taken of the sovereignty and interests of all States.

301 That there is a contradiction between the claims for sovereignty and/or equality of juridical capacities, on the one hand, and the cooperation requirements for environmental management, on the other, is argued for *e.g.* in "Introduction", Hurrel and Kingsbury, *op. cit.* esp. at 44-47; Kiss & Shelton, *op. cit.* at 20; P. Birnie & A. Boyle, *International Law and the Environment* at 85 (1992). These arguments, positing an antithetical relationship between sovereignty and environmental protection and/or sustainable development, implicitly identify or equate Third World claims to sovereignty over resources with the notorious conception of sovereignty asserted by the *Harmon* doctrine. (This doctrine was advanced by the United States in the late 19th century to provide basis for the argument that the US was not responsible for the river-borne water pollution suffered by Mexico if the pollution takes place in the territory of the US. The harm to Mexico was, therefore, political and not legal. *See* Kiss & Shelton, *id.*). It was already pointed out that the sovereignty claims of the developing States in UNCLOS III, and elsewhere, are founded on the twin principles of protection of resources from exploitation based on freedom *and* international cooperation, both intended to curb intrusions of that kind of cowboy sovereignty propounded by the *Harmon* doctrine.

not unfettered self-aggrandizing freedoms but powers shared between the holder of the power and the international community as a whole.[302]

In making the above cross-references to the "hard law" components of ocean governance,[303] and by synthesizing all the separate normative threads of co-operative activity in each of them into a more or less complete reinterpretation of rights and obligations for sustainable development in the ocean sphere, Chapter 17 possesses a normative status that transcends the "soft law" character of Agenda 21;[304] in reality Chapter 17 of Agenda 21 has become the most authoritative and comprehensive statement on the mandatory modes and practices of international cooperation[305] for sustainable development in the oceans.[306] Chapter 17 points to the fact that the legal framework for sustain-

---

302 Allot, *supra* note 3, at 77. Prof. Handl refers to this kind of sovereignty as a legal basis for inclusion, not exclusion, or for a commitment to cooperate for the good of the international community at large. Handl, *supra* note 250, at 87. The "sharing" or cooperation aspect of sovereignty under the LOSC is thus consistent with the theory of the Group of 77 regarding coastal State sovereignty in the EEZ as propounded at UNCLOS III. *See supra* Section E.

303 Chapter 17 also makes reference to other Chapters of Agenda 21 – *e.g.* radioactive and hazardous wastes, science for sustainable development, or conservation of biodiversity – which in turn refer to existing norms, treaties and other binding international regulations.

304 Chapter 17 of Agenda 21 could thus be imagined as a non-binding "framework" instrument whose binding "protocols" include the hard law outputs of UNCED as well as the 1982 Law of the Sea Convention.

305 It is also evident though that Chapter 17, Agenda 21 enunciates policy areas for international cooperation which are still wanting of positive law counterparts, justifying progressive development of law, *e.g.,* the *lex ferenda* of international cooperation to address land-based sources of marine pollution. *See* Washington Declaration on the Protection of the Marine Environment From Land-Based Activities, adopted 1 Nov 1995. Text in 26 EPL 37-51 (1996) [hereafter, Washington Declaration].

306 This it seems is the specific way by which the oceans output of UNCED can be related in a substantive way to the 1982 Convention on the Law of the Sea. Cicin-Sain and Knecht, *supra* note 236, at 341, seem to be at a loss on this point because "although references to the importance of the Law of the Sea Treaty as a basis for action on oceans and coasts abound in Agenda 21, nowhere is there an explicit discussion of how the UNCED provisions on oceans and coasts relate to or refine the treaty." *See also* Charney, *supra* note 126, at 882 note 11, stating that Chapter 17 of Agenda 21 is predicated upon the regime established by the 1982 Convention, but does not elaborate.

able development in the oceans had developed to such an advanced stage, definitively signalling the emergence of an "international law of cooperation on the basis of common but differentiated responsibilities" in the ocean sphere.

The implication of these observations on Chapter 17 with respect to the evolution of international law is clear. Universal agreement on the umbrella regime of international cooperation under Chapter 17, together with the consensus developed in particular "hard law" regimes of international cooperation in the ocean sphere – which includes the 1982 Convention's regime of cooperation in the EEZ – invariably supply a generalized *opinio juris sive necessitatis* behind a foundational obligation to cooperate for sustainable development. If this *opinio juris* element of the obligation to cooperate for sustainable development in the oceans is coupled with the growing and varied State practices thereon, at the bilateral and international organization levels, a strong case for the existence of a new customary norm can be argued.[307] The evidence of the specific components of this norm of cooperation for sustainable development in the oceans in terms of attributable State rights and obligations is shown not only by Chapter 17 of Agenda 21 but also by the various "hard law" components of ocean governance.[308] These rights and obligations are informed by,

---

307 *Cf.* Handl, *supra* note 250, at 80-81, who believes that "sustainable development" can turn into a peremptory norm of international law. But the initial challenge, he says, is to reach a clear international understanding on pathways to sustainable development and agreement on specific markers that lead to that goal; and then, the problem of the dispute settlement mechanisms to implement the *jus cogens* character of sustainable development should be dealt with. For a brief but insightful and far-sighted discussion on the legal status of sustainable development, *see* N. Singh, "Sustainable Development as a Principle of International Law" in de Waart, Peters & Denters, *op. cit.* 1-12.

308 *Cf.* H. Hohmann, *The Precautionary Legal Duties and Principles of Modern International Law* at 330 (1994). Although I agree with this author that sustainable development is a customary legal principle that needs to be reckoned with, his argument to support this proposition seems to hold loosely, apparently confusing law with policy, *lex lata* with *lex ferenda*:

Taking Agenda 21 into consideration as well, it can be concluded that the principle of sustainable development was specified to such a degree that it largely sets standards for the daily business of politics. Meant here are not legal but politically binding standards... The politically binding nature is *in reality* largely similar to a legally binding character. Due to political enforcement mechanisms, Agenda 21, which contains a consensus on most of the pressing problems of mankind, will determine the framework of environmental policy in the coming decades.

and at the same time interpret, the principle "common but differentiated responsibilities" of States for sustainable development, which is really the essential corollary of the general duty to cooperate for sustainable development.[309] Such principle was already anticipated in UNCLOS III in the context of a sectoral application of the standard "special interests and needs of developing States" in the protection and preservation of the marine environment. In the 1990s, the principle has acquired a wider strategic significance in the politics and discourse of sustainable development.[310] Under the principle of *common but differentiated responsibilities for sustainable development in the ocean sphere*, a developing State becomes the bearer of the "right to development" with respect to ocean and ocean-related undertakings, and a developed State is correspondingly duty bound to give assistance to the developing State to realize this right through various capacity-building initiatives. Both States are, however,

---

(emphasis in the original)

309 For a discussion of "the principle of common but differentiated responsibilities" as a general principle of "international environmental law", *see* M.T. Kamminga, "Principles of International Environmental Law" in P. Glasbergen & A. Blowers (Eds.), *Environmental Policy in an International Context* 111-131, at 126-128 (1995); SR Chowdhury, "Common But Differentiated State Responsibilities in International Environmental Law: from Stockholm (1972) to Rio (1992)" in K. Ginther, E. Denters & P.J.I.M. de Waart (Eds.), *Sustainable Development and Good Governance* 322-342 (1995). *See also* A. Adede, "International Protection of the Environment" in C. Tomuschat (Ed.), *The United Nations at Age Fifty: A Legal Perspective* 197-213, at 108 (1995).

310 Even before UNCED, the validity of the principle "common but differentiated responsibilities" as a treaty devise in international environmental law was already accepted. The Conclusions of the Sienna Forum, *supra* note 125, for example proposed that in international environmental protection, the special situation of the developing countries should be taken into account "through, e.g., financial and technical assistance to aid in implementing obligations; delayed compliance ('grace periods'); differentiated standards and objectives." More specifically, the successful consolidation of the "ozone regime", evolved since the 1985 Vienna Convention for the Protection of the Ozone Layer, may be credited to the serious consideration given by the parties to the special interests and needs of the developing countries, through provisions for delayed compliance and technical and financial assistance. *See* P. Szell "Ozone Layer and Climate Change" in Lang, Neuhold and Zemanek, *op. cit.* 167-178. For a further description of the controversy behind the precedent-setting obligation to give financial assistance to developing countries, *see* P. Szell, "Negotiations on the Ozone Layer" in G. Sjoestedt (Ed.), *International Environmental Negotiation* 37, 38 (1993).

equally and symmetrically bound by the *erga omnes* obligation to protect and preserve the marine environment.

A serious objection that may be raised against the existence of the principle "common but differentiated responsibilities" under the customary law of sustainable development in the ocean sphere should be considered. This objection posits that although the developed States have already accepted the positive obligation to give assistance to developing States to achieve sustainable development in the ocean sphere, particularly in relation to the latter's EEZs, the content of this obligation is too vague and indeterminate to possess normative identity, for it does not provide any guidance as to when and how this obligation is breached by the duty-bearer. Indeed, if the trends in ODA are at all any indication, assistance to developing countries had continually declined since UNCED,[311] rather than being multiplied in accordance with the principle of sustainable development.[312] As a complementary argument, some writers maintain that the financial assistance part of the North-South "global bargain" in UNCED (allegedly the heart of the new partnership for sustainable development) was not struck, simply because it was never put on the negotiating table in the first place,[313] thus warranting the assertion that there is no such thing

---

311 *See* UNGA Resolution of 19 December 1994, which notes the concern that there has been a 10% decrease in ODA since the conclusion of UNCED, with the grave possibility of undermining the basis of the global partnership forged at UNCED. *See* also *Chairman's Summary of the High Level Segment of the 3rd Session of the Commission for Sustainable Development*, 28 April 1995, noting the continuing concern over the declining trend in ODA, in absolute terms and as percentage of the donor countries' GNP.

312 The need for substantial "new and additional" financial resources to developing countries for sustainable development is stated in para. 1.4 (Preamble) and elaborated in Chapter 33 (Financial resources and mechanisms) of Agenda 21. For a backgrounder on "additionality", *see* P.S. Thacher, "The Role of the United Nations" in Hurrell and Kingsbury, *op. cit.* 183-211.

313 Johnson, *op. cit.* at 7, 443-450. This view is also shared by those who give a radically negative assessment of the UNCED, insisting that UNCED was really about the "environment" agenda and accomplished nothing by way of the "development" agenda. N. Middleton, P. O'Keefe & S. Moyo, *Tears of the Crocodile: From Rio to Reality in the Developing World* (1993). *Cf.* Cicin-Sain, *supra* note 299, at 138; and *The Declaration of the Ministers for Foreign Affairs of the Group of 77* at para. 33, asserting that "Agenda 21 and the Rio Declaration demonstrated a global commitment to assist the developing countries in both accelerating development and in improving their environment." Text in 1993 NILOS DOCUMENTARY YRBK

as a general Northern obligation to give assistance to the South under the principle of "common but differentiated responsibilities."

This objection, taken in perspective, raises the general question of standards of international responsibility or liability[314] – a subject that the International Law Commission had been wrestling with for a long time.[315] Specifically, the issue is to determine at what point in time international responsibility or liability attaches, in other words, when the obligation is breached, if the obligation in question is one to give assistance to prevent community harm.[316] In the context of the broad principle of sustainable development as well as the more specific principle of "common but differentiated responsibilities", the harm, injury or unreasonable risk contemplated is either the violation of the subjective right to sustainable development of developing States or, less im-

---

at 143- 147. *See also* Mr. Maurice Strong's closing speech to the Plenary Session of UNCED, 14 June 1992:

On finance, Mr. President, we must translate the good indications given here by many into specific commitments. And I would hope Mr. President, that a good many of the larger donor countries in particular will do this by the time the General Assembly considers this item in its next session. We must also start the process of developing new sources of funding, because the steps we have taken still do not promise to meet the larger needs.

Text in Johnson, *op. cit.* at 522. It is of course, obvious, that the provision for developing country assistance in the "hard law" output of UNCED entails binding legal obligations. In that sense, a North-South deal was struck.

314 Issues of dispute-settlement would not, conceptually, be part of the problem, inasmuch as the necessary mechanisms for dispute resolution are already in place in the "hard law" oceans output of UNCED, *viz.*, Part XV, CLOS; Art. 14, UNFCCC; Art. 27, UNCBD; and Part XIII, S&HMFS Agreement.

315 On the work of the ILC and the subject of international responsibility in relation to environment al concerns, *see* generally, F. Francioni & T. Scovazzi (Eds.), *International Responsibility for Environmental Harm* (1991).

316 This question is certainly different from the well-trodden issue in international environmental law about State liability for transboundary harm. *See* Principle 21, Stockholm Declaration and Principle 2, Rio Declaration. But the obligation to give assistance may be read as the broader, or even a stretched, interpretation of the familiar principle that States must answer for environmental damage caused by activities carried out or allowed within their jurisdiction and by activities that are under their control, *e.g.,* legislative authorization for Southern capacity-building. For a critical examination of this centerpiece principle in international environmental law, *see* K. Zemanek, "State Responsibility and Liability" in Lang, Neuhold & Zemanek, *op. cit.* at 187-198.

mediately but more dramatically, the ultimate catastrophe of planetary collapse, preceded as it were by distinct but interrelated processes of environmental decay in the world's coasts, oceans, forests, mountains, atmosphere, cities, etc. How can legal causation, or the existence of a legal nexus, be demonstrated between, on the one hand, failure of developed States to adequately cooperate for global sustainable development, and, on the other, the reality of retarded development on the part of developing countries, specifically, and impending oceans/planetary catastrophe, generally? The legal situation seems to lead to a *non liquet* dead-end,[317] summed up in a cynical way as "Sustainable development in the oceans. So what."

The above objection is indeed formidable, and the present law on international responsibility may supply no ground for resolving the kind of impasse it raises.[318] A system of redress that relies on reforming the current regime of international responsibility and liability to take into account notions of strict liability, communal harm, and compensation for immaterial damage[319] cannot surely explain at what precise point the present or on-going recalcitrance or delinquency of developed States to give adequate assistance to developing States for sustainable development in the oceans ripens into an actionable violation of the duty to cooperate for Third World capacity-building. In the same manner,

---

317 Those who advance the concept of "international environmental law" still retain some measure of confidence in, although are uniformly cautious about, the utility or limitation of the concepts of responsibility/liability for environmental protection. The possibility has not been conceived though, where Northern failure to cooperate for environmental protection by not giving "sustainable development" assistance to the South gives rise to legal responsibility. *See* Kiss & Shelton, *op. cit.* at Chapter VIII; Birnie & Boyle, *op. cit.* at Chapter 4; Zemanek, *supra* note 216, at 187; and F. Francioni, "International Cooperation for the Protection of the Environment: The Procedural Dimension" in Lang, Neuhold & Zemanek, *op. cit.* at 203. A perspective on the irrelevance of the doctrine of *non-liquet* in this contemporary context could be gleaned from a fresh reading of Professor J. Stone's *Non-Liquet and the Function of Law in the International Community* 39 BYIL 124-161 (1959).

318 *Cf.* O. Schachter, *The Emergence of International Environmental Law* 44 J INTL AFFAIRS 457 at 488 (1991), recognizing that it is not practicable to apply the law of liability to a situation where transboundary harm is caused by routine economic and social activities, and endorsing the proposal for the establishment of an international trust fund for reparation or prevention chiefly for the benefit of developing countries.

319 Zemanek, *supra* note 316, at 196-198.

those who would approach the problem from the point of view of determining due diligence "thresholds"[320] for responsibility or liability will certainly be at a loss in pinpointing the exact moment and the exact conditions as to when a breach is committed by this or that developed State with respect to this or that claimant developing State. And in the highly improbable case that the exact point of legal engagement is determined, the next legal issue that would await clarification will not be less insurmountable, namely, the nature and the size of compensation. If it is thus impossible to prove the dimensions of a breach of what clearly exists as a positive obligation to give assistance to developing States for sustainable development in a framework of State liability or responsibility, the entire edifice of the international law of cooperation under the oceans regime of UNCLOS and UNCED crumbles.[321] *Damnum absque injuria*?

On closer examination, the objection and its supporting arguments just outlined turn out to be largely misconceived. Far from invalidating the posited obligation in customary law to cooperate with and give assistance to developing countries under the principle of common but differentiated responsibilities, what this objection really brings to relief are the inherent limitations, and perhaps even the absurdity, of a rigid reliance on voluntaristic and neutralist/liberalist

---

320 *See* A. Springer, "Commentary" in Lang, Neuhold & Zemanek, *op. cit.* 199 and 201, who points out that the preferred approach to questions of state responsibility and liability for environmental damage is, assuming legal obligations already exist, to determine "threshholds": If one can accept the assumption that the State has a legal obligation to accept certain legal consequences of activities in or under its control which threaten or cause undesirable extra-territorial effects, the challenge is to give greater clarity to what those consequences are and the circumstances under which they can be invoked.

321 Birnie & Boyle, *op. cit.* at 186 and 213, partly recognize the difficulties involved with the admission that the "diversity of issues" needs to be emphasized in the resolution of environmental disputes, and that the balancing of interests inherent in the principle of sustainable development has implications for its translation into legal rights, and for that matter the juridical violation of these rights. *Cf.* Singh, in de Waart, Peters & Denters, *op. cit.* and also N. Singh, "Foreword" in Experts Group on Environmental Law of the WCED, *Environmental Protection and Sustainable Development: Legal Principles and Recommendations* (1987), esp. his note on "the problem of dispute settlement in relation to the law without sanctions."

assumptions of international co-existence[322] in solving what could best be described as a communal-ethical problem of international cooperation.[323] Without doubt, the posited principle of "common but differentiated responsibilities for sustainable development in the oceans" invites a deeper reflection on the methodology of international law, and forces a re-appreciation of concepts such as *"erga omnes* obligations", *"jus cogens"*, "sovereign equality", *"pacta sunt servanda"*, "the human right to development", "the principle of solidarity", "control and enforcement", "international security", the doctrine of *"non liquet"*,

---

322 *See* Weil, *op. cit.* 420-421, arguing that the essential features of international law in order to serve its functions meaningfully are voluntarism, neutrality and positivism. For a critical discussion of these values in the field of international relations, *see* D. Mapel, "The Contractarian Tradition and International Ethics" in T. Nardin & D. Mapel (Eds.), *Traditions of International Ethics* 180-200 (1992).

323 Weil, *id.* at 418 *et seq.*, argues that the essential functions of international law – *viz.*, co-existence and common aims – have not changed. Even if it is conceded that the features of "voluntarism", "neutrality" and "positivity" do work to preserve co-existence, it is not unlikely – and Prof. Weil seems to have ignored this – that these same features can be destructive of the equally if not more compelling purpose of achieving common aims, as shown quite persuasively by the "ideological" sustainable development argument. Professor Schachter has more recently observed the tendency to create principles on environmental liability such that "in moving beyond (or against) orthodox positive doctrine, the international law community has responded to a general perception of need." *See* O. Schachter, "The Greening of International Law" in *Humanité et Droit International Mélanges Rene-Jean Dupuy* 272 (Pedone, 1991). The need for a "paradigm shift", as this concept is used by Thomas Khun, *op. cit.*, is being acknowledged by authorities who discern an irreversible transition taking place in the field of international environmental law from one based on transborder interferences to another based on global/planetary threats. *See* for *e.g.*, Hohmann, *op. cit.* (from a "traditional", "anthropocentric" approach to a "modern", "ecological" approach); Birnie & Boyle, *op. cit.* 547 (neighborly relations to environmental trusteeship, in relation to the general shift from traditional to non-traditional/"soft law" sources of international environmental law). Kiss & Shelton, *op. cit.* (from juridical reciprocity to functional general interests of humanity). *See also* G. Porter & J.W. Brown, *Global Environmental Politics* (1991) (from an "exclusionist paradigm" in environmental politics to a "sustainable development paradigm"). *See also* P. Sand, *International Environmental Law After Rio* 4 EJIL 378 (1993). In the marine environment arena, a paradigm shift is advocated by, *e.g.*, B. Cicin-Sain, *Sustainable Development and Integrated Coastal Zone Management* 21 OCEAN & COASTAL MGMT at 12 (1993), and Cicin-Sain, *supra* note 299, at 142.

of "*non liquet*", the "precautionary principle", "inter-generational equity" and most certainly "the common heritage of mankind."³²⁴

Innovation and development of legal concepts, approaches, and strategies are needed if international law is to be made responsive and effective, in a most relevant and robust way, to the global ecological challenge that is engulfing humanity as a whole.³²⁵ The problem of vindicating the principle of "common but differentiated responsibilities" also directs legal technicians to apply themselves to the task of fulfilling the maxim *ubi jus ibi remedium* – that there ought to be a remedy behind every right.³²⁶ Once it is accepted that the imperatives of cooperation for sustainable development require more than ever the rule of law in international society, the basic obligation to cooperate must perforce assume a central remedial role in the legal framework to realize the right to sustainable development. This also suggests that the principle derives ultimately from a moral necessity to redress efficaciously and urgently at the normative level North-South imbalances, with more imagination and determination than in the past.³²⁷ Thus, far from merely projecting international law as an impersonal ordering tool, or a technician's instrument,³²⁸ the principle of common but differentiated responsibilities engenders the possibility that international

---

324 The literature on the re-evaluation and/or overhauling of international law or its concepts, norms and principles in light of the necessity of sustainable development is extensive. In addition to references cited in earlier footnotes, some other materials that relate a new view of international legal processes to the principle of sustainable development include E.B. Weiss, *In Fairness to Future Generations* (UNU, 1989) [on inter-generational equity]; V. Nanda, "Environment", in II Schachter & Joyner, *op. cit.* 631-669 [on prerequisites for effective environmental law making].
325 *Cf.* P. Birnie, "International Environmental Law: Its Adequacy for Present and Future Needs" in Hurrell & Kingsbury, *op. cit.*, for the argument that the present positivist structure of international law, through "an identifiable environment-specific regulatory regime" called International Environmental Law, is sufficiently ample and flexible "to meet all eventualities."
326 Singh, *supra* note 321 (1987) at xv, and *supra* note 307 (1988) at 12.
327 *See* Shue, *supra* note 243, for a strong statement of the view that issues of justice are integral to the quest for sustainable development.
328 *See* Weil, *op. cit.* 413 [International law is a tool, and ought to be of good quality, in governing international relations.]

law is "an international law of finalities",[329] as well as an international law that is continuously enmeshed in expanding human communication.[330] It is a facilitative international law, rather than a dominantly coercive one, that is perhaps called for by the new global partnership based on "common but differentiated responsibilities." It is an international law that can give expression to a new paradigm of North-South legal relations in the post-UNCED era: the International Law of Sustainable Development.

4. The International Law of Global Disparities versus the International Law of Sustainable Development

In spite of the fact that the system of redress under the prevailing structure and strictures of international law is incapable of fully vindicating the right of developing States to sustainable development in the ocean sphere, the case for international cooperation upon which this right is based cannot be seriously disputed.[331] Specifically, the existence in principle of the right or entitlement of developing States to be assisted for capacity-building in the ocean sphere, based on the treaty and customary standard of "common but differentiated responsibilities", is fully warranted by the evolution of international norms governing this sphere of human activities. With the entry into force of the 1982 UN Convention on the Law of the Sea, the framework of reciprocal political com-

---

329 M. Bedjaoui (Ed.), *International Law: Achievements and Prospects* at 14-17 (1991). From the perspective of sustainable development, the unrebuttable "finality" that simultaneously comprehends ideology, ethics, and science is the necessity for planetary survival. *Cf.* the finality of "human dignity" as postulated by the Policy-oriented School of International Law, *see* McDougal & Reisman, *supra* Chap. I note 44, at 123.

330 *See* Kratochwil, *supra* Chap. I note 44. In the language of the Commission on Population and Quality of Life, the concern should not only be on "carrying capacity" but also, more importantly, the "caring capacity" of the planet. *See* the Commission's Report, *Caring for the Future* (1996). From another perspective, the change of perspective is chronicled by Professor Douglas Johnston as the necessary transitions from a "classical" to the "neo-classical" and then "post-classical" periods of international relations. *See* Preface of D.M. Johnston, *The International Law of Fisheries A Framework for Policy-Oriented Studies* (1987 ed.).

331 *Cf.* Birnie & Boyle, *op. cit.* at 3-6, on the view that sustainable development is not yet a norm of international law and problems about its content will remain.

mitments for sustainable development contained in Chapter 17 of Agenda 21 is accorded normative recognition and is, on that account, stabilized as a detailed regime in programmatory law. On the assumption that these commitments partake of follow-up agreements envisioned by the 1982 Convention, the next logical step that now needs to be taken by the international community is the implementation and enforcement of these commitments.

The juridical model of international cooperation developed through the institution of the EEZ has proven extremely valuable in the search for a legal framework for sustainable development. By specifically attributing zone-specific as well as functional rights and obligations among States, and by providing for their balancing through institutional mechanisms of inter-State cooperation and dispute settlement, the EEZ is the most feasible legal apparatus that can serve to integrate a whole range of sustainable development concerns, including resource exploitation and conservation, scientific research, environmental protection, the development and transfer of technology, and human rights. It cannot be overemphasized that this integration respects and builds upon the principle of sovereignty (specifically, coastal State sovereign rights) and, by implication, the principle of equality of capacity for the exercise of rights and the assumption of obligations among States. For the developing countries, who introduced the EEZ concept in international law, the sovereign rights that characterize the EEZ is a sovereignty that is protective *and* at the same time custodial – emphasizing the inseparable community interest in the preservation, development, and sustainable use of this multifunctional zone.[332] The UNCED, through Chapter 17 of Agenda 21, reinforced the validity of this legal framework by unconditionally recognizing the constitutional role of the 1982 Convention in the pursuit and realization of the political commitments therein undertaken by all

---

332 The view that sustainable development is necessarily opposed to the principle of sovereignty is not entirely accurate, unless this notion of sovereignty is understood in its extreme sense as expressed by the *Harmon doctrine, supra* note 301. Even in the law of the sea, certain authors are tempted to generalize that coastal State sovereignty is a drawback to the realization of the purposes of the 1982 Convention, *see* Broadus & Vartanov (Eds.), *The Oceans and Environmental Security: Shared US and Russian Perspectives* at 227 (1994), albeit accepting the basic proposition, at 13 and 235, that the 1982 Convention is the most important basis for environmental security and a most viable framework for global assurance-building.

members of the international community as they embark on a global project of sustainable development.³³³

And yet a sense of failure and frustration creeps into the picture. Notwithstanding the formidable legal infrastructure of sustainable development developed for international cooperation in the ocean sphere, a vast majority of the world's peoples have not obviously enjoyed, much less started to benefit from, the regime in terms of cleaner seas and more bountiful oceans and coasts. On the contrary, the entire system of ocean governance premised on the principle "common but differentiated responsibilities" – the foundation for the new partnership between North and South for sustainable development – seems to be falling apart.³³⁴ It may be that this unfortunate situation is caused by the proverbial "lack of political will" on the part of governments in the North, or even the South, or both, to cooperate for capacity-building.³³⁵ But when the fundamental consensus on the principle of cooperation has been reached, when the modes to effectuate this cooperation have been identified, and when the direction and goals of cooperation have been firmly set, the complacency to implement sustainable development – particularly cooperation for sustainable development in the oceans – can no longer be brushed away as a failure of political will, and therefore relegated to the arena of international politics. To the extent that the global consensus on cooperation is governed by international law, and to the extent that the problem of growing North-South disparities in the ocean sphere is caused by a breakdown in the legal institutions of international cooperation, the lack of progress in ocean sustainable development is symptomatic of a structural failure of international law itself. If this is the case, the "international law of global disparities" once again rears its ugly head.

The much-needed transformation of international law that would make it more responsive to the requirements of capacity-building for sustainable development in the oceans awaits a committed intellectual effort on the part of international lawyers whose aim is the systematization of norms for sustainable development. It was already pointed out that the process of rethinking inter-

---

333 *See* para. 17.1, *Agenda 21*.
334 *See* Cicin-Sain, *supra* note 299, at 138-139, and 142.
335 *See* B. Kwiatkowska, "The Role of Regional Organizations in Development Cooperation in Marine Affairs" in A. Soons (Ed.) *Implementation of the Law of the Sea Convention Through International Institutions* at 130 (LSI, 1990); A. Rest, *Implementation of the Rio Targets – Preliminary Efforts in State Practice* 25 EPL 312-321 (Nov. 1995).

national law in this direction is underway, and the review and reassessment of fundamental concepts, principles and techniques of international law for this purpose have begun in earnest.[336] These are welcome developments that should be consolidated at every stage in the evolution of a truly effective "international law of cooperation" for sustainable development. It is not the intention of this thesis to describe in detail the progress that has so far been made in setting up this international law of cooperation in the global context of sustainable development. This chapter more particularly was simply aimed at verifying the hypothesis that the new international law of the sea had hitherto been ineffective in the resolution of global disparities within the traditional domains of North-South inequality in the oceans. With the demonstration that the current ocean regime is, at this point in time, only making slow progress towards its avowed aim of sustainable development, measures to remedy the situation should be in order. From the vantage point of an assessment of the doctrinal features of inequality in the new law of the sea, the remainder of this Chapter will consider one significant obstacle that stands in the way of establishing the principle of sustainable development in the ocean sphere. This major obstacle relates to the manner by which the concept of the "environment" is conceived and elaborated as a subject of international legal regulation.

If the paradigm of "sustainable development" in the oceans is to succeed as a policy instrument in overcoming the widening North-South gap, it must be able to regulate the ocean sphere in such a way that "environment" and "development" concerns are meaningfully integrated as a single arena for legal relations. This much is clear and uncontroversial. The problem arises though when, as is now apparently the case, an imbalance in normative focus occurs, whereby "environment" is seen as more primordial, more normatively mature, and a more valid object of legal relations, than "development." Definitions are thus crucial. It is interesting to note that in the process of definitional scoping necessarily undertaken by some analysts and legal technicians, the "oceans", or what I have referred to as the ocean sphere, as a subject of international legal regulation, is defined all too literally. It is reduced to its "physical environment" denotation, in disregard of the more amorphous "social development" element it possesses under the sustainable development equation. The relevant legal landscape defined is thus the marine environment *stricto sensu*, as a non-human medium rather than anything else. This reductive mind-set of defining the relevant "environment" as the physical environment *per se* could be traced

---

336 *See supra* note 323, on the paradigm shift in "international environmental law."

to an early tradition of the discipline "International *Environmental* Law".[337] In this tradition, the practice of defining the environment along literal lines assumes that, for instance, the sea "environment" is the physical ocean, much in the same way as the "environment" in the law of the atmosphere and outer space are the physical media of the atmosphere, or the ozone layer, or the moon and celestial bodies, or near-earth outer space, or the "environment" in the law of international watercourses is a transboundary river or a lake, or the "environment" in the law on conservation of living resources are the animals themselves – fish, birds, endangered species, etc.

Any legal definition of the "environment" would have critical implications at the normative level, inasmuch as its accepted definition would largely dictate the nature and scope of the regulatory regime as well as the application of legal techniques of which the "environment" will be subject. To the credit of the 1982 Law of the Sea Convention, the comprehensive ocean sphere which it regulates is conceived as *not* being limited to the physical "marine environment" as this term is used in its anti-pollution regime under Part XII.[338] The Convention also regulates non-sea physical media like rivers,[339] airspace,[340] and ice covered areas,[341] and is concerned with dominantly land-based concerns

---

337 For this early invocation of "International Environmental Law", *see* L.F.E. Goldie, "Development of an International Environmental Law – An Appraisal" in J.L. Hargrove, *Law, Institutions and the Global Environment* 104-165, at 104 (1972): ... an international environmental law should be a flexible instrument capable of protecting the environment at a number of levels of action. It should regulate government interactions, impose minimum standards for national legislation and administration, require all international agencies, be they regional or universal, to include the protection of the environment as an inherent and uncontrovertible measure of policy in the process of decision, build into regimes governing the exploration and exploitation of the seabed resources special standards and duties of environment protection, and establish international agencies which should flexibly impose minimum universal and regional standards for preventing further environmental degradation. It would be no part, however, of such an international environmental law's function to prevent absolutely the transformation of the environment into energy and useful or enjoyable commodities.

338 See definition of "pollution of the marine environment" in Art. 1 (4), CLOS in relation to Art. 194, CLOS.

339 Arts. 8 & 9, CLOS.

340 *E.g.*, Arts. 2 (2) and Art. 76, CLOS.

341 Art. 234, CLOS.

like rights of land-locked States,[342] land-based pollution activities,[343] cooperation in scientific research,[344] and technology transfer.[345] The reason for this expansive treatment and definition of the marine and/or ocean sphere as the "Law of the Sea" is stated curtly but elegantly in the Preamble of the Convention: "The problems of ocean space are closely interrelated and need to be considered as a whole." The marine environment under the 1982 Convention is, therefore, not merely confined to the medium of marine waters. An illustration of a subsequent interpretation or re-definition was already mentioned: even the specialized concern on protecting and preserving the marine environment under Part XII cannot, fundamentally, be dissociated from activities pertaining to the equally all-embracing MSR or the technology transfer provisions of the Convention.[346] Therefore, the definition of a proper environmental concern cannot be divorced from the realities of political decision-making in the international community.[347]

The UNCLOS III and UNCED were, therefore, landmark events in the evolution of "international law on the environment", for the chief reason that these fora generated an international consensus on what should be considered as "proper" environmental concerns. UNCLOS III successfully integrated "strictly environmental concerns" (*i.e.*, marine pollution) with the "developmental concerns" of the developing States through the EEZ regime, thus producing an authoritative definition of proper environmental concerns in the ocean sphere. In like manner, UNCED, through Chapter 17 of Agenda 21, expanded the idea of the ocean "environment" by embracing in its remit not simply marine waters – which was already done in UNCLOS – but coastal zones, entire land territories and nations called Small-Island Developing States (SIDS), and even the planetary geo-biosphere as a site of critical uncertainties in the management of climate change. More importantly, and in relation to its expanded definition of environmental

---

342 Part X, CLOS.
343 Arts. 207 and 213, CLOS.
344 Part XIII, CLOS.
345 Part XIV, CLOS.
346 *Supra* Section E.
347 For the argument on this point, *see* N. A. Robinson "Problems of Definition and Scope" in Hargrove, *supra* note 337, at 44-103, 45. *Cf.* Birnie & Boyle, *op. cit.* at 2-3, who at the beginning of their treatise pose the question "What is meant by 'the environment'?" but do not answer this question. Somewhat unbecoming of legal positivists, they endorse the view that "it is a term that everyone understands and no one is able to define."

concerns, Chapter 17 of Agenda 21 included as an inseparable ingredient of these concerns the economic and social "development" of States in the Third World under the concept of capacity-building for sustainable development in the oceans. Hence, the environmental law of the sea since UNCLOS III had always comprehended, by definition, equally pressing developmental matters in the ocean governance equation, *i.e.,* those relating to "the special interests and needs of developing States." The consequence of this reasoning on the old sectoral and segmented discipline of "international environmental law" is clear. Such orthodoxy should have to give way to a new "international law of sustainable development" plainly because the definition of the "environment" has changed.

One important consequence of the "international law of sustainable development", founded on a reoriented understanding of what constitutes "environmental concerns", is certainly a more affirmative and sympathetic interpretation of the Third World's historical claims for "development." Now that these claims have been recognized as legitimately part and parcel of global "environmental concerns", the framework for the international legal regulation of the "environment" must *ipso facto* be transformed. What should take place is a fundamental shift in the perception about the "environment" on the part of those who have hitherto regarded the "environment" as juridically outside and independent of the State and its institutions. The global "environment" cannot but include the world's poor – with all their needs, interests, aspirations, and potentials.[348]

---

348 The representation of the role of the Third World in the historical "sustainable development" movement is thus opposed to their representation in the traditional "international environmental law" movement. For instance, Kiss & Shelton, *op. cit.* 48-54, maintain that in the Stockholm Conference the developing States "did not favor the idea that cooperation of all countries was necessary to protect the environment"; that these countries wished to industrialize and "ignore the environmental costs"; that parts of the Stockholm Declaration reflected the agenda of the Third World rather than the agenda of environment; but that "Third World countries now largely accept the need for world cooperation to safeguard the planet" and that "developing countries today generally agree on the necessity of safeguarding the environment and integrating methods to protect it in the development process." These remarks suggest that the "integration" of environment and development – the main message of "sustainable development" – is still to take place in the minds of "environmental" lawyers. By assimilating "development" concerns as simply a historical add-on to the traditional epistemology of "international environmental law", the result is a truncated view of Third World "development" in relation to environmental protection, and a reification of the narrowly

"Environment" is not only colonial-state frontiers and panoramas but also entire populations of people struggling to be adequately clothed, sheltered, fed and educated.³⁴⁹ It is, in short, the "environment" that is *also* seen from the eyes and minds of the developing countries.³⁵⁰

---

    construed "environment" that is potentially bereft of human and humane elements:
    ... international environmental law developed more rapidly than international human rights law or the law of development, and its norms became less abstract than those principles governing outerspace or the oceans. In a sense, the law of nations was forced to mature and recognize the importance of developing formal sources of law for the identification of new rules.
    Kiss and Shelton, *op. cit.* 95. Birnie & Boyle, *op. cit.* 7, also fall into the same trap and misconstrue perceptions in the developing world about the relative importance of environmental concerns in relation to their development:
    greater involvement of developing states in conventions or codes concerning [international environmental] issues ... is likely to be dependent on further financial and technical and technological inducements or stimulation of greater public awareness in such states of their common interest in shared resources and surroundings and of the threats posed by environmental degradation, or over-exploitation, or both.
    Small wonder why these writers would wish to explain the ratifications to the 1982 Convention on the Law of the Sea that came exclusively from the developing States "because of its perceived economic benefits", even as "generally fewer developing States become signatories or parties to environmental treaties."

349 The need to reorient perceptions on problems like environmental protection before meaningful action can be pursued is argued in B. Ward "A New Creation? Reflections on the Environmental Issue" in *Tribute to Barbara Ward* (1987).

350 *Cf.* P. Sands, *Principles of International Environmental Law: Frameworks, Standards, and Implementation* 17-18 (1995) [adopting the UNEP definition of "environment" which includes "humans", but restricts the scope of his study to the non-human elements of the "environment"] Reference may also be made to a statement given by UN Secretary-General U. Thant in 1970:
    The developing countries are intimately concerned with these problems, which are crucial both to their own future and to the future of the environment. Their voices must be heard, and listened to, even if at the outset their technical contribution may be relatively small. Their confidence and their cooperation, as representing the largest part of the world's population, are vital. Otherwise we shall once again increase the gap between the advanced and developing nations which is already one of the major sources of tension in the world.
    Quoted in A. Chayes "International Institutions for the Environment" in Hargrove, *op. cit.* 1-26, at 5.

Unfortunately, the transformation of perceptions regarding what constitutes "the environment", impelled by the world consensus on "sustainable development" in both UNCLOS III and UNCED generally, and Chapter 17 Agenda 21, specifically, has barely taken place in the consciousness of Northern experts who write about the international law of the environment as though that environment was still the pre-UNCLOS "environment" *eo nomine*.[351] It is submitted that it is an outmoded view that asserts that the concept of "environment" is distinct and juridically independent from the existence of States, especially the majority of States in the South. It is also an outmoded view which argues

---

[351] Kiss & Shelton, *op. cit. See also* Birnie & Boyle, *op. cit.*, who are deeply ambivalent about an international environmental law that recognizes the perspectives of developing countries. First, they claim that despite economic, political and social problems raised by the developmental concerns of developing States (p. 6) there is now a distinct body of law for the protection of the environment which they call "international environmental law" (p. 1) although they hesitate to define what in their view constitutes the "environment" (p. 3). Secondly, the application of rules and principles of international environmental law is qualified by the "*different* priorities of southern hemisphere less-developed countries and their demands for 'special consideration.'" (p. 87 emphasis supplied); they, therefore, admit – quite appropriately – that their system of international environmental law is "based on precedents from the northern hemisphere industrialized States, and *reflect environmental concerns appropriate to their state of economic development.*" (p. 88, emphasis supplied). Thirdly, at the end of a textbook exposition of the "hard" as well as "soft" international environmental law – a "law" that expectedly does not address the central issue of the possibility of a legal framework for sustainable development – the conclusion is reached, at 547, that

... the problems of environmental law making and enforcement are essentially political and institutional in character. They are best seen as a reflection of the difficulties of securing international cooperation on global environmental management within a complex and diffuse structure of political authority and of the deeply conflicting priorities among developed and developing States.

The remark is of course an illustration of how the "law" of international lawyers of the positivist orientation succumbs to the realist/power politics approach to international relations. But the "realists" in international relations will perhaps be less cynical towards international law if international lawyers succeed in crafting a law not only for the environment but also for development, *i.e.,* the international law of sustainable development! For an initial exploration on the possibilities of the international law of sustainable development, *See* Ginther, Denters & de Waart, *supra* note 309. *See* also Sands, *supra* note 350 at 14, for the view that "international environmental law" is part of the "international law of sustainable development" but is narrower in scope.

that international cooperation and the performance of the duty to cooperate for environmental protection may conceptually set aside the social or "development" dimensions of sustainable development, because, if this view is accepted, the "environment" will always be regarded as threatened by people and States, rather than people and States, including their physical environment, threatened by environmental degradation.[352] The transition from "international environmental law" – a system of law that reinforces the construction and division of the world into advanced "environment-conscious" States and backward "development-conscious" States, and on this account participates in the "international law of global disparities" – to an "international law of sustainable development" is consistent with the transition that took place in the definition of the "marine environment" in the ocean sphere. Under the 1982 Convention and Chapter 17 of Agenda 21, the marine environment is not only water, coasts and the atmosphere, but also, more significantly, people.[353] The last element is perhaps the most crucial, since the deterioration, degradation, and thus demoralization and dehumanization of "people", or entire nation-States, is ultimately the worst type of environmental catastrophe, prefiguring all other corruptions of nature, that can possibly be imagined.

It is not certain at this point whether the North and the South will be able to persevere with the consensus on a new partnership based on the principle of sustainable development. If the dearth of political will is indeed the cause of this pessimism, perhaps the political will to escape from this quagmire is the political will on the part of international lawyers to systematically evolve, elaborate and oversee the implementation of the necessary legal framework upon which the details of the partnership can be transformed into effective cooperative projects, and upon which the urgent sense of partnership can be defended and kept alive. It is to be hoped that the international law of sustainable development will be recognized, developed and made fully operational in the near future. A central point is worth reiterating: some of the normative building blocks of this international law of sustainable development are already in place, thanks to the 1982 Convention and the oceans output of UNCED. These include the obligation to protect and preserve the marine environment; the obli-

---

352 By including in the definition of "State" the *a priori* element of "environment", as it is axiomatic in the juridical concept of "coastal State", *supra* Section E, it becomes clear why a threat to the environment becomes a threat to the State, its people, and its security. *Cf.* Broadus & Vartanov, *supra* note 332.
353 *Cf.* B. Ward & R. Dubos, *Only One Earth* at 295 (1972).

gation to cooperate on the basis of reciprocity or "common but differentiated responsibilities"; the obligation of developed States to assist developing States in the latter's capacity-building endeavors; the right and the duty of sustainable development for developing States; integrated and precautionary approaches; respect for sovereignty and equality of capacity for rights and obligations; compulsory dispute settlement mechanisms; and decision-making by consensus. One other important normative building block, which in itself potentially embodies a philosophy and a strategy on how all these elements of the emerging "international law of sustainable development" can be ordered into a unified architecture of international legal relations, should be identified. This is the principle of the "common heritage of humanity", to which our attention must now turn.

CONCLUSION

Two great upheavals in the post-war order have determined the overall shape and character of North-South legal relations: decolonization and the drive for sustainable development. In point of time, one came after another, like gigantic waves smashing onto the seeming stability of classical international law. In their substance, if not in purpose, these two upheavals share the common aim of questioning the abyss that exists in the international community between the few rich States and the many that are poor – akin to two immense rivers merging together into a grand onslaught – seeking to fulfill an objective that is yet uncharted in the history of the law of nations.

The oceans was the great normative battleground where the forces of decolonization and sustainable development were played out with much energy and creativity. For the poor developing States who propelled these forces in the hope of establishing a new international legal order sensitive to their needs and interests, the overhauling of an oceans regime as they found it in the aftermath of the colonial era offered an opportunity to lay the foundations of a more equal relationship with the rich countries. The train of events triggered by the 1967 speech of Ambassador Arvid Pardo in the United Nations attests to this determination, which bore fruit with the adoption and eventual entry into force of the 1982 UN Convention on the Law of the Sea. But even before the Convention entered into force in November 1994, another arena was opened up which enjoined a critical reappraisal of North-South legal relations in the ocean sphere, from which emerged what is now Chapter 17 of Agenda 21. On the whole, the two historical processes that culminated in the adoption of these texts – the "UNCLOS process" and the "UNCED process" – provided the political and diplomatic vehicles for the Third World to pursue the normative objectives of decolonization and sustainable development. The combined effect of these processes is the definition of the most detailed and the most advanced legal framework of contemporary North-South relations. Their inter-woven policy themes, mutually reinforcing norms, and overlapping implementation strategies and institutional mechanisms – at national, regional and global levels – formulate what can only be described as the most mature expression of ocean governance, and therefore planetary governance, in the context of decolonization and sustainable development.

To be sure, the normative outcomes of UNCLOS III and UNCED, if considered in isolation from one another, do not contribute in a meaningful way to the overall solution of narrowing the North-South gap. For instance, in the traditional domains of disparity in the ocean sphere between North and South, which this Chapter dealt with, the 1982 Convention on the Law of the Sea did not really come up with rigorous regimes that would meaningfully address the overriding standard "special needs and interests of developing countries, whether coastal or land-locked."[354] It was shown that the institution of the Exclusive Economic Zone, which recapitulates the position of the Group of 77 in UNCLOS III on the matter, is basically responsive to the "coastal State vs. non-coastal State" dichotomy, and was not meant to systematically address the North-South problematic. As a result, the developing LLGDS, whose members account for many of the poorest nations in the Third World, were effectively marginalized from the global sharing arrangements envisioned by the institution of the EEZ. Furthermore, to assert that the needs and interests of the developing countries were accorded positive recognition by way of enforceable units of rights and obligations in the crucial cross-cutting provisions of the Convention on environmental protection, marine scientific research, and transfer of technology is somewhat to exaggerate the achievements of the Convention in the positive law of decolonization.[355] Most of the *lex lata* provisions in the Convention

---

354 5th Preambular para., CLOS.

355 This is not to denigrate the contribution of UNCLOS III as a law-making exercise, which proved to be an exceptional "laboratory" of international law especially for the developing countries, not only in regard to the production of new concepts, new approaches, and new relationships in the legal ordering of the oceans but also in the development of unique techniques in international decision-making

that were intended to promote the cause of equality of capacity for rights and obligations between North and South were rightly described by commentators as overly broad *pacta de contrahendo* rules on international cooperation. It is in the prolific regime of international cooperation that the 1982 Convention excels as a constitutional document for North-South relations in the ocean sphere.

Similarly, the positive law output of UNCED in the ocean realm which can be relied upon as regimes within the ambit of "the special interests and needs of the developing countries" is minimal. From the perspective of the formal sources of international law, Chapter 17 of Agenda 21 is no more than a detailed commitment to ocean governance *de lege ferenda*, or "soft law." In a related way, the oceans provisions of the "hard law" outputs of UNCED that may be regarded as significant for the Third World agenda of development and global sharing – such as the UNFCCC, the UNCBD, and the S&HMFS Agreement – contain fundamentally hortatory rules on the general duty of States to cooperate – not unlike the 1982 Convention on the Law of the Sea, which is a paragon instrument on broadly-stated norms of international cooperation.

But international law, or the rules of global governance that figure in *lex lata* or *lex ferenda*, do not move in a vacuum, rarely unaffected by changes in the "environment" – historical, political, economic, social, and ecological. A separate, doctrinal reading of the 1982 Convention and Chapter 17 of Agenda 21 certainly yields a dismal picture of the North-South redistributive regime in the ocean sphere. But the historical linking of the two texts, which is rendered logical and inevitable by the real threat of impending planetary destruction produces what in effect is an outstanding, far-reaching regime that could be a model of all universal international law. This conclusion should not really come as a surprise. Like the molecular process of two unseen elements mixing together to produce visible water, the reasoning behind the paradigm of ocean governance is no less plain.

The catalyst that joins the 1982 Convention and Chapter 17, Agenda 21 is of course the duty to cooperate, which in a positivist universe of international law is really an obligation of *pacta de contrahendo* character. It was already indicated to what extent the 1982 Convention is replete with provisions on the duty to cooperate, especially in fulfillment of the North-South aims of the new

---

and North-South diplomacy.

regime on the oceans as enunciated in the Preamble to the Convention.³⁵⁶ What this means for the North-South dialogue is a continuing, possibly indefinite, mutual effort of arriving at a satisfactory *modus vivendi* on development and global sharing, a prospect that is not necessarily unfavourable to those countries which profit and prosper from the *status quo*. Without the necessary *quid pro quo* considerations that can drive the duty to cooperate forward and achieve results by way of concrete follow-up arrangements and agreements, the obligation to cooperate is of doubtful normative utility because of its very open-endedness. It is surely one of the sad legacies of a Eurocentric system of international law, which the developing States had to accept since decolonization, that constantly demands reciprocity³⁵⁷ and self-interested consent in the operations of inter-State legal relations.³⁵⁸

UNCED was a watershed event because it framed and articulated in the most dramatically compelling way the political terms of reciprocity for North-South legal relations: the North must assist the South to develop if the global ecology is to be preserved, and the South must assist the North in protecting this global ecology if it wishes to develop. Such is the "new global partnership for sustainable development" that was inaugurated at UNCED. The inclusive sweep

---

356 Or, a legal provision stipulating the duty to cooperate between parties is in reality a summary of the fact that the parties momentarily agreed to disagree, *i.e.*, that in relation to the subject on which they disagree, they will in good faith meet again at a later time to enter into an agreement that is more specific than their general duty to cooperate. An agreement to cooperate does not of course imply a duty to enter into an agreement later. *Cf.* Pinto, *supra* note 138.

357 Kiss and Shelton, *op. cit.* 15, argue that there were significant historical "exceptions" to the "principle of reciprocity", or for that matter consent, as basis of interstate legal relations: they cite freedom of navigation on international rivers and canals, prohibition of slave trading, protection of religious liberty, restriction on the means and methods of warfare, human rights, regulation and use of antarctica, outer space, and freedom of the seas. On closer inspection these are not really exceptions to, but affirmations of, the principle of reciprocity, but labeled as "nonreciprocal obligations" by the authors. What the authors were perhaps arguing is the existence of obligations *erga omnes*, which is conceptually distinct from the principle of consent in the conclusion of international agreements.

358 *Cf.* Birnie and Boyle, *op. cit.* 9, on this acceptance of international law in the field of "environmental law": "It is now well established and widely accepted that newly independent States have to take the previously Eurocentric international law as they find it but that they can then seek to change and influence its development."

of the reciprocity that is founded on the principle of sustainable development at once restructures North-South relations and the legal perspective that had hitherto governed the dominant conception of these relations. Crucial in this regard is the superimposition of the oceans output of UNCED on the 1982 Convention on the Law of the Sea. The legal framework of cooperation laid down in 1982 Convention is suddenly energized by UNCED's programme of North-South cooperation to save the oceans, a most critical "environment" in the total matrix of the planetary ecology. In turn, the very detailed political commitments crafted in the oceans output of UNCED, outlined particularly in Chapter 17 of Agenda 21, no longer need to await a normative underpinning, which has already been worked out in a previous consensus, namely the 1982 Convention on the Law of the Sea.

The impact of UNCED on the evolution of the obligation to cooperate in the 1982 Convention should be stressed. On the basis of the oceans output of UNCED – both in "hard law" and "soft law" – the duty to cooperate for sustainable development in the oceans is conferred the status of customary norm, with a quite specific content that is spelled out by the principle of "common but differentiated responsibilities." Under this principle rights and obligations of States in the EEZ are allocated in such a way that developed States are duty-bound to give assistance to developing States in the latter's capacity- building efforts, and developing countries are accorded the right and/or the duty to develop in a sustainable way according to the terms of Chapter 17, Agenda 21. Without the 1982 Convention, there is indeed no basis upon which to pursue the protection and sustainable development of the marine and coastal environment and its resources.[359] All said, the duty to cooperate for sustainable development in the oceans in the 1990s and beyond serves as the prism through which the preambular objectives of the 1982 Convention are converted into a variety of normative arrangements conducive to the equalization of capacities for rights and obligations on the part of developing and developed States alike.

It appears, however, that it might take some time before the obligation to cooperate for sustainable development in the oceans will be fully made operational. Already, there are tendencies that would wish to see this obligation conceived and practiced as narrowly as possible, to render it merely as an obligation to preserve and protect the environment *stricto sensu*, devoid of humans and human interference as far as politically feasible. This interpretation of the obligation to cooperate for sustainable development is inconsistent with

---

359 Para. 17.1, *Agenda 21*.

the global consensus on sustainable development – a legal principle pioneered by the 1982 Convention and strongly reaffirmed in UNCED. If allowed to prevail, this extreme but easy interpretation of the duty to cooperate for sustainable development will simply elevate the "international law of global disparities" to much more formidable heights, and further aggravate the North-South tensions that have already undoubtedly become an ultra-hazardous pollutant in the planet.

The "international law of sustainable development" which builds on a more inclusive interpretation of the obligation to cooperate for capacity-building in the developing world implies a difficult process of renewal and reconstruction in the normative ordering of the world. Establishing this international law of sustainable development would require a recasting of the legal position of States, individually as cooperating entities and collectively as North and South, more in keeping with the standard of "common but differentiated responsibilities" for sustainable development. This should lead to a jettisoning of the major tools and concepts of co-existence, like the freedom of the seas, which conflict with the demands of a thorough-going programme of international cooperation for sustainable development. At the same time, consolidating the normative and institutional elements of the international legal process supportive of the principle of sustainable development will have to involve a systematic re-examination of concepts about cooperation. Fortunately, there are already numerous building-block concepts which can be put to the service of an emergent international law of sustainable development. One such central concept that deserves clarification and re-appreciation is the principle of the "common heritage of humanity."

PART 2

THE COMMON HERITAGE OF HUMANITY AND WORLD INEQUALITY

III

THE COMMON HERITAGE OF HUMANITY: A LEGAL PRE-HISTORY

In his celebrated essay, *The Structure of Scientific Revolutions*,[1] Thomas Kuhn advanced the notion of "paradigm", meaning those exemplary achievements that for a time provide model problems and solutions to a particular scientific community. In the practice of what Kuhn calls normal science, a paradigm provides the community the foundations on which its members pursue puzzle-solving endeavors. When a paradigm no longer proves itself capable of solving the problems it defines on account of acute anomalies revealed in these endeavors, a crisis of expectations emerges, which seeks a resolution that demands nothing less than a revolutionary transformation of world views. The acceptance of an alternative, more legitimate paradigm – like the substitution of the Ptolemaic for a Copernican universe – signals the occurrence of a paradigm change, enabling the community to respond to, and once again practice a re-constituted normal science in, a totally different world.

In a very fundamental way, the rise of "sustainable development" thinking confirms the emergence of a new paradigm in global governance – one that may be initially imagined as totally incompatible with an older, heretofore predominant world-view which refuses to accept the essential validity and utility of merging environmental and development/economic policies.[2] To characterize

---

1 Originally published in 1962 and reproduced in Volume II of the *International Encyclopedia of Unified Science* (1969). My reference is to the 2nd enlarged edition, T. Kuhn, *The Structure of Scientific Revolutions* (1970). [Hereafter, Khun]

2 Although Kuhn, by and large, propounded his ideas on "paradigm change" with the history of the natural sciences in mind, the applicability and relevance of his theses to the practitioners of the social sciences could not be doubted. *See* Kuhn, at 208-209. *See also* for e.g., Porter & Brown, *op. cit.* at 26-33, on the observation of a "paradigm shift" that is taking place in environmental politics, which is described as a transition from an "exclusionist paradigm" to a "sustainable development paradigm." Cicin-Sain, *supra* Chap. II note 299, at 142 makes reference to

"sustainable development" as a paradigm in a Kuhnian sense is of course to uphold the purposes or operational roles of the sustainable development worldview, which simultaneously describe and prescribe the need for this paradigm.

As a description of its existence, the "paradigm of sustainable development" suggests a picture of people realizing a drastically and irretrievably altered view of the world simply because the idea of sustainable development has inevitably led them to this new consciousness. The experience, Kuhn would explain, is similar to being "suddenly transported to another planet where familiar objects are seen in a different light and are joined by unfamiliar ones as well."[3] The acceptance of the "sustainable development paradigm" necessitates the perception of a heretofore unrecognized "gestalt" of modern global existence. Once this gestalt has taken hold of a critical section of the international community, there is no way by which the global community as a whole can go back to the kind of existence dictated by the old paradigm.[4] The world never looks the same again after the paradigm of sustainable development triumphs over its old competitor.

As a prescription, the assertion of a "sustainable development paradigm" would imply the adoption of a world view on the part of the members of the international community which they believe to be superior and just.[5] This intellectual conviction is based on a kind of faith on the ability of the paradigm to generate the right kind of solutions to the problems it defines but cannot

---

a "new global paradigm of sustainable development." For a recognition of a paradigm change in the ocean sphere, *see* G. Noland, "Ocean Frontiers: Initiatives in the 21st Century" in Seung Yong Hong, E. Miles & Choon-Ho Park (Eds.), *The Role of the Oceans in the 21st Century* at 218-220 (LSI, 1995) [contrasting business practices and perceptions of the industrial revolution with emerging sustainable development philosophies].

3   Kuhn, at 111.
4   One metaphor reiterated by Kuhn to encapsulate the experience of paradigm change is "scales falling from the eyes." *Id.* at 122. Note that the conversion to a new paradigm is ill-described by the analogy, often used in other epistemological settings, of interpreting phenomena using alternative theoretical "lenses." *See id.* at 85.
5   *See* Shue, *supra* Chap. II note 243, for the argument that the question of justice is logically and practically inseparable from the new global consciousness that gives respect to the principle of planetary ecological integrity.

yet solve completely.⁶ Sustainable development is thus accepted as a sort of promise for a more reassuring mode of community life. It is a special promise which must be unconditionally embraced on the assumption that it will still have to be fully worked out in its details. Otherwise, it should not be embraced at all. While it is in competition with the older, established paradigm during the period of crisis, allegiance to the tenets of the sustainable development would require its proponents to earnestly strive for, if not induce, a paradigm change at the level of the community.⁷

What then does the paradigm of sustainable development exactly consist of? If the hypothesis of a Kuhnian "paradigm" is closely followed, it becomes readily evident that there cannot be a definite or easy answer to this question. The main reason for this is that a paradigm cannot be defined, or its existence proved, in any linguistic or sociological sense, but is simply practiced on the basis of knowledge embedded in shared exemplars.⁸ Comprehending the paradigm of sustainable development through its illustrative achievements, or the outstanding examples that prove its validity, is the only way to understand it as a historical phenomenon. The demonstration of these achievements is, in turn, closely related to a core methodological technique referred to by Kuhn as the problem of "paradigm choice" on the part of practitioners within a scientific community, whereby the competition between alternative paradigms is resolved through a paradoxical political process that involves persuasion and conversion but does not involve the giving of proofs for or against a particular

---

6   Kuhn, at 158:
    The man who embraces a new paradigm at an early stage must often do so in defiance of the evidence provided by problem-solving. He must, that is, have faith that the new paradigm will succeed with the many large problems that confront it, knowing only that the older paradigm has failed with the new. A decision of that kind can only be made on faith.
    The adoption of a new "paradigm of sustainable development" is also prescriptive on account of the unavailability of pure observation-language. *Id.* at 122, 126.
7   *Id.*, at 159.
8   *See id.*, at 141-143 and 187-198, esp. with reference to his discussion of the meaning of the expression $f=ma$ (Newton's Second Law of Motion). The paradigm of sustainable development, therefore, relies less on what is said about it by way of verbal definition than what is done on its behalf by way of alternative practices, projects and preoccupations in an emergent "normal science."

paradigm.⁹ In sum, the meaning of "sustainable development" as a paradigm is critically linked to its exemplary achievements, which cannot but be regarded as entirely inconsistent with the practices of a prior competing paradigm, giving rise to the problem of choosing between alternative modes of living and being.

It is submitted that the discipline or science of international law provides a most relevant background for the exploration, identification and elaboration of the exemplary achievements of the "paradigm of sustainable development." It is afterall in the expansive and expanding normative structure of international relations where the most significant and critical practices of global governance are manifested and carried out. Postulating the existence of an international law at the service of the "sustainable development paradigm" not only provides a platform where the cause of sustainable development as a world view could be advanced. The "international law of sustainable development", by necessary implication, also assumes the existence of an opposing paradigm of global governance, consisting of those countervailing or incompatible practices in the discipline of international law that are not in harmony with a world view based on sustainable development. I have proposed to describe this opposing paradigm as the "international law of global disparities", whose *status quo*-preserving regimes are generative of increasing global inequalities, and whose record is now being challenged by emerging alternative regimes in the ocean sphere. It is thus possible to specify more concretely the paradigm of sustainable development by clarifying the potentials of a normal science of international law build upon the strategic achievements of the "international law of sustainable development."

In the previous chapter, it was argued that the principle of "common but differentiated responsibilities for sustainable development" has virtually become a customary norm in international law. Nowhere is this more explicitly recog-

---

9   *Id.*, at Section IX. The irrelevance of "proofs" in paradigm choice is presupposed by the concept of "incommensurability" of competing paradigms. Kuhn speaks of a fundamental "incommensurability" between competing paradigms whereby the claims of one cannot be judged, through logic or experiment or otherwise, as necessarily superior with respect to the counter-claims of the other; and although the same vocabulary is used by the votaries of the competing paradigms to argue the validity of their respective world views, the opposing camps simply talk through each other with no meeting of minds occurring and no third force from above, as it were, to decide on the differences, *Id.*, at 94, 148-151, even if some role is played by the "translations" of each paradigm's claims in the process. *Id.*, at Section XII and 201-204.

nized than in the comprehensive regime of international cooperation in the ocean sphere, specifically in the EEZ, founded on the normative bedrock of the 1982 UN Convention on the Law of the Sea, in conjunction with the ocean-related outputs of UNCED. It was also pointed out that the egalitarian orientation of the principle, which is presupposed by a long-term North-South programme of capacity-building for developing States, confronts the operation of the "international law of global disparities" in the traditional domains of North-South inequality concerning the use and enjoyment of oceans. The imperative of planetary ecological integrity is ultimately what is sought to be fulfilled by the entrenchment of the reciprocity-based principle "common but differentiated responsibilities for sustainable development" in the corpus of international law. But for those who believe in its essential role in fostering the cause of humanity or humanism, the principle of more equality of capacity for rights and obligations between rich and poor States goes beyond serving utilitarian aims. It is a pre-eminent end in itself. The norm of "common but diffrentiated responsibilities" as defined in the sphere of ocean governance may thus be cited as one exemplary achievement in the new practice/science of international law under the paradigm of sustainable development.

It is submitted that the evolution of the new international law of the sea likewise saw the birth of what is potentially the most significant achievement under the paradigm of the international law of sustainable development. This is the "common heritage of humanity" principle. Like the principle of international cooperation in the EEZ, which it supplements and further refines, the common heritage principle operates as a pivotal normative devise in overcoming the multiplying historical disparities (certainly reflective of the deep crisis confronting the international community today) between developed and developing States. At the same time the principle establishes a model regime for global governance exemplifying a mini-paradigm, as it were, on an alternative mode of existence for the international community as a whole. The Common Heritage of Humanity principle embodied in the 1982 Law of the Sea Convention is undoubtedly a decisive testament to the depth and the richness of the "sustainable development paradigm." This is the argument that will defended in the remainder of this book. For those who are cynical about the global project of sustainable development, or only pay lip service to its cause, it may do well for them to reconsider the possibilities offered by the Common Heritage of Humanity.

The purpose of these Chapters in the Second Part of the thesis is to explore the contribution of the Common Heritage of Humanity principle in consolidating the paradigm of sustainable development. The subject of these Chapters is the elaboration of two closely associated profiles of the Common Heritage of Humanity principle in global governance: first, as a reaction to the "international law of global disparities" and, secondly, as an affirmative response to the "international law of sustainable development." Part Two of this thesis will thus consider the emergence and evolution of Common Heritage of Humanity principle from the viewpoint of North-South legal relations, currently governed by the "international law of global disparities." It is divided into three Chapters that each portray the three distinct stages in the development of the Common Heritage of Humanity principle in the Law of the Sea. These three stages, it will be submitted, translate as the conceptual or juridical elements of the Common Heritage of Humanity principle.

A caveat is in order before proceeding to a detailed examination of the Common Heritage of Humanity principle. To suggest that a new paradigm like sustainable development is in the offing is, of course, different from proclaiming that the world community is moving towards its progressive realization, or that a full scale paradigm shift is imminent. The paradigm of sustainable development, like any comprehensive world view invested in the minds of individuals and in the routine activity of societies, needs converts and adherents who are able and willing to lead the new paradigm to triumph over an old one. Thomas Kuhn alludes to the condition of a "war" or a "battle" in the competition of paradigms, although he would emphasize that the transfer of allegiance from one paradigm to another – the "revolution" itself – cannot in principle be coerced.[10] The new paradigm of sustainable development will, therefore, most likely prevail if its exemplary accomplishments, like the principle of international cooperation in the EEZ ("common but differentiated responsibilities") or the Common Heritage of Humanity principle, can be shown to be more sufficient, more consistent and more effective in overcoming the present puzzles and the on-going crises of global governance. It is truly an act of faith on the part of the paradigm's adherents to have even just the readiness to persevere in such protracted exercises of falsification and affirmation. Without doubt, their hope is surely that of seeing a much-awaited paradigm change come through before it is much too late for any kind of change.[11]

---

10 *Id.*, at 151.
11 *See* Porter & Brown, *op. cit.* 159, echoing a similar sentiment: "The issue, therefore, is not whether nation-states will move toward progressively more effective international cooperation on global environmental threats, but whether they would

This Chapter examines the environment surrounding the historical origins of the Common Heritage of Humanity as a fundamental principle of international law. It will be argued that as a paradigmatic instance of the international law of sustainable development, the Common Heritage of Humanity principle can be analyzed only through a detailed reconstruction of the seabed debates in the 1960s. This reconstruction will necessarily have to clarify the historical involvement of the Common Heritage of Humanity principle with the international law of global disparities. The first of three elements of the Common Heritage of Humanity as a paradigm will be analyzed. This element corresponds to the very first stage of normative elaboration that the Common Heritage of Humanity principle went through historically, namely (1) the object of the "common heritage of mankind" concept. The other two elements consist of the historical stages where (2) the Common Heritage of Humanity concept was advanced as a substantive legal principle, and (3) the institutional development the Common Heritage of Humanity principle was pursued. These last two elements will be considered in the next two Chapters. All these elements of the Common Heritage of Humanity "paradigm" find their counterpart in the three doctrinal aspects of the Common Heritage of Humanity as a formal legal principle (1) *ratione loci*, (2) *ratione materiae*, and (3) *ratione temporis*. Through these elements, it will be shown how certain forces in international society creative of global disparities contributed to the emergence of and the initial consensus on the Common Heritage of Humanity as a legal concept. This narration of genealogical and formal elements will also explain how and why the problematic concept of the Common Heritage of Humanity moved to become a central issue in North-South relations.

A. The Common Heritage of Humanity as an Invoked Principle in the 1982 UN Convention on the Law of the Sea

Article 136 of the 1982 Convention on the Law of the Sea provides: "The Area and its resources are the common heritage of mankind."[12] The term "common

---

do so rapidly enough."

[12] The term "Area" is defined in Article 1 (1), CLOS, as "the sea-bed and ocean floor and subsoil thereof, beyond the limits of national jurisdiction." "Resources" is defined in Article 133 (a), CLOS, to mean "all solid, liquid or gaseous mineral resources in situ in the Area at or beneath the sea-bed, including polymetallic

heritage of mankind"/"common heritage of humanity" is itself not defined in the Convention, although Article 155 of the Convention speaks of "the principle of the common heritage of mankind."[13] Since there is no provision that either explicitly defines this "principle", or at least identifies its definitive analytic components, the meaning of the term "the principle of the Common Heritage of Humanity" can only be derived inductively, or at least its elements surmised from a close appreciation of all the relevant provisions of the Convention, as well as other instruments where the concept is embodied.[14] This task of deriving a precise meaning through the text of the Convention, unfortunately, is quite oppressive, considering that the principle of the Common Heritage of Humanity is enmeshed in a complicated regime that is build on the normative structure comprehended by Part XI of the Convention,[15] including its Annex

---

nodules."
13 As noted in the subject index of the CLOS, at 198, the term "common heritage of mankind" occurs five times in the text of the Convention: Preambular paragraph 6; Art. 125(1), on rights of Land-locked States; Art. 136; Art. 155(2), on the Review Conference; and Art. 311(6), on the prohibition of amendments to "the basic principle relating to the common heritage of mankind set forth in article 136." It is significant to note that a closely-related term "benefit of mankind" is invoked five times in the Convention, mainly under Part XI: Preambular paragraph 6; Art. 140(1), on activities in the Area being carried out for the benefit of mankind as a whole; Art. 143(1), on marine scientific research in the Area; Art. 149, on archeological and historical objects in the Area; and Art. 150(i), on policies relating to activities in the Area, CLOS at 196.
14 Efforts to define the "common heritage of mankind" principle in such an inductive manner have been largely unofficial and originate from authorities who espouse a critical and creative role for the Common Heritage principle in international relations. *See* for *e.g.,* R.P. Anand, *Legal Regime of the Seabed and the Developing Countries* at 212 (1976); E.M. Borgese, "Expanding the Common Heritage of Mankind" in A. Dolman (Ed.) *Global Planning and Resource Management* (1980); A. Pardo & E.M. Borgese, "The Common Heritage of Mankind and the Transfer of Technology" in E.M. Borgese & P. White (Eds.) *Seabed Mining: Scientific, Economic, and Political Aspects An Interdisciplinary Manual* 366, at 370-373 (IOI Occasional papers No. 7.); D. Shraga, *The Common Heritage of Mankind: The Concept and its Application* 15 ANNALES D'ETUDES INTERNATIONALES 45-63 (1986); R.St.J. Macdonald, "The Common Heritage of Mankind" in *Festschrift fur Rudolf Bernhardt* 153-171 (1995).
15 Part XI is entitled "The Area." By the terms of the Preamble of the Convention, the normative definition of the Common Heritage of Humanity principle also includes necessary reference to the 1970 Declaration of Principles Resolution. *See*

III and Annex IV,[16] and Resolutions I and II of the Final Act of UNCLOS III,[17] as well as the recently concluded "Agreement Relating to the Implementation of Part XI of the United Nations Convention on the Law of the Sea of 10 December 1982."[18] The intricacies of the positive law regime will be made apparent in the discussions below. All these notwithstanding, one can be fairly confident in the following basic propositions: (1) there is a juristic phenomena, the general object of legal regulation, called "the area and its resources", (2) there is a legal principle denominated as the Common Heritage of Humanity, and (3) the Common Heritage of Humanity principle is applicable to "the area and its resources." These three broad premises in fact mark out three stages or episodes behind an oft-repeated "narrative" that accompanies every attempt to clarify the overall regime founded on the Common Heritage of Humanity principle. The first episode of this narrative, as presented in this Chapter, describes the origins of the "common heritage of mankind" as a unique object of international legal regulation.

B. A QUESTION OF FRONTIERS: THE AREA AND ITS RESOURCES

When the Maltese delegation in the United Nations requested the inclusion of an agenda item for the 1967 session of the General Assembly entitled "Declaration and treaty concerning the reservation exclusively for peaceful purposes of the sea-bed and of the ocean floor, underlying the seas beyond the limits of national jurisdiction, and the use of their resources in the interests

---

3rd quoted preambular para. in *supra* p.54.

16 Annex III, CLOS: "Basic Conditions of Prospecting, Exploration and Exploitation" and Annex IV, CLOS: "Statute of the Enterprise."

17 These Resolutions, entitled "Establishment of the Preparatory Commission for the International Sea-Bed Authority and for the International Tribunal for the Law of the Sea" (Resolution I) and "Governing Preparatory Investment in Pioneer Activities relating to Polymetallic Nodules" (Resolution II), and the 1982 Convention, according to the Final Act of UNCLOS III, form an integral whole. *See* CLOS at 168.

18 Text in LoS BULLETIN, 16 November 1994 (UNDOALOS, Special Issue IV). This Agreement is Annexed to UN General Assembly Resolution 48/263 which was adopted on 18 July 1994 on a recorded vote of 121 to 0, with 7 abstentions. It entered into force on 28 July 1996.

of mankind",[19] it was not at all certain whether there were indeed areas of the sea floor that could be considered as legally "beyond" or outside the limits of present national jurisdiction.[20] The seemingly factual assertion in the proposed agenda item that there exists, somewhere in the sea-bottom, a floor of the ocean beyond national jurisdiction turned out in fact to be a political desideratum on the part of Malta – a small, little-known country (once derisively referred to as "just a chunk of rock out in the Mediterranean"[21]) wishing to invite urgent global attention to the subject matter of its request. There was no hiding Malta's fears and apprehensions, were the premise of the existence of this deep ocean area to be proved incorrect. These fears where expressed initially in the explanatory memorandum accompanying its request,[22] and subsequently, in more vivid and dramatic terms, in the historic address delivered by Ambassador Arvid Pardo before the First Committee of the UN General Assembly in November 1967.[23] The phrase "seabed and ocean floor underlying the seas beyond the limits of present national jurisdiction" was not at all an innocuous description in oceanography, but a highly explosive political hypothesis.

If perceptions are never neutral, so it seems are the objects of perception. Even before Malta presented its "official perception" on the sea-bed and ocean floor beyond national jurisdiction, the existence of this particular submarine space was already subject to a variety of conceptions. At the "scientific" level

---

19 *Note Verbale* dated 17 August 1967 from the Permanent Mission of Malta to the United Nations Addressed to the Secretary General, in UN Doc. A/6695. UNGAOR 22nd Session Annexes, Agenda item 92. *See supra* Chap. II note 38.
20 For an early survey of views on this point, *see* G. Weissberg, *International Law Meets the Short-Term National Interest. The Maltese Proposal on the Sea-Bed and Ocean Floor – Its Fate in Two Cities* 18 ICLQ 41-102 (1969).
21 This was how Malta was described by US Congressman H. Gross of the House Committee of Foreign Affairs during congressional hearings on House Resolutions opposing Malta's move in the UN. *House Interim Report* at 22.
22 *Supra* note 19: "In view of rapid progress in the development of new techniques by technologically advanced countries, it is feared that the situation will change and that the sea-bed and ocean floor, underlying the seas beyond present national jurisdiction, will become progressively and competitively subject to national appropriation and use. This is likely to result in the militarization of the accessible ocean floor through the establishment of fixed military installations and in the exploitation and depletion of resources of immense potential benefit to the world, for the national advantage of technologically developed countries."
23 PV 1515-1516 (1 November 1967).

for instance, this immense part of the ocean, which putatively includes the geological shelf[24] – slowly being revealed as a vast storehouse of commercially valuable minerals – necessarily attracted the interests of profit-seeking psyches. Besides the familiar resources like sand, gravel, tin, coal, petroleum, or diamonds the ocean floor was also discovered as a plentiful source of glauconite, placer deposits, sea-floor phosphorite, red clay, calcareous deposits and oozes, siliceous oozes, and – most novel and interesting of all – manganese nodules.[25] The challenge was, therefore, to deploy available mining systems and related industrial and institutional infrastructures for the efficient extraction of these new riches from a frontier commercial environment.[26]

A closely-allied perception that would essentially treat the deep seabed as a sort of territorial frontier which had to be conquered came from those who viewed its acquisition for purposes other than mineral exploitation. Hence, it was considered that seamounts far out into the ocean were ideal sites not only for military activities – like the emplacement of weapons systems or the construction of undersea stations, for example[27] – but also for a host of scientific endeavors – like experiments and exotic investigations on radiology, genetics, submarine acoustics, seismic activity, and marine biology.[28] Thus viewed, the deep ocean floor potentially became a primordial base for the projection

---

24 There are 130,000,000 square miles of "deep ocean" lying beyond the 10,420,000 square miles of continental shelves up to the 200 meter isobath. Cited in L. Henkin, *Law for the Sea's Mineral Resources* 2 (1968). The sum of these areas represents about two-thirds of the earth's surface, the relative size of world's oceans.

25 J. Mero, "Review of Mineral Values On and Under the Ocean Floor" in *Exploiting the Oceans: Transactions of the 2nd Annual Marine Technology Society Conference* 27-29 June 1966, 61-78 (Washington, DC: MTS, 1966) [the volume will be referred to hereafter as *Exploiting the Oceans*].

26 See D. Brooks "Deep Sea Manganese Nodules: From Scientific Phenomenon to World Resources" in L. Alexander (Ed.), *The Law of the Sea The Future of the Sea's Resources* 32-41 (Proceedings of the 1967 Law of the Sea Institute Conference, 1968) [hereafter, *LSI 1967*]. *See also Exploiting the Oceans*.

27 W. Burke, "Legal Aspects of Ocean Exploitation – Status and Outlook" in *Exploiting the Oceans, supra* note 25, 1-23, at 18. *See also* A. Weber, "Our Newest Frontier: The Seabottom Some Legal Aspects of the Continental Shelf Status" in *id.*, 405-411 at 411.

28 Burke, *id.*, at 19.

of national power, national prestige,[29] and ironically – as exposed by Ambassador Pardo – national pollution.[30] This led, inescapably, to the perception of the remote seabed and/or its treasures as a prized object for political possession and pre-emption.

Lastly, and perhaps most importantly, the decisive reality of the deep ocean floor was brought home to legal consciousness when people started asking "Who owns it anyway?"[31] If indeed there were opportunities for new wealth, new knowledge, and new power lying on the deep oceans that were about ready to be tapped,[32] the calculating political gaze exploring the possibilities of "who gets what, when and how" had to be restrained by the cautioning voice of legitimacy. This time the critical dimension of "who gets where and under whose authority" was added to the focus. Henceforth, the physical phenomenon of the deep ocean floor and its resources became intertwined with the eminently political question of who has control, or who ought to have control, over it.

1. Towards Internationalizing the Deep Seabed

Even before Malta's proposed agenda was inscribed in the records of the United Nations, there were already competing policy proposals that sought to address the basic issue of who should control the deep seabed. These policy advocacies revealed the split that developed between those who argued for the "inter-

---

29　W. Burke, *Ocean Sciences Technology and the Future International Law of the Sea* (1966).

30　As reported by Ambassador Pardo, the deep ocean floor was also being accessed as a frontier ground for dumping toxic and radioactive wastes. PV 1515 at para. 73-87.

31　E. Luard, *The Control of the Seabed* at vii, 22, 29 (1977). The sense of urgency that made the deep ocean floor a momentous political question in the 1960s is seen in the contrast of responses to the query "whose is the bed of the sea" from the perspective of the 1920s and the 1960s. See the sober exposition of C. Hurst, *Whose is the Bed of the Sea?* 4 BYIL 34-43 (1923-24) and the highly-charged discussion in *Whose is the Bed of the Sea?* 1968 ASIL Proc 216-251. It will be recalled that the agenda item proposed by Malta was eventually allocated to the First (Political) Committee of the UN General Assembly, rather than to its Economic or Legal Committees.

32　See Burke, *supra* note 29, referring to "power, wealth, enlightenment, and skill" as the "base values" for authoritative decision-making in the oceans.

nationalization"³³ of the seabed, on the one hand, and those who opposed internationalization, on the other.³⁴ Internationalizing the deep seabed and its resources meant vesting their administration, control, or ownership in an international organization,³⁵ like the United Nations, such that their disposition would become subject to the political authority of an institution above any particular State.³⁶ In reaction, the negative view regarded internationalization as

---

33 E. Wenk, *Politics of the Oceans* (1972) at 255, on the origins of the internationalization debate:
 While speculation of commercial exploitability dates back to 1959, surprisingly it was neither nation-states nor industrial entrepreneurs who uncorked the economic prospects of the nodules and other seabed resources. Rather it was private individuals and organizations who idealistically coupled marine benefits to world order and institutions.
 See also Morell, *supra* Chap. II note 39, at 14 *et seq.*, for a discussion of the "movement toward internationalization" of the seabed.

34 Prior to the Malta initiative public debates on the deep ocean floor, specifically associated with the articulation of international ownership and control issues in the 1960s, were largely confined in the United States. Buzan, *supra* Chap. II note 45, at 62. The two most prominent public fora where the pros and cons of internationalization were keenly debated were the First Law of the Sea Institute Conference (Rhode Island, June 27 to July 1, 1966), proceedings in L. Alexander, (Ed.), *The Law of the Sea Offshore Boundaries and Zones* (1967) [hereafter, *LSI 1966*], and the American Bar Association National Institute on Marine affairs (California, June 7-10, 1967), whose proceedings were published in volume 1, numbers 2 and 3 of the journal NATURAL RESOURCES LAWYER published in 1968 [hereafter, NAT RES L). *See* S. Oda, *The Law of the Sea in Our Time – I. New Developments, 1966-1975* at 3-12 (1977).

35 The policy considerations regarding the question of installing an "international landlord of the seabotton" are summarized in C. Luce, *The Development of Ocean Minerals and the Law of the Sea*, Address by Under-Secretary of Interior Charles F. Luce, NAT RES L no. 3, at 29-37; *House Interim Report*, at 231.

36 For *e.g.*, in May 1966 the Commission to Study the Organization for Peace, reiterating its proposal first put forward in 1957, recommended the establishment of "a special agency of the United Nations ... to control and administer international marine resources; hold ownership rights; and grant, lease or use these rights..." *Seventeenth Report of the Commission to Study the Organization of Peace: New Dimensions for the United Nations* (1966). The Christian Science Monitor in 1959 also speculated that "an international agency, perhaps the UN might take over jurisdiction" of the ocean bottom. E. Wenk, *supra* note 33, at 257. A Report released on 20 February 1967 for the United States Senate Foreign Relations Committee filed by Senator Frank Church advocated United Nations ownership of the ocean's

inadvisable if not ill-timed, and preferred unilateral action by States in the meantime with respect to decisions on the legal and, hence, political question of ocean bottom control.[37]

---

mineral resources. *Id.*, at 259. *See also* contributions of Q. Wright, *LSI 1966* at 184; F. Christy, *id.* at 302; C. Eichelberger, *id.* at 299. The arguments are further developed in F. Christy, *Alternative Regimes for Marine Resources Underlying the High Seas* NAT RES L no. 2 at 63-77; C. Eichelberger, *A Case for the Administration of Marine Resources Underlying the High Seas by the United Nations, id.* at 85; R. Kreuger, *The Convention on the Continental Shelf and the Need for Its Revision and Some Comments Regarding the Regime for the Lands Beyond* NAT RES L, no. 3 at 1-11.

37 The argument against internationalization originally came from prominent American lawyers. *See* N. Ely, "The Laws Governing Exploitation of the Minerals Beneath the Sea" in *Exploiting the Ocean, supra* note 25, 373-378, who states, at 378, that:
... until enough international competition and friction develop to justify creation of some advance licensing scheme for administration by the United Nations, recognition of the flag of the craft or other surface mechanism from which the exploration is controlled sufficiently identifies the jurisdiction which ought to have plenary control over the exploration and over the exploitation of the resources so discovered.
This argument echoes and elaborates upon the "finders keepers" position adopted in J. Mero, *Mineral Resources of the Sea* 292-293 (1965). *See also* Burke, *supra* note 29, at 90, amplifying on the framework of analysis for ocean law laid down in M. McDougal & W. Burke, *The Public Order of the Oceans* specifically at 634 (1962), and argues that the problem concerning the allocation of seabed resources presented the United States with an opportunity – "through assertion of unilateral claim or, at least, influential pronouncement" – "of taking the lead in establishing a pattern of responsibility and restraint in the assertion of claim to newly available resources." For Prof. Burke's argument directed against the specific proposals of the Commission to Study the Organization for Peace, *supra* note 36, *see* W. Burke, "Law and the New Technologies" in *LSI 1966* 204-227, at 222-225. The arguments against internationalization were repeated and developed further in W. Burke, *A Negative View of a Proposal for United Nations Ownership of Ocean Mineral Resources* NAT RES L no. 2 at 42-62; N. Ely, *A Case for Administration of Mineral Resources Underlying the High Seas by National Interests, id.* at 78-84; M. McDougal, *Revision of the Geneva Conventions on the Law of the Sea. The Views of a Commentator* NAT RES L no. 2, at 99-100 & no. 3, 19-28. After Malta submitted its proposed UN agenda item, there were several moves in the US Congress to oppose "the vesting of title to the ocean floor in the United Nations." The reason for such opposition was put candidly by a US Congressional

Although attempts at the official inter-governmental level to pursue international administration of the deep seabed were rebuffed in the 1950s,[38] the call for internationalization in the 1960s acquired special cogency. The impact of advancing science and technology no doubt provided the most powerful stimulus for a wider consideration of the possibilities offered by the internationalization option.[39] In the first place, internationalization was viewed as a promising strategy to generate revenues for an increasingly financially embarrassed United Nations Organization.[40] Moreover, international control was strongly argued as the ideal institutional arrangement not only to assure the smooth and maximally efficient exploitation of seabed resources[41] but also to forestall the dangers of marine pollution or contamination.[42]

The most significant consideration that factored into the advocacy to internationalize the seabed was probably the window-of-opportunity argument for a more vigorous pursuit of the objectives of poverty alleviation and economic development in the less developed world. It was in the United Nations Economic and Social Council (ECOSOC) where this need was first expressed. Through

---

leader, Richard Hanna, in September 1967: "Until we have a better picture as to what the exploitative feasibility is within a developed technology that we not start talking about turning over sovereignty"; and, more animatedly: "My suggestion is that we haven't yet got the turkey." *See House Interim Report* at 18-19; Weissberg, *supra* note 20, at 43.

38 In the 1950s, in the context of its discussions on the continental shelf, the International Law Commission received various proposals from governments for the international administration of the seabed. M. Mouton, *The Continental Shelf* 309-312 (1952); Weissberg, *op. cit.* at 88; Buzan, *op. cit.* 45-46; Morell, *op. cit.* 16. Other bodies that put forward kindred proposals include the Institut de Droit International in 1934, the International Law Association in 1951, The World Association of Parliamentarians for World Government in 1951, and the Commission to Study the Organization for Peace in 1957. *See* Morell, *ibid.*

39 For an excellent account of US attitudes towards an internationalization policy dictated by marine science and technology developments during this period, *see* Wenk, *op. cit.*

40 *Seventeenth Report of the Commission to Study the Organization for Peace, supra* note 36. *See also* US Senate Report by Sen. Frank Church, *supra* note 36; and M. Eichelberger, *The Promise of the Sea's Bounty – How the Oceans' Enormous Riches can Contribute to Peace and Help Alleviate World Poverty – If they are placed under UN Administration Now* SATURDAY REVIEW 18 June 1966, excerpts in *House Interim Report* at 3-6, 10.

41 *See* Christy, in *LSI 1966* at 302-309. *See also* Christy, NAT RES L, *supra* note 36.

42 *See* Eichelberger, *supra* note 40.

ECOSOC Resolution 1112 of 7 March 1966,[43] the UN Secretary General was requested *inter alia* to make a survey[44] of the present stage of knowledge on the resources – mineral and food except fish – "beyond the continental shelf", and the techniques of exploiting these resource, and "to attempt to identify those resources now considered to be capable of economic exploitation, especially for the benefit of the developing countries."[45] But it was the Commission to Study the Organization for Peace which made explicit a direct link between the policy of internationalization and the necessity to foster and strengthen world peace through the economic upliftment of the poor countries.[46] Then, on 13 July 1967, the World Peace through Law Conference, a gathering of some 2,500 lawyers from over 100 countries, proclaimed a global humane cause behind internationalization and recognized the interests of developing countries in the resources of the deep seabed as the "common heritage of all mankind."

---

43 ECOSOC Off Rec, 37th Sess., Supp. no. 1 at 3. In introducing the Report of the Secretary General (on "Non-Agricultural Resources"), which recommended the mineral survey contemplated in this Resolution, the Under-Secretary General for Economic Affairs noted that the Report was written cognizant of the frustrations and disappointments in the United Nations on the failure of the First UN Development Decade at mid-point. ECOSOC Off Rec, 40th Sess., 1408th Mtg., 26 February 1966.

44 The UN General Assembly, though Resolution 2172 (XXI) of 6 December 1966, also requested the Secretary General to undertake a "comprehensive survey of activities in marine science and technology, including that relating to mineral resources development" and to formulate proposals for "ensuring the most effective arrangement for an expanded programme of international cooperation to assist in a better understanding of the marine environment through science and in the exploitation and development of marine resources..." The United States played a leading role in both these UN initiatives. *See infra*, pp. 175 *et seq.*

45 The preamble of this Resolution hints at a favored internationalist approach to the management of deep sea mineral resources in relation to economic development:

Considering that the mineral and food resources of the sea beyond the continental shelf, excluding fish, constitute reserves of raw materials which are yet not fully being utilized, and that the rational use of these resources to ensure optimum yield and minimum waste is of vital importance to all countries;

Being aware that the effective development of those resources can raise the economic level of peoples throughout the world, and especially the developing countries[.]

46 *See 17th Report, supra* note 36.

This Conference adopted a resolution[47] recommending that the UN General Assembly proclaim the deep seabed as appertaining to the United Nations.[48] Development and global sharing have thus become part and parcel of the early discourse to internationalize the deep seabed.

The strongest case for internationalization, made prior to the Maltese initiative, was no doubt pushed by the United States. The United States launched the biggest, most complex and outward-looking national programme on marine science and technology development in the 1960s.[49] A multinational, multilateral approach to the study of the oceans was embodied in the Marine Resources and Engineering Development Act of 1966[50] which declared the policy of the United States "to develop, encourage, and maintain a coordinated, comprehensive, and long-range national program in marine science for the bene-

---

47 This resolution was introduced in Geneva World Peace Through Law Conference by New York-based American lawyer Aaron Danzig. Wenk, *supra* note 33 at 259.

48 The Resolution invokes the term "common heritage of mankind":
Whereas, new technology and oceanography have revealed the possibility of exploitation of untold resources of the high seas and the bed thereof beyond the continental shelf and more than half of mankind finds itself underprivileged, underfed, and underdeveloped, and the high seas, are the common heritage of mankind,
Resolved, that the World Peace through Law Center:
(1) Recommend to the General Assembly of the United Nations the issuance of a proclamation declaring that the non-fishery resources of the high seas, outside of the territorial waters of any State, and the bed of the sea beyond the continental shelf, appertain to the United Nations and are subject to its jurisdiction and control. Text in *House Interim Report* at 8.

49 For an authoritative description of US ocean policy during this period, *see* Wenk, *supra* note 33, esp. at Chaps. 2 & 3. The US interest to assume a lead role in oceanography and deep ocean exploration, *id.* at 41-44, was an offshoot of the US response to perceptions of Soviet superiority in outer space technology in the late 1950s, more particularly to the Sputnik and Mutnik initiatives in 1957.

50 P.L. 89-454, signed into law 17 June 1966. Text in Wenk, *supra* note 33, Appendix 7. This legislation established a National Council on Marine Resource and Engineering Development, whose detailed career is given in *ibid*, and also created the Commission on Marine Science, Engineering and Resources (eventually known as the Stratton Commission), whose Report *Our Nation and the Sea* was released in January 1969.

fit of mankind."⁵¹ The United States' preeminent support of marine science initiatives in United Nations fora with respect to the deep seabed and its resources was consistent with the underlying philosophy of this Act.⁵² But no other historical event that emanated from the United States advanced the argument for internationalization more forcefully and urgently than the intervention from President Lyndon Johnson on 13 July 1966:

> Truly great accomplishments in oceanography will require the cooperation of all the maritime nations of the world. And so today I send our voice out from this platform calling for such cooperation, requesting it, and urging it...
>
> We welcome this type of international participation. Because under no circumstances, we believe, must we ever allow the prospects of rich harvests and

---

51 It is interesting to note that one of the declared objectives of US marine activities under the Act is "cooperation by the United States with other nations and groups of nations and international organizations in marine science activities when such cooperation is in the national interest." Wenk, *ibid*. As early as March 1961, Pres. J.F. Kennedy was already urging the imperative of a framework for international cooperation concerning marine science:
Oceanography is a natural area of opportunity for extensive international cooperation. Indeed, systematic surveys and research in all the oceans of the world represent tasks of such formidable magnitude that international sharing of the work is a necessity.
"Letter to the President of the Senate on Increasing National Effort in Oceanography" 29 March 1961. Text in Wenk, *id*., at Appendix 13.

52 Before ECOSOC Resolution 1112, *supra* note 43, was adopted, the US representative in the ECOSOC, Amb. J. Roosevelt, asserted that the "development of boundless food and mineral resources of the sea might make it possible to speed up economic development considerably and might even provide a source of international capital." ECOSOC Off Rec, 40th Sess, 1408 Mtg, 26 February 1966. *See also* his Statement in the Second Committee of the UNGA, reflecting on the need to learn to use deep seabed resources "to feed the hungry, clothe the naked, and even warm the cold"; inviting the Committee "to start dreaming and thinking exciting thoughts about the role of the UN can take"; and that an attack on the problem of the oceans "can be launched only if all the nations cooperate." *House Interim Report* at 8-9. The US Representative to the General Assembly also called support for UNGA Resolution 2172, *supra* note 44, on the strong belief that the international community should promote the "utilization of the sea for mankind." Morell, *op. cit*. 15. In the 1966 Report of the National Council on Marine Resources and Engineering Development, international cooperation was first on the priority list for a US marine science development programme, "particularly to reduce the resources gap between rich and poor nations." Wenk, *supra* note 33, at 115.

mineral wealth to create a new form of colonial competition among the maritime nations. We must be careful to avoid a race to grab and to hold the lands under the high seas. We must ensure that the deep seas and the ocean bottoms are, and remain, the legacy of all human beings.[53]

2. *The Stakes Behind Internationalization*

The message of internationalization to prevent a colonial-style all-out scramble among nations in the new frontier, especially the technologically powerful ones, was amplified and set in a comprehensive context in the monumental address of Ambassador Pardo to the United Nations on 1 November 1967.[54] For many who listened to this three-hour performance, it was perhaps only then that they came to realize the seriousness, the depth, and the urgency of the global cause behind the movement to internationalize the seabed. The novelty and multiplicity of the issues involved and the extensiveness and gravity of the interests at stake were presented with such political high-pitch that the General Assembly found itself suddenly faced with a new grand order of business, an exciting mission, never contemplated before.[55]

In this immensely important message to the United Nations, Ambassador Pardo drew out four major intricately-woven socio-political currents defining

---

53 "Remarks at the Commissioning of the Research Ship Oceanographer, 13 July 1966." Full text in Wenk, *supra* note 33 at Appendix 15. It is somewhat ironic, however, that in the 1966 Report of the National Council on Marine Resources and Engineering Development, President Johnson "had compared the exploration and development of the seas to the opening up of the American West", *id.*, at 116.

54 PV 1515 & 1516. In the Memorandum attached to the *Note Verbale* of Malta of 18 August 1967, *supra* Chap. II note 38, the proposal to internationalize via international agreement envisaged "the creation of an international agency (a) to assume jurisdiction as a trustee for all countries, over the seabed and the ocean floor beyond the limits of present national jurisdiction; (b) to regulate, supervise and control all activities thereon; and (c) to ensure that the activities undertaken conform to the principles of the proposed treaty." *See also* PV 1516, para. 8-10.

55 A new-found enthusiasm, particularly among developing countries, on the significant role of the United Nations in world affairs was evident from the interventions given by various delegations in the General Assembly to welcome the Maltese initiative. *See* UNGAOR, First Committee, 1524th-1530th Meetings (November 1967).

the contemporary condition of post-war international community – all converging into the question of who controls the deep seabed. First, above all, was the debilitating arms race between the superpowers which was turning the entirety of ocean space into an ultra-hazardous arena for cold-war confrontation. The rush to militarize the deep ocean floor was simply the latest phase in the heightening terror of superpower rivalry. Ambassador Pardo was convinced that international control of the seabed could stop a turn for the worse. This current may well be referred to as the *peace dimension* of the internationalization agenda.

Second, there were the rapid technological developments that have made accessible the deep seabed and its massive resources not only for military strategy but also for profitable commercial operations. In a world that was fragmented into the many poor and the few rich, it could not have been right that those countries which had the capability to subdue the deep seabed militarily would be the very same dominant countries which will exploit the vast resources of the seabed. International control of deep seabed resources thus meant no business-as-usual for business in the deep seabed. This is the *economic and technological dimension* of the internationalization issue with crucial implications on the long-term prospects for global progress or global scarcity.

Third, Ambassador Pardo was emphatic about preventing the further pollution of the seas through the disposal of radioactive wastes in the deep ocean – a practice by some technologically advanced countries that was putting at extreme risk not only the integrity of the marine environment but also the health of all people. Decisions to utilize the oceans in general, and the deep seabed in particular, as a waste dump cannot simply be left to the determination of individual States. The dilemmas inherent in the increasing contamination of the oceans constitute the *environmental dimension* of his internationalization proposition.

Lastly, the widening welfare gap between the rich and the poor nations, or the technologically-advanced and the technologically-handicapped States, was reiterated with a grave warning that the imminent competitive scramble for the wealth of the deep seabed would surpass in magnitude and implication the mischief of previous colonial aggressions in Asia and Africa. This current that highlights the "intolerable injustice that would reserve the plurality of the world resources for the exclusive benefit of less than a handful of nations" – the essence of a deepening North-South rift on the issue of global sharing – is the *development dimension* of the internationalization debate.

It is noteworthy that in their various reactions to Ambassador Pardo's presentation, the vast majority of delegations in the United Nations, from North and South alike, welcomed the multi-dimensional challenge presented by the deep seabed question. The consensus to establish an *"Ad Hoc* Committee to Study the Peaceful Uses of the Sea-Bed and the Ocean Floor beyond the Limits of Present National Jurisdiction"[56] was forged soon thereafter. This was the initial institutional response of the United Nations to grapple with the interconnected issues and concerns of the internationalization proposal in all its variety, depth and complexity. What is significant is that most of the developing countries represented in the UN were by then just beginning to absorb the reality and the implications of the deep seabed as a new domain of global disparity. They, therefore, emphasized the centrality of the development dimension in any overall framework of global endeavor to internationalize the deep seabed.[57] It was, however, clear to them that in this frontier of international relations, the increasingly acute "development gap" problem was indistinguishably merged with the equally compelling issues concerning demilitarization of the oceans, marine environmental protection and, sea-based economic growth and global technological advance. All issues – political, legal, economic, ecological, technical and strategic – were blended into one many-sided predicament, and all issues had somehow to be addressed simultaneously. As Ambassador H.S. Amerasinghe of Ceylon declared "the Maltese proposal presents us with the greatest opportunity we ever had of international cooperation on a grand scale."[58]

---

56 UNGA Res. 2340 (XXII) 18 December 1967. The Soviet block abstained. The relevant preambular clauses refer to "the common interest of mankind in the seabed and ocean floor"; the exploration and use of the deep sea-bed "in accordance with the purposes and principles of the Charter of the United Nations, in the interests of maintaining international peace and security and for the benefit of mankind"; and "greater international cooperation and coordination in the further exploration and use of the seabed and ocean floor."
57 *E.g.,* Venezuela (PV 1524); China, Somalia (PV 1525); Nigeria, Ghana, Trinidad and Tobago, Ceylon (PV 1526); Tanzania (PV 1527); Columbia, Sierra Leone, Turkey, Afghanistan (PV 1528); Mexico, Yugoslavia, Jamaica (PV 1529); India, Cyprus, Bolivia (PV 1530). Some of these developing countries include the landlocked States.
58 PV 1526 (13 Nov 1967).

3. *International Law on the Margins of the Deep Seabed*

Ambassador Pardo's profound thesis on the multidimensionality of an international control solution to the seabed problem rested on one fundamental but fragile assumption. Namely, that there is in fact a juridical phenomenon which he called "the seabed and the ocean floor, and the subsoil thereof, underlying the high seas beyond the limits of present national jurisdiction."[59] Malta's proposed programme for the United Nations to adopt a Treaty and General Assembly resolution[60] had as its major premise the existence of a physically submerged space outside national jurisdiction where an internationalization policy, and, therefore, where the future international law and rules for internationalization, should and must apply. If there is a technological frontier, and an economic frontier, as well as an international political frontier – as unquestionably there were such frontiers unfolding right before the United Nations – was there also a "legal" frontier in the deep ocean floor? In other words, was the deep seabed devoid of any law that would have necessarily governed it at the time Malta raised the question of the deep seabed? If there was a pre-existing normative structure already in place applicable to the deep seabed, how does this regime accommodate the desire to internationalize the control of this geographic space and its resources? These questions comprehend the *legal dimension* of the internationalization debate. The answers to these questions will soon prove decisive in the definition of the *élan* of the Common Heritage of Humanity principle.[61]

Ambassador Pardo and others who advocated international control of the deep seabed were all too aware that there was certainly no legal void, or *lacunae*, in the geophysical area of the deep ocean floor.[62] With reference particularly to the economic use/exploitation of the seabottom in question, the applicable law was actually very clear; in fact, it was the law's clarity and explicitness which appeared to be causing all the problems. The culprit was identified as the 1958 Geneva Convention on the Continental Shelf.[63] As Am-

---

59 Ambassador Pardo argued his case for "internationalization" in the context of what he observed were ominous "nationalization" trends that relied on the literal interpretation of, and expanding State practice based on, the 1958 Geneva Convention on the Continental Shelf. PV 1515, para. 56-72.
60 PV 1516, para. 10 & 12.
61 *See infra* Sec. B.4 & Chap. IV.
62 PV 1515, para. 56-70.
63 Text in 499 UNTS 312.

bassador Pardo explained, conceptions about the legal status of the deep seabed arise from this treaty, concluded barely a decade ago.[64] Article 1 of the 1958 Geneva Convention on the Continental Shelf provides:

> ... the term "continental shelf" is used as referring to (a) the seabed and the subsoil of the submarine areas adjacent to the coast but outside the area of the territorial sea, to a depth of 200 meters or, *beyond that limit, to where the depth of the superjacent waters admits of the exploitation of the natural resources of the said areas* ... (emphasis supplied)

In view of the rapid technological advances that have rendered the exploration, exploitation, and appropriation of the deep seabed resources feasible, it would seem reasonable and entirely common-sensical to infer from the very terms of the "exploitability clause" (italicized above) that the deep ocean floor would sooner or later assume the legal status of continental shelf.[65] But this conclusion – as a logical proposition or a legal technicality – was not at all so obvious. It was a conclusion that was regarded by many as highly contentious when Ambassador Pardo was already speaking before the General Assembly. It is even true to say that in some quarters in the United States, it had become heretical to believe in such a conclusion.[66] However, by hinting at the imminent reality of the deep ocean floor being turned into "continental shelf", Ambassador Pardo was simply adding fuel to the serious controversy that had already developed around the "exploitability clause" of the Continental Shelf Convention.

The provenance of the controversy involving the "exploitability clause" is often taken for granted, if not completely forgotten, by contemporary commentators on the Law of the Sea. It is submitted that a review of the origins of this controversy is of paramount importance in any investigation of the inter-

---

64 For an assessment of the continental shelf as a juridical concept, *see infra* Sec. B.4.
65 S. Oda, *The Geneva Conventions on the Law of the Sea: Some Suggestions for their Revision* 1 NAT RES L 103-105 (1968), at 103.
    It may be inferred that all the submarine areas of the world have been divided among the coastal states at the deepest trenches by the Convention on the Continental Shelf.
    The opinion of Professor Shigeru Oda in this article was quoted by Ambassador Pardo in PV 1515, para. 67.
66 *See infra*, Sec. B.4.

nationalization debate in the 1960s. This review should illuminate in more ways than one the decisive impact of the controversy surrounding the exploitability clause on the resolution (or non-resolution) of the basic issue of the legal status of the deep seabed at that time, and afterwards.

It could be supposed that any observant reader not familiar with the complicated career followed by the definition of the continental shelf in the 1950s and 1960s will readily appreciate the clear denotation of the afore-quoted "exploitability clause": it provides a *carte blanche* for coastal States to extend their continental shelves to an unspecified distance off shore up "to where the depth of the superjacent waters admits of exploitation of natural resources" of the seabed and its subsoil.[67] The inference of an elastic, open-ended definition of the physical extent of the legal continental shelf is authorized by the exploitability clause of the Convention.[68] It would thus seem perfectly logical to surmise from plain, unaffected literal reading of the above-quoted provision that the entirety of the ocean floor and all its resources[69] would, depending ultimate-

---

67 *See* S. Oda, *supra* note 65; *See also* S. Oda, *Proposals for Revising the Continental Shelf Convention* 7 COLUMBIA J TRANS L 1-31 (1968). Judge Oda's denotative reading of the Convention that "all the submarine areas of the world have been theoretically divided among the coastal states at the deepest trenches" is sustained by the tenets of treaty interpretation embodied in the 1969 Convention on the Law of Treaties, Art. 31 & Art. 32. Ambassador Pardo was obviously placing a political context to a literal reading of the Convention in his statement that "current international law encourages the appropriation of this vast area by those who have the technology to exploit it." PV 1515, para. 90.

68 For *e.g.*, Arthur Dean, head of the US delegation to UNCLOS I, states his first-impression understanding of the exploitability clause, A. Dean, *The Geneva Conference on the Law of the Sea: What was Accomplished* 52 AJIL 607, at 620 (1958) as follows:
The effect of the present language is that exploitability, and, therefore, the necessary control will be presumed to the depth of 200 meters, but must be shown beyond that point. Although the Conference showed themselves aware that technical advances may increase the depth to which control is possible, the 200 meter figure (655 ft.) serve to represent the greatest depth at which control is now thought possible.

69 Article 2(1) of the Convention provides that "The coastal State exercises over the continental shelf sovereign rights of the purpose of exploring and exploiting its natural resources", and in Article 2(4) "The natural resources referred to in this article consist of the mineral and other non-living resources of the seabed and subsoil together with living organisms belonging to sedentary species..."

ly on technological and economic considerations, eventually or potentially[70] fall within the regulatory ambit of the continental shelf regime.[71] It goes without saying that this rather straightforward understanding of the provision has absolutely nothing to do with the issue of whether the exploitability clause is good or bad, a prudent legislation or a short-sighted one.[72]

What cannot be over-emphasized is the fact that the exploitability clause, understood as such, was widely and unquestioningly accepted *de lege lata* in State practice from the time the Convention was adopted in 1958 up to the mid-1960s[73] – a relatively short span of time that spelled out all the difference

---

[70] "The concept of exploitability must be interpreted each time in terms of the most advanced standards of technology and economy in the world." Whatever seabed area that is not yet exploitable, howsoever "exploitability" is defined is, therefore, not regulated by the rules on the "continental shelf." See Oda, *supra* note 65 at 105. See also D. Bowett, *The Law of the Sea* 34 and 42 (1967). On "potential rights" under this definition, *see* F. Garcia-Amador, *The Exploitation and Conservation of the Resources of the Sea* at 110 (1960).

[71] An illustrative map of the world showing the division of the ocean floor among coastal States using hypothetical median lines, using the delimitation provisions of the Continental Shelf Convention, was produced by Dr. F. Christy in 1967. *See* insert in *LSI 1967*. The issue that arose by the mid-1960s was whether the International Law Commission which drafted Article 1 of the Continental Shelf Convention, and UNCLOS I which adopted it, "intended" this hypothetical division as a matter of law. From the standpoint of observers and commentators in 1958, there is strong evidence that this was part of the "legislative intent" of such a rule defining the continental shelf in an open-ended way, although many were agreed that such result was highly unsatisfactory. *See* R. Young, *The Geneva Convention on the Continental Shelf: A First Impression*, 52 AJIL 733-738 (1958); JAC Gutteridge, *The 1958 Geneva Convention on the Continental Shelf* 35 BYIL 102-123, esp. at 106-110 (1959). From the perspective of the mid-1960s, *see* Oda, *supra* note 65; LFE Goldie, in *LSI 1966* at 277-278; and Kreuger, *supra* note 36, at 7 esp. note 9 and at 36. For the debate about the "legislative intent" behind the "exploitability clause" in the US, *see* L. Henkin, *International Law and "The Interests": The Law of the Seabed* 63 AJIL 504 (1969); L. Finlay, *The Outer Limit of the Continental Shelf. A Rejoinder to Professor Louis Henkin* 64 AJIL 42 (1970); and L. Henkin, *A Reply to Mr. Finlay* 64 AJIL 62 (1970).

[72] As Professor Oda stated, in *supra* note 67, *lex ferenda* dictates that the "the regime of the ocean floor of the deep sea should be distinct from that of the continental shelf."

[73] As early as 1959, for instance, the State Department Geographer in the United States, G.E. Pearcy, interpreting the 1958 Convention, asserted that when the depth of exploitation is not limited by technology, the ocean bottom everywhere is sliced

up and defined as belonging to one or another coastal State. G.E. Pearcy, *Geographical Aspects of the Law of the Sea* 49 ANNALS, ASSOC. OF AMERICAN GEOGRAPHERS 1-23 (March, 1959), cited in Wenk, *supra* note 33, at 256. It is important to point out that Ambassador Pardo, at para. 68-69, cites the State practice of the developed countries as evidence of the literal application of the exploitability clause with respect to the "deep ocean floor" – then understood as the area geologically outside the continental margin: partitioning of the bed of the North Sea and the Baltic among the littoral States, and United States legislation acknowledging coastal State jurisdiction to any portion of the seabed accessible by current technology. For a description of the State practice up to 1966 relating to the continental shelf, and the sufficiency of the principles in the Continental Shelf Convention in supporting and expanding this State practice, *see* A.H. Dean, "The Law of the Sea Conference, 1958-1960, and its Aftermath" in *LSI 1966* at 244-264. *See also* Weissberg, *op. cit.* at 83. On US State practice, more particularly, the extension of US legislation to the deep seabed to accord with the "exploitability clause" of the Continental Shelf Convention is reiterated in the famous Memorandum of the Solicitor of the Department of Interior dated 5 May 1961, text in *House Interim Report*, at 165, 167:

The applicability of the Outer Continental Shelf Lands Act extends to all submerged areas lying seaward of the States' boundaries over the seabed and subsoil of which the United States has asserted jurisdiction. Since the United States has now asserted jurisdiction over the seabed and subsoil of the submarine areas adjacent to the coast of the mainland and islands as far as the depth of the superjacent waters permits exploitation of the natural resources, the Act is now applicable to those areas.

This official Interior Department opinion was later submitted to the Departments of State and Justice to determine whether the latter had objections, and they registered none. *See* F. Barry, *The Administration of the Outer Continental Shelf Lands Act* NAT RES L No. 3, 38-48 at 46 (1968). It should also be pointed out that the definition of the "continental shelf" in the 1958 Convention was a matter of indifference to the United States during UNCLOS I. A. Hollick, *US Foreign Policy and the Law of the Sea* at 125 note 86 (1981). Wenk, *supra* note 33 257, mentions that the US Senate casually ratified the Continental Shelf Convention on 26 May 1960, with scarcely a thought about any "ambiguities" in the Convention text or other implications, and that between 1960 and 1964, the year the Convention entered into force, the issue of the continental shelf's "outer limits" was completely quiescent. In 1965 and 1966, "only a few mild questions bubbled inconspicuously to the surface." As late as 1966, some US government functionaries were still asserting the view that the Convention on the Continental Shelf, with specific reference to the exploitability clause, was clear and self-explanatory – *i.e.,* that the continental shelf could reach as far as technology permits. E.F. Bennet, "Legal Climate for Undersea Mining" in *Exploiting the Oceans, supra* note 25, at 204, in regard to the question of the status of the deep seabed during this period and thereafter.[74] Even commentators were initially agreed that the exploitability clause, notwithstanding its hazy definition of the extent of the continental shelf under the exploitability clause, is part of a "moderate", "farsighted" or "flexible" approach taken by UNCLOS I in the drafting the Continental Shelf Convention.[75] There were, to be sure, already misgivings about the open-ended definition of the continental shelf even when the International Law Commission was studying the matter, but the concept of flexible limits was endorsed just the same.[76] When the Convention was adopted at UNCLOS I, the implications of the exploitability clause were discussed with much apprehension, but it passed all scrutiny, for two reasons. First, according to some delegations, the exploitability clause ensures that scientific and technological progress will not be hampered.[77] Second, and more importantly, the exploitability clause was adopted because all other alternatives failed.[78] In spite of its perceived shortcomings, associated

---

206-207. *See also* M. Belman, *The role of the State Department in Formulating Federal Policy Regarding Marine Resources* 1 NAT RES L 14, at 14 (1968), where it is stated that up to 1965, the US State Department was unaware of any need for study of international law or policy relating to the development of the natural resources of the ocean. Belman was with the US State Department's Office of the Legal Advisor when his remarks were given. L.F.E. Goldie, *LSI 1966* also agrees that the exploitability clause says what it means, but then should be deleted by way of amendment.

74 *See infra*, B.4.
75 Young, *supra* note 58, at 733; Barry, *supra* note 73, at 48. *See also* S. Bernfeld, *Developing the Resources of the Sea – Security of Investment* 1 NAT RES L 82-90 (1968): "the objective of the ILC was to divide the beds of the sea among coastal nations, for that was the real need if future conflicts were to be avoided." Dean, in *LSI 1966, supra* note 73, at 246-247, underscores the "prophylactic character" of the Continental Shelf Convention, its provisions being evidence of "a farsighted anticipation of and attempt to avoid certain areas of dispute which might arise in the future."
76 For a detailed treatment of the legislative background of Article 1, *see* B. Oxman, *The Preparation of Article 1 of the Convention on the Continental Shelf* (1969).
77 J. Symonides "The Continental Shelf" in Bedjaoui, *supra* Chap. I note 29, 871-884, at 872.
78 Young, *supra* note 71, at 733: The Continental Shelf Convention "leaves many serious uncertainties unresolved... This does not mean that it should be repudiated, but rather that its inadequacies should be promptly recognized for what they are. Some no doubt, can be objects of later improvement, others, it must be feared are now irreparable and must be viewed as part of the price to be paid for any

with ascertaining the mobile extent of the continental shelf, there was no question about what the exploitability clause exactly directed and authorized.[79] These findings strongly suggests that the "exploitability clause" had become an established norm even in the customary law of the continental shelf in the early 1960s.[80]

The reason why the exploitability clause became controversial is intimately connected with the question of *when exactly* it became controversial. It could be maintained that it was only when "manganese nodules" came up for policy discussion in the United States around the middle of the 1960s that the controversy over the Continental Shelf Convention – specifically, the exploit-

---

agreement at all." *See also* Gutteridge, *supra* note 71, esp. at 106-110, and at 122: the Continental Shelf Convention is "a substantial contribution to the progressive development of international law." Article 1 was adopted by 51 votes to 9, with 10 abstentions. VI UNCLOS I Off Rec at 47.

[79] In UNCLOS I, the Canadian Delegation outlined five possible methods of defining the continental shelf, one of which was to the effect that the extent be made coextensive with the exploitability of resources. This method was criticized by the Canadians because it was insufficiently objective, and was also objectionable because, in view of the rapid increase of scientific and technical knowledge, the limit based on exploitability would tend to expand continuously, thus creating more uncertainty. In spite of this lucid and well-understood clarification on the options concerning the definition of the legal continental shelf, the exploitability clause was adopted just the same. *See* Gutteridge, *supra* note 71, at 106; D.M. Johnston, *The International Law of Fisheries* at 238-239 (1965). As early as 1952, Professor Giddel commented on the clear meaning of an unclear continental shelf definition under the exploitability clause – "the extent of the continental shelf would be uncertain and varying: uncertain because it would depend on the degree of technical development of a given country and varying because the extent would change with technical developments." G. Giddel, "Le Plateau Continental", Fourth International Conference of the Legal Profession, IBA, Madrid, 1952, cited in Mouton, *op. cit.* 317. *Cf.* E.D. Brown, *The Legal Regime of Hydrospace* Ch. 1 (1971).

[80] *North Sea Continental Shelf Cases*, 1969 ICJ Rep 3, para. 63 [the seaward extent of the continental shelf defined in Article 1 reflects customary law]. Articles 1-3 inclusive of the Continental Shelf Convention are not subject to reservations. *See* Article 12(1), Continental Shelf Convention. It is also said that as early as 1956, when the definition of the continental shelf incorporating the exploitability clause was adopted by the American States in the Ciudad Trujillo Conference, the exploitability clause had become (regional) customary law. *See* Hollick, *op. cit.* 121.

ability clause – arose. The record is quite clear that prior to the widespread public knowledge of vast technologically accessible manganese nodule resources on the deep ocean floor, neither the exploitability clause nor the objective determination of the extent of the continental shelf thereunder was seen as contentious in any legal or politically-significant sense.

With manganese nodule mining on the policy horizon, a previously unheard-of issue had surfaced. This was the question concerning what was labelled as "the outer limits" of the continental shelf under the purview of the exploitability clause. This problem of "outer limits" began to invite a fair amount of comment when alleged uncertainties or misgivings about the legal regime governing the mining of manganese nodules were aired, at first by representatives of the commercial mining sector.[81] Calls and cries to amend or revise the Convention then became louder.[82] But the amendment of the Convention was not itself the subject of the controversy that was bound to be quite troublesome in the years to come. The gist of the debate turned on the issue of whether the definition of the extent of the continental shelf as provided for in the exploitability clause was to be taken as it was – plainly and literally. This issue introduced in a subtle way the advocacy for "outer limits" to the continental shelf under the exploitability clause, *i.e.*, that the exploitability clause must not be read literally.[83]

---

81 The publication of Mero's *Mineral Resources of the Sea, supra* note 37 (by Elsevier, 1965; the first edition was published in 1964), is historically significant in the evolution of thinking on the law of the continental shelf. Buzan, *op. cit.* 80, states that the seabed debate "was triggered by the impending creation of an active deep sea nodule mining industry."

82 *See LSI 1966* at 156, 172-187, 265-298; and NAT RES L (1968). According to the terms of reference in Article 13 of the Convention on the Continental Shelf, amendments to the Convention can only be formally entertained in 1969.

83 The change in usage, linguistically, of the phrase "uncertain continental shelf limits" in the context of controversy around the exploitability clause should be noted. In 1958, for instance, this phrase was used to signify the problem of fixing more precisely the extent or the limits of the continental shelf which was recognize as necessarily changing through time. *See* Young, *supra* note 71. In 1966, the phrase would now come to mean that there is, or there ought to be, a theoretically *"fixed outer limit" beyond which the continental shelf could not, or should not, extend – but this limit has been left uncertain. See LSI 1966.* This change in usage was also accompanied by the increasingly used terminology that sought to distinguish the "continental shelf" from the "deep seabed." For an historical overview of the issues involved, *see* D.N. Hutchinson, *The Seaward Limit to Continental*

In other words, when the industrial exploitation of manganese nodules became a serious proposition, it was only then that the argument was strenuously put forward that the Continental Shelf Convention did not actually mean what it said![84] That is, the exploitability clause must be read as a valid regime for the seabed only up to a restrained distance from the coast short of median-line boundaries, even if resource exploitation was possible beyond this distance[85]

Shelf Jurisdiction in Customary International Law 56 BYIL 111-188 (1985).

84 As far as I am aware, the pioneer argument that took this orientation was put forward by Professor W. Burke who, exploring the issue of the extent of the continental shelf in late-1965, imagined "counterclaims" against the claim for a literal interpretation of the exploitability clause. These counterclaims could be justified on the basis of the freedom of the seas doctrine, or on a demonstration that the policy of the Continental Shelf Convention was not to allocate deep ocean floor resources through exclusive coastal State control. Burke, *Ocean Sciences*, supra note 29, at 54-55. The "policy argument" was elaborated further in Burke, *Exploiting the Oceans*, supra note 25, at 10-14, 22. Professor Myres McDougal was insistent in his opinion, during the 1967 ABA Institute in Long Beach California, that there was nothing in the history of the Continental shelf convention to justify the view that the exploitability clause authorized coastal States to indefinitely extend their continental shelves to the depths of the oceans up to theoretical median lines. NAT RES L at 99 (no. 2) and 26 (no. 3). This opinion was of course openly at odds with the views expressed by US government representatives (Belman, *supra* note 73 and Barry, *supra* note 73) and other scholars (Oda, *supra* note 65 and Kreuger, *supra* note 36) during the same meeting. Professor Burke, at the first opportunity to comment on the implications of the Geneva Conventions on resource allocation way back in 1959, did not raise any doubts or notice any problems or ambiguities about the continental shelf or its definition in the Convention. W. Burke, *Some Comments on the 1958 Convention* [a reaction to the presentation of Arthur Dean on the Geneva Conventions], 1959 ASIL Proc 197-206.

85 *See* Burke, *LSI 1966* at 172 and 205. Northcutt Ely, in *id.* at 176-178, expressed his initially confusions about the "problem of limits", but in a different forum taking place elsewhere at the same time, *see* Ely in *Exploiting the Oceans*, supra 25, at 376, took the position that "at some point, at some great depth, at some great distance from land, the continental shelf must be presumed to end, even as a legal fiction" and an area beyond realized. For a similar view, *see* W. Tubman, "The Legal Status of Minerals Located On or Beneath the Ocean Floor Beyond the Continental Shelf" in *id.* at 379. Mero in 1964 asserted that the Continental Shelf Convention was "so clear so as to leave little maneuvering" on the question of limits, *supra* note 37, at 289; later on, he suggested that the "definitions in the convention should be tightened a little", *see* Mero in *LSI 1966, supra*

note 34, at 293-294; but in the following year Mero was categorical in his view that "I don't think that the Members of the Commission [*sic*: he was in this context referring to the 1958 Geneva Conference] had that in mind at all. They really felt that the boundaries concerning authority over exploitation of minerals from adjacent nations should stop some place at something that can be construed as the continental shelf." J. Mero, "Alternatives for Mineral Exploitation" in *LSI 1967, supra* note 26. Young, *supra* note 58, in 1958 thought that even if the Continental Shelf Convention (which was a moderate agreement) left much to be desired (*e.g.*, by way of certainty in the manner of defining the extent of the continental shelf) the Convention could be improved through time. Obviously he was referring to formal amendments as a modality of improving the text. By 1968, however, Young in his *The Limits of the Continental Shelf – and Beyond* 1968 ASIL Proc 229-236, at 231 took the view that an outer "seaward limit" was contemplated under Article 1 of the Convention "beyond which the continental shelf doctrine does not apply"; he was now suggesting that the continental terrace was the *ratione loci* of the exploitability clause.

It should be noted that the concern over limits coincided with the rising popularity of a topic which could have been unimaginable in the early 1960s: the "need for future modifications" of or "alternatives" to the Continental Shelf Convention. *LSI 1966, supra* note 34, at 265-298; *LSI 1967, supra* note 26, at 94 *et seq.;* Henkin, *supra*, note 24, at Chapters IV and V; Wenk, *supra* note 33 at 264. It was also suggested that the exploitability clause be deleted from the Convention. L.F.E. Goldie, *LSI 1966* at 278 and in *LSI 1967* at 101. It is furthermore significant to note that an apparent "change of mind" was happening in Europe. Thus, in acceding to the Continental Shelf Convention, France submitted a "Declaration" concerning Article 1 of the Convention (note that reservations are not allowed under the Convention), to the effect that:

In the view of the Government of the French Republic, the expression "adjacent" area implies a notion of geophysical, geological, and geographical dependence which *ipso facto* rules out an unlimited extension of the continental shelf.

See T. Kronmiller, *The Lawfulness of Deep Seabed Mining* at 125, (vol. I, 1980). France, it will be recalled, had consistently objected to the "exploitability clause" during the ILC and UNCLOS I deliberations on Article 1, but then urged that the draft Continental Shelf Convention be adopted by consensus to prevent further uncertainties. *See* Weissberg, *op. cit.* 70-74. The submission of the above-quoted declaration evidently proves *a contrario* that the notion of "unlimited extension of the continental shelf" was the prevailing understanding in the ILC and UNCLOS I, for otherwise, there would not have been any need to express a point so strongly emphasized by the French in voting *against* article 1 of the Convention when the articles were considered and voted upon one at a time. *See* VI UNCLOS I Off Rec at 2, 31-32, 43, 138.

– the "true" outer limits of the continental shelf do not really extend indefinitely to the deep ocean floor.[86]

The glare of manganese nodules, as it were, provoked a trend to re-interpret the "exploitability clause." The problem was no longer the *uncertain extent* of the continental shelf under the 1958 Continental Shelf Convention, but the *uncertain intent* of the exploitability clause itself. This "construction" of the exploitability clause was absolutely unheard of before and could have been dismissed outright as confused analysis or unsystematic thinking were it raised in 1958.[87] But what is interesting to note is that this became a fashionable interpretation in the United States, if not the most compelling view, of the Convention in the late 1960s and beyond.[88] This historical turn of events or

---

In the United Kingdom, the issues concerning the Continental Shelf Convention before public knowledge of the nodule phenomenon focussed largely on the nature of "sovereign rights" over the continental shelf. It is remarkable that there were at all no concerns raised or discussions made on the issue of the continental shelf's "outer limits." See G. Marston, *The Incorporation of Continental Shelf Rights into United Kingdom Law* 45 ICLQ 13-51 (1996). Thus, when the UK extended its continental shelf up to "half the North Sea" in 1964, no uncertainty or ambiguity was seen in the exploitability clause under which this extension was effected. In fact, it was fully acknowledged that the definition of the Continental Shelf under the 1958 Convention made allowance for developing exploitation techniques. See A. Samuels, "The Continental Shelf Act of 1964" in *Developments in the Law of the Sea 1958-1964* (British Institute of International and Comparative Law, 1965).

86 See Oxman, *supra* note 76; Tubman, *supra* note 85, at 379-392; E.D. Brown. "The Present Regime of the Exploration and Exploitation of Sea-Bed Resources in International Law and in National Legislation: An Evaluation" in *Symposium on the International Regime of the Sea-Bed Proceedings* 241-278 (Rome: 1970) [this volume will be referred to hereafter as *Rome Symposium*].

87 See *supra* note 79.

88 The issue of intent of the "exploitability clause" was closely associated with the new problem of interpreting the term "adjacent" in Article 1. Many arguments put forward in the later part of the 1960s in favor of a "reinterpreted" exploitability clause built their case on the basic contention that "adjacent" in this context means "exploitability near the shore" and not indefinitely up to mid-ocean. *See e.g.*, Tubman, *op. cit.*; Weissberg, *op. cit.*; E.D. Brown, *supra* note 86; Henkin, *supra* notes 24 & 71; Finlay, *supra* note 71. Apart from the question of vested interests having a stake in a "reinterpreted" exploitability clause, historical method in contemporaneous scholarship may be at issue here as well. Buzan, *op. cit.* 24, for instance, accepts it as obvious that the exploitability clause was not really

legal arguments needs to be examined more closely. I would argue most emphatically that the key to understanding more dispassionately the emergence of the Common Heritage of Humanity as a principle in international law lies in this inquiry.

Without doubt, it was in the United States where the subject of manganese nodule mining, along with its attendant legal infrastructure, was first given serious intellectual and policy consideration.[89] After the publication of John Mero's *Minerals of the Sea*, the legal considerations which the author drew in the concluding Chapter of this book concerning the mining of nodules became the special focus of attention by international lawyers and policy makers. With Mero's suggestion, arguably put forward on behalf of the US offshore minerals mining industry, that a high seas regime is the *preferred* legal setting for manganese nodule mining,[90] legal minds were immediately set to

---

intended to mean what it says; his rendering of the past, however, employs the tricky and misleading "whig" technique in narrating legal history. That is, the seeds of confusion on the intent of the exploitability clause in the late 1960s were already planted in 1958, because people in the late-1960s became "confused" about the intent of this provision. This version, which interprets the events in 1958 to accord with certain political preferences in the late 1960s, is reiterated in Morell, *op. cit.* 12-13. In the main, current literature accepts in a matter-of-fact manner the "dangerous imprecision", or "ambiguity", or unsatisfactory drafting of the exploitability clause. See Churchill & Lowe, *op. cit.* 125; Schmidt, *op. cit.* 19; T. Frank, *The Power of Legitimacy Among Nations* 53-54 (1990); E.D. Brown, *Sea-Bed Energy and Minerals The International Regime Vol. I The Continental Shelf* at 19 (1992); II COMMENTARY at 829; T. McDorman, *The Entry into Force of the 1982 LOS Convention and the Article 76 Outer Continental Shelf Regime* 10 IJMCL 165, at 175 note 41 (1996).

89 Buzan, *op. cit.* 62, 79-80.
90 Mero, *supra* note 37, at 289-293. After duly observing that the Continental Shelf Convention was clear as to the matter of continental shelf limits, and after noting the "major disadvantage" of this rule, Mero expressed his preference on the kind of legal regime that is ideal for deep sea mining: "it would appear to be of greater advantage to the ocean miner that the convention governing the high seas take control at the base of the continental slope" such that nodules are harvested in the same manner as fish in the open ocean.

work on the available possibilities[91] and, soon thereafter, policy makers began to examine the wider implications of deep ocean mining.[92]

Several factors came into play that militated against the continental shelf doctrine being utilized as the paramount legal framework for mineral extraction activities in the deep ocean. First, as indicated by Mero himself and eventually re-articulated by an industry lawyer, Northcutt Ely,[93] the requirement of exclusiveness of title or access over a particular deposit or mine site in such a high-risk, high-capital venture like deep sea mining[94] may be better assured if only a few relevant actors are involved in the whole business of manganese nodule mining. The few countries which possessed the technological capability for deep ocean mining, generally, and the deep ocean mining companies, specifically, were such relevant actors, for they were the only entities that have a direct interest in any likely disputes concerning mining projects and operations. The high seas regime for fisheries, Mero concludes, provides suitable rules that could be applied analogously to ocean mining operations.[95]

In wishing for a high seas regime option, however, what Mero clearly had in mind was a situation where the contemplated nodule mining activities will be be carried out in an area of the deep seabed that is actually or potentially within the extended continental shelf of *another* State which, ostensibly, was not the United States. He thus stressed that a "major disadvantage" of applying the law of the outer continental shelf according to the categorical terms of the exploitability clause was "the fee that would have to be paid to some nation for the privilege of mining the deposit and the time that would be lost in red

---

91 Professor Burke, in *Ocean Sciences*, *supra* note 29, at 14, thus entertained the feasibility of utilizing a "legal technicality" on the part of decision-makers for resolving future disputes, which he elaborates in his conclusions, at 87-91. Perhaps it was then still clear in his mind that the literal meaning of the exploitability clause had to be taken as a given. *Cf.* Burke, 1959 ASIL proc, *supra* note 84.
92 Wenk, *supra* note 33 at 262-265.
93 Ely, in *Exploiting the Oceans*, *supra* note 25.
94 *Id.*, at 377, the emphasis being on the legal pre-conditions for mining:
   The petroleum and mining industries, whether operating on dry land or beneath the sea, require two things above all to attract capital to the ultra-risky business of exploring for minerals: the discoverer's exclusive right to exploit the minerals discovered and security of tenure while he does so. At sea, these risks are multiplied.
   For the economic and institutional requirements of efficient manganese nodule mining, *see* Brooks, *supra* note 26, at 32-41.
95 Mero, *supra* note 37, at 290-293.

tape activities."[96] United States policy makers could not have been unsympathetic to this preference. For the major motivation of the United States in subsequently pressing for "continental shelf outer limits" was to prevent developing countries from nationalizing or confiscating foreign investments located in expanded areas off shore in which these countries might grant concessions.[97]

The problem raised by Mero regarding the drawbacks of mining nodules in the continental shelf of other coastal States, especially in the continental shelves of developing countries, is related to a second, more serious, problem about the implications of invoking the continental shelf regime for deep ocean mining. This is the follow-the-leader effect of probable US actions on the issue of the extent of the continental shelf. That is, whatever unilateral off-shore claims to mineral resources that will be made by the United States would have to be conceded on an equal or reciprocal basis to other States as well.[98] But the previous experience with other nations' claims that trailed the 1945 Truman Proclamation on the Continental Shelf was not at all very pleasant to the United

---

96 Mero, *id.*, at 290. Furthermore, were the operator to conduct mining activity close to the shore of another state, Mero, at 292-293, maintains that three alternatives are open to it: "(1) move to some other location, (2) pay the protection money, or (3) call on his sovereign for protection from interference in his activities on the high seas by a foreign sovereign." These alternatives were not hypothetical imaginings of Mero, for in his maps indicating the promising regions for mining nodules *id.* at 164 and 226, many of the nodule sites were located within the "extended" continental shelves of other States. On the option of "paying protection money" and a description of the "ethical problems" encountered by mining companies, *see* W. Bascom, "Mining the Sea" in *LSI 1966, supra* note 34, at 16-166. Ely, *LSI 1966* at 177, and Ely in *Exploiting the Oceans, supra* note 25, at 375-376, did not hide his apprehension with a touch of cynicism that mining could occur for example in the continental shelves of other States, "like Cuba or the Malagasy Republic." It is quite interesting to note that if the well-known Clarion-Clipperton Fracture Zone region were to be allocated as continental shelf via median lines between the relevant littoral States – the USA (Hawaii) and Mexico (Clarion Island) – most of the claims registered by the Preparatory Commission and assigned to Pioneer Investors, especially the claims of private consortia from the US and the UK, will fall within the area of sovereign rights appertaining to Mexico. *See* map in Glassner, *op. cit.* at 29.
97 *See* the recollection of Judge S. Oda in his dissenting opinion in the *Libya/Malta Continental Shelf Case*. 1985 ICJ Rep 4, at 152, para. 51.
98 Chapman, *LSI 1966, supra* note 34, at 125; McDougal, *supra* note 37, at 21.

States.⁹⁹ In the eyes of American policy-makers, the Latin American countries had already shown a brazen disposition to "better" the off-shore claims of the US. The prospect that other coastal States will claim for themselves, as the Latin American countries did earlier, not merely limited resource jurisdiction but full sovereignty over not only the advancing areas of continental shelf but also the superjacent waters was certainly most horrifying, not least to the US defense establishment which had consistently advocated maximum application of the freedom of the seas.¹⁰⁰ Considering that the sensitive issue of territorial sea limits, which had not been settled in UNCLOS I and II, and in light of the increasing sovereignty claims to bigger off-shore areas,¹⁰¹ implementing nodule mining projects under the juristic framework offered by the "exploitability clause" seemed ill-advised.¹⁰² A "preventative" approach to international law – directed specifically at that "the headache of jurisdiction below 200 meters"¹⁰³ – beckoned.¹⁰⁴

This points to a third factor which pulled the breaks on the seaward march of coastal State jurisdiction under the exploitability clause. Other competing

---

99 *Ibid.* For an account of the "extravagant demands" of the Latin American States and other national claims to off-shore areas that followed the US move to establish a continental shelf from the US perspective, *see* J. Kunz, *Continental Shelf and International Law: Confusion and Abuse* 50 AJIL 828-853 (1956); Hollick, *op. cit.* at Chap. 3, and 117 *et seq.*

100 W. Hearn, *The Role of the United States Navy in the Formulation of Federal Policy regarding the Sea* NAT RES L no. 2, 23-31. *See also* Hollick, *op. cit.* 183-187.

101 L. Alexander, "Offshore Claims of the World", *LSI 1966, supra* note 34, at 71-84, and 85.

102 Henkin, *supra* note 24, at 44.

103 Ely, *A Case for Administration of Mineral Resources Underlying the High Seas by National Interests* NAT RES L no. 2, at 82.

104 On the "preventative" concept, *see* Belman, 1 NAT RES J at 17, and the intervention of University of Miami Law School Dean Kelso, at 40. Belman's caution against embracing a "median-line" policy is stated as follows:
Our long coasts on two broad oceans would give us a good chance of striking rich. However since we know so little about the resources of the deep ocean seabed, it may be that our area of the ocean would be less rich than other areas which other countries would then assert jurisdiction ... [or] the wrong people from our point of view could end up with hitherto unsuspected resources to the exclusion of others despite having only at most a tenuous geographic connection with the location of those resources ... [or] this arbitrary system of distributing ocean resources could be unstable in the long run.

national interests necessarily intervened[105] – for example military, fishing, scientific research, and foreign policy[106] – that would have made further adherence to the open-ended definition of the continental shelf more a liability rather than an asset.[107] Thus, even before Ambassador Pardo made his move in the United Nations, the consideration by US decision-makers of the various interests affected by any policy of extending the continental shelf regime to the deep seabed had moved towards the development of policy that "initially rested on rejecting any belief that the 1958 Convention on the Continental Shelf was unambiguous in defining boundaries of national sovereignty."[108] By the fall of 1967, the United States' attitude on the question of continental shelf limits[109] sought to completely reverse the official US interpretation of the Continental Shelf that was favored up to the mid-1960s:[110]

> There should be deliberate policy decisions on the extent of the Continental Shelf; a precise definition of its seaward boundary seems desirable. A buffer zone might be established to bridge the boundary between the Shelf and the seabed with the coastal states' interests in the ocean floor given special protection in the Zone.[111]

---

105 For a historical survey of these domestic interests and their influence on the shaping of US policy, *see* Hollick, *op. cit.* Chaps. 6 & 7.
106 Henkin, *supra* note 24, at 8-12. Professor Henkin had consistently advocated an enlightened US foreign policy on the basis of a consideration of all relevant "voices" in national decision-making. *See also* Henkin, *supra* note 71.
107 *Cf.* Barry, *supra* note 73, for the view that the Convention's definition of the continental shelf is not flawed: "The existing body of law on the exploitation of ocean minerals is in itself a valuable resource. We discard it at our peril."
108 Wenk, *supra* note 33, at 264.
109 *See* testimony of D. Popper, Deputy Assistant Secretary of State for International Organization Affairs, for the view that the exploitability clause should imply outer limits. *See House Interim Report.* This and other opinions concerning the content and strategy of the US in the United Nations in response to the Pardo initiative (although the transcripts were full of security deletions) were thought to be representative of the views of the technologically developed countries on the seabed issue. Weissberg, *op. cit.* at 97.
110 *See supra* note 73.
111 This is stated in the 1968 Report of the US National Council on Marine Resources and Engineering Development as a finding in one study the Council had contracted, *i.e.*, Henkin, *supra* note 24. According to Wenk, *supra* note 33, at 205, this articulated position was favored by many, including the Stratton Commission, which eventually adopted it as its main recommendation on the issue of the deep seabed, in turn to become the basis of President Nixon's 1970 Statement of US

But even if no clear national, multi-sectoral consensus about the desirable limits to the continental shelf was yet on hand, or while this consensus was still being worked out, it was nonetheless essential that the *concept* – that the exploitability clause imposed limits – was maintained so that alternative policy options could be kept open.[112]

All these factors would prove that the advances in technology which made exploitation of the deep seabed a feasible proposition, if not an imminent reality, in the 1960s led to a redefinition of national interest on the part of the United States with respect to the conventional definition of the continental shelf. A flexible "outer limit" or the open-ended jurisdictional extent of the continental shelf was no longer serviceable and had become a threat to US national interests.[113] The new US position on the exploitability clause, therefore, demanded an ascertainable outer limit to the continental shelf, or a *de facto* inconclusiveness in the intent of the exploitability clause.[114] Efforts were consequently marshalled in developing the particulars of an alternative continental shelf regime embodying the concept of fixed outer shelf limits consistent with the evolving domestic consensus on a national marine policy.[115] The pith and core of any such consensus relied on tethering the exploitability clause of the Continental Shelf Convention. It should, however, be constantly borne in mind that any continental shelf regime embodying the concept of fixed outer limits short of hypothetically drawn median lines between bordering coastal States – by way of either "depth" or "distance" criteria – was *lex ferenda* to the extent

---

Policy on the Oceans.

112 E. Wenk, *A New National Policy for Marine Resources* 1 NAT RES J no. 2, 3-13, at 12, announcing that the US government was under the study mode on the implications of alternative regimes related to off-shore minerals.

113 After surveying the field, Northcutt Ely thought he "likes the suggestion that Article 1 [of the Continental Shelf Convention] be amended to define the boundary of the continental shelf." Ely, NAT RES L, no. 2 at 82. *See also* McDougal, NAT RES L no. 2 at 99.

114 *Ibid. See also* N. Ely, *American Policy Options in the Development of Undersea Mineral Resources* NAT RES L, no. 1, 91-95 (1968); Henkin, *supra* note 24, at Chap. V.

115 For a discussion of the resolution of the controversy on whether to adopt a "wide shelf" definition of continental shelf limits, as favored by the mining industry and the Interior Department, or a "narrow shelf", favored by Defense, *see* Wenk, *supra* note 33, at 268-271.

that it contradicted the previously upheld literal, plain, and straightforward[116] interpretation of the exploitability clause.[117]

Simultaneous with a policy strategy that would consider the formal amendment of the Convention, the assertion of a US policy interest in favor of installing fixed continental shelf limits also took the strange form of a conceptual attack against the exploitability clause itself. Accordingly, it was thought necessary that there should be *read into* the exploitability clause the concept of a fixed or maximum outer limit to the continental shelf, short of geographically delimited median lines.[118] The erstwhile clarity and transparency of the exploitability criterion in the determination of the extent of the continental shelf

---

116 It is interesting to note that a "literal" reading of the exploitability clause, regarded as "moderate" in the late 1950s and early 1960s, *see* Young, *supra* note 71, at 733, was already condemned as "extreme" in 1969. E.D. Brown, *supra* note 86, at 243. By 1969, there was no longer anyone in the US, inside or outside government, who was publicly associated with the "literal" interpretation of the exploitability clause. For the consensus on "adjacency" as the operative term in defining "exploitability", *see* Henkin, *supra* note 71 and Finlay, *supra* note 71. In the United Kingdom, the sea change in attitude was also evident. Thus, in 1959, a member of the UK delegation to UNCLOS I praised the exploitability clause, notwithstanding the uncertainty in the definition of the continental shelf, as "a substantial contribution to progressive development in international law" and "in step with the considerable technical advances on exploitation of the shelf, and with the needs of the international community." Gutteridge, *supra* note 71, at 122, 123. A decade later, Professor Jennings characterized the "exploitability clause" as a "puzzling provision" and would for practical purposes regard it as *functus officio*! R.Y. Jennings, *The Limits of the Continental Shelf Jurisdiction: Some Possible Implications of the North Sea Case Judgement* 18 ICLQ 819, at 831-832 (1969).

117 Oda, *supra* note 65; *See also* Vienna Convention on the Law of Treaties, Articles 31-32.

118 Note that after the nodule controversy arose, the issue defined during the early stages of the debate centred on the *equivocal* character of the exploitability clause – meaning, its amenability to two alternative interpretations; on whether a limit was intended or not. *See* LSI 1966, note 34. As the debate unfolded further, the disputed point had become the *ambiguity* of an assumed continental shelf outer limit: "there is an outer limit, but where does it lie?" *See* debate between Mr. Finlay, and Prof. Henkin, *supra* note 71. *Cf.*, the issue about the *uncertainty of the extent* of the continental shelf as indicated in Young, *supra* note 71 and Gutteridge, *supra* note 71.

somehow became a real threat to US national interest. The defenders of US policy interests thus argued that the exploitability clause – only recently regarded as self-explanatory international law governing the seaward extent of resource activities on the ocean floor[119] – was "ambiguous", "defective", "imprecise", "elusive", "inadequate", "uncertain", or did not correctly reflect the intention of its framers.[120] In practical effect, while formal amendments to the Convention were being considered, there was already an unofficial attempt to amend or repeal the exploitability clause by persistent and stubborn re-interpretation, such that the position in law invariably coincided with the position in policy: the exploitability clause does not permit an open-ended definition of the extent of the continental shelf.[121] Evidently, included in the range of "alternatives"[122] to address the policy question of limits was the option of obfuscation – or interpreting the exploitability clause against its own terms, or against the meaning previously accorded it in State practice.

---

119 *Supra* notes 74, 76, 78 & 79 and accompanying texts.
120 *See* Burke, LSI *1966 supra* note 34, at 204-205, Burke, *supra* note 27, at 13: UNCLOS I delegates "were without sure guidance" in drafting the Continental Shelf Convention and "hard mineral exploitation was not considered by them as having a bearing on expansion of shelf limits"; Ely, *Exploiting the Oceans, supra* note 25, at 375: there is a "built-in ambiguity" in the definition of the continental shelf, "compounded by the method of drawing boundaries on the shelf"; Tubman, in *id.* at 381: intent of the UNCLOS I delegates was to use adjacency as criterion; Henkin, *supra* note 24, at 24: on the law governing deep ocean mining, "no one knows what the law is"; Belman, *supra* note 73: the exploitability clause is "unambiguously ambiguous"; Statement of Mr. Popper, *House Interim Report* at 53-54. Present textbook writers echo this collective mental state of the late 1960s as gospel truth. *See* Churchill & Lowe, *op. cit.* 125 [the exploitability clause "was itself an elusive criterion"]; E.D. Brown, *supra* note 88, at 19 [on the "vague character of the rules" and the "difficulty" in interpreting Article 1 of the Continental Shelf Convention].
121 In 1968, the Committee on Deep-Sea Mineral Resources of the American Branch of the International Law Association (with Mr. Northcutt Ely as Chair and Prof. William Burke as rapporteur) suggested that the outer limits of the continental shelf extend to the submerged portion of the continental land mass, pointing out that this would result from the proper interpretation of the Continental Shelf Convention, and provisionally proposed a depth of 2,500 meters as outer limit. *See* Oda, *supra* note 34, at 28-30; *Cf.* Henkin, *supra* note 71.
122 Wenk, *supra* note 112, at 13, appropriately speaks of "implications of alternative regimes" and "springboards for policy decision."

199

It is certainly one thing to state that the extent of the continental shelf is unquantified and uncertain, which was – from all indications – the legislative effect considered by the ILC and UNCLOS I.[123] And it is another thing to claim that the *intent of the law* defining the extent of the continental shelf is altogether vague and anomalous.[124] As it was mentioned earlier, the Continental Shelf Convention, tested against State practice up to the mid-1960s, was clear and unequivocal *de lege lata* in its definition of the continental shelf,[125] by using the alternative criteria of depth and exploitability in defining the extent and scope of its application *ratione loci*. It goes without saying that if the exploitability clause was inadequate and unsatisfactory from the standpoint of evolving domestic policy, the remedy would have been obviously to "delete it" from Article 1 of the Continental Shelf Convention, as Professor Goldie and others rightly maintained.[126] This would naturally require an amendment to the Convention through the normal treaty-making process.[127]

The question arises: what was sought to be accomplished by the attempt to unilaterally "amend" the exploitability clause through its re-interpretation?

If the whole argumentative exercise is seen as a legal strategy to consolidate a preferred law or policy for deep ocean mining, the whole purpose it seems

---

[123] *Supra* note 79.

[124] On the meaning of an uncertain and varying extent as the intent of the exploitability clause, *see* also Giddel, *supra* note 79. In the same manner, the outer limits of the territorial sea were not defined and determinable in any precise way in the 1960s, but this uncertainty could not have implied that the law of the territorial sea was vague and uncertain.

[125] *See supra* note 73 and accompanying text; *See also* Weissberg, *op. cit.* 83, lamenting that early State practice disregarded the principle of adjacency or depth, which he believes is integral to the exploitability clause.

[126] Goldie, in *LSI 1966, supra* note 34, at 278; Oda, *supra* note 75 at 113; Kreuger, *supra* note 36, at 16-18; *See also* Young, *supra* note 71, at 733.

[127] Thus the Netherlands Branch of the International Law Association in 1966 advised that the application of the exploitability test under the Convention would lead to the division of the ocean floor among the coastal States, and that it would be desirable to devise a legal regime for the exploration and exploitation of the mineral resources of the ocean floor on the basis of an international treaty. *See* Oda, *supra* note 34, at 10. *See also* Article 13 of the Continental Shelf Convention, which lays down the procedure for its amendment.

behind the historical campaign[128] to cast a cloud over a clear provision of law, or to re-state the exploitability clause by putting a short leash to its seaward extent – that is, to delimit the scope *ratione loci* of the continental shelf consistent with the dictates of big power interest as this had developed since the mid-1960s – is to force a recognition of the existence of a juridical or conceptual entity called "seabed and subsoil beyond the limits of the continental shelf." This would validate the conclusion, for example, that "where the continental shelf ends the deep seabed begins",[129] instead of "where the continental shelf ends is somebody else's continental shelf." This is a conclusion that is in itself innocuous because the terms used are consistent with the vocabulary of the geologist. But when it is viewed in the context of a legal framework for manganese nodule mining, it becomes a potent premise for policy and for legitimizing this policy. The factual existence *de lege ferenda* of this juridical entity is only icing to the cake. Generally, many States were then willing to go along with the proposition[130] that there is a portion of the seabed, not covered by the continental shelf, beyond national jurisdiction.[131] The crucial and most essential point behind the argument that there must be a seaward limit to the continental shelf, notwithstanding the exploitability clause, was to emphasize the argument that the continental shelf, conceptually, cannot or can no longer move towards hypothetical median lines dividing the entire ocean

---

128 The aphorism "repetition of a lie does not make it truth" is perhaps applicable to the widely reiterated claim that the exploitability clause admits of unspecified near-shore outer limits. It is beside the point whether the "lie" was consciously orchestrated as a policy design or not.
129 Henkin, *supra* note 24, at 24; Ely, *Exploiting the Oceans*, *supra* note 25, at 376.
130 *See* Weissberg, *op. cit.*; and *infra* Chapter IV.
131 Even advocates of internationalization wanted to have the concept of a "seabed beyond national jurisdiction" firmly established. *See* Christy and Eichelberger, *supra* note 36; Weissberg, *op. cit. See infra* Section B.4, on Ambassador Pardo's relevant arguments. *See also, Report of the Ad Hoc Committee to Study the Peaceful Uses of the Seabed and Ocean Floor Beyond the Limits of National Jurisdiction* UN GAOR 23rd Sess. (1968), para. 86:
As was implied in the terms of resolution 2340 (XXII) [creating the *Ad Hoc* Committee] the *Ad Hoc* Committee recognized the existence of an area of the sea-bed and the ocean floor underlying the high seas beyond the limits of national jurisdiction.

floor among all coastal States.¹³² Once this derived assumption or hypothetical construct was converted into a conclusive interpretation and accepted as a jural norm, *de facto* exploitation beyond the imagined outer limits would preclude the application of the continental shelf regime – a regime that would have accompanied and automatically governed such exploitation by virtue of the unqualified operation of the exploitability clause.¹³³ What is more, and this point cannot be underscored too much, the portion of the seabed not "encroached"¹³⁴ upon by the de-fanged exploitability clause remains possessed of its status under classical or customary law – *i.e.,* as part of the high seas. Nodule mining outside the "seabed beyond the continental shelf" becomes an exercise of the freedom of the seas!¹³⁵

But re-interpretation to accord with desire, no matter how honest, can only go so far. For assuming *arguendo* that the exploitability clause means *de lege lata* that there is indeed a fixed outer limit to the continental shelf, the next logical and practical question was more insuperable, and if not addressed immediately will somehow make the re-interpretation self-defeating. The

---

132 Note that in interpreting the "Hypothetical Map" drawn by Christy and Herfindahl, insert in *LSI 1967, supra* note 26, Professor Alexander describes it as portraying "how the pattern of national ownership of the oceans would appear if all nations were *free to advance* their boundaries out to the median lines." (emphasis supplied) *Id.* at iii. Since the mid-1960s, the imagery of a *physical movement* of the *limits* of the continental shelf – from the land outward to the sea – did have a considerable influence on lawyers' understanding of the *conceptual extent ratione loci* of the continental shelf. Thus, E.D. Brown, *supra* note 79, at 40, Churchill & Lowe, *op. cit.* at 125, allude to technology pushing the limits of the continental shelf "farther and farther from shore."

133 *Cf.* Arangio Ruiz, "Reflections on the Present and Future Regime of the Seabed in the Ocean" in *Rome Symposium, supra* note 86, at 296-297.

134 The terms "creeping jurisdiction" or "encroachments into high seas", used as pejorative terms in the 1960s, denote a directional movement that could prove misleading in the analysis of *lex lata*. Hence, if it is the case that the Continental Shelf Convention, through the exploitability clause, subdivides *de jure* all the world's ocean floor along median lines, Oda, *supra* notes 65 & 67, the scope of coastal State jurisdiction *ratione loci* can no longer "creep" towards the open seas.

135 This result would coincide with arguments then put forward by a political analyst that an elitist/exclusionist concept of power, or the balance of power among the States which "can effectively participate in the mutation of the world ocean", is a preferred mode to create public order for the oceans. J.W. Oswald, "Toward a Political Theory of the Ocean" in *Exploiting the Oceans, supra* note 25, at 358-372.

relevant follow-up question is: where exactly does the continental shelf end? or, where exactly is the seabed under the high seas where nodule mining can take place absolutely unmolested by the continental shelf regime? Surely this problem can no longer be "fixed" by constructive re-interpretation.[136] It is a predicament that certainly vindicated the unpopular position advanced by Professor Shigera Oda: because there is no fixed outer limit to the continental shelf set by the exploitability clause, the shadow of the continental shelf regime will always follow any nodule mining activity anywhere in the oceans.[137] The Continental Shelf regime, to paraphrase US Justice Oliver Wendel Holmes, was a brooding omnipresence on the ocean floor. An actual limit, therefore, had to be set. The need for an international agreement – and by implication, the dangerous agenda of internationalization – was quite inescapable.[138]

---

136 An extraordinary attempt to unofficially amend the Continental Shelf Convention, employing a highly involved argument that "general principle of law should illuminate the Convention's definition [of the continental shelf] and not the other way around" is given in Jennings, *supra* note 116. Because the exploitability clause "provides no reasonably practical and clear outer limit, within limits laid down by general law and embodied in the Convention itself in the term 'adjacency'", Professor Jennings contends, "it may well be, therefore, that the exploitability clause could now for practical purposes be regarded as *functus officio*, and the extent of continental shelf jurisdiction governed by the Convention be regarded as approximating to that sanctioned by general law." *See id.* at 821, 832. For a critique, *see infra* Chap. IV.

137 Oda, *supra* note 65, at 106. In supporting the proposals to amend the Continental Shelf Convention, Judge Oda submitted: "Thus the concept of exploitability in the Convention is based upon an incorrect view that the exploitation of submarine resources, while having not been heretofore allowed, became permissible only in terms of the concept of the continental shelf." His use of "incorrect" in this context is not meant to interpret the intent of the exploitability clause but to suggest *de lege ferenda* the more accurate rendering of an amended continental shelf regime.

138 *Cf.* E.D. Brown, *supra* note 79, at 40, on the suggestion concerning "like minded States – perhaps in regional groups – to declare their interpretation of the law on the outer limit of the Shelf", in the event of a failure to agree on the universally valid conventional limit. It is of course, possible, that if this solution would have been thought out, say, in 1966 or early 1967, there may have been no need for a Seabed Committee. The resort to the devise of "like-minded States" as an approach to international law-making with respect to the seabed will, however, prove extremely useful to some industrialized States in the mid-1970s and the 1980s. *See infra* Chap. IV.

In the *interim*, if the hidden assumption behind the legal argument for fixed limits is not appreciated for what it is – that is, as a mere policy assumption that has no basis in positive law – the imagined "seabed beyond the continental shelf" will appear as a most compelling legal reality.[139] The consequences of this legal argument on the practical and programmatic pursuit of an internationalization policy for the deep ocean floor could be devastating indeed. Put simply, if the current policy proposals to internationalize the deep seabed fail, and for as long as any internationalization policy is not yet part of positive law, mining activities on the deep seabed "beyond national jurisdiction" will have to be governed, by default, by the customary regime of freedom on the high seas.[140] This was in fact the well-trodden argumentative tract that was officially advanced by the United States and some of its allies in the course of UNCLOS III,[141] and after UNCLOS III.[142] Nonetheless, if it is considered

---

139 It is interesting to note that Professor Jennings, in *supra* note 116, at 821, proves the objective existence of this seabed beyond the continental shelf by citing the Report of the *Ad Hoc* Committee, *supra* note 131, and divining that "this [para. 86: that there is a seabed outside the continental shelf] is a principle which can stand on its own feet and is not merely a deduction from a proper interpretation of Article 1 of the Convention...." The argument was evidently directed at Professor Oda's more simple argument that the exploitability clause means what it says, *i.e.*, there is no "seabed beyond the continental shelf." For a defence of the Report of the *Ad Hoc* Committee consistent with the thesis of Judge Oda, *see infra* Chap. IV.

140 This was the argument of E.D. Brown, in *supra* note 86, who thought that customary international law provides a bare but utilizable legal framework for seabed mining, based on the freedom principle, pending the amendment of the continental shelf convention. Professor McDougal, in 1 NAT RES L at 21, expressing his opposition to "great multilateral conventions" and the policy of internationalization, urged that "it would be best for us to continue in reliance upon traditional customary processes." *See also* K.R. Simmonds (Rapporteur), *The Resources of the Ocean Bed Report of a Conference at Ditchley Park*, 26-29 September 1969 (The Ditchley Foundation, 1969), at 38: "The international law which governs a regime of the ocean bed must be built upon existing law, with special reference to the law of the high seas."

141 *See* for *e.g.*, US Deep Seabed Hard Mineral Resources Act of 1980, Sec. 3 (a)(1), 19 ILM 1003 (1980); UK Deep Sea Mining (Temporary Provisions) Act of 1981, item 7 on "Freedom of the Seas." Text in II E.D. Brown, *The International Law of the Sea* 349 (1994).

that the entire deep ocean floor had the potential status of seamless continental shelf with respect to any resource activity therein – and that this was not only the conventional but also the customary law before the nodule controversy arose – there is actually no room for the operation of the freedom of the seas-doctrine.[143] Moreover, if it is recalled that this legal argument, historically, was based on the confusion of international law with domestic policy preference, or the unwarranted joinder of *lex lata* and *lex ferenda*, it surely loses much of its doctrinal integrity and objective persuasiveness.

Those who advocated internationalization could surely be said to have a radically different version or legal theory of how the "seabed beyond national jurisdiction" came to be realized as a juristic notion. This is explored in the next Chapter in relation to the evolution of the Common Heritage of Humanity principle as a jural postulate. It is a theory, sad to say, that has not been listened to hard enough, perhaps because of its non-systematic, non-aggressive articulation and slow evolution during the UN seabed debates in the late 1960s. This theory, in contrast to the US posture on the exploitability clause drawn above,

---

142 *See* Provisional Understanding Regarding Deep Seabed Matters among Belgium, Federal Republic of Germany, France, Italy, Japan, the Netherlands, the United Kingdom, and the United States, 3 August 1984, 23 ILM 1354 (1984). For a discussion of the "reciprocating States regime" based on the doctrine of freedom of the seas, *see* E.D. Brown, *Seabed Energy and Mineral Resources and the Law of the Sea* vol. II, at Chap. 8 (1986).

143 Dr. E.D. Brown in his major treatise on the subject in 1986 casually concluded that before Malta launched its initiative in 1967, seabed mining was a legitimate user of the high seas. He did not, however, make any reference to the intervention of the 1958 Continental Shelf Convention in his analysis of the pre-1967 regime, nor did he recall the difficulties he encountered in 1969 when he contemplated advocating a regime of freedom for deep seabed mining. These difficulties stemmed from the undefined "outer limits" of the continental shelf, and seemed insuperable because he justified his argument using the highly subjective and controversial "adjacency" thesis concerning the extent of the continental shelf under the exploitability clause. E.D. Brown, *id.*, at Chap. 2. *Cf.* E.D. Brown, *supra* note 86. In 1971, Dr. Brown, *supra* note 79, at 36, using a rather circuitous and evidently self-serving definition of "adjacency", reached the conclusion that the continental shelf beyond the territorial sea is "*Either* not more than 200 metres in depth *or, if greater than 200 metres, of such depth that the natural resources of the sea-bed and subsoil are exploitable*" (exploitability understood as "economically feasible exploitability") but that it should be "*not more than a reasonable, but yet to be defined, distance from the coast.*" (emphasis supplied)

accepts the necessity of dealing with the exploitability clause of the Geneva Continental Shelf Convention on its own terms, and recognizes the need to abandon or repeal the exploitability clause in an orderly and rational fashion – to have legal principle guide and direct national policy, and not *vice versa*.

4. The Omnipresence of the Continental Shelf

Ambassador Pardo shared the belief that the 1958 Continental Shelf Convention must be re-examined and accordingly formally revised if the internationalization project he proposed was to be successfully implemented.[144] He did not, however, take an explicit position on the question of "outer limits" of the continental shelf, but instead preferred to survey scholarly commentary and State practice on the subject[145] which, he argued, justify the conclusion that "current international law encourages the appropriation of this vast area by those who have the technical competence to exploit it."[146] Implied in his conclusion is the prominent thesis advanced by Professor Oda, quoted by Ambassador

---

144 The title of Malta's proposed Agenda item was "Declaration and Treaty concerning ..." but was changed to "Examination of the question of ..." to deflect the objections of the Latin American representatives who insisted that the item should be allocated to the Sixth (legal) Committee. UN GAOR Fifth Committee, 1224th Session. The full elaboration of Malta's proposal to adopt an appropriate UN General Assembly Declaration, and subsequently a treaty, that would effect an amendment to the 1958 Continental Shelf Convention was made by Ambassador Pardo in his November speech to the UN. PV 1515-1516, esp. para. 10 & 12. The changes in the wording of the agenda title put forward by Malta are, however, significant, with a three-fold effect:

... first of all, [the amendments] eliminated, at least for the time being, any possibility of change in positive law; as a result, the examination of the question was limited to a discussion of a political, or even socio-economic, nature; and lastly, it did not prejudice the possibility that States might extend the limits of their national jurisdiction.

See A. de Marffy, *supra* Chap. II note 37, at 143. Note also that while the original proposal refers to seabed "underlying the *seas* beyond the limits", the reworded item alluded to the seabed "underlying the *high seas* beyond the limits."

145 PV 1515, para. 63-69.
146 PV 1515, para. 56 & 90.

Pardo, that "all the submerged lands of the world are necessarily parts of the continental shelf by the very definition of the Convention."[147]

Professor Oda's assessment of the exploitability clause was a direct challenge to any proposition that there is an area of the seabed "beyond the continental shelf."[148] It is important to bear in mind that this assessment is true only in respect of resource jurisdiction on or under the seabed.[149] As Professor Oda explained, there certainly *is* a seabed outside or beyond national jurisdiction for military or non-resource purposes, which consists, technically, of the seabed that lies beyond the territorial sea – meaning, including the continental shelf.[150] This distinction between the *ratione loci* of the economic/continental shelf dimension of internationalization policy and the *ratione loci* of its peace dimension was never really appreciated in its fullness during the seabed debates in the late 1960s, and was largely forgotten thereafter. It is, however, a powerful distinction which, on hindsight, does clarify and strengthen the logic and essential legal argument for internationalization.[151]

In the context of a multi-dimensional programme for internationalization as proposed by Ambassador Pardo, the rationale for the distinction put forward by Professor Oda is to force a recognition that there are several functional regimes that are simultaneously operative in the deep seabed as a physical medium – what Northcutt Ely calls the "piece of real estate"[152] in question. In classical international law, the position was fairly straightforward, with jurisdiction or authority determined on the basis of locus: either an activity is covered by the regime of the territorial sea, or it is an exercise of the freedom of the high seas.[153] But the notion of the continental shelf introduced by the United States in 1945, which was eventually recognized in UNCLOS I, trans-

---

147 PV 1515, para. 67.
148 Another publicist supported this thesis. M. Sorensen, *Manual of Public International Law* (1968) at 40-41: "the continental shelf is part of the bed of the high seas bordering on the territorial sea."
149 The Continental Shelf is a special resource zone and non-resource oriented activities therein like the laying of submarine cables and pipelines are governed by the doctrine of freedom. *See* Art. 2(1) in relation to Arts. 3, 4, 5 (1), Geneva Convention on the Continental Shelf.
150 S. Oda, "Future Regime of the Deep Ocean Floor" in *Rome Symposium, supra* note 86, at 343-361.
151 *See* further below and, *infra* Chap. IV.
152 Ely, *LSI 1966* at 174.
153 Jessup, *supra* Chap. II note 64, at 5; Colombos, *supra* Chap. II note 64.

formed the classical neatness of customary law that had always relied on a uni-dimensional understanding of the law of the sea.[154] Co-existing with the territorial/locus system of jurisdictional allocation was now a special regime of the continental shelf that is justified on the theory that function determines authority.[155] Thus, beyond the territorial sea, if the activity involved is the

---

[154] F.A. Vallat, commenting on Sir Cecil Hurst's views on the horizontal delimitation of sovereignty effected via the continental shelf regime, states:
This horizontal division is a comparatively new idea, but there does not seem to be any compelling logical or practical reason why the earth, the sea and the surrounding space should not be divided horizontally as well as vertically. Indeed ... it is very likely that scientific progress will in time require a horizontal limitation on the extent of the space above the territory of a state which is subject to its sovereignty.
Quoted in Mouton, *supra* note 38, at 333.

[155] Noteworthy is an early comment by the US government in the International Law Commission in 1951, on the juridical nature of the continental shelf that defined its extent according to the test of exploitability:
"This Government wonders, accordingly, whether it would not be advisable to make it clear, at least in the commentaries, that controls and jurisdiction for the purpose indicated is the draft articles mean in fact an exclusive, but functional, right to explore and exploit."
Quoted in Mouton, *supra* at 331. *See also* Marston, *supra* note 85, at 47, for the view that the continental shelf is not a territorial but a functional regime ["the continental shelf is not territory but an extra-territorial area where the coastal state exercises certain functions in respect of certain resources"]. The "functional" approach to legal competence, dictated by what Professor Douglas Johnston aptly calls "hypertechnical logic" of the post-war "technological order of the sea", was seen as increasingly predominant in the international legal order. The social and strategic implications of this observation, in terms of the evolution of the structure of unshared authority at sea, is developed in D.M. Johnston, *supra* note 79, at 226 *et seq.* [the continental shelf doctrine implements the idea that substance is superior to form], and sharply extended in D.M. Johnston, *Law, Technology, and the Sea* 55 CALIF L REV 449-472 (1967).
The functional approach to maritime claims, which had blossomed into the "exclusive economic zone" in the new law of the sea, is traceable to the off-shore claims of the Latin American States in the later 1940s and 1950s – the progeny of the US continental shelf claim in 1945. Extavour, *op. cit.* 141. For a functional analysis of the 1958 Conventions *see* Garcia-Amador, *The Exploitation and Conservation of the Resources of the Sea* (1960), esp. the notion of "new specialized competences" at 67 *et seq.*

laying of submarine cables and pipelines on the seabed,[156] or the conduct of fundamental scientific research therein,[157] the applicable regime is freedom of the high seas. On the other hand, if the purpose is to explore and exploit resources on or under the same seabed,[158] coastal State authority, through the continental shelf doctrine is the operative rule.[159] If practical conflict en-

---

156 Art. 4, Continental Shelf Convention; Art. 2(3), Convention on the High Seas.
157 Article 5, *id.*, makes clear that exploration or exploitation activities in the continental shelf must not result "in any interference with fundamental oceanographic or other scientific research carried out with the intention of open publication."
158 Article 2(4) defines the resources covered by the continental shelf doctrine as including "mineral and other non-living resources of the seabed and the subsoil." The attempt to exclude manganese nodules as a type of seabed resource covered by the continental shelf regime on the ground that the ILC or the delegates of UNCLOS I were simply concerned with one type of exploitation – oil drilling from surface installations – and did not contemplate mineral exploitation is plainly contrary to this definition, and is inconsistent with the functional/non-vertical character of jurisdiction that underpins the continental shelf regime. Burke, *supra* note 27, at 13-14. *Cf.* literature cited in *supra* note 155.
159 "The nature of this [continental shelf] extension of State competence must be defined in the light of the purpose ['exploration and exploitation of the natural resources'] for which the rights are recognized." Garcia Amador, *op. cit.* 94. Dr. Colombos, using the traditional/vertical territorial conceptions of authority, *e.g.* appropriation by occupation, seems to be puzzled why the Continental Shelf Convention did not distinguish activities on the seabed and activities on the subsoil. Specifically, he claims that the status of the bed of the high seas is the same as the superjacent waters, and the legal position of the subsoil – which is capable of occupation through tunneling or directional drilling without interference to traditional freedoms – allows for exclusive appropriation. Properly understood as a functional regime, *supra* note 155, the continental shelf doctrine of course makes obsolete any distinctions of this kind offered by Dr. Colombos. See J. Colombos, *supra* at 67 *et seq.* Note that Colombos puts his discussion of the continental shelf under the heading "High Seas." This orthodoxy of analyzing the continental shelf as an areal grant of jurisdiction is carried over in Jennings, *supra* note 116, and E.D. Brown, *supra* note 79. Dr. Brown emphasized that in determining the "adjacency" of the continental shelf, the idea is to focus on *areas* rather than *points*, the latter being the test adopted by the International Court in the North Sea Continental Shelf Cases, *id.* at 34-35; the idea of *points* where sovereign rights could be exercised under the continental shelf doctrine is consistent with a functional definition of jurisdiction. Furthermore in *id.* at 31, Dr. Brown employs what he calls a "functional interpretation" to support his view that there is a necessity for "outer limits" to the continental shelf. He maintains that the

sues as a result of the superimposition of multiple regimes on the same space of the seabed, accommodation of uses based on the classical concept of reasonableness comes into play.[160]

It is this functional logic that underlies the exclusive allocation of authority or jurisdiction in the Convention on the Continental Shelf. From this functional perspective, it is therefore a mistake to say that the ILC or UNCLOS I was creating a paradox by providing rules for mineral exploitation in the continental shelf but not rules for mineral exploitation in the "subsoil" of the high seas.[161]

---

overriding aim of the Convention is to provide the necessary degree of security to exploiters. There seems to be a misleading analysis being made here, whereby "a condition for a function" is identified with the "function" itself underlying the regime, *i.e.*, the exploration and exploitation of resources. Moreover, there is at all no reason to believe why the literal interpretation of the exploitability clause means less security for exploiters, assuming proper delimitations lines are agreed upon. Again, there seems to be a self-serving interpretation of "functionalism" in this context that begs the whole question of what functionalism is. The purported argument seems to be: "if functionalism means security or title while this security means fixed limits, then functionalism means fixed limits."

160 Articles 4 and 5(1) of the Convention on the Continental Shelf, specifies the applicable concepts in the accommodation of uses, like "reasonable measures" or "unjustifiable interference." On the concept of "reasonableness", *see* Churchill & Lowe, *op. cit.* 166-168.

161 The existence of this "paradox" is alleged in Buzan, *op. cit.* 24, based on his interpretation of the oft-quoted commentary of the ILC to Article 2 of the 1958 High Seas Convention, which reads:

The Commission has not made specific mention of the freedom to explore or exploit the subsoil of the high seas. It considered that apart from the case of the exploitation of the soil or the subsoil of the continental shelf... such exploitation had not yet assumed sufficient practical importance to justify special regulation. II ILC YRBK at 278 (1956). It is significant to note that the high seas area referred to is only the "subsoil" of the high seas and does not refer to resources or nodules on the seabed. Morell, *op. cit.* 12-13, subscribes to the idea of a paradox by claiming that:

By distinguishing the continental shelf from the subsoil of the high seas and expressly leaving the latter area unregulated [sic], the [International law] Commission thus by implication confirmed the existence of a portion of the ocean floor which would remain beyond the limits of national jurisdiction, the exploitability clause notwithstanding.

Churchill & Lowe, *op. cit.* at 178-179, goes much further by claiming that the ILC regarded activities like nodule mining as subject to the general principle of the freedom of the high seas, and that this view was "widely accepted" in UNCLOS

While it is quite accurate to say that a "seabed beyond national jurisdiction" exists for activities such as the laying of submarine cables and pipelines, or military activities,[162] it is somewhat presumptuous to assume *a priori* the existence of a "seabed and subsoil beyond the continental shelf" for the purpose of exploring and exploiting the resources[163] of such seabed.[164] By virtue of its functional, rather than areal, scope, the application of the continental shelf doctrine under the Convention, specifically its exploitability clause, is informed by dynamic, potentially destabilizing technological facts as well as conditions of innovation and capability, and not static elements like depth or distance.[165] Within this normative conceptualization, it is logical to speak of the extent of the continental shelf and the problems associated with the uncertainties created by the stipulation of an open-ended spatial reach of the regime,[166] but it would

---

I – without, however, giving any corroborating evidence.

162 'Military activities' is not explicitly identified as a freedom of the high seas in the Geneva Convention on the High Seas or the 1982 Convention, but has been interpreted as covered by this regime via the *"inter alia"* clause in the definition of high seas freedoms. *See e.g., San Remo Manual on International Law Applicable to Armed Conflicts at Sea* 8 & 14 (L. Doswald-Beck, Ed., 1995) at Section IV, para. 10 and Section IV.

163 The exclusion of certain resources, notably living resources, from the continental shelf should be noted. Thus, as per Article 2(4) of the Convention, living resources that are not sedentary species are excluded from the regime.

164 Professor Scelle, in his criticism of the continental shelf doctrine, foresaw the futility of a freedom of the high seas regime for seabed natural resources beyond what was then understood as the continental shelf:
Adoption of the concept whereby the continental shelf extended as far as exploitation of natural resources of the seabed was possible would tend to abolish the domain of the high seas.
I ILC YRBK at 135 (1965).

165 *Supra* note 79, esp. Young, *supra* note 71, at 733 and 735; Gutteridge, *supra* note 71.

166 *Ibid.* As Young, *supra* note 71, at 735, considered, the uncertainty around the extent of the continental shelf can be cured by post-UNCLOS I administrative arrangements that would assist in ascertaining, verifying and publishing data about the latest exploitation limits, which would then lead to a determination of the outer limits of the Continental Shelf for all parties to the Convention. The commercial angle of this kind of uncertainty was considered by Ely when he was still in a ruminating mood concerning the exploitability clause:
If some stranger proves, by doing it, that wells can be drilled at very great depth at a distance of hundred miles from the nearest coast, then, if this language means

not make sense to talk about limits that would negate the very concept of open-endedness intended in the functional norm.[167] In familiar mathematical terminology, a "constant" is not a "function": there is no part of *juridical constant* (in this case the seabed beyond the territorial sea) that is unaffected by a *normative function* (in this case the technology or economics of resource exploration and exploitation).[168] More to the point, the applicable law had already been anticipated wherever the contemplated function is discharged or the relevant activity undertaken.

By the combined operation of the principle of inherent rights[169] and the principle of reciprocity, every coastal State is entitled "to assert rights off its

---

    what it says, he has automatically established, ex post facto, the exclusive jurisdiction of some coastal state which was incapable of this technical exploit itself, did not license this exploration, indeed, never heard about it, but now acquires sovereign powers to prohibit it, or police its operations, and collect taxes and royalties and control disposition of production. Is the coastal state bound to maintain order in this new outpost of its sovereignty and protect it from other powers? What are the limits, if any, on this ex post facto jurisdiction, if aimed away from any other islands below the horizon?

    Ely, *LSI 1966* at 177, and in *Exploiting the Oceans, supra* note 25, at 375. This quotation reveals the cynical attitude within the US mining industry, earlier expressed by Mero, about nodule mining taking place in the potential continental shelf of a coastal State other than the United States. *See supra* note 96 and accompanying text.

167 *See* Gutteridge, *supra* note 71; Young, *supra* note 71; and Kreuger, *supra* note 36, at 4, 7: there were no alternatives to exploitability, like a distance test or an 'adjacency' test, that could have been acceptable in the ILC and UNCLOS I. The "exploitability" alternative was employed precisely the avoid the difficulties associated with either a depth or a distance criterion. Barry, *supra* note 73, at 47.

168 Because of the dual criteria employed in Article 1 to define the continental shelf, the issue of outer limits *ratione loci* for economic purposes could be more accurately framed using the reference "seabed and subsoil beyond the 200-meter depth" rather than "seabed and subsoil beyond national jurisdiction." As Professor Oda states: "there can be no valid discussion of the *outer limits* of the continental shelf or of any areas *beyond* the continental shelf under the Geneva Convention." Oda, *supra* note 65, at 105. The only implied "outer limits" are, obviously, the delimitation lines drawn between opposite or adjacent States, in accordance Article 6 of the Convention.

169 Article 2(3), Continental Shelf Convention; *North Sea Continental Shelf Cases*, 1969 ICJ Rep at 3, para. 19.

shores out to the maximum depth for exploitation reached anywhere in the world, regardless of its own capabilities or of local conditions other than depth, which might prevent exploitation."[170] This consequence flowing from the exploitability clause surely had distributive implications, already discussed, that were found detestable in US policy.[171] Present-day commentators, however, ignore the egoistic basis of this policy interest, and instead direct their attention solely to the seemingly altruistic, publicly-stated reasons for the denunciation of the exploitability clause in the late 1960s – namely, that a mid-ocean division of the continental shelf by the outward push of actual continental shelf limits would have benefitted only a few technologically-advanced States.[172] In brief, the inequality flowing from the concept of exclusive jurisdiction under the Continental Shelf doctrine was sought to be replaced by the more assured inequality that was conceivable under a freedom of the seas regime.

In 1958 it was perhaps possible, for purposes of discussion, to refer to an actual, empirically verifiable seabed "beyond the continental shelf" for possible resource exploitation, simply because the capabilities for exploiting such areas were not yet there. The situation in law, however, was already settled inasmuch as "all the submerged lands of the world are necessarily part of the continental shelf by the very definition of the Convention."[173] This implicit normative framework for any seabed activity embedded in the functional logic of the exploitability clause was subjected to pervasive criticism only in the mid-1960s,[174] when the technology to exploit manganese nodules in the deepest

---

170 Young, *supra* note 71, at 735. This view is consistent with the inherent rights doctrine underlying the continental shelf: actual exploitation of resources beyond the 200-meter depth is not required for continental shelf rights to attach.
171 *Supra* at 192-196.
172 *See e.g.,* Churchill & Lowe, *op. cit.* 125-126.
173 Oda, *supra* note 65, at 105.
174 In the discussion of the legal status of the "seabed beyond national jurisdiction" for resource exploitation purposes, it is, therefore, more appropriate to focus on the technological/economic developments occurring in the early and the mid-1960s, than on the Maltese intervention of 1967 which had little to contribute by way of clarifying the *lex lata* of the continental shelf. *Cf.* E.D. Brown, *supra* note 142, at Chap 2.

parts of the ocean was already widely known to be as accessible.[175] Only then were political problems about actual and legal limits perceived because the possibility became very imminent that median lines will become *the* continental shelf outer limits. The issue, therefore, was no longer whether "exploitability" in the definition of the Convention was moving the continental shelf further seaward, or whether the continental shelf should be qualified henceforth as "economically feasible exploitability"[176] rather than "technological exploitability"[177] in order to fix the *transient* geographic limits of an uncertain continental shelf boundary. The main problem was that "exploitability" had reached its utmost *functional limits* brought about by the inescapable certainty that median lines will have to be drawn very soon as a result of exploration and exploitation of manganese nodules.[178] As it was already shown, what caused alarm in the United States was neither the hazily drawn outer limits of the continental shelf nor the hypothetical division of the seabed along median lines,

---

175 Mero's book is the best evidence to support the argument that manganese nodules have become exploitable in a technological sense, although the economics of the metal markets prevented their commercial exploitation. Mero, *supra* note 37, at 252-280. On the feasibility of deep sea mining from an engineering or technological standpoint, *see also* C.G. Welling & M.J. Cruickshank, "Review of Available Hardware Needed for Undersea Mining"; N.E. Montgomery, "Drilling in the Sea from Floating Platforms"; D.W. Clark, "Telemanipulator Systems for Deep-Sea Operations", all in *Exploiting the Oceans, supra* note 25.

176 E.D. Brown, *supra* note 86, at 244. The "economic" test to exploitability was perhaps advanced in the expectation that the outer limits of the continental shelf, short of median lines, could be restrained in their movement seaward by its invocation. This is surely unavailing, for a temporal delay in the implementation of a functional regime does not change the scope of this regime *ratione loci*.

177 This test was advanced by Young, *supra* note 71, at 745.

178 Outside of the vested interests that clamoured for the fixing of continental shelf outer limits, those who contemplated the "median lines" implication of the exploitability clause by late 1960s must have been extremely bothered by the prospects of overwhelming political problems and costs that will arise as a result of demands for continental shelf delimitation all over the world. The intricacies – and uncertainties – of delimitation, through the International Court (demonstrated by the *North Sea Continental Shelf* decision which was rendered by a majority of 11 to 6) or otherwise, may have greatly reinforced the urgent conviction to have fixed "outer limits" in both *lex ferenda* and *lex lata*. *See* for *e.g.*, E.D. Brown, *supra* note 79, at 70-71, on his assessment that the *North Sea* Judgement will "open the door to abusive and vexatious litigation in other parts of the world."

both of which were already accomplished way back in 1958 when the exploitability clause was approved as such in conventional law. Instead, it was the prospect of an imminent or actual delimitation of the deep seabed among all coastal States – an extremely dangerous development not only to US deep sea mining interests but also to US strategic interests as a whole. It was then that the functional language and spirit of the exploitability clause was sought to be modified by a proposed reinterpretation. The motivation, however, was the same as that when the United States unilaterally claimed a continental shelf in 1945: to obtain assured access, or practical access only by a very few technologically capable States, to resources; but this time under the regime of freedom of the seas.[179]

In closing, it is also important to point out one more obstacle, other than the trend already current in the United States, to reinterpret the Convention, that kept the legal status of the deep ocean bed from clear view. Ironically, this obstacle relates to the projection of a multi-dimensional internationalization programme by Ambassador Pardo himself – a projection which took as its starting point an unmitigated political assault against the exploitability clause. The effect could not have been more favourable to the preferred interpretation of the exploitability clause that elicited the demand for fixed "outer limits" before a formal amendment of the Convention was effected.

The almost unanimous excoriation of a "national lakes" approach to the division of the world's seabed areas – initially by the advocates of internationalization in the United States – had the effect, intended or not, of reinforcing the view that there *ought to be* limits to the actual seaward advance of the continental shelf.[180] It is thus not surprising that during the early stages

---

179 To paraphrase Professor Douglas Johnston, whether exclusive access is denominated as "sovereignty", or "sovereign rights", or "jurisdiction", or "freedom", or even "common heritage", from a functionalist perspective the substance of unshared authority is more important than form. D.M. Johnston, *supra* note 79, at 233.
180 Christy, *supra* note 36. Dr. Christy, himself not a lawyer, condemned the open-endedness of the exploitability clause and argued that there should be a limit to the continental shelf. On the assumption that there is a limit, he then guessed that there are no rules to govern the area behind the limit, at which point he suggested "alternatives that may be considered in the search for a regime to govern the minerals of the sea floor" – one of which he christened the "national lakes" approach. Unfortunately, in the terminological confusion that often takes place in the dialogue between lawyers and non-lawyers, and even among lawyers, pro-

of the nodule controversy in the US, a unique common ground was forged between those who favoured internationalization and those opposed to it: there was a consensus that the outer limits of the continental shelf should be specified.[181] Although their respective motivations for desiring a fixed limit and for wanting to wish away the exploitability clause may have been different,[182] the "realists" and the "idealists"[183] were joined in the shared cause of desiring fixed and ascertainable outer limits to the continental shelf.

This policy preference for fixed outer limits provided a silent major premise in Ambassador Pardo's presentation before the United Nations. But he took a further step and associated the Continental Shelf Convention, specifically the exploitability clause, with each and every evil that was sought to be overcome by his multi-dimensional internationalization agenda. On closer examination it would seem that this association, developed on a highly emotive plane, may have contributed to a confused and confusing legal assessment of the Continental Shelf Convention.

In the first place, Ambassador Pardo was emphatic that it was not in the best interest of the developing coastal States to have the ocean floor divided

---

fessor Oda's thesis – that the entirety of the world's seabed was by definition continental shelf *de lege lata* – was identified with the "national lakes approach" of Dr. Christy. Worse, Professor Oda's assessment was dismissed outright as an unacceptable option or policy alternative, rather than taken for what it is as a statement of positive law. *See* 1 NAT RES J 63-67, 99; *see also* Jennings, *supra* note 116, at 821, using the term "extension of national lakes" to dismiss outright a literal or denotative reading of the exploitability clause.

181 For e.g. *See* Christy, *supra* note 36; and Ely, in NAT RES L; Henkin, *supra* note 24. Mr. Danzig was also in favour of fixed outer limits, Weissberg, *op. cit.* 79 note 197.

182 Dr. Christy for instance, joins the "realists" (who according to Judge Oda are those who oppose internationalization *e.g.*, Mr. Ely and Prof. Burke) in his arguments against the "national lakes" approach: it is not good for US national interest. Kreuger, *supra* note 36, argues that the concept of a limit to the expansion of the continental shelf will assist in realizing the no-grab policy announced by President Johnson in his July 1966 statement. Ambassador Pardo's case against the "national lakes" approach is elaborated in PV 1515, para. 70-72.

183 Oda (1977), *supra* at 6, describes as "idealists" those proposing international control of deep seabed resources, and "realists" those opposing.

along median lines.[184] Fired by the conviction that the division of the deep ocean bed among littoral States would further aggravate the already serious gap between rich and poor nations, Ambassador Pardo may have unwittingly reinforced the belief, if not produced the impression, that the legal subdivision of the ocean floor envisaged by the Convention floor will still have to take place *in futuro* as a juridical fact. The message that the widening North-South gap could be stopped or reversed by stifling the forward march of the continental shelf seaward through the imposition of limits to its outward reach is certainly an acceptable statement *de lege ferenda*. But this hardly describes the situation in *lex lata*, inasmuch as the Convention, in principle, had already allocated the seabed among coastal States way back in 1958.[185] The coastal State "grab" was *fait accompli*.

Secondly, Ambassador Pardo gave the impression that the Continental Shelf Convention, or the progressive parcelling out of the seabed on account of the exploitability clause, would restrict the rights of the maritime powers in their defensive uses of the sea.[186] The reference to the Continental Shelf Convention was perhaps unnecessary and unwarranted in this context, because as a functional regime solely concerned with jurisdiction over resources, the continental shelf doctrine had only a minimal if not a non-existent connection to military activities at sea.[187]

---

184 "Under-developed states fronting on an ocean might believe that a division of the ocean floor of the world would be advantageous to them. This is a complete – and I should like to reinforce this – an utter illusion." PV 1515, para. 70.

185 Professor Scelle, in a 1955 article "Plateau Continental et Droit International" argued that:
The existence of the continental shelf is evidently bound to magnify considerably the de facto inequalities between States.... Some coastal States will be able to exploit it, while others will be unable to do so.
Quoted in de Marffy, *supra* Chap. II note 37, at 146. *See also* D.M. Johnston, *supra* note 155.

186 "It is even less credible that technologically advanced countries, encouraged by the terminology of the juridical masterpiece produced by the International Law Commission, would agree to adopt a restrictive interpretation of their rights under the Geneva Convention when their defense needs are directly involved." PV 1515, para. 71.

187 In addition, Ambassador Pardo stated that even the traditional freedom of the seas will be endangered by the militarization of the oceans encouraged by the Convention on the Continental Shelf. para. 71 & 72. This statement may have been made to recruit a wider base of sympathy and political support for Malta's initiative,

Lastly, even the problem of dumping of radio-active wastes on the ocean floor was blamed directly on the Continental Shelf Convention.[188] The role of the 1958 Convention on the High Seas was somehow minimized in the pollution problem,[189] although it could have been more logical to impute the responsibility for ocean contamination on those States which pollute the marine environment in their exercise, or abuse, of high seas freedoms.[190]

It then turns out that the "seabed beyond the limits of national jurisdiction" that should be put under the discipline of the peace, environmental, and (partly-) developmental dimensions of Malta's internationalization proposal consisted of the "seabed beyond national jurisdiction" that was then currently governed by the regime of the high seas. Any negotiated legal framework for the internationalization of the seabed underlying the high seas, therefore, should have contended with the established regime of freedom of the high seas.

On the other hand, internationalizing the "seabed beyond national jurisdiction" to address meaningfully the economic-cum-technical, developmental, and (partly) environmental dimensions of the project must also have been made to reckon with the regime of the continental shelf, and the notion of exclusive

---

especially from the traditional maritime States with an extreme sensitivity to the slightest threats against their traditional freedoms at sea. But as Professor Oda observed, an inaccurate legal assessment was being made here that tends mainly to confusion: the regime of the continental shelf is quite irrelevant to the military or non-military uses of the seabed beyond the territorial sea. It should also be remembered that it was precisely the regime of freedom of the seas that allowed the military powers to emplace offensive or defensive weapons on the continental shelves of other nations. Oda, *supra* note 150, at 343-344. *See also San Remo Manual on International Law applicable to Armed Conflicts at Sea*, *supra* note 162, at Sec. IV (36) & (37) on the concept of accommodation of military and other uses in the "high seas and the sea-bed beyond national jurisdiction."

188 "By encouraging the plurality of national jurisdictions on the sea floor, the Geneva Convention [on the Continental Shelf], unfortunately, also impedes a solution, beneficial to all countries, of the grave problems of disposal of radio-active wastes." PV 1515, para. 73.

189 PV 1515, para. 74.

190 Looking back at the Maltese move, Ambassador Pardo recalls that the real motivation behind his internationalization proposal was to attack the principle of freedom of the seas. A. Pardo, *The Origins of the 1967 Maltese Initiative* 9 INTERNATIONAL INSIGHTS 65, at 69 (1993). *Quarae*: whether it was a tactical move on his part to have presented the internationalization cause as a case exclusively against the exploitability clause embodied in the Continental Shelf Convention.

coastal State authority implicit in its functional definition of jurisdiction over the seabed. It turns out that the case against the exploitability clause was nothing more than a case against a special application of the principle of coastal State sovereignty.

Two general principles of regulation – formerly understood as mutually exclusive or even antithetical to each other – are thus surprisingly locked together as the operative norms in the same object, both preserving a *status quo* that was sought to be overturned by the movement of internationalization. Freedom and sovereignty – the two great pillars of the classical law of the sea – were simultaneously implicated as the normative regimes that stood in the way of realizing the vision to internationalize the deep seabed. It is an extraordinary ambition to challenge the authority and stature of both freedom and sovereignty at the same time. And there is nothing in the historical record to show that such an attempt had ever been undertaken. Is there an alternative principle of regulation in the law of the sea that does not rely, in one way or another, on either the fundamental doctrines of freedom or sovereignty? In short, a truly multi-dimensional internationalization programme would have to offer an alternative foundation to the international law of the sea. Could it be that the "common heritage of humanity" is such an alternative normative foundation? Ambassador Pardo hoped that the "new legal principle" will follow just that career:

> For my delegation, the common-heritage concept is not a slogan; it is not one or a number of more or less desirable principles; rather, it is the very foundation of our work; it is the key that will unlock the door to the future. It is a new legal principle which we wish to introduce into international law; it is a legal principle which we feel must receive recognition if the international community is to cope constructively and effectively with the ever more complex challenges which will confront us all in the coming decades.[191]

If a legal frontier is understood to mean not a *lacuna* or a legal "vacuum", but a yet-unknown community policy whose authority is not derived, nor is its justification deduced, from any general principle of law, then a policy that implements what is admittedly a noble and sensible multi-dimensional programme of internationalization is the crux of a legal frontier. It is submitted that it was the awareness and the experience of being in a legal frontier – the unique sense

---

[191] PV 1589, para. 52 (29 October 1968).

of searching for, and wanting to shape, a new policy for the deep ocean floor emerging as a new domain of disparity under the Law of the Sea – that moved many of the delegations in the United Nations in November 1967 to an unprecedented collective aspiration of a high order. The fate of that quixotic search for a new policy is known: Part XI of the 1982 United Nations Convention on the Law of the Sea. Its beginnings must again be re-told if only to appreciate more accurately the historical significance of what was then, and perhaps still, regarded as a policy for all frontiers of the international community – the principle of the Common Heritage of Humanity.

CONCLUSION

The 1960s may be regarded as a cross-road in the history of the Law of the Sea. It is a significant period not because a historic multilateral conference was held, nor a landmark legal instrument adopted, nor a novel customary norm crystallized – none of these took place and none was then expected to take place. It was a major turning point because the entire international community came to a sudden realization that there was need for a new law, or a new design for pre-existing law – a new policy for the international community – that will respond to a new need. This special need came about in the wake of technological advancements which made access to the deepest parts of the ocean possible. But the new law that was demanded involved less the perennial challenge of keeping the international normative system up-to-date in the face of rapid scientific and technological change than the recognition that a different way of *doing* international law, through pioneer legal institutions, was required.

Taking the historic 1967 address of Ambassador Arvid Pardo to the United Nations as a crucial point of departure, the deep seabed phenomenon provided the "anchoring ground" for the proposal to establish an ocean regime that would simultaneously address the major concerns of post-war international community: peace, economic growth, development, environmental protection, and the rule of law. The problems posed by the technological invasion of the deep ocean in the light of these concerns naturally called for a solution in international organization, as the suggestion to "internationalize" the deep ocean floor gained political momentum and increasing popularity. It speaks to the idealism of the period that international control of the deep seabed and its resources was seen as the most promising approach to break new and exciting ground in international law-making. As it was shown in this Chapter, the international community found itself face to face with a new frontier in international relations.

The movement to internationalize the deep seabed, at first spearheaded by non-governmental groups, necessarily provoked reaction and caustic opposition. In the United States where the internationalization issue was first thoroughly debated, the underlying economic, political, and global interests and implications were considered in the setting of an evolving domestic policy that was then in search of a durable orientation and direction with respect to the deep seabed. As the superpower that launched the most impressive national programme on marine science and development, and that possessed the most advance ocean technologies and capabilities, the United States was undoubtedly in a position to play the most critical role in deciding the fate of the internationalization movement.

It was also in the United States where the legal dimension of internationalization was first given the full attention it rightly deserved. The publication in 1964 of John Mero's *Mineral Resources of the Sea* served as a catalyst in the elaboration and detailed discussion of the international legal implications of the mining of manganese nodules – the new-found gold of the age lying abundantly on the deep ocean floor. Scientist-turned-entrepreneur, Mero did not hesitate to put forward his preferred view on the legal regime that should govern the mining of nodules: freedom of the seas. It did not take long for the real lawyers to peddle this preference in both public fora and within strategic policy circles.

Even before the UN General Assembly had any inkling about the arcane legal niceties of internationalization, the concept of nodule mining under a regime of freedom was already being defended as a *policy option* in the debates taking place in the United States concerning international control of the deep seabed. It had to be defended for two reasons: first, ocean mining industry interests had to be reconciled with other sectoral interests – like defense, foreign policy, petroleum interests, and fisheries – in the formulation of a national consensus on the law of the sea. Secondly, authoritative opinion as well as a powerful current of State practice have already developed around the notion that the entirety of the deep seabed, specifically the exploration and exploitation of its resources, was already under the regime of coastal State authority – the legal continental shelf. The first reason easily yielded to a policy outlook that would promote nodule mining under a legal regime of freedom. Meaning, it was widely perceived as ideal for the present and future national interests of the United States that deep seabed mining should take place on the basis of a legal framework dictated by the classical doctrine of freedom of the seas, pending the conclusion of international arrangements that could prove even more advantageous in promoting these national interests. The second above-mentioned reason, however, was more problematic, for the preferred seabed mining regime was not only contrary to consolidated US policy in the recent past but also subversive of a plainly-worded provision in a treaty to which the United States was a party.

From the literal terms of the 1958 Convention on the Continental Shelf, particularly the "exploitability clause", which gives an alternative definition of the extent of the continental shelf regime, coastal State authority – or "sovereign rights" – is automatically established over seabed resources wherever these resources as defined in the Convention admit of exploitation. It is a straightforward rule, although it is not perfect as would be any other contentiously negotiated compromise rule. It was, however, adopted in UNCLOS I and, from all appearances, was happily but quietly implemented by those coastal States who were fortunate enough to possess the off-shore resources and the technology to exploit these resources and take full advantage of its benefits – not least the United States. In 1969, the International Court of Justice, went so far as to declare that this rule had become part of customary law.

The "wisdom" of the exploitability clause, if one may refer to such attribute, resides in its functional character. Here is a radical departure from the traditional approach in the law of the sea, a law that had always conferred authority or defined jurisdiction on the basis of territoriality – with emphasis on the locus of activity – rather than the activity itself. The presence of jurisdiction, accordingly, was to be determined by the relevant activity *per se*, spelled out in the Convention as "exploration and exploitation of natural resources." This functional definition of the continental shelf explains the fact, confirmed by the International Law Commission that drafted the rule, that the "continental shelf" used in the Convention does not correspond to the layman's or scientist's understanding of the continental shelf. It is a legal definition that led Professor Shigeru Oda to conclude, quite correctly, that "all the submerged lands of the world are necessarily part of the continental shelf." Such a consequence, clearly recognized by those delegations that opposed it at UNCLOS I,[192] led Captain

---

[192] *See e.g.,* France, Netherlands, Pakistan, and United Kingdom. VI UNCLOS I Off Rec 1-48.

Mouton to condemn it, also quite correctly, as "a stupid definition that should be changed as soon as possible."[193]

Thus, if the entire area of the world's seabed outside of the territorial sea had, indeed, already been theoretically or potentially allocated as continental shelf for resource activity purposes, how could nodule mining operations be covered by a high seas regime? Two options, not necessarily mutually exclusive, commended themselves to US policy-makers beginning in the mid-1960s. First, create the seabed area for a high seas regime by revising the Convention on the Continental Shelf in order to delete the exploitability clause. The authorized procedure for this option, considered by many as the only option, was to be found in the formal provisions of the Convention. The second option was the more insidious, and the one that actually guided US policy strategy throughout: re-interpret the exploitability clause and make a legal chaos out of this norm, such that its *de facto* inconclusiveness could create a seabed area "outside the continental shelf" where the manganese nodules could be mined under the regime of freedom of the high seas.

The perversion of the literal meaning of the exploitability clause by its reinterpretation was given form through numerous discussions under the rubric of "outer limits of the continental shelf short of median line boundaries between bordering States." Outer limits of this sort are obviously diametrically opposed to the functional characterization of the continental shelf under the exploitability clause. Still, the campaign to create the impression that the continental shelf under the exploitability clause admitted of outer limits was largely successful. The reason for this success was partly due to the fact that even those promoting the cause of internationalization in the United States were convinced that there should be outer limits to the continental shelf. The concept of "outer limits" that was read into the re-construed exploitability clause, at first as a matter of policy suggestion but eventually as propagandized *lex lata*, was acceptable to, and became a shared stake of, the contending votaries of the internationalization debate.

But the "reinterpretation" option suffered from a fundamental difficulty. For where does the continental shelf exactly end and the seabed beyond this regime begin? This "headache of jurisdiction beyond the 200 meter depth", as the prominent mining industry lawyer Northcutt Ely described it, could not be resolved by a further denigration of the actual meaning of the exploitability clause. Unless international agreement was secured to fix, once and for all,

---

[193] Quoted in Kreuger, *supra* note 36, at 12-13.

the outer limits of the continental shelf, the mining of manganese nodules under a preferred high seas regime will have to wait for some more time. Should it be any wonder then why the United States and some industrialized countries were more eager to establish universal outer limits to the continental shelf rather than to assist in the effort of evolving substantive and innovative principles for the imagined area "beyond" the continental shelf during the days of the UN Seabed Committee? As yet, there was no ascertainable *ratione loci* for a high seas regime to cover manganese nodule mining.

Some observations about the social aspects of the international community policy underlying the continental shelf doctrine should be made at this point. It is surely not a secret that the United States advanced the idea of a legal continental shelf in 1945 in order to claim for itself exclusive control over the extensive petroleum deposits that were then found to lie under its vast continental shelves. This claim was considered by the United States as "reasonable and just."[194] However, those States which did not possess any significant geological shelves – the Latin American countries bordering the Pacific, for example – were obviously deprived of the benefits of a regime that accrued only to the naturally endowed, and it might be added technologically capable, coastal States. These less-capable States thus perceived the legal institution of the Continental Shelf as essentially arbitrary.[195] It must be noted that the inequality of capacity for rights and obligations produced by a regime that arbitrarily vests to a few countries the exclusive access to and enjoyment of the resources of the international commons tended to widen the gulf that already existed between the rich and the poor States. The continental shelf regime, not surprisingly, exemplifies once more the international law of global disparities.

The extension of Latin American off-shore claims that purportedly "exceeded" the US continental shelf doctrine,[196] by establishing wider resource competencies, may be regarded as simple extensions of the functional philosophy in the global distribution of resources through the customary process of unilateral action.[197] More significantly, these claims were meant to redress the inequality of well-being produced by the continental shelf doctrine, and

---

194 US Presidential Proclamation 2667 (Truman Proclamation on the Continental Shelf). Text in I J.N. Moore (Ed.), *International and United States Documents on Oceans Law and Policy* (1986).
195 *See* Garcia-Amador, *op. cit.* 74-75; Luard, *op. cit.* at 145.
196 Hollick, *op. cit.* 61.
197 Garcia-Amador, *op. cit.* 67 *et seq.*; Extavour, *op. cit.* 80 and 141.

were justified under a theory of international equality through non-symmetrical compensation in resource jurisdiction.[198] For them, the substance behind a claim to authority is more important than the juridical form it takes.[199] Most of these claims were, however, vigorously protested by the United States.[200]

When preparations were underway for UNCLOS I, the American States pushed for the inclusion of a juridical device in the doctrine of the continental shelf to counterbalance the geo-morphological criterion in the definition of the legal continental shelf. They advanced the "exploitability clause", which was not by its terms adverse to US interests.[201] The acknowledged purpose of the exploitability clause was, once more, to establish conditions of ostensible equality between coastal States with generous shelves and coastal States with little or insubstantial shelves.[202] The equality effected by the introduction of the exploitability clause, is largely formal[203] and potential[204] – for no substantive equality can result if the technology and the markets necessary for the economic exploitation of seabed resources in deeper waters are not possessed by the coastal State claiming to be compensated in its disadvantage *vis-à-vis* the broad-shelf State through the exploitability clause. Still, the exploitability clause was accepted in UNCLOS I, notwithstanding the known uncertainties in its application and, undoubtedly, in spite of its reinforcement of existing inequalities with respect to the enjoyment of rights and obligations.

The pattern of amplifying the gap between the rich and the poor States through the doctrine of the continental shelf was sustained in the 1960s. This

---

198 *See* Garcia-Amador, *id.*, at 74-75.
199 *See* 1952 Santiago Declaration by Chile, Ecuador and Peru, proclaiming that access to necessary food supplies and economic development, in addition to resource conservation, were the underlying motivations for their claim to extended maritime jurisdiction. Text in Moore, *supra* note 194.
200 Kunz, *op. cit.*; Hollick, *op. cit.* 67-80.
201 The first municipal legislation employing the "exploitability clause" as an alternative formula in the definition of the continental shelf was promulgated by Venezuela in 1956, and was not protested by any country. *See* Garcia-Amador, *op. cit.* 240. The adoption of the "exploitability clause" in the 1956 Ciudad Trujillo Conference, was fully supported by the United States. Hollick, *op. cit.* 121, maintains that the only area where there was substantial agreement in this conference was on the breadth of the continental shelf, reflecting the state of customary law in 1956.
202 Garcia-Amador, *id.*, at 110; Finlay, *supra*, note 71.
203 *Cf.* D.M. Johnston, *supra* note 79, at 233, 236.
204 Garcia-Amador, *op. cit.* 110.

time, the drive towards greater inequality was attempted, ironically, by curtailing the substantive jurisdictional reach of the continental shelf doctrine, particularly the exploitability clause. It is very clear from the evidence reviewed in this Chapter that the reason for reading "outer limits" into the text of the exploitability clause, contrary to its literal and material intent, was to aggrandize a particular configuration of national interest, with the likely effect of further widening the gap between the technologically superior States and the "have-not" States. In the case of the United States, this gap seemed better assured not by the "coastal lakes" approach provided by the exploitability clause – an approach which was publicly vilified as the consummate expression of the new colonialism – but through a high seas solution to the nodule mining problem. Only a high seas regime could effectively give the assurance that nodule mining will not have to take place in the continental shelf of inferior or enemy coastal States. What Professor Douglas Johnston calls the "hypertechnical logic" of the technological order of the sea continued more forcefully and with increasing efficiency in its reproduction and justification of global inequalities and inequities.

It would certainly have been preferable to see a consensus on the orderly formal amendment of the Continental Shelf Convention in the late 1960s. For one thing, the candid acknowledgement by the international community that the legal status of the deep seabed was governed by the inegalitarian Continental Shelf Convention, as *the* pre-existing law applicable to the question of nodule mining, would have rendered incongruous and unwarranted the subsequent claim made by the highly-industrialized States that a customary high seas right to nodule mining obtained prior to any agreement on an acceptable internationalization regime for the deep seabed. This claim, it must be emphasized, was founded on the belief that there was, for deep sea mining purposes, a "seabed and subsoil beyond the limits of national jurisdiction" – a juridical category that was in fact non-existent when the internationalization debate started, and arguably is not yet there for States which still have to ratify the 1982 Convention on the Law of the Sea.[205] It is a claim whose weakness as an assertion in positive law was inversely proportional to its toughness as a policy prefer-

---

205 *See* E.D. Brown, *supra* note 88, at 8: "States like the United Kingdom and the United States, which have not signed the [1982 Law of the Sea] Convention, may continue to rely upon the existing law, based upon international customary law and the Geneva Conventions, both now and also after the entry into force of the Convention for other States."

ence, being largely responsible for bringing about confusion, acrimony and divisive bitterness in the protracted debate to internationalize, and even humanize, the deep ocean floor.

A scrutiny of the original Maltese proposal to internationalize the seabed provides another reason – an affirmative one – why the continental shelf status of the deep seabed should have been accepted as it was. This reason relates to the pursuit of a unified multi-dimensional programme of internationalization, involving the institutionalization of controls covering military, economic, developmental, and ecological concerns. The simultaneous questioning of the regime of freedom and the regime of sovereign rights as concurrent regimes in the inegalitarian *status quo* of the deep seabed called for an alternative regime that relied neither on freedom nor sovereignty as a bottom-line philosophy. But was there a third conceptual alternative? Was not the law of the sea, overwhelmingly developed as a Euro-centric tradition, exclusively built upon the two and only two principles of "freedom" and "sovereignty" – principles which had hitherto imparted coherence and direction to its entire normative structure? Either this third alternative – which Malta initially designated as the "common heritage of mankind" – is a "utopic notion" that encourages people "to cherish an illusion", as the Soviet Representative in the United Nations alleged in 1968,[206] or – with reference to the epistemology of Thomas Kuhn – it signals the emergence of a new paradigm in the international law of the sea. The developing countries hoped and believed that the alternative offered by the "common heritage of humanity" concept should be pursued as a new departure in international law. The basis for this hope and prospects of the Third World's conviction on the Common Heritage of Humanity – as a fundamental principle in the law of the sea and as an embodiment of a new paradigm in international relations – will now be explored.

---

206 PV 1592, para. 36-37 (31 October 1968).

IV

BEYOND *MARE LIBERUM* AND *MARE CLAUSUM*: THE COMMON HERITAGE OF HUMANITY AS A FUNDAMENTAL PRINCIPLE OF INTERNATIONAL LAW

What purpose is served by adopting a fundamental principle for the "seabed beyond the limits of national jurisdiction" that does not ultimately derive from either the doctrine of freedom of the seas or the doctrine of coastal State sovereignty? And why should this fundamental principle – denominated as "common heritage of humanity" – be at all acceptable to those States, chiefly the most technologically advanced, whose immediate interests in the "Area" are better served by pursuing policies based on the age-old principle of freedom? Does the international community have urgent need of developing a novel principle in international law or, specifically, a new doctrinal approach to the problems of the law of the sea? How will this over-arching principle be evolved and realized in practice, and what implications does it carry for the production and distribution of power and well-being within international society?

Although these and other related questions have been deliberated upon, directly or tangentially, in the United Nations in the late 1960s it is worthy re-stating them once again from the vantage point of the 1990s. With the entry into force of the 1982 Convention on the Law of the Sea and the 1994 Implementation Agreement[1] (which effected substantial modifications to Part XI of the Convention) a fresh clarification of the substance of the principle of the Common Heritage of Humanity – a principle which is affirmed in both documents – is called for. To the extent that the political controversy that developed around Part XI of the 1982 UN Convention, together with its purported resolution through the 1994 Implementation Agreement, inquires into the substantive definition of the Common Heritage of Humanity, it repays to examine the principle and its underlying rationale. In addition, it may be useful to consider whether the original legislative objectives behind the introduction of the Common Heri-

---

1 UN Doc. A/RES/48/263 (17 August 1994).

tage principle are still relevant and significant to the public order of the oceans for the late 1990s and beyond.

The answers to the questions posed above do explore the *raison d'etre* of the Common Heritage of Humanity and provide the logical basis for an updated normative elaboration of its scope *ratione materiae*. It is submitted that the task of framing answers is perhaps rendered less difficult in light of the conclusion advanced in the previous Chapter: that an undistorted historical assessment of the legal situation in the 1960s would reveal that any deep seabed mining activity carried out at that time would have been under the inescapable purview of the 1958 Geneva Convention on the Continental Shelf. This conclusion is further defended in its microscopic details in the present Chapter. It is a conclusion, it should immediately be added, which was detested as a legal argument by many members of the international community – developed or developing – for different reasons of their own, thus rendering extremely difficult any clear and straightforward determination of the prevailing *lex lata*. The historic collective drive to excise the "exploitability clause" from the *lex scripta* provided fertile ground for a grand effort to alter a legal situation – for a purpose and in a direction not necessarily shared in common.

The introduction of the "common heritage of mankind" concept was a crucial part of the overall will to articulate a law *de lege ferenda* for the deep seabed. It was, in the first instance, an initiative aimed at clarifying the logic behind the proposition that there is an area of the seabed beyond national jurisdiction. Negotiations that initially centered on the Common Heritage concept were enlightening and useful to everyone concerned in this limited respect. More particularly, the foreign policy predicaments of the technologically advanced nations impelled the need to identify or establish definite geographic limits to continental shelf/national resource jurisdiction.

But the Common Heritage of Humanity, fundamentally, was not a concept that would rescind *simpliciter* the "exploitability clause" of the 1958 Continental Shelf Convention. It was imagined and elaborated as a substantive programme of internationalization whose main objective was the development of a system of community control over undersea resources. Since "freedom the seas" was a possible competing concept which was in fact simultaneously offered as a substitute for the continental shelf regime with respect to nodule mining in the deep ocean,[2] the Common Heritage of Humanity idea was advanced by the developing countries with a clear understanding that it was not simply going to be another name for freedom of the seas.[3] From the very start, one primordial purpose behind the will to develop the Common Heritage concept was to reject freedom as a conceivable alternative regime for harnessing deep seabed resources. The establishment of a regime in support of a pioneering policy to institutionalize the international control of ocean resources – unmolested by the imminence of mineral exploitation under the continental shelf regime, as the positive law in *status quo ante*, nor unthreatened by any future invocation of freedom of the seas as the "default" legal framework for seabed mining pending the elaboration of the new regime to govern the deep seabed – is a threshold proposition that must be maintained in any disquisition on the Common Heritage of Humanity as a fundamental principle in international law.

More was envisioned than just the simple replacement of one functional regime, *i.e.,* exploration and exploitation of seabed resources, for another. The Common Heritage of Humanity proposal was an invitation for the international community to emplace a comprehensive regime for *all*[4] human activities that may occur in an area that was yet to become a legal reality. What was contemplated was a completely new policy, an unprecedented legal postulate, for the deep seabed as a new maritime *space* that was to be governed *in toto*. Again the definition of this comprehensive areal regime was not supposed to reckon with the doctrine of coastal State authority nor take inspiration from the Grotian doctrine of freedom. A brief sketch of the broad historical picture that made this realization possible is in order.

---

2   Japan, for example, during the 1969 Seabed Committee discussions, advocated the position that the freedom of the high seas, or rules and regulations derived from the freedom of the high seas, is applicable to the exploration and exploitation of the deep ocean floor. S. Oda, *The Law of the Sea in our Time – II. The United Nations Seabed Committee 1968-1973* at 57 (1977). So did Australia, PV 1589 29 Oct. 1968. *See also* K.R. Simmonds, *supra* Chap. IV note 140, at 38, concluding that "the international law which governs a regime of the ocean bed must be built upon existing law, with especial reference to the law of the high seas."

3   *See* for *e.g.*, statements of Brazil, PV 1591 (30 Oct 1968); China, *ibid.*; Malta PV 1675 (3 Nov 1969). *See also* A. Pardo & C. Christol, "The Common Interest: Tension Between the Whole and the Parts" in MacDonald & Johnston, *op. cit.* 643-660.

4   *See* Statement of Ambassador S. Amerasinghe of Ceylon, PV 1673 (31 Oct. 1969); also statements of India, *ibid.*, and Cameroon, PV 1675 (3 Nov. 1969).

In the previous Chapter, it was explained how the notion of "the seabed and ocean floor and subsoil thereof underlying the high seas beyond the limits of national jurisdiction" became a problematical concern in the debate over the internationalization of the deep seabed. This debate was initially triggered by the discovery of a new source of undersea wealth in the form of manganese nodules lying abundantly on the deep ocean floor. The debate began with a straightforward and simple issue: should these resources be brought under international control and administration? On one side of the debate was the cause of the so-called "idealists", who saw in these nodules the promise of a radically strengthened United Nations Organization catering to the development needs of the poor countries; on the other side were the "realists", who advocated unilateral access and/or national control of the new-found resources. While both sides were differently motivated in their commonly-held assumption that the nodules must perforce be situated in a geophysical area beyond or outside of the jurisdictional reach of any State, the *lex scripta* of the day had nevertheless unconditionally provided for coastal State authority over activities directly related to exploration and exploitation of these mineral resources. It was argued earlier that through the functional regime embodied in the "exploitability clause" of the 1958 Geneva Convention on the Continental Shelf, the exploration and exploitation of manganese nodules anywhere in the oceans would have been governed by the doctrine of the continental shelf – a norm that was then tightly secured in conventional and customary law in the 1960s.[5]

The internationalization issue assumed enlarged proportions when the UN General Assembly was seized of the seabed controversy. With the inclusion of the "peaceful purposes" reservation for the deep seabed in the agenda of internationalization – a development that was provoked by the Maltese intervention in 1967 – the course was set for the elaboration of an ambitious multidimensional programme of internationalization. Henceforth, the mineral resources issue became entangled with the military and other pioneer uses of the deep seabed. In legal terms, the project of international/United Nations control of the deep seabed not only sought to contend with the policy question of dealing with the open-ended scope of the Continental Shelf regime, but also had to confront those kinds of potential undersea activities conducted within the dominant framework of the Grotian freedom of the seas, *e.g.*, the arms race in this frontier as well as its pollution or contamination. It is with reference to the "peace" and "environmental" dimensions of Malta's internationalization proposal

---

5   *See* Hutchinson, *supra* Chap. III note 83.

that the objective metes and bounds of the "seabed beyond national jurisdiction" were more or less ascertainable. As Professor Oda had accurately observed, this is the entirety of the area corresponding to the seabed outside the Territorial Sea.

The internationalization debate in the late 1960s thus made possible the simultaneous questioning of the functional continental shelf doctrine and the locational freedom of the seas regime as intertwined normative structures embedded on the same undersea space at the same historical time. Only the quest for a multi-dimensional solution to the internationalization challenge could have revealed the objective reality of a legal *status quo* perpetuated by the combined operation of the freedom and sovereignty norms. It was this reality that was meant to be overthrown by the introduction of a new concept in the law of the sea.

With this preliminary clarification, it is now possible to examine the Common Heritage of Humanity as a substantive principle in international law. The main argument put forward in this Chapter is that on the basis of a compelling need on the part of the international community to develop a new comprehensive policy for the deep ocean floor which had to be founded neither on the doctrine of freedom nor on the stricture of sovereignty, the Common Heritage of Humanity principle was consolidated as a fundamental norm in international law. The entry into force of the 1982 Convention on the Law of the Sea consolidates the normative status of the Common Heritage of Humanity principle, governing particularly and peremptorily "the Area and its resources." As a fundamental policy prescription, the Common Heritage of Humanity is an authoritative statement of a new form of governance in the public order of the oceans.

The present Chapter proceeds in five sections. The first Section will provide an overview of Part XI of the 1982 Convention on the Law of the Sea as the specific realization of the Common Heritage of Humanity as a fundamental principle of international law. The focus here will be on the "principles" governing the area and its resources. The second (historical) section will elaborate the overall development-cum-peace thrust of the Common Heritage concept. This section will show that the core motivation behind the introduction of the Common Heritage of Humanity principle is linked to a particular legal approach to the decolonization process, thus justifying the notion of a "programmatory law of the Common Heritage of Humanity." The debate over the issue of a precise definition of the seabed area beyond national jurisdiction in the context of elaborating the doctrinal elements of the Common Heritage concept will assume some importance in the discussion. The initial efforts at legal control to meet the challenge of demilitarization in the frontier will then be considered as a precursor element of the positive programmatory law of the Common Heritage of Humanity. In the third section, the pivotal concept of benefit-sharing is explored. The concept of "benefit for all humanity" in the international law governing common pool resources is without doubt a major point of reference for the Common Heritage of Humanity principle and a signal event that Part XI of the Convention responds in a quite revolutionary way to the interests and needs of developing States. Environmental protection in the Area is dealt with in the fourth Section. Indeed, the concern for the preservation of the ecological integrity of the common heritage as part of the environment to be managed for present and future generations has always been a critical part of the formulation of the Common Heritage principle since its introduction in the discourse of international relations. It is through the principle of environmental management that we are able to have a glimpse of the "sustainable development" programme behind the programmatory law of the Common Heritage. The last section of the Chapter will draw some conclusions, and will include a brief statement on the imperative of an institutional embodiment of the Common Heritage of Humanity principle through international organization, which is the subject of Chapter V.

A. THE COMMON HERITAGE OF HUMANITY PRINCIPLE AND PART XI OF THE 1982 CONVENTION

1. Textual Overview

The Preamble of the Convention foreshadows the regime embodied in its Part XI, entitled "The Area":

Desiring by this Convention to develop the principles embodied in resolution 2749 (XXV) of 17 December 1970 in which the General Assembly of the United Nations solemnly declared *inter alia* that the area of the seabed and ocean floor and the subsoil thereof, beyond the limits of national jurisdiction, as well as its resources, are the common heritage of mankind, the exploration and exploitation of which shall be carried out for the benefit of mankind as a whole, irrespective of the geographical location of States[.][6]

Part XI is subdivided into five Sections: (1) General Provisions,[7] (2) Principles Governing the Area,[8] (3) Development of Resources of the Area,[9] (4) The Authority,[10] and (5) Settlement of Disputes and Advisory Opinions.[11] Two Annexes to the Convention directly relate to the provisions of Sections 3 and 4 of Part XI: Annex III on Basic Conditions of Prospecting, Exploration and Exploitation, and Annex IV or the Statute of the Enterprise. Another annex, namely Annex IV, entitled the Statute of the International Tribunal for the Law of the Sea, has a section that treats of the "Sea-bed Disputes Chamber", and is therefore associated with Section 5 of Part XI.[12] Furthermore, three of the four Resolutions under the Final Act of UNCLOS III are relevant to the regime established in Part XI:[13] Resolution I on the establishment of the Preparatory Commission for the International Sea-bed Authority and the International Tribunal for the Law of the Sea; Resolution II governing Preparatory Investment in Pioneer Activities Relating to Polymetallic Nodules; and Resolution III relating to territories whose people have not obtained either full independence or some other self-governing status recognized by the United Nations or Territories under colonial domination.[14]

---

6   6th Preambular para., CLOS. "Area" is defined in Art. 1 (1), CLOS, as "the seabed and ocean floor and subsoil thereof beyond the limits of national jurisdiction." Its specific metes and bounds are delineated with reference to the outer limits of the continental shelf established by coastal States in conformity with Art. 76 of the Convention.

7   Arts. 133-135, CLOS.

8   Arts. 136-149, CLOS.

9   Arts. 150-155, CLOS.

10   Arts. 156-185, CLOS.

11   Arts. 186-191, CLOS.

12   The Annexes to the Convention, numbering nine, form an integral part of the Convention. Art. 318, CLOS.

13   Para. 42 of the Final Act of the UNCLOS III States that the Convention together with these Resolutions form an integral whole. CLOS at 168. These Resolutions took immediate effect upon signature of the Final Act. I E.D. Brown, *supra* Chap. II note 10, at 16.

14   The mandate of Resolution III is relevant to Art. 140 (1), CLOS, on "Benefit of Mankind", and Art. 156 (3), CLOS concerning observer status in the ISA.

234

The 1994 Implementation Agreement introduces adjustments[15] or amendments[16] to the provisions basically found under Sections 3 and 4 of Part XI of the Convention, including its related Annexes.[17] The provisions of Part XI intended to be adjusted or modified by this 1994 Implementation Agreement relate to nine substantive areas of concern as outlined in the Annex to the Agreement:[18] (1) Costs to States Parties and Institutional Arrangements, (2) The Enterprise, (3) Decision-Making, (4) Review Conference, (5) Transfer of Technology, (6) Production Policy, (7) Economic Assistance to adversely affected developing countries, (8) Financial Terms of Contracts, and (9) the Finance Committee.[19]

A question that must be raised at the outset concerns the overall nature of jurisdictional authority established by Part XI, *i.e*, whether, on the whole, it defines jurisdictional competence along the lines of a functional or a spatial regime.[20] In the previous Chapter it was shown that the law of the continental shelf established by the 1958 Geneva Convention embodied an alternative functional definition of the continental shelf, through the "exploitability clause." This regime, a post-war innovation in the public order of the oceans, is functional in character because it authorized the exercise of coastal State jurisdiction over a particular type of activity – the exploration and exploitation of seabed resources beyond the 200 meter isobath. The pre-existing classical law of the sea, in contrast, upon which the functional continental shelf regime was grafted, was built upon two fundamental and mutually exclusive jurisdictional principles whose application was based on the areal/territorial criterion. Coastal State jurisdiction prevailed over a narrow band of sea called territorial waters while

---

15 *See* M.H. Nordquist & J.N. Moore (Eds.), *Entry Into Force of the Law of the Sea Convention* (1995).
16 E.D. Brown, *supra* Chap. II note 10, at 11, 447.
17 Art. 2 (1) of the Implementation Agreement States that "The provisions of this Agreement and Part XI shall be interpreted and applied together as a single instrument. In the event of any inconsistency between this Agreement and Part XI, the provisions of this Agreement shall prevail."
18 The Annex forms an integral part of the Implementation Agreement. Art. 1 (2), 1994 Implementation Agreement.
19 On the entry into force of the Agreement and its "provisional application", *see* Arts. 6 & 7, 1994 Implementation Agreement.
20 *See* B. Chen, *The Legal Regime of Airspace and Outerspace: The Boundary Problem. Functionalism versus Spatialism: The Major Premises* 5 ANNALS OF AIR & SPACE LAW 323-361 (1980).

235

beyond this maritime belt lay the vast high seas, governed by the principle of freedom. The positioning of Part XI in the text of the Convention is interesting; it is preceded by the predominantly "areal", or zonal, regimes[21] and followed by the functional, or "activities", regimes.[22] The title of Part XI is also worthy of note: "The Area", as defined,[23] proves *ipso facto* that Part XI embodies an areal definition of jurisdictional authority.

Article 136 is of course conclusive on the point: "The Area and its resources are the common heritage of mankind." The simplicity and clarity of this short provision cannot be stressed too much. It enshrines a seminal principle that has gone through an embattled past and that has awaited full normative recognition for a period of over two decades.[24] In its definition of the scope of jurisdiction, a spatial criterion is employed, but added emphasis is also put on the "resources" aspects of jurisdictional authority exercised with respect to the physical area defined (*i.e.*, "its [or the Area's] resources"),[25] thereby indicating a particular functional (*i.e.*, "activities in the area")[26] definition of jurisdiction as well.[27] The mention of a special functional aspect (respecting mineral resources) of jurisdiction in the definition of jurisdictional authority based on

---

21 Part II of CLOS covers the territorial sea and contiguous zone; Part III is on straits used for international navigation; Part IV covers Archipelagic States; Part V is on the EEZ; Part VI is on the continental shelf; Part VII is on the high seas, Part VIII deals with islands; Part IX involves enclosed and semi-enclosed seas; and Part IX is on land-locked States.
22 Part XII is on protection and preservation of the marine environment; Part XIII deals with MSR; Part XIV covers development and transfer of marine technology; and Part XV is on settlement of disputes.
23 *See* Art. 1 (1), CLOS.
24 *See infra*, Sec. B.2 – B.4.
25 Under Part XI, "resources" is defined as "all solid, liquid or gaseous mineral resources *in situ* in the Area at or beneath the sea-bed, including polymetallic nodules." Art. 133 (a), CLOS.
26 "Activities in the Area" is defined as "all activities of exploration for, and exploitation of, the resources in the Area." Art. 1 (3), CLOS.
27 The spatial character of jurisdiction in the Area, defined in Part XI, is thus much broader in scope than the areal definition of jurisdiction in Part V, in which the EEZ is conceived as a multi-functional zone for coastal State authority with respect to its resources or economic uses only. *Supra* Chap. II note 81.

area or location seems somewhat superfluous,[28] since all activities conducted in the area, or any functional exercise of jurisdiction within the area, are deemed included in the omnibus grant of areal authority. That is, unqualified jurisdiction over an area necessarily includes jurisdiction over any object or activity therein. This phraseology is, however, perfectly understandable for it resolves the controversy that arose early on during the Seabed Committee debates on the matter. States were then divided on the question of whether the regime contemplated for the "seabed beyond national jurisdiction" should govern the area as a whole, *i.e.*, *all* activities therein (pan-functional) including resource activities (which was the position of the developing countries), or should only be limited in scope to the exploration and exploitation of resources in the area (which was advocated by the industrialized countries).[29] The averment of a functional scope of jurisdiction through the special mention of "resources" is also explained by the fact that the bulk of Part XI is concerned with the negotiated regime in UNCLOS III concerning regulation of mineral resources activities in the Area.[30] More importantly, though, Article 136 defines the scope of jurisdiction in Part XI in conjunction with its identification of the principle which shall govern[31] "the Area and its resources." This principle, applicable to *both* the

---

28   Compare Canada, PV 1779 (1 Dec 1970) [delegation finds difficulties with the statement that the area itself is common heritage; the language used "tends to imply that all uses of and all activities on the seabed beyond national jurisdiction should be regulated by the international regime to be set up"] vis-a-vis UK, PV 1799 (15 Dec 1970) [delegation does "not fully understand the necessity of specific mention of resources as an element distinct from area itself"].

29   *See* SBC Chairman Amerasinghe's summation of progress in the Seabed Committee, PV 1673, 31 October 1969; Oda, *supra* note 2, at 70; *See also* 1971 SBC Rep, para. 60.

30   Art. 134 (2), CLOS. *See* further below.

31   The title of Section 2 "Principles *Governing* the Area" is significant. The use of the term "governing" to qualify principles for the area was first used in the draft declaration of legal principles submitted by India to the *Ad Hoc* Seabed Committee. Annex III, 1968 Report of the *Ad Hoc* Committee. The United States supported by other developed States, preferring to use weaker language, subsequently submitted a "draft resolution containing statement of principles *concerning* the deep ocean floor" for the "guidance" of States. *Ibid.* Ambassador Amerasinghe emphasized the importance of legal principles "to govern" the area. PV 1588 (28 Oct. 1968); *cf.* statement of US representative, in PV 1590 (29 Oct. 1968), on the need to develop "principles which *may* ultimately serve as basis for an agreed regime" for the deep ocean floor. (All emphases mine)

area *and* its resources and, therefore, controlling as regards the exercise of spatial authority, generally, and functional jurisdiction, specifically, in the Area is denominated the "common heritage of mankind."

2. The Severability of the Common Heritage of Humanity Principle from the Seabed Mining Regime

It is important to highlight the areal scope of jurisdictional authority covered by the Common Heritage principle. This is often forgotten by textbook writers whose treatment of the Common Heritage of Humanity is solely focussed on the functional, *i.e.*, mineral resources, aspects of the regime developed in Part XI of the Convention.[32] It is true that Part XI of the Convention devotes considerable attention to the detailed rules and regulations governing the mining of mineral resources, specifically manganese nodules, in the Area.[33] And it is also not doubted that the long-drawn political controversy involving Part XI of the Convention had to do with some of its mining provisions. Yet there are other conceivable activities, and even other resources, whose particular regulation are equally under the ambit of Part XI simply on account of the full areal scope of jurisdictional authority stipulated in Article 136, that "the Area is the common heritage of mankind." It goes without saying that these other activities and resources, as long as they occur within the space defined as "the Area", are also "governed" by the Common Heritage principle. Their legal status is thus anticipated by Part XI, which advances the novel principle Common Heritage of Humanity.

Part XI mentions at least three other areas of functional regulation which are distinct from, but not as well-developed as, the mining regime in the Convention: (1) military uses of the Area, which are implied in the provision that "the Area shall be open to use exclusively for peaceful purposes";[34] (2) marine scientific research;[35] and (3) the disposition of archeological and historical objects in the Area.[36] Examples of mineral resources on or under the

---

32 *E.g.,* Churchill & Lowe, *op. cit.* 182 *et seq.*; E.D. Brown, *supra* Chap. II note 10, at Chap. 17.
33 *See* Sections 3 and 4, Part XI and related Annexes, CLOS.
34 Art. 141, CLOS.
35 Art. 143, CLOS.
36 Art. 149, CLOS.

seabed that are not encompassed by the manganese nodule mining regime under Section 3 of Part XI include recently discovered cobalt-rich manganese crusts or mineral deposits from sea-floor hot springs.[37] These resources are the "common heritage of mankind" as well. As for the living and other biotic resources in the Area,[38] there is likewise no question that Part XI provides the relevant legal framework for their regulation. Activities in the area relating to living resources may well come within the immediate purview of the Authority, which is tasked with a general duty concerning "the protection and conservation of the natural resources of the Area and the prevention of damage to the flora and fauna of the marine environment."[39] Some other imaginable activities that may take place in the Area not mentioned in the Convention, but are governed by the provisions of Part XI just the same, include "transfer of technology" for activities other than mining in the area[40] as well as tunneling and directional drilling in the Area. Apparently, the only single exception of an activity that takes place in the Area which is not governed by Part XI is the laying of submarine cables and pipelines – a function that was previously regulated by the freedom of the seas principle under the 1958 Geneva Convention on the High Seas.[41]

The indication of a zonal/multi-functional scope of special jurisdictional competence in Article 136 has a two-fold significance. First, since any and all activities that take place in the Area – with the exception of the freedom to law submarine cables and pipelines – whether expressly identified in the Convention or not, are to be "governed" by the principles laid down in Part XI, it can be maintained that these activities are thus within the regulatory domain of Part XI. The general principles stated in Part XI, specifically the

---

37 F.T. Manheim, *Marine Cobalt Resources* 232 SCIENCE 600-608 (2 May 1986); P.A. Rona, *Mineral Deposits from Sea-Floor Hot Springs* 254 SCIENTIFIC AMERICAN 84-92 (January 1986). *See* Art. 162 (2)(o)(ii), CLOS.
38 *See* V. Tunnicliffe, *Hydrothermal-Vent Communities of the Deep Sea* 80 AMERICAN SCIENTIST 336-349 (July-Aug 1992).
39 *See* Art. 145 (b), CLOS.
40 *Cf.* Art. 144, CLOS.
41 The reason for this single exception could be based on the notion of "prior rights" or "pre-exiting rights" in *jus communicationis*: the freedom to lay submarine cables and pipelines was explicitly recognized in the 1958 Geneva Convention on the High Seas, Art. 2 (3), 450 UNTS 82 (1963), thus preceding the seabed "common heritage" discussions which only began in the mid 1960s. *See also* Art. 87 (c) and Arts 112-115, CLOS and *infra* pp. 389 *et seq.*

principle that "The Area and its resources are the common heritage of mankind," would in this instance automatically apply to any legally-relevant fact in the Area. There is thus no room for the invocation or application of pre-Convention "general international law" with respect to any particular activity in the Area based on the proviso in the Preamble "that all matters not regulated by this Convention continue to be governed by the rules and principles of general international law."[42]

Secondly, and this should follow from the proposition just stated that Part XI regulates all activities but one in the Area, it can be said that the "principles governing the area" are applicable to each and every type of activity or function carried out in the area, and not only to the activity of deep seabed mining. Indeed it is evident that Section 2 of Part XI containing these principles is logically distinct and severable from the Sections dealing with deep seabed mining.[43] The principles in Section 2 are "generalizable"[44] in the sense that they do not only appertain to seabed mining as such but to every other activity that comes within the purview of "the Area." These principles may be likened to a "framework agreement", which then provides an umbrella regulatory regime for various "protocol" sub-agreements covering a range of activties; as it is the case today that the "protocol" relating to mining activities in the Area had already been established.[45] A "framework-protocol" approach to Part XI simply illustrates the fact that the scope of jurisdictional competence conceptualized in Article 136 adopts a general spatial orientation with specific functional dimensions.

3. The Special Legal Status of the Area and the Principles Governing the Area

It is, therefore, important to bear in mind the distinction between the general principles or provisions in Part XI applicable to the entirety of the Area as such

---

42 *See* last preambular para., CLOS.
43 *See* Morell, *op. cit.* 164.
44 *Ibid*; *cf.* C.A. Stephanou, "A European Perception of the US Rejection of the 1982 Convention" in C.L. Rozakis and C.A. Stephanou (Eds.), *The New Law of the Sea* 270-273 (1983).
45 Part XI is thus similar to Part XII of the Convention – an umbrella regime that provides some kind of a "constitutional" framework which becomes the basis for further legal development. For this characterization of Part XII, *see e.g.*, McConnell & Gold, *op. cit.*

and the rules that apply to particular functional interventions therein, like the detailed regime of mineral mining. In a practical sense, the specific rules that flow from negotiated functional regimes for the Area are the agreed applications or interpretations of these principles. Logically, however, particular regimes are founded on these principles, supplying the underlying legal justification for the evolution of these operational regimes in the Area. Certainly, a critical factor that enters into the calculation of the legitimacy[46] or acceptability of a specific regime for the Area is the degree to which this regime, or any of its rules, is perceived to be in harmony with the general principles that govern the Area.

These principles *de jure* that form the general management framework for the Area are, unfortunately, neither systematically nor unambiguously identified in Section 2 of Part XI.[47] The reference made to the 1970 Declaration of Principles resolution in the last-quoted paragraph of the Preamble of the Convention, gives more reason for segregating such principles. However, the enumeration of principles under Section 2 of Part XI should be presumed to yield the list of principles inasmuch as principles governing a novel object of international law, if they are to be authoritative at all, must ultimately find positive expression in the text of the Convention. There is no doubt that there are principles that govern the area as a whole, existing independently of their translation as the governing principles for the functional regime of seabed mining in the Convention. The main task is to single out each of these principles. What exactly are the general principles that govern the Area?[48]

The pivotal importance of an authoritative listing of principles governing the Area as a whole and applicable to every conceivable functional activity that takes place therein – whether seabed mining, or marine scientific research, or military activities, or ecological preservation – should be apparent. These principles make up the constitutional or "framework" legal prescriptions which

---

46 "Legitimacy" in the sense of "compliance pull" as defined by Professor Thomas Frank, *op. cit.* 24.

47 It will be noted that concerns which should properly be aligned to specific functional regimes in the Area are included under Section 2, *e.g.*, military activities in the Area (Art. 141, CLOS), MSR (Art. 143, CLOS), and preservation and disposition of historical and archeological objects (Art. 149, CLOS).

48 Some writers who have attempted to list these general principles on the basis of the text of the Declaration of Principles Resolution and the work of UNCLOS III include: R.P. Anand, *supra* Chap. III note 14, at 212; Borgese, in Dolman *supra* Chap. III note 14; Yuwen Li *op. cit.*

will have to guide the formation of future "protocols"/regulatory regimes for the Area. They elaborate a binding policy for all activities in the Area, giving a sense of unity and comprehensiveness to the zonal scope of jurisdictional competence achieved in Part XI.

The key concept which would throw light on the principles governing the area is found in the second half of Article 136: the "common heritage of mankind."[49] It is conceded that the legal status of the Area is summed up in this neologism in the law of the sea. There was a time, it may be recalled, when the term was deciphered as a politico-moral concept,[50] almost a poetic description that became fashionable in the law of the sea discourse.[51] With the entry into force of the Convention, there should no longer be any question about the normative standing of the Common Heritage concept. It is now a binding legal prescription that defines the legal status, according to Article 136 of the Convention, of "the Area and its resources."

As a description of the legal status of "the Area and its resources", the Common Heritage of Humanity is immediately comprehensible for *what it is not*. First, since the Area, as defined[52] is not within national jurisdiction, it follows that the concept of coastal State jurisdiction is not the concept of the Common Heritage of Humanity. Indeed the regimes of the EEZ or the Continental shelf, which exemplify this principle, are elaborated under separate Parts of the Convention.[53] The "common heritage of humanity" is, therefore, not "coastal State sovereignty" nor "sovereign rights." The mutual exclusiveness of the Common Heritage of Humanity and coastal State sovereignty is evident

---

49 The term "common heritage of mankind" is not defined in the Convention, but reference to "the principle of the common heritage of mankind" is made in Art. 155 (2), CLOS. Art. 311 (6) refers to "the basic principle relating to the common heritage of mankind set forth in Article 136." It does not appear that there was any initiative or formal proposal advanced in UNCLOS III to define the principle relating to the "common heritage of mankind."
50 S. Gorove, *The Concept of the Common Heritage of Mankind: A Political, Moral or Legal Innovation?* 9 SAN DIEGO L REV 390-403 (1972).
51 Professor Jennings once stated that his "only quarrel with the phrase 'the common heritage of mankind' is that it obscures the fact that it is the whole of the sea that is the common heritage of mankind." Jennings, in Churchill, Simmonds & Welch, *op. cit.* 15.
52 Art. 1 (1), CLOS.
53 *I.e.*, Parts V & VI, CLOS. Although it is not disputed that the EEZ is *sui generis*, it is a grant of jurisdictional (multi-functional) competence to the coastal State via the doctrine of "sovereign rights." *See* Art. 56, CLOS.

in the statement that the Area begins where the legal continental shelf ends. The point is clearly made in Article 137 (1) of the Convention:

> No State shall claim or exercise sovereignty or sovereign rights over any part of the Area or its resources, nor shall any State or natural or juridical person appropriate any part thereof. No such claim or exercise of sovereignty or sovereign rights nor such appropriation shall be recognized.

Secondly, and perhaps more significantly, the legal status of "the Area and its resources" as common heritage of humanity means that the Common Heritage concept is not the freedom of the seas concept. Again, the principle of freedom of the high seas[54] is found in another Part of the Convention[55] which does not purport to regulate the Area or its resources. With the single exception of the laying of submarine cables and pipelines, the concept of high seas freedoms is inapplicable to the Area and its resources. Article 135 suggests the mutual exclusiveness of the Common Heritage of Humanity concept and freedom of the seas concept when it distinguishes the legal status of the Area from "the legal status of the waters superjacent to the Area or that of the air space above those waters." With the adoption of the Convention in 1982, it was already widely recognized that the Common Heritage of Humanity and the freedom of the high seas are principles that cannot coexist or simultaneously apply in regard to the same object of legal regulation.[56]

In sum, the status of the Area and its resources as neither defined by the fundamental principle of coastal State sovereignty nor the principle of freedom of the seas arises not only from the arrangement of the major thematic Parts of the Convention but also from the text of Part XI itself. This legal status is *sui generis*, and upholds the original vision defended especially developing countries in the late 1960s that the traditional concepts of the law of the sea are not applicable to the Area and its resources.[57] In Ambassador Edvard Hambro's simple formulation, "new words are needed for new concepts."[58]

---

54 *See* Art. 87, CLOS.
55 Part VII, CLOS.
56 *See* J. Van Dyke & C. Yuen, *"Common Heritage" vs. "Freedom of the Seas": Which Governs the Seabed?* 19 SAN DIEGO L REV 493-551 (1982); E.D. Brown, *supra* Chap. III note 142, at Chap. 2.
57 *See* Anand, *supra* Chap. III note 14, at 208-210.
58 Norway, PV 1676 (4 Nov 1969).

The status of the Area and its resources as Common Heritage of Humanity has a further implication which flows from the fact that the Common Heritage of Humanity is neither the concept of coastal State sovereignty nor the concept of freedom of the seas. It is that the Common Heritage of Humanity lies on the same level of normative generality as the principles of coastal State sovereignty or freedom of the seas, assuming that norms in the international legal system admit of hierarchical classification.[59] Considering that "sovereignty" and "freedom of the seas" are regarded as "fundamental principles" of international law, it is only logical to treat "the common heritage of humanity" as equally seminal or fundamental.[60] By virtue of its position in the new normative order of the oceans as spelled out in the 1982 Convention on the Law of the Sea, the Common Heritage of Humanity may be regarded with confidence as a new fundamental principle of international law.

The fundamental or foundational character of the Common Heritage of Humanity principle has a direct effect on the identification and formulation of the "principles governing the area", as referred to above. Superficially, the Common Heritage of Humanity is, of course, by definition the sum of its component principles which, taken as a whole, govern the Area. But it can be inferred that these principles are not simply discrete doctrines that are listed to spell out a legal "framework" for the management of the Area. These principles combine and intersect in an organic fashion to form a *gestalt*, or a fundamental principle of international law. In an important way, therefore, the Common Heritage of Humanity principle is not merely a "short hand" expression of all the general principles taken together. Being a fundamental principle of international law, the Common Heritage of Humanity principle has an autonomous normative existence of its own[61] and, to the extent feasible, inspires

---

59 *See* Schwarzenberger, *supra* Chap. I note 51; Schachter, in MacDonald & Johnston, *op. cit.*

60 *See* Anand, *supra* Chap. II note 14, at 208, 210-211. E.D. Brown, *supra* Chap. II note 142, at II.2.1 makes reference to the Common Heritage of Humanity and the Freedom of the Seas as "fundamental principles in conflict."

61 *See* Art. 311 (6), CLOS.

if not guides the identification, the interpretation, and the application[62] of these analytic doctrines or sub-principles governing the Area and its resources.

The division of international legal prescriptions into "rules", "principles" and "ends", as suggested by Professor Oscar Schachter, may be usefully employed to recapitulate the legal structure of Part XI of the Convention.[63] In the governance of the Area and its resources, the statement of the authoritative goal or purpose for the Area is provided by the Common Heritage of Humanity as a fundamental principle of the law of the sea. The principles governing the area are the intermediate propositions that have a wide range of applications but are equally abstract or general as the Common Heritage of Humanity principle. Finally, the functional regimes that govern various activities in the Area – the protocols, as mentioned above – are the "rules" that dictate particular legal results. From the point of view of practical management of the Area, the "rules" are definitely the most interesting, supplying the degree of specificity that allows results to be achieved. However, from the standpoint of governance and comprehensive normative development, the most crucial aspect of the legal structure of Part XI lies in the inter-relationships among "rules", "principles", and the Common Heritage of Humanity as "end." To repeat, the principles, and by implication the Common Heritage of Humanity principle, stand as a framework deal, in relation to the rules that are constituted as implementing "protocols." A hierarchy of norms is thus established in Part XI.[64]

The logical inter-relationships among rules, principles and the Common Heritage of Humanity are, not surprisingly, illustrated most vividly and forcefully in the evolution of the regime governing mineral mining in the area. The history of the deep seabed mining regime embodied in Part XI is almost co-

---

62 Independently of the doctrinal meaning of the Common Heritage of Humanity principle, the words "common", "heritage" and "humanity" are discretely relevant in the determination of the meaning of the entire expression "common heritage of mankind." *See* A. Micoud, *Du "patrimoine naturel de l'humanité" considéré comme un symptome* 30/31 DROIT ET SOCIÉTÉ 265 (1995).
63 Schachter, *supra* note 59, at 758.
64 The "privileged" character of the "governing principles", particularly the fundamental principle of the Common Heritage of Humanity, is evidenced by the directives that the provisions embodying these prescriptions shall not be amended, repealed or rendered nugatory by States parties to the 1982 Convention. *See* Art. 155 (2) & Art. 311 (6), CLOS; *see also*, Art. 309, CLOS on the prohibition on reservations to the Convention.

extensive with the history of the Common Heritage of Humanity as a fundamental principle in international law. As it will be shown below, the "principles governing the area" – more general than the seabed mining rules but less abstract than the Common Heritage of Humanity – emerged as a result of the mutual and reciprocal (or dialectical) interaction of two developmental trajectories – one for the Common Heritage of Humanity norm and the other for the norms governing nodule mining in the Area. Consequently, an historical analysis of Part XI offers the most promising means of identifying the authoritative "list" of governing principles for the Area.

Before re-opening the historical discussion, a note on historical method is in order. It is of course true that advocates propounding particular interpretations of, or approaches to, Part XI, or any of its provisions, tend to highlight historical antecedents that would cast favorable light on their preferred legal positions on the subject, or else minimize if not obscure the importance of historical facts that would apparently argue against their case. Although a certain amount of selectivity and value orientation in historical narrative is inevitable, the consciousness that momentary legal advocacy affects historical perspective is rarely demonstrated in some of the available "authoritative" literature on Part XI of the Convention. The lessons from the arguments and clarifications that have been paraded as disinterested scholarship in the 1960s concerning the continental shelf regime are instructive. There is always the potential danger that through a variety of techniques in the verbalization of legal history, obdurate policy advocacies *de lege ferenda* can in fact be transmuted into magistral assertions of *lex lata*. In the historical recollection of events of such dramatic importance in the law of the sea, the perspective offered by a longer time frame of analysis could surely assist uncover the biases of historical interpretation in an earlier period.

As it was proposed above, the historical account that will be presented below concerning the substantive law aspects of Part XI of the Convention aims to extract the authoritative list of legal principles governing the Area as a whole. There is no question, in principle, that there are indeed "principles governing the Area." The language of the Convention says so. And if it were otherwise, the definition of the scope of jurisdictional competence in Part XI would not make any sense, and the conceptualization of the Common Heritage of Humanity as a fundamental principle of international law would not be possible. Because the list of such principles is not adequately systematized in Section 2 of Part XI – a formal defect which I believe needs to be glossed if the full scope and relevance of Part XI is to be ascertained – treaty interpretation is called for, requiring the examination of evidence given by the historical record.

It is, therefore, not pretended that the legal history of Part XI presented here will disclose the authoritative list of principles governing the Area. Some other interpretation of the history of Part XI may yield conclusions to the contrary. Moreover, the exercise is worthwhile in an additional sense. It will also serve as an opportunity to challenge certain fashionable impressions that have been propagated, and continue to be propagated, in the literature which, it is submitted, do prevent a meaningful dialogue on or a constructive approach towards Part XI of the Convention. A few not-so-innocent representations made in this respect, touching especially on the contribution of the Third World to the development of Part XI, which a more balanced legal history could rectify indeed may be cited: (1) the developing countries have always been motivated by the expectation of a financial bonanza from seabed mining, a highly-capital intensive undertaking involving sophisticated technology which they themselves do not possess or can ill-afford;[65] (2) The 1970 Declaration of Principles Resolution, upon which Part XI is based, illustrates how developing countries impose their wishes on a minority of States through paper majorities;[66] (3) the developing countries seek to establish, but are unable to pay for, a huge international bureaucracy aimed at controlling seabed mining initiatives, which is likely to be inefficient and would dissipate whatever common heritage income is generated by productive activity in the Area;[67] (4) either greed or short-sightedness on the part of developing countries have led them to advance and consolidate the expansive 200-mile EEZ, thereby reducing the amount of seabed resources that would have been allocated as part of the common heritage;[68] and (5) implementing the common heritage of mankind concept is part of the questionable agenda of the New International Economic Order (NIEO) movement, which caused so much divisiveness and confrontation in the international community when it was launched in the mid 1970s.[69] These and other[70] insinuations and argumentative assumptions could certainly lend support to a

---

65 Schmidt, *op. cit.* 16, 308.
66 Friedheim, *op. cit.* 234-235; Clingan, *supra* Chap. II note 26, at IV-V.
67 E.D. Brown, *supra* Chap. II note 10, at 460.
68 Schmidt, *op. cit.* 29; E.D. Brown, *supra* Chap. II note 10, at 10; Danilenko, *op. cit.* 299; Verwey, *supra* Chap. I note 29 at 848.
69 Schmidt, *op. cit.* 108-109, 161, 187-188, 192, 212; Friedheim, *op. cit.* Chap. 7.
70 *E.g.,* Hollick, *op. cit.* 264, avers that "The Group of 77 was not ready to begin serious negotiations on seabed issues until 1975."

particular view adopted concerning the interpretation of a rule or concept in Part XI of the Convention. It is however doubtful whether they are at all necessary or helpful not only in achieving the widely-shared goal of a stable and strengthened public order of the ocean miniaturized in Part XI but also, more broadly, in placing the increasingly marginalized North-South dialogue on a more reassuring pedestal. It is submitted that Part XI is, afterall, the most important manifestation, if not the essential core, of the North-South dialogue that had taken place in the normative sphere. The historical evaluation of Part XI will therefore begin by describing the North-South context that surrounded its beginnings – a context which cannot be allowed to fade into oblivion.

B. THE COMMON HERITAGE OF HUMANITY PRINCIPLE AS A PLEA FOR DEVELOPMENT AND PEACE

The internationalization debate that commenced in the United States in the mid-1960s was, on the whole, driven by the economics of deep sea resources. It should be recalled, however, that the economic issue that dominated the controversy at this early stage involved less the "production" aspects of newly discovered undersea wealth than its "distribution" on an international scale. Important as the technological and commercial possibilities of exploiting the newly discovered resources may be, the core problem that polarized opinion in the US essentially revolved around the issue "to whom should the new wealth accrue?" The book of Dr. John Mero, *Mineral Resources of the Sea* whose publication sparked this debate, did emphasize the "distributive" component in the equation of nodule mining by advocating that nodule resources should be treated in the same manner as fish on the high seas – free for anyone's taking. The only obstacle that stood in the way of realizing this preference, as he himself recognized, was the legal framework of resource allocation proceeding from the "exploitability clause" of the 1958 Continental Shelf Convention. From the very start, therefore, the regime of wealth distribution informed the problematical economics of manganese nodule mining. The political controversy over who controls the seabed projected, in the first instance, the acute disagreement on the matter of who ought to be materially enriched by, or should fundamentally enjoy the economic benefits of, the mines of Neptune.

1. New Deep Sea Resources and The Development Imperative

The views of those who advocated internationalization converged on the question of how the income or benefits derived from economic activities in the deep ocean should be used. Sharing in the profit derived from the exploitation of frontier resources by less developed countries and ensuring the financial independence of the United Nations were the two most-cited reasons given by various individuals and non-governmental groups in their defense of an internationalization policy. The Commission to Study the Organization for Peace, for instance, advanced these reasons as part of the rationale for a UN move to declare the title of the international community to the "uncommitted areas."[71] A "United Nations Marine Resources Agency", which the Commission proposed to be established, would then "distribute the returns from such exploitation in accordance with the directives issued by the United Nations General Assembly."[72] It will also be recalled that The World Peace Through Law Conference, which adopted a Resolution[73] that pioneered the use of the term "the common heritage of mankind", noted that "more than half of mankind finds itself underprivileged, underfed, and underdeveloped"; it was only logical that the economic development of mineral and food resources out in the seas beyond national jurisdiction "raise the economic level of peoples throughout the world, especially the developing countries."

The reaction of the so-called "realists" in the debate was predictably conservative on the central issue of who should benefit from resource exploitation of the deep seabed. The argument against internationalization was naturally propounded by those who believed that States must constantly strive to increase their power, wealth and skill[74] thereby justifying the primacy of intra-State

---

71 17th Report of the Commission, *supra* Chap. III note 36, at 37-39; *see also id.*, Chap. V. Other reasons for international control included prevention of military use and avoidance of contamination.

72 *Ibid*. In the United States Senate, Senator Frank Church reiterated the concept, already catching increasing public attention, that the United Nations be made financially independent through ownership of the oceans' mineral resources. Wenk, *supra* Chap. III note 33, at 259.

73 The Resolution called on the UNGA to proclaim "that the non-fishery resources of the high seas, outside of the territorial waters of any State, and the bed of the sea beyond the continental shelf deep seabed and its resources appertain to the United Nations and are subject to its jurisdiction and control."

74 Burke, *supra* Chap. III note 29; Oswald, *supra* Chap. III note 135.

decisions in the allocation of benefits derived from the ocean frontier. It was earlier shown that this view was welcomed by representatives of the emerging deep ocean mining industry in the United States, who wished for guaranteed exclusive access to the new ocean wealth through an exploitation regime founded on the concept of flag State supremacy.[75] Also in the United States, some quarters were opposed outright to internationalization on the ground that it gives away what was regarded as a "national birthright."[76]

It may seem paradoxical that the question òf how to distribute benefits and opportunities from the exploitation of resources in the new ocean frontier did not cause any major stir in the United Nations when the matter was first brought to its ken. There was in fact a straightforward consensus that easily emerged on the main objective of exploitation activity: new mineral and food resources in the oceans should be disposed for the purpose of economic development in the Third World. Thus, the Economic and Social Council, which launched the earliest initiative on marine resources exploitation in the UN, addressed the phenomenon of new marine resources through ECOSOC Resolution 1112 of March 1966,[77] whose underlying goals were to ascertain the nature of the opportunities that had to be tapped and to identify the new resources out there in the oceans that should be exploited especially for the benefit of developing countries.[78] The October 1965 statement of US Ambassador James Roosevelt before the UN expressed the high hope and noble aspiration that should have settled any doubts about the ultimate distributive/developmental aim of exploiting deep sea resources:

> The supply of marine life, not to mention mineral deposits, deep in the ocean and even near the surface is virtually endless. Learning to use it to feed the hungry, clothe the naked, and warm the cold could simplify if not solve many of the problems that now concern us and, I should emphasize, may well provide a source of international capital.[79]

---

75 Ely, *LSI 1966*, *supra* Chap. III note 34.
76 Wenk, *op. cit.* at 149; *See also* letters from several US Congressmen, the US Chamber of Commerce, and the American Legion expressing opposition to the vesting of seabed title to the UN. *House Interim Report* at 71-16.
77 *Supra* Chap. III note 43 and accompanying text.
78 *Id.*, para. (a) & (b).
79 UNGA Committee II speech excerpted in *House Interim Report* at 9. The move to generate policy-relevant information about deep sea resources gathered further momentum in the UN when the UN General Assembly, through UNGA Resolution

ECOSOC Resolution 1112, it cannot be forgotten, was part of a determined effort in the United Nations to vitalize the International Development Decade Programme,[80] which was perceived as having failed to produce meaningful results at the decade's midpoint.[81] The resolution requested the UN Secretary General "to identify any gaps in available knowledge which merit early attention by virtue of their importance to the development of ocean resource, and of the practicality of their early exploitation[.]" In the preliminary response of the Secretary General to this request, it is noteworthy that he identified two "major gaps", *viz.*, (a) the legal status of the deep sea resources and (b) ways and means of ensuring that the exploitation of these resources benefit the developing countries.[82] The first stated "gap" clearly suggested that the political issue of "who controls the seabed" was virtually inescapable from the agenda of the UN. The aim of exploiting deep sea resources for the benefit of developing countries was inextricably bound to the resolution of a prejudicial question regarding a proper legal framework to achieve this aim. More interestingly, the UN Secretary General revealed which side of the internationalization debate caught his sympathy when he proposed that the economic exploitation of deep sea resources for the benefit of developing countries not only required consideration of legal aspects but also inquired into the possibility of entrusting the deep sea resources to an international body.[83] By the time the Secretary-

---

2172 of December 1966, *supra* Chap. III note 44, called on the Secretary General to undertake a comprehensive survey of UN activities related to marine science and technology.

80   *See* UNGA Res. 1710 (XVI) 19 Dec. 1961.

81   *Supra* Chap. III note 43; *see also* agenda item discussions in the context of which US Ambassador James Roosevelt delivered his speech, *supra* note 79, before the UNGA Second Committee, UN Doc. A/C.2/PV (15 October 1965).

82   UN Doc. A/C.1/952 (31 October 1967).

83   *Id.* para. 9. The relevant observation that drives home the point that development concerns are ultimately tied up to the question of a "regime" and the "machinery" for the deep seabed – needs to be quoted in full:
     As pertains item (b), the Secretary-General will examine various alternatives, including the advisability and feasibility of entrusting the deep sea resources [*i.e.*, mineral and food excluding fish] to an international body. The General Assembly may consider it advantageous for the Secretary-General to prepare a more comprehensive report which would include a study of the legal framework which might be established for the deep sea resources, the administrative machinery which may be necessary for effective management and control, the possible system of licensing and various possible arrangements for distributing and/or utilizing

General made these observations, however, the delegation of Malta in the UN had already put on record its intention to speak on the serious and far-reaching political implications of the seabed question. Nonetheless, what the developments in the UN prior to the Malta initiative demonstrate conclusively was a strong international consensus that was building up to dispose of newly-discovered wealth in the oceans for the benefit of the developing countries.

2. Developing Countries and the "Race to Grab" the Deep Seabed

The International Development Decade project of the 1960s was indeed a fitting framework for the emerging marine resources agenda in the United Nations. It immediately supplied a broad up-front solution to the problem of how new ocean wealth should be distributed on an international basis, even if knowledge was still quite incomplete about the resources in question or the methods and costs of their exploitation. But apart from a clear identification at the outset of the proper beneficiaries of new ocean wealth, deliberations in the United Nations only vaguely hinted at the problem of participation of the beneficiary-developing countries in the policy process of distribution of new ocean wealth. Will the developing countries themselves have a decisive voice on how benefits from resource exploitation are to be allocated?

The enjoyment by developing countries of benefits that would accrue from potential economic exploitation of the deep oceans is logically distinct from the question of their involvement in the decision-making process concerning the distribution of those benefits. Furthermore, their participation in the decision process covering the distribution phase of economic activity is, likewise, logically separable from their participation in the production phase of the economic undertakings themselves. The conviction that developing countries should have a stake not only as passive recipients of post-production wealth in a new international endeavor but also as full-fledged participants in decision-making with respect to both production and distribution policy is exemplified in the 1966 Report of the Commission to Study the Organization of Peace. The Commission was certainly aware that the UN organs in the economic and social fields, especially the UN General Assembly which was thought to be the proper body that should declare title over the deep seabed, were dominated

---

the funds which would be derived therefrom, including those earmarked for the benefit of the developing countries.

by developing countries. By proposing to establish an international landlord called the UN Marine Resources Agency that would accept instructions from the UN General Assembly, the Commission was in effect proposing an extensive role for the developing countries in all phases of decision-making concerning the frontier.[84]

But it was US President Lyndon Johnson who articulated the most cogent and eloquent argument in support of the participation of the developing countries not only in the post-production benefit-sharing phase of undersea economic ventures but also, even more significantly, in the pre-production research and exploration stage of seabed activities undertaken on behalf of humankind. In his memorable remarks delivered during the commissioning of the US research vessel *Oceanographer*, he welcomed full international cooperation, including the participation of developing countries,[85] in marine scientific research – the very first activity that leads the way in the productive use of the oceans. Defending his vision of, or justification for, inclusive international participation in the new oceanographic endeavor, President Johnson announced:

> We welcome this type of international participation. Because under no circumstances, we believe, must we ever allow the prospects of rich harvests and mineral wealth to create a new form of colonial competition among the maritime nations. We must be careful to avoid a race to grab and hold the lands under the high seas. We must ensure that the deep seas and the ocean bottoms are, and remain, the legacy of all human beings.[86]

---

84 Professor Burke made a pointed objection to this proposition advanced by the Commission by asserting that the proposed UN Marine Resources Agency "has very little if any chance of birth unless the General Assembly is itself reconstituted so that its decision-making processes, especially those disposing of the new source of wealth to be placed in its control, more faithfully reflect the present distribution of power, wealth and skill among the members." Burke, *supra* Chap. III note 37.

85 India, Malaysia, Chile and Peru were among the countries invited to join the first global expedition of Oceanographer.

86 The first sentence of this landmark pronouncement, which provides the entire context of President Johnson's famous remarks, is almost always omitted when this part of the speech is quoted. Even the US delegation in the UN General Assembly in 1967 dropped the first sentence in the excerpt of President Johnson's speech. USA, PV 1527 (14 Nov 1967).

Reference to this curt statement had been repeatedly made as an endorsement of the substantive idea of the economics[87] of the common heritage, which it is.[88] But the statement was an articulation, above all, of a powerful argument on the procedural idea that all nations must be able participate in ocean activities that have become truly global in significance. The connection made between the policy of avoiding a "race to grab" colonial competition and the desire to recruit the participation and cooperation of all nations in the exploration and, logically, the exploitation of the deep seabed does reveal a policy framework behind the notion that the deep ocean floor and its resources are the legacy of all humankind.[89] Given that the "race to grab" the deep seabed can only be avoided if all nations participate in exploring and exploiting the new ocean frontier, the most rational and principled course to pursue is to involve all nations in the "conquest" of the new frontier. This policy position was advanced in support of the "statement of principles concerning the deep ocean floor" submitted by the United States to the *Ad Hoc* Seabed Committee.[90] In 1970, on the occasion of the adoption of the Declaration of Principles Resolution in the UN General Assembly, US Senator Claiborne Pell reiterated President Johnson's noble commitment for global, all-inclusive participation in the economic use and enjoyment of the "world last new frontier" and indicated a legal approach to achieve this aim:

---

87 The remarks are confined to the activity of exploration and exploitation of deep ocean resources, which is narrower in scope than the "exploration and use" language used in the preamble of UNGA Res. 2340 (XXII), which contemplated all types of activities in the area, including what is referred to in the dispositive part as "conservation".
88 *E.g.* H.S. Amerasinghe. "The Third World and the Seabed" in E.M. Borgese (Ed.), *Pacem In Maribus* 237-248, at 240 (1972).
89 The policy motivation underlying the "human legacy" concept of President Johnson is given in his 1968 Message to the US Congress on the International Decade of Ocean Exploration, text in Wenk, *op. cit.*, Appendix 16:
The task of exploring the ocean's depth for its potential wealth – food, minerals, resources – is as vast as the seas themselves. No one nation can undertake that task alone. As we have learned from previous ventures in ocean exploration, cooperation is the only answer.
90 UN Doc. A/AC.135/25 (28 June 1968), text in Wenk, *op. cit.* Appendix 17; 1968 Ad Hoc SBC Rep, Annex III.

> We do not want to see a "flag nations" rush towards new colonial empires. Rather we wish to see the ocean resources an usufruct available to all the world's peoples.[91]

President Johnson's inspiring call for expansive international cooperation in the new frontier of the deep oceans condemned *prima facie* the possible carving up the international seabed into exclusive economic or power enclaves among a few technologically advanced States. This policy attitude ruled out, by definition, the notion of unbridled freedom to explore and exploit the ocean bottoms akin in character to the divide-and-conquer techniques previously used by colonial marauders on land. His reference to the dangers of "new forms of colonial competition" in the new frontier was most appropriate in the context of the desire to include all nations – rich or poor, powerful or small – in a collective mission of discovery in the oceans. This certainly meditates on the sad epoch in human history when many nations under colonial rule were suppressed by a few gun-totting nations and forcibly excluded from decisions that mattered most to their own destinies – a point emphasized over and over again in the General Assembly after the Maltese initiative was launched. President Johnson's judicious remarks may well have recalled the 16th century sentiments of the Spanish jurist and theologian Francisco Vitoria who insisted that "other" peoples possessed legitimate legal status, and were entitled to have their views heard, their interests considered, and their needs humanely met by those who regard themselves as occupying a more privileged station.[92] The position is logical since it postulates the necessity of participation by all countries, including the developing countries, in a global endeavor that aspires to bring about material and moral well-being for all of humanity. It is also a claim that a valuable lesson of history had been learned: to avoid a repeat of colonialism, we must listen to its victims.

The intervention of President Johnson was made at a time when the UN was in the midst of searching for a meaningful way to achieve the goals of the UN Development Decade. His above-quoted remarks are significant because they somehow put forward a reinterpretation of the concept of decolonization in the context of implementing a meaningful international development policy in the 1960s. The programme of "decolonization" launched by the United

---

91 USA, PV 1774 (26 Nov 1970).
92 *See* A. Nussbaum, *A Concise History of the Law of Nations* 79-84 (1954).

Nations in the beginning of the 1960s[93] was primarily aimed at securing the political independence of nations that were still under colonial domination or administration. It was a policy for realizing political self-determination on the part of the Third World but lacked a corresponding economic programme which the first Development Decade project was hardly able to provide. The wide perspective adopted by President Johnson regarding international cooperation in ocean sciences, however, signalled a possible basis to realize the economic objective of decolonization. By denominating the "deep seas and the ocean bottoms" as "the legacy of all human beings", to be explored and exploited on this basis, he was in effect saying that all nations, including the newly emerged countries, can pursue economic development and safeguard their political independence on the basis of equality at the same time. The idea that the deep seabed was common human legacy justifies a most inclusive approach to its exploration, use and management, making possible the injection of a strong economic component into the international decolonization process.[94] For President Johnson, "universality" – as a pivotal feature of the new approach to the oceans – is the solution to the problematical relationship between decolonization and economic development. Fortunately, this principle of universality of participation in the exploration and use of the ocean was wholeheartedly endorsed by the international community when the UNGA adopted Resolution 2467D in December 1968 which launched the concept of an International Decade of Ocean Exploration.[95] The very first preambular paragraph of this Resolution reads:

> *Convinced* that the nations of the world should join together, with due respect for national jurisdiction, in a common long-term programme of exploration of the ocean as a potential source of resources, which should eventually be used for meeting the needs of all mankind with due recognition of those of developing countries and irrespective of the geographical location of States.[96]

---

93 *See* UNGA Res. 1514 (XV).
94 President Johnson's "heritage of mankind" concept was not, however, seriously pursued by the US State Department. Wenk, *op. cit.* 262, 267.
95 *See* 1968 Ad Hoc SBC Rep, para. 15-18; *Cf.* Danilenko, *op. cit.* [The Common Heritage of Humanity is a normative device claimed by the developing States to justify their participation in law making.]
96 The sad fate of the International Decade of Ocean Exploration idea in the US is chronicled in Wenk, *op. cit.* 262 *et seq.*

3. Global Distributive Justice and the Question of Continental Shelf Outer Limits

Ambassador Pardo, in his November 1967 address to the United Nations,[97] reiterated the anti-colonialism "race to grab" theme of President Johnson[98] but this time put heavy stress on the "intolerable injustice that would reserve the plurality of the world's resources for the exclusive benefit of less than a handful of nations."[99] The multi-dimensional programme of internationalization drawn by Ambassador Pardo was thus immediately thrown into the political cauldron of a North-South context that was quite unpronounced when the ECOSOC or the UNGA began deliberations on the question of deep sea resources the previous year.[100] The alarm was sounded on the imminent possibility that the North-South gap, which was already demoralizing the entire UN system in light of the mid-point assessment of the UN development Decade Programme, would further drastically deteriorate. The economic question of how to distribute the benefits from the exploitation of new ocean wealth on a global basis, which supplied the dominant theme of recent discussions on the seabed issue, was soon afterwards transformed into the terms of a grievance discourse that highlighted the issue of global distributive justice.

---

97 PV 1515 & 1516 (1 Nov 1967).
98 Ambassador Pardo in his well-researched and well-documented presentation did not see it fit to mention President Johnson's above-quoted remarks delivered at the commissioning of the *Oceanographer*. *Supra* at 252. He must not have been unaware of the President's remarks, whose prominent warning against the "new form of colonial competition" was also conveyed by Ambassador Pardo in the latter's reference to the "competitive scramble for sovereign rights over the land underlying the world's seas and oceans, surpassing in magnitude and its implication last century's colonial scramble for territory in Asia and Africa." PV 1515 para. 91. This paragraph contains a political high-point in the address. For an account of the research effort behind the Maltese initiative, *see* V. Gauci, "Personal Recollections and Reflections on a Major Initiative" in *Malta Review of Foreign Affairs Special Issue: Towards a Second Generation United Nations*, at 39-58 (Malta Ministry of Foreign Affairs & The Univ. of Malta, 1993).
99 PV 1515, para. 91.
100 *Cf.* Oda, *supra* Chap. III note 34, at 17-18 observing that when the Maltese item was being considered for allocation to the proper Committee of the UNGA, the Secretariat was somehow embarrassed because the economic motivation behind the Maltese proposal was already covered by on-going activities in the United Nations.

An examination of the general debates in the UN General Assembly that followed the historic address of Ambassador Pardo would show that the concerns expressed by most delegations about the economics of deep sea resource exploitation, especially those from the developing countries, followed a consistent orientation: urgent follow-up action on the Maltese move was necessary in order to prevent a horrendous aggravation of the North-South development "gap."[101] Deep ocean mineral resources, which were previously pictured in the United States and the United Nations as a delightful source of new wealth, were now perceived by developing countries as portending an ominous reality of multiplied global disparities.[102] It was the grave political tone set by the Pardo speech that left many countries to ask the question: will the technologically advanced States take advantage of the prevailing legal uncertainties and proceed to occupy the deep ocean floor and mine its riches?[103] The message of Ambassador Amerasinghe on the occasion of the submission of the Report of the *Ad Hoc* Seabed Committee to the General Assembly is exemplary, and marks out a permanent concern of the developing countries that lasted throughout the period of existence of the Seabed Committee and into UNCLOS III:

---

101 For the General Debate in the UN First Committee in November 1967, *see* PV 1524-1530.

102 The impression given by some writers that the representatives of developing countries in the UNGA had eyes gleefully flashing with dollar bonanza signs after Ambassador Pardo delivered his speech is grossly misleading. The more accurate depiction of events would show an overwhelming mood of fearful apprehension and distress on the part of developing States perceiving an accelerated deterioration of the North-South development gap. When the *Ad Hoc* Seabed Committee concluded its work in 1968, it was already clear to many countries, including the developing countries, that the prospects of a "pot of gold" from deep seabed mining is not likely to take place in the future. *See* US House of Representatives, Subcommittee on International Organizations and Movements, House Committee on Foreign Affairs, *The Oceans: A Challenging New Frontier*. "Report on the Work of the UN Ad Hoc Committee on the Seabeds" at 13R, 90th Congress, 2d Sess (Washington: 1968). The Ecuadorian representative in the UN as late as 1969 recognized that the "reality of bonanza" was indeed a "mirage." PV 1676 (4 Nov 1969). *Cf.* C.C. Joyner & E.A. Martell, *Looking Back to See Ahead: UNCLOS III and Lessons for Global Commons Law* 27 ODIL 73, at 83 (1996).

103 Ceylon, PV 1603 (8 Nov 1968), para. 5.

> The developing countries must adhere steadfastly to the pursuit of these two objectives of peaceful use and of economic exploitation for the benefit of mankind, with special regard to the interest and needs of the developing countries of the world. The wide disparity in economic standards between the developed and the developing countries will be further widened and the feeling of world-wide instability that arises from the existence of such a disparity will be intensified if the resources of the seabed and the ocean floor become the bounty of those who have the technological and financial capacity to exploit these resources and to convert them to their benefit.[104]

The most important motivation that stimulated the General Assembly to act urgently on the Maltese item, creating an *Ad Hoc* Committee for the purpose, was therefore negative in thrust: to prevent the few technologically advanced States from undertaking action with respect to resource exploitation on the deep seabed which in all likelihood "would result in widening the already considerable and dangerous [North-South] gap."[105] A national or unilateral approach to deep seabed mining, apart from its questionable status in law, was widely opposed because of its political identification with wilful action on the part of the technologically developed States to induce an irretrievably engulfing welfare gap between the developed and developing countries. At the time when the *Ad Hoc* Committee set out to consider the seabed question, there was no longer any question that there would be, in principle, international control or supervision of the deep seabed and its resources.[106] Two major questions remained to be addressed: (1) the nature or structure of international control over the deep seabed to be set up, and (2) what ought to be done in the meantime to protect or promote the acknowledged common interest of humankind in the deep seabed and its resources. However, the clarification of these questions took place in an atmosphere of pervasive apprehension created by the

---

104 Ceylon, PV 1588 (28 October 1968).
105 Belgium, PV 1596 (4 Nov 1968). It was through a Belgian proposal in the *Ad Hoc* Committee, Ad Hoc SBC Rep, Annex III, that led to the formation of the permanent Seabed Committee. PV 1588 (28 October 1968). *See also* statements from Yugoslavia, PV 1593 (31 Oct 1968); Libya, PV 1597 (4 Nov 1968); Poland, *ibid.*; Algeria, PV 1599 (5 Nov 68); Sierra Leone, PV 1600 (6 Nov 1968); Columbia, *ibid.*; Chile, PV 1602 (7 Nov 1968).
106 The crucial preambular items in Res. 2340 (XXII), creating the *Ad Hoc* Committee, recognize "the common interest of mankind in the seabed and ocean floor" as well as their exploration and use "in the interest of maintaining international peace and security and for the benefit of all mankind."

lurking suspicion that the technologically capable States will proceed to unilaterally mine the seabed.

It is in the context of this anxiety that the much-maligned Moratorium Resolution of 1969 should be understood.[107] The idea of a Moratorium on all exploitation activities on the seabed area "beyond the limits of national jurisdiction" was borne out of the perception, based on straightforward political suspicion, that anyone of the technologically advanced States might trigger the "race to grab" neo-colonial scramble by proceeding unilaterally to mine the seabed.[108] Unilateral exploitation while negotiations were taking place in the Seabed Committee for an acceptable regime to internationalize the seabed would, by the same token, indicate a blatant disregard for the serious international concern over the development gap problem. Pending the establishment of a seabed regime that will meaningfully respond to the problem of the North-South gap, Ambassador Sen of India reiterated that "no exploitation should take place before an international regime is established."[109]

The Moratorium Resolution is traceable to the idea of a "gentleman's agreement" on freezing the *status quo* on national claims, first proposed by Ambassador Alva Myrdal of Sweden in November 1967, the purpose being to forestall action that would impair the extent of the international area.[110] Although its proponents rightly pointed out that the resolution was not intended to have legally binding effect because it was merely an invitation for States to exercise political self-restraint[111] the Resolution was attacked on two

---

107 Resolution 2574D (15 December 1969). Of the 4 resolutions adopted by the UNGA in December 1969 related to the seabed item, this was the most controversial resolution where a recorded vote was taken: 62 to 28, with 28 abstentions. PV/1833 (15 Dec 1969). For a brief background, *see* Oda, *supra* note 2, at 90-94. *Cf.* Joyner & Martell, *op. cit.* at 76.

108 "The moratorium resolution was introduced because there was disturbing evidence that operational activities had already been initiated in the international area by States with advanced seabed technology, and it was feared that such operations were intended to and would forestall and thus jeopardize the efforts of the international community to establish international control over the exploitation of the resources of the area." H.S. Amerasinghe, "Key Issues in the Third United Nations Conference on the Law of the Sea" in Borgese & Krieger, *op. cit.* 332.

109 PV 1673 (31 Oct 1969); *see also* Brazil, PV 1674 (31 Oct 1969) and A/PV.1833 (15 Dec 1969).

110 Sweden, PV 1527 (14 Nov 1967), and PV 1596 (4 Nov 1968); Mexico, A/PV.1833 (15 Dec 1969). *Cf.* Oda, *supra* note 2, at 92.

111 Ceylon, PV 1708 (2 Dec 1969); Sweden, PV 1709 (2 Dec 1969).

grounds – one, political and the other, legal – both making reference to the "exploitability clause" of the Continental Shelf Convention. The political objection is interesting because it attempted to wrestle with the rationale for the moratorium proposal on its own ground. Thus, according to the United States – the most vociferous critic of the moratorium move – a call by the international community for a moratorium would actually encourage coastal States to maximize their claims through unjustifiable extensions of national jurisdiction offshore, defeating the very purported aim of the moratorium to preserve the integrity of the seabed area reserved for mankind.[112] In addition, it was argued that the moratorium would have the practical effect of retarding the development of sea-bed exploitation and accordingly the development of technological capacity for such exploitation."[113] These fears, nonetheless, did not materialize.

The second, legally-orientated, objection to the proposed moratorium resolution is more deserving of attention. This was the claim that the moratorium resolution is pointless and self-defeating because it begs the whole question of the "limits" of the continental shelf.[114] As the representative of Japan confidently asserted the proposed resolution, as worded, failed to set the concrete scope of its application.[115] Indeed, how can there be a moratorium on seabed exploitation "beyond the limits national jurisdiction" when no limits to the continental shelf have been agreed? Ambassador Phillips of the US, in the same vein, insisted that "there will be no [seabed exploitation] regime in fact until the area of its application is decided."[116]

There was, unmistakably, no rejoinder possible to the unassailable logic of this legal challenge. But it may well have been left unanswered, because

---

112 USA, PV 1709 (2 Dec 1969) and A/PV 1833 (15 Dec 1969); *see also* statements of Malta, Norway, Canada, Japan, and France, all in PV 1709 (2 Dec 1969).

113 USA, *ibid*. The US likewise sought to convince the General Assembly that present activities should not prejudice eventual location of the area, but that the seabed regime to be negotiated should provide protection for investments before the establishment of boundaries. PV 1709 (2 Dec 1969).

114 *See* statements of Malta, Norway, USA, Canada, Japan, UK, and France, all in PV 1709 (2 Dec 1969).

115 *Ibid*. Japan, therefore, suggested that the more sensible language to use would be a moratorium for the area beyond "the internationally recognized limits of national jurisdiction rather than "the area ... beyond the limits of national jurisdiction." The latter phrase was retained in Res. 2574 D.

116 PV 1709. *See also* United States Position on Moratorium, text in 9 ILM 831-832 (1970).

– to paraphrase US Supreme Court Justice Oliver Wendel Holmes – if there was at all any sound legal argument behind the Moratorium resolution, it lay not in logic but in "psychological" experience.[117]

The admission by those States who opposed the moratorium resolution that there was no concretely delimited area over which the suggested moratorium will be applied or, in other words, that the limits of national (continental shelf) jurisdiction are still undefined, is the very same proposition that would argue against the position that deep seabed mining, if carried out during that time, is within the scope of the freedom of the seas. The admission is, *mutatis mutandis*, itself an argument for the case that there is yet no specified area "beyond the limits of national jurisdiction" where any seabed exploitation activity under a regime of freedom of the seas can take place. We should note that *not one* of the countries voting against the moratorium resolution expressed opposition to the moratorium move on the basis of a conviction that seabed resource exploitation is – at that point in time when the moratorium resolution was being considered – an authorized freedom of the seas under the conventional or customary high seas regime embodied in the 1958 Geneva Convention on the High Seas. If it is really the case that deep seabed mining is part of the pre-existing freedom of the seas at the time when Ambassador Pardo delivered his monumental address in 1967 – as a handful of powerful industrialized nations, including so many writers sympathetic to their cause, had maintained in the 1970s and 1980s – the argument would have been to the effect that the proposed moratorium resolution was legally untenable because the General Assembly adopting a moratorium policy cannot alter or amend a right to mine the deep seabed on the basis of the freedom of the seas doctrine. But all the legal objections on record against the proposed moratorium were clearly, and rightly so, confined to the invocation of the exploitability clause of the Continental Shelf Convention which, without a scintilla of doubt, would indeed have applied to any exploitation activity on the deep seabed.[118]

---

117 Ambassador Amerasinghe, it will be recalled, reassured the UN General Assembly that the expected effect of the moratorium resolution was not legal but "purely psychological." Ceylon, PV 1708 (2 December 1969); also Sweden, PV 1709 (2 December 1969).
118 That the argument for the permissibility to mine manganese nodules under the freedom of the seas framework is a "political afterthought" is clear. It is fitting to make a few observations, in this connection, about the extent to which some authors have stretched their imaginations to make out a case for the freedom of the seas-basis of nodule mining. Take the case of the three-volume work, T.G.

Kronmiller, *The Lawfulness of Deep Seabed Mining* (1980). This opus claims to be "disciplined legal analysis" of the seabed debate which employs an "analytical method" (xi). That it is in many ways a lawyer's pleading does not seem to be denied, although the author at the same time states that the work is "academic in nature" which was supervised by the best minds in Cambridge and "reflects substantial independence of thought" (xv).

The achilles heel of this massively documented thesis is, as expected, the discussion on the limits of the continental shelf (pp. 108-131) where the author, in a rather unconvincing presentation, argues that the "exploitability clause" contemplated spatial "outer limits." After a selective marshalling of evidence, the blunt proposition is reached that: "Whatever uncertainty might have existed among minorities in the ILC and at the 1958 Conference, the issue should now be regarded as having been resolved" (p. 129). Further, perhaps in an effort to erase lingering doubts, it is then concluded that: "However, the point of law is sufficiently settled at this time [*i.e.*, 1978 or 1979] that there is no reason to belabor the matter by offering further evidence and arguments. There are far thornier issues requiring greater attention." When these statements were written, even the special negotiating group in UNCLOS III tasked to deal with the "hard core" issue concerning the definition of the continental shelf was still struggling to come up with a consensus text on the "outer limits" of the continental shelf. *See* II COMMENTARY at 833 *et seq.* and 856 *et seq.*; Hutchinson, *op. cit.*; and *infra* Secs. B.3 & B.4.

More revealing is that section of the work which addresses the question of "The Effect of the Moratorium Resolution" (pp. 224-234). Here it is reported, perhaps not without a trace of dishonesty, that

In the General Assembly First Committee and Plenary, during the consideration of the moratorium resolution, *the United States took the position that deep seabed mining is within the ambit of the freedom of the seas and that a legally binding moratorium could not be imposed by a U.N. General Assembly resolution.* (p. 227, emphasis supplied)

That part which narrates that the US was opposed to a "legally binding moratorium" could be the result of an honest mis-reading of the US statements referred to (*i.e.*, in Doc. A/C.1/PV.1709 of 2 Dec 1969 and Doc. A/PV.1833 of 15 Dec 1969), considering that nowhere did the US representative, or anyone else in the UN General Assembly, ever raised the issue of a "legally binding moratorium" being "imposed." But that part of the above-quoted statement which asserts that the US "took the position that deep seabed mining is within the ambit of the freedom of the seas" is a gross and inexcusable misrepresentation of facts. One can peruse the cited record forever to search in vain for the slightest reference being made by the US delegation to deep seabed mining and the freedom of the seas. The deceptive manipulation of the record is further shown in the text immediately following the one quoted above, where Dr. Kronmiller this time quotes the British representative: "We do not believe that the General Assembly can and should

263

One can only imagine the hypothetical situation that reversed the roles of the protagonists in the UN General Assembly where, say the US or the UK or Japan would have proposed a resolution to encourage deep seabed exploitation activities under an *ad interim* regime of freedom pending establishment of an international regime; this proposal would then invite the formidable refutation that such proposal is pointless because there is as yet no area clearly defined where an interim freedom to exploit seabed resources can possibly take place. The moral of the moratorium story is nothing more but the familiar "good faith" principle in general international law: *allegans contraria non est audiendus* – a person cannot affirm at one time and deny at another.[119]

It seems that the devastating logic of the moratorium resolution, not on the contemporaneous legal position of its supporters but on the future legal position of its opponents, was too consequential for the United States. For the US must have immediately realized its damning implications on the freedom of the seas framework as an available policy option for deep seabed mining. For the first time since the UN took cognizance of the seabed question, the United States averred, in no uncertain terms, its deep resentment on the handling of the seabed agenda by the General Assembly. Sufficiently provoked by the

---

by its recommendations purport to modify existing international law" (p. 27), where "existing international law" was somehow made to appear as "existing law on freedom of the seas." But the British representative was in fact alluding to the Continental Shelf Convention as the existing international law, because the British representative, in the paragraph that was only quoted partially by Dr. Kronmiller, was then expressing his agreement with the assessment previously made by Ambassador Amerasinghe about the relevant existing international law, which was the continental shelf regime.

Dr. Kronmiller's book was described by two very influential US Congressmen, John Murphy as Chairman of the House Committee on Merchant Marine and Fisheries and John Breaux as Chairman of the Oceanography Subcommittee, as the "most exhaustive and sophisticated analysis on the subject of the permissibility of deep seabed mining under international law" (p. xvii). The Congressmen admit that they relied heavily on Dr. Kronmiller's advise in framing the bill which eventually became the 1980 US Deep Seabed Hard Mineral Resources Act. 19 ILM 5 1003 (1980). Dr. Kronmiller chaired the Reagan Administration's policy review on the Draft 1980 Law of the Sea Convention. *See* D. Larson, *The Reagan Administration and the Law of the Sea* 11 ODIL 297, at 300 (1982).

119 On the application of the principle of "estoppel" in international law, *see* Bin Cheng, *General Principles of Law as Applied by International Courts and Tribunals* 141-149 (1987).

moratorium proposal the United States delegation, in a last ditch effort to prevent the resolution's adoption, intimated the accusation that the United Nations was now sending the "signal that it was willing to make fundamental decisions on the seabed issues through the politics of confrontation and paper majorities."[120] Understandably, there was a certain incoherence in the US stance taken then, for the US was fully aware that the resolution did not possess, and was not designed to possess, the least normative value to be anything but embodying a "fundamental decision" of the international community. Somehow, the US was actually forced to limit the flexibility of its national policy during the *interim* period, *i.e.*, pending the establishment of the new *lex lata* for the deep seabed and its resources. The Moratorium Resolution may be the first UN General Assembly Resolution, which created a binding rule of law, inspite of a prior unequivocal understanding that it was meant to be only recommendatory, and at the psychological level at that.

Beyond its legal environment, the debate on the Moratorium Resolution disclosed a more fundamental rift that had already plagued the United Nations. This relates to the serious disagreement on the practical terms of how to protect the "common heritage" while agreement was being sought on the regime to internationalize the deep seabed. It was already widely conceded in principle that a "race to grab" neo-colonial competition in the deep seabed was totally unacceptable to the international community. But could the threat to "race to grab" in the new frontier, widely perceived as a damocles sword over the UN deliberations, be removed while negotiations on the common heritage regime were in progress? The moratorium controversy dramatized the intricate dilemmas surrounding the quest for a necessary *modus vivendi* but, unfortunately, did not show any cues on how the *ad interim* difficulties could be overcome.

4. The Question of Limits (Again) and the Common Heritage of Humanity Principle

The decision to establish an *Ad Hoc* Committee[121] reflected the cautious attitude taken by many delegations in the UN General Assembly towards the internationalization proposal put forward by Malta. Undertaking a further study of the agenda item was a procedural move that basically allowed all countries more time to closely examine their interests and stakes in relation to the issues

---

120 Doc. A/PV 1833.
121 Res. 2340 (XXII), 18 Dec. 1967.

265

presented by the wet frontier, which they agreed were completely new and immensely complex. However, the general plan of action on the seabed item was evident: a special committee will first be constituted to study the item and afterwards prepare a draft declaration of principles, which will be recommended for adoption by the General Assembly as a formal resolution or declaration, and which, in turn, will provide the basis for the subsequent negotiation and conclusion of a treaty.[122] The precedent set by the adoption of the Outer Space Treaty[123] was seen by many delegations as highly significant in determining what general course of action should be taken on the deep seabed question.[124]

The 35-member *Ad Hoc* Committee organized itself into two working groups, an Economic and technical Working Group and a Legal Working Group, to consider "the scientific, technical, economic, legal and other aspects" of the seabed question. It could be said that the Committee successfully canvassed all the relevant issues touching on its mandate. Its work provided the necessary stimulus for the creation of a permanent UN Seabed Committee in 1968.[125] But it may be noticed as somewhat strange that no finding or recommendation in substantive law was arrived at by the *Ad Hoc* Committee. Apart from providing a chronicle of its deliberations and the points of discussion in its two working groups, the Report of the *Ad Hoc* Committee did not state or endorse any legal conclusion of the Legal Working Group. Various draft declarations on legal principles were submitted to the Legal Subcommittee for adoption at various stages in the Committee's work.[126] Unfortunately, efforts made during the last session of the Committee to produce a consensus text on legal

---

[122] For the Maltese proposal on a strategy of action, *see* PV 1516, para. 8-15.
[123] *Treaty On Principles Governing the Activities of States in the Exploration and Use of Outer Space, including the Moon and Other Celestial Bodies*, 610 UNTS 205, opened for signature 25 January 1967 and entered into force 10 October 1967. The item on outer space was first placed on the agenda of the UN in 1958. An *Ad Hoc* Committee was established thereafter but was unable to embark on its work; in 1961 a Permanent Committee on Peaceful Uses of Outer Space was established. The 1967 Treaty was preceded by a unanimously-adopted UN General Assembly *Declaration on Legal Principles Governing the Activities of States in the Exploration and Use of Outer Space* on 13 December 1963. By 1995 ninety-one States had become parties to this treaty. *See* M. Lachs, "Outer Space, the Moon and Other Celestial Bodies" in Bedjaoui, *supra* Chap. I note 29, 959-947.
[124] *See* PV 1524-1530, 1542-1544 (November 1967).
[125] Res. 2476A (XXIII), 21 Dec. 1968.
[126] *See* Ad Hoc SBC Rep, Annex III.

principles concerning the deep seabed were not successful. As a consequence the Report presents the two sets of proposed "principles"[127] which were not reconciled, reflecting the different formulations of two interest groups that had emerged in the *Ad Hoc* Committee. These two groups, it must be noted, corresponded to major geographic alignments in the UN: the developing countries of the Asian, African and Latin American regions, on one side, and the "Western European and others" group of countries, on the other.

Prior to discussions in the *Ad Hoc* Committee on the legal aspect of the seabed agenda item, there was widespread expectation that the formulation of relevant legal principles, or the drafting of a declaration of principles, would become the principal preoccupation of the *Ad Hoc* Committee. It was Ambassador Pardo who called the attention of the General Assembly to what he called "generally acceptable principles" or "long-term objectives" for the internationalization of the deep seabed,[128] which was really an enumeration of general statements that envisioned a minimum normative framework for the new frontier.[129] A survey of the Secretary General on the views of member

---

127 *See id.*, para. 88.
128 PV 1516, para. 10.:
(a) The sea-bed and the ocean floor, underlying the seas beyond the limits of national jurisdiction as defined in [a treaty clearly defining the outer limits of the continental shelf subject to national jurisdiction], are not subject to national appropriation whatsoever.
(b) The sea-bed and the ocean floor beyond the limits of national jurisdiction shall be reserved exclusively for peaceful purposes.
(c) Scientific research with regard to the deep seas and ocean floor, not directly connected with defence, shall be freely permissible and its results available to all.
(d) The resources of the sea-bed and ocean floor, beyond the limits of national jurisdiction, shall be exploited primarily in the interests of mankind, with particular regard to the needs of poor countries.
(e) The exploration and exploitation of the sea-bed and ocean floor beyond the limits of national jurisdiction shall be conducted in a manner consistent with the principles and purposes of the United Nations Charter and in a manner not causing unnecessary obstruction of the high seas or serious impairment of the marine environment.
129 In the Maltese scheme, these "principles" are proposed to be incorporated in a treaty that would create a special agency to administer the deep seabed and that would clearly define the outer limits of the continental shelf. The negotiation of this treaty will be preceded by the adoption of a resolution by the General Assembly embodying three concepts. The first is a substantive concept, quoted below

States on the seabed question conducted prior to the convening of the *Ad Hoc* Committee also revealed the preferences of not a few governments for certain legal principles, more or less sympathetic with the principles advanced by Malta, that should govern the deep seabed.[130] The "legal principles" facet of the study to be undertaken by the *Ad Hoc* Committee was likewise stressed by UN Secretary General U Thant who, addressing the opening session of the Committee, expressed his view that the deep ocean floor was the common heritage of all humanity.[131] Finally, the "programme of work" adopted by the Legal Working Group specifically sought a comprehensive inquiry into the legal principles relating to the deep seabed, both *lex lata* and *lex ferenda*.[132] The cardinal emphasis on legal principles in the framing of the overall mission the *Ad Hoc* Committee and, later, the permanent Seabed Committee,[133] throws

---

in full, and the other two are procedural suggestions, *viz., ad interim* freezing of sovereignty claims and the creation of a study group. *Id.*, para. 12-15. The first concept, which attempts to encapsulate all the "long term objectives" proffered, reads: ... the seabed and ocean floor are a common heritage of mankind and should be used and exploited for peaceful purposes and for the exclusive benefit of mankind as a whole. The needs of poor countries, representing that part of mankind which is most in need of assistance, should receive preferential consideration in the event of financial benefits being derived from the exploitation of the sea-bed and ocean floor for commercial purposes.
See also para. 3 of the Memorandum attached to the *Note Verbale* of Malta of 18 August 1967, *supra* Chap. II note 38.

130 Oda, *supra* note 2, at 8-10.
131 *Id.*, at 13.
132 "Examination of the legal principles relating to the sea-bed and the ocean floor, and the subsoil thereof, underlying the high seas beyond the limits of present national jurisdiction, including: (a) Existing regulations in this field; (b) Consideration of legal principles which should govern international co-operation with a view to the preparation of an agreement on the use of the sea-bed and the ocean floor, and the subsoil thereof, exclusively for peaceful purposes; (c) Consideration of legal principles which should govern international co-operation in the use, in the interests of mankind, of the resources of the seabed and the ocean floor and the subsoil thereof, underlying the high seas beyond the limits of present national jurisdiction." 1968 Ad Hoc SBC Rep, Annex II, para. 5.
133 *See* Res. 2467 (XXIII), 21 Dec. 1968, para. 2, instructing the permanent Sea-Bed Committee "to study the elaboration of legal principles and norms which would promote international cooperation in the exploration and use of the sea-bed and the ocean floor, and the subsoil thereof, beyond the limits of present national jurisdiction and the ensure the exploitation of their resources for the benefit of

into sharp relief the North-South character of the primal dissention on seabed principles in the *Ad Hoc* Committee.

This original disagreement on principles, or more accurately, on a correct approach to the formulation of principles for the deep ocean floor in the *Ad Hoc* Committee, between the rich countries, on the one hand, and poor countries, on the other, merits careful attention. Hindsight indeed shows that the protracted North-South debate on the seabed issue began with an initial failure of the international community to agree on principles for the deep ocean floor. But it is not enough to simply note that the disagreement was between rich and poor countries, and leave it at that.[134] Inasmuch as the disagreement was on *legal principles*, what should be scrutinized is the structure of legal reasons, methods and considerations that would distinctly characterize this disagreement as not merely a political disagreement but, more importantly, as a disagreement in law between North and South. It is submitted that the key to understanding the Common Heritage of Humanity as a substantive legal principle for present-day purposes lies in the analysis and synthesis of the North-South legal issues that were originally ventilated in the *Ad Hoc* Committee.

The two sets of principles outlined in the Report of the *Ad Hoc* Committee consist of the so-named "Set A" principles, which was supported by most developing countries in Asia, Africa and Latin America, and the "Set B" principles, submitted by the "Western Europe and Others" group including Japan.[135] There is undoubtedly valid ground for the belief that there is a substantial divergence between the "Set A" principles and the "Set B" principles. By simply juxtaposing the first-stated legal principles indicated in both sets of proposals, the most fundamental difference between them becomes all too evident. The first item under the "Set A" principles reads:

---

mankind, and the economic and other requirements which such a regime should satisfy in order to meet the interests of humanity as a whole[.]" *See also* Res. 2547B (XXIV), 15 Dec. 1969, para. 3 & 4.

134 *Cf.* Luard, *op. cit.* 92; Churchill & Lowe, *op. cit.* 180.

135 For an overview, *see* Oda, *supra* note 2, 30-34. Some countries – Malta, Pakistan and Kenya – expressed support for both sets of principles, while France, Kenya, and Yugoslavia pointed out that two sets of principles were not basically very different. As the debate progressed, however, these countries aligned their positions along the North-South divide. The Soviet block countries took the position that it is was beyond the competence of the *Ad Hoc* Committee to adopt a draft declaration of legal principles. *Id.* 30-31, 35.

269

(1) The sea-bed and the ocean floor, and the subsoil thereof, as referred to in the title of the item, are the common heritage of mankind and no State may claim or exercise sovereignty over any part of the area mentioned in resolution 2340 (XXII)[.]

On the other hand, the opening two items stated under the "Set B" text read:

(1) There is an area of the sea-bed and ocean floor and the subsoil thereof, underlying the high seas, which lies beyond the limits of national jurisdiction (hereinafter described as "this area");
(2) Taking into account the relevant dispositions of international law, there should be agreed a precise boundary for this area[.][136]

For convenience, we may refer to these propositions as the contending "first principles" for the deep seabed. Evidently, while the developing countries wished to accord prominence and legal significance to the expression "common heritage of humanity", the developed countries thought that the most salient legal consideration that should appear at the forefront of any "agreed principles" for the deep seabed is the assertion that there is a deep seabed area beyond national jurisdiction which should have a precise boundary.[137] Evidently, what the developing countries had in mind in their formulation was to impart a

---

136 The original language of item (2) reads "Taking into account article 1 of the Continental Shelf Convention ..." but was modified to "Taking into account the relevant dispositions in international law ..." as an alleged compromise move by the developed countries to bring the "Set B" principles closer to the "Set A" principles of the developing countries. Oda, *supra* note 2, at 33-34.
137 I do not agree with Luard's assessment that the North-South disagreement in this case is between "maximalists" (*i.e.*, "Set A" proponents) "who wanted a set of much more ambitious and controversial proposals with specific content" and "minimalists" (*i.e.*, supporters of "Set B") who "wanted a set of harmless statements" or "pious platitudes." Luard, *op. cit.* 92. As it was shown, the postulation of continental shelf "outer limits", which in itself is a "maximalist" position, is not at all innocuous. Churchill & Lowe's characterization of the North-South divergence, which highlights a difference in "pace" and "direction", is more satisfactory but is not entirely accurate either, *op. cit.* at 180:
The [industrialized States], wishing to build upon the 1958 Conventions, which they considered broadly satisfactory, favoured a cautious approach to the question with a view to the eventual enunciation of agreed principles concerning the exploitation of the seabed; the [developing States] preferred more rapid progress towards the establishment not only of agreed principles but an international organization with wide powers to regulate deep seabed mining.

special legal status to the deep ocean floor as the "common heritage of mankind."[138] However, the developed countries wanted to pronounce as a lead principle the certainty of the bounded existence of the area.

The political motivations that would justify these "first principles" become apparent if we examine their respective legal implications and consequences. Each of these "first principles" does reveal a specific assessment of the prior or pre-existing legal situation and shows a particular preference concerning a future legal dispensation for the deep seabed *de lege ferenda*. Moreover, it is quite interesting to note that, by postulating a "dialogue" or interaction between these two "first principles", a completely different legal approach to the 1970 Declaration of Principles Resolution, or for that matter Part XI of the 1982 Convention on the Law of the Sea, is made possible. As it will be shown below, the not-frequently-remembered controversy regarding the "priority" of issues that emerged in the Seabed Committee – namely, whether precedence should be given to the establishment of the substantive "regime" or the determination of the "limits" or "boundaries" of the area – is largely a consequence of the historical interaction of, or negotiations surrounding, these competing "first principles."

There was a single point, of direct relevance to the legal status of the deep seabed, which seemed to have received unanimous acceptance in the *Ad Hoc* Committee. This was the proposition that there exists an area of the seabed beyond the limits of national jurisdiction. The report of the *Ad Hoc* Committee puts it forthrightly: "As was implied in the terms of Resolution 2340 [which established the *Ad Hoc* Committee] the *Ad Hoc* Committee recognized the existence of an area of the seabed and the ocean floor underlying the high seas beyond the limits of national jurisdiction."[139] Indeed, this proposition serves as the shared premise of the contending "first principles" mentioned above.[140] But it is significant to note that although the developing countries chose to take for granted this "fact" that "seemed obvious"[141] the developed countries wanted to recognize the existence of the area in more explicit and authoritative terms. Thus, the developing countries preferred that the proposition should be mentioned in a matter-of-fact fashion in the preamble of a draft declaration

---

138 *See* Ad Hoc SBC Rep, para. 15.
139 Ad Hoc SBC Rep, para. 86.
140 *See* statement of *Ad Hoc* Committee Chairman Amerasinge, PV 1588 (28 Oct 1968), para. 151.
141 Ad Hoc SBC Rep, Annex II para. 40.

of principles,[142] reserving the operative part of a declaration to the elaboration of substantive principles, the cornerstone of which would be the "common heritage of mankind."[143] The developed countries thought otherwise, and instead preferred to see the "common heritage of mankind" formulation in the preamble of a draft declaration of principles[144] while putting the statement of the existence of the area in the operative part.[145] Clearly, the placement or positioning of any of these "first principles" in any agreed declaration of principles – namely, whether a "principle" should find expression as a preambular clause or in the operative part of a document – already suggests legal consequences. Given these two "first principles", which one of them is the statement of fact that should find expression in the preamble, and which is the "true" legal principle that should find its place in the operative part, of a UN Declaration of Principles?

The "existence of the area", whether as a fact or a legal principle, is obviously an innocuous proposition in itself. What really mattered was the kind of conclusion sought to be derived from this proposition. For the developing countries under the "Set A" principles, accepting the "existence of the area" as a fact led them to the conclusion that this area must be governed by norms, which are presently either too inadequate[146] or completely non-existent.[147]

---

142 Brazil, PV 1674 (31 Oct 1969).
143 Some middle powers, like Sweden, PV 1596 (4 Nov 1968), Norway, PV 1676 (4 Nov 1969), New Zealand, PV 1677 (5 Nov 1969), and Denmark, PV 1683 (10 Nov 1969) supported the position of developing countries.
144 *E.g.* France, PV 1680 (7 Nov 1969); Italy, PV 1681 (7 Nov 1969).
145 1969 SBC Report, para. 74. *See also e.g.*, Canada, PV 1779 (1 Dec 1970); Belgium, PV 1788 (8 Dec 1970).
146 *See e.g.* Malta, PV 1589 (19 Oct 1968); Ceylon, PV 1673 (31 Oct 1969); Sweden, PV 1680 (7 Nov 1969).
147 Reference may be made to the "legal vacuum" theory behind the Set A "first principle", for what was sought to be accomplished was to fill a notional space *tabula rasa* with an innovative regime build upon the Common Heritage of Humanity concept. *See* Chile, PV 1602 (7 Nov 1968) on behalf of delegations of Asia, Africa and Latin America. *See also* Brazil, 1591 (30 Oct 1968) & 1708 (2 Dec 1969); Yugoslavia, PV 1593 (31 Oct 1968); Chile, PV 1601 (6 Nov 1968); and Belgium, PV 1588 (28 Oct 1968) that there is "no body of law covering the subject of the item in question" and that there is need to agree "on a statement of principles upon which such body of law might be based"; Anand, *supra* Chap. III note 14, at 267; F. Paolillo, *The Institutional Arrangements for the International Seabed* 188 RECUEIL DES COURS 135, at 198 (1984). Although there may be

New norms must, therefore, be developed for the Area. This required an unprecedented exercise in international law-making, providing an "active workshop of common endeavor."[148] Moreover, this experiment in collective imagination "to devise in advance an international structure for the greatest untapped area of planetary resources"[149] would eventually lead to the practical setting up

---

doctrinal doubts about the phenomenon of *lacunae* or "legal gaps" from the standpoint of international adjudication, *see* H. Lauterpacht, *The Function of Law in the International Community* Part II (1966), the concept of a *lacunae* or "legal vacuum" could prove useful in the context of a political solution to novel international problems that are widely regarded as barely regulated by law and thus requiring new norms and unprecedented community policies. *See* J. Stone, *Non-Liquet and the Function of Law in the International Community* 35 BYIL 124-161 (1959). In this general sense, since it was imagined that the UN was embarking upon a collective law-making exercise for a frontier, undeterred by any the restraints raised by existing norms, the "legal vacuum" theory is a tenable outlook. From a functional perspective, however, the "legal vacuum" theory used to support the Common Heritage of Humanity as first principle is only partly true. As it was shown in the previous Chapter, the seabed "beyond the limits of national jurisdiction" does not exist as a legal fact if reference is made to the exploration and exploitation of the natural resources of the seabed, by virtue of the open-ended definition of the continental shelf under the 1958 Geneva Convention on the Continental Shelf. It exists, however, for all other purposes, *e.g.* military uses of the seabed beyond the territorial sea. *Cf.* Canada, PV 1599 (5 Nov 1968), para. 55. There then emerges a legal or legislative "gap" with respect to one particular use of the seabed but not with respect to other uses. If the community policy is to establish the precise boundaries of an area of the deep seabed that will be unaffected by national resource jurisdiction, there will surely be a "legal vacuum" if the delimitation of this area by conventional law is not accompanied by a stipulation of the substantive norms to be applied. With respect to other uses of the seabed, however, like military uses or laying of submarine cables and pipelines, a "legal vacuum" cannot be presupposed for the seabed "beyond national jurisdiction", because the high seas regime for these functions is already in place in such area. Naturally, those States who do not agree that the pre-existing law for a particular use of the deep seabed should be changed will not submit to the view that there is a "legal vacuum" with respect to such use. All in all, the "legal vacuum" theory for the Common Heritage of Humanity "first principle" is valid and appropriate only if there is a universal or near-universal agreement that innovative legislative policy for the deep seabed, either as an entire geographic-legal zone or as a functional legal reality, is required.

148 Norway, PV 1593 (31 Oct 1968).
149 New Zealand, PV 1677 (5 Nov 1969).

of a regime ideally built upon the "common heritage of mankind" concept.[150] This eminently teleological, policy-oriented position adopted by the group that supported the Set A first principle explains how the Common Heritage of Humanity was conceptualized as a functional "first principle" for the seabed.

The developed countries, on the other hand, would reach a totally different conclusion from the proposition that the area exists. If there is an area beyond national jurisdiction, then "there should be agreed a precise boundary for this area." But it should immediately be added that the conclusion – that there should be a precise boundary for the area – is made synonymous with the unarticulated proposition that no coastal State is authorized to extend the continental shelf to an indefinite distance from the shore into the deep ocean floor. Accordingly, the "principle" that the area exists, from the viewpoint of the developed countries, "amounted to acknowledging that claims cannot be unlimited under the Continental Shelf Convention or under general international law."[151] The proposition that "the area exists" is, in this context, understandably a "legal principle" rather than a statement of fact, because it is being equated to a normative prescription that coastal State claims offshore – functionally by way of the Continental Shelf Convention or in a zonal sense under the law of territorial waters – can not be unlimited under international law. This Set B "first principle" unreservedly warrants further comment.

It is admittedly not difficult to discern the verbal sleight-of-hand involved in the conceptualization of the Set B "first principle." If the eminent western philosophers (such as David Hume and Immanuel Kant) are right in their understanding that an "ought" proposition cannot be derived from an "is" statement, and *vice versa*, it is surely a good strategy in advocacy to transform the "existence of an area" into a normative "ought" proposition so that the transition to other "ought" propositions – *e.g.* that the precise boundary of the area should be determined, or, which is not really the same thing, that national maritime jurisdiction has precise "outer limits" – is easily facilitated.[152] The subtle aim was thus to commit the Seabed Committee and the UN General Assembly

---

150 Malta, PV 1589 (29 Oct 1968); Algeria, PV 1599 (5 Nov 1968); Ceylon, PV 1673 (31 Oct 1969); India, PV 1673 (31 Oct 1969); Brazil, PV 31 1674 (31 Oct 1969).
151 *See* Ad Hoc SBC Rep, Annex II para. 40; also 1969 SBC Rep para. 74. On Malta's support for this interpretation, *see* further below.
152 For the application of this argumentative strategy, *See* Jennings, *supra* Chap. III note 116, at 821 & 832, asserting that the exploitability clause should be regarded as *functus officio* because paragraph 86 of the Report of the *Ad Hoc* Committee, *supra* Chap. III note 131, which embodies a "general principle of law", says so.

to a particular interpretation of the Continental Shelf Convention. There are three distinct but interwoven intellectual operations involved – unambiguously revealing the relationship of the Set B "first principle" to pre-existing international law. First, rationalize that the proposition "the area exists" is a normative proposition; secondly, justify that this first normative proposition necessarily entails another normative statement that would command the immediate delimitation or precise definition of the area; and thirdly, equate the delimitation of the area with a prohibitory norm that coastal States cannot extend their continental shelf indefinitely.

The first argumentative step – establishing the area's existence as a norm – is directed solely at the Continental Shelf Convention,[153] because the "exploitability clause" supplies *carte blanche* authority that potentially exterminates the notion of a seabed "beyond national jurisdiction." The acknowledgement of the "existence of the area" as a fact, either notionally or empirically, which is its characterization under the Set A principles, cannot accomplish the purpose of curtailing, qualifying or manipulating the open-ended definition of the continental shelf under the plain terms of the exploitability clause. However, if the existence of the area is accepted, not as a mere fact, but as a legal principle – even just in the realm of *lex ferenda* – then there is a basis for the creation of customary law, or maneuvering room for an argument that the customary norm of the "existence of the area" had modified the conventional definition of the continental shelf under the exploitability clause. As it will be further explained below, the "existence of the area" as a legal principle was never accepted in the Seabed Committee, or in the United Nations for that matter. Its inscription under a *proposed* set of principles, however, indubitably proves one thing: the *fact* that the statement "there is an area" was *offered* by the industrialized countries to the international community *for acceptance as a legal principle* proves that the status of this alleged norm of international law at the time it was put forward in the *Ad Hoc* Committee was uncertain at best.

The second pillar of the Set B "first principle", which says that agreement on the precise boundaries of the area *necessarily and peremptorily* follows from the existence of the area, is clearly open to grave doubt. As the Latin Americans then quite correctly pointed out, the "territorial sea" or the "high seas" or other recognized maritime spaces exist, but their precise boundaries have never been determined.[154]

---

153 *See* USA, PV 1590 (29 Oct 1968); Belgium, PV 1673 (31 Oct 1969).
154 *See* Ad Hoc SBC Rep, Annex II para. 78.

The third, most critical and decisive, step in the argument – that the "existence of the area" is tautologically equivalent to, or an inevitable corollary of, a prohibitory norm for coastal States not to extend their continental shelf indefinitely up to mid-ocean – obviously needs more justification if it is at all to be convincing. Can such prohibition be deduced from the principle that there is an area, assuming *arguendo* a valid acceptance of this principle? The arguments – substantive and procedural – that emerged from the seabed deliberations in the UN questioning the validity and propriety of this inference embodied in the Set B "first principle" may be recalled.

The substantive argument that overthrows the logic of an imagined injunction on continental shelf "outer limits" was raised by Ambassador Kaplan of Canada. He put forward a bold suggestion that aimed to prevent a selective reading of the Continental Shelf Convention and that certainly conceived of a "new departure" in the definition of the area beyond national jurisdiction. If the question is "Can the precise boundaries of the area be established without reference to the continental shelf convention?", then the Canadian response was "yes": assuming that there is an area of the seabed beyond national jurisdiction, a novel "principle" that may be considered in the definition of the area is that "every ocean basin and every seabed of the world should have similar percentages of its underwater acreage reserved for the benefit of mankind." In other words, the determination of the precise boundaries of the area might just as well "begin from the center of the sea proceeding landward."[155] This would render unnecessary any interference with the exploitability clause of the Continental Shelf Convention!

The more politically formidable, and assuredly fatal, refutation against the concept of a prohibition being drawn from the Set B "first principle" issued from the Latin American countries. This took the form of a procedural objection that the *Ad Hoc* Committee, or for that matter the United Nations General Assembly, did not possess any competence to consider or decide upon the question of the outer limits to national jurisdiction.[156] Neither the *lex ferenda* nor the *lex lata* of the definition of the continental shelf was thus open for discussion. The Latin American position is not at all surprising. Recall that the Latin American countries successfully moved to amend the proposed agenda item of Malta in 1967 in order not to bring within the ambit of deep seabed discus-

---

155 *See* Canada, PV 1682 (10 Nov 1969) & PV 1779 (1 Dec 1970).
156 *See* Ad Hoc SBC Rep, Annex II para. 40; 1969 SBC Rep, Report of Legal Sub-Committee, para. 76-77. Ireland, supported this view. PV 1679 (6 Nov 1969).

sions questions bearing on the limits of their maritime boundaries.[157] Their position, not altogether unsound, was that under international law or, specifically, under the exploitability clause of the Continental Shelf Convention a coastal State has the basic right to determine its own maritime boundaries[158] – a contentious matter which they claimed should be under the cognizance of the Sixth (legal) Committee of the General Assembly if it was to be discussed at all, and which, in any case, could be reviewed in the context of an international conference on the law of the sea if and when such a conference was called for.[159] The inference on (1) the need for a precisely delimited area, and (2) the prohibition on indefinite extensions of the continental shelf, as principles flowing from the "existence of the area", were, thus, never legally recognized nor established in any normative sense during the UN deliberations on a draft declaration of principles for the deep seabed.[160] The representative of Belgium

---

157 *Supra* Chap. III Secs. B.3 and B.4. It is important to reiterate the keen observation of A. De Marffy, *supra* Chap. II note 37, that the Latin American amendments to the title of the proposed agenda item by Malta had a three-fold effect: "first of all, they eliminated, at least for the time being, any possibility of a change in positive law; as a result, the examination of the question was limited to discussion of a political, or even economic, nature; and lastly, it did not prejudge the possibility that States might extend the limits of their national jurisdiction."

158 The underlying motivation for this position, rooted in a historical appreciation of the national socio-economic development imperative, had sometimes been misunderstood. *See e.g.* Luard, *op. cit.* 144, observing that the Latin American countries were not being logical when they resisted calls to establish continental shelf outer limits, or that "they had not correctly calculated their own national interests in the matter."

159 *See* statements of Brazil, PV 1674 (31 Oct 1969); Guatemala, PV 1676 (4 Nov 1969); Chile, PV 1679 (6 Nov 1969), PV 1682 (10 Nov 1969), and PV 1708 (2 Dec 1969); Peru, PV 1682 (10 Nov 1969); *See also* 1969 SBC Rep, Report of Legal Sub-Committee, para. 74-80.

160 A fascinating but misleading account of the evolution of the existence of the area as an alleged "truism" was given by the representative of Belgium, PV 1788 (8 Dec 1970): "The Seabed Committee proceeded on the working hypothesis that there is such an area, and as the discussions and consultations gradually evolved, that hypothesis became a generally accepted postulate, to be finally established as a juridical principle. That truism is not without some importance because it is tantamount to rejecting the elastic interpretation of the definition which the Convention of 1958 gives to the coastal States." The Belgian representative then went on to say that the "truism" should have been placed in the operative part of what became the 1970 Declaration of Principles Resolution.

was almost bitter in his assessment that the Seabed Committee was unable to discharge its mandate ever since it was established "because one group of countries interpreted this mandate as precluding discussion of the question of the definition of the extra-jurisdictional area."[161]

From a procedural standpoint, it is clear that the battle between the "first principles" was won by the developing countries. Since the official mandate of the Seabed Committee encouraged and emphasized more the positive consideration of teleological internationalization principles, less than a backward-looking rectification of established legal principles, the progressive development of the "common heritage of humanity" principle *de lege ferenda* took off without legal obstructions. Also from this point of view, it could be said that the evolution in customary law, or progressive development, of the Common Heritage of Humanity "first principle" was commenced given the significant number of countries which accepted it as a working hypothesis for a draft declaration of principles. One cannot fail to note that a proper appreciation of the work of the permanent Seabed Committee, which was established precisely "to study the elaboration of legal principles and norms" for the deep seabed would automatically rule out a norm-creating function for the Set B "first principle", as conceived by its proponents in the *Ad Hoc* Committee.

The resistance to the Common Heritage of Humanity framework for elaborating principles and norms was, by and large, political in origin and orientation but had definite legal consequences. Thus, when the Soviet block countries argued that the Common Heritage of Humanity principle was altogether vague and lacked clarity from the standpoint of pre-existing international law[162]

---

[161] Belgium, PV 1799 (15 December 1970). *See also* Netherlands, PV 1801 (16 Dec 1970), decrying the "time-consuming and fruitless discussions" held in the Seabed Committee because its terms of reference did not authoritatively include the question of boundaries. However, it was not only the Latin American countries which opposed implied amendments to the Continental Shelf Convention. See for *e.g.*, Ireland, PV 1648 (19 Dec 1968) & PV 1679 (6 Nov 1969); United Arab Republic, PV 1676 (4 Nov 1969); Yugoslavia, PV 1677 (5 Nov 1969); Portugal, PV 1798 (15 Dec 1970). Romania, PV 1682 (10 Nov 1969), declared that "If the Continental Shelf Convention need to be clarified, the procedure to be followed should be that provided in the Convention itself."

[162] But the Representative of Brazil correctly brushed aside this objection because "before their adoption, all legal concepts are devoid of legal content." PV 1674 (31 Oct 1969); *see also* Kuwait, PV 1675 (3 Nov 1969): "if the common heritage of mankind has no legal content, nothing need prevent us from giving it content."

or that it connoted a form of collective property that would encourage rather than deter "unobstructed looting by capitalist monopolies of the deep seabed",[163] they were claiming that the Common Heritage of Humanity concept was politically unacceptable as a new normative basis for international relations. In legal effect, this complaint was a threat made by these countries that their consent would be withheld on any Common Heritage of Humanity-based rule for the area, because they would be either "persistent objectors" in the formation of a customary norm or future non-parties to a conventional regime on the Common Heritage of Humanity. It is of course well known that the Soviet block countries reversed their legal posture towards the Common Heritage of Humanity in the mid-1970s and henceforth embraced the Common Heritage as a useful legal concept.[164]

In a similar manner, although the major Western developed countries did not have any objections to the use of the term "common heritage of mankind" in a political or moral sense,[165] they sought to minimize the future normative significance of the concept, if not permanently deny it of legal content altogether. Canada, for instance, which took the most moderate position among the "skeptics" to the Common Heritage of Humanity, accepted the terms of the "common heritage of mankind" as a "first principle" but proposed that its scope be limited to the resources of the area only, and should not be applied to the area as a whole or to all uses and activities that are possible in the area.[166] But the attempt to relegate the "common heritage of humanity" terminology to the preambular section of any draft declaration of principles for the area[167] would surely have achieved a debilitating effect on this proposed principle. The French representative thus regarded the Common Heritage of Humanity concept as the "synthesis of the different elements composing the body of a declaration of principles."[168] This "inductive approach" to the Com-

---

163 *See* USSR, PV 1592 (31 Oct 1968), PV 1679 (6 Nov 1969) & PV 1798 (15 Dec 1970); Bulgaria, PV 1683 (10 Nov 1967); Byelorussian SSR, PV 1790 (2 Dec 1970).
164 *See* Andreyev, *et al., op. cit.* 25, 87-93; V. Postyshev, *The Concept of the Common Heritage of Mankind: From New Thinking to New Practice* (1990).
165 USA, PV 1590 (29 Oct 1968) & PV 1774 (26 Nov 1970).
166 Canada, PV 1779 (1 Dec 1970); *cf.* UK, PV 1775 (27 Nov 1970).
167 France, PV 1680 (7 Nov 1969); Italy, PV 1681 (7 Nov 1969).
168 France, PV 1680 (7 Nov 1969). No mention of "the common heritage of mankind" is made in the proposal of France on the "Establishment of a regime for the exploration and the exploitation of the Sea-Bed" submitted to the SBC in 1970. The principles or "basic requirements" of the regime are "efficiency" and "inter-

mon Heritage of Humanity was also favoured by the United States, whose position was that the meaning of the Common Heritage of Humanity is "indicated by the principles which follow it and will be elaborated in an agreed regime to be established."[169] A last argumentative technique employed to cast cloud over the identity of the Common Heritage of Humanity as an independent principle *de lege ferenda* was the devise of a self-fulfilling prophesy: the Common Heritage of Humanity is a political or poetical concept because it has unclear legal implications and is incapable of precise legal definition.[170] No doubt, the vagueness of the Common Heritage of Humanity as a legal neologism will persist as long as the States raising the issue of vagueness do not have the political will to accept the status of the Common Heritage of Humanity as a potential legal principle and cooperate in good faith towards its more precise definition as such. As Ambassador Myrdal of Sweden asserted:

> ... we have noticed with regret a tendency on the part of some industrialized countries to avoid expressing the same conviction as representatives from the less privileged countries do, namely, that the supreme principle to acknowledge on this issue must be that the sea-bed is "the common heritage of mankind." Well, Sweden definitely shares that conviction.... But we must honestly recognize that we stand at a crucial crossroads. If different positions were taken on this fundamental principle, it would amount to more of a parting of ways than is generally thought possible. In its turn it will entail differences on practically all the remaining issues, however technical they have appeared in the discussion.[171]

All in all, the indifference if not scorn of some industrialized countries towards the Common Heritage of Humanity as a proposed legal principle in its own right betrayed their lack of interest in a concept that aimed at fundamental

---

national equity." Text in 1970 SBC Rep, Annex VII.
169 US, PV 1799 (15 Dec 1970). *See* "Draft United Nations Convention on the International Sea-Bed Area" 1970 Working paper submitted by the USA. Text in 1970 SBC Rep, Annex V.
170 *See* Australia, PV 1777 (30 Nov 1970); UK, PV 1799 (15 Dec 1970). The term "common heritage of mankind" is nowhere used in the Working Paper "International Regime" submitted by the UK to the SBC in 1970. Text in 1970 SBC Rep, Annex VI.
171 Sweden, PV 1680 (7 Nov 1969), para. 25-26. *See also* statements of Ambassador Amerasinghe, Ceylon, PV 1673 (31 Oct 1969), and Ambassador Hambro, Norway, PV 1676 (4 Nov 1969).

doctrinal innovation in the law of the sea. They believed that there was no need for any new fundamental legal concept for the new frontier, specifically, or for improving the public order of the oceans, generally. Somehow, it was obvious to them that the substantive law for the deep seabed will in due course issue from a creative application and recombination of existing legal tools and norms.[172] According to them, the main point was first to make sure that the area was precisely defined.

And yet the debates in the *Ad Hoc* Committee or the Seabed Committee and in the First Committee of the UN General Assembly made it abundantly clear that the Common Heritage of Humanity principle that was insisted upon by the developing countries was not going to be understood according to the terms of the traditional concepts in the law of the sea. Neither the ancient doctrines of *res communis* or *res nullius* nor the modern principles of coastal State sovereignty or freedom of the seas was particularly useful in engineering a legal structure of governance for the deep seabed.[173] The rejection by the poor countries of the familiar normative building blocks in the development of a regime to internationalize the deep seabed did not make any sense to the industrialized countries, whose understanding of the law of the sea did not and could not go beyond the universe drawn by the traditional doctrines[174] and, more importantly, whose national interests have always found satisfaction in

---

172 USSR, PV 1592 (31 Oct 1968): "A prime requirement is that in this work the United Nations must not ignore the rules of law which already apply, and should most certainly not contradict them, but should rather build on what has been done before."

173 *See* for *e.g.*, Brazil, PV 1591 (30 Oct 1968); Libya & Ireland, PV 1597 (4 Nov 1968); Honduras, PV 1600 (6 Nov 1968); Congo, PV 1708 (2 Dec 1969); Ecuador, PV 1676 (4 Nov 1969); Yugoslavia, PV 1677 (5 Nov 1969); Iceland, PV 1678 (6 Nov 1969); Chile, Uruguay & Thailand, PV 1679 (6 Nov 1969); Iran, PV 1682 (10 Nov 1969). *See also* Oda, *supra* note 2, at 102.

174 *See e.g.* USSR, PV 1592 (31 Oct 1968); Australia, PV 1589 (29 Oct 1968). Scholarly writings on the regime of the deep seabed, likewise, continually refer to the concepts of *res nullius* or *res communis* in explaining the Common Heritage of Humanity, inspite of the statements from its original proponents in the UN that these concepts are inadequate and absolutely inappropriate for the purpose. *See* Kronmiller, *op. cit.* 243-244; A. Post, *Deep Sea Mining and the Law of the Sea* (1983); L. Sohn & K. Gustafson, *The Law of the Sea* at Ch. IX (1984); Morell, *op. cit.* 173 *et seq.*; Joyner & Martell, *op. cit.* 75-76.

these pre-existing norms and concepts.¹⁷⁵ This irreverence towards established norms and legal concepts, however, was seen by the developing countries as fully justified in light of the requirements of decolonization, development and disarmament.¹⁷⁶ For them, what was more disturbing was the patent lack of sympathetic response on the part of the industrialized countries towards a legal concept which they thought was just, progressive and promised so much for humanity – rich and poor, present and future.¹⁷⁷

From among the developed countries, however, it was the old seafaring nations of Scandinavia who grasped the significance, necessity and urgency of evolving a new conceptual universe for the law of the sea.¹⁷⁸ The unambiguous language of their interventions could not have failed to convey to the industrialized countries the basic message of the Common Heritage of Humanity principle. Ambassador Hambro of Norway understood the reasons for an irreverent attitude towards established doctrine and explained the rationale behind a new fundamental principle in the law of the sea. His 1969 intervention is one of the most balanced and authoritative statements on the Common Heritage of Humanity, and should be quoted to its fullest extent:

---

175 *See* discussion on the move of the UK and the Netherlands to limit the scope of UNCLOS III only to matters not settled by the 1958 Geneva Conventions. PV 1799-1801 (15-16 Dec 1970).
176 Ceylon, PV 1588 (28 Oct 1968); Malta, PV 1589 (19 Oct 1968); Brazil, PV 1591 (30 Oct 1968); India, PV 1591 (30 Oct 1968) & PV 1673 (31 Oct 1969); Yugoslavia, PV 1593 (31 Oct 1968); Ecuador, PV 1594 (1 Nov 1968); Algeria, PV 1599 (5 Nov 1968); Chile, PV 1602 (7 Nov 1968)(on behalf of delegations from Asia, Africa and Latin America); Guatemala & United Arab Republic, PV 1676 (4 Nov 1969); Trinidad-Tobago, PV 1677 (5 Nov 1969); Venezuela, PV 1678 (6 Nov 1969); Columbia & Argentina, PV 1680 (7 Nov 1969); Afghanistan, Mauritius, Ghana & Kenya, PV 1681 (7 Nov 1969); Jamaica, PV 1782 (3 Dec 1970).
177 The delegation of Ecuador, therefore, lamented that there must have been a dialogue of the deaf taking place because the developed countries just did not seem to comprehend what the developing countries were saying when the latter insisted that the Common Heritage of Humanity was a legal principle, inspite of years of discussion. PV 1782 (3 Dec 1970).
178 Iceland, PV 1589 (29 Oct 1968), PV 1678 (6 Nov 1969), PV 1778 (1 Dec 1970); Norway PV 1592 (31 Oct 1968) & PV 1676 (4 Nov 1969); Sweden, PV 1596 (4 Nov 1968), PV 1709 (2 Dec 1969), PV 1680 (7 Nov 1969), PV 1775 (27 Nov 1970); Denmark, PV 1683 (10 Nov 1979).

... the objective is to reserve the riches of the bottom of the sea for humanity as a whole and not only for the fortunate few who have the technological skills to exploit the sea-bed beyond the limits of national jurisdiction.

... I think it is clear that if we are to reach an understanding among us on this issue, we must raise our eyes above national horizons. After discussing those problems for two years, we should also conclude that the time for sweeping general statements is over.

... I am convinced that [Ambassador Amerasinghe's] proposal for a set of principles, which in fact coincides to a great extent with the basic principles already proposed in the standing [Seabed] Committee by my delegation, will prove to be a solid basis for our future work in arriving at a set of principles to which, I hope, we can all agree.

... There seems to be common agreement at least that the seabed and ocean floor and subsoil thereof, beyond the limits of national jurisdiction, shall not be subject to national appropriation and that no State shall exercise or claim sovereignty or sovereign rights over any part of it. This is all very well as far as it goes, but what is much more important is to reach agreement on the central and basic question, namely, that this area is the common heritage of mankind and as such should come under international control and authority and that exploitation of the area should be carried out in accordance with the rules and regulations of the regime to be established for such an area.

There are those who maintain that the sea-bed and ocean floor outside the boundaries of national jurisdiction is free for all and should continue to be so. Typical of this is the following – and I quote from a recent statement by a leading industrialist:

> "There is no reason why a State cannot license a firm to mine anything on the deep sea-bed anywhere under existing international law in the same manner as it licenses vessels wearing its flag specifically to engage in the mackerel trade."

This statement is clearly in line with the view that there is no general division for juridical purposes in international law between the water column of the high seas, the air column above it and the solid earth column below it. My delegation cannot agree with this, and I want to make it quite clear that it is the Norwegian Government's view that the deep ocean floor is not a free-for-all where anybody can do what he wants for various purposes. Basic principles of law exist governing those areas, but those principles are so rudimentary in substance and general in form that they obviously must be further elaborated and supplemented to suit the host of problems which the technical revolution has created and will continue to create in those areas. The main task of the Sea-bed Committee will be to work even harder on the elaboration of a set of principles for the sea-bed, and I repeat that the fundamental principle in the regime of the sea-bed and ocean floor beyond the limits of national jurisdiction must be that this area is the common heritage of mankind and as such must come under international control and authority.

Some have remarked that the term "common heritage of mankind" is not an established term in the vocabulary of international law. That may be, but the problems with which we are confronted are novel and the solutions we must offer in this area in order to establish international justice and maintain international peace can hardly be found on the bookshelves of international law libraries. We must not be afraid of new concepts or of new terms to explain them. New words are needed for new concepts.

The term "common heritage of mankind" points to something valuable, referring to the past as well as to the present and the future, emphasizing that those areas and the riches contained therein with their possibilities and problems, have been passed on to the present international community as a heritage of mankind and for the common benefit as a whole, not to any individual nation or group of nations.

... It has been stated by some people that it is perhaps somewhat premature to draw precise boundaries at the present stage because such a delimitation may to a great extent be dependent upon the substance of the matter, that is, upon the nature and the extent of the rights of exploitation in the deep ocean floor. Such a line of reasoning might easily lead to a vicious circle, namely, that we do not want to define the nature and contents of the rights pertaining to the deep ocean floor until we have obtained a more exact definition of the geographical extent of those areas, and so on.

On the other hand, there are obvious merits in the thought that we should move with a certain caution in this respect until the problems and our answers to them have matured somewhat. But it ought to be clear to all of us that sooner or later we shall have to face this problem. If we let it drift, the area of the sea-bed and ocean floor beyond national jurisdiction will gradually become smaller and smaller. The concept of non-appropriation will become meaningless in the end, because the outer limits of the continental shelf are determined on the basis of the criterion of exploitability. Even the concept of adjacency is so vague and unclear that we cannot expect it to play any role in checking the gradually extending continental shelves. We should bear in mind that the continental shelf today in our terminology is no longer a geological concept but a legal one.

> The most important task of the Sea-Bed Committee is to work out a set of principles essential to the legal structure of a system for exploring and utilizing the sea-bed and ocean floor beyond the limits of national jurisdiction. To administer such a regime, some form of machinery or authority will have to be established.[179]

Still, notwithstanding this formidable argument in law, was there any compelling political reason why the developed countries should accept the Common Heritage of Humanity as a new fundamental doctrine in the law of the sea, and for them to assist in its elaboration as a unique normative system in which the internationalization programme for the deep seabed could be firmly anchored? What would it take for the industrialized countries to accept the legal proposition that "The area and its resources are the common heritage of humanity", knowing fully well that the implications of this principle on the existing legal order of the oceans – a legal order which on the whole served their national interests quite faithfully – are potentially revolutionary? Since a change of heart was not forthcoming on the part of the industrialized countries, the solution had to be found in the "relations of forces" obtaining in the day. The North-South bargaining situation unmistakably supplied the answer: the developed countries can have their continental shelf "outer limits" if the they would enter into negotiations to conclude a seabed regime based on the Common Heritage of Humanity principle. Conversely, the developing countries can have their Common Heritage of Humanity principle and regime recognized by the developed countries if a universal agreement was concluded to permanently fix the limits or boundaries of national jurisdiction. The legal underpinnings of this "Faustian bargain" – the original package deal that underpins the work of UNCLOS III – need to be fully explored.

As Ambassador Hambro of Norway indicated in his afore-quoted clarification, the consideration of principles under the "Set A" framework of legal principles would sooner or later have to tackle the issue of a precise definition of the area. Likewise, the developing countries, including the Latin American States it must be emphasized,[180] did recognize early on that the issue of

---

179 Norway, PV 1676 (4 Nov 1969).
180 The Latin American States agreed in principle that the deep seabed as common heritage must be precisely delimited, but they believed that the precise definition of the area must be considered in another forum and only *after* the substantive principles to govern the area have been more or less determined. Obviously, that position was not inconsistent with their support for a moratorium on seabed claims. *See* 1969 SBC Rep, Report of Legal Sub-Committee, para. 77-80. Brazil, PV 1674

285

"limits" or "boundaries" was an indispensable part of the Common Heritage, or internationalization, agenda.[181] The boundaries of the area must be determined not only to impart reality to the new principle of the Common Heritage of Humanity but also to protect this principle and the regime it supports against the encroachments of the continental shelf regime. From the logic of this outlook, it should be noted that the necessity of establishing limits or boundaries flows from a prior conceptual commitment to the Common Heritage of Humanity principle.

The problem of defining the prospective scope of the Common Heritage of Humanity *ratione loci* necessarily brought into the discussion the main interest of the industrialized countries, which was the precise definition of the outer limits of the continental shelf, or the modification of the exploitability clause of the Continental Shelf Convention. Undoubtedly, there was a coincidence of objectives pursued by developed and developing countries, namely, to come up with a precise definition of the Area. But the motivations for this common objective were apparently divergent as seen from the alternative legal frameworks within which this objective was sought to be discussed by both groups. On the one hand, the developing countries appreciated the issue of boundaries from the standpoint of implementing a substantive regime defined beforehand by the Common Heritage of Humanity "first principle" through the Seabed Committee deliberations. The developed countries, on the other hand, saw the precise delineation of the continental shelf as an end in itself. However, as it was shown earlier, this concern *per se* was not within the purview of the Seabed Committee's competence, unless its mandate were accordingly adjusted.

The growing impatience of a number of States, especially the industrialized countries, over the issue of boundaries led Malta to launch in 1969 a less-well-known initiative whose legal impact was far more consequential than the 1967 intervention of Ambassador Pardo. Malta, moved by the perception that the "race-to-grab" competition is on the brink of reality, and hoping to end once and for all the uncertainty over "outer limits", proposed in October 1969 a draft resolution which would have asked the Secretary General to ascertain the views

---

(31 Oct 1969); Chile, PV 1682 (10 Nov 1969), PV 1708 (2 Dec 1969); Guatemala, PV 1676 (4 Nov 1969); Peru, PV 1682 (10 Nov 1969).
181 *See* Malta, PV 1516 (1 Nov 1967), PV 1675 (3 Nov 1969); Ceylon, PV 1588 (28 Oct 1968), PV 1603 (8 Nov 1968) & PV 1673 (31 Oct 1969); Kuwait, PV 1675 (3 Nov 1969); Kenya & Sudan, PV 1681 (7 Nov 1969). *See also* Iceland, PV 1678 (6 Nov 1969); Canada, PV 1682 (10 Nov 1969).

of member States on the desirability of convening a "conference particularly for the purpose of arriving at a clear, precise and internationally acceptable definition of the area of the deep ocean floor."[182] The draft resolution, which was, not surprisingly, supported by many developed States,[183] invited swift criticism from developing countries who thought that the conference, if it was to be convened at all, should not be restricted or exclusively devoted to a revision of the 1958 Continental Shelf Convention.[184] Peru[185] in particular scoffed at the draft proposal for raising "in obvious haste, a question that has not yet matured" and which "approaches a global problem ... in a tangential manner, isolating one single aspect."[186] Indeed, if the time had come to look back and reform pre-existing law for the sake of a forward-looking principle to internationalize the deep seabed, then the international community should not only review one aspect of this pre-existing law but examine all other unresolved issues in the law of the sea. And for the developing countries, the list of "unresolved" issues was certainly very long. This reasoning did not sit well with the countries which believed in the virtue of resolving law of the sea issues in "manageable packages."[187] They did not wish to de-stabilize the traditional law already codified in the 1958 Geneva Conventions. Nevertheless, reiterating the main reason for a broader approach, Ambassador Maurtua

---

[182] Doc. A/C.1/L.473, see PV 1673 (31 Oct 1969). Malta also entertained the possibility that the UN General Assembly would proclaim the minimum limits of the area. PV 1675 (3 Nov 1969).

[183] Oda, *supra* note 2, at 84.

[184] India and Brazil, PV 1674 (31 Oct 1969); Ecuador, PV 1676 (4 Nov 1969); Chile, PV 1679 (6 Nov 1969); Columbia, PV 1680 (7 Nov 1969); Kenya and Sudan, PV 1681 (7 Nov 1969); El Salvador, PV 1709 (2 Dec 1969).

[185] PV 1682 (10 Nov 1969).

[186] "Thus quite clearly, what the Maltese draft proposes is not the technical improvement of international law but simply the limitation of the continental shelf in favour of the sea-bed area.... I wonder, therefore, are we proposing to initiate a movement to revise the Geneva Convention with a view to limiting the jurisdiction of States as recognized in that Convention? Or are we proposing to extend that jurisdiction? Or are we proposing to amend the Convention half-heartedly or radically? Has the Convention fulfilled its legislative role? Have there been difficulties in applying it? Has it even acquired great universal force by being accepted and ratified? In short, are we dealing with well-established law or half-baked law – an instrument that was still-born?" *Id.* para. 111, 113.

[187] *E.g,* USSR, PV 1708 (2 Dec 1969); USA, PV 1709 (2 Dec 1969); Malta, Doc. A/PV 1833 (15 Dec 1969).

of Peru stressed that "all problems relating to the sea are closely bound up together and are legally and physically indivisible."[188]

Initially through Jamaica and Trinidad-Tobago, amendments to the Maltese draft were subsequently proposed to include the other Geneva Conventions within the purview of any forthcoming international conference.[189] These amendments were voted into Malta's draft resolution which was eventually approved by the General Assembly as Resolution 2574 A (XXIV), requesting the Secretary General

> ... to ascertain the views of Member States on the desirability of convening at an early date a conference on the law of the sea to review the regimes of the high seas, the continental shelf, the territorial sea and contiguous zone, fishing and conservation of the living resources of the high seas, particularly in order to arrive at a clear, precise and internationally accepted definition of the area of the sea-bed and ocean floor which lies beyond the limits of national jurisdiction, in light of the international regime to be established for that area.[190]

This Resolution supplied the strategic opportunity to open up the seabed deliberations to other law of the sea issues which the developing countries regarded as deserving an omnibus review.[191] On the basis of the results of the consultations undertaken by the Secretary General pursuant to this Resolution, the General Assembly carried forward the momentum of the "comprehensive conference" initiative in the following year and adopted Resolution 2750 C which called for the convening of a Third United Nations Conference on the Law of the Sea in 1973.[192] This Conference on the Law of the Sea

---

188 *Supra* note 185, at para 108.
189 Oda, *supra* note 2, at 83-85.
190 It should be noted that Ambassador Pardo strongly condemned the re-wording of Malta's draft resolution and expressed the fear that the adoption of Res. 2574 A "will make the entire effort of establishing an international regime for the seabed ... unrealizable except on paper." Doc. PV/1833 (15 Dec 1969).
191 *See* "Lusaka Declaration on Peace, Independence, Development Co-operation and Democratization of International Relations and Resolutions of the Third Conference of Heads of States of Government of Non-Aligned Countries" (8-10 Sept 1970) excerpt in I JN Moore, *International and United States Documents on Ocean Law and Policy* (1986).
192 Res 2750 C (17 Dec 1970), adopted by a vote of 109-7-6, with the Eastern European block voting against.

... would deal with the establishment of an equitable international regime – including an international machinery – for the area and the resources of the sea-bed and the ocean floor, and the subsoil thereof, beyond the limits of national jurisdiction, a precise definition of the area, and a broad range of related issues including those concerning the regimes of the high seas, the continental shelf, the territorial sea (including the question of its breadth and the question of international straits) and contiguous zone, fishing and conservation of the living resources of the high seas (including preferential rights of coastal States), the preservation of the marine environment (including *inter alia*, the prevention of pollution) and scientific research[.]

This resolution to convene a Conference on the Law of the Sea with a comprehensive agenda was accepted with much hesitation on the part of some developed countries which did not see any reason why the 1958 Conventions should be reviewed afresh.[193] But they had to agree with the broad terms of reference of the Conference because otherwise, the majority of nations in the international community would not agree to a precise definition of "outer limits." Moreover, in the face of strong suggestions that the conclusion of "an equitable international regime – including machinery" for the deep seabed should have "priority" in the preparatory process leading to the conference and/or in UNCLOS III itself,[194] there was strenuous objection from the developed countries that the issue of "limits" should *not* have any *less priority* than any subject covered by the Conference. This was an important procedural point, for the acceptance of the industrialized countries of Resolution 2750 C was conditioned on the widely-shared and explicit understanding on record that the negotiations on all issues, including agreement on the central issues of the "international regime" and "precise limits", were to take place concurrently, with no one issue having "priority" over the rest.[195] This was the only way to overcome the

---

193 *See* New Zealand, PV 1786 (7 Dec 1970); Japan, PV 1787 (7 Dec 1970); Poland, PV 1798 (15 Dec 1970); Australia, USSR PV 1800 (16 Dec 1970); Ireland, PV 1801 (16 Dec 1970), and discussion on the UK & Netherlands joint-proposal to amend the terms of reference of the draft resolution, PV 1799-1801 (15-16 Dec 1970).
194 Chile, PV 1775 (27 Nov 1970); Argentina, PV 1779 1 Dec 1970); Cameroon, PV 1783 (3 Dec 1970); Canada, PV 1799 (15 Dec 1970). *See also* Peru, Doc. A/PV1933 (17 Dec 1970).
195 UK, PV 1775 (27 Nov 1970); Brazil, PV 1777 (30 Nov 1970), Iceland, France, and USA, PV 1778 (1 Dec 1970); France, PV 1778; Canada, PV 1779 (1 Dec 1970) [final settlement of both questions – definition of limits and nature of regime – should be reached at the same conference]; Madagascar PV 1779 (1 Dec 1970);

289

"procedural issue of chicken-egg"[196] meaningfully and pragmatically. The procedural agreement reflected in Resolution 1750 C, indicating the trade-off of values and the essential reciprocity of interests between developed and developing countries at a critical juncture in the evolution of the Common Heritage of Humanity principle, was best summarized by United States Ambassador Stevenson as follows:

> On the subject of priority, it is our view that all subjects should be given equal and simultaneous treatment and that no country should be expected to reach a final decision with regard to any of the matters before the conference until it is satisfied with respect to the treatment of all such matters.[197]

> The nature of the regime and the limits of the area to which it applies must be negotiated and resolved together... It should be clear from this dilemma that there can be no real progress on either issue if it is addressed in isolation.[198]

In the same manner the developing countries made it very clear that there would be no agreement on a precise definition of "outer limits" until agreement was simultaneously reached on the international regime and machinery for the

---

Spain, PV 1780 (2 Dec 1970); Kuwait, PV 1780 (2 Dec 1970) [Regime and limits are two facets of the same process and should be simultaneously considered]; Ghana, PV 1785 (4 Dec 1970); United Arab Republic, PV 1787 (7 Dec 1970); Portugal, PV 1788 (8 Dec 1970); USA, Ethiopia, and UK, PV 1794 11 Dec 1970); Singapore, PV 1796 (14 Dec 1970); Belgium, PV 1796 (14 Dec 1970); Pakistan, PV 1796 (14 Dec 1970)[on balance considering the fears of the developed and developing countries, regime, machinery and limits of the area should be taken up simultaneously]; Netherlands, PV 1796 (14 Nov 1970); USA, PV 1799 (15 Dec 1970); Malta, PV 1799 (15 Dec 1970); Belgium, PV 1799 (15 Dec 1970) & PV 1800 (16 Dec 1970); Peru, PV 1799 (15 Dec 1970); El Salvador, PV 1800 (16 Dec 1970); China, PV 1800 (16 Dec 1970); Peru, PV 1800 (16 Dec 1970); Australia, PV 1800 (16 Dec 1970); Canada, PV 1800 (16 Dec 1970); New Zealand, PV 1800 (16 Dec 1970); France, PV 1801 (16 Dec 1970); Netherlands, PV 1801 (16 Dec 1970); UK, PV 1801 (16 Dec 1970). *See also* Japan & Belgium, A/PV.1933 (17 Dec 1970).

196 USA, PV 1799 (15 Dec 1970).
197 PV 1794 (11 Dec 1970).
198 PV 1799 (15 Dec 1970).

area.[199] The broader bargaining picture defined under the terms of Resolution 2750 C was, of course, equally unambiguous: no negotiations leading to an agreement on precise "outer limits" was possible without undertaking at the same time negotiations on all other unsettled issues (from the developing country standpoint) in the law of the sea – such as fisheries, resource conservation and environmental protection, and marine scientific research.

What is the legal status of this bargain, or this original "package deal" on substantive priorities, as embodied in Resolution 1750 C? Is the agreement to negotiate and conclude an agreement on the "regime" as well as the "limits", and all other law of the sea issues besides, simultaneously and organically, binding in international law? Is it lawful for one group of countries to run off from the Conference negotiations as soon as a semblance of consensus on the "limits" question has emerged somewhere in the conference hall corridors while leaving a counterpart consensus on the "regime" astray in mid-ocean, as it were, and then claim that the "limits" thus defined constitutes a customary law resolution?

Time and again, it is said that General Assembly resolutions are not a source of international law, and that the General Assembly can only pass recommendations in discharging its political functions,[200] unless its members expressly acknowledge that a resolution or a part of a resolution, constitutes an independent statement of customary law. It is, however, equally true, that within a narrow band of concerns, chiefly on internal, procedural or budgetary matters,[201] decisions of the General Assembly are unconditionally binding upon its members.[202] Resolution 2750 C is embraced within this narrow sphere

---

199 *See supra* note 195, esp. Peru, PV 1777 (30 Nov 1970) inasmuch as "there is no guarantee that the international regime will be established" coastal jurisdiction must be protected, for "national jurisdiction cannot be reduced by the establishment of the area" alone; Trinidad-Tobago, PV 1778 (1 Dec 1970): "we feel that it is the establishment of precise maritime boundaries in the absence of an equitable international regime for the area that will create a free-for-all and cause a new scramble for colonies on the deep sea-bed." Venezuela, PV 1788 (8 Dec 1970) [rights under the continental shelf convention are not prejudiced until agreement is reached on the regime]; *see also* Portugal, PV 1798 (15 Dec 1970).

200 *See* Art. 10, UN Charter.

201 *See* Arts. 16-22, UN Charter.

202 The most authoritative statement of the rule on the competence of the General Assembly is given by Judge Lauterpacht in his Separate Opinion in the *South-West Africa – Voting Procedure* Advisory Opinion, 1955 ICJ Rep 67, at 115:

291

of authoritative decision. As a resolution that lays down a procedural decision for the orderly conduct of business in a forthcoming conference under United Nations auspices,[203] it is obviously a positive rule of international law. A procedural decision of the General Assembly is compelling in its legal effects and cannot be disregarded by a member State lest an international obligation is breached, or the constitutional rights of other States in the organization violated.[204]

A General Assembly resolution may also achieve legally binding effect if this is so provided in a treaty. Significantly, Article 13 (2) of the 1958 Geneva Continental Shelf Convention[205] illustrates just such situation. This article provides that the General Assembly of the United Nations shall decide upon the steps to be taken with respect to any request for the revision of the Continental Shelf Convention. It is very strange indeed why this provision of law had not been given the amplification it deserves during the seabed debates in the 1960s and 1970s. But if it is remembered that the entire seabed question was – from a procedural standpoint – all about revising or amending the Continental Shelf Convention, the full authority of the General Assembly thereunder must be recognized. Resolution 2750 C (and arguably all other related resolutions, including the Moratorium Resolution, which may constructively fall

---

Although *decisions of the General Assembly are endowed with full legal effect in some spheres of the activity of the United Nations*, and with limited legal effect in other spheres, it may be said by way of a broad generalization, that they are not legally binding upon the Members of the United Nations. *In some matters*, such as the election of the Secretary-General, election of Members of the Economic and Social Council, *the adoption of rules of procedure*, admission to, suspension from and termination of membership, and approval of the budget and apportionment of expenses – *the full legal effects of the Resolutions of the General Assembly are undeniable.* (Emphasis supplied)

203 "Procedural decisions: include adoption of rules of procedure, inclusion of items in an agenda, decisions to convene an extraordinary session, putting a draft to a vote, placing a time-limit on speeches, etc. Many procedural decisions are also organic decisions, such as the referral of a question to an ad hoc committee, the convening of an intergovernmental conference on a particular topic, etc." *See* M. Virally, "Unilateral Acts of International Organizations" in Bedjaoui, *supra* Chap. I note 29, 241-263, at 245.
204 *See* Art. 2(2), UN Charter.
205 499 UNTS 312.

within the scope of Article 13 of the Geneva Convention) is a law-creating, obligation-producing act of the General Assembly.[206]

The procedural obligation that underlies Resolution 2750 C was reiterated and formally articulated by the General Assembly in 1973 when it adopted Resolution 3067 (XXVIII) – the resolution that abolished the Seabed Committee and finally convened UNCLOS III. This was effected through a "gentleman's agreement" among the members of the UN General Assembly[207] which in turn was adopted by the Conference as its "gentleman's agreement" and appears as an Appendix to its Rules of Procedure:[208]

> Bearing in mind that the problems of ocean space are closely interrelated and need to be considered as a whole and the desirability of adopting a Convention on the Law of the Sea which will secure the widest possible acceptance,
>
> The Conference should make every effort to reach agreement on substantive matters by way of consensus and there should be no voting on such matters until all efforts at consensus have been exhausted.[209]

The gentleman's agreement, according to UNCLOS III Chairman Amerasinghe forms an integral part of the "package deal" of rules that constitute the decision-making/voting regime for the Conference.[210] It was the "very foundation of the rules of procedure" of UNCLOS III.[211] It also conveys the basic idea that the envisioned Law of the Sea Convention to be negotiated[212] must itself be an indivisible agreement consisting of all the substantive matters it deals with. This is the same "package deal" notion that was stressed explicitly and

---

206 *See* further, *infra* note 263 and accompanying text.
207 Adopted by consensus by the UN General Assembly upon recommendation of the First Committee. *See* A/PV 2169 (16 Nov 1973). For the debate on the gentleman's agreement in the First Committee, *see* PV 1924-1933, 1936, 1937 & 1939 (15-26 Oct 1973).
208 I UNCLOS III Off Rec at 52. Further on the view that the package deal is a binding rule of law, *see* J. Evensen, *Working Methods and Procedures in the Third United Nations Conference on the Law of the Sea* 199 RECUEIL DES COURS 415 (1986-IV).
209 Adopted by consensus. Text in Annex of UNCLOS III Rules of Procedure, March 6, 1980, UN Doc. A/CONF.62/30/Rev.3 (1980).
210 I UNCLOS III Off Rec at 51.
211 Statement of Ambassador Yankov of Bulgaria, I UNCLOS III Off Rec at 46.
212 Res. 3067 (XXVIII) 16 Nov 1973, para. 2, provides that the mandate of UNCLOS III is to adopt one convention dealing with all law of the sea matters.

unambiguously in the discussions on Resolution 2750 C of 1970.²¹³ In the context of UNCLOS III, the "gentleman's agreement" was based on the belief that neither a majority nor a minority should be allowed to impose its will on the other on any matter of substance through the tricks of decision-making formalities, and yet it also recognized the fact that resort to voting is proper only when the worse turns to worst. As Ambassador Amerasinghe suggested, although the gentleman's agreement is necessarily vague, it definitely encourages and ultimately assumes mutual trust, mutual confidence and mutual goodwill.²¹⁴

That the draft Law of the Sea Convention had to be finally adopted by a vote rather than by consensus,²¹⁵ is admittedly a sad testament to process of consensus building on the Law of the Sea by the international community, which had so much promise when the Conference started. The reason why consensus failed is well known. The United States eventually became intransigent on its ideological views regarding Part XI²¹⁶ leaving no opportunity for further principled negotiations on the part of the vast majority in the international community. The United States defected from the negotiations in 1982 on the ground that it was dissatisfied with the "regime" for the deep seabed laid down in Part XI of the Convention text; however, it claimed at the same time to benefit from the consensus agreements reached in the Conference with regard to, *inter alia*, the "limits" of national jurisdiction.²¹⁷

---

213 The over-emphasized "navigation for nodules" trade-off, which is affirmed by some writers, *see* Sebenius, *op. cit.* and Morell, *op. cit.*, but denied by others, *see* Schmidt, *op. cit.* and Friedheim, *op. cit.*, Miles, *supra* Chap. II note 7, is admittedly only a minor part of the UNCLOS III package-deal. It is submitted that a more accurate and positive law-based assessment of the negotiation history of the 1982 Convention on the Law of the Sea should refer instead to the "Common Heritage of Humanity Regime for Continental Shelf/coastal State jurisdictional limits" trade-off.
214 Ceylon, PV 1936 (25 Oct 1973).
215 After a determination was made that all efforts at reaching general agreement has failed, a recorded vote was taken at the request of the United States on 30 April 1982, resulting in the adoption of the Convention 130 in favour, 4 against with 17 abstentions. CLOS at 168.
216 *See infra* Chap. V.
217 *See* statement of Ambassador T. Clingan, Head of US delegation at Final Session of UNCLOS III, 9 Dec. 1982:
The result is that consensus eluded us on deep seabed mining. Each nation must now evaluate how it must act to protect its interests in the years to come.

So the questions come marching in. What about the mutual undertaking of the developed and developing countries to negotiate the "international regime" and the issue of "limits" simultaneously, and their procedural commitment to reach agreement on these and other issues at the same time? Could the *bona fides* of the United States and other industrialized countries be questioned on the basis of the international obligation of States to negotiate in good faith under the procedural terms of Resolution 2750 C? Were these States claiming in effect that the "exploitability clause" of the Continental Shelf Convention was already rescinded or amended when they decided not to carry on with further negotiations on the international regime to govern the Area? By voting against the 1982 Convention on the Law of the Sea, was the United States still bound by the terms and definitions of the regime under the 1958 Continental Shelf Convention? Considering that there was technically no high seas-regime for deep seabed mining before UNCLOS III was convened, could it be validly supposed that a high seas regime for nodule mining was created while UNCLOS III negotiations were in progress? If the position of the United States and some of its allies – that there exists an *interim* high seas freedom to mine the deep seabed – is regarded as illogical and illegal, what consequences flow from this recognition from the standpoint of the 1990s, and what sanctions or remedies – legal, political, even moral – are available to the rest of the international community? Last but not the least, could it then be maintained that, for all intents and purposes, the 1982 Convention was indeed adopted by consensus, thereby finally consolidating the Common Heritage of Humanity regime for the deep seabed as of 1982?

These are some of the questions that the "regime versus outer limits" debate in the late-1960s brings to light – questions that were never asked and are perhaps still timely to be asked. Be that as it may, it is submitted that the present law governing the deep seabed could be understood more meaningfully and

---

We need not fear the future. In particular those elements which promote the general community interests with respect to navigation, and conservation and utilization of resources within national jurisdiction, reflect long-standing practice. The expectations of the international community in these areas can and should be realized because we recognize that certain practices are beneficial to the community as a whole .... The rules that reflect the international community's expectations are sound and, therefore, they will endure.

Text in M. Nordquist & Choon-ho Park, *Reports of the United States Delegation to the Third United Nations Conference on the Law of the Sea* (LSI, 1983). [Hereafter, *Reports of US Delegation*]

critically with these unanswered questions on the background, questions whose legal consequences or political implications must be addressed before the international community could honestly look forward to a brighter future for the law of the sea with any confidence and faith in the international legal process. For the purposes of this book, however, these questions are simply being posed in order to demonstrate more persuasively the moral force as well as the normative integrity of the principle of the Common Heritage of Humanity.

5 The Programmatory Law of the Common Heritage of Humanity

UNCLOS III was the procedural device employed by the international community to overcome what US Ambassador Stevenson in 1970 referred to as the dilemma[218] on priorities involving the twin issues of the "regime" and "limits." By the terms of Resolution 1750 C, UNCLOS III was also intended to serve as the forum where the international community's expectation regarding the establishment of a regime for the deep seabed was sought to be realized. The recognition made in Resolution 2750 C that the UNCLOS III will

> deal with the establishment of an equitable international regime – including an international machinery – for the area and the resources of seabed and ocean floor and subsoil thereof, beyond the limits of national jurisdiction

definitely marks a culmination in the work of the United Nations on the seabed item. If the fact is considered that international supervision or United Nations control of the deep seabed was regarded as a highly controversial proposition only three years earlier,[219] the acceptance in principle by the international community of the internationalization concept in 1970 is truly a signal achievement. What is more, the specific mention of "an international machinery" to be established together with the "international regime" suggests a forthright community expectation that a relatively strong system of international control will have to be negotiated.[220] In addition, the defined scope of the inter-

---

218 USA, PV 1799 (15 Dec 1970).
219 *See* debates and discussions in *LSI 1966*, & NAT RES L, *supra* Chap. III note 34.
220 Only the Eastern European countries were opposed to any suggestion of international regulation or control. The Communist block accounts for all the dissenting votes and half of the abstaining votes on Res. 2750 C.

national regime tabled for future discussion covered not only resources in the area but likewise the area as a whole.

The obligation to concurrently negotiate and simultaneously reach agreement on the triad of issues – *viz.*, the international regime, the international machinery, and precise limits for the area[221] – is a major step forward in the movement to internationalize the deep seabed. Laying down the procedural framework of this obligation to negotiate in good faith was the pre-eminent accomplishment of Resolution 2750 C. But agreement on the procedural approach to internationalize the deep seabed did not necessarily imply that an agreement on the substance of internationalization would be reached. What Resolution 2750 C did was merely to identify the forum, set the agenda, indicate a time-table, and establish preparatory mechanisms for agreement.[222] The substance and the details of an internationalization agreement will still have to be worked out in UNCLOS III. Fortunately for the Seabed Committee and the Conference, however, the international community did not have to start from scratch in negotiating such an internationalization agreement, because the broad structural outlines of the international regime have already been drawn by another UNGA resolution adopted on the same day as Resolution 2750 C. This is the epochal Declaration of Principles Resolution (no. 2749), which was adopted by a vote of 108 in favor, none against, with 14 abstentions.[223]

Resolution 2749 marks the apogee of five years of work in the United Nations that began when the Economic and Social Council, in early 1966, first took cognizance of the role of deep sea resources in the economic development of poor countries. For a time, it appeared that consensus on a declaration of principles was impossible to achieve, given the way fundamental interests were contraposed in the Seabed Committee, even as it laboured arduously to define areas of agreement among various options and proposals. The incommensurable perceptions of the industrialized and developing countries on what should constitute "principles", as against factual premises for these principles, as shown earlier, illustrate the difficulties involved. The Seabed Committee adjourned

---

[221] These three issues have been generally considered as distinct subjects in the Seabed Committee discussions. In defending the position that these three issues should be considered organically, the delegation of Belgium, for instance, argued that if the machinery is part of the regime, then it is also true that the question of limits is part of the regime. PV 1799 (15 Dec 1970).

[222] Res 2750 C at para. 5-6, enlarged and reconstituted the Seabed Committee as a preparatory body for UNCLOS III.

[223] Most of the abstentions were from the Eastern European block.

its 1970 session with no draft declaration to boast.[224] It was through the wide, intensive and informal consultations conducted shortly thereafter, spearheaded by SBC Chairman Amerasinghe, that finally produced a "comprehensive and balanced"[225] draft declaration which was presented to the First Committee in late November of that year.[226] Because of the relative mystery surrounding the informal negotiations of the draft declaration, the delegation of New Zealand referred to it as an "enigmatic text."[227] But the Declaration's virtue may very well lie in its enigma, for the absence of any official references as to prior documentary sources, author's intentions, or contextual motivations[228] makes it a work that should be understood and appreciated purely on its own terms. One fact was granted to those who facilitated its conclusion: the draft declaration of principles was earnest toil to memorialize the 25th anniversary year of the United Nations.[229] The mystical collective authorship[230] of the draft declaration, its auspicious debut as a hallmark of the jubilee year of the United Nations, as well as its re-dedication to the cause of the Second UN Development Decade[231] exactly mirror the idealism of the very first operative paragraph of the Declaration: 'The area and its resources are the common heritage of humanity.' Enigmatic indeed!

From a legal standpoint, there can be no discussion about the recommendatory status of the Declaration of Principles Resolution. Although Ambassador Evensen of Norway described the principles as "indications of the rules and the provisions of international law, present and future", the Declaration is a non-binding decision of the General Assembly. And apart from the question of the subsequent normative evolution of the principles themselves, the resolution has no legal value as such. Some delegations, quite legitimately,

---

224 The Seabed Committee was requested to submit a draft declaration to the General Assembly for its twenty-fifth session. Res. 2574 B, para. 4.
225 Ceylon, PV 1773 (25 Nov 1970).
226 Ceylon, PV 1773 (25 Nov 1970).
227 PV 1786 (7 Dec 1970).
228 Ambassador Amerasinghe pointed out that "there is no single author to this draft." Ceylon, PV 1773 (25 Nov 1970).
229 *See* statement of Ambassador Amerasinghe, UN Doc. A/PV1933 (17 Dec 1970).
230 Or, to use the terms exchanged in the verbal spar between delegations of Kuwait and the USA, "The common heritage of mankind is not a gift from coastal States." PV 1780 (2 Dec 1970).
231 *See* statement of UN General Assembly President Hambro, PV 1933 (17 Dec 1970).

cautioned that the Declaration does not create legal consequences.[232] And SBC Chairman Amerasinghe underlined the fact that the Declaration "cannot claim the binding form of a treaty but is a definite step in that direction." The undisputed view which emerged was that the Declaration serves as an important basis for negotiating a new legal order for the deep seabed, and consequently a new public order for the oceans.[233]

If the "psychological impact" of the 1969 Moratorium Resolution was only grudgingly accepted by the developed countries, this cannot be said of the Declaration of Principles Resolution. Notwithstanding all the reservations noted on record concerning the merits or demerits of the Declaration, it met with near-unanimous acceptance[234] and was welcomed as a persuasive basis for norm-building and norm-creation. Since substantive ideas were laid down in the Declaration, future negotiations will then have to refer to these ideas not as bland concepts merely put forward by delegations but as "principles" or fundamental arguments that possess the political or moral authority of the international community. It is against this background that the real impact and success of the Declaration should be measured. For the first time since the *Ad Hoc* Committee began its quest for legal principles to govern the deep seabed, there was now an identifiable stock of shared principles which will be drawn upon in the progressive development of the law of the sea.

---

232 Australia, PV 1777 (30 Nov 1970); USSR, PV 1798 (15 Dec 1970); UK, PV 1799 (15 Dec 1970).

233 *See e.g.*, Chile, PV [the Common Heritage of Humanity embodied in the Declaration is a new and revolutionary concept]; Sweden, PV 1775 (27 Nov 1970) [a futuristic Declaration]; Iceland, PV 1778 (1 Dec 1970) [Declaration as basis for future work and true and effective internationalization]; El Salvador & India, PV 1781 (2 Dec 1970) [Declaration as a step towards the regime but not yet the regime]; Denmark, PV 1782 (3 Dec 1970) [Declaration a useful basis for drafting legal provisions]; Romania, PV 1784 (4 Dec 1970) [Declaration as step towards complete demilitarization]; Iraq, PV 1785 (4 Dec 1970) [Declaration as solid foundation for complete and balanced international regime]; Japan, PV 1787 (7 Dec 1970) & PV 1798 (15 Dec 1970) [the epoch-making significance of Declaration and a decisive turning point]; Barbados, PV 1787 (7 Dec 1970) [with Declaration, international community is in the beginning stages of a revolution in the law of the sea]; USA, PV 1799 (15 Dec 1970) ["Declaration is a useful basis for negotiations"].

234 Only the Soviet Union registered what could be considered a protest against the "seriously deficient" draft declaration. USSR, PV 1798 (15 Dec 1970).

The most momentous principle emblazoned in the Declaration is, most assuredly, that which is stated first in its operative part: "The Sea-bed and the ocean floor, and the subsoil thereof, beyond the limits of national jurisdiction, as well as the resources of the area, are the common heritage of mankind." As the foremost dispositive statement, this proposition sets forth the core substantive argument behind the Declaration. Being at the threshold of a solemn enactment, it provides the pivotal and most critical point of reference – in political, psychological, moral, or even formal linguistic terms – in the Declaration of *Principles*. The form which was given to the Declaration thus upholds and sustains the approach that was all along advocated by the developing countries in the *Ad Hoc* Committee in the formulation of legal principles for the deep seabed. The main point was to have all States accept the proposition that "the area and its resources are the common heritage of humanity", and whatever consequences flow from that recognition will then have to be worked out later. This was the perspective or the attitude *de lege ferenda* which the industrialized countries refused to acknowledge earlier.[235] In the struggle for "first principles" alluded to earlier, it could be maintained that the "first principle" advanced by the developing countries had won the day – which ought to put to rest the conceptual chaos that had obtained concerning the policy strategy of the international community for the deep seabed.[236] When the UNCLOS III opened its first substantive session in Caracas in 1974, all delegations that referred to Resolution 2749 took it for granted that the principles and rules for the international regime will have to be built upon, and be in accordance with, this "first principle", whatever meanings that can be read into the principle.[237] In more symbolic terms, the "common heritage of humanity" was finally appreciated as the seed that will give life to the regime, the cornerstone upon which an edifice will be built, a first definitive step towards a clearcut goal. Creating a system of norms that derives from the common heritage *grundnorm* (to borrow a term from Professor Kelsen) translates as the program-

---

235 *E.g.*, The following remark of US Ambassador Stevenson is clearly at odds with the "first principle" taken by the developed countries in the *Ad Hoc* Committee: the meaning of the common heritage of humanity "is indicated by the principles which follow it and will be elaborated in the internationally agreed regime to be established." PV 1799 (15 Dec 1970).
236 *See* Luard, *op. cit.* 135-138.
237 *See* general statements of delegations, I UNCLOS III Off Rec 59 *et seq.*, and opening statements on regime and machinery in the First Committee, II UNCLOS III Off Rec 5-36.

matory law behind the principle that "the area and its resources are the common heritage of mankind." It accomplishes what ICJ Judge Bedjaoui will later on refer to as "international law in the service of a design."[238] This is no mean achievement. It bears emphasizing that it took over three years for the developing countries to have this teleological point of view, this "obvious" principle, accepted in the Seabed Committee and acknowledged by the international community as a whole.[239]

At the risk of missing out the subtle points in the text, a convenient summary of the Declaration's contents is in order. (The full text of Declaration of Principles Resolution is appended to this book.)

The Declaration has six preambular statements and 15 operative paragraphs.

The first preambular item recalls the previous General Assembly Resolutions that dealt with the seabed agenda item. The second affirms that there is an area of the seabed beyond national jurisdiction whose precise limits are yet to be determined. In the third preambular item, it is recognized that the existing legal regime of the high seas does not provide substantive rules for regulating the exploration and exploitation of the area's resources, while the fourth says that the area shall be reserved exclusively for peaceful purposes, and resource activities therein shall be for the benefit of humanity as a whole. The belief that an international regime and machinery are essential and should be established as soon as possible is expressed in the fifth paragraph. Finally, the sixth item in the preamble states that development and use of the area and its resources shall be undertaken in such a manner as to foster the healthy development of the world economy and the balanced growth of international trade, and to minimize adverse economic effects of these activities.

The first operative paragraph asserts that the area as well as its resources are the common heritage of humanity. The second provides that the area is not subject to appropriation and no State shall claim or exercise sovereignty or sovereign rights therein. It is pointed out in the third that no State or person shall have rights with respect to the area and its resources incompatible with the regime to be established and Resolution 2749. The fourth paragraph stipulates that all resource activities and other related activities in the area shall be governed by the international regime

---

238 Bedjaoui, *supra* Chap. II note 25, at 111.
239 As Ambassador Amerasinghe remarked, the Common Heritage of Humanity concept was not so long ago regarded as a chimerical dream. Doc. A/PV 1933 (17 Dec 1970).

to be established. The fifth posits that the area shall be used exclusively for peaceful purposes in accordance with the international regime to be established.

The sixth dispositive paragraph provides that in the area, States shall act in accordance with the UN Charter and the 1970 UNGA Friendly Relations Resolution. The seventh paragraph avers that exploration and exploitation shall be for the benefit of humanity as a whole, whether land-locked or coastal, and taking into particular consideration the interests and needs of developing countries. The reservation exclusively for peaceful purposes of the area in relation to the arms race is provided for in the eight paragraph. The ninth says that on the basis of Resolution 2749, the international regime and machinery for the area and its resources shall be established by an international treaty of a universal character generally agreed upon. It also indicates some elements of this regime. The tenth paragraph enjoins States to promote international cooperation in scientific research and provides the measures to be taken towards this end.

The eleventh operative item refers to environmental protection and conservation of resources in the area. In the twelfth paragraph, the rights and interests of coastal and other States with respect to activities in the area are recognized. The thirteenth paragraph provides that Resolution 2749 does not affect the legal status of the superjacent waters and airspace above those waters as well as the rights of coastal States to act in order to prevent pollution or other hazards caused by activities in the area. The fourteenth provides for the responsibility of States and international organizations to ensure that activities in the area, done by them or on their behalf, shall be carried out in conformity with the regime to be established. Finally, in the fifteenth paragraph, reference is made to the principle of peaceful settlement of disputes concerning activities in the area.

On the question of the "proper" interpretation of the Declaration of Principles Resolution, consensus developed around two major themes when the Resolution was adopted. The first is the "package deal" nature of the Declaration. The second is the understanding that the Declaration does not lay down an *interim* regime for the seabed. It is submitted that these themes are the most critical features of the programmatory law of the Common Heritage of Humanity.

On the "package deal" character of the Declaration, it was generally agreed that the principles in the Declaration constitute an integral whole – a delicately balanced compromise reflecting the highest degree of agreement attainable at that time.[240] Ambassador Evensen pleaded to the delegations not to submit formal amendments to the draft resolution but instead to simply make necessary oral reservations on record so as not to disturb the fragile, if not "brittle",[241] balance achieved in the document. Each principle was organically linked to the others as well as to the whole. The Declaration was, therefore, to be interpreted as a whole.

If it was agreed from the very beginning that the substantive principles for the deep seabed, as formulated, are closely interwoven and form an organic indivisible unity, for conceptual or normative purposes, it may be asked: what consequences follow if this "substantive package deal" embodied in Resolution 2749 is juxtaposed with the "procedural package deal" mandated under Resolution 2750 C. Considering that the principles for the deep seabed would provide the normative foundations for the regime to be established and in view of the fact that the regime will have to be negotiated in the context of all issues and problems relating to the law of the sea – covering not only "outer limits" but also fisheries, MSR, environmental protection, etc. – it is reasonable to conclude that the principles for the regime governing the area and its resources must be inseparable from, and treated as a whole in conjunction with, the principles underlying the regimes for fisheries, territorial sea, marine conservation, MSR, etc. What also logically emerges from this analysis is that the so-called traditional or classical principles in the law of the sea, must be adjusted somehow in light of the introduction in the new ocean order of a new regime founded on the fundamental principle of the Common Heritage of Humanity. The programmatory law of the Common Heritage cannot but entail the "re-programming" of the classical law of the sea.

On the basis of the "package deal" character of the principles governing the seabed, the procedural integration of law of the sea issues into a single negotiation framework called for in Resolution 2750 C inevitably requires the substantive harmonization of all principles in the law of the sea. Arguably, this conclusion preempts a situation where a State or group of States, for political reasons or otherwise, chooses to abide by those principles or regimes in the new ocean order that it likes, and disregards those which it dislikes. This is clearly not allowed under the combined operation of "package deal" commitments under both Resolution 2749 and Resolution 2750 C. The message is

---

240 *See* remarks of Ambassador Amerasinghe, Ceylon PV 1773 (25 Nov 1970) and Ambassador Evensen, Norway, PV 1774 (16 Nov 1970).
241 UK, PV 1799 (15 Dec 1970).

simple: if the problems of ocean space are closely interrelated and need to be considered as a whole,[242] then the principles of ocean law are closely interrelated and need to be adopted and interpreted as a whole. The formal undertaking to negotiate only one Law of the Sea Convention[243] would ensure that this would be the case.

The holistic "package deal" nature of the new public order of the oceans to be negotiated in UNCLOS III as mandated in Resolution 2750 C is without doubt an ambitious objective. There could be no denying the fact that negotiating this package Convention on the Law of the Sea will be extremely complex and difficult. More practically, it will take time. The question that arises then is this: pending the establishment of the new comprehensive regime for the oceans, what legal framework for the Area obtains in the meantime? Specifically, if the problem presented by the seabed issue is urgent, what measures, from a legal standpoint, should be installed to ensure that the regime for the deep seabed contemplated by the Common Heritage of Humanity principle is not overrun by *interim* developments? The response of the international community to this query lies in the second theme that underlies the universal acceptance of the Declaration of Principles Resolution.

A caveat which was made absolutely clear when Resolution 2749 was adopted was that the Declaration does not provide for an *ad interim* regime for the area and its resources.[244] This follows from the fact that the Declaration, like any other substantive UN General Assembly resolution, does not have binding legal effect but only serves as the basis or a persuasive guideline for negotiating the regime. This is also consistent with the "package deal" procedural agreement in Resolution 2750 C, which proclaimed that there shall be no international regime unless agreement is also reached on, among other matters to be considered in a forthcoming Conference, the precise definition of the Area.[245]

---

242 Res. 2750 C, 2nd preambular para.
243 Res. 3067 (XXVIII), para. 2, provides that UNCLOS III "shall adopt a convention dealing with all matters relating to the law of the sea taking into account the subject-matter listed in paragraph 2 of General Assembly resolution 2750 C." Res. 2749, para. 9, speaks of "an international treaty of a universal character, generally agreed upon."
244 *E.g.*, Peru, PV 1777 (30 Nov 1970); El Salvador, PV 1781 (2 Dec 1970); UK, PV 1799 (15 Dec 1970).
245 *Cf.* France, PV 1778 (1 Dec 1970) [the regime cannot be decided in the abstract unless the continental shelf is delimited]; Belgium, Doc. A/PV1933 (17 Dec 1970) [the extra-jurisdictional area is an integral part of the regime itself].

It is, therefore, only logical that *any* kind of *interim* regime *de lege lata* cannot be presupposed for the "seabed beyond national jurisdiction" at the time when the Declaration was adopted – for the obvious reason that an *interim* regime would have as yet no known area of application. The urgency for the immediate conclusion of an international regime was precisely due to the absence of an *interim* regime on resource exploitation in the deep seabed, outside of the "exploitability clause" of the 1958 Continental Shelf Convention which the international community was eagerly wanting to abandon once and for all.

Only the United States had specific views about the possibility of an *interim* regime, or more specifically an *interim* resources regime, pending the conclusion of the "international treaty of a universal character" embodying a definitive regime for the area and its resources. The evolution of an *interim* policy for the deep seabed in the US must be examined closely, because it is this policy that has been regarded as undermining the "package deal" integrity not only of the UNCLOS III negotiations but also the new regime of the oceans produced by UNCLOS III.

The first US *interim* regime proposal was announced by US President Nixon in May 1970 in his Statement on United States Policy for the Seabed.[246] This Statement, it will be recalled, advocated a deep seabed regime that included an intermediate "trusteeship" or buffer zone beyond the 200-meter depth line off shore.[247] The Statement recognized, however, that negotiations on such a complex regime will take quite some time. Thus, an *interim policy* was proposed:

> ... I do not, however, believe it is either necessary or desirable to try to halt exploration and exploitation of the seabeds beyond a depth of 200 meters during the negotiating process.
>
> Accordingly, I call on other nations to join the United States in an interim policy. I suggest that all permits for exploration and exploitation beyond 200 meters be issued subject to the international regime to be agreed upon. The regime should accordingly include due protection for the integrity of investments made in the interim period. A substantial portion of the revenues derived by a state from

---

246 Text in Wenk, *op. cit.* at Appendix 19.
247 The concept was originally conceived by Prof. Henkin in 1967, *supra* Chap. III note 24; Wenk *op. cit.* 276. *See* "Draft United Nations Convention on the International Sea-Bed Area" Working Paper submitted by the USA. Text in 1970 SBC Rep, Annex V.

exploitation beyond 200 meters during this interim period should be turned over to an appropriate international development agency for assistance to developing countries. I would plan to seek appropriate congressional action to make such funds available as soon as a sufficient number of other states also indicate their willingness to join this interim policy.[248]

This proposal for an *interim* regime did not attract as much comment or negative reaction as the "trusteeship" proposal did,[249] but met the same political fate as the latter: it was practically ignored[250] and overtaken by the events in the UN leading to the decision to convene a Law of the Sea Conference with a comprehensive agenda.[251] The idea of an *interim* regime was resurrected by the United States when the substantive session of UNCLOS III began in 1974. This time the proposal was for "the provisional application of the permanent regime and machinery."[252]

In the domestic struggle in the US that accompanied the formulation of the Nixon Statement, it was the US mining industry which bitterly lost.[253] It will be remembered that previously, in the internationalization debate in the US, the nascent nodule mining industry was already too adamant in its view that a "freedom of the seas" regime was the most ideal legal framework for deep seabed mining.[254] Finding little support from the US Executive Department, the industry turned to more sympathetic ears in the US Congress for its freedom-

---

248 The treaty details of this interim policy were defined in Chapter VI "Transition" of the "Draft United Nations Convention on the International Sea-Bed Area" Working Paper submitted by the USA. Text in 1970 SBC Report, Annex V. Neither the Working Paper of the UK, *id.* Annex VI nor the Proposal of France, *id.*, Annex VII on the regime made reference to interim arrangements.
249 *See* summary of criticisms aired at the *Pacem in Maribus* Conference held in Malta in 1970, E.M. Borgese (Ed.), *Pacem In Maribus* xxxi-xxxii (1972).
250 Even the US delegation was not very keen on pushing the US Draft Convention, which was the subject of very serious controversy in the US. Hollick, *op. cit.* 232-234, 262.
251 In stating the US position on Resolution 2749, Ambassador Stevenson stated that "our views on the problem of interim activities are clearly indicated in President Nixon's statement of 23 May last." USA, PV 1799 (15 Dec 1970).
252 Address by US Amb. J. Stevenson to the First Committee, UNCLOS III, Caracas, 27 July 1974. Text in *UN Source Documents on Seabed Mining* 342, at 348 (Wa. DC: Nautilus Press).
253 Hollick, *op. cit.* 262.
254 *See supra* Chap. III Sec. B3.

of-the-seas cause.²⁵⁵ Draft legislation sponsored by mining interest were then introduced starting in 1971, providing for deep seabed mining under a national/unilateral licensing system pending the establishment of an international regime.²⁵⁶ These draft legislation in the US Congress took the position that an *interim* mining regime for the "seabed area beyond national jurisdiction" is supportable by the freedom doctrine. This was a position that was motivated by nothing less than an industry's appetite for "gold rush" style profit. In any case, this position was doctrinally suspect from the standpoint of international law as it stood during that time.

The legal stance of the US Executive Department somehow began to shift and tow the industry line around 1973. Dr. John Norton Moore, as Chairman of the US National Security Council Interagency Task Force on the Law of the Sea and Deputy Special Representative of the US President for the Law of the Sea Conference, testifying before the US Senate, defended the mining industry's theory of an *ad interim* regime founded on the precept of freedom:

> It is certainly the position of the United States that the mining of the deep seabed is a high seas freedom and I think that would be a freedom today under international law. And our position has been that companies are free to engage in this kind of mining beyond the 200-meter mark subject to the international regime to be agreed upon, and of course, assured protection of the integrity of the investment in that period.²⁵⁷

---

255 Hollick, *op. cit.* 263.
256 *Ibid.*; *See also* JG Laylin, "Interim Practices and Policy for the Governing of Seabed Mining Beyond the Limits of National Jurisdiction" in L. Alexander, *supra* Chap. II note 51, 25 at 26; Morell, *op. cit.* 45.
257 Hearings before the Senate Subcommittee on Minerals, Materials and Fuels, 93rd Congress, 1st Sess at 247 (1973). Quoted in "Notice of Discovery and Claim of Exclusive Mining Rights, and Request for Diplomatic Protection and Protection of Investment, by Deepsea Ventures, Nov 1974." Text in C.J. Joyner (Ed.), *International Law of the Sea and the Future of Deep Seabed Mining* Proceedings of the J.B. Moore Society of International Law Symposium and the American Society of International Law Regional Meeting, Virginia, 16 Nov 1974, at 25 (1975). *See also* J.N. Moore, "The Law of the Sea: An Overview", *ibid.*, and Statement of JN Moore in the Hearings Before the Senate Subcommittee on Minerals, Materials and Fuels, 93rd Cong, 2nd sess (1974), quoted in Kronmiller, *op. cit.* 232. Similarly, Dr. Bernard Oxman, Assistant Legal Adviser in the US State Department, in 1973 hinted that the US may resort to the "procedural" solution of unilateral action as a "method of developing law" if reasonable alternatives do not emerge from

307

These less than conciliatory and palpably arbitrary[258] overtures by some US government officials on the question of an *interim* regime did not bode well for UNCLOS III which was then just about to begin its sessions. Ambassador Thompson-Flores of Brazil put it frankly when he asserted in February 1973:

> Pending the decision on the type and powers of the future international machinery, any initiative towards the creation of an interim operating procedure would amount to an unacceptable attempt to exercise a biased pressure on the preparatory work of the future Conference on the Law of the Sea.
>
> ... I might say that to even consider at this stage any interim policy would, beyond being objectionable from an ethical or juridical point of view, certainly turn out as an unproductive exercise.[259]

Throughout UNCLOS III, there was no hiding the fact that the threat of unilateral *interim* legislation based on the freedom of the seas-doctrine was being usefully deployed by the United States and its allies as a tactical ploy to gain concessions.[260] The structure of the threatened interim regime was ominous, contemplating a leviathan of concerted unilateral seabed mining legislation on the part

---

UNCLOS III. He did not however, explicitly refer to a "freedom of the seas" regime as an *interim* or permanent policy option for the US. *See* B. Oxman, "The US Position" in Alexander, *supra* Chap. II note 51, at 156.

258 Under this "interim regime theory", the freedom of the seas regime for deep seabed mining was thought to begin beyond the 200-meter isobath.

259 S. Thompson-Flores, "Remarks" in Alexander, *supra* Chap. II note 51, at 41. The threat of unilateral seabed mining was also condemned in the Seabed Committee in 1972. Schmidt, *op. cit.* 99.

260 *See* Morell, *op. cit.* 45; Schmidt, *op. cit.* Chap. 3. The US delegation in UNCLOS III did not categorically state the official US view concerning *interim* measures until the Seventh Session of the Conference in August 1978, when Ambassador Richardson, in a short debate that took place in the General Committee, "stated that the common heritage of mankind never meant that resources of the deep seabed would have to remain unexploited in the absence of a new international regime" and that "States and their nationals have the legal right to explore and exploit deep seabed minerals and that such activities constitute freedom of the high seas which have not been abridged by any treaty or any customary international law." Kronmiller, *op. cit.* at 83. This position was reiterated publicly during the full debate on the matter in Plenary on 15 September 1978. *See* further discussion below.

of "reciprocating" technologically-advantaged States.[261] This proposed *interim* regime became *de facto* reality with the passage of the Deep Seabed Mineral Resources Act in 1980. Thereafter with the adoption of the "package deal" Convention on the Law of the Sea in 1982, this domestic legislation was transformed into a bizarre regime with extra-territorial effects through the "mini-treaty" among several industrialized States.[262]

The wisdom of the policy behind the Declaration of Principles resolution – that it in no way stipulates an *interim* regime, and this was accepted even by the western industrialized States – becomes even more apparent if we consider the method of revising the 1958 Convention on the Continental Shelf as provided for in this Convention. Article 13 of the Continental Shelf Convention states that "the General Assembly of the United Nations shall decide upon the steps, if any, to be taken" in respect of a request for the revision of the Convention.[263] It could be assumed that Resolution 2750 C, and all subsequent UNCLOS III-related Resolutions passed by the UN General Assembly, have outlined the definitive steps and binding procedures to be taken by the international community in reviewing and repealing the "exploitability clause" of the Convention. And the measures to be followed for this purpose took the form of the "package deal" agreement. By virtue of this procedural agreement, and as a matter of orderly process, no "outer limits" shall be conclusively established until an international (not unilateral) regime for the deep seabed was finally concluded. Bearing in mind the issue of "priorities" concerning the regime

---

261 Morell, *op. cit.* 44; Schmidt, *op. cit.* 98; Hollick, *op. cit.* at 263. The concept of co-ordinated legislation by like-minded States to support a particular design of customary law development concerning seabed resource exploitation was also put forward in E.D. Brown, *supra* Chap. III note 138.

262 For a detailed description of the "Reciprocating States regime" as a contrast to the "UN Convention regime", *see* E.D. Brown, *supra* Chap. III note 142. The UN General Assembly, starting with Resolution 37/66 (3 Dec 1982), continually stressed the unified character of the 1982 Law of the Sea Convention and called on the industrialized States to refrain from further action directed at undermining the Convention or defeating its object and purpose.

263 Art. 13 (2). The first paragraph of Article 13 provides that "After the expiration of five years from the date on which this Convention shall enter into force, a request for the revision of this Convention may be made at any time by any Contracting Party by means of a notification in writing addressed to the Secretary-General of the United Nations." *Cf.* Hutchinson, *op. cit.* at 131, suggesting several modes of repealing or amending Article 1 but without making reference to Article 13 of the 1958 Continental Shelf Convention. *See supra* Section B.4.

versus limits, this solution is not only just but also pragmatic. It takes more time to develop and establish principles and substantive norms for the international regime than to define a precise and quantitative definition of the Area.

The General Assembly-sanctioned procedure for amending the Continental Shelf Convention is significant in the context of the supervening emergence of the 200-mile EEZ regime as a customary law institution during UNCLOS III. While it cannot be denied that the EEZ resource regime establishes some type of "outer limits" to national resource jurisdiction, the EEZ cannot be regarded as formally rescinding the "exploitability clause" of the Continental Shelf Convention.[264] It, therefore, smacks of opportunism on the part of the industrialized States to regard the emergence and consolidation of the EEZ as a warrant for unilateral seabed mining beyond the EEZ.[265] On the part of parties or signatories to the 1958 Continental Shelf Convention, it is legally impermissible to establish a provisional regime for seabed mining outside the EEZ as such while UNCLOS III was in progress because the Continental Shelf Convention had not yet been validly revised according to the procedure that was prescribed for this purpose by the UN General Assembly.

When the issue of unilateral deep seabed mining was debated at UNCLOS III in 1978, not one of principal industrialized States supporting this kind of *interim* regime made reference to the issue of "outer limits" under the Continental Shelf Convention.[266] How could they, when the prime target of convenient attack was Resolution 2749, which they maintained did not and could not prohibit *interim* unilateral mining activities. But the issue was not whether Resolution 2749 was binding or has normative value during the *interim* period. That question was already settled way back in 1970. The real issue was whether

---

[264] *See* Hutchinson, *op. cit.* The argument is corroborated by the fact that certain broad-shelf States expressed reservations on the EEZ if its delimitation prejudiced their vested rights to the continental shelf that extends farther than 200 nautical miles. *See* Canada, I UNCLOS III Off Rec at 97. For a description of how the "outer limits" of the continental shelf was negotiated in UNCLOS III, *see also* II COMMENTARY at 837 *et seq.*

[265] It will be noted that the policy preference of the US Executive Department for an *interim* regime founded on the freedom of the seas-doctrine was initially made public at the time when the overall outlines of a "package deal" had already emerged in UNCLOS III, to include the widely-accepted 200-mile economic zone. *See* JN Moore, *supra* note 257, at 86.

[266] France, Belgium, Federal Republic of Germany, Italy, UK, USA & Japan; *see* IX UNCLOS III Off Rec at 106, *et seq.*

it at all made any sense to talk about an *interim* resources regime for the "seabed beyond national jurisdiction" when this area did not exist and could not have existed except through the "package deal" procedure prescribed in Resolution 2750 C. It is easy to forget that the reasons which render legally improper the adoption by the majority in the UN General Assembly of a Moratorium or temporary freeze on seabed mining activities are the very same reasons which render legally impermissible the adoption by a minority of a transitional operational regime for deep seabed mining.

On the other hand, the legal position of the Group of 77 on the issue of unilateral seabed mining was summarized in a Letter dated 24 April 1979 from the Chairman of the Group of 77 Addressed to the President of the Conference.[267] In this exposition, the Group of Legal Experts of the Group of 77 argued that the principles set out in Resolution 2749 prohibited a unilateral mining regime for the area. This argument was heyday for Third World critics who readily joined the crowd that pilloried General Assembly resolutions before the altar of positivist purity.[268] The weakness of the Group of 77 position is evident. First, on the political plane, it was a position that deepened the involvement of Resolution 2749, or the Common Heritage of Humanity principle, in the explosive controversy surrounding the "New International Economic Order" – an international social movement commenced in the mid-1970s built upon the tenuous normative foundation of a coordinated series of General Assembly Resolutions.[269] Since, historically, it is the developed countries which ultimately decide whether the substantive contents of any General Assembly resolution should be regarded as binding law or not, the argumentative path taken by the Group of 77 was much too bold and risky, indicative of the deep

---

267 XI UNCLOS III Off Rec 80-82. *See also* Statement of Ambassador Nandan (Fiji) on behalf of the G-77 in IX UNCLOS III Off Rec 103-104 (15 Sept 1978). The inadvisability of *interim* legislation, either on legal or pragmatic-political grounds, was also stressed by the USSR, China, Romania, Norway (on behalf of Finland, Norway and Sweden) Canada, The German Democratic Republic, and Poland. New Zealand and Australia equivocated. *See* IX UNCLOS III Off Rec 105-108.
268 Kronmiller, *op. cit.* 318 et seq.; E.D. Brown, *supra* Chap. III note 142, at II.2.28 *et seq.*
269 The 1974 Charter of Economic Rights and Duties of States includes a provision reiterating principles found in Resolution 2749, *see* A/RES/3281 (XXIX), 12 Dec 1974, Art. 29. *See also* UNCTAD Resolution on "The Exploitation of the Seabed beyond the Limits of National Jurisdiction" of 17 September 1978. UNCTAD Doc. TD/B (XVIII)/SC.1/L.2. On the NIEO debates, generally, *see supra* Chap. II, note 25.

political confrontation at the time. Secondly, The Group of 77 position against an *interim* unilateral regime, somewhat prematurely, distinguished the principles embodied in Resolution 2749 from the Resolution itself, arguing that the former have binding character as customary norms.[270] As it was stated earlier, Resolution 2749 only served as the basis for negotiating an international regime. It is only when this regime is finally established in a universal Law of the Sea treaty that the principles in Resolution 2749 crystallize as norms of customary law, or at least become binding on account of their expression in conventional law. This result follows from the premise that it is through the adoption of a Law of the Sea Convention as prescribed in Resolution 2750 C, that the "Area", with its precise delimitation, becomes a legal reality.

It is submitted that the sustained political intimidation through the threat of *interim* unilateral legislation throughout UNCLOS III as well as the subsequent actualization of this threat in municipal law, including the creation of the "reciprocating-States" regime, were unlawful and unwarranted. These interventions achieved what UNCLOS president Amerasinghe described as "disastrous psychological effects" that could only have pressed negotiations to proceed on the basis on "coercion."[271] With this in mind, the parallelism between the 1969 Moratorium Resolution and the move to establish an *interim* regime comes to an end. The former did not pretend to be a non-binding call for moral restraint; the latter had all the arrogant pretensions of positive law. While the former was a plea made by the majority for patience and empathy on the part of a minority, the latter was an aggressive imposition by a profit-seeking coterie on the overwhelming number of nations. The former strove for a cost-effective and orderly development of the legal infrastructure for the deep seabed, but the latter precipitated a costly "chaotic situation with regard to the law of the sea."[272] And while the "psychological effect" of the former amounted to no more than unwelcome admonition of the poor to the rich; the "psychological effect" of the latter devastated the hopes of the vast majority of States whose

---

270 "Consequently, any unilateral act or mini-treaty is unlawful in that it violates these principles [laid down in Resolution 2749], for the legal regime, whether provisional or definitive, can only be established with the consent of the international community as a whole representative of mankind and in conformity with the system determined by the international community." G-77 position, *supra* note 267, under item 5.
271 *See* IX UNCLOS III Off Rec at 108.
272 Fiji (on behalf of Group of 77), IX UNCLOS III Off Rec at 104.

only claim to the seabed was the hope that it will someday, somehow assist them alleviate the poverty in their societies.

Consequently, it is difficult to deny that the *de facto interim* seabed mining legislation consolidated by a handful of industrialized countries introduced a grave distortion into the programmatory law of the Common Heritage of Humanity. The assault on the Common Heritage of Humanity through the brazen policy of "interim regime" power politics seriously impaired the work of UNCLOS III, not least the 1982 UN Convention on the Law of the Sea. This policy, it must be repeated, is without foundation in international law. The alleged "freedom the seas" underpinning of this policy was nothing more but the wishful gloss by the US mining industry, if not the ideological afterthought of certain governments intent on pleasing narrow industry interests in their own polities. Apart from the issue of whether these governments did in fact negotiate in bad faith, the realization that the community effort to establish a comprehensive, unified, and more stable public order of the oceans was compromised in UNCLOS III should put into question those tendencies in the international community which permit narrow private interests to dictate upon international law-creating processes of truly universal significance.[273]

Although the programmatory law of the Common Heritage of Humanity is yet to fulfill its agenda, it had at least illuminated the darker, less dignified side of classical international law, a law that breeds upon the chicanery by the powerful and perpetuates a baffling indifference to the needs of people and humanity as a whole.[274] The underlying cause of the protracted conflict concerning the deep seabed is less the inability of international law to keep pace with advances in technology than the old problem of the international community coming to terms with its transformed self and with its past so that it could address more effectively the changing needs and interests of all its members.[275] The Common Heritage of Humanity is a crucible on the maturity of the international community to deal with the outstanding issues between

---

273 In the domestic political process in the US, authoritative views have been put forward warning against narrow industry agendas dictating on US foreign policy. *See* W. Scholz, "Observations on the Draft Agreement reforming the Deep Seabed Mining Provisions of the Law of the Sea Convention" in Nordquist & Moore, *op. cit.* 69-82; and L. Henkin, *supra* Chap. III note 71.
274 *See* Bedjaoui, *supra* Chap. I note 29, at 5-13.
275 *See* I. Brownlie "The Expansion of International Society: The Consequences for the Law of Nations" in H. Bull & A. Watson (Eds.), *The Expansion of International Society* 357-369, at 368-369 (1984).

313

the rich and the poor States. The exuberant words of Ambassador Amerasinghe ring ever loudly: the gigantic endeavor that the international community has undertaken in the ocean sphere will test us to the limits; and the only instrument at our disposal is a non-binding Declaration of Principles Resolution, whose real virtue lies simply in its moral force.[276]

6. The Reservation of the Common Heritage for Peaceful Purposes

If the Declaration of Principles resolution does not provide for an *interim* regime on resource exploitation in the Area, it does, however, make reference to an *interim* or transitory regime of a different kind. Paragraph 8 of the Declaration states:

> The area shall be reserved exclusively for peaceful purposes without prejudice to any measures which have been or may be agreed upon in the context of international negotiations undertaken in the field of disarmament and which may be applicable to a broader area. *One or more international agreements shall be concluded as soon as possible in order to implement effectively this principle and to constitute a step towards the exclusion of the sea-bed, the ocean floor and the subsoil thereof from the arms race.* (emphasis supplied)

The 1971 Treaty on the Prohibition of the Emplacement of Nuclear Weapons and Other Weapons of Mass Destruction on the Sea-Bed and the Ocean Floor and the Subsoil Thereof[277] should be considered as an agreement envisaged in this paragraph.[278] The purpose of this section is to briefly explain how this Treaty fits into the programmatory law framework of the Common Heritage of Humanity.

The principle of reservation exclusively for peaceful purposes stated in paragraph 8, which is also found in paragraph 5 of the Declaration, is immediately traceable to the first part of the agenda item proposed by Malta in

---

276 Ceylon, PV 1799 (15 Dec 1970) & A/PV.1933 (17 Dec 1970).
277 Concluded at London, Moscow and Washington on 11 February 1971. Text in 955 UNTS 115. [Hereafter, Sea-Bed Treaty] As of 1995, The Sea-Bed Treaty had received 90 Ratifications. 20 UN DISARMAMENT YRBK 248 (1995).
278 B. Vukas, "Peaceful Uses of the Sea, Denuclearization and Disarmament" in Dupuy & Vignes, *op. cit.* 1233-1320, at 1236.

1967. That part, according to Ambassador Amerasinghe, constitutes the pith and centre of the agenda item, for the exploration and exploitation of ocean floor resources cannot proceed unless the area is reserved exclusively for peaceful purposes.[279] In the internationalization project envisioned by Ambassador Pardo, the idea of reserving the area exclusively for peaceful purposes – the peace dimension of a multi-dimensional internationalization programme – was specifically aimed at achieving a negative objective: to prevent the use of the deep seabed as an arena for the arms race.[280] Many countries welcomed the concept that the seabed beyond national jurisdiction should be devoted exclusively to peaceful purposes, but differences instantly surfaced about what this concept entailed, *e.g.*, whether it meant "non-military" purposes.[281]

In the *Ad Hoc* Committee, the two superpowers – the US and the USSR – to whom the peace reservation theme was at once directed, submitted draft resolutions for consideration by the General Assembly.[282] While the USSR proposal sought complete prohibition of the use of the seabed area beyond territorial waters for military purposes, the US proposal contemplated the prevention of the emplacement of weapons of mass destruction on the seabed and ocean floor. Both proposals, however, did refer to the Geneva-based Eighteen-Nation Committee on Disarmament (ENCD) as the proper forum where the necessary decisions must be taken. It should be mentioned that the Antarctic Treaty of 1959 and the 1967 Outer Space Treaty were considered as significant precedents in tackling the question of peaceful use of the seabed.[283]

While the Seabed Committee deliberated on the matter, the US and the USSR, within the framework of the ENCD, were able to reach agreement on a draft treaty in October 1969. This draft treaty was based on the aforesaid US proposal

---

279 Ceylon, PV 1588 (28 Oct 1968).
280 PV 1515, para 91.
281 Ad Hoc SBC Rep, Annex II, para. 20-22.
282 *See* Ad Hoc SBC Rep, Annex III.
283 1969 SBC Rep, Report of the Legal Subcommittee, para. 42. It should be noted that the while Antarctic Treaty aims at complete demilitarization by interdicting "any measures of a military nature" in Antarctica, the Outer Space Treaty, Art. IV, is more limited in scope, directing States "not to place in orbit around the Earth any objects carrying nuclear weapons or any other kinds of weapons of mass destruction, install such weapons on celestial bodies, or station weapons in outer space in any other manner." *See* Vukas, *op. cit.* 1235.

which had restricted its scope of application to weapons of mass destruction.[284] The draft was initially rejected by the UN General Assembly because of its extremely inadequate provisions, *viz.*, the hazy definition of area of application, the fact that it aimed only at partial demilitarization, and its insufficient provisions on control and verification. After exhaustive diplomatic activity, the superpowers agreed to modify their original draft and to assure the UN that, *inter alia*, the proposed treaty will only serve as a first step towards complete demilitarization. The scope of weapons covered, however, remained unchanged.[285] On 17 November 1970 the General Assembly, adopted and recommended to States the Sea-bed Treaty.[286]

The Sea-Bed Treaty, as its title suggests, interdicts implanting or emplacing on the seabed and ocean floor "any nuclear weapons or any other types of nuclear weapons of mass destruction as well as structures, launching installations or any other facilities specifically designed for storing, testing or using such weapons."[287] Its area of application corresponds to the seabed and ocean floor beyond an off-shore zone of 12 miles.[288] There are provisions that stipulate what are basically national measures of verification with the possibility of international control included.[289] Most significantly, largely on account of Swe-

---

284 The USSR dropped its demand for complete demilitarization in exchange for the US' agreement to have the treaty apply to the entire seabed beyond 12 miles from the coast. A. Pardo. *Development of Ocean Space – An International Dilemma* 31 LOUISIANA L REV 45-72, at 67 (1970).
285 *See* USSR & US, PV 1748 (2 Nov 1970). France expressed the most serious misgivings about the scope of the returned draft. PV 1754 (9 Nov 1970).
286 The Treaty was adopted by a vote of 102 in favor, 2 against (Peru and El Salvador) and 2 abstaining. PV 1763 (17 Nov 1970).
287 Art. I, Sea-Bed Treaty.
288 Art. II, *id*. It should be noted that the "12-miles limit" corresponds to what the US and USSR considered as the maximum breadth of the territorial sea, but did not use the expression "territorial sea" because of objections from the Latin American States. The treaty however confirms the thesis of Professor Oda, *supra* Chap. III note 150, that for military purposes, the "seabed beyond national jurisdiction" is the seabed area beyond territorial waters. The conclusion of the Sea-Bed Treaty with the precise definition of its area of application was instrumental in the move of the US Department of Defense to support the narrowest definition of the continental shelf possible, Hollick, *op. cit.* 214-215, thus reinforcing the emergent thrust of US policy to re-interpret the "exploitability clause" in the most restrictive fashion.
289 Art. III, *id*.

den's insistence,[290] there was included an express undertaking by the Parties "to continue negotiations in good faith concerning further measures in the field of disarmament for the prevention of an arms race on the seabed, the ocean floor and the subsoil thereof."[291] Finally, and related to the last-mentioned provision, the treaty contains a review mandate so that five years after the entry into force of the Treaty, a conference or a series of conferences of States parties will be held "to review the operation of this Treaty with a view to assuring that the purposes of the preamble and the provisions of the Treaty are being realized."[292]

When the General Assembly considered the draft Declaration of Principles Resolution, many countries reiterated the conviction that the Sea-Bed Treaty is *only an initial step* towards complete demilitarization of area.[293] The insistence on the preliminary character of the Sea-bed Treaty was stressed because everyone understood that the Treaty, from a military point of view, did not mean anything to the Superpowers.[294] It is perhaps true that by consenting to the step-by-step process of seabed demilitarization, the international community missed a singular opportunity to adopt once and for all a policy of total

---

290 *See* Sweden, PV 1750 (4 Nov 1970).
291 Art. V, Sea-Bed Treaty.
292 Art. VII, *id.* The supporting preambular paragraphs read:
Convinced that this Treaty constitutes a step towards the exclusion of the seabed, the ocean floor and the subsoil thereof from the arms race;
Convinced that this treaty constitutes a step towards a treaty on general and complete disarmament under strict and effective international control, and determined to continue negotiations to this end[.]
293 *E.g.*, Chile, PV 1775 (27 Nov 1970) [Endorsement of the Treaty is a concession made by the developing countries for the commitment to negotiate total demilitarization]; Sweden, PV 1775 (27 Nov 1970) [agrees with the Norwegian interpretation that the Seabed treaty is only a first step, that it is part of the regime of resource exploitation, and that international procedures of completion should be followed]; Romania, PV 1783 (3 Dec 1970) [Sea-Bed Treaty as first step towards complete demilitarization]; Yugoslavia, PV 1783 (3 Dec 1970)[Treaty as introduction to full demilitarization]. One of the stated objections of the USSR to the Declaration of Principles Resolution was that it did not categorically state a ban on all military activities in the Area. USSR, PV 1798 (15 Dec 1970).
294 *See* for *e.g.*, E.M. Borgese, "Introduction" *Pacem In Maribus* at xxvi (1972); S. Hirdman, "Prospects for Arms Control in the Ocean" in Borgese & Krieger, *op. cit.* at 80-99; J.-P. Cot & P. Boniface, "Disarmament and Arms Control" in Bedjaoui, *supra* Chap. I note 29, at 811-821, at 818.

ban on all military activities and installations in the area.²⁹⁵ But since the Treaty was evidently the best deal that could be obtained under the circumstances,²⁹⁶ the complete demilitarization of the area remained an unsettled issue – a "live item" on the agenda of international organizations that must work to complete the internationalization of the deep seabed under the Common Heritage principle.²⁹⁷

In the preparations leading to UNCLOS III, several draft proposals were submitted in pursuit of the "reservation for peaceful purposes" principle under Resolution 2749. The working paper submitted by the Latin American States on an international regime, as well as the Draft Ocean Space Treaty submitted by Malta, granted to the international organizations proposed to be created extensive authority to implement this principle.²⁹⁸ Less directly, the USSR's "Provisional draft articles of a treaty on the use of the sea-bed for peaceful purposes" prohibits the use of the area for military purposes and adds that further international agreements should be concluded for this purpose.²⁹⁹ On the UNCLOS III agenda, the item "peaceful uses of the ocean space; zones of peace and security" was allocated to the Plenary as well as to the three main Committees in so far as it was relevant to their mandates.³⁰⁰ Suggestions to elaborate more precise rules on the subject did not prosper in Plenary,³⁰¹ but the First Committee was able to work out provisions on the peaceful uses of the Area.³⁰²

Part XI of the 1982 Convention contains four provisions which mentions the "peaceful purposes" clause: Article 141, confirming the principle in para-

---

295 J. Andrassy, "Present Regime of the Military Uses of the Seabed: Possible Regimes to be Envisaged" in *Rome Symposium, supra* Chap. III note 86, 501-511 at 504-505.
296 Statement of Ambassador Amerasinghe, PV 1773 (25 Nov 1970).
297 *See* Sweden, PV 1750 (4 Nov 1970); A. Myrdal, "No Arms on the Ocean Floor" in Borgese, *supra* note 88, at 322-327.
298 1971 SBC Rep, Annexes I.8 & I.11.
299 1971 SBC Rep, Annex I.3.
300 I UNCLOS III Off Rec 40.
301 In April 1976, the delegations of China, Ecuador, Iraq, Madagascar, Pakistan, Peru, the Philippines, Romania and Somalia favoured incorporation in the future LOS convention of measures aimed at limiting military activities at sea. Bulgaria, Cuba, the USSR and the US did not want any negotiations on the subject. Vukas, *op. cit.* 1237.
302 *See* Vukas, *ibid.*

graph 5 of the Declaration of Principles Resolution that the Area shall be used exclusively for peaceful purposes; Article 143(1) providing that MSR in the Area should be carried out exclusively for peaceful purposes and for the benefit of humanity as a whole;[303] Article 147(2)(d) providing that the use of installations for carrying out activities in the Area shall be exclusively for peaceful purposes; and Article 155(2) instructing the Review Conference to maintain the principle of the use of the Area exclusively for peaceful purposes.

An examination of the circumstances surrounding the adoption by the UN General Assembly of the Sea-Bed Treaty reveals that the principle "reservation exclusively for peaceful purposes" had entered the corpus of international law. With the inclusion of this principle in Article 141 of the 1982 Convention and its perpetuation in the regime contemplated under Part XI[304] it could even be argued that this principle had acquired the character of *jus cogens*, whose derogation is not permitted under international law.[305] Its elements as a peremptory norm, it is submitted, are gleaned from the 1982 Convention, the Sea-Bed Treaty itself, the Declaration of Principles Resolution, and the 1970 deliberations of the General Assembly.

First, at the most general level, the principle of peaceful use for the area reiterates a basic principle under the UN Charter through Article 301 of the 1982 Convention.[306] Under the Heading "peaceful uses of the seas", article 301 provides:

> In exercising their rights and performing their duties under this Convention, States Parties shall refrain from any threat or use of force against the territorial integrity of political independence of any State, or in any other manner inconsistent with the principles of international law embodied in the Charter of the United Nations.

Secondly, there seemed to have been no disagreement over the proposition initially enunciated by Ambassador Pardo that the Area should be saved from the superpower "scramble." Although the ending of the cold war may have mooted this element of the principle, the prohibition of an arms race in the area remains a most significant facet of the internationalization policy for the Area and its resources. This leads to a third element that establishes the norm

---

303 *Cf.* Art. 240 (a), CLOS.
304 *See* Art. 155(2), CLOS.
305 *See* Art. 35, 1969 Vienna Convention on the Law of Treaties.
306 Vukas, *op. cit.* 1238-1239.

of complete demilitarization of the Area. This norm under the peaceful purposes reservation principle directly arises from the Sea-Bed Treaty, and its main thrust is recapitulated by Ambassador Myrdal: "National militarization and international peaceful exploitation of the riches of the seabed simply cannot co-exist"[307] – an insight whose profound relevance today is most clearly dramatized by the tragic phenomenon of land-mines.[308] The progammatory law of the Common Heritage of Humanity principle is informed by the principle of complete interdiction of military activities on the deep ocean floor.

The fourth and most crucial aspect of the principle of complete demilitarization of the seabed in the period following the entry into force of the 1982 Convention of the Saw of the Sea is its institutional definition. Specifically, it may be asked: what institutional mechanisms are available to pursue the goal of complete demilitarization in the post UNCLOS III and post-cold war era? If it is conceded that the "first step" had already been taken towards the complete demilitarization of the seabed through the 1971 Sea-Bed Treaty, there must be, in principle, further steps that should be adopted towards this objective. Although the Sea-Bed Treaty identifies the periodic review-conference of States Paries as the means to keep alive the issue of seabed demilitarization, it should be noted that the scope of the seabed area covered by the Sea-Bed Treaty is broader than and includes the "Area" as defined under the 1982 Convention. Moreover, it is conceivable that the International Seabed Authority (ISA) established under the Convention, which acts on behalf of humanity as a whole with respect to the Area's resources,[309] will have a direct interest in the demilitarization of the Area to the extent that this affects, directly or incidentally, the exercise of its powers and functions.[310] It is, therefore, very likely that the Review Conference mechanism under the Sea-Bed Treaty will interface with the ISA with respect to the implementation of the total demilitarization policy in the area. It is not certain whether adjustments to the Sea-Bed Treaty in terms of, for example, scope of weapons/military activities covered or conduct of verification procedures, will be needed. But it certainly can be maintained that the international community is one step closer to the realization of

---

307 Myrdal, *supra* note 297, at 327.
308 *See e.g.* K. Anderson & M. Schurtman, *The United Nations Response to the Crisis of Landmines in the Developing World* 36 HARV INTL L J 359-371 (1995).
309 Art. 137 (2), CLOS.
310 *See* Art. 157, CLOS. Necessarily, the activities under the Nuclear Test Ban Treaty will also be of interest to the International Seabed Authority. *See infra* Sec. D.4.

the objective of general and complete disarmament under strict and effective international control[311] with the entry into force of the 1982 UN Convention on the Law of the Sea.

C. The Common Heritage of Humanity and the Principle of Benefit-Sharing

Article 140 of the Convention, under the heading "Benefit of Mankind", applies the seventh operative principle in the Declaration of Principles Resolution which reads:

> The exploration of the area and the exploitation of its resources shall be carried out for the benefit of mankind as a whole, irrespective of the geographical location of States, whether land-locked or coastal, and taking into particular consideration the interests and needs of the developing countries.

A closely related provision under the Declaration is paragraph nine, concerning the establishment of an international regime and machinery through a generally accepted treaty of universal character:

> ... The regime shall, *inter alia*, provide for the orderly and safe development and rational management of the area and its resources and for expanding opportunities in the use thereof, and ensure the equitable sharing by States in the benefits derived therefrom, taking into particular consideration the interests and needs of the developing countries, whether land-locked or coastal.

It would not be an exaggeration to say that the business of UNCLOS III, particularly the work of its First Committee, was all about translating these rather vague and general principles into the operational regime now found in Part XI. But it would be simplistic to assume that the mining regime in Part XI was in fact inspired by or logically deduced from these principles. The negotiation environment in UNCLOS III was much too checkered and complicated for that conclusion. From the perspective of the progmatory law of the Common

---

311 For national views on the relationship between international control of the seabed and its resources and an effective regime of disarmament, *see* Poland, PV 1748 (2 Nov 1970); Norway, PV 1775 (10 Nov 1970); Sweden, PV 1775 (27 Nov 1970); Yugoslavia, PV 1784 (4 Dec 1970).

Heritage of Humanity the importance of these principles lies less in their subsequent execution or application as doctrine in the design of a specific functional regime for the Area than in their political pronouncement that certain legal doctrines and principles have come to an end.

In the internationalization debate that transpired in the US in the 1960s, it will be recalled that there was a very strong current of opinion which defended the harvesting of manganese nodules using the exclusive framework of municipal law. This municipal law approach to nodule mining was to be based either on the doctrine of the continental shelf or the flag-state mechanism of the freedom of the seas. In the context of US policy, it was realized that the former regime, constitutive of *lex lata*, was not politically feasible and although the latter option was legally impossible, this was nonetheless entertained as worth a gambit to be pursued through the aggressive assertion of US foreign policy. When the General Assembly took cognizance of the seabed issue, it was almost certain that international, rather than national, control of the deep seabed would be the rule. The use of the words "common heritage of mankind" by Ambassador Pardo to describe an all-inclusive, multi-dimensional outlook of internationalization, guaranteed that the wealth resulting from the exploitation of manganese nodules was removed from the exclusive claims of national jurisdiction. Principles 7 and 9 of the Declaration of Principles Resolution, in conjunction with principles 2 and 3 thereof (which rule out the doctrines of coastal State sovereignty and freedom of the seas, respectively), mark the crowning victory for the individuals and groups (like President Johnson, or the Commission to Study the Organization of Peace, or the lawyers attending the 1966 World Peace through Law Conference – the "idealists") who advocated internationalization. These principles proclaim that, henceforth, the exploration of the area and the exploitation of its resources shall be under international or United Nations control, supervision and direction and that no one country or nation shall be permitted to take these resources without the permission of the international community. Elsewhere, this has been described as the peremptory norm of multilateral regulation of activities in the Area.[312] From this vista, the principles enunciated in the Declaration unconditionally decided the political

---

312 *See* Morell, *op. cit.* at 183-189.

issue of who controls the seabed, and are therefore neither vague nor abstract in that regard.³¹³

The "common heritage of mankind", according to Roderick Ogley, "has always had a ring to it ... an idea on the borderline between dream and reality."³¹⁴ Intuitively, the partisans for internationalization thought that if the deep seabed and its resources are to be regarded as the common heritage of all humanity, it seemed unnecessary to further justify and explain why the new wealth must be used for the economic development of the poor countries, or why the United Nations should have title to these resources and profit from it, or why some novel form of international organization should be set up to administer or defend the "common heritage." The negative implications from the invocation of the phrase were no less significant: direct or indirect enjoyment of the common heritage should not be confined to a few; treating the resources as common heritage should preclude conflict and competitive struggle among nations; and the common heritage should not encourage the conduct of international relations on a business-as-usual individualistic basis.

These hunches about what lay behind the expression "common heritage of humanity" converged in the consolidated "Set A" Principles put forward by the developing countries in the *Ad Hoc* Committee. Accordingly, an international regime was envisaged for the exploration, use and exploitation of the area and its resources "for the benefit and in the interest of humanity." The establishment of this regime shall be for the purpose of, *inter alia*, promoting economic development "particularly that of the developing countries, whether coastal or land-locked."³¹⁵ Significantly, it should be noted that the "Set B" draft principles proposed by the developed countries, without resorting to the terminology of the "common heritage of mankind", also advocated internationalization, or "an international regime governing the exploitation of resources in the area" with the added proviso that "exploration and use of this area shall

---

313 It is often mentioned that the Declaration of Principles Resolution is susceptible to a wide variety of conflicting interpretations, rendering its intent almost impossible to determine. See for *e.g.*, L.M. Alexander, "Future Regimes: A Survey of Proposals" in Churchill, Simmonds & Welch, *op. cit.* 119-133, at 130; Buzan, *op. cit.* at 110; S. Mahmoudi, *The Law of the Deep Seabed Mining* at 134 *et seq.* (1987); Churchill & Lowe, *op. cit.* 181; Schmidt, *op. cit.* at 39. This is no doubt true if and only if the Declaration is seen as some kind of a specific blueprint for any *future* regulatory regime, *e.g.*, on seabed mining.

314 Ogley, *supra* Chap. II note 75, at 41 & 42.

315 *See Ad Hoc* SBC Rep, para. 88, items 3 & 4.

be carried on for the benefit and in the interest of mankind, taking into account the special needs of the developing countries." With respect to the economic use and exploitation of the resources of the deep seabed, therefore, there was a consensus from the very beginning about what internationalization entailed: (1) that economic activities in the area shall be conducted for the benefit and in the interest of humanity, and (2) the special needs of the developing countries shall assume special importance with respect to these activities.

1. "Benefit of Humanity" as a Rule of Decision

Professor Jean-René Dupuy must be credited with his pioneering conceptualization of what is meant by "mankind" in the context of Part XI.[316] Mankind or humanity, according to him, has a twofold meaning, both of which are enshrined in the provisions of Part XI:

- it is interspatial and includes all persons living at a given time, irrespective of where they are established;
- it is intertemporal in scope, since humanity consists not only of the people living today but also of those who will come later. Humanity is envisaged as going beyond those now alive.

There are two implications arising from a "transspatial" conception of humanity. First, all peoples are grouped together as a single sovereign or collective owner without discrimination. Second, there is general participation in the joint-management of the area and its resources at the level of decision-making institutions, at the operational level of economic activities, and at the level of sharing financial and other benefits. The notion that humanity is transspatial, therefore, fulfills a universalist and egalitarian function whereby wealth is destined to be shared equitably by everyone. On the other hand, Professor Dupuy would continue, the transtemporal characterization of humanity suggests that, first, the international community – conceived as either the United Nations or the International Seabed Authority – is merely a manager whose tasks should be the conservation of the domain and long-term programming of activities

---

316 J-R Dupuy, "The Area as the Common Heritage of Mankind" in Dupuy & Vignes, *op. cit.* at 579-586; also in Rozakis & Stephanou, *op. cit.*

therein. Secondly, the manager is accountable. A transtemporal humanity, in a word, will have an eternal value.

I agree with Professor Dupuy that the debate over the issue whether "mankind" or humanity is a new subject of international law is largely pointless.[317] The resolution of this issue, one way or another, cannot change the fact that under the Convention practical and operational decisions with respect to the governance of the Area and its resources are made by the institutions and agencies assigned to act on behalf of humanity. And when they do so, the decisions taken are by definition in the interest of humanity as a whole.[318] Nevertheless, what the notion of "benefit of humanity" does offer is the difficult challenge for those making the decisions to take the widest possible perspective and consider the most inclusive of all interests – transtemporal and transspatial humanity – in the governance of the Area and its resources, transcending loyalties as to flag, regional affiliation, or transient socio-political and cultural memberships. It urges the adoption of a world-view which would encourage those entrusted with the common heritage to discharge their obligations as "trustee" or "manager" with a view to promoting humanity's interests in intra- and inter-generational terms.

The riposte in terrestrial realism is whether the present crop of leaders and policy makers had developed or will soon develop – or will ever develop – that kind of transcendence called for by the new political programme on international control of resources. Judge Oda would, therefore, ask: has international society developed at such a high level of responsibility or harmony that we

---

317 *See* Bedjaoui, *supra* Chap. II note 25, at 236 ["mankind" is a new subject of international law]; W. Verwey, *The Establishment of a New International Economic Order and the Realization of the Right to Development and Welfare – A Legal Survey* 21 INDIAN J INT L 1 at 2 (1981) [reporting that the Common Heritage of Humanity partakes of a "third generation" of human rights]. *Cf.* P. Alston, *A Third Generation of Solidarity Rights: Progressive Development or Obfuscation of International Human Rights* 29 NETH INT L REV 307-322 (1982); R. Wolfrum, "Law of the Sea: An Example of the Progressive Development of International Law" in Tomushchat, *op. cit.*, 309-327, at 324.
318 This is corroborated by the absence of a general "judicial review" concept under Part XI. *See* Art. 189, CLOS concerning the limitations on the jurisdiction of the Sea-Bed Disputes Chamber with regard to decisions of the Authority.

could talk with common understanding of the "common heritage of humanity?"[319] Indeed, Judge Bedjaoui would add, simply positing the concept of "the common heritage of humanity" already exposes it to risk of being "co-opted", if it had not already been "co-opted", by the great powers for their own advantage.[320] "Co-optation" or "recovery" of the concept in this context means that the legal notion of "benefit of humanity" will simply be read or reinterpreted by the great powers in a way that would aggrandize their self-interest, as this has usually been done in the past. For example, it will be recalled that the USSR delegation, in explaining its vote on Resolution 2749 took the position that as far as the USSR was concerned the common heritage of humanity "means that the sea-bed is at the general disposal of all States and not subject to appropriation by any State, body or individual"[321] – much to the chagrin of those who laboured long and hard for internationalization. Also, the delegation of Ecuador once had to put on record, not without a hint of cynicism, its views against the prevailing US position that the term "benefit of humanity" means participation in benefits or resources by developing countries, and not that whatever increases wealth or industrial output is indirectly in the interest of humanity.[322] These attempts at "co-optation" serve as a warning that a haughty and narrowly-conceived national view of what constitutes humanity, or "benefit of humanity", is always a policy option for the warriors of *raison d'Etat*. The possibility of "co-optation" should also serve as reminder of what is principally at stake in the implementation of the "benefit of humanity" principle: *i.e.*, an abiding political interest in the unity and identity of humanity. Under the 1982 Convention on the Law of the Sea, what specifically are those

---

319 S. Oda, "Sharing of Ocean Resources – Unresolved Issues in the Law of the Sea" in J.-R. Dupuy (Ed.), *The Management of Humanity's Resources: The Law of the Sea* 49 at 61 (Workshop, Hague Academy of International Law & UNU, 1982).
320 Bedjaoui, *supra* Chap. II note 25, at 222-228.
321 USSR, PV 1798 (15 Dec 1970). *See also Message from the President of the United States and Commentary Accompanying the United Nations Convention on the Law of the Sea and the Agreement Relating to the Implementation of Part XI Upon their Transmittal to the United States Senate for its Advice and Consent*. Text in 7 GEORGETOWN INTL ENVIR L REV 77-194, at 152 (1994): "[The Common Heritage of Humanity] principle reflects the fact that the Area and its resources are beyond the territorial jurisdiction of any nation and are open to use by all in accordance with commonly accepted rules."
322 Ecuador, PV 1594 (1 Nov 1968). *Cf*. Ad Hoc SBC Rep, Report of the Economic and Technical Working Group, para. 52.

interests or needs which should underlie the decisions made on behalf of humanity? And how inclusive or representative of humanity are these interests?

2. Benefit of Humanity and the Special Needs and Interests of the Developing Countries

The reassuring conception of "humanity" advanced by Professor Dupuy must unavoidably be appreciated in the historical setting of a world acutely divided between haves and have-nots. Fortunately, Part XI of the Convention fully acknowledges the reality of the North-South division in the international community and stipulates outright that the interests and needs of developing States, as well as peoples who have not attained full independence or other self governing status, shall be taken into particular consideration when taking decisions bearing on the "benefit of mankind" element of the Common Heritage of Humanity regime.[323] The notion of "humanity" in the Convention is thus inseparably linked to the favoured status of the overwhelming majority of present day humanity – the developing States, or the "have-nots" – when it comes to the practical application of the principle that economic activities in the Area shall be conducted in the interest of all humanity.[324]

It would be a mistake to regard the favoured treatment of the developing countries under Part XI as some kind of exceptional rule of "positive discrimination." The entire history of Part XI of the Convention, as elaborated by the "first principle" of the Common Heritage of Humanity, testifies to the fact that the law governing the Area and its resources is a law for and on behalf of the developing countries, based on the principles of reciprocity and equality. The concept of the favoured standing of developing countries is inherent in the international regime itself and pervades the entire structure of Part XI. To interpret the principle of "benefit of humanity" as some version of transient "affirmative action" would certainly lead to undesirable consequences – as seen in the application of the "benefit of mankind" principle by industrialized States through their unilateral seabed mining legislation.

---

323 Art. 140, CLOS. *See also* Art. 148, CLOS, providing for the participation of developing States in activities in the Area.
324 M.C.W. Pinto, "Mineral Resources" in Dupuy, *supra* note 319, at 19-32.

327

The *interim* seabed mining legislation unilaterally adopted by some industrialized countries uniformly implements a peculiar and rather condescending notion of "benefit sharing." Under the terms of these statutes, national "revenue-sharing funds" consisting of levies from licensed mining activities were established and earmarked for international aid purposes.[325] The "revenue sharing" arrangements were cited by the reciprocating States as evidence that their *interim* seabed regime was compatible with the UNCLOS III mining regime. Thus, the German legislation purported to be "a contribution to the development of the common heritage of mankind ... and not in contradiction to the common heritage of mankind principle."[326] In this scheme, therefore, the principle of "benefit for humanity" under the Convention was understood as denoting a principle of "revenue-sharing", if only to express these States' "good intent towards the wider international community, and in particular the developing countries."[327]

"Benefit sharing" through the concept of passive receipt of token revenue under the interim regime executed by the industrialized countries was precisely that eventuality which the developing countries have constantly dreaded since the UN embarked on the project of formulating principles for the deep seabed. Ambassador Njenga of Kenya had, for instance, deplored the outlook which could lead some States to believe that they can bequeath the common heritage of humanity to the United Nations, and categorically asserted that the developing countries were not negotiating for charity.[328] International distribution of what are essentially treated as national revenues, *i.e.*, foreign aid, can never be reconciled with international control of the Area and its resources under any stretch of the imagination. The *interim* division of the ocean floor effected by the technologically advanced States so that they may, incidentally, be able to raise revenue for "development" purposes amounted to nothing more but the neo-colonial "scramble" which, it would be supposed, had ran out of fashion in the aftermath of the 1967 Maltese initiative. "Benefit sharing" under the Reciprocating States regime, so similar in intent and design to the orderly parceling out of Africa by the colonial powers in the 1885 Berlin Conference, is diametrically opposed to the active concept of benefit sharing favoured by the developing countries, which required participation not only in decision-

---

325 For details, *see* E.D. Brown, *supra* Chap. II note 141, at II.8.23-29.
326 *See id.* at II.8.25.
327 To use the words of a British Minister of Parliament. Quoted in *ibid*.
328 Kenya, PV 1781 (2 Dec 1970).

making but also in the full range of deep seabed governance.³²⁹ Added to the injury inflicted by the coercive *interim* legislation of some industrialized States is the insult to the majority in the international community occasioned by the industrialized States' conscience-saving "revenue-sharing" schemes.

The repulsive provisions on "benefit sharing" under the unilateral seabed mining legislation were premised on the revival of an oligarchic international law (to use a label of Judge Bedjaoui) which divides international society into the "civilized" and "all the rest."³³⁰ The ultimate justification for this type of international social stratification is, admittedly, not difficult to discern: the political interests of a few States are more worthy of protection under international law. The point of departure is the pronouncement made by the International Court in the 1969 *Continental Shelf* cases: the validity or development of a norm of customary law depends upon its acceptance by "States whose interests [are] specially affected."³³¹ This pronouncement immediately afforded ammunition to the defenders of unilateral legislation who were convinced that the industrialized countries *must be* the "specially affected States" entitled to have the last word on the evolution of customary law for deep seabed mining. The aim was to accord preferential status to these countries as "vitally affected States" which can claim superiority on the basis of technological capability to mine the seabed.³³² The question perforce must be raised once again: in the context of economic activities in the area, are there particular States or categories of States which are in some way "specially affected?" If so, who are such States – or, which fragments of humanity, as it were, must be regarded

---

329 E.M. Borgese, "A Constitution for the Oceans" in Borgese & Krieger, *op. cit.* 340-352, at 346. For a contrary view, *see* A. Kiss, *The Common Heritage of Mankind: Utopia or Reality* 60 INTERNATIONAL JOURNAL 423-441 (1985) [benefit sharing is not an essential element of the Common Heritage of Humanity].

330 Bedjaoui, *supra* Chap. I note 29, at 6.

331 *North Sea Continental Shelf Cases*, 1969 ICJ Rep 42, para 73.

332 *See* Kronmiller, *op. cit.* 295, 337; D. Arrow, *The Proposed Regime for the Unilateral Exploitation of Deep Seabed Mineral Resources by the United States* HARV INT L J 337-417, at 371, 379 (1980); II E.D. Brown, *supra* Chap. II note 141, at II.2.35 [special status of western countries derives from percentage of their contribution to UN Budget]. For a refutation of the favoured standing of the industrialized States in the law of deep seabed mining, *see* Morell, *op. cit.* at 167-169.

as distinctly "specially affected" and be given favoured status in the practice and implementation of the norm "benefit sharing for humanity?"

The "specially affected States" rule under the imagined "customary law" of deep seabed mining was no doubt put forward to counter the doctrinal and historical definition of the "benefit of humanity" principle found in the 1982 Convention. This is the reason why the alleged customary freedom to mine the deep seabed was put forward in the context of serious reservations to Part XI, as conventional law, expressed by the industrialized countries. "Benefit-sharing" under customary law, howsoever gilded with benign trappings was totally inconsistent with and absolutely outside the framework of "benefit sharing" in the deep seabed mining regime under Part XI of the Convention. In the doctrinal scheme of the common heritage, the "specially affected States" for the purposes of benefit-sharing are no less than the developing countries, coastal and land-locked, as well as the people who have not attained full independence or other self-governing status.[333] This conventional definition of "specially affected States" is unequivocally inspired by the principle of decolonization; it reflects upon what President Johnson at one time referred to as the policy against the neo-colonial "race to grab" the ocean bottoms. Under the 1982 Convention on the Law of the Sea, the "benefit of mankind" principle cannot be understood except in relation to the special interests and needs of people in the developing countries.

3. The Interests and Needs of Developing Countries under Part XI of the 1982 Convention

The concept of "special interests and needs of developing countries"[334] is necessarily a dynamic one. These special interests and needs, understandably, change over time as would the membership in the category "developing countries", which is an extremely heterogenous and fast-differentiating group of States. The volatility of the pertinent "interests and needs" or for that matter the "developing countries" does not, however, change the doctrinal thrust of the concept under Part XI of the Convention. It consists of two broadly defined

---

333 Art. 140, CLOS.

334 It is in the setting of Part XI where the term "developing countries" or "developing States" is used most pervasively in the Convention, occurring at least 38 times in the text. *See* subject index CLOS at 200, and 201-202.

elements: first, functionally-orientated interests and needs, *e.g.*, in scientific research and training, seabed exploitation activities, protection for land-based production, and transfer of technology; and second, special interests and needs with respect to the governance of the area and its resources, *e.g.* representation in the Council of the ISA. These interests and needs are to be addressed by the system of international cooperation established under the regime.

The general position of developing States in relation to the mining regime embodied in Part XI of the Convention may be summarized as follows. Activities in the Area, including marine scientific research, which are to be carried out for the "benefit of humanity", shall take into consideration the interests and needs of developing States,[335] including their participation and over-all economic development.[336] Any future amendments of the regime shall not modify this norm established in favour of developing countries.[337] Moreover, developing States shall avail of a programme for transfer of seabed mining technology[338] while producer developing States whose export earnings or economies are adversely affected by mineral production in the Area shall benefit from a compensation package to help them ameliorate their hardships.[339] In the decision-making processes of the International Seabed Authority – the organization through which the States Parties organize and control activities in the Area[340] and which thereby acts on behalf of humanity as a whole with respect to the resources in the Area[341] – developing countries shall be effectively represented as a "special interest" constituency, particularly in the Council as the executive organ of the Authority.[342] It may be mentioned that the Authority is given the additional task of receiving payments and contributions from broad-shelf coastal States with respect to the exploitation of the continental shelf beyond 200 nautical miles off shore; the Authority shall then distribute these payments and contributions to States Parties "on the basis of equitable

---

335 Arts. 140(1), 143(3), CLOS.
336 Arts. 148; 150, CLOS.
337 Art. 155 (2), CLOS.
338 Arts. 144, 273 & 274; Art. 15, Annex III, CLOS. *Cf.* Section 5, Annex, 1994 Implementation Agreement.
339 Art. 151 (10), CLOS; *Cf.* Section 7, Annex, 1994 Implementation Agreement.
340 Art. 157 (1), CLOS.
341 Art. 137 (2), CLOS.
342 *See* Arts. 152, 160 (f)(i); Art. 161 (1)(c), (d) & (e); *cf.* Section 3, para. 15, Annex, 1994 Implementation Agreement; Art. 162 (2)(d); Art. 163 (4); Art. 164 (1); Art. 163 (2)(b) & (d), CLOS.

sharing criteria, taking into account the interests and needs of developing States, particularly the least developed and the land-locked among them."[343] The land-locked and geographically-disadvantaged developing countries shall also be given special consideration in the exercise of the powers and functions of the Authority.[344] Lastly, pending the entry into force of the Convention, a signatory developing State, including its enterprises or nationals, may be registered as a pioneer investor;[345] in the meantime the problems which would be encountered by developing land-based producer States as a result of mineral production in the Area shall be studied by the Preparatory Commission.[346]

Viewed from the perspective of implementing the programmatory law of the Common Heritage of Humanity, the principle of "benefit-sharing" for humanity as a whole is certainly to be welcomed as a concept for the empowerment of developing States and nations. To be sure, there may not be any seabed mining activity in the near or distant future for the international community to ever come close to the "revenue sharing" phase of benefit-sharing. But this is not really what matters. The most crucial point is that Part XI had succeeded in establishing a regime that at least *recognizes in principle* that international law can be primarily devoted to meeting the special interests and needs of developing countries – as determined, by and large, by the developing countries themselves. And it is immaterial whether "developing countries" are in the majority or minority in the international community. That a *lex specialis* in international law exists which refutes the "international law of global disparities" is a paramount achievement in itself for the international community as a whole.

This achievement is what the mining companies of the industrialized countries vehemently abhorred, perceiving Part XI as encouraging "discrimination in favor of developing countries" and establishing "an untested international organization possessing very broad discretionary powers, partially controlled by countries whose interest is to make seabed mining impossible."[347] With the entry into force of the Convention, it seems that some mining companies

---

343 *See* Art. 82 in relation to Art. 162 (2)(o)(i), CLOS.
344 Arts. 152; 160 (2)(k); 161 (1)(d) & (2)(a); and 274 (a), CLOS.
345 *See* para. 1 (a)(iii), Resolution II, Final Act, CLOS.
346 *See* para. 5 (i) & 9, Resolution I, Final Act, CLOS.
347 C. Welling, "The Views of the United States Ocean Mining Licensees on Trends in the Negotiation to Make the United Nations Convention on the Law of the Sea of 1982 Universally Acceptable" in Nordquist & Moore, *supra* note 15, at 255-263.

will have to continue to fight their unprincipled battle with more creativity. For they can only successfully excise Part XI from the 1982 Convention on the Law of the Sea at the cost of irreparably destabilizing the entire public order of the oceans.[348]

In the meantime, the institutional mechanisms for benefit-sharing under the Convention must be set to work. However, the broad picture of implementing the "benefit of mankind" principle in the full range of all economic activities in the Area should not be forgotten. The functional regime of sea-bed mining developed in detail under Part XI of the Convention is just one specialized regime that derives from the spatial regime governing the Area as a whole founded upon principle of the Common Heritage of Humanity. Just like the 1971 Sea-Bed Treaty, therefore, benefit-sharing under the mining regime established in Part XI should be regarded as but a first step, although a highly significant one, in realizing the principle of the Common Heritage of Humanity whose ultimate goal is sustainable development in a decolonized world.

The goal of development for all humanity in an inter-generational context, *i.e.*, "sustainable development", brings to the fore another juridical pillar of the Common Heritage of Humanity principle. This relates to the principle of protection of the Area as an environmental resource within the total ecology of ocean – and planetary – space.

D. THE COMMON HERITAGE AS ENVIRONMENT

The environmental dimension of Ambassador Pardo's proposed internationalization programme vividly drew the picture of an ocean floor heaped with radioactive wastes and other pollutive refuse while the international community desperately stood on the side with no solutions to offer.[349] It was, however, the danger of marine pollution resulting from new industrial activities of resource exploration and exploitation on the deep seabed which caught the immediate attention of the General Assembly. Specifically, the permanent Seabed Committee was instructed "to examine proposed measures of co-operation to be adopted by the international community in order to prevent the marine pollution which may result from the exploration and exploitation

---

348 *See* intervention of Professor E. Miles in Hong, Miles & Park (Eds.), *The Role of the Oceans in the 21st Century* 381-382 (1995). *See also supra* Chap. V.
349 PV 1515, para.73-87.

of resources of this area."[350] In 1970 the spoliation of the ocean floor through uncontrolled dumping practices was once more brought to the fore with the news that the United States dumped a certain quantity of nerve gas in the Atlantic. The response of the Seabed Committee to the incident, in view of its tethered mandate, was to issue a moderately-worded statement of concern accompanied by an appeal to governments to refrain from using the seabed as dumping ground for toxic wastes.[351]

As is well known, the international regime which addresses the practice of ocean dumping was only agreed upon in December 1972, with the adoption of the global Convention for the Prevention of Marine Pollution by Dumping of Wastes and Other Matter.[352] It is significant to note that the preamble of this Convention makes reference to UN General Assembly Resolution 2749, presumably acknowledging the status of a portion of the ocean floor that could be seriously affected by dumping as the common heritage of humanity. The treaty also stipulates that nothing in the Convention shall prejudice the codification and progressive development of the law of the sea in UNCLOS III.[353]

The exclusion of dumping from the terms of reference of the Seabed Committee illustrates the application of a sectoral approach to environmental protection which, by and large, characterized international environmental regulation in the 1960s and 1970s.[354] By confining the Committee's "environmental protection" study mandate to a single activity likely to contaminate the marine environment, namely, the exploration and exploitation of seabed mineral resources, the United Nations decided that pollution from this one source posed the most urgent threat to the marine environment and, by inference, to the ecology of the new frontier. More particularly, as revealed by the discussions in the General Assembly, the preoccupation with this source of pollution stemmed from the concern voiced by coastal States that seabed mining activities will inevitably interfere with their fisheries. Iceland, for instance, whose economy

---

350 Res. 2467 A, para. 2(d). *See also* Res. 2467 B.
351 1970 SBC Rep, para. 25.
352 For the text and a brief description of this Convention, as amended up to 1993, *see* P. Birnie & A. Boyle, *Basic Documents on International Law and the Environment* 174-188 (1995).
353 Art. XIII, *id.*
354 For a discussion of the sectoral development of environmental law, *see* A. Adede, "International Protection of the Environment" in Tomuschat, *op. cit.* at 197.

heavily depended on its off-shore fisheries led the initiative to have the UN examine the impact of seabed mining on the health of coastal fisheries.[355]

The emphasis on down-stream pollution likely to be caused by seabed mining operations gives the impression that the Seabed Committee was less interested in the conservation of the deep seabed and its resources *per se* as a subset of the total marine ecosystem than in the environmental preservation of the superjacent waters, its living resources, as well as adjacent coastal areas.[356] The intrinsic ecological worth of the deep seabed as such was least on the agenda of international deliberations. This apparent lopsidedness reflected the rudimentary state of scientific knowledge on the deep seabed at that time and the prevailing optimism that subordinated any interest in the ecology of the deep seabed to the prospects of generating new wealth from the internationalized frontier.[357] From the more ecologically-conscious stance of the 1990s, it would appear that the international community in the late 1960s neglected the identity of the deep seabed environment itself – or that part of the marine environment which they were about to proclaim as the common heritage of humanity.

1. Overcoming a Sectoral Approach to Marine Environmental Protection

Notwithstanding the rather narrow conception of the "seabed environment" in the mandate of the Seabed Committee, an integrative and holistic approach to the protection of this environment was indicated, somewhat surprisingly, in the 1970 Declaration of Principles Resolution. In the Declaration, the Area is recognized not only as an integral part of the larger marine ecosystem but also as a distinct environment in its own right. Paragraph 11 provides:

> With respect to activities in the area and acting in conformity with the international regime to be established, States shall take appropriate measures for and shall

---

355 Iceland, PV 1589 (29 Oct 1968). Iceland was the sponsor of Resolution 2467 B which was unanimously adopted.
356 *See* Reports of Economic and Technical Subcommittee in the 1969 and 1970 SBC Reps.
357 Even the concept of an International Decade of Ocean Exploration, announced in Resolution 2467 D, was geared to a study of the ocean as a potential source of resources.

cooperate in the adoption and implementation of international rules, standards and procedures for, *inter alia*:

(a) The prevention of pollution and contamination, and other hazards to the marine environment, including the coastline, and of interference with the ecological balance of the marine environment.
(b) *The protection and conservation of the natural resources of the area* and the prevention of damage to the flora and fauna of the marine environment.[358] (Emphasis supplied)

It should be stressed that the term "activities in the area" as used in the Declaration literally meant all activities that can conceivably take place in the Area – including resource exploration and exploitation, scientific research, and military activities.[359] The Declaration, therefore, takes a comprehensive multi-functional or inter-sectoral approach to environmental protection of the Area and its resources, covering not only all possible sources or causes of environmental degradation (and not merely pollution) of the seabed beyond national jurisdiction but also every adverse ecological impact of any seabed activity on the larger marine environment.

The above-quoted principle in the Declaration, or its expansive intent, found its way in the "Draft articles considered by the [First Committee of UNCLOS III] in its informal meetings" of August 1974.[360] It is worth quoting the relevant provision of this draft *in extenso*, for it reveals the initial perspective of UNCLOS III on what should constitute an adequate regime of environmental protection for the Area:

With respect to [all] activities in the Area, appropriate measures shall be taken for the adoption and implementation of international rules, standards and procedures for, *inter alia*:

(a) The prevention of pollution and contamination, and other hazards to the marine environment, including the coastline, and of interference with the ecological

---

358 The text of this principle, particularly sub-paragraph (b), appears to have been adopted from a proposed draft resolution submitted by Norway in 1970. 1970 SBC Rep, Appendix II.
359 *See e.g.*, usage of term in para. 4, 10, 12 & 14, Res. 2749.
360 III UNCLOS III Off Rec 157-164.

> balance of the marine environment, particular attention being paid to the need for protection from activities such as drilling, dredging, excavations, disposal of waste, construction and operation or maintenance of installations and pipelines and other devices related to exploration of the area and exploitation of its resources.
> (b) The protection and conservation of the natural resources of the Area and the prevention of damage to the flora and fauna of the marine environment.[361]

Article 145 of the 1982 Convention on the Law of the Sea retained the elaboration that follows the term *"inter alia"* in the above draft but the *chapeau* was changed to read:[362]

> Necessary measures shall be taken in accordance with this Convention with respect to activities in the Area to ensure effective protection for the marine environment from harmful effects which may arise from such activities. To this end the Authority shall adopt rules, regulations and procedures for *inter alia* ...

The one crucial difference between the 1982 Convention, on the one hand, and the Declaration of Principles Resolution, on the other, is the scope of activities covered by the envisioned environmental protection regime: the Convention defines "activities in the area" restrictively to mean only the activities of exploration and exploitation of mineral resources in the Area.[363] This restrictive definition, it will be recalled, was insisted upon by the industrialized countries which wanted to see the Authority possess as little discretionary powers as possible.[364] The Convention thus retreats from the comprehensive environmental protection regime envisaged by Resolution 2749 and goes back to the uni-sectoral approach to marine environmental protection originally spelled out in the mandate of Seabed Committee.

The uni-sectoral definition of environmental protection under Part XI of the Convention, elaborated in the legal regime to prevent, reduce or control

---

361 Article 13, *ibid.* The bracketed word "all" appears in the original text.
362 The wording of Article 145, CLOS first appeared in the 1975 Informal Single Negotiating Text.
363 Art. 1(1), CLOS.
364 *See infra* Chap. V.

marine pollution from mining activities in the Area,[365] raises the question: How can the Area *in toto* – as an ecological space and a discrete environmental resource beyond national jurisdiction – be conserved and protected from all forms of environmental degradation? Stated differently, does its status as "common heritage of mankind" entitle the Area and its resources to a composite environmental protection and conservation regime distinct from the environmental regimes governing other marine jurisdictional zones in the Law of the Sea?

2. Existing Environmental Law for the Area and its Resources

Apart from the provisions under or deriving from the mining regime in Part XI of the Convention, which define the regulatory framework of environmental protection for the Area,[366] there are no other international environmental norms applicable to the Area that are not also applicable to the marine environment as a whole.[367] The environmental protection regime for the Area is, therefore, indistinguishable from the environmental protection regime for the entire

---

365 For an overview of the emerging regime on pollution control under Part XI of the Convention, *see* Consolidated Provisional Final Report of the Preparatory Commission, Draft Provisional Report of Special Commission 3, UN Doc. LOS/PCN/ 130 (17 Nov 1993); A. Nollkaemper, *Deep Sea-Bed Mining and the Protection of the Marine Environment* 15 MARINE POLICY 55 (1991); J.E. Hardes, in Wolfrum *supra* 431-454; E.D. Brown, *supra* Chap. III, note 141, at II.9.11-19. The rules and regulations are restricted to the exploration and exploitation stages of mining activities, and excludes from the ambit of environmental regulation pre-prospecting activities, like commercially-oriented scientific research, and post-exploitation undertakings, such as transport and on- or near-shore processing.

366 *See* Arts. 139, 145, 147, 150 (b), 162 (2)(x) CLOS; Arts. 2 (1)(b), 4 (4), 17 (1)(b)(xii) & (1)(f) Annex III, CLOS. *See also* Churchill & Lowe, *op. cit.* 276-277.

367 The environmental norms embodied in the *interim* seabed mining legislation of some industrialized States do not derive from Part XI, and cannot, therefore, be considered in relation to this framework. The environmental protection provisions in these statutes would, however, assume significance in relation to Arts. 139 and 145, CLOS, generally and Art. 4(4), Annex III, CLOS, specifically, when those States ratify the Convention. *Cf.* Art. 7 (2), 1994 Implementation Agreement, on the provisional application of these legislation. For the environmental protection rules of national legislation under the *interim* regime, *see* E.D. Brown, *supra* Chap. III note 141, at II.9.19-35.

marine environment, as laid down in Part XII of the Convention (on the Protection and Preservation of the Marine Environment).

A description of this general framework will show the limitations of the current regime in protecting and preserving the Area and its resources. The comprehensive framework of marine environmental protection laid down in Part XII is "comprehensive" only with respect to its identification of all sources of marine pollution.[368] Under the "umbrella" provisions of Part XII, measures to prevent, reduce and control marine pollution[369] are directed at the following exhaustive sources of pollution: pollution from land-based sources, from sea-bed activities, from activities in the Area, pollution by dumping, pollution from or through the atmosphere, and pollution from vessels. By inference, these are the types of pollution against which the Area and its resources are protected. *Pari passu* with the comprehensive framework of environmental protection for the marine environment, the framework for the prevention, reduction and control of pollution in the Area is all-embracing.

Some general provisions in Part XII may also be noted for their relevance to the protection and preservation of the Area and its resources. Hence, States are obliged to take all necessary measures to ensure that pollution arising from incidents or activities under their jurisdiction or control does not spread beyond the areas where they exercise sovereign rights.[370] States are also duty-bound not to transfer damage or hazards to the Area or, generally, transform one type of pollution into another.[371] In addition, they are required to take all measures to prevent, reduce and control pollution of the Area resulting from their use of technologies under their jurisdiction or control, or the intentional or accidental introduction of species, alien or new, to the Area, which may cause significant and harmful changes thereto.[372]

In light of recent discoveries of unique life forms and rare ecosystems on the deep ocean floor[373] singular importance may be attached to Article 194 (5) of the Convention. This provision requires States to take measures necessary to protect and preserve rare or fragile ecosystems as well as the habitat of

---

368 *See* E.D. Brown, *supra* Chap. II note 10, at Chap. 15; Gold & McConnell, *op. cit.*; Churchill & Lowe, *op. cit.* Chap. 15.
369 "Pollution of the marine environment" is defined in Art. 1 (4), CLOS.
370 *See* Art. 194 (2), CLOS.
371 *See* Art. 195, CLOS.
372 *See* Art. 196, CLOS.
373 *See supra* note 38. *See also* L. Glowka, *The Deepest Ironies: Genetic Resources, Marine Scientific Research and the Area* 12 OCEAN YRBK 154-178 (1996).

depleted, threatened or endangered species and other forms of marine life. This provision complements in a significant way the recently concluded UN Convention on Biological Diversity which provides norms to protect and conserve the earth's biodiversity resources in areas beyond national jurisdiction.[374]

Outside the framework of Part XII of the Convention, international agreements relating to military activities in the Area may also be cited as having a direct bearing on the environmental protection of the Area. Mention was already made of the 1971 Sea-Bed Treaty which prohibits emplacement of weapons whose presence in the Area certainly jeopardizes its environmental integrity. The 1963 Treaty Banning Nuclear Weapon Tests in the Atmosphere, in Outer Space and Under Water, whose interdictions should apply to nuclear weapons testing in the Area, is also significant in this respect.

Not surprisingly, the implementation of the environmental law governing the Area and its resources takes place under the same institutional conditions as the enforcement and implementation of the environmental law of the sea in general. The problem of implementation is broadly indicated in Article 194 (1) of the 1982 Convention, which provides that in taking all measures to prevent, reduce and control pollution from all sources, States are in general required to use the best practicable means at their disposal and in accordance with their capabilities, endeavoring to harmonize their policies for this purpose.[375] The characteristic fragmentation and dispersion of international institutions and agencies as well as the variety of national policies and priorities which bear on the management of the marine environment is equally present in the management of the Area and its resources. The multiplicity of institutions or machineries that oversee the ecological integrity of the Area – *e.g.*, the International Seabed Authority and sponsoring States for mining activities *per se*; Flag State and/or coastal state control for post-mining activities; the Consultative Meetings of the Parties to the London Dumping Convention for dumping activities; Meetings of States Parties to the 1971 Sea-Bed Treaty for military

---

374 Art. 5 of the UN Convention on Biological Diversity provides for a best-efforts obligation to protect and conserve biodiversity in the Area:
Each Contracting Party shall, as far as possible, and as appropriate cooperate with other Contracting Parties, directly or, where appropriate, through competent international organizations, in respect of areas beyond national jurisdiction and on other matters of mutual interest, for the conservation and sustainable use of biological diversity.
375 Art. 194 (1), CLOS.

activities; the IMO for vessel-source pollution; UNEP for land-based pollution; the FAO for fisheries; and States, regional organizations, and international agencies for biodiversity preservation – hardly distinguishes the Area with a unique status as common heritage of humanity from the superjacent waters, governed as it were by the free-for-all doctrine of freedom of the seas. Considering the multitude of uncoordinated institutional competencies in the environmental governance of the Area and its resources, the current situation is perhaps no different from the one deplored by Ambassador Pardo in 1967: "Plurality of jurisdiction, fragmentation of competence, a general lack of a sense of urgency, have unfortunately not resulted in effective international action to contain the massive problem of marine pollution."[376]

3. International Responsibility under the Environmental Law of the Area and its Resources

A problem that is peculiar to the application and enforcement of environmental law in the Area pertains to the rules on international responsibility or liability for serious harm or damage caused to the environment of the Area. The general rule in customary law is that States have the responsibility to ensure that activities within their jurisdiction or control do not cause damage to the environment of other States or of areas beyond the limits of national jurisdiction.[377] With respect to actionable harm originating within areas of national jurisdiction which adversely affects the Area, the 1982 Convention provides for the basic obligation of States to take all measures necessary to prevent this harm, their failure to do so being the basis for incurring international responsibility.[378] The rules on liability and compensation for transboundary environmental damage will thus apply. On the other hand, the situation involving damage to the environment of the Area arising from activities conducted outside of national jurisdiction would, however, present some interesting problems.[379] How can responsibility be enforced if serious environmental damage is inflicted on the Area or any part of the Area as a result of any illegal or hazardous activity within that zone under the supervision and control of any particular State,

---

376 PV 1515, para. 87.
377 Principle 2, Rio Declaration.
378 *See* Art. 194 (2) in relation to Art. 235, CLOS.
379 *See* Principle 13, Rio Declaration.

assuming under the circumstances that no transboundary effects occur in the territory of any other State?

If the environmental harm to the seabed beyond national jurisdiction arises from mining activities in the Area, then the ISA would unquestionably have the right to define relevant environmental standards, including standards for acceptable environmental harm in the Area itself. The ISA, through its rules, regulations and procedures, in cooperation with its member States, would have the authority to enforce compliance with these standards, and presumably the standing to initiate redress proceedings if and when these are called for.[380] As regards the capacity to bring suit, States Parties to the 1982 Convention have also been recognized by the International Law Commission as having an independent right to initiate action against any other State Party which may have infringed on the collective interest of maintaining a healthy environmental state for the common heritage.[381]

But what if serious damage occurs as a result of some other activities in the Area – such as naval operations that involve ultra-hazardous activities to the seabed environment, or dumping of environmentally deleterious materials not controlled by international convention, or nuclear weapons testing by a non-signatory State to the Test Ban Treaty; or destructive and unsustainable harvesting of living resources and other life forms in the Area? Who defines the standards? What is the basis for these standards? And how is international responsibility to be established? If it is true that actual mineral mining operations in the Area are still decades if not generations away, the most pressing environmental threats to the Area and all its natural resources will surely come from these other activities as potential sources of ecological harm. Because the powerful industrialized countries in UNCLOS III had insisted on a narrow ISA competence to safeguard the environmental integrity of the Area, Part XI of the Convention is silent on how the international community should cope with these other threats. It is clear, however, that the common heritage of humanity should be protected from all environmental threats on account of the express directive in Principle 11 of the 1970 Declaration of Principles Resolution. If it is accepted that the protection of the ecological integrity of the entire Area is an indispensable part of what the International Law Commission calls the "collective interests" in the common heritage of humanity, and there

---

[380] Art. 139 & 145 in relation to Art. 157 (1) & (2). See Nollkaemper, *supra* note 365.
[381] II ILC YRBK, part 2 at 25 & commentary 27 (1985); Nollkaemper, *op. cit.*

is no reason to believe otherwise because the Convention expressly states that the Area – and not only its mineral resources – is the common heritage of humanity, the programmatory law of the Common Heritage of Humanity principle is once more proven in the environmental field. There is clearly a need to expand and consolidate the environmental norms under Part XI of the Convention.

The ISA, as the agency that has been practically designated as the "trustee" or the "manager" of humankind with respect to the mineral resources of the Area, could and should play an important role in the development of baseline environmental standards against which the impacts of any activity in the Area other than mineral mining may be assessed. In the process of determining what constitutes an acceptable level of harm to the marine environment beyond which causative mining activities must be prohibited, the ISA would in effect be providing reference points for determining the acceptable level of environmental harm that may be applicable to other activities likely to adversely affect the Area. While the issue of what is an acceptable, as opposed to an unacceptable, harm ultimately hinges on political choice inherent in any act of standard-setting, the scientific input used in the determination of acceptable or unacceptable impacts remains a persuasive basis for a comprehensive environmental protection regime for the Area. Thus, the threshold issue of international responsibility – the level of significant harm that should not be reached – leads our inquiry into the nature and the institutions of scientific research in the Area, specifically, and in the marine environment, generally.

4. Scientific Research and the Environmental Protection Regime for the Area

The long-drawn consideration of the seabed question had always confronted the dilemma of decision-making in the face of scientific uncertainty. The combination of resolutions passed by the General Assembly in 1968 – consisting of the decision to establish a permanent Sea-Bed Committee to elaborate a set of legal principles for the seabed; a call for a deeper study of environmental consequences of economic activity on the deep seabed; the request to study the appropriate international machinery for resource activities in the Area; and the inauguration of the decade-long programme of scientific research of the marine environment[382] – provides an excellent encapsulation of the elements of what we call today the "precautionary principle."[383] These closely interrelated elements are: international norms of a substantive character; international institutions; and scientific research, both applied (concerning the nature of environmental impacts of economic activities) and fundamental. The three way interaction of "norms", "institutions", and "science" lies at the heart of decision-making in the face of scientific uncertainty, and it is in this interaction that we see the promise of the programmatory law of the Common Heritage of Humanity principle in the environmental field.

It was just mentioned that standard setting on the important question of what constitutes "acceptable harm" to the environment of the Area is a political process which relies on substantial scientific input. In the case of deep seabed mining, the political process occurs within the framework of the ISA, which has the responsibility, with respect to mining activities in the Area, of adopting rules, regulations and procedures for the protection of the marine environment.[384] However, with respect to the conduct of marine scientific research the authority of the ISA is area-wide, and is not at all confined to MSR relevant to "activities in the area":

> The Authority may carry out marine scientific research concerning the Area and its resources, and may enter into contracts for that purpose. The Authority shall promote and encourage the conduct of marine scientific research in the Area, and shall coordinate and disseminate the results of such research and analysis when available.[385]

---

382 Resolution 2467 A, B, C & D (XXIII).
383 Principle 15 of the Rio Declaration provides:
In order to protect the environment, the precautionary approach shall be widely applied by States according to their capabilities. Where there are threats of serious of irreversible damage, lack of full scientific certainty shall not be used as a reason for postponing cost-effective measures to prevent environmental degradation.
384 Art. 145, CLOS.
385 Art, 143 (2), CLOS. Cf. E.D. Brown, *supra* Chap. II note 10, at 430. Although Professor Brown accepts that *all* scientific research is embraced in Article 143, CLOS, he would, nonetheless, maintain that "the scope *ratione materiae* of Article 143 is not beyond doubt."

The competence of the ISA on MSR is complemented by the participation of States in MSR in the Area. On the part of State Parties to the Convention undertaking MSR in the Area, these States

> ... shall promote international co-operation in marine scientific research in the Area by:
>
> (a) participating in international programmes and encouraging co-operation in marine scientific research by personnel of different countries and of the Authority;
> (b) ensuring that programmes are developed through the Authority or other international organizations as appropriate for the benefit of developing States and technologically less developed States with a view to:
> (i) Strengthening their research capabilities;
> (ii) training their personnel and the personnel of the authority in the techniques and applications of research;
> (iii) fostering the employment of their qualified personnel in research in the Area;
> (c) effectively disseminate the results of research and analysis when available, through the authority or other international channels when appropriate.

All States shall have the obligation to carry out MSR in the Area exclusively for peaceful purposes and for the benefit of humanity as a whole.[386]

The framework of international cooperation for MSR in the Area as laid down in the Convention thus enables the Authority to interact with all States and international organizations, and also private institutions, which carry out any and all forms of scientific investigation in the Area. How this interaction will be worked out in practice remains to be seen, but its potentials for the

---

[386] Art. 143 (1), CLOS. It should be noted that the right of non-parties to the 1982 Convention to conduct MSR in the Area, *see* Art. 256, CLOS, does not constitute a high seas freedom in view of the qualification "for the benefit of mankind as a whole" that was added to Article 143; this qualification does not appear in the general provisions on MSR under Part XIII nor under Art. 87 (f). The "benefit of mankind" principle, whose doctrinal significance derives from Art. 136 and 140, CLOS, with reference to which, *see* discussion on "benefit-sharing", *supra* Sec. C, should distinguish the MSR in the high seas from MSR in the Area. *See also* Principle 10, Declaration of Principles Resolution. *Cf.* Soons, *op. cit.* at 224-229.

progammatory law of the Common Heritage of Humanity are enormous.[387] In the first place, through the circulation, the constant exchange and the continuous refinement of scientific research findings pertaining to the Area, the Authority would be in a position to consider the latest environmental variables that should be imputed in its determination of "acceptable impacts." The Authority's standard-setting role would not only be enhanced by the best or most recent scientific knowledge or advise available but would also possess a fair amount of legitimacy on account of the inclusiveness of participation that is achieved in the scientific phase of standard-setting. Through the "democratization" of MSR in the Area, the entire global scientific community vouches for the environmental regime governing seabed mining implemented by the ISA.

The more crucial aspect of the Authority's mandated interaction with States and other international organizations concerning scientific research in the Area concerns the practice of international cooperation itself which is or will have to be generated by this MSR. The nature of the international cooperation conceived under Article 143 is a broad process that has far-reaching implications not only on the governance of the seabed and its resources but also on ocean governance as a whole. Scientific research in the Area, as seen in Article 143, strives to accomplish a variety of goals which are fully consistent with the principles of "non-military use" and "benefit sharing" under the Common Heritage of Humanity principle: (1) the participation of personnel of different countries and of the Authority; (2) strengthening research capabilities of developing countries and the "technologically less developed States", including the employment of personnel and their training in the techniques and applications of research; and (3) coordination and dissemination of MSR results. The mechanisms envisioned may well constitute a fulfillment of the "transfer of technology" provision under Part XI.[388] Since the phrase "marine scientific research in the area", from an environmental standpoint, is rarely if ever to be understood and practiced as research "in and of the Area" exclusively, but involves the research about the Area in its relation to the marine environment or even to the global environment as a whole,[389] a comprehensive concept

---

387 *See* E.M. Borgese, *An International Sea-Bed Authority for the 21st Century* (forthcoming)[copy on file with author].
388 Art. 144, CLOS. Annex III, Art. 5 (8), CLOS defines "technology" not only as hardware but also technical knowhow, training and technical advise and assistance, and the legal right to use these items on a non-exclusive basis.
389 *See* Borgese, *supra* note 387.

of marine technology cooperation could be put in place by the International Seabed Authority. A proposal on how this could initially be done by the ISA was put forward in 1992 by the German delegation to the Preparatory Commission:

> Since the United Nations is expected at some point to function in a regulatory capacity, controlling the exploitation of natural resources in that part of the ocean that has become widely accepted as the "common heritage of mankind", it would also be the logical choice as organizer and sponsor of a coordinated, worldwide ocean mining risk assessment and impact evaluation program. Such a program, although primarily of an applied science nature, would at the same time elucidate many basic science questions on the deep sea. The use of a global cost- and effort-sharing approach would satisfy the needs of the environment, involve all interested parties on a more equitable basis, benefit the interest of furthering our basic knowledge and understanding of the deep sea, and serve as a much needed hallmark of international cooperation.[390]

The ISA, with the legitimacy that its universal or near-universal membership brings, could indeed assume a leadership or catalytic role in any future initiative to coordinate, harmonize, or consolidate all scientific research[391] in the Area.[392] The multiplicity of States, international agencies, and other actors concerned with or undertaking marine scientific research in the Area requires this kind of institutional integration if the programmatory law of the Common Heritage of Humanity principle in the environmental field is to be realized.

---

390 H. Thiel, E.J. Forell, G. Schriever, *Potential Environmental Effects of Deep Seabed Mining* (University of Hamburg, 1992). This document was submitted by Germany to the PrepCom as LOS/PCN/SCN.3 (14 Aug 1992). *See* Borgese, *supra* note 387.

391 *Cf.* Art. 143 (2), CLOS, which accords to the Authority a coordinating function with respect to results of research.

392 The political and even moral authority of the ISA, as the very first institution in international law to administer the common heritage of humanity, must be assumed in this regard. The successful catalytic role of UNEP in building the momentum towards the adoption of the 1992 UN Biodiversity Convention may be cited as precedent. This contrasts with the failed attempt by the FAO to provide the forum for the conclusion of a multilateral treaty on tropical forests; the objection being that FAO could not deal with the problem of forests in all its aspects – as a source of energy, a carbon sink, home for indigenous peoples, source of export lumber, source of biodiversity, etc. *See* Adede, *supra* note 354, at 210.

5. Institutional Aspects of Sustainable Development of the Area and its Resources

If it is admitted that sustainable development in the ocean sphere requires a high level of institutional integration or harmonization in the implementation of international norms[393] this should be no less true for the sustainable development of the Area and its resources. In the absence of a well-coordinated and harmonized effort to preserve and conserve the totality of the Area and its resources it would be difficult to imagine the promise of intra- and intergenerational equity that is thought to be fostered by the Common Heritage of Humanity principle.[394] The rationale balancing of conservation needs, on the one hand, and optimum utilization of the Area and its resources, on the other, is possible only if all institutions – including the ISA, the IMO, the IOC, the UNEP, FAO, the consultative parties under the 1971 Sea-Bed Treaty and the 1972 Dumping Convention, broad-margin coastal States, and possibly the great naval powers – get their act together and implement common strategies, or a common plan of action, for the common heritage. If the future agenda of international action is put in these terms, the notion that the Area and its resources is a "trust", or should be held and managed in the concept of a trust for all humanity,[395] acquires special significance. The governance of the area and its resources as an environment with a distinct legal status demands nothing less.

Fortunately, the imperative of harmonization of institutional activities bearing on marine scientific research in the Area has been recognized in the 1982 UN Convention on the Law of the Sea.[396] Through the opportunity for institutional cooperation offered by the regime of international cooperation for scientific research under Part XI, the fruits of marine science cooperation will likely be shared on the most equitable and inclusive basis. Was this not the essence of the message of President Johnson in 1966 when he invited all nations

---

393 See Payoyo, *supra* Chap. II note 235; also para. 1, Chapter 17, *Agenda 21* on the need for an "integrated" approach to marine management.
394 See Weiss, *supra* Chap. II note 325, at 48-49 & 144.
395 "We envisage such an agency as assuming jurisdiction, not as a sovereign, but as a trustee for all countries over the oceans and the ocean floor." Malta PV 1516, Para. 8. *See also* Dupuy, *supra* at 555 and at note 316, on the notion of the international community being a "manager"; and Wenk, *op. cit.* at Chap. 10, on his concept of "alternative marine futures" based on the management theme advanced by the Common Heritage of Humanity.
396 Art. 143, CLOS.

of the world to participate in a collective expedition of ocean discovery?[397] It is also through this functional integration of institutional activities that the environmental protection of the Area is best assured. Cooperation in scientific research in the Area brings the international community closer to the goal of comprehensive environmental protection envisioned by Principle 11 of the Declaration of Principles Resolution.

The "evolutionary approach" in the setting up and functioning of the organs of the International Seabed Authority as directed by the 1994 Implementation Agreement[398] affords the Authority the time and breathing space needed to study and elaborate the requirements of institutional integration in order to fulfil the objective of sustainable development more meaningfully. Specifically, the mandate of the Authority to promote and encourage MSR in the Area and to acquire scientific knowledge in connection with the protection and preservation of the marine environment[399] can provide the Authority a basis for coordinating a host of endeavors that involve many agencies inside and outside of the UN system. These endeavors include development of human resources, technology cooperation, study on long-term environmental impacts, and enhancement of biodiversity.[400] Benefit-sharing under the Common Heritage of Humanity principle can, therefore, be realized in the meantime even if mining activities in the Area are still years away – or, even if no manganese nodules will ever be mined from the deep seabed.

In closing, it can be said that the actualization of the principle of environmental protection for the Area and its resources, depends on the critical leadership role that the International Seabed Authority will assume in the field of marine scientific research in the very near future. The Convention provides the Authority with the broad competence and flexibility, neigh the obligation, to govern the Area through the modality of marine scientific research. Through its role in promoting scientific research the Authority, in a very pivotal way, can demonstrate the validity, the necessity or timeliness, and the fairness of the principle that "the problems of ocean space are closely interrelated and need to be considered as a whole."[401] The Authority will fail in its mission to act

---

397 *See supra* note 86 and accompanying text.
398 Sec. 1(3), Annex, 1994 Implementation Agreement.
399 Sec. 1 (5)(h) & (i), in relation to (5)(g) & (k), Annex, 1994 Implementation Agreement.
400 Borgese, *supra* note 387.
401 Third Preambular para., CLOS.

349

on behalf of humanity, and it will betray the lofty aims of the Common Heritage of Humanity principle, if it does not harness to its full advantage the regime of international cooperation for marine scientific research in the Area.

CONCLUSION

This Chapter began by posing some questions on the need for and the nature of a new fundamental principle in international law, the Common Heritage of Humanity. The hope expressed was that these questions will assist in illuminating more clearly and dispassionately the meaning and significance of the Common Heritage principle in the period following the entry into force of the 1982 Convention on the Law of the Sea. We are now in a position to offer some answers to these questions.

First, why the need for a new fundamental principle in the Law of the Sea?

Decolonization and development were the great political themes in international relations in the 1960s. They capture the political objectives of an international social movement articulated and advanced by an increasingly self-conscious and organized group of new "have-not" States – the developing countries. It was in the United Nations where these countries found the most important forum to express and pursue their collective objectives. In the search for possible avenues to overcome what was believed to be a desperate deadlock in the development decade, it was the promise of ocean wealth to which the significant attention of the international community was directed. In the UN Economic and Social Council, for instance, the developing countries were made to believe that the resources of the deep sea might soon rescue the cause of economic development. The optimism was such that even US President Lyndon Johnson denounced a neo-colonial "race to grab" the abundant harvest of the undersea.

Hopes were raised but a significant quantum of optimism was dashed when one small newly independent State, Malta – which also happened to be associated with the "Western Europe and Others" group in the regional typology within the United Nations – raised other agendas that were about to envelop the mysterious depths of oceans. Ambassador Pardo reminded the United Nations that some other issues of great moment other than decolonization and development, were involved in the project to tap the vast resources of the deep ocean. He pointed out that the imminence of an arms race in the ocean bottoms as well as the "race" already started to pollute and contaminate the ocean environment were outstanding predicaments which must be urgently addressed if the promise of the frontier were to be realized. Malta released the internationalization genie out of the UN General Assembly lamp.

From a legal point of view, the international control of the deep seabed was caught in the complex web of the pre-existing international law of the deep seabed. The freedom to pollute the seabed and to navigate it via military devices coexisted with the open-ended definition of the legal continental shelf to explore and exploit its resources.

The developing countries have never been at home with the *laissez faire* regime of freedom in classical international law. It was the abhorrent freedom of the seas doctrine which, in the first place, made them victims of a terrestrial colonial scramble in the past. They had good reason to believe that this doctrine of freedom will induce another colonial "grab and scramble" at sea. The industrialized countries, on the other hand, saw expanding coastal State sovereignty as anathema to their interests. Their navies and their fishermen were hampered by the "crawl and creep" of coastal State jurisdiction. More interestingly, their new deep seabed mining industries wanted to exploit the continental shelves of other States without paying tribute to coastal State authority.

The concept that the deep seabed was "common heritage of mankind" meant just that: everyone – rich or poor, coastal or land-locked States, industrialized or less industrialized nations, present humanity and future humanity – partake of the patrimony equitably. Ambassador Hambro of Norway stressed that it was a new term that was needed in order to affirm a new concept, and hopefully to inaugurate a new practice of international cooperation. An overwhelming number of countries represented in the United Nations agreed that the vagueness, or poetic justice, of the new terminology can be worked out through patient dialogue and multilateral cooperation – an enterprise that was found either too comical or too taxing by the industrialized States of capitalist and communist orientation. But this was a new terminology that suddenly destabilized the neat and predictable conceptualizations made in the law books, which for a long time explained the split and oftentimes schizophrenic personality of the law of the sea according to the twin criteria of freedom, or "inclusive interests", and sovereignty, or "exclusive interests."[402] For the developing countries, however, the neologism faithfully reflected their desire for a "freedom from..." and opposed the incessantly self-centred drive of the rich countries

---

402 Colombos, *op. cit.*; McDougal & Burke, *op. cit.*

for a "freedom to...."[403] Furthermore, the concept represented for them a new legal order for the seas, or at least for the deepest, most inaccessible and mysterious part of ocean – mysteriously symbolizing humanity's conscience. Then was their chance to get involved, to particulate meaningfully, and to have their voices heard in, and perhaps to materially benefit from, the process of law-making in an expanded international society.

The opportunity of the developing countries to participate in the exercise of international *law-making* was, however, less important from the viewpoint of the industrialized States than the involvement of the developing countries in a *law-repealing* exercise: the industrialized countries wished to repeal or omit the "exploitability clause" from Article 1 of the 1958 Geneva Convention on the Continental Shelf, and they needed legitimacy – or the sanction of the international community. The involvement of the entire international community in the revision of the Continental Shelf Convention was found to be necessary at two levels: legal and practical. On the legal plane, Article 13 of the Continental Shelf Convention required the procedural authorization of the UN General Assembly in the revision of the Convention. More importantly though, on the practical level, the international community's agreement was needed in order to come up with a precise – specifically, a numerically precise – definition of the "outer limits" of national jurisdiction. For the industrialized countries, the political exercise should be able to stop the "creep", and perhaps also lead to the formulation of operational rules (not principles) for the orderly exploitation of the seabed beyond national jurisdiction by the technologically advanced countries. This leads us to the second question which I attempted to throw some light in this Chapter.

Why should the Common Heritage of Humanity principle be at all acceptable to the industrialized maritime powers whose immediate interests in the deep seabed are better catered for under the freedom of the seas principle?

It is not really very clear whether some of the principal industrialized States whole-heartedly and in good faith welcomed the primordial legal principle of the Common Heritage of Humanity in their midst, although the records would show that they *had to* accept it, or the representatives of the developed countries at least happily said they accepted it, pursuant to a "package deal" concluded in 1970. The package consisted of a historic trade-off in the law of the sea,

---

403 *See* J. Davis, "Confrontation or Community? The Evolving Institutional Framework of North-South Relations" in M. Wright (Ed.), *Rights and Obligations in North-South Relations: Ethical Dimensions of Global Problems* 159-188 (1986).

where the developed countries would have their precise "outer limits" defined (thus mollifying their "creep" concerns) in exchange for their consent to establish the "international regime, with appropriate international machinery" for the deep seabed (therefore meeting the needs of the rest of the international community for international control of a portion of the seabed). A "bonus" for all sides in concluding this package deal was also realized: the definition of outer limits and the establishment of an international regime for the deep seabed will be negotiated along with all other outstanding issues in the law of the sea. This "bonus" may have proven to be a most complicating factor in subsequent negotiations at UNCLOS III, but it was crystal clear that the substantive order of the law of the sea had to be re-examined *in toto* if the seabed question were to be resolved with complete satisfaction. The safeguard clause to guarantee that the "limits" question was concluded *at the same time* as the "international regime" question was innocuously called a "gentleman's agreement" – consistent with the tradition of civilized behaviour in classical *jus gentium*. This "gentleman's agreement" was really a *modus vivendi* secured by a binding procedural resolution of the UN General Assembly.

The high level of apparent goodwill that surrounded the historic "package deal" just mentioned did provide occasion for the international community to adopt the 1970 "Declaration of Principles Governing the Sea-Bed and the Ocean Floor, and the Subsoil Thereof, beyond the Limits of National Jurisdiction." This unanimously accepted resolution of the General Assembly contained a long list of rather general and architectural ideas which UNCLOS III was to develop and consider in the negotiations on the international regime for the deep seabed. Politically, its significance lay in its affirmation that the deep seabed and its resources were to be subject to international control or supervision according to the fundamental principle of the Common Heritage of Humanity. With the adoption of this Resolution, "the seabed", in the felicitous language of UN General Assembly President Ambassador Hambro of Norway, "is being decolonized before it is colonized."[404] Politically, if not legally, the Declaration of Principles resolution, established a commitment on the part of all States to the "programmatory law" of the Common Heritage of Humanity.

The notion of a "programmatory law" behind the Common Heritage of Humanity principle answers our third question is: how will the new principle be realized in practice? It is important in this regard to bear in mind that the

---

404 Doc. A/PV.1933 (17 Dec 1970).

Common Heritage of Humanity principle does not only proffer substantive doctrine but also entails its own realization, procedurally and institutionally.

Professor Roscoe Pound's idea of "legal engineering" may have found exemplary fulfillment at the international level when the United Nations set out to work on a comprehensive regime for the oceans in UNCLOS III. The agenda was dense, the issues complex, and the interests involved so multitudinous and conflicting that it at first looked extremely idealistic for the international community to have embarked on such a grand exercise. But the effort was crowned when the United Nations, although not in the best of moods, finally adopted the 1982 Convention on the Law of the Sea. The fact that UNCLOS III was concluded at all is testament to the operational validity and practical wisdom of the proposition that "the problems of ocean space are closely interrelated and need to be considered as a whole."

The reason why the atmosphere in the United Nations was not totally celebratory when the Convention was adopted is well know: some gentlemen in a few famous capitals in the world chose not to believe in the 1970 "gentleman's agreement." The unkindest cut of all was the adoption by some industrialized States of unilateral legislation on seabed mining applicable beyond what was already textually established as outer limits of the continental shelf, pending the establishment of what would be acceptable to them as an international regime for seabed mining. Are these States culpable only for paying lip service to the cause of the new principle of the Common Heritage of Humanity? Was it a doctrinaire faith in the continuing and abiding utility of the "Grotian heritage", or of international liberalism, which led those countries to torment the rest of the international community with the politics of *interim regime-formation*?[405] Or was the violence done to the old-fashioned norm of *pacta sunt servanda* simply a consequence of the unenlightened profit motive extolled in the corporate board rooms of the deep seabed mining industry? The burden of conscience, if there is any under the circumstances, is with the industrialized States whose fealty to the programmatory law of the Common Heritage of Humanity is yet to be clearly demonstrated.

---

405 For a defense of the "Grotian Heritage" in the law of the sea post-UNCLOS III, *see* W.E. Butler, "Grotius and the Law of the Sea" in H. Bull, B. Kingsbury & A. Roberts (Eds.), *Hugo Grotius and International Relations* 209-220 (1992); for a general criticism of liberalism in the international legal order, *see* M. Koskenniemi, *From Apology to Utopia: The Structure of International Legal Argument* (1989).

For the developing countries and a host of middle powers, the commitment to the Common Heritage of Humanity principle – no matter how hazy a concept in law this initially appeared – was shown way back in the late 1960s. Concretely, this was expressed when the policy of total demilitarization of the deep seabed was vigorously insisted upon. The programmatory law of the Common Heritage of Humanity in fact started with the principle that the deep ocean floor should be reserved *exclusively* for peaceful purposes. The principle of banishing all military uses of the deep seabed – uses that are almost always unilateral in orientation and purpose, inconsistent with the notion of international control underlying the Common Heritage of Humanity principle – is the very first conceptual step in the historical execution of the programmatory law behind the Common Heritage of Humanity. The irrelevance of the "Grotian Heritage" – in the small, through the freedom of the seas, and more interestingly in the large, through the notion of *jus in bello* and *jus ad bellum* – is apparent.[406] In principle, there is no longer any "law of war" that obtains on the deep seabed. This is an idea that is perennially expounded by the International Ocean Institute's annual conference that started in 1970 aptly called *Pacem in Maribus*, or "peace in the oceans." Above all, the programmatory law of the Common Heritage is solely concerned with the *temperamenta pacis* (a term I should employ as a contrast to the Grotian idea of *temperamenta belli*, *i.e.*, "moderation in war" or the rules for "civilized warfare") on the deep seabed. The Common Heritage of Humanity is a strategy and a method to realize international peace, and together with it, sustainable development.

The *temperamenta* of the common heritage should evince the answer to our last question: how does the new fundamental principle of the Common Heritage of Humanity affect the distribution of power and well being in international society?

The seminal principle bannered in Part XI of the 1982 Convention on the Law of the Sea, that "The Area and its resources are the common heritage of humanity", conveys the "first principle" which the developing countries struggled hard to be recognized in the Seabed Committee. In the context of an international programme for decolonization and development in the United Nations, which provided the germinal environment for the introduction and elaboration of this principle, the message behind the "first principle" of the developing

---

406 For an updated account of Hugo Grotius' ideas on war, *see* B. Kingsbury & A. Roberts "Grotian Thought in International Relations" in Bull, Kingsbury & Adams, *id.*, at 1-64.

countries is fairly straightforward: the new undersea wealth and the benefits deriving therefrom must be shared as widely and as equitably as possible. "Benefit of Humanity" is the specific expression given to this conviction in Article 140 of the Convention. The normative effect of the benefit-sharing principle is to ensconce the "special interests and needs of the developing States", as well as the interests and needs of the "have-not" nations which are not (yet) States, in the substance of decisions taken by the agency representing transspatial and transtemporal humanity. Specifically under the regime of manganese nodule mining developed Part XI of the Convention, these interests and needs are to be attended to through the substantive output of decisions of the ISA and through the process of decision-making in the ISA itself.

The principle of benefit-sharing, which by definition takes into particular consideration the inclusive participation of developing States, inevitably assumes a programmatory character. It has to be developed and expanded as a normative underpinning of the Common Heritage of Humanity principle in two ways. First, the scope of benefit-sharing is conceived as applying to the entirety of the Area, and not merely to activities relating to manganese nodule mining. Regimes involving other activities in the Area must therefore be evolved through an "umbrella-protocol" approach to legal development. The ultra-narrow interpretation being propagated by some scholars[407] and some developed countries[408] that the Common Heritage of Humanity principle, or Part XI of the Convention, is concerned only and exclusively with a mineral mining (unifunctional) regime in the Area is not historically accurate and flies in the face of the spatially-orientated provision of law which plainly and clearly says that "the Area" is "the common heritage of humanity." The application of the benefit sharing principle in the whole space of the Area is a *de jure* definition that has been won normatively, but still needs to be pursued institutionally and politically. The "Area" – as a legal reality and a physical space – is not an empty

---

407 *See infra* Chap. V, notes 87 and 293.
408 *See e.g. Message from the President of the United States and Commentary Accompanying the United Nations Convention on the Law of the Sea...*, *supra* note 321, at 153:
Other activities on the deep seabed, including military activities, telecommunications and marine scientific research, may be conducted freely in accordance with principles of the Convention pertaining to the high seas, including the duty to have reasonable regard to other uses.
See further *infra* Chap. V.

category and its further interpretation has a direct bearing on the way power is deployed and social life structured at the international level.[409]

Secondly, and more urgently, the expansive application of the benefit-sharing principle occurs in the setting of developing a programme of "sustainable development" for the Area and its resources. "Sustainable development" is a term that has not been frequently invoked in the context of Part XI of the Convention, but as Ambassador Christopher Pinto of Sri Lanka had pointed out, the regime established in Part XI foreshadows the concept of "sustainable development" in many significant ways.[410] The notion of sustainable development of the Area and its resources starts, obviously, from the principle that the Area, as a bio-physical environment, must be protected from all sources of environmental degradation and that the optimal utilization of its resources must be guided by the wise rule of conservation. This principle is liberally expressed in the 1970 Declaration of Principles Resolution but watered down in its institutional application in Part XI of the 1982 Convention. As a consequence, Part XI deals with an environmental protection regime covering deep seabed mining activities only.

It is through the comprehensive regime of marine scientific research for the Area, however, that the goal of sustainable development could be pursued under the mining regime established in Part XI. Article 143 of the Convention accords a central role to the ISA in marine scientific research. Through the active and determined intervention of the ISA in scientific research pending the first mining operation on the deep ocean floor, a host of notable objectives consistent with the principle of benefit-sharing could already be achieved. These include the increase of publicly-available knowledge on the marine environment, participation of developing countries in scientific research together with the training of their nationals in marine environmental management as a form of technology transfer and technology development, and the conservation of the biodiversity resources of the deep seabed. An activist posture on the part of the ISA in the realm of scientific research and marine environmental protection is absolutely necessary if this international organization is to be instrumental in solving the problems of ocean space – recognized as clearly interrelated and in need of holistic consideration. The path of desuetude is not an option for the institution to whom the common heritage of humanity had been entrusted.

---

409 For the critical elaboration of this proposition in the municipal law context, *See* N.K. Bromley, *Law, Space and the Geographies of Power* (1994).
410 Pinto, *supra* Chap. II note 292.

It is, therefore, the institutional translation of "benefit-sharing" which proves to be the most crucial element in the programmatory law of the Common Heritage of Humanity. If international control of the Area and its resources requires international institutions, with all the more reason should international control effected under the terms of the Common Heritage of Humanity principle demand a durable and potent international institution or institutions. The principle of international control through institutional development is, hence, another main pillar of the programmatory law of the Common Heritage of Humanity. This principle of institutional development renders the pursuit and attainment of the other principles of the Common Heritage of Humanity feasible: (1) the principle of peaceful use, (2) the principle of benefit sharing, and (3) the principle of environmental protection/sustainable development of the Area and its resources. Without the fourth principle of institutional development, the Common Heritage of Humanity, to paraphrase Ambassador Amerasinghe, will remain a chimerical dream.[411]

We now turn our attention to the principle of institutional development, the most practical element of the programmatory law behind the Common Heritage of Humanity principle.

---

411 Doc. A/PV.1933 (17 Dec 1970).

V

THE INSTITUTIONAL ELEMENT OF THE COMMON HERITAGE OF HUMANITY PRINCIPLE: TOWARDS AN INTERNATIONAL ORGANIZATION FOR SUSTAINABLE DEVELOPMENT?

Regime-building for the deep seabed in the last quarter of the century no doubt proves the essential interlinkage between the foundational norms that conceive and consolidate a political vision for the deep seabed, on the one hand, and the institutional operations that impart concrete meaning to these more or less abstract norms, on the other. Indeed the early internationalization debate in the United States already demonstrated the diametrically opposed institutional conceptions generated by the contraposition of a unilateral flag-nations approach to nodule mining defended by the so-called "realists" and the international control or "United Nations title" approach to seabed exploitation advanced by the "idealists."[1] Not until the adoption of the 1970 Declaration of Principles Resolution was the doctrinal controversy momentarily (or superficially) resolved in favor of the idealists. The formal acceptance by the international community of the notion that the Area and its resources have a special legal status as the Common Heritage of Humanity set the official tone for subsequent negotiations on the international regime to govern the deep seabed. It was left to UNCLOS III to spell out the precise terms of international control, with the Declaration of Principles Resolution serving as main point of reference.[2]

The national control versus international control debate, however, re-emerged much later in the aftermath of the adoption of the 1982 UN Convention

---

1   See Oda, *supra* Chap. III note 34.
2   See for *e.g.*, UN Doc. A/AC.138/SC.1/L.18/Add.3 in the 1972 SBC Rep 81-108; UN Doc. A/AC.138/SC.1/94/Add.1 in the 1973 II SBC Rep 39-166; UN Doc. A/CONF.62/C.1/L.3 in III UNCLOS III Off Rec 157-164, on the work of the special Working Group on the International Regime created by Sub-Committee I of the Expanded Seabed Committee, headed by Ambassador Christopher Pinto of Sri Lanka.

on the Law of the Sea, this time in an actual confrontation between two extant institutional regimes on deep seabed mining. One was concerted by the reciprocating legislation of a few industrialized States which believed that they were entitled to unilaterally exploit the Area under a customary *interim* regime of freedom. The other proceeded from the internationalization framework drawn under the 1982 Convention on the Law of the Sea which established the ISA. The ISA's institutional precursor, the Preparatory Commission (PrepCom), claimed exclusive competence to administer mining activities in the Area. The resulting impasse which lasted for about a decade was overcome through a series of "informal consultations on outstanding issues" under the auspices of the UN Secretary General begun in 1990, culminating in the adoption of the 1994 Implementation Agreement by the UN General Assembly.

The 1994 Implementation Agreement may properly be viewed as a second historical attempt to establish a definitive political and juridical basis for international control over the Area and to banish, once and for all, unilateral approaches to the governance of the deep seabed. The 1994 Implementation Agreement re-packaged the package deal agreement originally achieved in UNCLOS III by modifying the scheme of international control for the deep seabed developed under the Convention's Part XI.[3] The adjustment of the regime laid down in Part XI of the Convention, however, did not purport to alter the basic policy of internationalization set forth therein, nor did it disturb the fundamental principle of the Common Heritage of Humanity as the acknowledged governing norm for this policy.[4] This was to be expected. The necessity or inevitability of international control was no longer questioned when the informal consultations began. The bottom line for a universal accommodation, as PrepCom Chairman Ambassador Jose Luis Jesus asserted, was that "there is no alternative to the international regime other than an improved international regime."[5] The real question that needs to be addressed is whether the new understanding on the terms of international control had indeed improved the international regime governing the Area and its resources – or, did it simply improve the terms of

---

3   For a description of the impact of the 1994 Agreement on Part XI of the Convention from the US point of view, *see* B. Oxman. *The 1994 Agreement and the Convention* 88 AJIL 687-696 (1994). *See* further *infra* Secs. C.2 & C.3.
4   Preambular para. 2, UNGA Res. 48/263 (28 July 1994); Preambular para. 2, 1994 Implementation Agreement.
5   J.L. Jesus, "Statement on the Issue of the Universality of the Convention" in R. Wolfrum (Ed.), *Law of the Sea at the Crossroads: The Continuing Search for a Universally Accepted Regime* 21-30 at 24 (1991).

national access within an international framework of control? It is submitted that one crucial factor to consider in this regard is the extent to which the renegotiated system of international control, as embodied in the 1994 Implementation Agreement, takes full account of the original doctrinal intent and programmatory thrust of the Common Heritage of Humanity principle.

This Chapter will explore the institutional element behind the doctrine of international control of the Area and its resources. It takes off from the premise that a unilateral or an exclusive national approach to the governance of the Area and its resources is now politically and legally unacceptable to the international community.[6] The question that it attempts to clarify relates to the institutional consequence of an internationalization policy for the Area and its resources based on the Common Heritage of Humanity principle. Specifically, it aims to link the efforts to establish institutions of international control for the deep seabed with the historical perceptions about the normative goals of internationalization. As it will be made evident, notwithstanding broad agreement on the novel legal status of the Area and its resources, a fundamental contradiction of perspectives – basically along the North-South divide – had persisted with regard to the pace, direction, and ultimate goals of internationalization. In strictly legal terms there was a profound dispute over the scope *ratione temporis* of the Common Heritage of Humanity principle, or its evolutionary essence as a programmatory norm. It would seem that this dispute has found some weird kind of resolution in the 1994 Implementation Agreement – which effectively put a stop to the normative evolution of the Common Heritage of Humanity principle itself.

The main discussion in the present Chapter will be divided into two parts, corresponding to the two identifiable periods of "progressive institutionalization" (to borrow a phrase from Professor Felipe Paolillo)[7] of an international regime for the deep seabed. The first period started with the adoption of the Declaration of Principles Resolution, spanning the UNCLOS III decade of the 1970s and

---

[6] For the thesis that international control under a modified Part XI regime has become inevitable, and even desirable, for the industrialized countries, *see* contributions in the "International Symposium on Implementing the United Nations Convention on the Law of the Sea", 27 January 1995, Georgetown University Law Center, reprinted in 7 GEORGETOWN INTL ENVIR L REV No. 3 (1995); *Law of the Sea Forum: The 1994 Agreement on the Implementation of the Seabed Provisions of the Convention on the Law of the Sea* 88 AJIL 687-714 (1994). *See* further *infra.* Sec. C.1

[7] Paolillo, *supra* Chap. IV note 147, at 157.

extending to 1980s. The second period was ushered in by the informal consultations held under the auspices of the UN Secretary-General beginning July 1990. During each of these periods, there was an apparent collective will to pursue the basic policy of international control for deep seabed activities, accompanied by a determination to establish appropriate institutions to carry this basic policy forward. Both periods throw light on the on-going international workshop to design an institutional structure for a regime that has become the most innovative but contentious hallmark of the new Law of the Sea. Both periods also show a contrast in the achievements of the international community with respect to the establishment of a universal legal order for ocean space.

The first section of this Chapter will compare the original visions or expectations held by the developed and the developing countries in the project of internationalization. These original expectations, as it will be argued in the second section, defined the polarized positions of these two groups of States on the most fundamental problem of institutionalizing a seabed regime, namely, the meaningful surrender of sovereignty, especially on the part of the developed States, to an international seabed agency that will have sole authority to act on behalf of humanity on all matters within its assigned sphere of competence. The historical polarization of the international community on this critical problem will be shown by re-tracing the evolution of States' expectations, or divergent perceptions, in the context of the negotiations over the "machinery" for an international seabed regime in UNCLOS III. This polarization will also be explained in terms of the disagreement about the role of the ISA – the sole institutional pillar of the deep seabed regime – in the progressive development of the Common Heritage of Humanity principle. In an effort to further appreciate the meaning and institutional significance of the Common Heritage of Humanity principle as a fundamental norm of international law, the third section of the Chapter will then highlight the transformation of the ISA in the 1990s, making specific reference to the impact of the 1994 Implementation Agreement on the scope *ratione temporis* of the Common Heritage of Humanity principle – or on its evolution and vitality as a fundamental norm of international law. The concluding section will, *inter alia*, evaluate the prospects of pursuing sustainable development under the subsisting institutional regime for the deep seabed.

A. The Institutional Significance of the Common Heritage of Humanity Principle

In any analysis of the Common Heritage of Humanity principle, very much depends on the definition given to the terms "internationalization" or "international control." But as the complex and tortuous negotiating history of Part XI of the 1982 Convention would reveal, agreement on a common meaning is difficult to find, if not altogether elusive. The institutional significance given to these concepts refers us to the underlying practical objectives of international control as expounded by its various advocates who may not necessarily share the same perceptions on the political or strategic goals of internationalization.

1. Pre-1970 Developments: The Basic Issue in International Organization Defined

At the height of the debate between the "nationalists" and "internationalists" in the US (or what Professor Oda referred to as the "realists" and "idealists", respectively) the advocates of international control were unambiguous in their view that some form of supranational management was necessary to administer and regulate the exploitation of deep seabed resources and to distribute benefits arising from exploitation activities. Administration and regulation of the deep seabed through an appropriate international organization was logical. It was a necessary means to an end that cannot be realized in any other way. The ultimate goal was the utilization of the seabed and its resources for the benefit or betterment of all countries, especially the developing States. A functional international organization called upon to address this huge challenge was, however, fundamentally opposed to the deep sea management regime that would be implemented exclusively by flag-state or intra-national institutions, which was supported by the "realists."

Thus, in initially recommending that the United Nations take title to the sea resources beyond national jurisdiction, the Commission to Study the Organization for Peace in 1966 advocated the creation by the United Nations General Assembly of a "United Nations Marine Resources Agency" to administer these resources on behalf of the international community.[8] In the same manner, the proposed "Treaty Governing the Exploration and Use of the Ocean Bed" drafted in 1968 by the United Nations Committee of the World Peace through Law Center conceived of an international Ocean Agency on the basis of the concept that humanity has a common interest in the exploration and use of the ocean bed and the utilization of its resources for peaceful purposes and for the benefit of all peoples.[9] Earlier in the same year, US Senator Claiborne Pell proposed the establishment of a powerful Licensing Authority under the United Nations in keeping with the primordial idea of the "common heritage of mankind" and humanity's common interest in the exploration of ocean space and the exploitation of its resources for peaceful purposes.[10] Last but not the least, Professor Elisabeth Mann Borgese, building upon these previous initiatives, developed a comprehensive "draft statute" for an international organization that will, *inter alia*, "regulate, supervise, and control all activities on the high seas and on or under the seabed." Among the fundamental guiding principles she proposed for the "International Regime" are the ecological indivisibility of ocean space, the common heritage of humanity, and the reservation for peaceful purposes of the seabed.[11]

Some "realists" had in the meantime come to terms with the practical inadequacies of a purely national approach to nodule mining.[12] It was recognized that a "flag nations" regime was a highly precarious framework that would not guarantee the security of title or the exclusiveness of any claim to mine sites on the deep seabed.[13] An international mechanism was, therefore, needed, if only to act as the sole authority that will unconditionally assure miners of

---

8 *17th Report*, *supra* Chap. III note 36, note at 39 *et seq*. The *1969 Report of the Commission*, likewise, made suggestions concerning "an international authority for the sea", but it was in the Commission's *1970 (21st) Report* that a detailed description of a "United Nations Seabed Authority" was given.
9 For a summary of this proposed treaty, also known as the Aron Danzig draft, *see* Oda, *supra* note 1, at 35-37.
10 For a description of Senator Pell's draft "Treaty on Principles Governing the Activities of States in the Exploration and Exploitation of Ocean Space", *see id.*, 37-40.
11 E.M. Borgese, *The Ocean Regime: A Suggested Statute for the Peaceful Uses of the High Seas and the Sea-Bed Beyond the Limits of National Jurisdiction* (1968).
12 *See* contributions of N. Ely in NAT RES J, *supra*. Chap. III note 34.
13 S. Oda, *International Law of the Resources of the Sea* 118 (1979).

exclusive tenure to mining claims, prevent claim jumping, and permit the orderly commercial development of deep sea minerals. Such was the objective of the "registration system" initially favoured by the developed States in the Seabed Committee. Its main feature was a legitimizing international institution that basically attends to the requirements of resource exploitation conducted under national control. This was the orientation of several proposals that neither took inspiration from the broad cosmopolitan theme "benefit of humanity" nor motivated by the superior ethical demands of development and global sharing. The obvious starting point was an exact definition of the outer limits of the continental shelf and, beyond those limits, the assurance of orderly and commercially-viable access to nodules on the part of States or entities which possessed the capital and technology to mine the new frontier. It is fair to say that these proposals, which were developed *in reaction* to the internationalization concept advanced by the "idealists", sought to annul the element of moral consciousness, or awareness of global social conditions, which was the driving force behind the international control position of the "idealists."[14]

Hence, the Deep Seabed Mining Committee of the International Law Association prepared a preliminary report in February 1968 which suggested the establishment of an international body that would be given the special task of only granting concessions.[15] In the recommendations of the 1968 Stockholm International Peace Research Institute Symposium prepared by Professor Burke, the advisability and feasibility of establishing a new international structure dealing with ocean uses were contemplated. Pending the introduction of this new structure, an *ad interim* system of registration was proposed to encourage further investment and economic activity as well as momentarily quiet possession.[16] Also in 1968, Dr. E.D. Brown advanced the idea of an Ocean Agency, consisting of three main organs: a Registrar of Claims, an International Inspectorate, and an Arbitral Board. States may apply for deep seabed leases from the Agency, which should not necessarily be a UN specialized agency; the object

---

14 *Cf.* Mahmoudi, *op. cit.* 204.
15 Oda, *supra* note 1, at 51. The revised ILA Report of 1970 made provision for an International Registration Agency, and International Mining Supervisory Agency, and an Ocean Floor Tribunal, and a previously proposed clause on "needs of developing countries" was deleted in this Report. *Id.*, at 54.
16 *Id.*, at 45-46.

of the proposed scheme was *not* certainly to guarantee the finances of the United Nations.[17]

From this summary account of the earliest proposals on the institutional aspects of internationalization, what comes out in bold relief are the two competing trajectories – or two contradictory "visions" – of international control. One sees international control or regulation of the deep seabed as the mission of a unique and hitherto untried international organization primarily constituted to promote an ideal of social justice at the global level. The global social imperative is suggested by the term "common heritage of mankind" which was the rallying cry of the advocates of this version of internationalization. Ambassador Pardo referred to this international agency as a "trustee" for all States with respect to the deep ocean floor,[18] implying a permanent inter-generational mandate on the part of the international agency that executes a multidimensional internationalization programme.[19] The underlying social and moral theme is the key element in this outlook, because the purpose of the institutional regime, as the Iranian delegation in the UN would later declare, surely goes beyond the creation and implementation of rules for an orderly gold-rush in the frontier.[20]

But an "orderly gold rush" it was which preoccupied those whose sights were mainly focussed on the prospects of manganese nodule mining in the deep ocean. The *raison d'etre* of this other version of international control is the assured access of miners to new mineral resources on the seabed. And since the objective is simply to install a viable *sui generis* regime that would allow and encourage cost-effective nodule mining operations, they took the familiar service role of an international agency as given.[21] There was obviously no need to resort to transcendental-sounding principles or abstract purposes in ar-

---

17 See *id.*, at 56-57.
18 Malta Note Verbale, Doc. A/6695, *supra* Chap. II note 38.
19 The exemplary role of the international agency is commended in the proposed institutional regime of Prof. Borgese: "The International Regime shall provide a framework for the future pattern of international organization." Art. II (14), *supra* note 11. Prof. Henkin, noting the merits of the "licensing system", observes: "It would be a critical step toward isolating the seas as a special environment subject to a new departure in international living that seems worth trying." Henkin, *supra* Chap. III note 24, at 73.
20 Iran, PV 1682 (10 Nov 1969). *See also* Ceylon, PV 1603 (8 Nov 1968).
21 *See* J. Barkenbus, *Deep Seabed Resources: Politics and Technology* 104-105 (1979).

ticulating the functions of the international agency contemplated.²² On this view, the role of the international seabed institutional mechanism is a narrow and technical one: to facilitate. To paraphrase a straightforward metaphor used by a US Congressman, its capacity should not basically be to draw up recipes on how to cook a turkey, but to have somebody get the turkey first.²³

This clash of perceptions on the proper role of international organization for the seabed suggests the key terms behind the basic issue involved: altruism versus aggressive acquisition, global amelioration versus national ambition, allocation versus access, principle versus power. At one level of analysis, these competing themes may indeed be regarded as self-interested positions in a complex negotiating environment. But at another level, the differences that obtain between them are not likely to be susceptible to negotiation, because they comprehend political outlooks that are in fact logically incommensurable. The only variance that existed between these two outlooks is historical: one seeks to be recognized and established in practice while the other proceeds from a dominant established pattern of relationships.

It is thus more appropriate to describe the two competing visions of internationalization as illustrative of two "paradigms" (in a Kuhnian sense)²⁴ that are locked in battle in a contest that will confirm whether a "paradigm shift" will take place, or is already taking place, in the practice of international organization. The incompatibility of these two paradigms of international control, or original outlooks concerning the institutional underpinning of international control, must be seen in the broader context of the transformation of international relations and international organization in the second half of the twentieth century.

In the contemporary historical setting, the proposition that an international seabed agency should assume the role of a vanguard in the promotion of supranational interests and global moral values is hardly surprising. It confirms the need for intensive and extensive cooperation by a growing number of States especially in the post-War and post-cold war period, which has given rise to a multiplicity of cooperative endeavors at the level of international organization²⁵ – a trend that directly challenges the resilience of the classical political

---

22 *See* B. Oxman, *The Third United Nations Conference on the Law of the Sea: The 1976 New York Sessions* 71 AJIL 247-269 (1977).
23 Remarks of Congressman Richard Hanna, in *House Interim Report* at 18-19.
24 *See supra* 159, *et seq.*
25 *See* Friedmann, *op. cit.*

conception of international organization as a platform for the unmitigated projection of State power and national self-interest.[26] A claim to retool international organizations as more effective instruments for realizing the common long-term interests of all States is, thus, a consequence of the deepening fissures in the current structure of international law as well as in the prevalent system of international organization founded on the simple co-ordination of juxtaposed sovereignties. These are structural fissures which have become more apparent given the progressive diminution of the scope of the so-called domestic domain of legal competence reserved exclusively for the application of territorial State power.[27] More and more, the primacy of values, or what Professor Charles de Visscher calls the "human ends of power",[28] as bases for the redefinition of the international legal community, would reinforce the evolution of, and lend legitimacy to, international institutions which advance the moral infrastructure of international law. In the functionalist perspective propounded by Professor Johnston, the assumption by international organizations of corrective and developmental functions is informed by the historical movement towards a cooperative ethic that had become dominant in contemporary post-classical international law.[29]

An institutional structure for the deep seabed regime that derives from the perceived ascendancy of social and ethical values in the international normative sphere is fundamentally at odds with a seabed regulatory mechanism that at its core preserves, and is in turn justified by, an international legal order without moral inspiration or teleological direction, governed solely by the norms of competition and coordination of national political ends among co-existing sovereignties. It is easy to see that the former entails the surrender, as it were, of a significant amount of national freedom of action in favor of an international organization for the deep seabed. The latter, on the other hand, calls for the greatest possible projection of national sovereignty and national interest in and through seabed international institutions. And while the balancing of these political claims necessarily requires dialogue and negotiation, the final historical outcome of the encounter cannot but be an either-or result. In consequence, there is a war being played out between two incompatible "paradigms" of inter-

---

26 I. Claude, *Swords into Plowshares* 403 (1964).
27 *See* de Visscher, *op. cit.*
28 *Id.*, in his Chap. IV.
29 D.M. Johnston, *Functionalism in the Theory of International Law* 26 CAN YRBK INT L 3 (1988).

national law, where one or the other will have to emerge as clear winner. This, it is submitted, is the crux of the tension between the two original conceptions of international control. As it will be shown below, the weight of evidence suggests that the paradigm for the *status quo* has prevailed, so far. The official negotiations on the purposes, powers, and the destiny of the ISA may have come to a stop; but at the level of practical politics the contest of paradigms continues.

From a legal standpoint, the idealists' and realists' definitions of international control have two things in common. First, both original competing versions of international control required a definitive clarification or authoritative determination of the legal status of the deep seabed and its resources over which an international agency will assume some juridical competence. It should be noted in this regard that international control or supervision rules out, by definition, the concept of coastal State jurisdiction or territorial sovereignty as the controlling norm for institutional development. This is the reason why it was relatively easy to come to an agreement on the non-susceptibility of the Area to national appropriation and to claims of sovereignty or sovereign rights.[30] Moreover, as some realists have themselves conceded, the doctrine of freedom of the seas, or flag state jurisdiction, is an insufficient normative framework that cannot be conceptually nor practically reconciled with the efforts to evolve a minimum institutional response to address deep seabed mining requirements at the international level. Adequately empowering an international organization as the indispensable vehicle for the attainment of the goals of international control, howsoever these goals are conceived or expressed, would involve the elaboration of a *sui generis* regime that governs the object of international control. It was the UN Seabed Committee which was given the initial mandate to develop and negotiate the legal principles and norms for this regime.

A second overlapping concern of both these original conceptions of international control is the resolution of the issue of exact boundaries that will delineate the seabed area where the policy of international control will have to apply. This commonality implies the abandonment of the "exploitability clause" in the 1958 Continental Shelf Convention which defines the outer limits of the continental shelf in an open-ended manner. It is not certain at what exact point in historical time was the exploitability clause excised from the corpus of international law. But there is no doubt that the "limits" problem had to await resolution at the UNCLOS III, which supplied the procedural framework for its

---

30 Principle 2, Declaration of Principles Resolution.

authoritative consideration. As it was argued in the previous Chapter, the Seabed Committee was not the competent forum where the question of the precise delimitation of the Area could have been settled.

2. The Issue of International Machinery in the Seabed Committee

In the United Nations, the relationship between a supranational form of international management and the normative framework of multilateral control for the deep seabed was first noted by the UN Secretary General in his preliminary response to the directive contained in ECOSOC resolution 1112 of 1966. He observed "two major gaps" that warranted attention. First, there was a gap concerning the legal status of deep sea resources, and second, there was also a gap in the ways and means of ensuring that the exploitation of the new deep sea resources will benefit the developing countries. He consequently suggested fuller examination of the prospects of entrusting these resources to an international body.[31] The intricate interweaving of legal norms and their institutional aspects had at once become evident.[32]

In Ambassador Pardo's famous speech, strong emphasis was given to "the creation of a special agency with adequate powers to administer in the interests of humanity the oceans and the ocean floor beyond national jurisdiction."[33] The indispensable institutional element behind the common heritage concept should undoubtedly be highlighted as the central thesis of Ambassador Pardo's presentation. But the relationship between the establishment of a special inter-

---

31 UN Doc. A/C.1/952 (31 October 1967).
32 *See* Henkin, *supra* Chap. III note 24, at 59: "In the end, the international body that is established will reflect – and in turn shape – the legal regime that is to govern, in particular the distribution between national autonomy and international control."
33 PV 1515, para. 8. And in para. 10: "We believe that the existence and powers of the suggested agency should be founded on a treaty clearly defining the outer limits of the continental shelf subject to national jurisdiction, and establishing generally acceptable principles with regard to the use of the deep seas and of the ocean floor." *See also* para. 4 of the Memorandum attached to Malta's Note Verbale, Doc. A/6695 (18 Aug 1967), *supra* Chap. II note 38: "the proposed treaty should envisage the creation of an international agency (a) to assume jurisdiction, as a trustee for all countries, over the seabed and the ocean floor, underlying the seas beyond the limits of present national jurisdiction; (b) to regulate, supervise and control all activities thereon; and (c) to ensure that the activities undertaken conform to the principles and provisions of the proposed treaty."

national agency and the Common Heritage of Humanity as a proposed substantive principle was not simply incidental or merely imagined. What should be underscored is the assertion of a direct cause-effect relationship between norms, on the one hand, and institutional arrangements for the deep seabed, on the other.[34] This perceived causal relationship was affirmed by the General Assembly when it established the permanent Seabed Committee to study the elaboration of legal principles and norms for the deep seabed.[35] Procedurally, therefore, the General Assembly took a decision to resolve the fundamental question of the legal status of the deep seabed first before embarking on the resolution of the machinery issue. The priority of an international agreement on legal principles and norms over agreement on institutional matters relating to the regulatory regime for the deep seabed was aptly summed up by Belgium:

---

34 "...the notion of property that cannot be divided without the consent of all and which should be administered in the interests and for the benefit of all is also a logical extension of the common heritage concept." Malta, PV 1589 (29 October 1968).

35 Res. 2467 A (21 Dec 1968). A separate resolution, Res. 2467 C, requested the Secretary General to undertake a study on the question of "machinery." Resolution 2467C, adopted 85 to 9 with 25 abstentions, requested the "a study on the question of establishing in due time appropriate international machinery for the promotion of the exploration and exploitation of the resources of this area, and the use of these resources in the interests of mankind, irrespective of the geographical location of States, and taking into special consideration the interests and needs of the developing countries." The communist block voted against this Resolution and the countries from "Western Europe and Others" abstained. Apparently, the indifferent attitude of the Western group of States towards institutional questions was abandoned the following year, when Resolution 2574 C was adopted by a vote of 100 to 0, with 11 Eastern European States abstaining. Resolution 2574 C requested "a further study on various types of international machinery, particularly a study covering in depth the status, structure, functions and powers of an international machinery, having jurisdiction over the peaceful uses of the seabed and the ocean floor, and the subsoil thereof, beyond the limits of national jurisdiction, including the power to regulate, coordinate, supervise and control all activities relating to the exploration and exploitation of their resources, for the benefit of mankind as a whole, irrespective of the geographical location of States, and taking into special consideration the interests and needs of the developing countries, whether coastal or land-locked." The opposition of the communist block against consideration of institutional issues was based on the resigned belief that any international machinery will be "controlled and operated by imperialist monopolies." USSR, PV 1679 (6 Nov 1969).

"there can no longer be any question of discussing the superstructure before the foundation has been made secure."[36]

Notwithstanding the "secondary" nature of the machinery issue *vis-à-vis* the primary mandate of the Seabed Committee to formulate legal principles and norms, the development of a strong political focus on the institutional aspects of a *sui generis* deep seabed regime, chiefly on account of the initial insistence by the developing countries on the importance of a machinery for the new regime,[37] not only led to UN General Assembly requests for the Secretary General to undertake various studies on the matter of "machinery."[38] This also encouraged the Seabed Committee to discuss institutional matters whose detailed clarification was regarded as relevant to its mandate.[39] It was in fact in these deliberations in the UN prior to the adoption of the 1970 Declaration of Principles Resolution where we see most clearly the North-South divergence of views concerning the relationship of preferred norms to envisaged international institutions for the deep seabed. These positions reiterate the two original visions or approaches to internationalization described above and basically echoed in negotiating outlooks on machinery issues during the UNCLOS III and beyond.

3. The Developing Countries: The Common Heritage of Humanity Principle as a New Modality of International Organization

The previous Chapter described the emergence of two alternative and incommensurable "first principles" for the deep seabed in the *Ad Hoc* Seabed Committee. On the one hand, the developing countries of Asia, Africa and Latin America espoused the Common Heritage of Humanity principle *de lege ferenda* as the foundational norm that governs a hypothesized seabed beyond national jurisdiction. On the other hand, the industrialized countries propounded as their desired "first principle" the existence of the seabed beyond national jurisdiction and, by necessary implication, the existence of outer limits to the continental

---

36 PV 1602 (7 Nov. 1968).
37 *Infra* Sec. A.3.
38 Res. 2467 C (1968) and Res. 2574 C (1969).
39 *See* Report of the Economic and Technical Sub-Committee, 1969 SBC Rep 43, *et seq.*; 1970 SBC Rep 37.

shelf. It is worthwhile to recall the institutional norms that were thought to derive from each of these two "first principles" from the perspective of their respective proponents.

It was in the *Ad Hoc* Committee where the developing countries first expressed the need for an "international machinery" which shall be an inherent part of a novel "international regime" for the undersea frontier. The argument in favor of a regime realized through a special type of international machinery appeared as a proposed general principle in the Working Paper submitted to the *Ad Hoc* Committee by representative countries from Asia, Africa and Latin America:

> The international regime to be established shall also consider the way for the most appropriate and equitable application of benefits obtained from the exploration, use and exploitation of the sea-bed and ocean floor and the subsoil thereof, as referred to in the title of the item, through a suitable international machinery, for the economic, social, scientific and technological progress of developing countries[.][40]

The fundamental importance of the "machinery" in the process of evolving legal principles founded on the common heritage concept was never lost in the agenda of the developing countries.[41] The unity of the Common Heritage of Humanity "regime" and its corresponding "machinery" – or the *legal principle de lege ferenda* that an international machinery shall be an indispensable component of the common heritage regime for the deep seabed – was reiterated by many of their delegations.[42] The underlying conviction was that the machi-

---

40 Working paper on the draft declaration of General Principles proposed by Argentina, Brazil, Ceylon, Chile, Ecuador, El Salvador, India, Kenya, Liberia, Libya, Pakistan, Peru, Thailand, United Arab Republic and United Republic of Tanzania. Text in Ad Hoc SBC Rep at 62. *See* also Draft Declaration of General Principles proposed by developing countries, in para. 88, Ad Hoc SBC Rep at 18.
41 Pinto, "The Structure and Functions of the International Seabed Authority" in Borgese & White, *op. cit.* 316: "An administrative organization, or Authority is an essential part of the 'common heritage' concept."
42 *E.g.* Venezuela, PV 1593 (31 Oct 1968) and PV 1678 (6 Nov 1969); Libya, PV 1597 (4 Nov 1968); Kuwait, PV 1598 (5 Nov 1968) and PV 1675 (3 Nov 1969); Ceylon, PV 1603 (8 Nov 1968); Brazil, PV 1674 (31 Oct 1969); Nigeria, PV 1674 (31 Oct 1969); Cameroon, PV 1675 (3 Nov 1969); Guatemala, PV 1676 (4 Nov 1969); United Arab Republic, PV 1676 (4 Nov 1969); Trinidad & Tobago, PV 1677 (5 Nov 1969); Liberia, PV 1679 (6 Nov 1969); Thailand, PV 1679 (6 Nov 1969); Argentina, PV 1680 (7 Nov 1969); Congo, PV 1681 (7 Nov 1969); Af-

nery to implement the novel seabed regime is the concrete means of realizing a multidimensional internationalization programme as originally proposed by Malta.[43] Specifically, the machinery of the proposed Common Heritage of Humanity principle was conceived as the means through which the widening welfare gap between rich and poor countries will have to be redressed. In this sense, the institutional fulfillment of the Common Heritage of Humanity principle will also be a practical fulfillment of the UN Charter goal "to employ international machinery for the promotion of the economic and social advancement of all peoples."[44]

The developing countries' preference for a "strong" international organization – or an international seabed agency with extensive powers to which States surrender a fair modicum of national prerogative – was made evident with the adoption of the 1969 General Assembly resolution 2574 C, which requested a follow-up study by the UN Secretary General on the question of international machinery. In the first study undertaken by the Secretary General,[45] three types of international machinery were identified, indicating the range of functions which could be assumed by an international agency that will have some form of jurisdiction over the exploration and exploitation of deep seabed resources: registration, licensing, and a fully operational agency. While this Report exhaus-

---

ghanistan, PV 1681 (7 Nov 1969); Kenya, PV 1681 (7 Nov 1969). *See also* Sweden, PV 1596 (4 Nov 1968); Poland, PV 1597 (4 Nov 1968); Norway, PV 1676 (4 Nov 1969); Canada, PV 1682 (10 Nov 1969); Denmark, PV 1683 (10 Nov 1969).

43 *See supra* Chap. III, Sec. B.2.

44 *See* Canada, PV 1682 (10 Nov 1969). Notwithstanding this posited interpretation of Common Heritage of Humanity principle, the industrialized countries would later argue that each State can unilaterally have the right to administer the common heritage under the doctrine of *dedoublement fonctionnel*. Mahmoudi, *op. cit.* 256. *See e.g.*, R. Wolfrum, *The Principle of the Common Heritage of Mankind* 43 ZaöRV 313, at 317 (1983):

To avoid any misunderstanding it should be emphasized that the establishment of an international organization empowered with resource jurisdiction is no peremptory consequence derived from the common heritage principle. It would have been possible to stick to a solution more in line with the existing structure of the international community of states which results in leaving the administration of the common heritage to individual states. The states would then act not on their own but – in the absence of an international organization – in the capacity of an organ of the international community.

See also Kiss, *supra* Chap. IV note 329, at 435.

45 *See* 1969 SBC Rep, Annex II at 81.

375

tively described the potential models of machinery possessed with a functional jurisdiction over deep sea mineral resources, the developing countries insisted that the scope of powers of the envisaged international machinery, consistent with the emerging elements of the Common Heritage of Humanity principle, should cover *all* possible activities in the frontier, *i.e.*, its competence will not be limited to mineral resource activities of exploration and exploitation.[46] Resolution 2574 C, thus, emphasized the contemplated jurisdiction of the international organization over all the peaceful uses the deep seabed, in addition to its resource jurisdiction.

In keeping with the preference of the developing countries for an equitable system of management that should cover not only resources but also the entire Area itself,[47] the Secretary-General's report[48] elaborated the spatial scope of the machinery's jurisdiction. With respect to it resource jurisdiction, the report outlined a continuum of four main forms of possible international machinery: machinery for exchange of information and preparation of studies; machinery with intermediate powers, *i.e.*, a forum for discussion; machinery for registration and licensing; and machinery having comprehensive powers. The last mentioned form of international machinery would not only have the power to regulate, coordinate, supervise and control all resource activities in the area[49] but would also exercise jurisdiction over all other peaceful uses of the seabed – such as laying of submarine cables and pipelines, military uses, and scientific research. This type of machinery will, likewise, have functions with respect to the prevention of pollution, protection of living resources, safety at sea, settlement of conflicting uses, and legal liability. For the developing countries, which envisaged the establishment of an "international sea-bed authority" (rather than an "international sea-bed resource authority") only the comprehensive model of international machinery with an autonomous and universal character

---

46 *See e.g.*, Ceylon, PV 1673 (31 Oct 1969) & PV 1708 (2 Dec 1969); Nigeria, PV 1674 (31 Oct 1969); Cameroon, PV 1675 (3 Nov 1969); Kuwait, PV 1675 (3 Nov 1969).
47 *See* 1970 SBC Rep at 17, para. 46-47.
48 *Id.*, Annex III.
49 The Report classifies "resources" into mineral, living, and other resources. The resource-related functions of the machinery include licensing, direct exploitation, role with respect to fluctuation of prices, collection of fees and royalties, and training programmes.

would correspond to the basic concept that the Area and its resources are the common heritage of humanity.[50]

It is also significant to note the commitment of the developing countries to the effectuation of the broad principle of equality of States with the setting up of an international machinery. The participation of all States on the basis of equality in the system of management to be established was regarded as a corollary of the Common Heritage of Humanity principle.[51] In practical terms, the Common Heritage of Humanity principle implied that the norm of one-State-one-vote should apply to all decisions of the international organization to be established and there should be no system of weighted voting or veto.[52] In sum, the result desired was the equality of capacity for rights and obligations on the part of all States with respect to the regime that will govern the Area and its resources.

4. The Industrialized Countries: An International Agency to Promote and Guarantee Assured Access to Seabed Mineral Resources

The initial nonchalant attitude if not outright opposition of the developed States towards the initiative of the developing countries to request the Secretary General to undertake a study on the issue of international machinery[53] partly reflected the preoccupation of those States with the issue of delimitation of

---

50 *See* 1970 SBC Rep 17.
51 India, PV 1673 (31 Oct 1969); Trinidad & Tobago, PV 1677 (5 Nov 1969) [advocating equitable participation by all States in administration of area]; Venezuela, PV 1678 (6 Nov 1969) [administration of area must be entrusted to an organ that is representative of humanity]; Uruguay, PV 1679 (6 Nov 1969) [Common Heritage of Humanity means participation in administration and benefits earned]; Thailand, PV 1679 (6 Nov 1969) [all States participate in the administration of the common heritage]; Kenya, PV 1681 (7 Nov 1969) [in the absence of an international machinery, developing countries will be in a very disadvantaged position in relation to the developed States]; Brazil, PV 1777 (30 Nov 1970) [every State has an equal right to participate in policy-making as well as in regulating coordinating and supervising activities of the machinery]; Yugoslavia, PV 1784 (4 Dec 1970) [Common Heritage of Humanity means common management in order to achieve a higher level of genuine equality].
52 Pinto, *supra* Chap. II note 51, at 11.
53 *E.g.* US & USSR, PV 1648 (19 Dec 1968); Oda, *supra* Chap. IV note 2, at 79.

the Area, which they considered as the most critical matter needing international attention in regard to the evolution of a legal regime for the deep seabed.[54] But when the second study to be undertaken by the Secretary General was commissioned in 1969, there was already a realization on the part of the western industrialized states that the exploration and exploitation of new mineral resources on the seabed beyond the postulated limits of the continental shelf would require a minimum system of international control that would guarantee the orderly commercial exploitation of these resources.[55] Since the first report of the Secretary General revealed that this minimum international machinery could take the form of an international registry of claims,[56] this model was generally endorsed by the western developed States.[57] Under this clearing house or ticketing system, inasmuch as each State would retain control over operations registered in its name, the functions of the registry would be quite limited and its discretionary authority strictly defined.[58] A minimum international mechanism, in brief, was the most advantageous to the technologically developed States, for this will most likely maximize the goal of national access.[59]

Unlike the developing countries which had put forward the concept of the Common Heritage of Humanity as the supreme governing norm behind the establishment of an international machinery, the developed States did not identify with, nor present a unified stand on, any doctrinal concept or normative framework that would support their preference for a minimum order of international control in the deep seabed.[60] The resistance of the developed States

---

54 US, PV 1590 at 8 (29 Oct 1968); France, PV 1591 (30 Oct 1968); Italy, PV 1593 (31 Oct 1968); UK, PV 1676 (4 Nov 1969).
55 Oda, *supra* note 13, at 116-119; Belgium, PV 1673 (31 Oct 1969); France, PV 1680 (7 Nov 1969).
56 1969 SBC Rep at 102-108, Annex II.
57 *See* US, PV 1673 (31 Oct 1969).
58 1969 SBC Rep at 103, 107, Annex II.
59 Oda, *supra* note 13, at 118.
60 Japan, which expressly took the position *de lege ferenda* that the freedom of the seas principle is applicable to the exploration and exploitation of the area, Oda, *supra* Chap. IV note 2, at 57, nonetheless supported an international machinery which would assure orderly exploitation of the area, with the proviso that a portion of the value of the recovered resources be dedicated to international community purposes. Oda, *Id.* at 80. The USSR, in a similar manner, asserted that the applicable law for the deep seabed includes the Geneva Convention on the High Seas, but it was however absolutely opposed to the setting up of international

in welcoming the Common Heritage of Humanity concept as a possible framework of normative and institutional development for a deep seabed regime, together with the absence of a clearly posited doctrinal view at the level of *lex ferenda* concerning the legal status of the deep seabed which would undoubtedly assist the developed States clarify their own notion of an adequate international machinery that ought to facilitate the exploration and exploitation of deep sea mineral resources, accounts for the perception that the few technologically advanced States were bent on pursuing a "primitive registration service [that] would do very little apart from paying lip service to the thought of internationalization of the area."[61] It was, therefore, widely felt that unless the *bona fide* commitment of the highly developed States to the Common Heritage of Humanity principle was secured, their choice of an international machinery would continue to be dictated by the standard of national interest to exclusive and unimpeded access to deep seabed resources.[62]

The primacy of the developed States' national claims to assured access in any scheme of international control – as opposed to any comprehensive social conception of community interests on the deep seabed projected by the Common Heritage of Humanity concept – is well illustrated by the specific proposals on a seabed regime put forward by the US, the UK and France in the Seabed Committee in 1970. A common trait of all these proposals is the establishment of an international machinery with a restrictively defined resource jurisdiction that leaves technologically advanced nations with a wide latitude of freedom concerning the exploration and exploitation of the resources in question.

The US "Draft UN Convention on the International Seabed Area"[63] divides the seabed beyond national jurisdiction into an "international trusteeship area" (seabed beyond the 200 meter isobath up to the edge of the continental margin), which is basically controlled by a management regime defined by the "Trustee" coastal State, and the seabed area beyond the trusteeship zone, which is under the purview of an International Seabed Resource Authority. This Authority is tasked with the issuance of exploration and exploitation licenses for mineral

---

machinery. USSR, PV 1592 (31 Oct 1968).
61 *See* Norway, PV 1676 (4 Nov 1969): The registration system "would not protect the international community against an exploitation race, nor would it promote or guarantee world peace or the exploitation of these riches for the benefit of mankind."
62 Sweden, PV 1680 (7 Nov 1969).
63 Doc. A/AC.138/25, in Annex V, 1970 SBC Rep 130.

resources using facilitative criteria and guidelines that are spelled out in clear detail in the Draft Convention. When called for, the exercise of discretion by the Authority is done through a decision by its executive organ, the Council, consisting of 24 States parties divided into two categories of members: six industrially advanced countries and 18 developing countries. Decisions by the Council require a double majority, or a system of "chambered voting": the approval of a majority of its members, including a majority of members of each of the aforementioned two categories of members. Pending the entry into force of the Draft Convention, a contracting party may authorize exploration and exploitation of the international seabed area; there is provision for the integrity of investments already made. Notwithstanding these prominent features in "national control", the Draft Convention ironically puts forward the "basic principle" that "the International Seabed Area shall be the common heritage of all humanity." The invocation of the Common Heritage of Humanity concept in this context is thus purely rhetorical.

The Working Paper submitted by the UK on an International Regime[64] covers the mineral resources as well as the sedentary living resources of the area. The regime contemplates the division of the entire seabed area beyond national jurisdiction into blocks allocated to States on the basis of licenses peremptorily issued by an international body. The nucleus of this international body is a Board of Governors whose limited membership "should reflect a balance which would inspire confidence and would reflect the interests of, and the technical contribution which could be made by, the developed and developing countries, both land-locked and maritime."

The Proposal submitted by France[65] would seem to lie closest to the registration system that was modelled in the report of the Secretary General. Under this scheme, two kinds of international machinery were proposed depending on whether the mineral resources to be mined can be exploited using mobile equipment, such as manganese nodules, or fixed installations, like hydrocarbons. In the case of the former, a registration system would be the appropriate machinery. In the case of the latter, States would be granted by an international organization areas within which they would issue licenses. Such international organization, when it is unable to take simple decisions, will be a forum for exchange of views, negotiation, and possible arbitration.

---

64 Doc. A/AC.138/26, in 1970 SBC Rep at 177.
65 Doc. A/AC.138/27, in 1970 SBC Rep at 185.

A perusal of these proposals would thus prove that the industrialized States were not ready to concede to a principle of international organization which would effectively put them individually at par with the other members of the international community. The underlying fear, justified or not, was the domination of the future institutions of international control by the developing countries as well as their "irresponsible majority vote."[66] They were not willing to submit to an international organization that would not somehow acknowledge their superior capacity for rights and obligations, or translate this superiority into the freedom of national action to which they have always been accustomed. Except perhaps the consolidation of a rule on the more precise delimitation of the area, no doctrinal consideration, much less the development of a fundamental norm in international law, was thought of as being implicated in the setting up of an international machinery for deep seabed mining. For the industrialized States international organization based on the emerging norms of the radical Common Heritage of Humanity principle was definitely unnecessary. This was highly inimical to the established distribution of power among States on the international plane.

5. The Impact of the Declaration of Principles Resolution on the Original Positions on International Machinery

Ambassador Amerasinghe attributed the real virtue of Resolution 2749, on the occasion of its adoption by the United Nations, to its simple "moral force"[67] – a message clearly understood by the developing countries who had all along sought universal recognition of a "first principle" for the deep seabed which they initially articulated in the *Ad Hoc* Seabed Committee, namely, that the Area and its resources are the common heritage of humanity. It took three years of difficult and complex negotiations to produce this Declaration, which the developing countries assumed had definitively and finally upheld their "new thinking", or political cosmology, on the need for international control of the seabed as common heritage. The enthronement of the Common Heritage of

---

66 *See* E.D. Brown, "Our Nation and the Sea: A Comment on the Proposed Legal-Political Framework for the Development of Submarine Mineral Resources" in L. Alexander (Ed.), *Law of the Sea: National Policy Recommendations* 10 (1969 LSI Conference Proceedings, 1970).

67 Doc. A/1933 (17 Dec 1970).

Humanity principle in this document would have meant, among other things, that the original perception of the developing countries on the institutional aspects of this "moral" principle – which in the meantime had come to be understood by them as a fundamental norm of international law encompassing progammatory elements in the normative realms of peace, development and environmental protection – became *the shared perception* on the meaning of international control, and will, therefore, be the legitimate basis for further good faith bargaining and negotiation in legal development.[68] Paragraph 9 of the Declaration links the "first principle" of the Common Heritage of Humanity to the elaboration of an international regime and international machinery for the deep seabed:

> On the basis of the principles of this Declaration, an international regime applying to the area and its resources, and including appropriate international machinery to give effect to its provisions, shall be established by an international treaty of a universal character, generally agreed upon. The regime shall, *inter alia*, provide for the orderly and safe development and rational management of the area and its resources and for expanding opportunities in the use thereof, and ensure the equitable sharing by States of benefits derived therefrom, taking into particular consideration the interests and needs of developing countries, whether land-locked or coastal.[69]

Apart from the question of whether peremptory legal consequences flow from the Declaration of Principles Resolution, there is no doubt that the Declaration, in general, and the Common Heritage of Humanity "first principle", in particular, dispose of a moral and political authority that should not be disregarded in the subsequent negotiations on a regime and machinery for the deep seabed. The Declaration, without purporting to establish immediately binding legal rules,

---

68 *Cf.* L. Ratiner, "Reciprocating State Arrangements: A Transition or An Alternative?" in A. Koers & B. Oxman (Eds.), *The 1982 Convention on the Law of the Sea* 195, 201 (LSI, 1984) [on the "ethical principle of obligatory redistribution of global wealth"].

69 Upon the insistence of developing countries, the "international machinery" concern also figured prominently in the package deal agenda of the Third UN Conference on the Law of the Sea, Para. 2, Res. 2750 C (17 Dec 1970) – explaining the high importance that they attached to the institutional or "machinery" issue *vis-a-vis* the "regime" and "limits" issues as preparations got underway for UNCLOS III. On the interrelationship of the triad of deep seabed issues involving "machinery", "regime" and "limits", *see* Ceylon, PV 1673 (31 Oct 1969); Malta, PV 1675 (3 Nov 1969); and Canada, PV 1682 (10 Nov 1969).

thus creates a strong expectation that members of the international community will abide by the political settlement reached with respect to the direction, goals, and framework of international control.[70] From the viewpoint of reconciling radically opposed conceptions of international control, it is the consensus on the unimpeachable moral and political authority of the Declaration[71] that in fact proves to be the most significant factor in the process of reaching agreement on an international regime and machinery for the common heritage, providing as it does the *shared value system* without which no legislative activity in a pluralist society is possible.[72] The constellation of values formed around nucleus of the Common Heritage of Humanity concept, consisting of a multidimensional programme of internationalization that was initially conceived by Malta in 1967,[73] should have dispelled any doubts about the moral and political orientation of the regime for the deep seabed as well as its institutional superstructure. The adoption of the Declaration of Principles Resolution is a landmark political and moral victory for the developing world as well as for the entire international community, and a milestone in UN diplomatic history, precisely because it enunciates the Common Heritage of Humanity principle as the paramount value premise in the development of a regime for the deep seabed – upholding the view on the need for a new approach to the worsening North-South development gap through a fundamental reorientation of international law and international organization. The Resolution signifies *prima facie* the recognition or solemn acceptance by the entire international community that social justice or international amelioration, rather than rapid commercialization or assured access, should be the main assumption and political *weltanschauung*, or "ideology" if one prefers that term, behind any technical elaboration of international control.[74]

If Resolution 2749 is thus to have any meaning from the standpoint of a rational parliamentary process of legal development and international regime formation in the law of the sea – and the idea of legal development for the

---

70 *Cf.* Brown, *supra* Chap. III note 142, at II.2.18-19.
71 Gorove, *op. cit.*
72 *Cf.* W. Brewer, *Deep Seabed Mining: Can an Acceptable Regime Ever be Found?* 11 ODIL 25, at 52 (1982).
73 On the view that the Common Heritage of Humanity includes values, *see* A. Pardo & E.M. Borgese, *The Common Heritage: Selected Papers on Oceans and World Order* 1967-1974 at xi (1975).
74 *Cf.* Friedheim, *op. cit.* 247, for the view that the Common Heritage of Humanity is the "formula notion" to "confirm or tame in the later phases of negotiation."

deep seabed was indeed the paramount concern in the UN from the time the Seabed Committee was constituted up to the time of the Resolution's adoption – the Resolution must perforce be understood as laying down a shared value system, or a common set of political perceptions and negotiating referents, which becomes the agreed ideological backdrop[75] through which meaningful communication and dialogue between parties holding different opinions become possible. At least, this was how the developing countries appreciated Resolution 2749 as a collective act of political will. It implied a crucial political concession on the part of the industrialized States for them to accept the requirement of a moral dimension as well as a holistic approach to international control – an imperative that was nurtured and persistently argued by the developing States since 1967. It was certainly a concession that the industrialized countries had to give, for the internationalization of the deep seabed on the basis of the Common Heritage of Humanity principle was to be traded-off with the specification of precise limits to national jurisdiction off shore.[76]

But how did the developed States, on their part, come to appreciate the political significance of Resolution 2749? Was Ambassador Amerasinghe's message of a "moral force" behind Resolution 2749 comprehended by them in the same way that the developing countries understood the Common Heritage of Humanity principle as a modality of pursuing international social justice? Was there actually a meeting of the minds – or what regime theorists would call convergence of significant expectations – between North and South on the political and moral significance of the Declaration of Principles Resolution?

After the adoption of Resolution 2749, the spate of draft proposals on a seabed regime that followed suit reveals the *unchanged* attitude of industrialized States with respect to the political implications of the Common Heritage of Humanity principle. While the developing countries were putting forward bold if not altogether radical proposals experimenting with the idea of an unprecedented international organization with powerful territorial jurisdiction over the Area in keeping with the grand normative intent of the Common Heritage of Humanity concept,[77] the developed countries held strongly to "assured access"

---

75 *Cf. id.*, at 350-352.
76 *Supra* Chap. IV Sec. B.3-B.5.
77 *See* Doc. A/AC.138/33 (Tanzania) [establishing an International Sea-bed Authority with extensive resource jurisdiction including powers to explore and exploit its resources; and with authority over scientific research, military-oriented activities, safety, and environmental protection]; Doc. A/AC.138/49 (Chile, Columbia,

to nodules as the overriding value-assumption in the negotiations on the institutional design for a deep seabed regime.

The United Kingdom, for instance, reiterating its earlier notion of an "International Seabed Resource Authority", conceived of an international agency whose sole justification is the issuance of licenses – a function that is to be seen as "primarily administrative."[78] The USSR similarly proposed the creation of an International Sea-Bed Resources Agency that will supervise the implementation of the treaty in regard to the industrial exploration and exploitation of the area.[79] Canada, in its analytic working paper that takes off from Resolution 2749,[80] confines the nature of the machinery to be created to a "seabed resource management system" that will encourage continuing investment. Notwithstanding its recognition that the nature of the tasks of the international machinery "is so radically different from anything now being undertaken in the UN System that this new institution will require a new approach not tied to traditions and practices intended for wholly different purposes", the most significant inference

---

Ecuador, El Salvador, Guatemala. Guyana, Jamaica, Mexico, Panama, Peru, Trinidad & Tobago, Uruguay, and Venezuela) [establishing an International Seabed Authority with equally ample powers and setting up the "Enterprise" as operational organ of the Authority]; Doc. A/AC.138/53 (Malta) [proposing "a total and comprehensive approach to the marine environment and to the international regulation of its problems" by establishing an ambitious "international ocean space institutions" with supranational authority over marine space outside national jurisdiction]. The Working paper submitted by several land-locked and geographically-disadvantaged States, Doc. A/Ac.138/55, also proposed an innovative International Authority on whose behalf the exploration and exploitation of deep seabed mineral resources are to be conducted, with the proviso that the representation in its organs will be equally divided between coastal and non-coastal States. The texts of all these proposals are annexed to the 1971 SBC Rep.

78 Doc. A/AC.138/46, in 1971 SBC Rep at 83. The concept of representation in the executive organ of this Authority under this proposal – making special provision for "States with an established sea bed technology, who have a special contribution to make in organizing seabed activity and without whose support no international regime in this field would be viable" – is no different from the UK proposal made before the adoption of UNGA Resolution 2749. *See supra* note 64 and accompanying text.

79 Doc. A/AC.138/43, 1971 SBC Rep at 67. The Working Paper submitted by Poland, Doc. A/AC.138/44, 1971 SBC Rep at 76, adopts an equally restricted view of the functions of a seabed organization, proposing a resource authority whose functions include ensuring for all States equal access to the Area's resources.

80 Doc. A/AC.138/59, in 1971 SBC Rep at 205.

made was that the international machinery should have the capacity to be sued.[81] Last but not the least, Japan in its "Outline of a Convention on the international seabed regime and machinery",[82] defended the idea of mineral exploration and exploitation by States under licenses issued to them on a first-come-first-served basis by an International Seabed Authority, which would assume a supervisory and regulatory role in keeping with its position as "guardian of the common heritage of humanity."[83]

If subsequent behaviour is the best indicator of the seriousness which a State gives to any of its political commitments, it is clear that the developed States failed to exhibit political fealty to the "moral force" espoused by the developing countries as embodied in Resolution 2749. And if they did so, this commitment was selectively focused on a particular and partial feature of this "moral force" that would make the basic postulate of assured access look more palatable to the developing countries. In all the proposals emanating from the developed States, the only institutional reference made to the "needs and interests of developing countries" is to be found in the marginal provisions on the allocation of revenues from seabed exploitation – stipulated as a secondary or incidental function of an international seabed agency.[84] Here, the general role of developing countries is pictured as passive recipients of a portion of the net profits from seabed exploitation, not different from the essential role conceived for them by the developed States before the passage of Resolution 2749.[85] Hence, the political concession made by the developed States – which

---

81 *See* Paolillo, *op. cit.* 324, note 89.
82 Doc. A/AC.138/63.
83 *See* Oda, *supra* Chap. IV note 2, at 193-194.
84 The USSR draft makes one general reference to interest and needs of developing countries, and would encourage States to cooperate with developing States concerning scientific research against the stated premise that scientific research is a freedom of the high seas. The provision on "distribution of benefits" is left blank. In the UK proposal, the developing countries would be represented in the institutions of the Authority set up for the purpose of distributing the surplus from seabed revenues. And while Canada puts emphasis on the interests and needs of developing countries with respect to the distribution of revenues, Japan would also like to see developing countries enjoy "equal opportunity to participate in exploitation" through their sub-licensing of invited foreign entities.
85 *See* Appendix D of the 1970 US Draft and item 10 of the UK Working Paper, *supra* notes 63 & 64. Item IV of the French proposal, *supra* note 65, pondered on a tax on mineral exploitation levied by mining States and distributed as foreign aid to developing countries.

was implicit in the adoption of the historic Declaration of Principles Resolution and explicit with respect to the acknowledgement of the Common Heritage of Humanity as "first principle" for any deep seabed regime – is more apparent than real. Consistent with the claim of the developed States that the meaning of the term "common heritage of mankind" is either non-existent or will still be elaborated in a regime that is yet to be established,[86] the only concession made by these States on the occasion of the adoption of Resolution 2749 was a rhetorical one, bereft of moral, political, and much less legal, connotations. Evidently for the industrilaized States, Resolution 2749 neither generated shared substantive values nor occasioned a convergence of crucial political expectations and philosophical assumptions on international control. This convergence would have been a desirable development if the North-South dialogue that was commenced in the Seabed Committee were to advance to a more meaningful problem-solving phase.[87] If this was the case, Resolution 2749 was simply a paper victory for the Common Heritage of Humanity principle as an emerging fundamental norm of international law.

The difficult if not impossible task of reconciling the original positions of the developing States and industrialized countries on the question of institutionalizing an international regime for the seabed – philosophical positions that were not at all bridged by the adoption of Resolution 2749 – fell initially on the Working Group on the International Regime. The Working Group was established by Sub-Committee I of the enlarged Seabed Committee in 1972 with the mandate to identify areas of agreement and disagreement on the various issues involved.[88] The Working Group, which was headed by Ambassador Pinto of Sri Lanka, produced a series of informally negotiated documents that neatly outlined the various areas of agreement and disagreement, using the text of

---

[86] *See e.g.* USSR, PV 1798 (15 Dec 1970) and US, PV 1799 (15 Dec 1970).
[87] *Cf.* Friedheim, *op. cit.* 231 *et seq.*, 315 *et seq.* periodizing the negotiation history of Part XI into three phases – diagnosis, formula, and detail, but withholding comment on the significance of Resolution 2749 in the "diagnostic" phase of the negotiations, in keeping with the author's unarticulated "diagnosis" of the overall negotiation problem as simply one involving manganese nodule mining.
[88] *See* 1972 SBC Rep at 22-23. The Working Group continued to work as "informal meetings of the whole" during UNCLOS III and was disbanded at the end of the 1975 session. Schmidt, *op. cit.* 119, 123.

Resolution 2749 as a point of departure.[89] When UNCLOS III convened for its first substantive session in 1974 (Caracas), the Working Group had a fairly clear idea about the fundamental differences of views regarding the scope of an international regime that will *pro tanto* define and delimit the powers of a new international organization for the deep seabed. Ambassador Pinto summarized these differences under two headings: (1) those relating to the fundamental principles of the international regime, and (2) those relating to the structure and functions of the international authority.[90]

Under the first heading, the two major issues that basically reiterate the original North-South positions on international control pertain to (a) the activities that should be governed by the regime, and (b) the system under which the area may be explored and exploited. As regards the former the developing countries favoured the view that all activities of whatever nature and scope – not merely confined to commercial mineral exploitation – should be covered by the regime. The developed countries on their part generally held the view that exploration and exploitation of the resources of the area should be the only relevant activities to be governed by the regime. As regards the latter issue on the system of exploitation, the developing countries preferred an organization with wide powers that would not only include the issuance of licenses but also the authority to engage in exploration and exploitation activities itself. The developed countries, however, defended the idea of an administrative authority that would simply issue licenses to the entities which will in turn be given great latitude in exploration and exploitation activities. This issue on the system of exploitation, as Ambassador Pinto put it, "lies at the very heart of our work":

---

89 The relevant documents considered by the Seabed Committee were Doc. A/AC.138/ SC.I/L.18/Add.3, *Texts illustrating areas of agreement and disagreement on programme of work, item 1, 'Status, scope and basic provisions of the regime, based on the Declaration of Principles'*, in 1972 SBC Rep at 81; and the more exhaustive Doc. A/AC.138/94/Add.1, *Texts illustrating areas of agreement and disagreement on items 1 and 2 of the Sub-Committee's programme of work: Item 1. 'Status, scope and basic provisions of the regime, based on the Declaration of Principles'; Item 2. 'Status, scope, functions and powers of the international machinery'*, in 1973 II SBC Rep at 39. See also "Draft Articles" on the principles for regime, Doc. A/CONF.62/C.1/L.3 (15 Aug 1974), in III UNCLOS III Off Rec at 157.

90 *See* Statement by C.W. Pinto (Sri Lanka), Committee I, 11 July 1974. Text in *UN Source Documents on Seabed Mining*, supra Chap. IV note 252. *See also* J. Stevenson & B. Oxman, *The Preparations for the Law of the Sea Conference* 68 AJIL 1-32, at 5 (1974).

> ... there is one essential respect in which the proposals differ from one another: *the degree to which the new organization, through its appropriate organ, will control the activities of the entity actually carrying out exploration or exploitation.* This is, in our opinion, the central issue: To what extent should the organization penetrate the actual operation of a particular project? Or to give the question a slightly different twist, to what degree should the organization establish and exercise control over an entity in the interest of obtaining the maximum benefit for, and maximum protection of the interests of, mankind as a whole? (emphasis in the original)

The central issue under the heading of "structure and functions of organs of the new organization" relates to the differences of approach on the "location of executive power" in the organization to be set up. For the developing countries, power should be concentrated in the plenary organ of the new organization, the Assembly. The developed countries, on the other hand, opted for an organ with limited membership – the Council, adequately representing the special claims of the technologically advanced countries – to be the locus of executive power.

The institutionalization of a regime for the deep seabed as clarified and conceptualized in the Seabed Committee after the adoption of Resolution 2749, therefore, leads us to inquire into three specific issues whose resolution in UNCLOS III practically decided the contest between the two original positions on international control that were advanced by the developed and developing countries, respectively. These three issues – (1) the scope of activities covered by the regime that would dictate the range of powers available to the seabed authority, (2) the system of exploration and exploitation, and (3) the disposition of executive power in the new international organization – mark out the field of dialogue and accommodation, or conflict and combat,[91] between two apparently irreconcilable and incommensurable forces: assured national access versus reassuring international amelioration. The following section will explain how UNCLOS III, by and large, succeeded in upholding the case for assured access.

---

91 The Chairman of Committee One, Ambassador Engo of Cameroon, conveniently describes these issues as "battlegrounds." P.B. Engo, "Issues of the First Committee at UNCLOS III" in Koers and Oxman, *supra* note 68, at 33, 41-47.

B. Institutional Development and Innovation for the Area in UNCLOS III: Eroding the Moral Force of the Common Heritage of Humanity Principle

The negotiation history of Part XI of the 1982 Convention on the Law of the Sea is a subject that has received substantial treatment in scholarly commentary and writing.[92] The object of the present section is not to go into the twists and turns involved in the complex work of Committee One in UNCLOS III, the details of which are well narrated elsewhere, but to draw out the most salient features of Committee One negotiations bearing directly on the question of how the two competing original positions on the institutionalization of international control were threshed out in UNCLOS III. Specifically, my purpose is to reflect on how UNCLOS III considered the three major issues which define the essence of the institutional regime laid down in Part XI of the Convention, in order to arrive at a judgement on the question of which side, as between the two paradigms of international control, prevailed. These issues cover the scope of activities subject to international control, the system of exploration and exploitation of resources, and the nature of the executive process in the seabed organization.

1. Activities Contemplated by the Regime

The reason why the developing countries insisted that *all* activities that may conceivably take place in the Area should be subject to the international regime was a simple one: since the "Area", which is the common heritage of humanity, is a territorial/areal concept, it follows that all activities that occur within this geographic or geologic space should be governed by the new regime to be negotiated. The territorial basis of the Common Heritage of Humanity regime follows from the need to agree, in the very first instance, on the "limits of the area" – which is the subject of the very first stipulated provision in the draft articles prepared by the Working Group headed by Ambassador Pinto.[93] This territorially-grounded conception of the regime is of course not inconsistent

---

92 The major works post 1982 include Friedheim, *supra* Chap. II note 16; Mahmoudi, *supra* Chap. IV note 313; Morell, *supra* Chap. IV note 39; Ogley, *supra* Chap. II note 76; Paolillo, *supra* Chap. IV note 147; Schmidt, *supra* Chap. II note 76; Sebenius, *supra* Chap II note 12.

93 For the alternative formulations, *see* Art. I, Doc. A/CONF.62/C.1/L.3.

with a multi-functional regime that regulates and coordinates all the traditional as well as new uses of the Area, such as the laying of submarine cables and pipelines, scientific research, military uses, environmental enhancement, and resource exploitation,[94] giving rise to a management system for the common heritage that implies "management not only in the sense of management of resources, but management of all uses."[95]

The 1975 Informal Single Negotiating Text (ISNT)[96] that was issued at the end of the third Session of UNCLOS III (Geneva) essentially adopts the territorial/spatial concept of a Common Heritage of Humanity regime. It, therefore, projects the position of the developing countries insofar as the management system conceived therein embraces all types of functional uses of the area. The comprehensive character of institutionalized activities under the regime is indicated in the first paragraph under Article 21 of the ISNT, entitled "Nature and fundamental principles of the functioning of the Authority":

> The Authority is the organization through which States Parties shall administer the Area, manage its resources and control the activities of the area in accordance with the provisions of this Convention.[97]

In contrast to a territorial or multi-functional denotation of activities to be covered by the new regime is the definition of 'activities in the area' which implements what Professor Borgese once decried as the "single-function regime governing only the mining of manganese nodules, at least for the next few decades."[98] This definition found expression in the 1976 Revised Single Nego-

---

94 *See* 1972 SBC Rep at 20-21.
95 Pardo & Borgese, *supra* note 73, at xi.
96 Doc. A/CONF.62/WP.8 (7 May 1975), in IV UNCLOS III Off Rec at 137.
97 "Activities in the area" is defined as "all activities of exploration or the area and of the exploitation of its resources, as well as other associated activities in the Area, including scientific research." Art. 1 (ii), ISNT. The term "resources" which is distinguished from the term "mineral resources" is broadly defined as "resources *in situ*." Art. 1 (iii) & (iv), ISNT. The Assembly, which is organized according to the principle of sovereign equality/one-State-one-vote, is given powers commensurate with its designation as "the supreme policy-making organ of the Authority", Arts. 21(2), 25 and 26, ISNT.
98 Statement before the First Committee, 12 July 1974, in *UN Source Documents on Seabed Mining, supra* Chap. IV note 252, at 336-341; II UNCLOS III Off Rec at 12-13.

tiating Text (RSNT),[99] a negotiating document that perfectly accommodated the interest of the developed States on a seabed organization conceived with a narrow technical purpose and with suitably circumscribed functions.[100] Under the RSNT, "activities in the area" came to mean "all activities of exploration for and exploitation of resources [*i.e.*, mineral resources] in the area",[101] such that the Authority, in this definitional context, becomes "the organization through which States Parties shall organize and control activities in the Area, particularly with a view towards the administration of the resources of the area, in accordance with this Part of the Convention."[102] The 1982 Convention literally follows the RSNT in its definition of the activities subject to international control, which in turn provides the rationale for the International Seabed Authority.[103]

In explaining the major change in the scope of activities to be brought under international control, Chairman Engo of the First Committee clarified that other activities – for *e.g.* scientific research, transfer of technology, and the protection of the marine environment and human life – would still be covered or governed by the regime; but in these cases the Authority would have a "special role to play" such that "the Authority is required to take specific measures to fulfil its role."[104]

"Other activities" are thus effectively removed from the main control regime of the Authority, or from its assigned field of supranational discretion.[105] In effect, what the modification in the RSNT brought about is a kind of variable or differential institutionalization, where various shades of power and entitlement, or different degrees of authority, are drawn up for an international organization. International control in this case is made to depend on what specific

---

99 Doc. A/CONF.62/WP.9 (31 March 1976).
100 Why this drastic shift was made in the regime's definition of relevant seabed activities subject to international control or regulation from the ISNT to the RSNT is not entirely settled, although the predominant explanation points to the idiosyncratic behavior of the Chairman of the First Committee in the negotiation or non-negotiation of these texts. See Hollick, *op. cit.* 303 and 315; Schmidt, *op. cit.* 121-135; Morell, *op. cit.* 59; Miles, *supra* Chap. II note 7. *Cf.* Engo, *supra* note 91.
101 Art. 1 (ii) and (iii), RSNT.
102 *Id.*, Art. 21(1).
103 *See* Arts. 1(3), 133, 137(2), and 157(1)(2), CLOS.
104 V UNCLOS III Off Rec at 126.
105 J. Evensen, Keynote Address, in Koers and Oxman, *supra* note 68, at xxxvi.

functional use of the Area is involved: a higher degree of international control for mineral resource activities (and as will be seen below, a further differentiation of this control authority with respect to identifiable mineral resource-related activities or operations in the Area), a lesser regulatory competence for the Authority over certain other activities like environmental protection,[106] and the absence of any articulated role for the Authority in yet some other activities, like the preservation of archeological objects[107] or military activities in the area. The dilution of the scope of institutional power available to the Authority that results from this differential application of institutional competence over activities in the Area goes against the idea of an international organization yielding unified powers over a particular territory. On this count, therefore, it is clear that the view of the developed countries prevailed in UNCLOS III. The successful confinement of the powers of the seabed authority to a single function confirms an important negotiating strategy employed by the developed States in the course of Committee One negotiations at UNCLOS III: using the threat of defection, force the majority to accept modifications, alterations, and obfuscations in the detailed provisions intended to carry out the Common Heritage of Humanity idea, eventually rendering this concept a hollow shell.[108]

The diminution of the scope of potential powers of the Authority through the narrowing down of relevant activities subject to its control or regulation is more vividly demonstrated in the negotiations on the system of exploitation of resources in the area, the most crucial issue where the internationalization

---

106 The regulatory powers of the Authority over living resources may be inferred from the environmental protection powers conferred on it. M.C.W. Pinto, "Scope of Operations in the Area", in Borgese & White, *supra* note 41, at 303.
107 *See* Art. 149, CLOS.
108 Friedheim, *op. cit.* 225 and 236. This tactic, Friedheim maintains, was possible because if the developed States could not get acceptable modifications on important provisions, "they could always defect", *i.e.*, proceed to unilaterally mine the deep seabed. *See also* E. Richardson, "Changing Circumstances Bring New Opportunities for Agreement on the Law of the Sea Convention" in Nordquist (Ed.), *17th Annual Seminar of the Center for Oceans Law and Policy* (Univ. of Va., 1993) at 7:
The only real bargaining asset of the United States was that when the Conference concluded we could refuse to go along with the result, whatever it was. I had to sell that horse over and over again, as it was about the only thing we had to work with. Beyond that, we were effectively limited to whatever we could present persuasively and reliably.

agenda of the developed and the developing countries logically converged.[109] The initial position of the Group of 77, consistent with its view that a strong international organization is warranted by the Common Heritage of Humanity principle, took the orientation that all operations related to the exploration and exploitation of seabed mineral resources should be under the control of the Authority.[110] These operations include scientific research, general survey, exploration, evaluation, feasibility study, construction, exploitation, processing, transportation and marketing. The developed countries, on the other hand, wanted the Authority to enter the picture with a specified active role only at the evaluation and exploitation stages.[111]

With the well-known compromise on the "parallel system" – which basically divides the exploitable portions of the Area into two sides: one "private" side allowing for the assured access to nodules by States and their corporations, and the other "Enterprise" side being reserved for direct or indirect exploitation by the Authority[112] – the industrialized countries essentially won their bid for a greatly-reduced profile of the Authority with respect to the mineral resource operations conducted on the "private side" of the exploitation system. Under the 1982 Convention, the Authority will be able, in specifically prescribed fashion, to "organize and control" exploration and exploitation, and to a lesser extent prospecting, activities carried out in the non-reserved sites by States and other entities. However, the ISA will certainly be able to "organize, control and conduct" all operations – *viz.*, scientific research; prospecting; exploration and exploitation; transportation, processing, marketing and waste disposal – by or through the Enterprise.[113] It will be noted that the developing countries, in exchange for agreement by the developed countries to provisions

---

[109] On this shared interest on the system of exploitation, specifically on Article 9 of the Draft Articles prepared by the Working Group, entitled "Who may exploit the area", *see* A.O. Adede, *The System of Exploitation of the "Common Heritage of Mankind" at the Caracas Conference* 69 AJIL 31-49 (1975).

[110] Conditions of Exploration and Exploitation submitted by the Group of 77, Doc. A/CONF.62/C.1/L.7 (16 August 1974), VI Platzoder, *UNCLOS III Documents* at 450.

[111] For a tabular comparison of the position of the G-77 and the developed countries, *see* Doc. CP/CAB.10 (17 August 1974), in VI Platzoder at 64-70. The position of the developing countries was generally upheld in the early negotiated texts, *see* Doc. CP/CAB.12 (9 April 1975); CP/CAB.12/REV.1 (7 May 1975) and Art. 1 (ii), ISNT, but was reversed under the RSNT.

[112] The parallel system was embodied in the RSNT and upheld in the 1982 Convention.

[113] *See* Paolillo, *op. cit.* 195-209; Pinto, *supra* note 106, 302-313.

on technology transfer, gave up their claim for the Authority to have exclusive competence over scientific research in the Area.[114]

In relation to the limited discretionary powers of the ISA over exploration and exploitation activities conducted by States and other entities on the private side of the parallel system, mention should be made of one more major concession made by the developing countries in favor of "assured access." This concerns the protection of pioneer investments in the Area through Resolution II of the Final Act of UNCLOS III "governing preparatory investment in pioneer activities related to polymetallic nodules."[115] In a last minute attempt at UNCLOS III to convince the United States and a few other industrialized countries to desist from further unilateral action and subscribe to the Convention framework for seabed mining, the developing countries agreed to assure automatic access to nodule resources to the first generation of miners, effectively "grandfathering in" the claims of those entities which have already made some investments in nodule exploration before the entry into force of the Convention.[116] Provided potential investors, whether as States or private corporations, meet certain minimum requirements, they would be registered as pioneer investors by the Preparatory Commission and be entitled to "have the exclusive right to carry out pioneer [*i.e.*, pre-production] activities"[117] in specific areas. After entry into force of the Convention, pioneer investors are entitled to be given priority in the allocation of production authorizations from the ISA,[118] which is duty-bound to recognize and honour rights and obligations arising from the PIP resolution as well as the decisions of the PrepCom taken pursuant to this

---

114 Morell, *op. cit.* 69. Although the Authority is divested with the power to regulate and control scientific research, it does not thereby follow that scientific research in the Area becomes – by some kind of juridical default mechanism – an activity subject to the freedom of the high seas doctrine, although the effect may be the same in practice. It is submitted that the Common Heritage of Humanity principle still governs, only that its present institutionalization with respect to scientific research is different from its institutionalization with respect to manganese nodule mining. *Cf.* Paolillo, *supra* at 208; Soons, *op. cit.* 224-229.
115 CLOS at 177-182. On the negotiation background of the Preparatory Investment Protection, or "PIP", resolution, *see* Schmidt, *op. cit.* 169-176.
116 *See* L. Ratiner, *The Law of the Sea: A Crossroads for American Foreign Policy* 60 FOREIGN AFFAIRS 1014 (1982).
117 Para. 6 in rel. to Para. 1(b), Res. II, Final Act, CLOS.
118 Resolution II., para. 9, CLOS.

resolution.[119] The PIP resolution virtually guarantees pioneer investors all the seabed mineral production possible in the next fifty years or so.[120] In sum, through the regime of "pioneer activities" implemented by the PrepCom, acting as the institutional precursor of the ISA, the fundamental objective of assured access by the developed States was met.

The powers of the ISA are, therefore, delineated according a graduated scale of international control over activities and mineral resource operations in the Area. At the high end of this normative scale of control are the mineral resource activities it undertakes through the Enterprise. However, as it will be shown later, the 1994 Implementation Agreement will further circumscribe the scope of powers of the ISA in this regard. At the other, very heavy, end of the spectrum are activities over which the Authority possesses no regulatory role. These activities include military uses of the Area or the transport and processing of manganese nodules mined from the Area by others.

With the quiet elimination of so many deep seabed activities from the actual and potential control functions of the Authority though the RSNT, negotiations in UNCLOS III shifted focus to the issue that was dearest to the industrialized States: their guaranteed orderly access to manganese nodules through appropriate international institutions. When this point was reached, the negotiations in UNCLOS III turned into bargaining discussions over the practical arrangements for mining manganese nodules as a resource beyond national jurisdiction. It could be said that these discussions were far removed from the basic substantial interest of the developing countries in the establishment of an institutional regime for the entirety of the Area as common heritage of humanity.

2. Assured Access to Nodules Under the Parallel System

The issue concerning the system of exploitation for deep seabed resources quickly became the arena where the two competing views of international control were placed in virtual combat. Conceptually, the initial negotiating positions on this issue at UNCLOS III were difficult if not impossible to reconcile. The bargaining positions held by the Group of 77, on the one hand, and industrialized countries, on the other, only allowed a certain degree of modi-

---

119 *Id.*, para. 13.
120 *See* P. Bruckner, "Preparatory Investment Under the Convention and the PIP Resolution" in Koers & Oxman, *supra* note 68, at 181-194.

fication and adjustment beyond which one can be deemed to have succumbed to the other.

Always mindful of their interest in the practical realization of a hitherto theoretical Common Heritage of Humanity principle, the developing countries reasoned out that since humanity through an International Seabed Authority is the title-holder of the resources of the seabed, the ISA should have the corollary right to determine how these resources should be exploited, and by whom. The Authority may, therefore, in its discretion directly exploit the common heritage on behalf of humanity as a whole, or it may enter into contracts with natural or juridical persons in the conduct of resource operations in the Area, with the Authority maintaining effective control over these operations at all times.[121]

The industrialized States, on the other hand, could not imagine the Authority possessed of operational powers, either directly or indirectly through service contracts and joint ventures.[122] The proper role of the Authority, in their view, was simply to license qualified operators, the implication being that license holders have more autonomy than an entity maintaining a joint arrangement with the Authority.[123] The minimal discretionary powers or control functions on resource operations exercised by the Authority is consistent with what the developed countries understood as their "right"[124] flowing from the common heritage concept, *i.e.*, provided it meets the obligations imposed by the treaty, each State has a "right of access" to seabed resources.

At the level of conference diplomacy, no progress in the negotiations on the system of exploitation was possible if either side of the issue remained inflexible in its philosophical conviction, or if either group did not offer to make major adjustments in its rigidly defined position. But it must be asked: Was it at all possible for both sides to somehow "meet halfway" in order to come up with a compromise political solution to the problem of "who may exploit the Area?" Considering that there were no shared substantive values that could serve as a common negotiating backdrop where an intelligent process of give-and-take may have taken place, is it feasible to imagine or define a "golden mean" between these two negotiating positions that would balance the interests

---

121 Doc. A/CONF.62/C.1/L.7.
122 Mahmoudi, *op. cit.* 181.
123 CP/Cab.11 (19 March 1975).
124 Address of US Ambassador J.R. Stevenson before Committee One, Caracas, 17 July 1974, *supra* Chap. IV note 252, at 345.

involved? What could be regarded as pragmatic and moderate under the circumstances, in light of the absence of, what Dr. Henry Kissinger calls, the "agreement on the intangibles" – a necessary element in the stability of any legal and historico-political order in the international community?[125]

From the point of view of the industrialized countries, there was certainly a middle course that could break the deadlock on the issue about the system of exploitation. At the early stage in UNCLOS III, separate proposals by the US and USSR advanced the "parallel system" of exploitation.[126] The basic thrust of these proposals was the division of all potential mine sites on the seabed into two areas for simultaneous development: one where States and private entities enjoyed unobstructed access to resources under national licensing regimes, and the other area being "banked" or reserved for the Authority such that all activities therein would be under the effective control of the Authority.[127] The idea of a dual or parallel system of access was discussed in the Working Group headed by Ambassador Pinto[128] but was subsequently rejected by the Group of 77 as an unsound proposal.[129] The re-introduction of the parallel system in the RSNT, made possible through secret negotiations by "a group of a self-styled 'interested delegations'", was not at all appreciated by the developing countries.[130]

For the developing countries, the "parallel system" was not only a serious threat to the doctrinal integrity and identity of the Area as common heritage

---

125 H. Kissinger, *Diplomacy* 27 (1994).
126 During the Caracas session of UNCLOS III, however, the US unequivocally rejected the idea of a parallel system. "We support [the] rejection [of the parallel system]. We are here to find a single system for exploration and exploitation which will accommodate the interests and needs of all countries." Address of Ambassador Stevenson before Committee I, Caracas, Venezuela, 17 July 1974, *supra* note 124, at 348.
127 For a discussion of the origins of the parallel system, *see* Barkenbus, *op. cit.* 116-119; Mahmoudi, *op. cit.* 183; Schmidt, *op. cit.* 124-125.
128 *See* para. 7, Doc. CP/Cab.12 (9 April 1975).
129 The revised negotiated document of the Working Group, Doc. CP/Cab.12/Rev.1 (7 May 1975) dropped the idea of a parallel system of access. The contents of this document were carried over in the Annex of the ISNT. *Cf.* Friedheim, *op. cit.* 242.
130 *See* Engo, *op. cit.* at 43 and his references; Morell, *op. cit.* 59; Schmidt, *op. cit.* 126-128.

of humanity.[131] More seriously, the parallel system would also in effect obliterate the capacity of the Authority to carry out exploitation itself, directly because it would not have the requisite technological and financial resources to undertake operational functions, and indirectly because mining companies would be in no hurry to operate under the control of the Authority while they enjoy liberal access to an indefinite number of mine sites through the private side of the system.[132] In short, there was in truth no concession, or movement towards a middle ground negotiating position, being made by the developed States.[133]

The "unitary system" of exploitation[134] defended by the developing countries entailed the creation of an "Enterprise" – the operational organ of the Authority with monopoly over resource activities in the Area[135] – which will be subordinated to the Council, just as the Council is subordinated to the Assembly of the Authority.[136] Indeed, it is the institution of the Enterprise which makes the Authority more than just a familiar intergovernmental body; its establishment affirms an innovative approach to international organization, in keeping with the revolutionary spirit of the Common Heritage of Humanity principle.[137] For the developing countries, the impasse could be overcome not basically by giving in to the demand for a parallel system but in the accom-

---

131 As the delegation from Algeria remarked: "Are we here to reserve 50 per cent of the sea bed area for private corporations?" The delegate from Barbados, however, believed that 75 per cent of the Area would really be given to the control of developed States or multinationals because the Authority would contract with these entities in the exploitation of the reserved areas. *See* Barkenbus, *op. cit.* 118; E. Miles, *An Interpretation of the Geneva Proceedings* 3 ODIL 187, at 199-200 (1975-76).
132 Barkenbus, *op. cit.* 119; Morell, *op, cit.* 56.
133 *Cf.* Mahmoudi, *op. cit.* 183. It does not seem accurate or fair, therefore, to castigate the developing countries which have vigorously opposed the idea of a parallel system as outright "radicals" and those who were willing to entertain the concept of the parallel system as "moderate." *See* Barkenbus, *op. cit.* 118 and Miles, *supra* note 131.
134 *See* Art. 22, ISNT.
135 The idea of the "Enterprise" is traceable to the 1971 proposal of 13 Latin American countries in the Seabed Committee. Doc. A/AC.138/49, 1971 SBC Rep at 93.
136 AO Adede, *The Group of 77 and the Establishment of the International Sea-Bed Authority* 7 ODIL 31-64 at 42 (1979).
137 *See* Paolillo, *op. cit.* 178 *et seq.*, 212 *et seq.*

modation of the interests of the developed States within a unitary system.[138] The concessions which the Group of 77 perceived as just and reasonable from their philosophical standpoint were indicated in the ISNT. It provided, *inter alia*, that the Enterprise may not refuse to enter into a contract for resource operations in the Area with any State or entity if certain well defined criteria have been met;[139] that the Council, rather than the Assembly, will "exercise direct and effective control over activities in the Area";[140] and that the representation of special interests in the Council, especially for the States with substantial investment and advance technology, would be permitted.[141]

A turning point in the negotiations on the system of exploitation was reached when US Secretary of State Henry Kissinger intervened in 1976 to break the deadlock in Committee I.[142] Secretary Kissinger's aim, essentially, was to make the parallel system acceptable to the Group of 77, deploying the usual carrots-and-sticks tactic for this purpose. The stick, which should be mentioned first because it provoked a sense of extreme urgency in UNCLOS III, was the loud and unambiguous threat that the US will proceed to unilaterally mine the deep seabed if the Group of 77 did not accept the concept of assured access through the parallel system.[143] "The time has come", Secretary Kissinger an-

---

138 Statement of Singapore, in Miles, *supra* note 131, at 207.
139 Sec. 8, Annex I, ISNT.
140 Art. 28 (x), ISNT.
141 Art. 27(1)(a), ISNT.
142 Kissinger launched his high-profile high-level intervention in UNCLOS III with a speech delivered before the Foreign Policy Association on April 8, 1976: *The Law of the Sea: A Test of International Cooperation*. Text in 74 Dept of State Bul 533-542, 26 Sept. 1976. Copies of this speech were circulated to all UNCLOS III delegations.
143 "If the deep seabeds are not subject to international agreement, the United States can and will proceed to explore and mine on its own"; "But if agreement is not reached this year, it will be increasingly difficult to resist pressure to proceed unilaterally." 74 Dept of State Bul at 539 and 541, 26 April 1976. "But we have come to the point where rapid, responsible and cooperative progress is indispensable. The world community now faces the possibility that domestic pressures of many nations may set into motion unilateral national moves which could gravely impair the chances of achieving a treaty in the near future, if at all. Thus it is vital that this current session of the Conference be successful." Letter of Secretary H. Kissinger to UNCLOS III President Shirley Amerasinghe dated 3 August 1876, in 75 Dept of State Bul at 327-328, 6 Sept 1976; "despite – indeed, because of – these tendencies [in many nations towards unilateral tendencies],

nounced, "to put aside the theoretical debates."[144] The parallel system of access was an irreducible, non-negotiable element in US seabed policy that must be acknowledged by everyone concerned as an integral part of the new regime, lest the US would go it alone:

> I must say candidly that there are limits beyond which no American Administration can, or will, go. If attempts are made to compel concessions which exceed those limits, unilateralism will become inevitable. Countries which have no technological capacity for mining the seabeds in the foreseeable future should not seek to impose a doctrine of total internationalization on nations which alone have this capacity and which have voluntarily offered to share it.[145]

It must be noted in this regard that Secretary Kissinger took the "concept" of the common heritage of humanity to mean that "humanity has a responsibility to the world community in the deep seabeds"[146] – a clear indication that there was at all no comprehension of the fundamental position in the 1970 Declaration of Principles Resolution as defended by the developing countries which would have maintained instead that the "principle of the common heritage of humanity means that the present world community has a responsibility to humanity as a whole, especially to the disadvantaged nations and to future generations." The inherent 'right of access' of all States to the seabed, rich or poor alike, was the basic postulate reiterated by Secretary Kissinger. The parallel system of exploitation was thus seen as a "self-imposed sacrifice" made by the US "which represented significant restrictions on [its] freedom of action."[147]

The "carrots" in the diplomatic offensive of Secretary Kissinger consisted of a "package"[148] of assurances calculated to make the parallel system appear to be the lesser of two evils for the Group of 77, the alternative evil being the

---

it is imperative that this session make significant progress on all the remaining major issues still in contention." Remarks to US Delegation, 75 Dept of State Bul at 333, 13 Sept 1976; *See also* Dept of State Bul at 399, 452-453 and 508.

144 Remarks of 1 Sept 1976, 75 Dept of State Bul at 398, 27 Sept 1976.
145 H. Kissinger, *Towards a New Understanding of Community*, address before the 31st UNGA, 30 Sept 1976, in 75 Dept of State Bul 497-510, at 497, 25 Oct 1976. *See also* 75 Dept of State Bul at 333, 336, 370, 395-396, 399, 452-453.
146 75 Dept of State Bul at 335.
147 *See id.*, at 398, 399 and 508.
148 *Id.*, at 452.

consummation of the threat of unilateral exploitation. There were three specific assurances offered in this regard. The first was the proposal on financing the Enterprise so that it could begin its mining operation simultaneously or practically concurrently with mining operations on the private side of the system.[149] Secondly, and closely related to the purpose of the first, Kissinger agreed to "provisions for the transfer of technology so that the existing advantage of certain industrialized States would be equalized over a period of time."[150] Lastly, the US proposed for periodic review conferences, say every 25 years, in which the system of exploitation would be continually re-examined.[151]

As a result of the Kissinger intervention, the developing countries were generally willing to make adjustments in their original position with respect to the *form* of the system of exploitation in favor or a dual mode of access.[152] Although they were prepared, albeit reluctantly,[153] to acknowledge the distinct roles of the Enterprise and private entities in a parallel system of exploitation, it was less certain whether the Group of 77 was willing to agree, in principle, to the concept of permanent automatic access by States and private corporations to resources on the private side of system.[154] The *interpretation* of the parallel system that was incorporated in the 1977 Informal Composite Negotiating Text (ICNT),[155] which *inter alia* gave the Authority powers of control on both sides of the parallel system by stipulating that resource activities in the Area shall be "carried out on the Authority's behalf",[156] was vehemently rejected by the United States because the goal of assured access was not clearly recog-

---

[149] *Id.*, at 398.

[150] *Ibid.* "The United States is prepared to make a major effort to enhance the skills and access of developing countries to advanced seabed mining technology in order to assist their capabilities in this field." 74 Dept of State Bul at 540.

[151] 75 Dept of State Bul at 398.

[152] *See* Report of the Chairman of the First Committee on the work of the Committee, Doc. A/CONF.62/L.16 (6 Sept 1976), VI UNCLOS III Off Rec 130, at 131.

[153] Schmidt, *op. cit.* 130.

[154] *See* discussion on "the issues of exploitation" in the Statements of the Chairman of the First Committee, Docs. A/CONF.62/C.1/L.20 (26 May 1977) and A/CONF.62/C.1/L.21 (16 June 1977), in VI Platzoder, *supra* note 110, at 499-508.

[155] Doc. A/CONF.62/WP.10 (15 July 1977), in VIII UNCLOS III Off Rec.

[156] Art. 151, ICNT.

nized.[157] For the industrialized countries the parallel system was designed precisely to bring about unhampered access – a message that was sorely missed by the ICNT. The angry response of the United States to the ICNT included bolstering the "stick" that Kissinger warned about earlier. This time, however, the threat took the alarming form of unilateral action based on a "mini-treaty" by potential seabed mining States.[158]

Removing the regulatory discretion of the Authority over access by States and corporations to the private side of the parallel system as demanded by the US would definitely put the Enterprise in the awkward position of competing with these other mining entities. It was a consequence that potentially makes the parallel system highly inefficient from a management perspective, if not completely unworkable from an economic perspective.[159] Still, the view of the US prevailed. The officers of the Conference determined that the parallel system received widespread and substantial support which offered a substantially improved prospect of consensus.[160] It was in the special Negotiating Group presided over by Ambassador Njenga[161] where the developing countries finally acquiesced to the "assured access" element of the parallel system of exploitation. The ICNT was amended such that entities which met the requirements stipulated in the Convention will be given automatic access to the Area.[162]

The major concession on the parallel system entailed a heavy and somewhat stultifying burden on the United States and its allies. This was drawing up the specifics of the regime to make it absolutely certain that the idea of assured

---

157 For an account of the US response, *see Report of the US Delegation*, Sixth Session, New York, May 23-July 15, 1977, *supra* Chap. IV note 217, 161, *et seq.*
158 *Cf.* Schmidt, *op. cit.* 136-138.
159 *See* E.M. Borgese, *The Enterprises: A Proposal to reconceptualize the operational arm of the International Seabed Authority to manage the common heritage of mankind* (IOI Occasional Papers No. 6, November 1978).
160 M.C.W. Pinto, "'Common Heritage of Mankind': From Metaphor to Myth, and the Consequences of Constructive Ambiguity" J. Makarczyk (Ed.), *Essays in Honour of Krzysztof Skubiszewski* 249-268, at 259 (1996).
161 Seven Negotiating Groups (NGs) were established during the 7th session of UNCLOS III to deal with the "hard-core" issues. Three of these Negotiating Groups tackled the Committee I hard-core issues: NG1 – system of exploitation; NG2 – Financial Arrangements; and NG3 – Organs of the Authority, their composition, powers and functions. *See* Doc. A/CONF.62/61 (11 April 1978), in X UNCLOS III Off Rec 1.
162 *See* revision of Art. 151, ICNT in Doc. NG1/10/Rev.1, X UNCLOS III Off Rec at 21.

access through the parallel system was implemented to the last detail. They, therefore, had to draft an elaborate mining code that would leave the Authority with a minimum of discretion on matters related to qualification and selection of applicants, terms and conditions of contracts, procedure and criteria for their approval, security of tenure, etc. The exercise was obviously overwhelming, and proved quite oppressive to the delegates at UNCLOS III who called for "simplification" of many detailed and highly technical draft provisions.[163] It is against common sense, the developing countries protested, to write in stone the minutiae of a regulatory regime intended to govern activities that have no precedent and an industry that has barely started. Simplification notwithstanding, the United States was able secure at least 130 changes to the seabed mining provisions of the ICNT,[164] specifying in advance the complex details of the "right" of technologically advanced countries to mine the seabed.

However, the acceptance by the international community of the parallel system with its corollary standard of assured access rested on an arduously-negotiated consensus package.[165] There were two very critical elements of this package, eventually incorporated in the 1982 Convention. The first is the transient nature of the parallel system secured through a provision for its experimental operation during an *interim* period of 20 years. The second pertained to the arrangements that will ensure the viability of the Enterprise during the *interim* period.[166] A perusal of the overall package on the system of exploitation leads to the conclusion that although the industrialized States won their battle for assured access, such "right" of unhampered access to nodules

---

163 Reports of the Chairman of the First Committee, IX UNCLOS III Off Rec at 98, 15 Sept 1978, and Doc. A/CONF/62/L.36 (26 April 1979), XI UNCLOS III Off Rec 96, at 97. For a discussion of "simplification", *see* S. Allen & J.P. Craven (Eds.), *Alternatives in Deepsea Mining* 5-11, 20-22 (LSI Workshop, 1979); *Cf.* Schmidt, *op. cit.* at 140-141.
164 Of the 138 modifications to seabed provisions of the ICNT made from July 1977 to August 1980, only 7 were in favor of developing countries, according to US Ambassador Richardson, in Koers and Oxman, *op. cit.* 15.
165 On the "package" character of the agreements relating to the system of exploitation, *see* Engo, *op. cit.* 44.
166 The elaboration of a "production limitation" policy may be considered as another element of the package, *see* Art. 151, CLOS. However, because there was a sustained North-South consensus at UNCLOS III on the need to protect adversely affected land-based producers by seabed mining, Mahmoudi, *op. cit.* at 185-186, this matter will not be considered as part of the basic issue involving the competition of institutional visions for the system of exploitation.

was not meant to be permanent. Notwithstanding the parallel system, the developing countries did not completely abandon the cause of a unitary system of exploitation which they understood as a necessary offshoot of the Common Heritage of Humanity principle.[167]

Articles 154 and 155 of the 1982 Convention concerning the review mechanisms under Part XI explain the precarious normative pedestal upon which the parallel system was placed. Article 154 provides that the Assembly of the ISA shall conduct periodic 5-year reviews in order to take or recommend measures to improve the operation of the international regime established. These periodic reviews would afford opportunities for critical assessment of the parallel system.[168] The review momentum culminates after some time as indicated in Article 155 (the more important article) which provides that after the first fifteen years of commercial production in the Area, the Assembly shall convene a review conference to consider in detail the following issues:

a) whether the provisions of [Part XI] which govern the system of exploration and exploitation of the resources of the Area have achieved their aims in all respects, including whether they have benefitted mankind as a whole;
b) whether, during the 15-year period, reserved areas have been exploited in an effective and balanced manner in comparison with non-reserved areas;
c) whether the development and use of the Area and its resources have been undertaken in such a manner as to foster a healthy development of the world economy and balanced growth of international trade;
d) whether monopolization of the activities in the Area has been prevented;
e) whether the policies set forth in articles 150 and 151 [on general policies and specific production policies] have been fulfilled; and
f) whether the system has resulted in the equitable sharing of benefits derived from activities in the Area, taking into particular consideration the interests and needs of the developing States.[169]

The review mechanism is consistent with the vision of institutionalization founded on the Common Heritage of Humanity principle *ratione temporis* in

---

167 As NG1 Chairman Njenga maintained, the predicament surrounding the system of exploitation "is more a question of finding a balance between the various interests than of reconciling radically opposed philosophies." Doc. NG1/12, in X UNCLOS III Off Rec at 19.
168 *See* Art. 314, CLOS precluding modifications to the parallel system before the Review Conference.
169 Art. 155(1), CLOS.

at least four ways. First, it is the Assembly – the most representative and democratically constituted organ of the ISA – which has competence over the review process. Second, detailed substantive consideration of the subjects covered by the review conference promotes the idea of normative/programmatory law development and progressive institutionalization under the Common Heritage of Humanity principle; third, the review conference is expressly mandated to ensure the maintenance of, *inter alia,* the Common Heritage of Humanity principle; and fourth, if no consensus on the system of exploitation is reached five years after the commencement of the review conference, changes thereto shall be binding on all States parties if approved by three fourths of their number.[170]

The other critical element in the package of negotiated agreements on the system of exploitation would seek to strike a proper balance between the two sides of the parallel system, in order to make it truly "parallel."[171] The objective was to ensure the viability of the Enterprise as an effective operator and to be able to engage in exploitation *concurrently* with States or corporations on the private side of the system. This brings to fulfillment the commitment of Secretary Kissinger to make the parallel system work. More particularly for this purpose, the financing of the Enterprise's mining operations in a first mine site, principally through the contributions from States parties, was provided for in the Convention.[172] "Transfer of technology" to support nodule exploitation by the Enterprise had also been agreed,[173] with the important caveat that absent the consent of the industrialized States which become members of the Authority, there shall be no obligation to transfer technology to the Enterprise on the part of a contractor.[174] Other measures provided in the Convention that are intended to assist the Enterprise overcome the enormous problems it will face as an operator in the Area include a token priority to be given production authorizations during the *interim* period, and a tax holiday of ten years within which period the Enterprise will be exempted from making payments to the Authority.[175]

---

170 Art. 155, CLOS. *See also* Art. 151 (3), CLOS.
171 Report of the Chairman of Negotiating Group 1, Doc. A/CONF.62/L.35, in XI UNCLOS III Off Rec at 86.
172 *See* Art. Article 170(4) & 173(2)(c), CLOS and Art. 11, Annex IV, CLOS.
173 Art. 144(2), CLOS and Art. 5, Annex III, CLOS.
174 M.C.W. Pinto, "The United Nations Convention on the Law of the Sea and the New International Economic Order: Interdependence and International Legislation", in Koers & Oxman, *op. cit.* 224-235 at 230-231; Paolillo, *op. cit.* 264-267.
175 *See* Paolillo, *op. cit.* 267-268.

Overall, the system of exploitation established in the 1982 Convention upholds the goal of assured access as the overriding objective of the resources regime for the deep seabed. There is, however, an underlying paradox, or internal contradiction, behind the victory of the "parallel system" as the practical means of achieving assured access to manganese nodules. In the first place, the insurmountable problems of capitalization of, and transfer of technology to, the Enterprise, coupled with the cost-ineffectiveness of managing the system[176] may not altogether be in complete harmony with free market principles[177] as the champions of assured access may want to think. The concession that the Enterprise should be economically viable – a logical and political consequence of the parallel system – translates into an encouragement of unhealthy economic competition between the Authority and an established industry.[178] Rather than being harnessed by the institutions representing transspatial and transtemporal humanity, private enterprise initiative – undoubtedly the most powerful productive force in a globalized economy – is instead set up against these institutions. If the Enterprise becomes truly viable would this not spell out the destruction of the private side of the parallel system?

But what if the operators on the private side of the system – regulated essentially by *national* control regimes – become the dominant economic force in the system? The contradictions in the parallel system would now go deeper because according to the Convention, this success during the *interim* period will have to be assessed according to *international* control standards or criteria, listed above, for detailed consideration by the Review Conference. Since it is to be expected that activities in the non-reserved sites will likely not measure up to the "Common Heritage standards" enforced in the review process, the success of assured access, based as it is on the logic of national aggrandizement, would truly be short lived. The genius of the Review Conference is precisely its prediction that the parallel system will self-destruct sooner or later, and the wisdom of the 1982 Convention lies in its practical translation of the patient but determined "moral force" behind the Common Heritage principle that would grant a pyrrhic or conditional victory to the compulsive "right" of assured access.

---

176 Borgese, *supra* note 159, at 97; A. Pardo, *The Convention on the Law of the Sea: A Preliminary Appraisal* 20 SAN DIEGO L REV 489 (1983).
177 *See* Pinto, *supra* note 174, at 231.
178 Borgese, *supra* Chap. II note 204, at 97.

3. Decision-Making in the Execution of a Design

The developing countries entered the UNCLOS III negotiations with a very strong position on the issue of decision-making and voting in the new international organization for the deep seabed. Since the "Area" as a notional entity is a conventional legal fiction that can only be established *de jure* with the consent of States, particularly States with a stake in the revision of the exploitability clause of the 1958 Continental Shelf Convention, all coastal States would therefore be "equally affected" or "equally interested"[179] in the internationalization of the Area and its resources. Without the consent of these affected States, it will not be possible to establish an international regime or its machinery "by an international treaty of a universal character, generally agreed upon."[180] The inclusive interpretation given by the developing countries to the Common Heritage of Humanity principle as foundational norm for internationalization, however, led them to promote the equal stake and interest of the land-locked States in the management of the common heritage.[181] The concept of "benefit of humanity" demanded nothing less than the parity of all States – big or small, rich or poor, land-locked or coastal, island States or continental States, old States, new States or States yet to be – in the process of precise delimitation of the Area, in the development of norms and principles to govern the Area, and in the progressive institutionalization of a Common Heritage regime. All States enter the "frontier" at the same time with equal legal capacities. This arises from an historic *modus vivendi* which says that they will all behave as "gentlemen" who do not "race to grab" the wealth of the new frontier lest they re-create the colonial evils of the past. All States collectively act as agents, trustees, or instruments of humanity in the realization of the teleological ends of the Common Heritage of Humanity principle. Recalling the transition from a "state of nature" to civilized polity, the whole situation captures an ideal setting for the full application of the doctrine of sovereign equality of States, giving unqualified recognition to the equal capacity of all States for rights and obligations. From this perspective, the distribution of power in the new inter-

---

179 *Cf. North Sea Continental Shelf Cases* 1969 ICJ Rep. 3, at 42, para 73. *See supra* Chap. IV note 331 and accompanying text.
180 Para. 9, Declaration of Principles Resolution.
181 Chile, on behalf of the delegations from Asia, Africa and Latin America, PV 1602 (7 Nov 1968).

national organization for the seabed will be dictated by the principle "one State, one vote" – as the Group of 77 argued in UNCLOS III.[182]

On the other hand, the major industrialized countries which have chosen to limit their view of the seabed problematic to the practical and technical challenge of manganese nodule mining, notwithstanding the adoption of the 1970 Declaration of Principle Resolution, were insistent on preserving the notion of "a privileged few" in the system of decision-making within the seabed organization to be created.[183] In their view, the reason why certain States should be treated as superior to, or "more equal" than, others in a regime for deep seabed mining was obvious: since only these States or their nationals possessed the capital and the technology to extract the nodules, they must have a proportionately bigger influence in the development of the regime. By definition, the spectators who just stood on the sidelines and simply waited for the nodule resources to be exploited cannot be deemed their equals. The few technologically advanced States were, therefore, the "most vitally affected States" from such normative standpoint, whose participation in the regime was either a necessary or sufficient condition for legal development.[184] In addition, the new international organization cannot be too prone to the whims of an "irresponsible majority vote."[185] "A fair and thoughtful decision making process" in the International Seabed Authority should be supported by "realistic voting arrangements."[186]

The conflict of views regarding the basis and orientation of decision-making in the new international organization was brought to bear on the negotiations concerning the distribution of power within the International Seabed Authority, as the new international organization came to be known. The structure of the ISA was more or less decided when UNCLOS III was convened, broad agreement having been reached on the ISA's main organs constituting the machinery of the regime. These organs are the Assembly as the plenary organ, the Council as executive organ with limited membership, the Enterprise as the operational

---

182 Adede, *supra* note 136, at 35.
183 *See* US, UK and French proposals in the Seabed Committee, *supra* notes 63, 64 and 65, and accompanying texts.
184 *See* Kronmiller, *op. cit.*
185 E.D. Brown, *supra* note 66, at 10.
186 Statement of US Ambassador Stevenson before Committee I, Caracas, 17 July 1974, *supra* note 124, at 348.

arm of the ISA, and the Secretariat.[187] Furthermore, there was also a clear consensus on the need to institutionalize a system for the compulsory settlement of disputes arising from the seabed regime.[188] It should be noted that the Enterprise is the organ that makes the ISA the only international organization with an operational capability – a unique feat in the history of international organization.[189] It should also be pointed out that the system of dispute settlement for seabed disputes, through the Sea-Bed Disputes Chamber of the International Tribunal for the Law of the Sea established under the 1982 Convention,[190] follows a unique procedure in the determination of legality that defines in unprecedented ways the relationships among States, international organizations, and private entities in the context of compulsory dispute resolution.[191] Nevertheless, the competence of the Enterprise and the Sea-Bed Disputes Chamber, or for that matter their functions and internal constitutions,[192] were subjects which were not as bitterly contested in UNCLOS III as the allotment of powers to the Assembly and the Council of the ISA. The "battleground" of decision-making in the new international regime for the deep seabed[193] inquires into the scope and density of institutional power disposed by these two organs of the Authority.

It is a fact that the major issue of decision-making, deliberately left out for negotiation until the last stage of UNCLOS III, had lost much of its importance as the two other main issues in Committee I – the nature of activities covered by the regime and the system of exploitation – were resolved.[194] It was only after restricting the relevant activities over which the ISA assumes regulatory competence to the exploration and exploitation of manganese nodules, as the industrialized countries have desired, and after accepting the parallel system of exploitation that would meet the imperative of assured access, again

---

187 Statement of Ambassador Pinto, Sri Lanka, before Committee I, 11 July 1974, *supra* note 90, at 309.
188 *Id.*, at 312; *see also* Adede, *supra* note 136, at 33.
189 Paolillo, *op. cit.* Ch. 1, 168-175, and Chap. IV.
190 Art. 186, CLOS.
191 Paolillo, *op. cit.* Chap. V. *See also* L.C. Caflisch, "The Settlement of Disputes Relating to Activities in the International Seabed Area" in Rozakis & Stephanou, *op. cit.* 303-344.
192 On the relatively uncontroversial adoption of dispute settlement procedures under Part XI in UNCLOS III from a North-South perspective, *see* Mahmoudi, *op. cit.* 290.
193 Engo, *op. cit.* 46.
194 *See ibid.*

to the liking of the industrialized States, that the Conference was able to move to the issue of decision making. Not surprisingly, when the issue of decision-making was up for hard-bargaining,[195] the cogency of the "one State, one vote" thesis initially put forward by the G-77 had lost much of its stature. Without doubt, the consensus on an international organization that would be concerned, on the whole, with the assured access of States and their nationals to manganese nodule resources on the seabed beyond national jurisdiction[196] placed a heavy burden of argument on the proponents of "sovereign equality" as the operative principle of institutional decision-making. The dilution of the principle of sovereign equality at the later part of UNCLOS III occurred in several stages.

The first decisive step that was taken in the direction of weakening the "sovereign equality" provision of the ICNT[197] involves the restrictive definition of the "express" and "implied" powers of the ISA. Narrowing the powers of the ISA as far as feasible was in line with the position of the industrialized countries that conceived of an ISA with no discretionary powers, or with very strictly defined discretionary powers. One of the very first modifications introduced by the WG-21 to the ICNT provided that the "powers and functions of the Authority shall be those expressly conferred upon it", and it shall have "incidental powers as are implicit in and necessary for the performance of these powers and functions with respect to activities in the area."[198] By confining the express and implied powers of the ISA to "activities in the area", the intended effect of this compromise provision was to confirm the very limited functional competence of the ISA. If exceeded, the procedures for dispute settlement regarding *ultra vires* acts of the ISA will be triggered.[199]

The tethering of institutional competence to "activities in the Area", likewise, implies that decision-making with respect to these activities would be based on a system of representation that reckons with interests that are directly

---

195 Although special Negotiating Group 3, with open-ended membership, was tasked to deal with the hard-core issue "Organs of the Authority, their composition, powers and functions", it was the Working Group of 21 (WG-21) – set up during the Eighth Session (Geneva) in 1979 consisting of 10 developing States, 10 industrialized States and China – which served as the forum for negotiations on the question of decision-making in the ISA.
196 Art. 153, CLOS.
197 Art. 155(2), ICNT. *See* Art. 157(3), CLOS.
198 Doc. WG21/2 (18 Aug 1979), in VI Platzoder, *supra* note 110, 364 at 374. *See* Art. 157(2), CLOS.
199 *Report of the US Delegation*, 8th Session (Resumed) *supra* note 157, at 327.

411

affected by the conduct of these activities. The representation of special interests in the decision-making institutions of the ISA, like States with the largest investments in these activities or States importing and exporting mineral resources that are the object of these activities, becomes unavoidable. The minor concession made by developing countries in the ISNT which recognized the legitimacy of special interests representation in the Council of the ISA[200] was turned into a principal norm of decision-making in the ISA: the tail that eventually wagged the dog. The result of special interest representation in any of the political organs of the ISA is far reaching. By virtue of the primary recognition given to "special interests" in respect of "activities in the Area" in the decision-making process of the ISA, a very partial definition of "humanity" has emerged. "Transspatial" and "transtemporal" humanity,[201] on whose behalf the ISA shall act,[202] is no longer as inclusive as the developing countries would have wished. "Humanity" had been effectively truncated into an aggrupation of "specially affected States" entitled to promote and protect manganese nodule mining-related interests.[203] To amplify the observation of Professor Borgese:

> ... it is questionable whether the introduction of interest representation is the best way to serve the real interests of a progressive international community. It might have been better to confine interest representation in the Enterprise, which should be a business, based on sound financial criteria. The Council, in contrast, should be a political body, based on democratic and permanent principles. Interest groups tend to shift over time, to freeze them in a constitution may cause long term problems. Straight regional representation (the criterion underlying the composition of the General Committee of the Preparatory Commission) would have been far more appropriate.[204]

The test of participation in the ISA's decision making process is this: "does a State have a vital interest with respect to the mining of manganese nodules?"

---

200 Art. 27, ISNT.
201 *See* Dupuy, *supra* Chap. IV note 316.
202 Art. 137(2), ICNT; Art. 137(2), CLOS.
203 The "specially affected States" that represent special interests are identified in Art. 159(1), ICNT and Art. 161(10, CLOS: States which are largest consumers/importers of the categories of minerals derived from the area; States with the largest investments respecting activities in the area; major net exporters of the categories of minerals derived from the area; and developing countries.
204 Borgese, *supra* Chap. II note 204, at 96.

This is a test that is far removed from the criterion of inclusive reciprocity in decision-making introduced by the 1970 Declaration of Principles Resolution: "does a State have an interest in the precise delimitation and legal definition of the Area as the common heritage of humanity?"

A second step taken in the process of establishing the ISA that mocks the principle of sovereign equality is the organic de-linking of the Assembly from the Council. This development proceeds from the fundamental premise of interest representation, which is certainly antithetical to any notion of democratic control based on the rule "one State, one vote." Since the Assembly as a plenary organ was ill-suited for interest representation, ways and means were devised to concentrate institutional power – power to effectively bring about the goal and secure the "right" of assured access to manganese nodule resources – on the Council. Because the Council by definition is an organ of limited membership, it became the appropriate institutional vehicle for the realization of the ends of special interest representation. Several changes to the ICNT were negotiated in WG-21 that led to the abandonment of the position of developing countries which would have made the Assembly the supreme policy-making organ of the ISA.

Mention should be made first of the characterization of the Assembly in the ICNT as "the supreme organ of the Authority."[205] While a literal substantive supremacy was intended in the ICNT, the WG-21 negotiated a watered-down concept of supremacy. The ICNT provision was accordingly revised so that the sources of Assembly's supremacy would "lie in its membership consisting of all members of the Authority, in its accountability for the other principal organs of the Authority," and in its "incidental" and "residual" powers.[206] Considering the balance of expressly identified powers attributed to the Assembly, on the one hand, and the Council, on the other, there is no doubt that *de jure* and *de facto* supremacy belongs to the Council.[207]

Further on the question of the interrelationship between the Assembly and the Council, mention should also be made of the doctrine of strict separation of powers between the Assembly and the Council.[208] To achieve this, the

---

205 Art. 158(1), ICNT. *See* Art. 160(1), CLOS.
206 Doc. A/CONF.62/C.1/l.26 (21 Aug 1979), XII UNCLOS III Off Rec at 77.
207 *See* Paolillo, *op. cit.* 242-250.
208 Pinto, *supra* note 41, at 318.

413

WG-21 agreed on the following provision, which was carried over to the 1982 Convention:[209]

> The principal organs shall each be responsible for exercising those powers and functions which have been conferred upon them. In exercising those powers and functions, each organ shall avoid taking any action which may derogate from or impede the exercise of specific powers and functions conferred upon another organ.[210]

The developed countries would interpret this rule to mean that the Assembly cannot, by the exercise of its express or implied powers, interfere with the Council's exercise of powers and functions conferred to it under Article 162 of the Convention[211] – a provision which gives a very long enumeration of the Council's functions, proving beyond a scintilla of doubt that it is indeed the locus of executive and policy-making power in the Authority.[212] It is significant to note that the strict separation of powers implemented by the Convention was a concession that exceeded somewhat the original demand by the industrialized countries which had argued earlier for "an appropriate system of checks and balances among organs of the authority."[213] To illustrate, reference may be made to scope of general competence allocated to the Assembly *vis-à-vis* the Council. While the Convention recognizes that the principal function of the Assembly is "to establish general policies"[214] and the main function of the Council is to establish "specific policies",[215] there is no legal means of invalidating the adoption and implementation of specific policies by the Council which are inconsistent with the general policies laid down by the Assembly.[216] More concretely, a situation could be imagined where the specific rules, regulations and procedures adopted by the Council relating to activities in the Area may be contrary to the general policies adopted by the Assembly which, under the Convention, has the power to consider and approve these rules,

---

209 *See* Art. 158(4), CLOS.
210 Doc. WG21/2, IV Platzoder, *supra* note 110, at 375.
211 *Report of US Delegation*, Eighth Session (Resumed), in *supra* note 157, at 327.
212 Paolillo, *op. cit.* 227 and 250, makes the apt observation that the list of powers under Article 162 (2) exhausts the letters of the alphabet.
213 Address of US Ambassador Stevenson, *supra* note 124, at 348.
214 Art. 160(1), CLOS.
215 Art. 162(1), CLOS.
216 Paolillo, *op. cit.* 248-249.

regulations and procedures;²¹⁷ pending approval by the Assembly or amendment by the Council, these rules, regulations and procedures as adopted by the Council shall remain in effect and be applied provisionally.²¹⁸

A third and final stage in the progressive impoverishment of the principle of sovereign equality in the Authority refers to the pivotal issue of decision-making in the Council. Once it was determined that the real center of political power in the ISA was with the Council, intensive negotiations gravitated on the problem of how this paramount power was to be distributed within this organ. Efforts to untangle this difficult problem were, specifically, addressed at the twin issues of composition and voting in the Council. The resolution or non-resolution of these issues spelled out the fate of UNCLOS III.

The composition of the Council was an issue that directly emanated from the recognition that the Council was to represent special interests. The ICNT contemplated a Council of 36 members divided equally into the category of members representing special interests and the category of members chosen on the basis of equitable geographical distribution.²¹⁹ While the make-up of the second mentioned category did not present any difficulties, the composition of the category representing interest groupings proved more controversial. For instance, although three groups of countries – the Group of 77, the Socialist States, and the industrialized States – were given permanent representation as special economic interests, the less industrialized States, consisting of countries like Austria, Finland, Spain and Sweden, complained that they were underrepresented.²²⁰ However, their attempts to increase the size of the Council failed, leaving them with no choice but to accept the system of 'common heritage' representation for the sake of saving a fragile consensus.²²¹

The issue of guaranteed representation of groups of countries, either on a geographical or special interest basis, was not as insoluble as the problem of guaranteed representation of *specific* countries. What comes to mind in this case was the insistence by the United States that it be given a guaranteed seat

---

217 Art. 160(f)(ii), CLOS.
218 Art. 162 (2)(o)(ii), CLOS.
219 Art. 159(1), ICNT. *See also* Art. 308(3), CLOS, on the constitution of the First Council after entry into force of the Convention.
220 *See* Mahmoudi, *op. cit.* 263-264.
221 *See* Doc. A/CONF.62/L.43 (29 August 1979), para. 21, explaining why certain special interests – like island States, countries with migrant workers, and the less industrialized among the developed States – should be accommodated in the framework of Council composition established in the revised ICNT.

in the Council. In principle guaranteed representation of a specific country in the Council is inconsistent with the communitarian idea of equality of access to the common heritage. Even the traditional "freedom of the seas" principle, in theory, does not admit of the notion which accords preferential treatment to any particular State in the use and enjoyment of the high seas. Nevertheless, the desire of the US for a guaranteed seat was duly accommodated by the provision[222] which gave each interest and regional group entitled to representation the right to select its own representatives.[223] It should, however, be recalled that in spite of this indirect arrangement to assure the US a guaranteed seat in the Council, the Reagan Administration subsequently expressed its displeasure over the solution arrived at of an indirectly guaranteed seat for the US.[224] The US had changed its mind. It wanted instead to have not merely a politically guaranteed seat but a legally recognized permanent seat in the Council. In other words, the State which championed the cause of non-discriminatory access to nodule wealth since the time the UN Seabed Committee embarked on its mandate[225] wanted a rule of positive discrimination in its favour! Without doubt, institutional discrimination in favour of the most powerful country with respect to resources declared as common heritage of humanity was an enormous demand. Although the developing countries, especially the Africans, were against the institution of permanent seats in the Council as much as they were opposed to weighted voting and veto,[226] the guaranteed permanent seat of the US, as unquestionably "the largest consumer"[227] of metals derived from manganese nodules,[228] was agreed upon during the last days of the Conference. Still, it is well known that this concession was not good enough for the Reagan Administration. The alleged failure of the Convention to assure the US adequate

---

222 *See* Art. 161(2)(c), CLOS.
223 Schmidt, *op. cit.* 184-185; *Report of the US Delegation*, Ninth Session (Resumed) 1980, in *supra* note 157, at 435.
224 *See Report of US Delegation*, 1981 Tenth Session (Resumed), *supra* note 157, at 515.
225 "There shall be no discrimination in the availability of the deep ocean floor for exploration and use by all States and their nationals in accordance with international law." US Draft Resolution containing statement of principles concerning the deep ocean floor. Doc. A/AC.135/25, Ad Hoc SBC Rep at 54.
226 *See* Schmidt, *op. cit.* 183.
227 Art. 161(1)(a), CLOS.
228 Sanger, *op. cit.* 184; Mahmoudi, *op. cit.* 274; Schmidt, *op. cit.* 185-186.

representation in the Council was one reason given by the US for voting against the 1982 Convention.[229]

With respect to the rules on voting to be followed in the Council, the Convention embodies a unique voting system that attempted to bridge the negotiating positions of the Group of 77 and the industrialized countries.[230] It would seem that the view of the Group of 77 that all members of the Council should have equal votes, *i.e.*, there should be no weighted vote and no veto, could not possibly have been reconciled with the position of the industrialized countries which supported standard weighted voting in the Council proportional to the economic and technological power of States represented therein. The WG-21 easily reached a consensus that the traditional veto system as known in the United Nations was not acceptable.[231] The WG-21 also reached the conclusion that the proposal to establish a system of "chambered voting"[232] which would allow identified interest categories to veto or block Council decisions, was widely rejected.[233] The impasse on weighted voting was less easy to crack.

The scheme of voting in the Council preferred by the developing countries was straightforward: a simple majority vote for the adoption of procedural decisions and a two-thirds majority vote for substantive decisions.[234] However, the opposition of the developing countries to giving weighted votes to either special interest or geographic groupings in the Council did not mean that they did not recognize the need for some form of protection for the various special interests represented in the Council.[235] The need to protect special interests,

---

229 *See* Statements of US Ambassador Malone, *Report of the US Delegation*, *supra* note 157, at 559 & 596.
230 For a review of the voting procedure in the Council, *see* Paolillo, *op. cit.* 233-242; Mahmoudi, *op. cit.* 275-278.
231 Doc. A/CONF.62/C.1/L.26, XII UNCLOS III Off Rec at 77.
232 The idea "Chambered voting", initially broached by the US in its 1970 Draft Treaty, *supra* note 63, denotes decision-making based on double majorities, where in addition to an overall majority, a majority should also be attained in any of the special interest categories in the Council. For an account of the negotiations concerning "chambered voting" *see* Doc. NG3/2, in X UNCLOS III Off Rec at 78-80; *Report of US Delegation*, 1980, Ninth Session, *supra* note 157, at 433, 435-436; Schmidt, *op. cit.* 179.
233 Doc. A/CONF.62/C.1/L.26.
234 Paolillo, *op. cit.* 233.
235 Doc. NG 3/2 at 79 ; *Cf. Report of US Delegation*, 1980, Ninth Session, *supra* note 157, at 380.

in principle, follows from the concession made by Group of 77 in the ISNT to establish a system of special interest representation in the Council. The problem which confronted the WG-21 was, therefore, the mutual accommodation of the need to protect special interests, as conceded by the Group of 77, and the requirement of the industrialized countries for them to be able to prevent decisions in the Council adverse to their economic and political interests.[236]

The reason why the industrialized countries took the bottom-line negotiating position that argued for their ability to prevent or veto inimical Council decisions is apparent: since the detailed rules for a seabed mining regime negotiated thus far (and eventually incorporated in the Convention) were already in their favour, i.e., the right of assured access had been effectively secured constitutionally, they simply needed to possess the voting facility to prevent the substantive rules from being changed. The voting system, from the standpoint of the developed countries, should therefore offer them a procedural devise to preserve the regime (or, the "default" regime) and shield it from unwarranted modifications that could potentially be introduced by way of the derivative law of the ISA. There was no need for affirmative action on the part of the Council to sustain the regime of assured access that was already grafted into the constitutional framework of the ISA.[237]

The pragmatic solution that reconciled the "one State, one vote with provision for protection of special interests" stance of the Group of 77 and the "blocking/veto vote" position of the industrialized States was found in the identification of a list of "special or sensitive issues."[238] What are those concerns meant to protect the special interests of the industrialized countries and at the same time are also the concerns which the industrialized States would seek a blocking vote? The so-called "three-tiered" system of majority voting was the answer to this problem – the result of a breakthrough in the negotiations on this list in 1980.[239] Under this system, the majority vote required for the purpose of taking substantive decisions in the Council would depend on the degree of "sensitivity" of the substantive question involved. Three kinds of majorities are envisioned depending on the sensitivity of the decision to be taken:[240] for "least sensitive" questions, a two-thirds majority of members

---

236 *Id.*, 433-436.
237 *Cf.* Schmidt, *op. cit.* 184.
238 Doc. A/CONF.62/C.1/L.26.
239 *See* Schmidt, *op. cit.* 182-184.
240 Art. 161(8), CLOS.

present and voting; for "less sensitive" questions, three-four majority of members present and voting; and for "sensitive" questions, by consensus[241] but with provision for conciliation if this was not initially achieved.[242]

Matters under the least sensitive category of issues include those relating to the general administration of the ISA (which range from reviewing payments by and to the ISA to entering into agreements with the UN or other international organization), adoption of directives for the enterprise, requesting advisory opinions, and recommending a system of compensation or other measures of economic assistance and adjustment to developing countries adversely affected by activities in the area. Most of the decisions calling for the adoption of "specific policies" by the Council, however, fall under the second category of less sensitive issues. Notably, decisions concerning the supervision and coordination of the implementation of Part XI would require a three-fourths majority vote. Finally, attention should be drawn to the decisions requiring consensus. Five important questions appertain to this category:[243] (1) the taking of measures to protect adversely affected developing land-based producers; (2) recommending rules, regulations and procedures for the equitable sharing of benefits derived from activities in the Area; (3) adopting and provisionally applying rules, regulations and procedures relating to activities in the Area and the financial management and internal administration of the ISA; (4) adopting amendments to the Convention, and (5) *disapproving* plans of work recommended for approval by the Legal and Technical Commission[244] and previously subjected to a conciliation procedure in the Council.[245] Decision-making by consensus concerning the last mentioned item, not surprisingly, was devised in order to restrict the exercise of discretion by the Council in denying access.

---

241 "Consensus" is defined as "absence of any formal objection." Art. 161(8)(e), CLOS.
242 For a discussion of the three-tiered system, *see* Mahmoudi, *op. cit.* 275-278; Paolillo, *op. cit.* 233-237.
243 *See* Art. 161(8)(d) and Art. 162(2)(j)(i), CLOS.
244 The Legal and Technical Commission is an organ of the Council, Art. 163(1), performing various tasks to assist the Council discharge its functions under the Convention, including the important function of granting access. *See* Art. 165, CLOS.
245 The Convention is silent on the possibility of a recourse to voting in case of failure to secure consensus, when this is called for. Some authors see this as a potential source of paralysis in the Council's decision-making system. Paolillo, *op. cit.* 240-241; Mahmoudi, *op. cit.* 278; Sanger, *op. cit.* 184. *Cf. Report of the US Delegation, 1980, supra* note 157, at 434-436.

419

In sum, applicants with the qualifications set forth in the Convention will have assured access to the Area.[246]

Short of explicitly recognizing the principle that the industrialized States should be able to defeat Council decisions inimical to their interests, the Convention adopts a complex voting system that effectively grants minority groups in the Council, in this particular case the industrialized countries, the power to veto decisions affecting the most vital interest of these countries in the regime, *i.e.*, assured access. "Rare indeed will be those situations where a determined minority would not be able to halt an action to which it is opposed, given the Council composition."[247]

But the veto or blocking vote has been described as a "double-bladed sword"[248] available not only to the industrialized countries but to the developing countries as well. This conclusion arises from the very nature of consensus as a decision-making technique, which the G-77 accepted "because it does not discriminate among nations."[249] Decision-making by consensus-oriented rules is afterall consistent with the "international law of social interdependence" advocated by the developing countries.[250] Thus, notwithstanding the fact that the constitutional dice of assured access, so to speak, had been loaded in favor of the industrialized States, a parity of voting power is established in circumstances where the Council needs to take affirmative action on questions relating to access. The institutionalization of equality between rich and poor countries in this limited sense, hardly a victory for the cause of global amelioration that proceeds from an action-oriented Common Heritage regime, again invited the displeasure of the Reagan Administration. Just as the finely tuned compromise on the voting system was about to see the light of day, the negotiating position of the US drastically changed, largely for ideological reasons.[251] In addition to its earlier demand for a "blocking vote", the new requirement of the US was a decision-making system which "should provide

---

246 Paolillo, *op. cit.* 240. *Cf.* Schmidt, *op. cit.* 184 reporting that the voting system was based on optimistic assumptions held by US negotiators that the PrepCom will succeed in producing rules and regulations that would obviate the need for affirmative action on the part of the Council.
247 *A Quiet Revolution* (Department of Public Information, United Nations, 1984) at 46.
248 Engo, *op. cit.* 46.
249 Quoted in Morell, *op. cit.* 128.
250 *See* Pinto, *supra* note 174, at 227.
251 *See* Schmidt, *op. cit.* 257-260.

that, on issues of highest importance to a nation [*i.e.*, the US], that nation will have affirmative influence on the outcome."[252] Without doubt, had the international community acquiesced to this extreme demand, the result would have been the granting to some self-appointed States the power to exercise sovereignty or sovereign rights in the Area under the institutional cover of the ISA!

In conclusion, the meticulously negotiated decision-making system for the ISA as outlined in the 1982 Convention on the Law of the Sea had been molded to the narrow technical requirements of assured access. The strategic steps taken at the UNCLOS III to secure the imperative of assured access – from restricting the scope of discretion by the organs of the Authority, especially the Assembly, to suppressing the effective exercise of initiative by the majority of developing countries in the Council – amply illustrate the predominance of the industrialized countries' agenda with respect to the evolution and further development of the seabed regime. Still, collective decision-making under the framework of the Convention contained some egalitarian features. The "three-tiered" majority system of decision-making in the Council is a particularly notable expression of mutuality and equality in international law, representing an advance in the progressive institutionalization of the new law of the sea, specifically, and of international law, generally.[253]

Unfortunately, the entire structure of decision-making developed in Part XI of the Convention was repudiated as "fundamentally flawed"[254] by a few industrialized States, led by the United States. Worse, the detailed and carefully-crafted compromises on the institutional regime in Part XI – compromises which worked largely in favour of the industrialized States and which these countries themselves had a big hand in shaping – were considered as the ultimate incarnation of the Third World's New International Economic Order.[255] The adoption of a Reciprocating States Agreement by the industrialized countries meant, among other things, that they were not prepared to share with the rest of the international community, even only minimally, the power to decide the present and future disposition of the common heritage of humanity. On a more basic psychological level, the rejection by the industrialized countries of the insti-

---

252 Statement of US Ambassador Malone, 23 February 1982, *Reports of US Delegation*, *supra* note 157, at 560. *See also* Doc. A/CONF.62/L.121 (13 April 1982).
253 *See* Pinto, *supra* Chap. II note 293.
254 J. Breaux, "The Case Against the Convention" in Koers and Oxman, *op. cit.* 10-14.
255 *Cf.* Schmidt, *op. cit.* 248, 259 & 308.

tutional regime in Part XI of the Convention, betrays a deep-seated distrust against the institutions that promote universal control and democratic participation by developing States in international organization.[256] The assumption was that inter-state relations *should* continue to be governed by the values of individualism, co-existence and realist power play in international law. Unilateralism could not but have undermined – philosophically and practically, the Convention's institutional regime for deep seabed mining, including whatever enfeebled institutional expression had been given to the Common Heritage of Humanity principle in the Convention. The net result of the impasse on Part XI as a consequence of the defection of the US and its allies from the Convention regime was the retrogression of the international community back to the position where it started in 1970. After the adoption of the 1982 Convention the international community was still hoping that "an international regime applying to the area and its resources and including appropriate international machinery to give effect to [the Declaration of Principles Resolution] provisions shall be established by an international treaty of a universal character, generally agreed upon."[257]

C. THE 1994 IMPLEMENTATION AGREEMENT: UNIVERSALITY AND SACRIFICE IN THE LAW OF THE SEA

The confrontation between two institutional regimes for deep seabed mining in the 1980s, involving the regime implemented by the PrepCom under the 1982 Convention, on the one hand, and the Reciprocating States regime, on the other, demonstrates a curious turn of events in the history of seabed politics. It will be recalled that the deep seabed problem began with the debate in the US between those who advocated internationalization based on the Common Heritage of Humanity concept and those who defended a "flag nations" or national control approach to seabed mining. The adoption in 1970 of the Declaration of Principles Resolution shifted the emphasis of the debate to the terms of international control; the contestants involved were those who wanted maxi-

---

256 "...my concept of manoeuvering in an organization could in fact be destroyed if the organization is too large. In the Council I can see effective coalitions building; in the Assembly I see mob voting." L. Ratiner, quoted in Sanger, *op. cit.* 183.

257 Para. 9, Declaration of Principles Resolution.

mum international control to meet the multi-dimensional objectives of the Common Heritage of Humanity principle, on the one hand, and those who preferred a minimalist regime of international control sufficient to realize the "right" of some States to assured access to manganese nodules, on the other. After the adoption of the 1982 Convention on the Law of the Sea, the controversy was refocussed on a new tract altogether. This time the battle was fought between those who supported a rough but widely accepted international regime of assured access exclusively under the framework of Part XI of the Convention, as described above, and those who wanted to pursue the same goal of assured access but under national legislation coordinated under a reciprocating States regime concluded by a few industrialized States.[258]

The reason why the industrialized countries denounced Part XI of the Convention is summed up in the six objectives of the United States which that country alleged were not met by Part XI.[259] The US wanted a regime that

- Will not deter development of any deep seabed mineral resources to meet national and world demand;
- Will assure national access to these resources by current and future qualified entities to enhance US security of supply; to avoid monopolization of the resources by the operating arm of the international Authority, and to promote the economic development of the resources;

---

258 See *Agreement Concerning Interim Arrangements Relating to Polymetallic Nodules of the Deep Seabed among France, Federal Republic of Germany, United Kingdom, and the United States*, 2 Sept 1982, 21 ILM 950-962 (1982) and modified by the *Provisional Understanding Regarding Deep Seabed Matters among Belgium, Federal Republic of Germany, France, Italy, Japan, the Netherlands, the United Kingdom and the United States*, 3 Aug 1984, 23 ILM 1354-1360 (1984). The national legislation coordinated by these two Agreements purport to justify seabed mining as a freedom of the high seas. It will be noted that even signatories to the 1982 Convention, *e.g.*, France [for the defense of the position of France as signatory to both the Convention and the Reciprocating States Agreement, *see* P. Manin, "The Viability of a Dual Approach: The French Position" in R. Krueger & S. Riesenfeld, *The Developing Order of the Oceans* 206-213 (LSI, 1985)], are parties to the 1984 Reciprocating States Agreement. The position of the G-77 is that the Reciprocating States regime is subversive of the 1982 Convention and is "wholly illegal." For an overview of the debate *see* Schmidt, *op. cit.* 277-288; Krueger & Riesenfeld, *op. cit.*

259 *See* Statement of US Ambassador Malone, 30 April 1982, UNCLOS III Plenary, in *Reports of the US Delegation, supra* note 157, at 594-597.

- Will provide a decision-making role in the deep seabed regime that fairly reflects and effectively protects political and economic interests and financial contributions of participating States;
- Will not allow for amendments to come into force without approval of the participating States, including in our case the advise and consent of the Senate;
- Will not set other undesirable precedents for international organizations; and
- Will be likely to receive the advise and consent of the Senate. In this regard, the Convention should not contain provisions for the mandatory transfer of private technology and participation by and funding for national liberation movements.[260]

A point-by-point refutation of these claims had been undertaken elsewhere and will not be repeated here.[261] It would suffice to state, following Professor Borgese, that the overall complaint of the US against the 1982 Convention was not founded on a technically accurate appreciation of the Convention but was simply politically and ideologically motivated: the whole idea of the Common Heritage of Humanity and of a new type of relationship with the developing countries was opprobrious to the Reagan Administration.[262] Analysis of developments leading to the US rejection of the 1982 Convention from a domestic politics standpoint also reveals that the above objections were maintained as a pretext to justify the pursuit of the old "flag nations" approach to nodule mining through a reciprocating States regime on the part of a government that was determined to establish an alternative seabed regime.[263]

As some authorities had predicted, the legal framework to nodule mining embodied in the Reciprocating States regime did not succeed in attracting commercial ventures in the deep seabed under its auspices.[264] For one thing, banks were certainly not willing to extend financing to potential seabed projects that are politically clouded and legally infirm, or not minimally possessed with the requisite security of title which could only have been conferred by an inter-

---

260 Statement by President Reagan, 29 January 1982, text in *Reports of the US Delegation, supra* note 157, at 554-555.
261 *See* Morell, *op. cit.* Chap. 4.
262 Borgese, *supra* note 178, at 98. *See also* comment of Elliot Richardson that "the foremost objections were to the very idea of a multilateral body purporting to exercise supranational regulatory authority", *supra* note 108, at 12-13.
263 *See* Schmidt, *op. cit.* Chap. 7 & 277-288.
264 *See e.g.*, Borgese, *supra* note 178, at 98-99; Schmidt, *op. cit.* 288; Morell, *op. cit.* 205.

national body.²⁶⁵ In contrast, the PrepCom had certainly succeeded in laying down a viable basis for activities in the Area through the registration of pioneer investors, which even included the multinational consortia that have been licensed by the industrialized countries under the reciprocating States regime. No one disputes the fact that the historic breakthrough in the registration of pioneer investors was due to the professionalism, flexibility and constructive approach which the PrepCom consistently displayed in discharging its mandate under Resolution II of the Final Act.²⁶⁶

The non-participation of a few industrialized States in the Convention regime did, however, pose problems concerning the maintenance of what the UN General Assembly has repeatedly referred to as the "unified character" of the 1982 Convention.²⁶⁷ For the overwhelming number of countries represented in the PrepCom, the danger lay less in the destruction of the "common heritage" framework to nodule mining under Part XI of the Convention through unilateral seabed mining regimes than in the unravelling of the delicately balanced package of compromises embodied in the entirety of the Convention itself, as a consequence of its non-ratification by the industrialized countries.²⁶⁸ Indeed, if some countries chose to stay out of the Convention altogether and persisted in their attitude of unilateralism not only with respect to activities in the Area but also with respect to the interpretation of the rule of law in the non-seabed portions of the Convention, the stability of the entire ocean order spelled out in the 1982 Convention and painstakingly negotiated in UNCLOS III was in grave danger. Was there not a distinct possibility that broad shelf States, for example, will likewise seek refuge in the same unilateralism in order abandon the obligation to share resources beyond their

---

265 Morell, *op. cit.* 205; Richardson, *supra* note 108, at 15.
266 *See* S. Nandan, "The United Nations Convention on the Law of the Sea: Resolving the Problems of Part XI" in Nordquist, *supra* note 108, at 57, 58-61; L.D.M. Nelson, "The Preparatory Commission for the International Sea-Bed Authority and the International Tribunal for the Law of the Sea: An Evaluation" in Wolfrum, *supra* note 5, 31 at 32-37; C. Maquieira, "Statement on the Implementation of resolution III of the Third United Nations Conference on the Law of the Sea by the Preparatory Commission for the International Sea-Bed Authority" in Wolfrum, *id.*, at 45-57.
267 *See* annual Law of the Sea resolutions of the UN General Assembly starting 1983, *e.g.*, Res. 38/59 A (14 Dec. 1983) and Res. 50/23 (5 Dec 1995).
268 *See* Jesus, *supra* note 5, at 22; *Cf.* E.D. Brown, *supra* Chap. II note 10, at 445-446.

Exclusive Economic Zone with the international community?[269] And for the same reason, would not the generality of coastal States be more readily predisposed to extend their functional and areal jurisdiction off-shore as a means of getting parity with the industrialized States – "creeping jurisdiction" to compensate for the "race to grab" by the powerful members of the international community? Simply put, the unilateral action of the industrialized States in the Area was one good reason why coastal States should be forced to abolish its precise limits altogether. This was the problematic situation that the UN General Assembly exactly sought to overcome as far back as 1970 when it called for the convening of a Third UN Conference on the Law of the Sea. There was no doubt that without the commitment of the industrialized countries to the Convention as a whole, and precisely because of their non-adherence to the 1982 Convention, the potential for legal chaos in the oceans akin to that obtaining in the 1960s has reached new heights, most assuredly to the prejudice of all States.

It was not at all clear whether the United States and its few allies throughout the 1980s completely understood the implications of their non-participation in the Convention, or their very partial commitment to the Convention, in this way. But the message that the "unified character" of the Convention must also be in the interest of the industrialized countries had to be delivered sooner or later.[270] The position firmly held by them that there can be two alternative regimes for the seabed coexisting with only one regime for all other matters under the law of the sea[271] was not sustainable;[272] there can be no "unitary" Convention on the law of the Sea alongside a dual system of competing seabed mining regimes. Either there is only one "unified" Convention on the Law of the Sea or there was none at all.

---

269 *See* Jesus, *id.*, at 23.

270 By 1988, scholars in the US were urging general adherence to the 1982 Convention to preserve the benefits deriving from the non-seabed portions of the Convention. *See Statement by Expert Panel: Deep Seabed Mining and the 1982 Convention on the Law of the Sea* 82 AJIL 363 (1988). *See also* G. Galdorski, "The United States and the Law of the Sea: Decade of Decision" in *The United States and the Law of the Sea Convention: The Cases Pro and Con* 7-71 (LSI Occasional Paper No. 38, 1994).

271 *See* Statement of US Ambassador Clingan UNCLOS III Plenary 192nd Meeting, 9 Dec 1982, *supra* Chap. IV note 217.

272 *Cf.* A. D'Amato, *An Alternative to the Law of the Sea Convention* 77 AJIL 281-285 (1983).

Protecting the unified character of the Convention entailed the affirmation of the wise counsel of the Convention that "the problems of ocean space are closely interrelated and need to be considered as a whole."[273] More specifically, it meant renewed efforts to realize the mandate of the Declaration of Principles Resolution that the regime for the seabed should be "established by an international treaty of a universal character, generally agreed upon."[274]

1. Towards a Universal Interest in the Universality of the Convention

The Group of 77 made a series of unilateral concessions in favor of the US and other industrialized countries during the last days of UNCLOS III in the hope of attracting universal support for the Convention.[275] These concessions, however, proved unavailing because the principal industrialized countries decided to stay out of the Convention regime anyway, to such an extent that the US even boycotted the Preparatory Commission. This notwithstanding, the quest for a unified and a universally accepted Convention remained an outstanding challenge to the Group of 77.

After the adoption of the 1982 Convention, major efforts on the part of the developing countries to convince the parties to the reciprocating States regime that the unified character of the Convention was worth saving occurred within the framework of PrepCom activities. The commitment to universality was demonstrated in various ways. For example, decision-making in the PrepCom was structured in such a way as to follow consensus techniques in the widest possible terms. The PrepCom/Group of 77 thus adopted a policy of practically giving full rights of participation to the observers in the PrepCom,[276] although Resolution I of the Final Act did not entitle observers to participate in the taking of decisions.[277] But it was in the complex process of registering pioneer investors under Resolution II that the PrepCom demonstrated its abiding commitment to universality. By accommodating the interests of all potential pioneer investors, including the multinational consortia of the industrialized

---

273 3rd Preambular para., CLOS.
274 Para. 9, Res. 2749.
275 *See* Report of the President of the Conference, Doc. A/CONF.62/L.141 (29 April 1982).
276 Intervention of Ambassador Jose Luis Jesus, in Wolfrum *supra* note 5, at 495-496.
277 Resolution I, Final Act, CLOS at 175.

countries licensed under the reciprocating States regime, the PrepCom proved that the task of registration could be responsibly carried out and fulfilled to the satisfaction of all parties concerned, including the non-signatory States to the Convention.[278] Again, concessions on the part of the Group of 77 were involved here inasmuch as the successful registration of pioneer investors with overlapping claims meant departures from, or "creative interpretations" of, the strictures in the Convention regime.[279]

With the registration of pioneer investors in the late 1980s securely in place under the Convention regime, bold steps were further taken by the Group of 77 to make the Convention universally acceptable. In September 1989 the developing countries opened a new door towards universality, with the announcement of an invitation to all concerned States, especially the United States, for a dialogue with a view to resolving the latter's outstanding concerns on the Convention. Chairman Kapumpa of the Group of 77 declared:

> ... I wish to state that the Group of 77 has always been ready, and continues to be ready, to hold discussions, within the context of the Preparatory Commission, with any delegation, or group of delegations, on any issues relating to the Convention and the work of the Preparatory Commission.
>
> Our willingness to discuss is born out of a genuine desire to ensure the universality of the Convention, because the universality of the Convention has always been the objective of the Group of 77. Any delegation, or group of delegations, be they currently involved in the work of the Preparatory Commission or not, whether signatories or non-signatories to the Convention, are welcome to open a dialogue with the Group of 77.
>
> This we declare without any pre-conditions, other than that those willing to talk must indicate a positive approach to serious and meaningful talks. This has been our position and shall continue to be our position.[280]

---

278 Nandan, *supra* note 278, at 58 & 61. *See also infra.* note 279.
279 *See* Maquieira, *op. cit.*, and intervention of Amb. Ballah, in Wolfrum, *supra* note 5, at 77. For an assessment of the achievements of the PrepCom from a skeptical perspective, *see* E.D. Brown, *supra* Chap. II note 10, at 448-456.
280 Text in LOS Bulletin 55 (No. 15, May 1990). For further discussion on the role of the Group of 77 in opening avenues for dialogue regarding Part XI, *see* L.D.M. Nelson, "Issues in Amending Part XI of the LOS Convention: Renewing the Dialogue" in M. Nordquist (Ed.), *15th Annual Seminar of the Center for Oceans Law and Policy, supra* Chap. II note 11, at 51-52 (Univ. of Va., 1991); W.S. Scholz, "The Consistent United States Policy for Acceptable Seabed Mining Provisions in a Universally Accepted Law of the Sea Convention" in Nordquist,

This historic move by the Group of 77 to welcome a dialogue with the US in any forum[281] was endorsed by the UN General Assembly which adopted a Resolution in 1989 inviting all States "to make renewed efforts to facilitate universal participation in the Convention."[282] On the basis of this Resolution, UN Secretary General Perez de Cuellar launched the initiative for informal consultations on outstanding issues relating to Part XI on 19 July 1980.[283] Notwithstanding these gestures, the United States did not show interest to earnestly engage in the dialogue and find solutions to what that country considered were its problems concerning Part XI of the Convention.[284]

Eventually, the United States under the newly-elected Clinton Administration adopted a policy of "reengagement"[285] and fully supported the Secretary General's informal consultations beginning in April 1993.[286] With the active participation of the US in the dialogue concerning outstanding issues relating to Part XI, the road was paved for the realization of a universally accepted Convention on the Law of the Sea. The 1994 Implementation Agreement, which came out of the Secretary General's informal consultations, represents a significant

---

supra note 108, 51, at 53-54.

281 The Group of 77 preferred that the forum for dialogue concerning Part XI should be the PrepCom, *see* statement of PrepCom Chairman J.L. Jesus, *supra* note 5, but maintained an open-ended view on this question, *see* Intervention of Amb. Kapumpa, in Wolfrum, *supra* note 5, at 503-504. The US strongly held to the view that the PrepCom could not "fix" Part XI, *see* Statement of US President on Withholding of United States Funds, 18 WEEKLY COMP Pres Doc 1674 (30 Dec 1982); L.D.M. Nelson, *supra* note 280, at 55.

282 Res. 44/26 (20 Nov 1989). *See* intervention of Amb. Zegers Santa Cruz, in Wolfrum, *supra* note 5, at 493.

283 M. Hayashi, "Effect of the Entry into Force of the UN Convention on the Law of the Sea" in Koh, Beckman & Chia Lin Sien, *supra* Chap. II note 237, at 72. The informal consultations were continued by UN Secretary General Boutros Boutros-Ghali in 1992.

284 Nandan, in Nordquist *supra* note 280, at 236, 238.

285 Colson, in Norquist, *supra* note 108, at 21-28.

286 W. Scholz, *The Law of the Sea Convention and the Business Community: The Seabed Mining Regime and Beyond* 7 GEORGETOWN INTL ENVIR L REV 675, at 678; C. Joyner, *The United States and the New Law of the Sea* 27 ODIL 41, at 46 (1996).

milestone in the quest for universality by the international community as a whole.[287]

2. Stability and Change in the Deep Seabed Regime

In considering the substantive content of the Implementation Agreement, it would be appropriate to first of all consider the general background of events that induced the search, which began in the late 1980s, for a new approach to Part XI. For this purpose, attention is called to the two generally acknowledged factors which have contributed to an acceptable renegotiation of Part XI of the Convention. The first factor, just referred to, is the emergence of a political will on the part of the international community to achieve "universal participation" in the Convention. As the UN General Assembly noted "the objective of universal participation in the Convention may best be achieved by the adoption of an agreement relating to the implementation of Part XI."[288] The second factor that accounts for the modifications made in Part XI is identified in the 1994 Implementation Agreement as the "political and economic changes, including in particular a growing reliance on market principles."[289] We may properly refer to these factors as the "subjective" and "objective" reasons, respectively, for the adjustment of Part XI of the Convention. The relationship between these two main factors or reasons for the renegotiation of the Convention regime deserves to be examined closely. As it will become clear, the "subjective", rather than the "objective", reason was the essential driving force behind the recent modifications of Part XI of the Convention.

It is easy to appreciate the role of the "political will" to achieve a universally accepted Convention in the renegotiation of Part XI. The subtlety and force of this subjective reason is delivered by the cliché "where there's a will, there's a way." But the "objective" reason for renegotiating Part XI is less easy to grasp. What, it may be asked, is in the "political and economic changes, in-

---

287 *See* "Report of the Secretary General: Consultations of the Secretary-General on outstanding issues relating the deep seabed mining provisions of the United Nations Convention on the Law of the Sea", in LoS BULLETIN 1-5 (Special Issue IV, 16 Nov 1994).
288 9th preambular para., Res. 28/263 (28 July 1994); preambular para. 6 & 7, 1994 Implementation Agreement.
289 6th preambular para., Res. 48/263; 5th preambular para., 1994 Implementation Agreement.

cluding market-oriented approaches" which supervened in the 1980s that *necessitated* a renegotiation of Part XI?

The "objective" reason was initially identified by the Secretary General as follows:

> ... in the eight years that had elapsed since the Convention was adopted, certain significant political and economic changes had occurred which had had a marked effect on the regime for deep seabed mining contained in the Convention. Prospects for commercial mining of deep seabed minerals had receded into the next century, which was not what was envisaged during the negotiations at the Third United Nations Conference on the Law of the Sea. The general economic climate had been transformed as a result of the changing perception with respect to the roles of the public and private sectors. There was a discernible shift towards a more market-oriented economy.[290]

There are thus two developments related to the "objective" reason for renegotiation: (1) the fact that commercial seabed mining had become a remote, if not an improbable, prospect, and (2) the ascendancy of market approaches to economic development world-wide. Was it necessary and urgent to renegotiate Part XI on the basis of these developments? If so, how were their various requirements translated into the stipulations of the 1994 Implementation Agreement?

The consensus that nodule mining activities will not take place until well into the future, if at all,[291] must surely have wrecked havoc and devastation to the theory of "assured access" developed for the mining regime in Part XI of the Convention. The economic feasibility of nodule mining, which was assumed in UNCLOS III, provided a justification to spell out the details for a regime of assured access which the industrialized countries strove hard to establish in UNCLOS III. Now that this economic rationale had vanished, the narrow regime of seabed mining in the Convention, particularly the rules related to the post-exploration phase of activities in the Area, had all but become a paper regime, with the least chance of ever becoming operational. The absurdity of legally assured access in an economic environment that precludes this access puts into question the very normative foundation of Part XI as perceived by

---

290 *See* Report of the Secretary-General, *supra* note 287, para. 2.
291 Statement of Expert Panel, *supra* note 270, at 363.

the developed States, subjecting it to the crisis of *reductio ad absurdum*.[292] It is, therefore, not surprising why there were suggestions made in the early 1990s to "split" Part XI from the rest of the Convention, *i.e,* "separate Part XI from the rest of the Law of the Sea Convention, to move forward with ratifying the remaining provisions of the treaty, and to agree to a renegotiation of Part XI."[293] The proponents of "splitting" did not appreciate any redeeming value to Part XI of the Convention outside of its provisions that secured the "right" of assured access. Professor T. Treves, thus, asked: "If there is no sea-bed mining, what is the purpose of the Authority?"[294]

It will be noted that all along, the impact of changes in the economic climate for seabed mining was viewed differently by the developing States. Reiterating their interpretation of the Common Heritage of Humanity principle as requiring institutions representing and acting on behalf of humanity as a whole, they argued that the proper response to economic conditions affecting seabed mining lay not in "splitting" or "freezing" Part XI but in allowing the ISA to deal with the challenge posed by the shifting economics of seabed mining. Part XI is not just about the *function* of seabed mining but about the *functions* of the ISA as a representative or embodiment of humanity.[295] Thus, the "ameliorative" as opposed to the "acquisitive" model of institutional development was reiterated in a very decisive way. Any renegotiation of Part XI in light of changing economic conditions should, therefore, have to consider how to make the ISA a viable institution in spite of the dim prospects of commercial seabed activities – "viable in the sense of accomplishing the goals for which it was created and viable also in the sense of generating resources that

---

292 *Cf.* T. Iguchi, "Perspectives on Proposed Revisions in Part XI" in Nordquist & Moore, *op. cit.* 133: "... some provisions of Part XI and related Annexes are a nightmare.... The difficulties, as we all know by now, were created by the lack of understanding on the part of the Group of 77 regarding the problems of deep seabed mining and the position of pioneer investors...."
293 J.N. Moore, "Renegotiating Part XI: Ensuring an Effective Seabed Mining Regime" in Nordquist, *supra* note 280, 239 at 246; A. Sagurian, "Excision of the Deep Seabed Mining Provisions from the 1982 Law of the Sea Convention" in J.M. van Dyke, D. Zaelke & G. Hewison (eds.), *Freedom for the Seas in the 21st Century* 379-397, at 386 (1993). *See also* intervention of Prof. Treves defending the "splitting" concept, in Wolfrum, *supra* note 5, at 505.
294 *Id.*, at 522.
295 Kapumpa, in Wolfrum, *supra* note 5, at 522. *See* Paolillo, *op. cit.* 182-188.

could be shared among all nations."²⁹⁶ On this view, streamlining the elaborate provisions of Part XI, adjusting the institutional regime established in Part XI on the basis of maximum effectiveness, and maintaining the normative framework under the Common Heritage of Humanity principle, are some consequences flowing out of a meaningful consideration of the changing economics of nodule mining.

In regard of the second "objective" development affecting Part XI – namely, the growing world-wide reliance on market principles – it is interesting to note that what had come under intense attack in the wake of this development was the entire notion of the "Enterprise", the operational arm of the ISA. The US in particular sought to eliminate the institution of the Enterprise on the ground that "it is an outdated relic of the past which is inconsistent with the growing acceptance of free market principles."²⁹⁷ As in UNCLOS III, the Enterprise was seen by the US as the evil embodiment of the Third World's demand for a New International Economic Order. With "market" approaches in currency, the argument was made that the Enterprise could now be dispensed with because the NIEO is "totally dead."²⁹⁸ The historical association of the NIEO to the international oil cartels in the 1970s is valid,²⁹⁹ but the assumed antithetical relationship between market principles and the institution of the Enterprise is perhaps reading too much in the negotiation history of Part XI. The Enterprise in the context of a unitary system of exploitation can be made to operate on the basis of market principles,³⁰⁰ but the Enterprise in a "parallel system" is truly a dirigistic nightmare.³⁰¹ The US mining companies were more forthright in their reasons for opposing the Enterprise as an institution for the 1990s: it was a formidable rival that had to be obliterated in the re-

---

296 Jesus, *supra* note 5, at 27. "In the end, what matters most is that the resources of the common heritage of mankind be exploited in such a way as to generate the highest income possible for the benefit of all States." *Ibid.*
297 Scholz, *supra* note 286, at 683.
298 Richardson, *supra* note 108, at 8.
299 E. Richardson, Remarks in 7 GEORGETOWN INT ENV L REV at 642 (1994). *See supra* Chap. II, note 25.
300 Borgese, *supra* note 159.
301 *See* P.N. Kirthisingha, *The Enterprise: An Expendable Triumph* 5 MARINE POLICY 252-256 (1982). *Cf.* Ogley, *op. cit.* at 245.

negotiations.³⁰² This opposition is now largely moot and academic, because an economic competitor cannot exist where there is no economy to begin with.

It is submitted that the campaign against the Enterprise *per se* had nothing to do with the increasing recognition of market approaches to economic and resource development. It bears reiterating that the idea of an operational arm for the ISA advanced by the Group of 77 at UNCLOS III was conceived as an organ that would monopolize resource activities in the area under a unitary regime – initially or permanently through joint undertakings with States and/or private enterprises.³⁰³ A congruence between the conduct of activities solely by or through the Enterprise and the carrying out activities in a free market economy is conceivable if, as Ambassador Zegers Santa Cruz argued, humanity is conceived as the owner of the resources in question. The ISA and the Enterprise – which will act on behalf of humanity, similar to the situation where the State acts on behalf of its nationals at the municipal level – will then be in the best position to develop a resource policy as well as general policy strategy for the area.³⁰⁴ However, the issue of "who owns" the seabed resources – an issue whose definitive resolution comes before a market-based solution to the issue "who may exploit such resources" can be meaningfully clarified – was successfully evaded by the industrialized countries at UNCLOS III. In truth, if one admits hypothetically the elimination of the private side of the parallel system, a free market system for activities in the Area could still be sustained.³⁰⁵

It is thus evident that what the US was seeking to eliminate in the renegotiation of Part XI was not the "Enterprise" as such but the very institution of the parallel system which that country was largely responsible in setting up at UNCLOS III. If successful, the result would have been not only the repudiation of the Kissinger compromise in the mid-1970s but also the absolute institutionalization of "assured access" as the sole basis for the regime to govern

---

302 *See* C. Welling, "The Views of the United States Ocean Mining Licensees on Trends in the Negotiation to Make the United Nations Convention on the Law of the Sea of 1982 Universally Acceptable" in Nordquist & Moore, *op. cit.* 255-263.
303 *See* Pinto, *supra* note 90, at 308.
304 Zegers Santa Cruz, in Wolfrum, *supra* note 5, at 517.
305 *See* Borgese, *supra* note 159. The triumph of economic liberalism at the national level during the 1980s did not mean complete *laissez-faire* policies but involved pervasive government interventions to encourage private sector and export-driven growth. *See* E.H. Preeg, *Traders in a Brave New World* 18-20 (1995.)

the Area. This would be a cruel irony, considering that "assured access" had just been indefinitely invalidated by the economics of seabed mining. It is not far fetched to conclude that the US objection to the Enterprise was inspired less by the dictates of a free market approach to resource management and development than the old political imperative of assured access to resources in the Area.[306]

The developing countries and all other States did not support the move to eliminate the Enterprise.[307] For the Group of 77, the Enterprise is the practical venue where all States, especially the developing countries, could participate in the commercial development of the Area through joint ventures in particular. It was also, more crucially, an important expression of the Common Heritage of Humanity principle which they wished to retain.[308] Rather than eliminate the Enterprise, members of the Group of 77 have proposed at the PrepCom to strengthen the Enterprise by reinterpreting the relationship between the Enterprise, on the one hand, and the Assembly and Council, on the other, so that the Enterprise will not have too many bosses as defined in the Convention.[309]

The "objective" reason for renegotiating Part XI thus offered an opportunity less to "split" Part XI than to modify it in the direction of promoting and consolidating the "common heritage" approach – rather than an "assured access" approach – to legal development in the Area. Neither the poor prospects of commercial seabed mining nor the ascendancy of market approaches to resource management could be seen as a warrant to further strengthen and institutionalize the concept of assured access that had pervaded the mining regime in Part XI. Instead, these developments raise a serious challenge to the relevance of the

---

306 The Implementation Agreement "guarantees the United States and other nations access to the mineral resources of the seabed on acceptable terms that will permit mining to take place when and if economic conditions warrant." W. Scholz, in Nordquist & Moore, *op. cit.* at 75.

307 The other industrialized countries did not favour the total elimination of the Enterprise on the ground that they could be able to prevent it from becoming operational anyway. Scholz, *supra* note 286, at 683.

308 K. Rattray, "Assuring Universality: Balancing the Views of the Industrialized and Developing Worlds" in Nordquist & Moore, *op. cit.* 55, at 59-60; L.F. Ballah, "The Universality of the 1982 Convention on the Law of the Sea: Common Heritage or Common Burden?" in Najeeb Al-Nauimi & R. Meese (Eds.), *International Legal Issues Arising Under the United Nations Decade of International Law* 339-365, at 362-363 (1995).

309 *See* Nelson, in Wolfrum, *supra* note 6, at 43.

ISA as an institution solely concerned with deep seabed mining, vindicating the doctrinal position of the developing countries in UNCLOS III that the ISA should have sufficient powers coextensive with its role as "trustee" of humanity in the management of the common heritage Area as a whole.

The tension between the "objective" reason for renegotiating Part XI and the "subjective" reason for the exercise should now be apparent. For while the objective reason supported the adjustment of Part XI in favor of the common heritage stance of the developing countries, the subjective reason – *i.e.*, the will to universalize participation in the Convention – required accommodating the views of the few non-signatory industrialized States to an adjusted Part XI to make it acceptable to them. If this is correct, another major concession on the part of the developing countries would have been made in the renegotiation of Part XI. This concession involved foregoing the objective grounds for adjusting Part XI so that the subjective reason for renegotiation – achieving universal participation in the Convention – would prevail.

That universality was to be the primordial goal of renegotiation is seen in the catalytic move by the Chairman of the Group of 77 in 1989, quoted above, to welcome a dialogue with States which have not participated in the Convention.[310] The aim, specifically, was to improve the existing provisions of Part XI "with a view to finding a suitable accommodation for the problems that the United States and other industrialized countries have."[311] When the Secretary General began his informal consultations on "outstanding issues" concerning Part XI, it was understood that the "outstanding issues" sought to be addressed were basically and fundamentally the outstanding issues as perceived by the industrialized countries.[312] The agenda on the table, in other words, was the renegotiation agenda of the industrialized States.

The developing countries recognized that renegotiating Part XI to achieve universality will be most likely a success if certain sacrifices were made on their part on two sets of substantive issues. The first relates to the non-seabed provisions of the Convention that were not to be opened up for discussion. Many developing countries had of course realized, as confirmed by the reports of the Secretary General issued during the early stages of the informal consul-

---

310 Rattray, *supra* note 308, at 57.
311 Jesus, *supra* note 5, 24.
312 Report of Secretary General, *supra* note 287, para. 1; D.H. Anderson, *Resolution and Agreement Relating to the Implementation of Part XI of the UN Convention on the Law of the Sea: A General Assessment* 55 ZaöRV 275, at 274 (1995).

tations,[313] that they had not significantly or materially benefitted from the non-seabed regimes of the Convention, chiefly from the institution of the EEZ. The explanation for this failure was elaborated later at UNCED generally, and Chapter 17 of Agenda 21, specifically: the framework of sustainable development and the concept "common but differentiated obligations" – both embodied in the 1982 Convention – did not provide for concrete obligations on the part of developed States to assist the international community realize a comprehensive and binding regime of international cooperation for sustainable development in the oceans.[314] The developing countries would have been in a legitimate position to demand from the industrialized countries, in exchange for a renegotiation of Part XI, a simultaneous renegotiation of the sustainable development provisions of the Convention to effect a strengthening of the regimes relating to international cooperation in the EEZ as expressed in Parts XII, XIII and XIV of the Convention. Such a demand by the developing countries to adjust the non-seabed provisions of the Convention for the purpose of bolstering the legal framework of sustainable development in the 1982 Convention could have been eminently just and reasonable in the context of the ascendancy of "sustainable development" approaches in the 1990s. But this demand was not pursued by the Group of 77 for the sake of "universality."

The second level of sacrifice incurred by the developing countries, which paved the way for an acceptable renegotiation of Part XI, relates to the interests of the developing countries in the seabed regime itself. As mentioned earlier, the indefinite postponement of commercial seabed mining operations on account of adverse economic conditions was in itself an excellent argument for a fundamental reorientation of the resources regime under Part XI in favor of an areal or territorial, as opposed to an extremely narrow functional, competence for the ISA. Since the adoption of the Convention in 1982, important scientific and commercial developments pertaining to sustainable development in the Area could not have escaped the Group of 77, which could have indeed provided justification for their insistence on a zonal or multifunctional definition of competence for the Authority as was done previously in the ISNT or ICNT. For example, biotechnology companies have been making significant revenues in

---

313 UN Doc. A/45/712 (16 Nov 1990) & Doc. A/46/722 (4 Dec 1991) entitled "Law of the Sea – Realization of benefits under the United Nations Convention on the Law of the Sea: Need of States in regard to development and management of ocean resources, and approaches for further action."

314 *See supra* Chap. II, Secs. E & F.

commercially exploiting unique life forms found in the Area.[315] These and other biodiversity resources of the deep seabed are as much a part of the common heritage of humanity as manganese nodules. And yet the ISA under the Convention was not provided with the power to manage these resources on behalf of humanity as a whole. A fresh look at the concept of international control under Part XI to render it a truly relevant and pivotal instrument for the sustainable development of the Area, as well as *all* resources in the Area, would have been a great advance for the international community. But this option – a golden opportunity to launch a fresh career for the Common Heritage of Humanity principle, or to install what Dr. James Morell describes as the peremptory requirement of a multilateral regulatory regime for common pool exhaustible resources[316] – was not pursued by the Group of 77, again for the sake of remaining true to their offer of achieving a universally accepted Convention on terms acceptable to the industrialized countries.

The scope of substantive discussions in the consultations held under the aegis of the Secretary General was defined by a list of "hard core" issues introduced by the United Kingdom.[317] These issues were:

1. Cost to State Parties
2. The Enterprise
3. Decision-making, particularly in the Council
4. The Review Conference
5. Transfer of Technology
6. Production Policy
7. Compensation Fund ("economic assistance") and
8. Financial terms of Contract.[318]

---

315 Communication from Professor William Burke to author, 21 October 1994. *See also* Glowka, *op.cit.*
316 *See* Morell, *op. cit.* 176-189. This *jus cogens* norm of multilateral control recalls the thesis of F. Christy, in *supra* Chap. III note 36, concerning the rational economic basis of international control of marine resources.
317 D.H. Anderson, *Efforts to Ensure Universal Participation in the United Nations Convention on the Law of the Sea* 42 ICLQ 654, at 657 (1993); E.M. Borgese, *Ocean Governance and the United Nations* 43 (1995).
318 It must be noted that a ninth item, "Environmental Considerations", was dropped from the list in 1992 since "it was no longer considered to be a controversial issue in the context of deep seabed mining." Report of the Secretary General, *supra* note 287, para. 9; L.D.M. Nelson, *The New Deep Seabed Mining Regime* 10 IJMCL 189, at 191 (1995). However, the topic resurfaced again at a relatively late stage

It is evident that not one of these issues was new in the context of international seabed negotiations. They were earlier raised by President Reagan as the unredressed concerns of the United States[319] defining the obstacles to ratification of the Convention by the industrialized countries.[320] However, these issues – no more and no less – were accepted by the international community as setting the definitive agenda for the renegotiation of Part XI. These were the same issues that were resolved to the satisfaction of the industrialized States in the 1994 Implementation Agreement.[321]

3. The 1994 Implementation Agreement as Process

For the developing countries, the commitment to a universal Convention did not only mean deference to the substantive terms of renegotiation, the framework of which was already drawn by the industrialized States. It also involved a readiness, especially on the part of the overwhelming number of developing States which have already ratified the Convention, to relinquish rights and obligations – substantive as well as procedural – that have already accrued in their favor as a result of ratification. What comes immediately to the fore in this connection are their normative expectations as States Parties to a package-deal Convention – a treaty that purportedly allows no reservations and exceptions.[322] There is no doubt that these legitimate expectations had to be abandoned. Also, the principle that Part XI of the Convention shall be modified only

---

in the consultations. D.H. Anderson, *Further Efforts to Ensure Universal Participation in the United Nations Convention on the Law of the Sea* 43 ICLQ 886-893, at 891 (1994). It is also interesting to note that there was a suggestion from the industrialized countries to delete the term "common heritage of mankind" from Part XI, but this was naturally rejected by the Group of 77. Conversation with Ambassador Hasjim Djalal, Dec. 1994.

319 Borgese, *supra* note 317, at 43; Nelson, *id.*, at 191; Hayashi, *supra* note 283, at 72.
320 *See* Anderson, *supra* note 317, at 654.
321 *See Law of the Sea Forum: the 1994 Agreement on the Implementation of the Seabed Provisions of the Convention on the Law of the Sea* 88 AJIL 687-714 (1994); Anderson, *supra* note 318, 886-893, esp. note 18 (1994); J.N. Moore, *The United Nations Convention on the Law of the Sea and the Rule of Law* 7 GEORGETOWN INT ENV L REV 645, at 648 (1995); J. Koch, "Revisions in Part XI: A Necessary Compromise" in Nordquist & Moore, *op. cit.* 151, at 152.
322 *See* Arts. 309 & 310, CLOS.

according to the review and amendment clauses of the 1982 Convention[323] had to be set aside. The methodology adopted by the informal consultations to establish the temporal relationship between the original Part XI of the Convention and the substantive consensus on a renegotiated Part XI, which needs to be briefly described, is testament to yet another huge concession made by the majority of developing countries in favor of the industrialized States in order to seal universal participation in the 1982 Convention.[324]

From the standpoint of the industrialized States, it was crucial to embody the terms of a renegotiated Part XI in a binding legal instrument – a demand that easily met with general approval when the participants in the Consultations began deliberations on the subject of procedural/operational approaches to the amendment of Part XI.[325] It was also essential that such binding agreement precluded a duality of regimes, *i.e.*, the situation where the original Part XI

---

323 *See* Arts. 154, 155, 314 & 316(5), CLOS.
324 For a full discussion of the procedural questions involved *see* M. Hayashi, *The 1994 Agreement for the Universalization of the Law of the Sea Convention* 27 ODIL 31-39 (1996); A. De Marffy-Mantuano, *The Procedural Framework of the Agreement Implementing the 1982 United Nations Convention on the Law of the Sea* 89 AJIL 814-824 (1995); T. Treves, "Entry Into Force of the United Nations Convention on the Law of the Sea: The Road Towards Universality" in Najeeb Al-Naumi & Meese, *supra* note 308 at 445-480; G. Jaenicke, "The United Nations Convention on the Law of the Sea and the Agreement Relating to the Implementation of Part XI of the Convention. Treaty Law Problems in the Process of Revising the Deep Seabed Mining Regime" in *Festschrift Rudolf Bernhardt* 122-134 (1995); LB Sohn, *International Law Implications of the 1994 Agreement* 88 AJIL 696-705 (1994).
325 *See* Report of the Secretary General, *supra* note 287, para. 10-12; Jaenicke, *op. cit.* 123. Upon request of the participants in the Consultations, the Secretariat prepared an Information Note in April 1993 which identified four such approaches: (1) A contractual instrument such as a protocol amending the Convention, (2) An interpretive agreement consisting of understandings on the interpretation and application of the Convention, (3) An interpretive agreement on the establishment of an initial Authority and an initial Enterprise during an interim regime accompanied by a procedural arrangement for the convening of a conference to establish the definitive regime for the commercial production of deep seabed minerals when such production became feasible, and (4) An agreement additional to the Convention providing for the transition between the initial phase and the definitive regime, in particular, the Authority would be mandated to develop solutions for issues still outstanding on the entry into force of the Convention.

regime would exist alongside the renegotiated Part XI regime.[326] This was a more difficult matter to deal with, considering the following two possibilities: (1) a State which had already ratified the Convention would be bound by the original Part XI regime until such time that it ratifies or becomes Party to the amending regime, and (2) a State which has still to ratify the 1982 Convention may decide to be a Party to an unmodified Convention, but not to any agreement amending the Convention's original Part XI. Indeed, respect for the position of States which have already ratified the Convention, coupled with crucial considerations of timing, would make it impossible to avoid the emergence of a dual normative regime, even if this duality would transpire for only a brief period of time.[327] For the participants in the Consultations, however, it became more important to supress the emergence of a dual *institutional* regime, even if a dual substantive regime involving Part XI of the Convention proved to be inevitable.

The solution which assured that there was to be only one objective institutional regime after the entry into force of the Convention was proffered by the what came to be known as the "boat paper" – initially an anonymous document circulated during the later stages of the Consultations.[328] At that time, notification on the 60th ratification to the Convention – which determined the exact date when the Convention would enter into force[329] – was imminent.[330] Since the entry into force of the Convention would trigger into *de jure* operation the institutional provisions of the Convention, it was necessary that the alternative institutional provisions for Part XI under the amendatory agreement be put into effect before, or, at the latest, at the same time as, the entry into force of the Convention, such that the latter practically supersedes, or overtakes *de facto*, the former. The main challenge was to forestall the establishment of the institutions contemplated under the original Part XI regime by the pre-emptive operation, as it were, of the institutional regime conceived

---

326 Report of the Secretary General, *id.*, para. 12.
327 *See* De Marffy-Mantuano, *supra* note 324; Jaenicke, *op. cit.* 128.
328 Report of Secretary General, *supra* para. 13. On the "boat paper" see literature cited in note 324.
329 The Convention enters into force 12 months after the deposit of the 60th instrument of ratification. *See* Art. 388(1) CLOS.
330 54th ratification, Saint Kitts & Nevis (7 Jan. 1993); 55th Zimbabwe (24 Feb. 1993); 56th, Malta (20 May 1993); 57th, Saint Vincent & the Grenadines, (1 Oct. 1993); 58th, Honduras, (5 Oct 1993); 59th, Barbados (12 Oct 1993); 60th, Guyana (16 Nov 1993).

under the amendatory agreement. As a result, the institutional regime defined under the original Part XI of the Convention will be indefinitely suspended, if not "stillborn", upon the entry into force of the Convention. This was the effect that the "boat paper" was uniquely designed to achieve.

The "boat paper", in its evolved form as the binding amendatory agreement to Part XI of the Convention, has three parts: (1) UN General Assembly Resolution 48/263; (2) the Agreement Relating to the Implementation of Part XI of the UN Convention on the Law of the Seà of 1982, which is annexed to UNGA 48/263; and (3) the substantive amendments to Part XI by way of specific resolutions to the "hard core" issues settled in the Consultations, which form an annex to the Agreement.[331] It is submitted that the major impact of the boat paper lay in its redefinition, if not annulment, of the scope *ratione temporis* of the Common Heritage of Humanity principle. This it did in two ways: first, bind as many States as possible to its procedural and substantive provisions; and second, have the substantive and institutional regime of the "boat paper" take effect as soon as possible, or at the earliest possible opportunity before the Convention entered into force.[332]

The strategy behind the boat paper for the recruitment of a wide base of State consent is indicated in the provisions on how States and other entities establish their "consent to be bound" to the renegotiated terms of Part XI. Article 4 of the Implementation Agreement thus provides that "after the adoption[333] of this agreement, any instrument of ratification or formal confirmation of or accession to the Convention shall also represent consent to be bound by this Agreement."[334] It also provides that "no State or entity may establish its consent to be bound by this Agreement unless it has previously established or establishes at the same time its consent to be bound by the Convention."[335] Consent to be bound, in turn, is to be expressed by:

---

331 *Cf.* Report of Secretary General, *supra* note 287, para. 14.
332 *See* UNGA Res. 48/265, para. 8-12.
333 Note that the adoption of the Agreement was effected through UNGA Res. 48/263, para. 3. UNGA Res. 48/263 was adopted by a vote of 121 to nil, with 7 abstentions. 56 UNGA members were absent or did not cast votes. LoS Bulletin, *supra* note 287 at 7. States which consent to the adoption of the 1994 Implementation Agreement are called upon to refrain from any act which would defeat its object and purpose. UNGA Res. 48/263, para. 6.
334 Art. 4 (1), 1994 Implementation Agreement, *See also* UNGA Res. 48/263, para. 5.
335 Art. 4(2), *id. See also* UNGA Res. 48/263, para. 5.

a) Signature not subject to ratification, formal confirmation or the [simplified procedure set out in Art. 5];
b) Signature subject to ratification and formal confirmation, followed by ratification and formal confirmation;
c) Signature subject to the [simplified procedure set out in Art. 5]; or
d) Accession.[336]

The "simplified procedure" of establishing tacit or implied consent to be bound is an option given to a State which had already ratified the Convention before the adoption of the Implementation Agreement (28 July 1994): that State shall *be considered* to have established its consent to be bound by the Agreement 12 months after 28 July 1994, *unless* it gives notification before 28 July 1995 that it is *not* availing itself of this simplified procedure.[337] Overall, all States and entities which have voted in favor of UNGA Resolution 48/263, or which have signed the Implementation Agreement, or which have established their consent to be bound by the Agreement, are bound by the rule that "the provisions of this Agreement and Part XI shall be interpreted and applied together as a single instrument. In the event of inconsistency between this Agreement and Part XI, the provisions of this Agreement shall prevail."[338]

The operationalization of the substantive terms of the "boat paper" as early as possible is the task of Article 7 of the Implementatiopn Agreement – stipulating its "Provisional Application." Accordingly, if the Implementation Agreement has not entered into force on 16 November 1994 (the date of entry into force of the Convention) it shall be provisionally applied effective that date[339] pending its entry into force by:

a) States which have consented to its adoption [in the UNGA], except any such State which before 16 November 1994 notifies the depositary in writing either that it will not so apply this Agreement or that it will consent to such application only upon subsequent signature or notification in writing;
b) States and entities which sign this Agreement, except any such State or entity which notifies the depositary in writing at the time of signature that it will not so apply this Agreement;

---

336 Art. 4(3), *id.*
337 Art. 5(1), *id.*
338 Art. 2(1), *id. See also* UNGA Res. 48/263, para. 4.
339 Art. 7(2), *id.*

c) States or entities which consent to its provisional application by so notifying the depositary in writing;
d) States which accede to this Agreement.[340]

All States and entities applying the Agreement provisionally shall do so "in accordance with their national or internal laws and regulations."[341] In addition, a State applying the Agreement provisionally becomes a member of the ISA and may sponsor an application for a plan of work for exploration in the Area.[342] After the entry into force of the Implementation Agreement,[343] a State which has been applying the Agreeement provisionally and for which it is not in force may continue to be a member of the ISA on a provisional basis pending its entry into force for that State,[344] with the same rights and duties as other members of the ISA.[345]

When the 1982 UN Convention on the Law of the Sea entered into force on 16 November 1994, the UN Division of Ocean Affairs and the Law of the Sea reported that the "International Seabed Authority" had 136 members, divided into three categories: States which have ratified the Convention or acceded or succeeded to it; States or entities which are not parties but have consented to the adoption of the Implementation Agreement; and States or entities which have signed the Agreement.[346] For the overwhelming number of members, this "International Seabed Authority" was the institutional entity envisioned by the "boat paper" – or the ISA under the renegotiated Part XI regime.

---

340 Art. 7(1), *id.*
341 Art. 7(2), *id. See also* Sec. 1 (12)(c), Annex, 1994 Implementation Agreement.
342 Sec. 1 (6)(a)(iv), Annex, 1994 Implementation Agreement.
343 The Implementation Agreement shall enter into force 30 days after the date on which 40 States have established their consent to be bound, provided that such States include at least 7 pioneer investor States and that at least five of those States are developed States, *i.e.*, on 28 July 1996. *See* Art. 6(1), 1994 Implementation Agreement.
344 *See* Sec. 1(12), Annex, 1994 Implementation Agreement.
345 Sec. 1(12)(c), *id.* Provisional membership cannot extend beyond 16 November 1998. Sec. 1 (12)(a)(b) & (e), *id.*
346 LoS Bulletin, *supra* note 287 at 48-49. As of 11 February 1997, the 1982 Convention has received 113 ratifications/accessions, with 74 States having ratified/acceded to/participated in the 1994 Impementation Agreement. From the *DOALOS internet database, http://www.un.org/depts/los.*

The ISA under the original Part XI of the Convention was, objectively, no longer there.[347]

4. A Renegotiated Part XI and the Old Politcs of Assured Access

Instead of re-stating how the 1994 Implementation Agreement addressed each of the substantive issues listed above,[348] this section will describe the main features of the Agreement that bear on the principal issue, identified earlier, of competing institutional visions for the deep seabed regime. Obviously, on account of the basic framework of unilateral concession inherent in the move by the Group of 77 to secure universal participation in the Convention, the substantive contents of the 1994 Implementation Agreement would reflect less the competition between the original visions of international control than the further accommodation of the paradigm of assured access in the seabed regime. As will be made abundantly clear in the immediately following discussion, the 1994 Implementation Agreement deepened the institutionalization of assured access in the three "battlegrounds" (to recall the expression of Ambassador Engo) defining the international machinery issues at UNCLOS III: (1) activities covered or the scope of functional competence of the ISA (2) the system of exploitation, and (3) decision-making. This was the cost paid by the Group of 77 to achieve the goal of universal participation in the Convention.

The most significant change to the Convention regime that directly impinges on the content and the exercise of powers of the ISA relates the adoption of

---

347 By 16 November 1994, the States which may be deemed to be members of the "substituted" ISA – *i.e.*, the ISA contemplated under the original, unmodified terms of Part XI of the 1982 Convention – included Angola, Costa Rica, Djibouti, Dominica, the Gambia, Mali, Saint Kitts & Nevis, Sant Lucia, Saint Vincent & the Grenadines, Sao Tome & Principe, Somalia, Yemen, Yugoslavia, and Zaire. *See* LoS Bulletin, *id.*, at 29-39. These few States – which ratified the Convention before the adoption of the implementation Agreement by the UNGA, which were absent/did not cast any vote when UNGA Res. 48/263 was adopted, and which were non-signatories to the Implementation Agreement as of 16 November 1994 – were not technically bound by the "boat paper" in any way when the 1982 Convention entered into force and were, theoretically at that point in time, in a unique position to repudiate the Implementation Agreement as an unauthorized concurrent regime under the 1982 Convention.

348 *Supra* p. 437. For a description and assessment of these issues as reflected in the 1994 Implementation Agreement, *see* Oxman, *supra* note 3; Nelson, *supra* note 318; Hayashi, *supra* note 283, at 69-85, Jaenicke, *op cit.* 123-128.

an "evolutionary approach" in the setting up and functioning of the organs and subsidiary bodies if the ISA.[349] The requirement that the organs and bodies of the ISA shall only be able to discharge their full functions in stages or when there is a need to do so reiterates the concept of an ISA with limited functional and discretionary competence. The actual exercise of powers and functions of the ISA is keyed to developments and possibilities solely associated with "activities in the area" (exploration and exploitation of mineral resources).[350] A streamlined ISA as a result of an "evolutionary approach" in the discharge of its functions was also dictated by considerations of cost-effectiveness.[351]

Some developing countries voiced their concern that the zeal to pursue cost-effectiveness might lead to a very restrained ISA, paralyzing it altogether.[352] This notwithstanding, the issue of whether the organs and bodies of the ISA have adequate resources at any particular point in time to exercise their respective functions is to be addressed by a Finance Committee of 15 members, a super-powerful body established under the Implementation Agreement.[353] Recommendations of the Finance Committee on, *inter alia*, "the financial management and internal financial administration of the Authority" shall be taken into account by the Assembly and the Council.[354] Significantly, the Implementation Agreement provides that until the Authority has sufficient funds, membership in the Finance Committee shall include representatives of the five largest financial contributors to the administrative budget of the ISA.[355] Because, the Finance Committee is to take decisions by consensus,[356] the industrialized countries are accordingly given a quite extensive influence in the evolution of the ISA, for they can "ensure that the budget of the Authority remains reasonable in relation to the tasks that it must perform."[357]

It is in the Convention provisions relating to the system of exploitation that radical adjustments were introduced by the Implementation Agreement. First,

---

349 Sec. 1(3), Annex, 1994 Implementation Agreement.
350 Sec. 1(1) & (3), *id.*
351 Sec. 1(2), *id.*
352 Rattray, *supra* note 308, at 59.
353 Sec. 9, Annex, 1994 Implementation Agreement.
354 Sec. 9(7)(a), *id.*
355 Sec. 9(3), *id.*
356 Sec. 9(8), *id.*
357 D. Colson, *United States Accession to the United Nations Convention on the Law of the Sea* 7 GEORGETOWN INT ENV L REV 651, at 656 (1995).

the "Enterprise" side of the parallel system had been virtually abolished.[358] Its functions shall initially be performed by the Secretariat[359] and will become fully operational only when the Council takes the affirmative decision to make it so[360] – an event that will not come to pass without the approval of the industrialized States.[361] If and when the Enterprise becomes operational, it shall conduct is initial mining operations through joint ventures, with the original applicant that had contributed the reserved area having the right of first refusal with respect to a joint venture proposal in that area.[362] It should also be mentioned in this connection that the Implementation Agreement removes what the detractors of the Enterprise perceived as its competitive advantage *vis-a-vis* the private side of the parallel system: the obligation of States to fund one integrated mining operation by the Enterprise under the 1982 Convention "shall not apply";[363] the Convention provision on the transfer of technology to the Enterprise, already toothless as it was, also "shall not apply";[364] and the obligations applicable to contractors shall also be made applicable to the Enterprise.[365]

Secondly, assured access on the "private side" of the parallel system is reinforced by the Implementation Agreement in several ways: the regime governing financial terms of contract established under the Convention was adjusted to make the system "fair both to the contractor and the Authority";[366] the system of production controls have been eliminated;[367] and most importantly, the industrialized States applying the Implementation Agreement on a provisional basis[368] have been given the right to sponsor applications for approval of a plan of work for exploration.[369] The US-led multinational consortia in particular had their claims "grandfathered in" on terms no less favourable than

---

358 Borgese, *supra* note 317, at 45.
359 Sec. 2(1), Annex, 1994 Implementation Agreement.
360 Sec. 1(2). *id.*
361 Scholz, *supra* note 286, at 683.
362 Sec. 2(2) & (5), Annex, 1994 Implementation Agreement; Scholz, *id.*, at 683.
363 Sec. 2(3), *id.*
364 Sec. 5(2), *id.*
365 Sec. 2(4), *id.*
366 Sec. 8, particularly (a), *id.*
367 Sec. 6, *id.*
368 *See* Art. 7, 1994 Implementation Agreement.
369 Sec. 1(12)(c)(ii), Annex, 1994 Implementation Agreement; *see also* Sec. 1(6) & (8)-(12), *id.*

the best granted to the previously registered Pioneer Investor under Resolution II.[370] For all qualified applicants in the future, automatic access has been given them on a first come, first served basis.[371] It is not an exaggeration to say that the system of access installed under the Implementation Agreement revives the "registration system" which was rejected by the international community in the late 1960s.

Lastly, the Implementation Agreement drastically revises the review and amendment provisions applicable to the system of exploitation as established by the 1982 Convention. It is submitted that it is in this normative area where the Implementation Agreement effects the most serious and far-reaching surgical adjustment to the Convention regime. Recall that the Review Conference under Article 155 of the Convention was designed to give the Assembly, as the most democratic organ of the ISA, the power to evaluate, alter, or redirect the system of exploitation installed in Part XI according to "common heritage" criteria. Article 155 embodied the only seed of hope, or the only defensive shield, for the developing countries to promote an institutional regime for the deep seabed not on the basis of the stifling structures of assured access but on the basis of a unitary system of resource development. From the point of view of the Group of 77 at UNCLOS III, the Review Conference was a compromise that would allow the vindication of their vision of internationalization, openning up a more mature stage of normative development for the Common Heritage of Humanity principle. It was the only saving grace of the system of exploitation build upon the predominant force of assured access.[372]

The Implementation Agreement provides that the Convention provisions on the Review Conference[373] "shall not apply."[374] More particularly, the power of the Assembly to convene a Review Conference as well as the consensus approach to decision-making in the Review Conference and in the amendatory process have been nullified. As an alternative to a displaced Review Conference, it is provided that "the Assembly, *on the recommendation of the Council*, may undertake at any time a review" of the resources regime in Part

---

370 Scholz, *supra* note 306, at 72.
371 Oxman, *supra* note 3, at 692.
372 Prominent G-77 representatives who took active part in the renegotiation of Part XI did not, however, register strong views on the elimination of the Review Conference institution. *See* Valle, in Nordquist & Moore, *op. cit.*; Rattray, *op. cit.*; Nandan, *supra* note 266, at 127; Ballah, *op. cit.* 358-359.
373 Specifically, Art. 155, para. 1, 3 & 4, CLOS.
374 Sec. 4, Annex, 1994 Implementation Agreement.

XI.[375] For the United States, the significance of this adjustment made by the Implementation Agreement is clear: "Amendments to the deep seabed mining regime could not be adopted without US consent."[376]

The final set of changes introduced by the Implementation Agreement for our consideration relates to the issue of decision-making in the ISA. Since this outstanding issue goes to the heart of governance in the ISA, it is not surprising that it figured as the most prominent concern of the industrialized countries in the renegotiation of Part XI.[377] In general, the modifications made to the Convention regime were designed to erase the discretionary competence of the Assembly and to establish the dominance of the industrialized countries in the Council, where the real locus of the ISA's institutional powers resides.

The Implementation Agreement thus categorically rejects the unqualified power of the Assembly under the Convention "to establish general policies" through the stipulation that "the general policies of the Authority shall be established by the Assembly in collaboration with the Council."[378] Hence, decisions of the Assembly on which the Council also has competence, including administrative, budgetary, and financial matters, shall be based on the recommendations of the Council.[379] As a further check on the exercise of competence by the Assembly, Assembly decisions that have budgetary and financial implications shall be based on the recommendations of the powerful Finance Committee,[380] dominated by the industrialized States.[381] Since any decision of moment would unavoidably have financial and budgetary implications, there is no way by which the Assembly, simply on the basis of the one-nation, one-vote principle which safeguards its institutional integrity, can dispose of independent judgement. The "problem" – that policy-making in the ISA will be carried out by a one-nation, one-vote assembly – no longer exists.[382] The

---

375 *Ibid.* Emphasis supplied.
376 Oxman, *supra* note 3, at 695.
377 Nelson, *supra* note 318, at 197.
378 Sec. 3(1), Annex, 1994 Implementation Agreement.
379 Sec. 3(4), *id.* If the Assembly does not accept the recommendation of the Council, the matter is returned to the Council for further consideration. If the Council persists in its original recommendation, the next step is not specified and is therefore uncertain. Nelson, *supra* note 318, at 198.
380 *Supra* 651 *et seq.*
381 Sec. 3(7), Annex, 1994 Implementation Agreement; *See* Borgese, *supra* note 317, at 45.
382 Oxman, *supra* note 3, at 689.

other direct effect of such adjustment, undoubtedly, is to reconfirm the supremacy of the Council – not because the Council had gained more powers, but because the feeble and extremely limited system of checks and balances that existed between the Assembly and the Council in Part XI had now completely vanished.

The reformatting of the decision-making regime applicable to the Council is a spectacular event that repays attention. On the question of its composition, the major change – which is really cosmetic – relates to a guaranteed permanent seat given to the State that has "the largest economy in terms of gross domestic product on the date of entry into force of the Convention."[383] But it is in the arena of decision-making and voting procedures where the Implementation Agreement creates quite dramatic changes. The "three-tiered" system that was arduously negotiated in UNCLOS III has been replaced by the "chambered" voting system, which UNCLOS III rejected.[384] All Council decisions, whether involving substantive of procedural matters, will now be taken by consensus.[385] However, if all efforts to reach consensus have been exhausted,

> decisions on questions of substance, except where the Convention provides for decisions by consensus,[386] shall be taken by a two third majority of members present and voting, provided that such decisions are not opposed by a majority in any one of the chambers referred to [in the Implementation Agreement].[387]

The Council was, therefore, reorganized into four chambers corresponding to the special interest groupings recognized under the Convention: (1) a four-member chamber of States that qualify as the largest consumers or importers of commodities produced from the categories of minerals derived from the Area, (2) a four-member chamber representing the eight States parties which are the largest investors concerning activities in the Area, (3) a four-member chamber of States which are the major net exporters of the categories of minerals derived from the Area, and (4) the chamber consisting of all the representative of developing countries in the 36-member Council.[388]

---

383 Sec. 3(15)(a), Annex, 1994 Implementation Agreement.
384 *Supra* note 232 and accompanying text.
385 Sec. 3(2), Annex, 1994 Implementation Agreement.
386 *See supra* note 243 and accompanying text.
387 Sec.3(5), Annex, 1994 Implementation Agreement.
388 *See* Sec. 3(9) & (15), *id.* 19 developing country representatives were elected to the first Council in 1995. Borgese, *supra* Chap. IV note 387.

The purpose of the shift to a chambered voting system was no doubt to institutionalize the concept of group veto which was not formally acknowledged in the "three tier" system of Part XI. Under the Implementation Agreement, the industrialized countries could more easily block undesirable decisions in the Council because two of the four-member chambers (1 and 2 above) are likely to be under their effective control.[389] It takes only three votes in either chamber to prevent a decision from being taken, which would certainly not be difficult for the industrialized States to muster.[390] On the other hand, the numerical majority of the developing counties in the Council had been turned into a potential disadvantage – because as a Chamber, they would need to gather a bigger number of votes to block decisions adverse to their interests. The rationale for the new system is, however, no different from that of the laboriously developed three-tiered system, built as it was on the negative notion of a "blocking vote." Parenthetically, it may be noted that given the group veto in the Chamber of developing countries, the US did not fully succeed in adjusting the voting system to satisfy the claim of the Reagan Administration that the US should have an "affirmative influence" in decision-making on issues of highest importance to it.[391]

In closing, a preliminary balance sheet of the costs and benefits of "universal participation" in the Convention may be drawn. For the industrialized countries, the weight of advantages is indeed a substantial one. In addition to the enthronement of their right of assured access to the mineral resources of the seabed, which may or may not bring practical benefits to the world in the medium to long term, their leadership in the modes of enjoyment of the non-seabed regimes of the Convention is already well-secured.[392] The 1994 Implementation Agreement, in many ways, is their license to assume this leadership since the multilateralism required to stabilize the deep seabed regime is the same multilateralism that they will need to further their interests with respect

---

389 Oxman, *supra* note 3, at 690.
390 Scholz, *supra* note 306, at 79. During the election of the first Council, the United States did not want China and India to be both members of the chamber of biggest investors, although these two countries were qualified for membership. To have China and India in one of the 4-member Chambers would have meant a reduced ability of the industrialized countries to block decisions. For an account of the first Council election, *see* Borgese, *supra* note 388.
391 *Cf.* Oxman, *supra* note 3, at 690.
392 *See* Galdorski, *supra* note 270, at 68-70; K. Davidson, *Comment* 55 ZaöRV 290-297 (1995).

to the non-seabed regimes in the Convention – which have become acutely vital in terms of a stable legal order for naval mobility, navigation and commerce, resource development, and environmental protection.[393] The cost of multilateralism in the deep seabed regime is without doubt far outweighed by the benefits of multilateralism in the non-seabed regimes under the Convention. For the United States in particular, the cost is an initial annual outlay of about $650,000, as its contribution for the budget of the ISA.[394] This limited amount, which the Finance Committee of the ISA can adjust accordingly, serves as the "insurance premium" to ensure and stabilize the vast benefits from the non-seabed regimes of the Convention that will accrue to its nationals[395] – not at all a bad deal for the world's superpower.

On the other hand, the cost-benefit ledger for the developing countries as a whole does not look as bright. With a "lean and mean" ISA set up under the 1994 Implementation Agreement, it is doubtful whether immediate benefits for them can be realized from the operations of the new international organization. Since no seabed mining is forthcoming, and assuming the ISA chooses to confine the exercise of its competence to the demands or non-demands of this narrow function, the participation of the developing countries in the "common heritage" institutions of the ISA will likely prove to be more of a "common burden" for the vast majority of them, especially the land-locked and geographically disadvantaged. In this sense, their financial contributions to help run the ISA, no matter how small, would appear less as an "insurance premium" paid for an elusive future security than an on-going "subsidy" in favor of the States which are presently reaping the benefits of a universally accepted Convention. Is this not a new form of wealth transfer from the poor to the rich? This is a tragic result, especially because, as I have argued in Chapter II of this book, sustainable development realized through the non-seabed provisions of the Convention remains a distant dream for many developing countries.

The cost of universal participation in the convention is thus unevenly and lopsidedly distributed in the international community. While the industrialized countries have already ascertained the amazing benefits of their accession to

---

393 *See* "Message from the President of the US and Commentary Accompanying the United Nations Convention on the Law of the Sea and Agreement Relating to the Implementation of Part XI Upon their transmittal to the United States Senate for its Advice and Consent" in 7 GEORGETOWN INT ENV L REV at 77 (1994).
394 Colson, *supra* note 357, at 655-656.
395 *Id.*, at 655.

452

the 1982 Convention, it is difficult to deny that not many developing countries are able to pinpoint qualitatively and quantitatively any increase in national advantage as a result of the adoption of 1994 Implementation Agreement. Did the 1994 Implementation Agreement "for the universalization of the Law of the Sea"[396] justify the extraordinarily enormous amounts of money, energy and human resources which the developing countries expended in negotiating a Law of the Sea Convention and in bringing it into force on a universal basis? The answer may not be forthcoming but already there is sadness being expressed.[397] Somehow, the developing countries have won their symbols – "sustainable development", the "unified character" of the Convention, and the "common heritage of humanity." But these hard won symbols have still to find a home in the living institutions of the Law of the Sea.

CONCLUSION

Putting into practice one of the most ambitious and revolutionary ideas in postwar international relations – the Common Heritage of Humanity – is a hallmark of contemporary law-making in the international community. The cost and complexity of the process that lasted for at least a quarter of a century should drive home the point that there is a formidable gap that separates an egalitarian norm of international law from its actual realization in a world of disparities. Even before Ambassador Pardo put the United Nations on notice that the Common Heritage of Humanity principle is an idea whose time had come, the forces of reaction and opposition have made it clearly known that the realization of the Common Heritage of Humanity principle will not be a picnic. In this Chapter, I have attempted to show that although the normative idea of the Common Heritage of Humanity had been successfully embodied in a binding instrument of international law, the 1982 UN Convention on the Law of the Sea, it has still to find its rightful place in the everyday practice of living law.

The key aspect of the legal principle that deserves our closest attention is without doubt its operational value, or its self-defined ability to create an impact in the behaviour of States and individuals. When the Common Heritage of Humanity principle was under consideration in the UN Seabed Committee the

---

396 *See* Hayashi, *supra* note 324, at 31.
397 For a pensive assessment of the 1994 Implementation Agreement, *see* Pinto, *supra* note 160.

developing countries were steadfast in their conviction that the principle required a new type of international organization which will have to bring it to life and develop it to full maturity. The essential element which imparts practical significance to the principle is its institutional definition. Without an international organization that will carry out programmes with respect to the environments and the resources that are declared to be the common heritage of humanity, the new fundamental legal principle – which is programmatory in this sense – will simply be locked up in the law books. Functional international institutions are the only guarantee to ensure that these frontier environments and resources will be assured of their "common" character, will be conserved and managed as a "heritage", and will be disposed on behalf of "humanity" as a whole – special consideration being given to the needs and interests of poor nations.

Dreams, as a poet said, are the stuff of which life is made of. Those who have opposed the idea of the Common Heritage of Humanity were similarly poised to breathe life into an idea which was, also from the very beginning, just a dream. The dream was for them to have the proverbial place in the sun – that is, a "place" beyond the limits of national jurisdiction, yet undefined and vigorously contested, where they could have adequate freedom to enjoy its untold riches. Putting this dream into practice, or bringing it into the realm of operative norms and international legal procedures, did not obviously require the setting up of an international organization. It required, in the first instance, an unimpeachable international consensus on the precise geographic delimitation of the place where dreams become reality, and where reality can churn out material wealth.

But the dreamers of wealth, principally in the industrialized countries, were also practical people. The legal fiction of an "area beyond the limits of national jurisdiction" was surely a necessary but not a sufficient condition in the grand movement from dreams to riches. More critically, it was important for them to be assured that if and when the boundaries are established, the dreamers do not "rush to grab" the riches of the legal frontier. A minimum order in "the Area" was definitely called for, lest the dream become an all too familiar nightmare. That nightmare, it will be recalled, occurred because the dreamers, in the not too distant past, had to wage brutal wars on each other and on some others as well in the recovery of other kinds of riches in what were then other legal frontiers. International arrangements should, therefore, be set up to ensure "an orderly gold rush" in the frontier.

When the UN General Assembly adopted the historic Declaration of Principles Governing the Sea-Bed and Ocean Floor and the Subsoil thereof Beyond the Limits of National Jurisdiction in 1970, one would have imagined that the developing countries won their cause to evolve, programmatically, international institutions for the Area on the basis of the Common Heritage of Humanity principle. The Declaration afterall asserts in its crowning statement the fact that "the Area and its resources are the common heritage of humanity." Its political significance lay in the presumed acceptance by the entire international community of the principle that the development and the structure of institutions, particularly an unprecedented form of international organization, for the deep seabed should be founded on the normative dictates of the Common Heritage of Humanity. For this purpose, the Declaration laid down the strategy to be followed by the international community: "On the basis of the principles of the Declaration, an international regime applying to the area and its resources and including appropriate international machinery to give effect to its provisions shall be established by an international treaty of a universal character, generally agreed upon."

The acceptance by the industrialized countries of the principle that the Area and its resources are the common heritage of humanity did not, however, induce an adjustment of the attitudes they previously held with respect to the goals and purposes of international control of the deep seabed. Notwithstanding the neologism "common heritage of humanity" boldly asserted in a document of high political and moral importance, the industrialized countries clung to their belief, already well articulated before the adoption of the Declaration of Principles Resolution, that international regulatory bodies with competence over deep seabed resources should be constituted for no other purpose but the institutionalization of a regime for the "orderly gold rush" into the Area. What is more, the proposed standard of non-discriminatory "assured access" to the resources of the Area (particularly manganese nodules) which the industrialized countries thought was reflected in the language in the Declaration, had become a "right" which should therefore be catered for by the international institutions to be evolved.

While the doctrine of international control of the Area could be regarded as having become a generally accepted principle of law as a consequence of the adoption of the 1970 Declaration of Principles Resolution, the implications of this doctrine on institutional development are difficult to ascertain. The work of the First Committee of UNCLOS III, which should be considered in this light, proves the depth and extent of the difficulties involved. Given the competing visions of institutional development for the Area, advanced respectively by the developing and industrialized States in the negotiating environment of UNCLOS III, a pragmatic meeting of minds was an extremely agonizing prospect. Notwithstanding the Declaration of Principles Resolution as a common working document, there was really no value of fundamental importance which the two camps shared in common. The contrast of negotiated solutions discretely embodied in the ISNT and RSNT demonstrates that the institutional translation of the multi-functional Common Heritage of Humanity principle, which was done in the ISNT on the one hand, is totally incompatible with the institutional expression of the alleged "right to assured access", which is reflected in the RSNT on the other. It is thus more accurate to maintain that there was a competition of "paradigms" on international control in UNCLOS III. Since paradigms engage in battle, there cannot be a win-win situation in the historical context of UNCLOS III. Either the institutional paradigm of Common Heritage of Humanity principle wins, or the *status quo* maintaining paradigm of assured access prevails. Only one side must win at the expense of the other. And this determines whether a paradigm change will take place. Moreover, the war of paradigms had more at stake than just the control of an international law "machinery." Perhaps, more importantly, a moral or ethical dimension in the development of international law was at stake. For the victory for the Common Heritage of Humanity paradigm was also a moral victory for the developing countries. In a world deeply divided between rich and poor, the attitude of individualistic ambition and acquisitiveness cannot coexist with the attitude of altruism and social amelioration. Either seabed institutions come to the service of a jealously guarded national "right to assured access", or they discharge an obligation attendant to the care of an all-inclusive "trust", or what is now referred to as the "right to sustainable development." The institutional regime for the deep seabed must choose which attitude to adopt.

It was shown in this Chapter how the paradigm of assured access "won" recognition at UNCLOS III. The 1982 Convention established an International Seabed Authority that will have to respond, by and large, to the alleged "right" of States to mine mineral resources in the Area. For this purpose, the "parallel system" of exploitation was designed to facilitate and promote the assured access of industrialized States to manganese nodules, with the least interference from "irresponsible majorities" in the Authority. In the political environment of UNCLOS III, the "parallel system", as an institutional mechanism for assured access, was a compromise formula that had to be accepted if meaningful progress in negotiations were to be realized. In the first place, its acceptance was based on the condition that the assured access paradigm on which the parallel system was based must surrender to a Common Heritage paradigm of resource development in about twenty years time. In the second place, the offer to the international community of the parallel system "package" was accompanied by a threat of unilateral exploitation under the access regime justified by the freedom of the high seas argument in the event of its non-acceptance. The strategy of reasoned persuasion based on the "moral force" of the Common Heritage of Humanity principle could only have gone so far in the face of a pervasive coercive element throughout the negotiations.

As negotiated in UNCLOS III, Part XI of the 1982 Convention on the Law of the Sea may very well be considered as a *normative argument* in favor of global amelioration, institutional altruism, and international allocation of values based on the Common Heritage principle. It is, in other words, a victory for the Common Heritage paradigm of institutional development. Part XI acknowledged assured access as a framework of institutional operations only for a limited period of time, after which it will have to reckon with performance standards dictated by the Common Heritage principle – not unlike the day of judgement in an eschatological context. The conditional recognition of assured access as an experimental paradigm with a fixed term of twenty odd years is wholly consistent with the "moral force" of Common Heritage of Humanity principle as embodied in the 1970 Declaration of Principles Resolution. Thus, the programmatory character of the Common Heritage of Humanity principle, as a strategy for the multi-dimensional internationalization of the Area, is affirmed. The scope *ratione temporis* of the Common Heritage of Humanity principle is clearly defined in the timetable of institutional progress under Part XI.

Developments in the decade following the adoption of the 1982 Convention on the Law of the Sea would show that the institutional regime in Part XI meant to foster the "right of assured access" had become largely dysfunctional and irrelevant. The most significant intervening event in this regard is the realization that seabed mining will not be economically viable for a long time to come. The dream became an illusion. This meant that there was no longer any urgent reason why the industrialized States, which have expressed dissatisfaction with Part XI, should continue to stay out of the 1982 Convention which afterall was not merely a seabed mining treaty but the Constitution for the entirety of ocean space.

The ascendancy of "market oriented approaches" to economic development in the setting of growing "sustainable development" thinking had also refuted the philosophy of "assured access" as embodied in parallel system under Part XI. Efficiency in the development of resources coupled with equity and sharing in an intra- and inter-generational context was the central theme of the UNCED held in 1992. It should be noted that this theme was already well developed in the deep seabed context when the 1970 Declaration of Principles Resolution was adopted. The vindication of the Common Heritage paradigm on institutional development for the deep seabed on account of sustainable development imperatives in the 1990s would have given an excellent argument for the adjustment of the institutional provisions of Part XI to render Part XI an exemplary regime to sustainable development. The passage of time had proven that the "right of assured access" must give way to the "right of sustainable development."

The renegotiation of Part XI through the informal consultations of the UN Secretary General did not, however, lead to an adjustment of Part XI according to the imperatives of sustainable development. The main agenda of the renegotiations was eminently political: how to accommodate the objections of the industrialized States to Part XI so that universal participation in the 1982 Convention will be achieved. It was an agenda that was offered by the Group of 77 and welcomed by the industrialized countries. This time, the international community was ready to renegotiate Part XI and Part XI alone in order to realize the goal of a universally accepted Convention.

When the informal consultations were over, the international community had before it the so-called "boat paper", the composite legal technique behind the 1994 Implementation Agreement. Here was the vehicle that will deliver the goal of universality. It was also the instrument that silenced the normative argument in Part XI for a Common Heritage approach to institutional development for the deep seabed. According to the 1994 Implementation Agreement, the Review Conference established under Part XI, or the day of judgement for assured access under the parallel system, "shall not apply." And for this purpose, a "new" International Seabed Authority must be born after the entry into force of the 1982 Convention. It was an imaginative formula that practically extinguished the *ratione temporis* of the Common Heritage of Humanity principle. The rest of the adjustments made on the original Part XI were designed to further promote assured access – like strengthening the private side of the parallel system, redesigning decision-making to protect this access, and installing more institutional checks to make sure that "irresponsible majorities" in the new ISA maintained proper discipline.

If it is considered that the dim prospects of seabed mining are here to stay, the renegotiation of Part XI which took off from the familiar premise of securing further the "right" of assured access would indeed appear very strange and anomalous. But for the votaries of the "assured access" paradigm, the 1994 Implementation Agreement does make sense. That a "paradigm shift" in international organization is *not* likely to take place in the near or distant future is itself an achievement for those who profit much from the *status quo*. And it would certainly not hurt if, just in case, the dream of mining deep seabed minerals will become vivid again. The universalization of the 1982 Convention on the Law of the Sea is a happy ending for the paradigm of assured access.

On the other hand, the vital clock of the Common Heritage of Humanity paradigm seems to have been set back by at least 25 years, returned to its original normative and political position in the 1970 Declaration of Principles Resolution. The question should of course be asked, especially on the part of the leaders of the Group of 77, whether the major one-sided sacrifice was worth the goal of achieving universal participation. Was the abandonment of the institutional cause of the Common Heritage of Humanity principle, including the long years of effort and struggle to give it practical definition in the 1982 Convention, justified by the political will to achieve universal participation in the Convention? Did the pragmatism behind the political will to pursue universal participation imply a relinquishment of the moral force behind the Common Heritage of Humanity principle? And will there be a stronger political will on the part of the Group of 77 to re-negotiate universally accepted institutions inspired by the Common Heritage of Humanity paradigm?

Is there any hope then that the Common Heritage of Humanity principle which follows the paradigm of international social justice will find adequate institutional expression under Part XI again? It is not likely that an international organization responsive to the doctrinal requirements of the Common Heritage of Humanity will emerge from the terms of the 1994 Implementation Agreement. It is also not likely that the North-South dialogue on sustainable development will take place on the basis of reciprocity in and through the new International Seabed Authority. The most significant reason for this is the control by the industrialized countries of the ISA's financing, which may not create the best environment conducive to dignified *quid pro quo* negotiations in the areas of normative development and institutional innovation. Additionally, it is difficult to find a bargaining leverage for the developing countries which they will need if only to induce a future discussion on constitutional matters – except perhaps its group veto in the ISA Council, which may never be invoked in practice.

All hope, however, is not lost. The normative framework for the Common Heritage regime still exists. It is only the institutional infrastructure that needs to be re-adjusted, or perhaps reinvented again altogether. This, no doubt, is a gigantic task. But it is one that need not be foreclosed even if the opportunity to do so is not yet, tragically, in sight. The optimism of Professor Borgese is worth sharing, in full:

> ... The practical task now is not to lament the past but to regain lost momentum, to encourage ratifications, and to see what can be done to make this new International Seabed Authority as useful as possible to the international community, especially developing countries, and to revive the flagging spirit of the common heritage of mankind.
>
> The first point that should be noted is that what has been changed once most certainly can be changed again. If the Authority turns out to be dysfunctional at the time seabed mining becomes economically and environmentally sustainable, its structure can and will have to be changed again, inspite of the fact that the Agreement abolishes the Review Conference mandated by the Convention. The review and revision will have to take account of economic, scientific, technological and political circumstances which we cannot predict today. Hopefully, future changes will conform more closely to the highest standards of international law than the "Implementation Agreement" of 1994.
>
> Second, if our purpose is, on the one hand, to enhance international cooperation in seabed mining activities and, on the other, to make the Authority useful to the international community, we should stress two principles built into the Agreement: the principle of cost-effectiveness and the evolutionary approach. That is, we will have to evolve an agenda that will contribute to making the Authority economically self-reliant. This would mean widening the scope of the activities as they are circumscribed initially.[398]

---

398 Borgese, *supra* note 317, at 46.

VI

GENERAL CONCLUSIONS:
The International Law of Sustainable Development and the Future of the Common Heritage of Humanity Principle in a World of Growing Disparity

THE ARGUMENT IN BRIEF

This book proceeded from the fundamental premise that the international law in force in the past fifty years had been instrumental in creating the highly inegalitarian international community that we have today. Post-war international law contributed a not so insignificant role in the ever-growing disparities among nations, chiefly between the "developed" countries of the North and the "developing" States of the South – in the affirmative sense that its norms and institutions have materially favoured certain States to the exclusion of others and in a negative sense insofar as its effects and consequences have been largely indifferent to the demands for less inequality between North and South. The "international law of global disparities", as I have referred to this disposition of the international legal order, operates in many important branches of, or "domains of inequality" (old and new) in, international law: like the law of international organization, or the law for particular environments like the oceans or for that matter the deep seabed. This international law of disparities is a consequence of activities or practices governed by and generative of international rules, such as the exploitation and enjoyment of world resources, participation and influence in global decision-making, military power exercises, and burden-sharing in manifold global endeavors. Although the fundamental principles and doctrinal underpinnings of international law *in abstracto* are putatively neutral – and in this work I have mainly touched base with the fundamental principle of sovereign equality of States – the historical realization or concrete operationalization of these principles, in varying degrees of intensity, have on the whole resulted in widening material disparities among States. The operation of the legal principles also tended to be suppressive of normative demands for balance, development, and global sharing in a world divided into rich nations and poor nations. International law it seems is truly incapable of removing old inequities, but is eminently adaptable in generating new ones. Countervailing norms and institutions meant to correct these disparities by equalizing the capacities of States for rights and obligations have had only minimal success in reversing the trend of widening disparities. Indeed, such disparities, measured in terms of the much belaboured gap in standards of living among countries, have legitimized and perpetuated the intellectual construction and actual division of the world, legally and politically, into developed and developing States. This division is acknowledged in the 1982 United Nations Convention on the Law of the Sea.

Sustainable development, both as an approach to the reconstitution and advancement of international relations and as a critique of the "international law of global disparities", is a promise to deliver a new material and legal equilibrium between the North and the South. It is built on the concept of interdependence in a decolonized world but enriches the content of this interdependence by positing the centrality of interconnectedness and active cooperation at all levels of governance – national, regional, and global – in political and ecological terms. A legal framework for sustainable development is possible not only because "sustainable development" is now recognized as a "right." It is also widely acknowledged that a normative infrastructure, both in hard law and soft law, is integral to the maintenance and promotion of reciprocity-based cooperative endeavors aimed at maintaining the most vital value worth preserving in a sustainable international community – humanity's survival itself. Thus, sustainable development inevitably forces a re-examination of inter-State interactions and human relationships at the global level which perpetuate legal and material inequalities among nations. The imperative of sustainable development cannot but compel a reformatting of the normative structure upon which these interactions and relationships rest. It is a foregone conclusion that the norms and standards of "an international law of sustainable development" demand a fundamental adjustment of North-South relations on the basis of the objective of equality, or less inequality, between these two worlds that unfortunately co-exist in the same planet. For the first time since decolonization the terms of sovereign equality between States across the North-South divide are being subject to radical review and fresh redefinition. The aggravation of material inequalities between the rich nations and poor nations is now adjudged unsustainable. This bodes ill for the future of the *status quo*-preserving "international law of global disparities."

Nowhere is the clash between the "international law of sustainable development" and the "international law of global disparities" exposed more vividly in the normative arena than the Law of the Sea. There is no question that material inequality among States in the maritime sphere is unavoidable. For how can, say, an island State ever claim to be equal with a large continental State, or a naval power with a land-locked State? But the inequalities arising from political geography precisely provide a reason why the progressive legal order for the oceans must evolve normative devices for the equalization of capacities for rights and obligations among all States in the use and enjoyment of the "commons", notwithstanding the diversity and configuration of national territory. The movement towards equality of capacity for rights and obligations within the international community is a necessary, although it may not be a sufficient, condition for material equality among nations.

It fell on the Third United Nations Conference on the Law of the Sea to frontally engage the issue of North-South inequality in the legal order of oceans. As it should be expected, the developing countries raised the question of equality as the main point on the agenda, or the central prize in the arena. For them, the classical law of the sea – built upon the central pillar of the "international law of global disparities": the freedom of the seas principle – did not square with the demands of decolonization and economic development. It had to be restructured or accordingly reoriented if the widening material inequality between North and South was to be reversed. In a critical sense, the decade-long Third United Nations Conference on the Law of the Sea proved to be a real test on the part of the international community to recast existing ocean regimes that perpetuate North-South disparities and create new regimes that will enhance equality.

An examination of the achievements, or non-achievements, of the Third UN Conference on the Law of the Sea as embodied in 1982 UN Convention on the Law of the Sea in regard to its positive law contribution intended to overcome the international law of global disparities, in both old and new domains of inequality, would generally disappoint. The relationship between the international law of global disparities and the 1982 Convention on the Law of the Sea could be assessed in terms of the output of the Law of the Sea Conference in positive law and in the actual practice of States. The main question for consideration is whether in the two domains, the "special needs and interests of the developing countries" have been adequately secured in legal rights and obligations. The corollary question that needs to be raised is whether, in evolving a normative system that meets the "special needs and interests of developing countries" in the ocean realm, the international community moved closer to realizing the "international law of sustainable development."

In the traditional domain of inequality in the oceans between the North and the South – which includes concerns such as access to fisheries, marine resources development and conservation, navigation, and the conduct of scientific research – the provisions of the Convention are, on the whole, on the short end of positive law with respect to the amelioration of inequalities in legal capacity between developed and developing States. The most adversely affected States in the new distribution of rights and obligations, and in the actual enjoyment of these rights and obligations, are certainly the developing countries, especially the land-locked and geographically disadvantaged among them. Under the 1982 Convention, the important terms of North-South amelioration are couched in the language of *pacta de contrahendo*, rarely an acknowledgement that the problem of growing disparities exists. The solution proffered by the Convention to the "international law of global disparities" in the ocean sphere is to be found in a framework of rules governed by "the obligation to cooperate" – a legal obligation which *prima facie* lacks a fair degree of specificity.

The rise of "sustainable development" thinking in the late 1980s and the 1990s undoubtedly recasts the outlook on the 1982 Convention on the Law of the Sea. The United Nations Conference on Environment and Development held in 1992, with its prime focus on intra- and inter-generational equity, may be regarded as a historic boost towards the operationalization of regimes in the 1982 Convention which enhance the prospects of reducing inequality among States. More particularly, Chapter 17 of Agenda 21 – a comprehensive action plan for sustainable development in the oceans – transformed the general regime of cooperation under the 1982 Convention into a powerful normative framework for the realization of inter-State equality. The *jus cogens* principle of sustainable development would demand nothing less than the equalization of legal capacities across the North-South divide based on the norms founded on reciprocity and cooperation between the developed and the developing States. One such norm is the principle of "common but differentiated responsibilities" elaborated in Chapter 17 of Agenda 21 and foreshadowed by the concept of the EEZ as a zone of international cooperation in the 1982 Convention on the Law of the Sea. On the whole, these norms constitute the building blocks of the "international law of sustainable development."

The evolution and consolidation of "the international law of sustainable development" in the traditional domain of inequality in the law of the sea is, however, dependent on the more precise understanding of the normative properties of "sustainable development" as a systemic approach to global problems. The challenge is thus to encrust the ethos of sustainable development into the entire corpus of international law. Unless there is agreement on the exact practices and interactions constitutive of sustainable development that must perforce be translated into norms and legal institutions, the international law of sustainable development – as the paradigmatic antidote to the international law of global disparities – will remain as an equivocal response to the gross predicament of international legal inequality.

On the other hand, the implications of the "new" domain of disparity in the ocean sphere on sustainable development are more straightforward. It will be recalled that the negotiations on this domain during the Third UN Conference on the Law of the Sea centered chiefly on the regime governing the deep seabed. North-South inequality in this normative arena is, in particular, dictated by the functional regime on deep seabed mining under Part XI of the Convention. There is much evidence to prove that Part XI, in all its detailed provisions, reinforces the inegalitarian concept of "assured access" to the mineral resources of the deep ocean floor. The 1982 Convention on the Law of the Sea, in a word, extended the norms and practices of the "international law of global disparities" to human operations on the deep seabed.

But unlike the regimes in the 1982 Convention that appertain to the traditional domain of North-South disparity, Part XI of the Convention did not undergo a reevaluation, nor was it subjected to a "sustainable development" critique, at the UNCED. The omission is understandable in view of the deep political controversy that had engulfed Part XI since the Convention was adopted in 1982. However, it should be noted that the negotiations on Part XI at UNCLOS III did exemplify the North-South debate on legal equality in its sharpest form. Paradoxically, notwithstanding the *status quo*-preserving features of Part XI, it was the displeasure of the industrialized States over Part XI itself that caused these countries to reject it.

The tangled situation involving Part XI is more than meets the eye. The reason why the industrialized countries denounced Part XI had everything to do with the *overall* normative framework set forth in Part XI to govern the deep seabed. This general normative framework, as I have shown, developed to the fullest extent the idea of "the international law of sustainable development." While the functional regime of deep seabed mining favoured the interest of the industrialized countries, this regime – or the "international law of global disparities" which it projects – was captured into the overall framework, or timetable, of sustainable development as defined in Part XI.

The normative approach that addresses the overall problem of North-South legal inequality in the domain of the deep seabed is a startling achievement of Part XI, with far-reaching implications. This approach, which anticipates the principle of "sustainable development" – imparting conceptual coherence and a progammatory method to its pursuit and practical realization – is encoded in the Common Heritage of Humanity principle. Small wonder the institutional element of the Common Heritage of Humanity principle was the most controversial and most arduously negotiated issue in UNCLOS III. Part XI of the 1982 Convention, in brief, spells out a normative paradigm of sustainable development. In part XI lies the formula for the "international law of sustainable development" as a decisive response to the "international law of global disparities."

The amendements to Part XI introduced by the 1994 Implementation Agreement depict the phenomenon of how the "international law of global disparities" manifests itself at the level of institutional development. Notwithstanding the formula for sustainable development already embodied as a norm in Part XI of the Convention, the 1994 Implementation Agreement succeeded in indefinitely postponing the institutionalization of the Common Heritage of Humanity principle by demolishing the scope of the principle *ratione temporis*. This it did specifically by the *de facto* establishment of a "new" International Seabed Authority when the 1982 Convention entered into force on 16 November 1994. The ISA originally contemplated under the original Part XI of the Convention was stillborn – the cost of universal (or near-universal) participation in a "new" Convention on the Law of the Sea.

When a detailed historical consideration is given to the evolution of the Common Heritage of Humanity principle in the new law of the sea, we gain a clear view not merely of the brilliant possibilities of "the international law of sustainable development" but also of the disheartening operations and schemings of "the international law of global disparities." The examination of the arena where the struggle between these competing paradigms took place – inside or outside the United Nations, as well as inside or outside law journals – discloses the facts at the level of human drama. Here paradigms cease to be mere intellectual constructs but become enmeshed in the politics of advocacy and in the aesthetics and ethics of scholarship. Hope and expectation, deceit and manipulation, selfishness and sacrifice, expediency and foresight, human sensitivity and indifference: all these are on record to testify to the emergence and evolution of the Common Heritage of Humanity principle.

The spectacular clash of paradigms for ocean and global governance, made abundantly clear in the development of the Common Heritage of Humanity principle as a fundamental principle of international law, is an on-going process. However, the battle of paradigms in the "Area", ultimately, has no spectators. In a very real sense each and everyone of us is involved in the struggle to realize or defeat the materialization of the international law of sustainable development, be it through the Common Heritage of Humanity principle or otherwise. There is, in truth, an inevitable choice to be made which in the end will either oppress or uplift the "moral force" behind the international law of sustainable development. That, I believe, is the crux of the principle of the Common Heritage of Humanity.

Lessons in Legal Development

Governance for sustainable development at the global level requires an infrastructure of norms and institutions in public international law. These norms and institutions, it must be stressed, are not solely nor primarily addressed to the preservation or restoration of natural resources and physical ecosystems but are mainly directed at overcoming the problem of growing North-South disparities. The integration of "environment" and "development" – the theme of the international community consensus in UNCED – is very much a challenge for international law as it is for international relations. It is in this context that the 1982 United Nations Convention on the Law of the Sea leads the way in the grand effort to restructure and transform the ever-present "international law of coexistence" to an "international law of sustainable development."

As a model for a comprehensive legal approach that strives towards the goal of a less unequal international community, the new Law of the Sea establishes two pioneering legal institutions around which the specific norms of sustainable development merge. These are the "exclusive economic zone" (EEZ) as a zone of international cooperation, one the one hand, and "the Area" as Common Heritage of Humanity, on the other. As we have seen, both the EEZ and the Common Heritage of Humanity define regimes that are spatial in scope and multi-functional in orientation. Both were originally broached by the developing countries to carry forward the North-South dialogue in the negotiations leading to the historic 1982 Convention. Each of these regimes, as a normative formulation of strategy to meet the "special needs and interests of developing countries", was introduced in relation to the demands of development and global sharing in the law of the sea.

What distinguishes the regime of the EEZ from the regime of the Common Heritage for the purpose of analyzing the legal framework of sustainable development under the Convention is simply this: the former is a regime applicable "within" the bounds of national jurisdiction while the latter is applicable "outside national jurisdiction." The distinction is crucial, since the Convention adopts different normative approaches to the equalization of legal capacities among States, or between the North and the South, in these discrete regions of the ocean. These normative approaches to the equalization of legal capacities "within national jurisdiction" as well as "outside national jurisdiction" certainly deserve very careful consideration. With this distinction, there emerges not one but two models of governance embodied in the 1982 Convention which could potentially be extended to, or developed for, other areas of global concern, depending on whether a particular area of concern falls within the remit of matters "within national jurisdiction" or "without national jurisdiction." The dichotomy is a meaningful and exhaustive one, because in a decentralized system of international relations consisting of sovereign but highly unequal States, there seems to be no other way of conceiving global ecological space for the purposes of governance than through its division into a sphere "within national jurisdiction" and a sphere "outside national jurisdiction."

Within the sphere of national jurisdiction, the equalization of capacities for rights and obligations among States across the North-South divide takes place through the operation of the general obligation of States to cooperate on the basis of their common but differentiated responsibilities. In the EEZ as a zone of cooperation, the exercise of "sovereign rights" by a developing coastal State becomes the vehicle for "capacity-building" in the context of the implementation of Part XII, Part XIII, and Part XIV of the Convention – all taken together in relation to Chapter 17 of Agenda 21. The "right to sustainable development" in this case is buttressed by the obligation of developed States to assist developing States increase the latter's capabilities to discharge effectively their basic obligation to protect and preserve the marine environment. Thus, through the operationalization of the principle of common but differentiated responsibilities, sustainable development "within national jurisdiction" is realized.

On the other hand, the Common Heritage of Humanity without doubt stands as the exemplary normative approach to the equalization of legal capacities among States in the sphere "outside national jurisdiction." The 1982 United Nations Convention on the Law of the Sea identifies the exhaustive elements of this normative approach: reservation for exclusively peaceful uses, inclusive benefit sharing, environmental protection, and institutional development for international control. The unconditional repudiation of the doctrine of freedom as the operative rule of governance in this sphere must be emphasized. The freedom of the seas principle is inconsistent with the sustainable development of spatial or functional areas outside national jurisdiction, just as the traditional freedom of access of the powerful maritime nations to the coastal resources and near-shore environments of other States under the classical law of the sea is inconsistent with sustainable development within national jurisdiction.

The EEZ and the Common Heritage of Humanity, therefore, suggest complementary but asymmetrical approaches to the equalization of capacities for rights and obligations among all States, developed and developing. This means that the dividing line between these two approaches must be maintained and constantly borne in mind if the lessons on legal development offered by the international experience on the new Law of the Sea are to be appreciated. A clear and definite consensus on whether a particular space, resource or function falls "within" or "outside" national jurisdiction is a necessary condition for its governance based on alternative norms of sustainable development.

In the past, political difficulties have arisen because of attempts to extend the Common Heritage of Humanity principle to areas that are clearly "within national jurisdiction." For instance, at the height of the oil crisis and the debate on the New International Economic Order in the 1970s, the industrialized countries argued that hydrocarbon resources within national jurisdiction should be declared common heritage of humanity. This was rightly rejected as a "co-optation" of the Common Heritage of Humanity principle that would likely have led to an exacerbation of the North-South gap.[1] Also, the developed countries and their pharmaceutical companies had at one time argued that biodiversity resources within national jurisdiction were the common heritage of humanity. The developing countries at UNCED recounted their experience on this treatment of resources, and arrived at the conclusion that the Common Heritage Principle had been invoked by the developed countries to gain untrammelled access to

---

1   *See* Bedjaoui, *supra* Chap. II note 25, at 229.

these resources within national jurisdiction.² The UN Convention on Biodiversity had rectified the situation with its policy statement that biodiversity is a "common concern" of humanity, governed by cooperative norms based essentially on the principle of common but differentiated responsibilities.³ The case of Antarctica should be mentioned as a last illustration of the predicament involving the delineation of "areas within national jurisdiction" and "areas outside national jurisdiction." It could be maintained that until there is reached a clear international consensus on the legal status of Antarctica, including its metes and bounds as an environment or a resource outside any national jurisdiction – an extremely unlikely prospect considering the history and complexity of territorial claims in the region – it will not be possible to extend the full normative potential of the Common Heritage of Humanity principle to the functional or areal governance of Antarctica.⁴

The governance of outer space, the celestial bodies, and the moon – environments which clearly lie beyond national jurisdiction – including the use of related resources deemed outside national jurisdiction like the radio frequency spectrum or the geostationary orbit, may well be advanced with the consistent application of the Common Heritage of Humanity principle as a basis for nor-

---

2   See F. Hendrickx, V. Koester & C. Prip, *Convention on Biological Diversity. Access to Genetic Resources: A Legal Analysis* 23 EPL 250-258, at 250 (1993); For a more general discussion, *see* V. Sanchez & C. Juma (Eds.), *Biodiplomacy: Genetic Resources and International Relations* (1994). Mention should be made of the recent efforts of the Maori people to establish a "life-form patent free zone" in the South Pacific as a response to the commercial patenting of natural components and life forms taken in the region. Australian Broadcasting Corporation Documentary, re-broadcast via Canadian Broadcasting Corporation radio, 13 Feb. 1996.
3   See A.E. Boyle, "The Rio Convention on Biological Diversity" in M. Bowman & C. Redgewell (Eds.), *International Law and the Conservation of Biological Diversity* 33-49, at 40 (1996).
4   For an overview of the issues associated with the potential applicability of Part XI to the Antarctic, *see* C. Joyner, *The Antarctic Treaty System and the Law of the Sea – Competing Regimes in the Southern Ocean?* 10 IJMCL 301-331 (1995). For a more general discussion, *see* R. LeFeber, *The Exercise of Jurisdiction in the Antarctic Region and the Changing Structure of International Law: The International Community and Common Interests* 21 NETHERLANDS YRBK INT L 81 (1990); E.S. Tenebaum, *A World Park in Antarctica: The Common Heritage of Mankind* 10 VA ENV L J 109-136 (1990).

mative development.⁵ The law of the sea experience concerning normative and institutional development in the Area can surely provide specific insights on the further evolution of law and institutions governing these areas from the standpoint of sustainable development.

A normative approach to the sustainable development of global resources that combines the "EEZ model" and the "Common Heritage of Humanity model" of governance while maintaining the juridical distinction between areas of national jurisdiction and areas outside national jurisdiction is illustrated in the recently adopted Agreement for the Implementation of the 1982 UN Convention on the Law of the Sea Relating to the Conservation and Management of Straddling and Highly Migratory Fish Stocks.⁶ By providing for "compatible" regulatory regimes for the fisheries in question within and outside national jurisdiction, by empowering regional fisheries organizations to control access to and the exploitation of these fisheries, and by stipulating assistance to developing countries in the overall programme of sustainable development for these fisheries, the Agreement effectively regionalizes the Common Heritage of Humanity principle, even if the term "common heritage of humanity" nowhere appears in the text of the Agreement.⁷ The regime governing straddling and highly migratory fish stocks developed under the new law of the sea may indeed provide valuable cues on how other resources which "straddle" or "migrate across" the boundary that separates the concerns "within" and the concerns "outside" national jurisdiction may be governed to achieve the specific goals of sustainable development. These other "straddling" concerns, which have been thought of as properly the subject of an evolving or aspirational Common Heritage regime include the world's cultural heritage,⁸ knowledge

---

5   For a discussion of the main issue of distributional equity in relation to sustainable development in this new domain of inequality in international law, *see* R. Steinhardt, "Outer Space" in Schachter & Joyner, *op. cit.* 753-787.
6   Text in 34 ILM 1542-1580 (1995).
7   For a discussion of the common heritage approach to these fisheries, *see* P. Payoyo, *Fishing for the Common Heritage in Straddling and Highly Migratory Fish Stocks* (Lecturer's Paper in the IOI Training Programme Course Book, Halifax, 1994). *See also* S. Oda, *Fisheries under the United Nations Convention on the Law of the Sea* 77 AJIL 739 (1983).
8   *See* A. Strati, *The Protection of Underwater Cultural heritage: An Emerging Objective of the Contemporary Law of the Sea* 11 (1995); P. O'Keefe & J. Nafziger, *The Draft Convention on the Protection of Underwater Cultural Heritage* 25 ODIL 391 (1994); A. Monden & G. Wills, *Art Objects as Common Heritage of Mankind*

resulting from marine scientific research,[9] industrial technology,[10] world food supplies,[11] and the planetary atmosphere.[12]

Overall, the normative framework of sustainable development drawn by the 1982 UN Convention on the Law of the Sea has a wide scope of feasible replicability. It is for this reason that the Convention is not only a "constitution for the oceans" but a potential constitution for the entirety of the human environment as well. The 1982 UN Convention on the Law of the Sea does establish the basis upon which the international community can build and pursue the "international law of sustainable development."

EQUALITY IN THE HUMAN SPHERE

This book began by posing the question whether less inequality among States, in a legal as well as in a material sense, is worth aspiring for as a set goal by the international community. We are now in a position to offer an unambiguous answer based on the experience of international law-making at sea. There is no doubt that in a world that is acutely divided into rich nations and poor nations, and in a world where more and more people are recognizing the virtues of a sustainable quality of life in an intra- and inter-generational sense, the equalization of actual capacities among States to enjoy rights and assume obligations under the 1982 Convention on the Law of the Sea is an absolute good to be desired. It should be stressed furthermore that equality, or less disparity, is not only a desiderata for the poor States but a necessity for all members of the international community – rich, or less rich, or the poorest alike. The imperative of sustainable development at the global level is nothing more but the imperative of equality in the 21st century.

It should now, likewise, be clear that the "international law of sustainable development" is much more than just a structure of equality-generating norms and institutions. The message of equality, as the late Ambassador Amerasinghe

---

19 REVUE BELGE DE DROIT INTERNATIONALE 327 (1986).

9 *See* Canada Working Paper, Doc. A/AC.138/SC.III/L.18, in 1972 SBC Rep at 203.

10 G. Piel, "The Right to Development" in II *Federico Mayor: Amicorum Liber* 699-701, at 701 (1995).

11 M. Bedjaoui, "The Right to Development" in Bedjaoui, *supra* Chap. I note 29, 1177-1204, at 1196.

12 J. van Ettinger, A. King & P.B. Payoyo "Ocean Governance and the Global Picture" in Payoyo, *supra* Chap. II note 235, 247-277, at 263-265.

noted with respect to General Assembly Resolution 2749, has an abiding moral force that cannot be ignored. From the standpoint of the late 1990s, the moral force behind the "international law of sustainable development" is not an abstract ethical proposition in development and global sharing. It is, to paraphrase US Justice Oliver Wendell Holmes, the life of this law that is based not on logic but on experience.

For the developing countries, the moral force behind the Common Heritage principle implies the constant striving to express and overcome the hideous gap in standards of living between the rich North and the poor South. In the Law of the Sea context, the developing countries succeeded in responding to this challenge by playing the lead role as the "voice of conscience" of the international community in the cause against worsening global disparity. It was a role which these countries strenuously and consistently upheld during the long years of difficult negotiations on a new ocean order following the historic address of Ambassador Pardo in 1967. And it was this same role which saw the adoption and, eventually, the entry into force of the 1982 UN Convention on the Law of the Sea, as well as the conclusion of the UN Conference on Environment and Development in 1992.

A wavering in the Third World's commitment to sustainable development for a less unequal world was, however, revealed with the adoption of the 1994 Implementation Agreement. It is submitted that this lapse must not be allowed to remain unredressed. In this regard, the principal task of the leadership as well as the rank and file of the Group of 77 – a fast differentiating group that should, nevertheless, be united in the cause for a less unequal world – is to remain steadfast in their disciplined adherence to the moral force behind the Common Heritage principle. This is the only resource that had kept their solidarity alive and fruitful in the Seabed Committee, at UNCLOS III, and in the PrepCom. It is a resource that is worth sustaining in a world that has still to recover its humanity through the moral outrage that is continuously provoked by the never-ending inhumanity of growing world inequality.

For the industrialized countries, the challenge of the Common Heritage principle should lie in the great potential that this principle offers them for leadership and bold initiative at the global level. The universal acceptance of the 1982 Convention is a real opportunity for these countries to lead the world community towards a sustainable future, beginning with implementation of a stable legal order for the entirety of ocean space.

For the United States, in particular, the ideologically-motivated opposition to the principle of the Common Heritage of Humanity must now cease. The interest of the United States in the Common Heritage principle is in fact inseparable from its present-day interests in maintaining and promoting peace, orderly development, international comity, and environmental values in the oceans. That interest, it must be stressed, simply harks back to the grand vision of President Lyndon Johnson – true harbinger of the Common Heritage spirit – who, in 1966, called upon all the nations of the world to join in a exemplary common endeavor on the oceans and conquer the deeply-entrenched selfishness and destructive ambitions of nation-States. His words have not lost their resonance and incisiveness. The central role that the United States can and must assume in the new sustainable ocean order will only command the respect and admiration of the international community if it proceeds from the moral leadership that is inspired by the justice of the Common Heritage principle. It is a hoped-for justice which, under the present circumstances, can only be claimed by the United States: "The supernatural virtue of justice consists of behaving exactly as though there were equality when one is stronger in an unequal relationship."[13]

---

13 S. Weil, *Waiting for God* 143 (Harper Colophon Ed., 1973).

APPENDIX

Declaration of Principles
Governing the Sea-bed and the Ocean Floor
and the Subsoil Thereof
Beyond the Limits of National Jurisdiction

United Nations General Assembly Res. no. 2749 (XXV)
17 December 1970

25 UNGAOR Suppl no. 28, at 24; UN Doc. A/8028 (1970)

The General Assembly,

Recalling its Resolution 2340 (XXII) of 18 December 1967, 2467 (XXIII) of 21 December 1968 and 2574 (XXIV) of 15 December 1969, concerning the area to which the title of the item refers,

Affirming that there is an area of the sea-bed and the ocean floor, and the subsoil thereof, beyond the limits of national jurisdiction, the precise limits of which are yet to be determined,

Recognizing that the existing legal regime of the high seas does not provide substantive rules for regulating the exploration and exploitation of the aforesaid area and the exploitation of its resources,

Convinced that the area shall be reserved exclusively for peaceful purposes and that the exploration and exploitation of its resources shall be carried out for the benefit of mankind as a whole,

Believing it essential that an international regime applying to the area and its resources and including appropriate international machinery should be established as soon as possible,

Bearing in mind that the development and use of the area and its resources shall be undertaken in such a manner as to foster healthy development of the world economy and balanced growth of international trade, and to minimize any adverse economic effects caused by fluctuations of prices of raw materials resulting from such activities,

Solemnly declares that:

1. The sea-bed and ocean floor, and the subsoil thereof, beyond the limits of national jurisdiction (hereinafter referred to as the area), as well as the resources of the area, are the common heritage of mankind.

2. The area shall not be subject to national appropriation by any means by States or persons, natural or juridical, and no State shall claim or exercise sovereignty or sovereign rights over any part thereof.

3. No State of person, natural or juridical, shall claim, exercise or acquire rights with respect to the area and its resources incompatible with the international regime to be established and the principles of this Declaration.

4. All activities regarding the exploration and exploitation of the resources of the area and other related activities shall be governed by the international regime to be established.

5. The area shall be open for use exclusively for peaceful purposes by all States whether coastal or land-locked, without discrimination, in accordance with the international regime to be established.

6. States shall act in the area in accordance with the principles and rules of international law including the Charter of the United Nations and the Declaration of Principles of International Law concerning Friendly Relations and Cooperation among States in accordance with the Charter of the United Nations, adopted by the General Assembly on 24 October 1970,[1] in the interest of maintaining international peace and security and promoting international co-operation and mutual understanding.

7. The exploration of the area and the exploitation of its resources shall be carried out for the benefit of mankind as a whole, irrespective of the geographical location of States, whether land-locked or coastal, and taking into particular consideration the interests and needs of the developing countries.

8. The area shall be reserved exclusively for peaceful purposes, without prejudice to any measures which may have been or may be agreed upon in the context of international negotiations undertaken in the field of disarmament and which may be applicable to a broader area. One or more international agreements shall be concluded as soon as possible in order to implement effectively this principle and to constitute a step towards the exclusion of the sea-bed, the ocean floor and the subsoil thereof from the arms race.

9. On the basis of the principles of this Declaration, an international regime applying to the area and its resources and including appropriate international machinery to give effect to its provisions shall be established by an international treaty of a universal character, generally agreed upon. The regime shall, *inter alia*, provide for the orderly and safe development and rational management of the area and its resources and for expanding opportunities in the use thereof and ensure the equitable sharing by States in the benefits derived therefrom, taking into particular consideration the interests and needs of developing countries, whether land-locked or coastal.

10. States shall promote international cooperation in scientific research exclusively for peaceful purposes:

(a) By participation in international programmes and by encouraging cooperation in scientific research by personnel of different countries;

(b) Through effective publication of research programmes and dissemination of the results of research through international channels;

---

[1] Resolution 2625 (XXV).

(c) By cooperation in measures to strengthen research capabilities of developing countries, including the participation of their nationals in research programmes.

No such activity shall form the legal basis for any claims with respect to any part of the area or its resources.

11. With respect to activities in the area and acting in conformity with the international regime to be established, States shall take appropriate measures for and shall cooperate in the adoption and implementation of international rules, standards and procedures for, *inter alia*:

(a) Prevention of pollution and contamination, and other hazards to the marine environment, including the coastline, and of interference with the ecological balance of the marine environment;

(b) Protection and conservation of the natural resources of the area and prevention of damage to the flora and fauna of the marine environment.

12. In their activities in the area, including those relating to its resources, States shall pay due regard to the rights and legitimate interests of coastal States in the region of such activities, as well as of all other States which may be affected by such activities. Consultations shall be maintained with the coastal States concerned with respect to activities relating to the exploration of the area and the exploitation of its resources with a view to avoiding infringement of such rights and interests.

13. Nothing herein shall affect:

(a) The legal status of the waters superjacent to the area or that of the air space above those waters;

(b) The rights of coastal States with respect to measures to prevent, mitigate or eliminate grave and imminent danger to their coastline or related interests from pollution or threat thereof resulting from, or from other hazardous occurrences caused by, any activities in the area, subject to the international regime to be established.

14. Every State shall have the responsibility to ensure that activities in the area, including those relating to its resources, whether undertaken by governmental agencies, or non-governmental entities or persons under its jurisdiction, or acting on its behalf, shall be carried out in conformity with the international regime to be established. The same responsibility applies to international organizations and their members for activities undertaken by such organizations or on their behalf. Damage caused by such activities shall entail liability.

15. The parties to any dispute relating to activities in the area and its resources shall resolve such dispute by the measures mentioned in Article 33

of the Charter of the United Nations and such procedures for settling disputes as may be agreed upon in the international regime to be established.

REFERENCES

Books

Alexander, L. (Ed.), *The Law of the Sea Needs and Interests of Developing Countries* (RI: Law of the Sea Institute, 1973)

Alexander, L. (Ed.), *The Law of the Sea: A New Geneva Conference* (RI: Law of the Sea Institute, 1971)

Alexander, L. (Ed.), *National Policy Recommendations* (RI; Law of the Sea Institute, 1969)

Alexander, L. (Ed.), *The Law of the Sea The Future of the Sea's Resources* (RI: Law of the Sea Institute, 1968)

Alexander, L. (Ed.), *The Law of the Sea Offshore Boundaries and Zones* (Ohio State Univ. Press, 1967)

Allen, S. & Craven, J.P. (Eds.), *Alternatives in Deepsea Mining* (Hawaii: 1978 Law of the Sea Institute Workshop, 1979)

Anand, R.P. *International Law and Developing Countries* (Dordrecht: Martinus Nijhoff, 1987)

Anand, R.P. *Origin and Development of the Law of the Sea* (The Hague: Martinus Nijhoff, 1983)

Anand, R.P. *Legal Regime of the Seabed and the Developing Countries* (Leiden: Sijthoff, 1976)

Andryev, E.P., *et al. The International Law of the Sea* (USSR: Progress, 1988)

Axelrod, R. *The Evolution of Cooperation* (NY: Basic Books, 1984)

Barkenbus, J. *Deep Seabed Resources: Politics and Technology* (NY: Free Press, 1979)

Bedjaoui, M. (Ed.), *International Law: Achievements and Prospects* (Paris: UNESCO, 1991)

Bedjaoui, M. *Towards a New International Economic Order* (Paris: UNESCO, 1979)

Bernhardt, R. (Ed.), *Encyclopedia of International Law* Vol 9 (Netherland: Elsevier, 1986)

Beyerlin, U. *et al.* (Eds.), *Festschrift fur Rudolf Bernhardt* (Berlin: Springer-Verlag, 1995)

Bin Cheng, *General Principles of Law as Applied by International Courts and Tribunals* (Cambridge: Grotius Publications, 1987)

Birnie, P. and Boyle, A. *International Law and the Environment* (Oxford: Oxford Univ. Press, 1992)

Borgese, E.M. *Ocean Governance and the United Nations* (Halifax: Dalhousie Univ. Centre for Foreign Policy Studies, 1995)

Borgese, E.M. *The Future of the Oceans: A Report to the Club of Rome* (Montreal: Harvest House, 1986)

Borgese, E.M. & White, P. (Eds.), *Seabed Mining: Scientific, Economic, and Political Aspects An Interdisciplinary Manual* (Malta: IOI Occasional papers No. 7)

Borgese, E.M. & Krieger, D. (Eds.), *Tides of Change* (New York: Mason/Charter, 1975)

Borgese, E.M. (Ed.), *Pacem In Maribus* (NY: Dodd, Mead, 1972)

Bos, A. & Siblesz, H. (Eds.), *Realism in Law Making* (The Hague: TMC Asser Instituut, 1986)

Bowett, D. *The Law of the Sea* (UK: Manchester Univ. Press, 1967)

Bowman, M. & Redgewell, C. (Eds.), *International Law and the Conservation of Biological Diversity* (UK: Kluwer Law International, 1996)

Broadus, J.M. & Vartanov, R.V. (Eds.), *The Oceans and Environmental Security: Shared US and Russian Perspectives* (Washington, DC: Island Press, 1994)

Brown, C. *International Relations: New Normative Approaches* (NY: Columbia Univ. Press, 1992)

Brown, E.D. *The International Law of the Sea* 2 Vols. (UK: Dartmouth Publishing, 1994)

Brown, E.D. *Sea-Bed Energy and Minerals: The International Regime, The Continental Shelf* Vol. I (Dordrecht: Martinus Nijhoff, 1992)

Brown, E.D. *Seabed Energy and Mineral Resources and the Law of the Sea* Vol. II (London: Grahan & Trotman, 1986)

Brown, E.D. *The Legal Regime of Hydrospace* (London: Stevens, 1971)

Brownlie, I. *Principles of International Law* 4th Edition (Oxford: Clarendon Press, 1990)

Bull, H. *The Anarchical Society: A Study of Order in World Politics* (NY: Columbia Univ. Press. 1977)

Bull, H. & Watson, A. (Eds.), *The Expansion of International Society* (UK: Oxford Univ. Press, 1984)

Bull, H., Kingsbury, B. & Roberts, A. (Eds.), *Hugo Grotius and International Relations* (UK: Oxford University Press, 1992)

Butler, W. (Ed.), *Control Over Compliance With International Law* (Dordrecht: Martinus Nijhoff, 1991)

Buzan, B. *Seabed Politics* (NY: Praeger, 1976)

Cassese, A. *International Law in a Divided World* (Oxford Univ. Press, 1986)

Chowdhury, S.R., Denters, E. & de Waart, P. (Eds.), *The Right to Development in International Law* (Dordrecht: Martinus Nijhoff, 1992)

Churchill, R.R. & Lowe, A.V. *The Law of the Sea* 2nd Edition (Great Britain: Manchester Univ. Press, 1988)

Churchill, R.R., Simmonds, K.R. & Welch, J. (Eds.), *New Directions in the Law of the Sea* Vol. III (London: The British Institute of International and Comparative Law, 1973)

Clingan, T. *The Law of the Sea: Ocean Law and Policy* (SF: Austin & Winfield, 1994)

Colombos, C.J. *The International Law of the Sea* 6th Edition (London: Longman, 1967)

The Commission on Global Governance. *Our Global Neighborhood* (UK: Oxford University Press, 1995)

The Commission on International Development Issues, *North-South: A Programme for Survival* (Mass.: MIT Press, 1980)

The Commission on Marine Science, Engineering, and Resources, *Our Nation and the Sea* (Washington: U.S. Government Printing Office, 1969)

The Commission on Population and Quality of Life, *Caring for the Future* (Oxford: Oxford Univ. Press, 1996)

The Commission to Study the Organization of Peace, *Building Peace. Reports of the Commission* (NJ: Scarecrow Press, 1973)

Couper, A. & Gold, E. *The Marine Environment and Sustainable Development: Law, Policy, and Science* (Honolulu: LSI, Univ. of Hawaii, 1993)

Danilenko, G.M. *Law-Making in the International Community* (Dordrecht: Martinus Nijhoff, 1993)

Developments in the Law of the Sea 1958-1964 (London: British Institute of International and Comparative Law, 1965)

DeWitt Dickenson, E. *The Equality of States in International Law* (Cambridge, Mass: Harvard Univ. Press, 1920)

Dolman, A. (Ed.), *Global Planning and Resource Management* (UK: Pergamon Press, 1980)

Dolman, A. & van Ettinger, J. (Eds.), *Ports as Nodal Points in a Global Transport System* (UK: Pergamon Press, 1992)

Dominice, C., Patry, R. & Reymond, C. (Eds.), *Etudes de Droit International en L'Honneur de Pierre Lalive* (Geneva: Institut de Hautes Etudes Internationales; Editions Helbing & Lichtenhahn, 1993)

Dupuy, R.-J. & Vignes, D. (Eds.), *A Handbook on the New Law of the Sea* 2 Vols. (Dordrecht: Martinus Nijhoff, 1991)

Dupuy, R.-J. (Ed.), *The Management of Humanity's Resources: The Law of the Sea* (Workshop, Hague Academy of International Law & UNU, 1982)

van Dyke, J.M., Zaelke, D. & Hewison, G., *Freedom for the Seas in the 21st Century* (Washington DC: Island Press, 1993)

Experts Group on Environmental Law of the World Commission on Environment and Development, *Environmental Protection and Sustainable Development* (Dordrecht: Martinus Nijhoff, 1987)

Exploiting the Oceans: Transactions of the 2nd Annual Marine Technology Society Conference 27-29 June 1966 (Washington, DC: MTS, 1966)

Extavour, C. *The Exclusive Economic Zone* (Geneva: GIIS, 1979)

Fanon, F. *The Wretched of the Earth* (C. Farrington trans., NY: Gorove Press, 1963)

Federico Mayor: Amicorum Liber Vol. II (Bruxelles: Bruylant, 1995)

Fox, H. (Ed.), *International Economic Law and Developing States* (London: British Institute of International and Comparative Law, 1992)

Francioni, F. & Scovazzi, T. (Eds.), *International Responsibility for Environmental Harm* (London: Kluwer, 1991)

Frank, T. *The Power of Legitimacy Among Nations* (Oxford: Oxford Univ. Press, 1990)

Friedheim, R. *Negotiating the New Ocean Regime* (USA: Univ. of South Carolina Press, 1993)

Friedmann, W. *The Changing Structure of International Law* (London: Stevens, 1964)

Fukuyama, F. *The End of History and The Last Man* (NY: The Free Press, 1992)

Garcia-Amador, F.V. *The Emerging International Law of Development* (USA: Oceana, 1990)

Garcia-Amador, F.V. *The Exploitation and Conservation of the Resources of the Sea* (Leyden: Sijthoff, 1960)

Ginther, K., Denters E. & de Waart, P.J.I.M. (Eds.), *Sustainable Development and Good Governance* (Dordrecht: Martinus Nijhoff, 1995)

Glasbergen, P. & Blowers, A. (Eds.), *Environmental Policy in an International Context* (UK: Open University of The Netherlands, 1995)

Glassner, M.I. *Neptune's Domain* (Boston: Unwin Hyman, 1990)

Gorbachev, M. *Perestroika: New Thinking For Our Country and the World* (NY: Harper & Row, 1987)

Hargrove, J.L. *Law, Institutions and the Global Environment* (NY: Oceana, 1972)

Herr, R. (Ed.), *The Forum Fisheries Agency: Achievements, Challenges and Prospects* (University of South Pacific, 1990)

Hohmann, H. *Precautionary Legal Duties and Principles of Modern International Law* (London: Kluwer, 1994)

Hollick, A. *United States Foreign Policy and the Law of the Sea* (Princeton: Princeton Univ. Press, 1981)

Hossain, K. (Ed.), *Legal Aspects of the New International Economic Order* (NY: Nichols Publishing, 1980)

Humanité et Droit International Mélanges René-Jean Dupuy (Paris: Pedone, 1991)

Hurell, A. and Kingsbury, B. (Eds.), *The International Politics of the Environment* (Oxford: Clarendon Press, 1992)

International Organizations and the Law of the Sea Documentary Yearbook 1990 to 1993 Vols. (Netherlands Institute for the Law of the Sea)

Jackson, R. *Quasi-States: Sovereignty, International Relations, and the Third World* (Great Britain: Cambridge University Press, 1990)

Jennings R. & Watts, A. *Oppenheim's International Law* 9th Edition, Vol. I, (Essex: Longman, 1992)

Jessup, P. *The Law of Territorial Waters and Maritime Jurisdiction* (NY: Jennings, 1927)

Johnson, S.P. *The Earth Summit* (London: Graham & Trotman, 1993)

Johnston, D.M. *The International Law of Fisheries: A Framework for Policy-Oriented Studies* (Dordrecht: Martinus Nijhoff, 1987 ed.)

Johnston, D.M. (Ed.), *Marine Policy and the Coastal Community* (London: Croom Helm, 1976)

Jones, C.A. *The North South Dialogue: A Brief History* (NY: St. Martins Press, 1983)

Joyner, C.J. (Ed.), *International Law of the Sea and the Future of Deep Seabed Mining* Proceedings of the J.B. Moore Society of International Law Symposium and the American Society of International Law Regional Meeting, Virginia, 16 Nov 1974 (Va. Accent Printing, 1975)

Kiss, A. & Shelton, D. *International Environmental Law* (London: Graham & Trotman, 1992)

Kissinger, H. *Diplomacy* (NY: Simon & Shuster, 1994)

Koh, K.L., Beckman, R.C. & Chia Lin Sien (Eds.), *Sustainable Development of Coastal and Ocean Areas in Southeast Asia: Post-Rio Perspectives* (National University of Singapore, 1995)

Koers, A. & Oxman, B. (Eds.), *The 1982 Convention on the Law of the Sea* (Honolulu: LSI, Univ. of Hawaii, 1984)

Kooijimans, P.H. *The Doctrine of the Legal Equality of States* (Leiden: Sythoff, 1964)

Koskenniemi, M. *From Apology to Utopia: The Structure of International Legal Argument* (Helsinki: Lakimioliiton Kustannus, 1989)

Kratochwil, F. *Rules, Norms, and Decisions: On the Conditions of Practical and Legal Reasoning in International Relations and Domestic Affairs* (UK: Cambridge University Press, 1989)

Kreuger, R. & Riesenfeld, S. (Eds.), *The Developing Order of the Oceans* (Honolulu: LSI, Univ. of Hawaii, 1985)

Kuhn, T. *The Structure of Scientific Revolutions* (Univ. of Chicago Press, 2nd Ed.: 1970)

Kronmiller, T. *The Lawfulness of Deep Seabed Mining* (NY: Oceana, 1980)

Kwiatkowska, B. *The 200 Mile Exclusive Economic Zone in the New Law of the Sea* (Dordrecht: Martinus Nijhoff, 1989)

Lang, W., Neuhold, H. & Zemanek, K. (Eds.), *Environmental Protection and International Law* (London: Kluwer, 1991)

Lauterpacht, H. *The Function of Law in the International Community* (Conn.: Archon Books, 1966).

The Law and the Sea: Essays in Memory of Jean Carroz (Rome: FAO, 1987)

The Law of the Sea: Priorities and Responsibilities in Implementing the Convention (Gland: IUCN, 1995)

Lowe, A.V. & Warbrick, C. (Eds.), *The United Nations and the Principles of International Law: Essays in Memory of Michael Akehurst* (London: Routledge, 1994)

Luard, E. *The Control of the Seabed* (NY: Taplinger, 1977)

Lyotard, J.F. *The Post-Modern Condition: A Report on Knowledge* (C. Benington & B. Massumi trans., Minneapolis: Univ. of Minnesota Press, 1984)

Macdonald, R.St.J. (Ed.), *Essays in Honour of Wang Tieya* (Dordrecht: Martinus Nijhoff, 1994)

Macdonald, R.St.J. & Johnston, D.M. (Eds.), *The Structure and Process of International Law: Essays in Legal Philosophy, Doctrine, and Theory* (Dordrecht: Martinus Nihhoff, 1986)

Macdonald, R.St.J., Johnston D.M. & Morris G.L. (Eds.), *The International Law and Policy of Human Welfare* (The Netherlands: Sijthoff & Noordhoff, 1978)

MacIntyre, A. *Whose Justice? Which Rationality?* (Notre Dame: University of Notre Dame Press, 1988)

Mahmoudi, S. *The Law of Deep Seabed Mining* (Sweden: Almquist & Wiksell, 1987)

Makarczyk, J. (Ed.), *Theory of International Law at the Threshold of the 21st Century: Essays in Honour of Krzystof Skubiszewski* (The Hague: Martinus Nijhoff, 1996)

Makarczyk, J. *Principles of a New International Economic Order: A Study of International Law in the Making* (Dordrecht: Martinus Nijhoff, 1988)

McDougal, M. & Burke, W. *The Public Order of the Oceans* (Yale Univ. Press, 1962)

Meadows, D., *et al. The Limits to Growth* 2nd Edition (USA: Universe Books, 1974)

Mero, J. *Mineral Resources of the Sea* (The Netherlands: Elsevier, 1965)

Middleton, N., O'Keefe, P. & Moyo, S. *Tears of the Crocodile: From Rio to Reality in the Developing World* (London: Pluto Press, 1993)

Morell, J. *The Law of the Sea: An Historical Analysis of the 1982 Treaty and its Rejection by the United States* (North Carolina: McFarland & Co., 1992)

Morgenthau, H.J. *Politics Among Nations: The Struggle for Power and Peace* 6th Edition (NY: Knopf, 1985)

Mouton, M. *The Continental Shelf* (The Hague: Martinus Nijhoff, 1952)

Nadjeeb Al-Nauimi & Meese, R. (Eds.), *International Legal Isues Arising Under the United Nations Decade of International Law* Proceedings of the 1994 Qatar International Law Conference (The Hague: Martinus Nijhoff, 1995)

Nardin, T. & Mapel, D. (Eds.), *Traditions of International Ethics* (Cambridge Univ. Press, 1992)

Nordquist, M.H. & Moore, J.N. (Eds.), *Entry Into Force of the Law of the Sea Convention* (The Hague: Martinus Nijhoff, 1995)

Nordquist, M.H. (Ed.), *New National Perspectives on the Law of the Sea Convention: 17th Annual Seminar of the Center for Oceans Law and Policy* (Univ. of Va.: 1993)

Nordquist, M.H. (Ed.), *Issues in Amending Part XI of the Convention: 15th Annual Seminar of the Center for Oceans Law and Policy* (Univ. of Va.: 1991)

Nordquist, M. (Ed.-in-chief), *United Nations Convention on the Law of the Sea 1982: A Commentary* Vol. 1 (Va.: Center for Oceans Law and Policy, Univ. of Va., 1985)

Nordquist, M. (Ed.-in-chief); Nandan, S., Rosenne S. & Grandy N. (Eds.), *United Nations Convention on the Law of the Sea: A Commentary* Vol. 2 (Va.: Center for Oceans Law and Policy, Univ. of Va., 1993)

Nordquist, M. (Ed.-in-chief); Rosenne, S., Yankov A. & Grandy N. (Eds.), *United Nations Convention on the Law of the Sea: A Commentary* Vol. 4 (Va.: Center for Oceans Law and Policy, Univ. of Va., 1991)

Nordquist, M. & Choon-ho Park (Eds.), *Reports of the United States Delegation to the Third United Nations Conference on the Law of the Sea* (Hawaii: LSI, 1983)

Nussbaum, A. *A Concise History of the Law of Nations* (NY: MacMillan, 1954)

O'Connell, D.P. *The International Law of the Sea* 2 vols. (Oxford: Clarendon Press, 1982-1984)

Oda, S. *International Law of the Resource of the Sea* (The Netherlands: Sijthoff & Noordhoff, 1979)

Oda, S. *The Law of the Sea in Our Time - I. New Developments, 1966-1975* (Leyden: Sijthoff, 1977)

Oda, S. *The of the Sea in our Time - II. The United Nations Seabed Committee, 1968-1973* (Leyden: Sijthoff, 1977)

Ogley, R. *Internationalizing the Seabed* (USA: Gower, 1984)

Olson, R. *United States Foreign Policy and the New International Economic Order: Negotiating Global Problems 1974-1981* (Boulder: Westview Press, 1981)

Oxman, B. *The Preparation of Article 1 of the Convention on the Continental Shelf* (Va.: National Technical Information Service, 1969)

Pardo, A. & Borgese, E.M. *The Common Heritage: Selected Papers on Oceans and World Order 1967-1974* (Malta Univ. Press, 1975)

Payoyo, P.B. *Ocean Governance: Sustainable Development of the Seas* (Tokyo: UNU Press, 1994)

Payoyo, P.B. *Port State Control in the the Asia-Pacific. An International Legal Study of Port State Jurisdiction* (University of the Philippines, Institute of International Legal Studies, 1993)

Porter, G. & Brown, J.W. *Global Environmental Politics* (Boulder: Westview, 1991)

Post, A.M. *Deep Sea Mining and the Law of the Sea* (Martinus Nijhoff, 1983)

Postyshev, V. *The Concept of the Common Heritage of Mankind: From New Thinking to New Practice* (Moscow: Progress Publishers, 1990)

Preeg, E.H. *Traders in a Brave New World* (University of Chicago Press, 1995)

Rembe, N. *Africa and the Law of the Sea* (The Netherlands: Sijthoff & Noordhoff, 1980)

Rozakis, C.L. & Stephanou, C.A. (Eds.), *The New Law of the Sea* (NY: Elsevier, 1983)

Rousseau, J. *Discourse on the Origin and Foundations of Inequality among Men* (Second Discourse) in *Collected Writings of Rousseau*, Vol. 3 (Dartmouth College: University Press of New England, 1992)

Sachs, W. (Ed.), *The Development Dictionary: A Guide to Knowledge as Power* (London: Zed Books, 1992)

Sahović, M. (Ed.), *Principles of International Law Concerning Friendly Relations and Cooperation* (NY, Dobbs Ferry: Oceana, 1972)

Sanchez, V. & Juma, C. (Eds.), *Biodiplomacy: Genetic Resources and International Relations* (Kenya: African Centre for technology Studies, 1994)

Sands, P. *Principles of International Environmental Law: Frameworks, Standards and Implementation* (UK: Manchester Univ. Press, 1995)

Sanger, C. *Ordering the Oceans: The Making of the Law of the Sea* (Toronto: Toronto Univ. Press, 1987)

San Remo Manual on International Law Applicable to Armed Conflicts at Sea (L. Doswald-Beck, Ed.; Cambridge Univ. Press, 1995)

Sauvant, K.P. & Hasenpflug, H. (Eds.), *The New International Economic Order: Confrontation or Cooperation between North and South?* (Boulder: Westview Press, 1977)

Schachter, O. *Sharing the World's Resources* (NY: Columbia Univ. Press, 1977)

Schachter, O. & Joyner, C. (Eds.), *United Nations Legal Order* 2 Vols. (Cambridge Univ. Press and ASIL, 1995)

Schaar, J.H. *Legitimacy in the Modern State* (New Jersey: Transaction Books, 1981)

Schmidt, M.G. *Common Heritage or Common Burden?* (Oxford: Clarendon Press, 1989)

Sebenius, J. *Negotiating the Law of the Sea* (Mass.: Harvard University Press, 1984)

Seoung-Yong Hong, Miles, E. & Choon-Ho Park (Eds.), *The Role of the Oceans in the 21st Century* (Honolulu: LSI, Univ. of Hawaii, 1995)

Sjoestedt, G. (Ed.), *International Environmental Negotiation* (Laxanberg, Austria: IIASA, 1993)

Sinjela, A.M. *Land-Locked States and the UNCLOS Regime* (NY: Oceana, 1983)

Snyder, F. & Slinn, P. (Eds.), *International Law of Development: Comparative Perspectives* (UK: Professional Books, 1987)

Snyder, F. & Sathirathai, S. (Eds.), *Third World Attitudes Towards International Law* (Dordrecht: Martinus Nijhoff, 1987)

Sohn, L. & Gustafson, K. *The Law of the Sea* (USA: West Publishing, 1984)

Soons, A. *Marine Scientific Research and the Law of the Sea* (The Hague: T.M. Asser Institute, 1982)

Soons, A. (Ed.), *Implementation of the Law of the Sea Convention Through International Institutions* (Honolulu: LSI, Univ. of Hawaii, 1990)

Sorensen, M. *Manual of Public International Law* (USA: MacMillan, 1968)

The South Commission, *Challenge to the South* (Oxford: Oxford Univ. Press, 1990)

Strati, A. *The Protection of Underwater Cultural Heritage: An Emerging Objective of the Contemporary Law of the Sea* (The Hague: Martinus Nijhoff, 1995)

Susskind, L. *Environmental Diplomacy* (Oxford: Oxford University Press, 1994)

Symposium on the International Regime of the Sea-Bed Proceedings (Rome: Accademia Nazionale Dei Lincei, 1970)

Thucydides, *The Peloponnesian War* The Thomas Hobbes Translation (Ann Arbor: Univ. of Michigan, 1959)

Tomuschat, C. (Ed.), *The United Nations at Age Fifty* (The Hague: Kluwer Law International, 1995)

Tribute to Barbara Ward (Ottawa: World Media Institute, 1987)

Tucker, R. *The Inequality of Nations* (NY: Basic Books, 1977)

Vasciannie, S.C. *Land-Locked and Geographically-Disadvantaged States in the International Law of the Sea* (Oxford: Clarendon Press, 1990)

Verwey, W.D. *Economic Development, Peace and International Law* (Assen: Van Gorcum, 1972)

de Visscher, C. *Theory and Reality in Public International Law* Revised Ed. (NJ: Princeton University Press, 1968)

Vukas, B. (Ed.), *Essays on the New Law of the Sea* (Zagreb: S. Liber, 1985)

de Waart, P., Peters, P. & Denters, E. (Eds.), *International Law and Development* (Dordrecht: Martinus Nijhoff, 1988)

Wallerstein, I. (Ed.), *World Inequality* (Montreal: Black Rose Books, 1975)

Ward, B. & Dubos, R. *Only One Earth* (London: Andre Deutsch, 1972)

Weil, S. *Waiting for God* (Trans. by Emma Crauford, NY: Harper Colophon Edition, 1973; originally published by Putnam's Sons, 1951)

Weiss, E.B. *In Fairness to Future Generations. International Law, Common Patrimony, and Intergenerational Equity* (Tokyo: UNU Press, 1989)

Wenk, E. *Politics of the Ocean* (Wa.: Univ. of Washington Press, 1972)

Wolfrum, R. (Ed.), *Law of the Sea at the Crossroads: The Continuing Search for a Universally Accepted Regime* (Berlin: Duncker & Humblot, 1991)

The Work of the International Law Commission (UN Sales E.88.V.1, 1988)

World Commission on Environment and Development, *Our Common Future* (UK: Oxford University Press, 1987)

Wright, M. (Ed.), *Rights and Obligations in North-South Relations* (NY: St. Martins Press, 1986)

Yuwen Li, *Transfer of Technology for Deep Seabed Mining: The 1982 Law of the Sea Convention and Beyond* (Dordrecht: Martinus Nijhoff, 1994)

Zammit-Cutajar, M. (Ed.), *UNCTAD and the North-South Dialogue: The First Twenty Years* (UNCTAD: 1985)

ARTICLES

Adede, A.O. *The System of Exploitation of the "Common Heritage of Mankind" at the Caracas Conference* 69 AJIL 31 (1975)

Adede, A.O. *The Group of 77 and the Establishment of the International Sea-Bed Authority* 7 ODIL 31 (1979)

Adede, A.O. "International Protection of the Environment" in C. Tomuschat (Ed.), *The United Nations at Age Fifty: A Legal Perspective* 197 (Kluwer, 1995)

Adelman, S. & Paliwala, A. "Law and Development in Crisis" in S. Adelman & A. Paliwala (Eds.), *Law and Crisis in the Third World* 1 (London: Hans Zell Publishers, 1993).

Ajomo, M.A. "Third World Expectations" in III R. Churchill, K. Simonds & J. Welch, (Eds.), *New Directions in the Law of the Sea* 302 (UK: BIICL, 1973)

Alexander, L.M. "Offshore Claims of the World" in Alexander, L.M. (Ed.), *The Law of the Sea Offshore Boundaries and Zones* 71 (Ohio State Univ, Press, 1967)

Alexander, L.M. "Future Regimes: A Survey of Proposals" in III R. Churchill, K. Simonds, & J. Welch (Eds.), *New Directions in the Law of the Sea* 119 (London: BIICL, 1973)

Allot, P. *Power Sharing in the Law of the Sea* 77 AJIL 1 (1983)

Alston, P. "The Right to Development at the International Level" in F. Snyder & S. Sathirathai (Eds.), *Third World Attitudes Towards International Law* 811 (Dordrecht: Martinus Nijoff, 1987)

Alston, P. *A Third Generation of Solidarity Rights: Progressive Development or Obfuscation of International Human Rights* 29 NETH INT L REV 307 (1982)

Amerasinghe, H.S. "The Third World and the Seabed" in E.M. Borgese (Ed.), *Pacem In Maribus* 237 (NY: Dodd, Mead, 1972)

Amerasinghe, H.S. "Key Issues in the Third United Nations Conference on the Law of the Sea" in Borgese E.M. & Krieger D. (Eds.), *Tides of Change* 328 (NY: Mason/Charter, 1975)

Anand, R.P. *Sovereign Equality of States in International Law* 197 RECUEIL DES COURS 99 (1986-II)

Anand, R.P. "Winds of Change in the Law of the Sea" in R.P. Anand (Ed.), *Law of the Sea: Caracas and Beyond* 36 (The Hague: Martinus Nijhoff, 1980)

Anderson, D.H. *Resolution and Agreement Relating to the Implementation of Part XI of the UN Convention on the Law of the Sea: A General Assessment* 55 ZaöRV 275 (1995)

Anderson, D.H. *Further Efforts to Ensure Universal Participation in the United Nations Convention on the Law of the Sea* 43 ICLQ 886 (1994)

Anderson, D.H. *Efforts to Ensure Universal Participation in the United Nations Convention on the Law of the Sea* 42 ICLQ 654 (1993)

Anderson K. & Schurtman, M., *The United Nations Response to the Crisis of Landmines in the Developing World* 36 HARV INT L J 359 (1995)

Andrassy, J. "Present Regime of the Military Uses of the Seabed: Possible Regimes to be Envisaged" in *Symposium on the International Regime of the Sea-Bed Proceedings* 501 (Rome: 1970)

Arangio Ruiz, "Reflections on the Present and Future Regime of the Seabed in the Ocean" in *Symposium on the International Regime of the Sea-Bed Proceedings* 296 (Rome: 1970)

Arrow, D. *The Proposed Regime for the Unilateral Exploitation of Deep Seabed Mineral Resources by the United States* 21 HARV INT L J 337 (1980)

Babović, B. "The Duty of States to Cooperate in Accordance with the Charter" in M. Sahović (Ed.), *Principles of International Law Concerning Friendly Relations and Cooperation* 277 (NY: Oceana, 1972)

Baker, P.J. *The Doctrine of Legal Equality of States* 4 BYIL 1 (1923/24)

Ballah. L. "The Universality of the 1982 Convention on the Law of the Sea: Common Heritage or Common Burden?" in Nadjeeb Al-Nauimi & R. Meese (Eds.), *International Legal Isues Arising Under the United Nations Decade of International Law* 339 (The Hague: Martinus Nijhoff, 1995)

Balton, D.A. *Strengthening the Law of the Sea: The New Agreement on Straddling Fish Stocks and Highly Migratory Fish Stocks* 27 ODIL 125 (1996)

Barry, F. *The Administration of the Outer Continental Shelf Lands Act* 1 NAT RES L, No. 3, 38 (1968)

Barry, F. *Administration of Laws for the Exploitation of Offshore Minerals in the United States and Abroad* 1 NAT RES L, No. 1, 48 (1968)

Barsch, R.L. *The Rights to Development as a Human Right: Results of the Global Consultation* 13 HUMAN RIGHTS QRTLY 322 (1991)

Bascom, W. "Mining the Sea" in L.M. Alexander (Ed.), *The Law of the Sea Offshore Boundaries and Zones* 160 (Ohio State Univ. Press, 1967)

Belman, M. *The Role of the State Department in Formulating Federal Policy Regarding Marine Resources* 1 NAT RES L, No. 2, 14 (1968)

Bennet, E.F. "Legal Climate for Underseas Mining" in *Exploiting the Oceans: Transactions of the 2nd Annual Marine Technology Society Conference 27-29 June 1966* 204 (Washington, DC: MTS, 1966)

Bennouna, M. "The Multidimensional Character of the New Law of the Sea" in R.-J. Dupuy & D. Vignes (Eds.), *A Handbook on the New Law of the Sea* Vol I, 3 (Dordrecht: Martinus Nijhoff, 1991)

Bernard, H.R. "Restrictions on Oceanic Research: An Anthropologist's View" in L. Alexander (Ed.), *The Law of the Sea Needs and Interests of Developing Countries* 206 (Law of the Sea Institute, 1973)

Bernfeld, S. *Developing the Resources of the Sea - Security of Investment* 1 NAT RES L, No. 1, 82 (1968)

Bernhart, J. *A Schematic Analysis of Vessel-Source Pollution: Prescriptive and Enforcement Regimes in the Law of the Sea Conference* 20 VA J INT L 265 (1980)

Berthoud, P. "UNCTAD and the Emergence of International Development Law" in M. Zammit Cutajar (Ed.), *UNCTAD and the North-South Dialogue: The First Twenty Years* 71 (UNCTAD, 1985)

Bin Chen, *The Legal Regime of Airspace and Outerspace: The Boundary Problem. Functionalism versus Spatialism: The Major Premises* 5 ANNALS OF AIR & SPACE LAW 323 (1980)

Birnie, P. *Law of the Sea and Ocean Resources: Implications for Marine Scientific Research* 10 IJMCL 229 (1995)

Birnie, P. "International Environmental Law: Its Adequacy for Present and Future Needs" in A. Hurell and B. Kingsbury (Eds.), *The International Politics of the Environment* 51 (Oxford: Clarendon Press, 1992)

Boczek, B.A. *Ideology and the New Law of the Sea: The Challenge of the New International Economic order* 7 BOSTON COLLEGE INT & COMP L REV 1 (1984).

Boczek, B.A. *The Transfer of Marine Technology to Developing Nations in International Law* (Law of the Sea Institute Occasional Paper no. 23, 1982)

Bodansky, D. *Protecting the Marine Environment from Vessel-Source Pollution* 18 ECOLOGY L QTLY 719 (1991)

Borgese, E.M. "A Constitution for the Oceans" in E.M. Borgese & D. Krieger (Eds.), *Tides of Change* 340 (New York: Mason/Charter, 1975)

Borgese, E.M. *The New International Economic Order and the Law of the Sea* 14 SAN DIEGO L REV 584 (1975)

Borgese, E.M. "Expanding the Common Heritage of Mankind" in A. Dolman (Ed.), *Global Planning and Resource Management* (Oxford: Pergamon Press, 1980)

Borgese, E.M. *The Enterprises: A Proposal to reconceptualize the operational arm of the International Seabed Authority to manage the common heritage of mankind* (Malta: IOI Occasional Papers No. 6, November 1978)

Borgese, E.M. *An International Seabed Authority for the 21st Century* (forthcoming)

Bos, M. "Will and Order in the Nation-State System: Observations on Positivism and International Law" in R.St.J. MacDonald & D.M. Johnston (Eds.), *The Structure and Process of International Law: Essays in Legal Philosophy, Doctrine, and Theory* (Dordrecht: Martinus Nihhoff, 1986)

Boutros-Ghali, B. "Foreword" to the *Symposium on The United Nations: Challenges of Law and Development* 36 HARVARD INT L J 267 (1995)

Boutros-Ghali, B. *Agenda for Peace - One Year Later* 37 ORBIS 323 (1993)

Boyle, A.E. "The Rio Convention on Biological Diversity" in M. Bowman & C. Redgewell (Eds.), *International Law and the Conservation of Biological Diversity* 33 (UK: Kluwer Law International, 1996)

Boyle, A.E. *Marine Pollution under the Law of the Sea* 79 AJIL 347 (1985)

Brewer, W. *Deep Seabed Mining: Can an Acceptable Regime Ever be Found?* 11 ODIL 25 (1982)

Breaux, J. "The Case Against the Convention" in A. Koers & B. Oxman (Eds.), *The 1982 Convention on the Law of the Sea* 10 (Honolulu: LSI, Univ. of Hawaii, 1984)

Broadus, J. "Introduction" in Seung-Hong, E. Miles & Choon-ho Park (Eds.), *The Role of the Ocean in the 21st Century* 329 (Honolulu: LSI, Univ. of Hawaii 1995)

Broms, B. "States" in M. Bedjaoui (Ed.), *International Law Achievements and Prospects* 60 (UNESCO, 1991)

Brooks, D. "Deep Sea Manganese Nodules: From Scientific Phenomenon to World Resources" in L. Alexander (Ed.), *The Law of the Sea: The Future of the Sea's Resources* 32 (RI: Law of the Sea Institute, 1968)

Brown, E.D. "Maritime Zones: A Survey of Claims" in III R. Churchill, K. Simonds & J. Welch (Eds.), *New Directions in the Law of the Sea* 157 (London: BIICL, 1973)

Brown, E.D. "The Present Regime of the Exploration and Exploitation of Sea-Bed Resources in International Law and in National Legislation: An Evaluation" in *Symposium on the International Regime of the Sea-Bed Proceedings* 241 (Rome: 1970)

Brown, E.D. "Our Nation and the Sea: A Comment on the Proposed Legal-Political Framework for the Development of Submarine Mineral Resources" in L. Alexander (Ed.), *National Policy Recommendations* 2 (RI; Law of the Sea Institute, 1969)

Brownlie I. "The Expansion of International Society: The Consequences for the Law of Nations" in H. Bull & A. Watson (Eds.), *The Expansion of International Society* 357 (UK: Oxford Univ Press, 1984)

Bruckner, P. "Preparatory Investment Under the Convention and the PIP Resolution" in A. Koers & B. Oxman (Eds.), *The 1982 Convention on the Law of the Sea* 181 (Honolulu: LSI, Univ. of Hawaii, 1984)

Burke, W. "Commentary" in A. Soons (Ed.), *Implementation of the Law of the Sea Convention Through International Institutions* 539 (Honolulu: LSI, 1990)

Burke, W. *1982 Convention on the Law of the Sea: provisions on conditions of access to fisheries subject to national jurisdiction* FAO Fisheries Report No. 293, Annex I (1983)

Burke, W. *A Negative View of a Proposal for United Nations Ownership of Ocean Mineral Resources* 1 NAT RES L, No. 2, at 42 (1968)

Burke, W. "Legal Aspects of Ocean Exploitation - Status and Outlook" in *Exploiting the Oceans: Transactions of the 2nd Annual Marine Technology Society Conference 27-29 June 1966* 1 (Washington, DC: MTS, 1966)

Burke, W. *Ocean Sciences, Technology and the Future International Law of the Sea* (Ohio State University, 1966)

Burke, W. *Some Comments on the 1958 Conventions* 1959 ASIL Proc. 197

Caflisch, L.C. "The Settlement of Disputes Relating to Activities in the International Seabed Area" in Rozakis, C.L. & Stephanou, C.A. (Eds.), *The New Law of the Sea* 303 (1983)

Carty, A. *Critical International Law: Recent Trends in the Theory of International Law* 2 EJIL 66 (1991)

Charlesworth, H. *The Public-Private Distinction and the Right to Development in International Law* 13 AUSTRALIAN YBIL 190 (1992)

Charney, J. *The Marine Environment and the 1982 United Nations Convention on the Law of the Sea* 28 INTERNATIONAL LAWYER 879 (1994)

Charney, J. *Universal International Law* 87 AJIL 529 (1993)

Chayes, A. "International Institutions for the Environment" in J.L. Hargrove (Ed.), *Law, Institutions and the Global Environment* 1 (NY: Oceana, 1972)

Chemillier-Gendreau, M. "Relations between the Ideology of Development and the Development of Law" in Snyder & Slinn (Eds.), *International Law of Development: Comparative Perspectives* 63 (UK: Professional Books, 1987)

Childers, E. & Urquhart, B. *Renewing the United Nations System* 1994 DEVELOPMENT DIALOGUE (no. 1, special issue)

Chinkin, C., *The Challenge of Soft Law: Development and Change in International Law* 38 ICLQ 850 (1989)

Chowdhury, S.R. "Common but Differentiated State Responsibility in International Environmental Law: from Stockholm (1972) to Rio (1992)" in K. Ginther, E. Denters & P.J.I.M. de Waart (Eds.), *Sustainable Development and Good Governance* 322 (Dordrecht: Martinus Nijhoff, 1995)

Christy, F. *Marine Fisheries and the Law of the Sea Special (Revised) Chapter of the State of Food and Agriculture 1992* FAO FISHERIES CIRCULAR No. 853 (1993)

Christy, F. *Alternative Regimes for Marine Resources Underlying the High Seas* 1 NAT RES L, No. 2, 63 (1968)

Cicin-Sain, B. *Earth Summit Implementation: Progress Since Rio* 20 MARINE POLICY 123 (1996)

Cicin-Sain, B. *Sustainable Development and Integrated Coastal Zone Management* 21 OCEAN & COASTAL MGMT 12 (1993)

Cicin-Sain, B. & Knecht, R. *Implications of the Earth Summit for Ocean and Coastal Governance* 24 ODIL 323 (1993)

Clark, D.W. "Telemanipulator Systems for Deep-Sea Operations" in *Exploiting the Oceans: Transactions of the 2nd Annual Marine Technology Society Conference 27-29 June 1966* (Washington, DC: MTS, 1966)

Colson, D. *United States Accession to the United Nations Convention on the Law of the Sea* 7 GEORGETOWN INT ENV L REV 651 (1995)

Cot, J.-P. & Boniface, P. "Disarmament and Arms Control" in M. Bedjaoui (Ed.), *International Law: Achievements and Prospects* 811 (UNESCO, 1991)

Crawford, B., Cobb, JS & Freidman, A. *Building Capacity for Integrated Coastal Zone Management in Developing Countries* 21 OCEAN & COASTAL MGMT 311 (1993)

D'Amato, A. *An Alternative to the Law of the Sea Convention* 77 AJIL 281 (1983)

Danzig, A. *A Funny Thing Happened to the Common Heritage on the Way to the Sea* 12 SAN DIEGO L REV 655 (1975)

Davidson, K. *A Comment* 55 ZaöRV 290 (1995)

Dean, A. *The Geneva Conference on the Law of the Sea: What was Accomplished* 52 AJIL 607 (1958)

Dempsey, P. *Compliance and Enforcement in International Law - Oil Pollution of the Marine Environment by Ocean Vessels* 6 NORTHWESTERN J INTL L & BUS 459 (1984)

Douglas Lummis, C. "Equality" in W. Sachs (Ed.), *The Development Dictionary: A Guide to Knowledge as Power* 38 (London: Zed Books, 1992)

Dupuy, R.-J. "The Sea Under National Competence" in R.J. Dupuy, & D. Vignes, (Eds.), *A Handbook on the New Law of the Sea*, Vol. I, 247 (Dordrecht: Martinus Nijhoff, 1991)

Dupuy, R.-J. "The Area as the Common Heritage of Mankind", in R.J. Dupuy, & D. Vignes, (Eds.) *A Handbook on the New Law of the Sea*, Vol. I, 579 (Dordrecht: Martinus Nijhoff, 1991)

Dupuy, R.-J. "The Notion of the Common Heritage of Mankind Applied to the Seabed" in Rozakis, C.L. & Stephanou, C.A. (Eds.), *The New Law of the Sea* 199 (1983)

van Dyke, J. *Modifying the 1982 Law of the Sea Convention: New Initiatives on Governance of the High Seas Fisheries Resources in the Straddling Stocks Negotiation* 10 IJMCL 219 (1995)

van Dyke, J. & Yuen, C. *"Common Heritage" vs. "Freedom of the Seas": Which Governs the Seabed?* 19 SAN DIEGO L REV 493 (1982)

Eichelberger, C. *A Case for the Administration of Marine Resources Underlying the High Seas by the United Nations* 1 NAT RES L, No. 2, 85 (1968)

Eichelberger, M. *The Promise of the Sea's Bounty - How the Oceans' Enormous Riches can Contribute to Peace and Help Alleviate World Poverty – If they are placed under U.N. Administration Now* excerpts in *House Interim Report* 10

Ely, N. "The Laws Governing Exploitation of the Minerals Beneath the Sea" in *Exploiting the Oceans: Transactions of the 2nd Annual Marine Technology Society Conference 27-29 June 1966* 373 (Washington, DC: MTS, 1966)

Ely, N. *A Case for Administration of Mineral Resources Underlying the High Seas by National Interests* 1 NAT RES L, No. 2, 78 (1968)

Ely, N. *American Policy Options in the Development of Undersea Mineral Resources* 1 NAT RES L, No. 1, 91 (1968)

Engo, P.B. "Issues of the First Committee at UNCLOS III" in A. Koers & B. Oxman (Eds.), *The 1982 Convention on the Law of the Sea* 33 (Honolulu: LSI Univ of Hawaii, 1984)

van Ettinger, J., King, A. & Payoyo, P.B. "Ocean Governance and the Global Picture" in P.B. Payoyo (Ed.), *Ocean Governance: Sustainable Development of the Seas* 247 (Tokyo: UNU Press, 1994)

Evans, G. *All States are Equal, But..* 7 REVIEW OF INTERNATIONAL STUDIES 59 (1981)

Evensen, J. *Working Methods and Procedures in the Third United Nations Conference on the Law of the Sea* 199 RECUEIL DES COURS 415 (1986-IV)

Evensen, J. "The Effect of the Law of the Sea Convention Upon the Process of International Law: Rapprochement Between Competing Points of View" in R. Krueger & S. Riesenfeld (Ed.), *The Developing Order of the Oceans* 23 (Hawaii: Law of the Sea Institute, 1985)

Fatouros, A. "Developing States" in R. Bernhardt (Ed.), *Encyclopedia of International Law*, Vol. 9, 71 (The Netherlands: Elsevier, 1986).

Finlay, L. *The Outer Limit of the Continental Shelf. A Rejoinder to Professor Louis Henkin* 64 AJIL 42 (1970)

Flory, M. "Adapting International Law to the Development of the Third World" in F. Snyder & S. Sathirathai (Eds.), *Third World Attitudes Towards International Law* (Dordrecht: Martinus Nijoff, 1987)

Fleischer, C.A. "Fisheries and Biological Resources" in R.-J. Dupuy, & D. Vignes, (Eds.) *A Handbook on the New Law of the Sea*, Vol. II, 989 (Dordrecht: Martinus Nijhoff, 1991)

Flory, M. "A North-South Legal Dialogue: The International Law of Development" in F. Snyder & P. Slinn (Eds.), *International Law of Development: Comparative Perspectives* 14 (UK: Professional Books, 1987)

Fons Buhl, J. "Development and Transfer of Marine Technology" in R.-J. Dupuy & D. Vignes, (Eds.), *A Handbook on the New Law of the Sea*, Vol. II, 1146 (Dordrecht: Martinus Nijhoff, 1991)

Francioni, F. "International Cooperation for the Protection of the Environment: The Procedural Dimension" in W. Lang, H. Neuhold & K. Zemanek (Eds.), *Environmental Protection and International Law* 203 (Kluwer, 1991)

Fye, P. "Scientific Research in the Oceans" in E.M. Borgese & D. Krieger (Eds.), *Tides of Change* 306 (New York: Mason/Charter, 1975)

Galdorski, G. "The United States and the Law of the Sea: Decade of Decision" in *The United States and the Law of the Sea Convention: The Cases Pro and Con* 7 (LSI Occasional Paper No. 38, 1994)

Gauci, V. "Personal Recollections and Reflections on a Major Initiative" in *Malta Review of Foreign Affairs* Special Issue: Towards a Second Generation United Nations, 39 (Malta: Ministry of Foreign Affairs & The Univ. of Malta, 1993)

Glowka, L. *The Deepest Ironies: Genetic Resource, Marine Scientific Research and the Area* 12 OCEAN YRBK 154 (1996)

Gold, E. "The Rise of the Coastal State in the Law of the Sea" in D.M. Johnston (Ed.), *Marine Policy and the Coastal Community* 13 (London: Croom Helm, 1976)

Goldie, L.F.E. "Development of an International Environmental Law - An Appraisal" in J.L. Hargrove (Ed.), *Law, Institutions and the Global Environment* 104 (NY: Oceana, 1972)

Gorove, S. *The Concept of the Common Heritage of Mankind: A Political, Moral or Legal Innovation?* 9 SAN DIEGO L REV 390 (1970)

Griffith, M.D. *The South and the United Nations Conference on Environment and Development: The Dawn of a Probable Turning Point in International Relations Between States* 18 OCEAN & COASTAL MGMT 55 (1992)

Gundling, L. *Compliance Assistance in International Environmental Law: Capacity-Building Through Financial and Technology Transfer* 56 ZaöRV 796 (1996)

Gunter, M. *What Happened to the United Nations Mini-State Problem?* 71 AJIL 110 (1977)

Gutteridge, J.A.C. *The 1958 Geneva Convention on the Continental Shelf* 35 BYIL 102 (1959)

Handl, G. "Environmental Security and Global Change: The Challenge to International Law" in W. Lang, H. Neuhold & K. Zemanek (Eds.), *Environmental Protection and International Law* 85 (London: Kluwer, 1991)

Handl, G. *Environmental Protection and Development in Third World Countries: Common Destiny - Common Responsibility* 20 NYU J INT L & POL 603 (1988)

Hayashi, M. *The 1994 Agreement for the Universalization of the Law of the Sea Convention* 27 ODIL 31 (1996)

Hayashi, M. "Effect of Entry into Force of the UN Convention on the Law of the Sea" in K.L. Koh, R.C. Beckman & Chia Lin Sien (Eds.), *Sustainable*

Development of Coastal and Ocean Areas in Southeast Asia: Post-Rio Perspectives 59 (National University of Singapore, 1995)

Hearn, W. *The Role of the United States Navy in the Formulation of Federal Policy regarding the Sea* 1 NAT RES L, No. 2, 23 (1968)

Hendrickx, F., Koester V. & Prip, C. *Convention on Biological Diversity. Access to Genetic Resources: A Legal Analysis* 23 EPL 250 (1993)

Henkin, L. "Old Politics and New Directions" in III R. Churchill, K. Simonds & J. Welch (Eds.), *New Directions in the Law of the Sea* 3 (London: BIICL, 1973)

Henkin, L. *Law for the Sea's Mineral Resources* (NY: Columbia Univ., 1968)

Henkin, L. *International Law and "The Interests": The Law of the Seabed* 63 AJIL 504 (1969)

Henkin, L. *A Reply to Mr. Finlay* 64 AJIL 62 (1970)

Hirdman, S. "Prospects for Arms Control in the Ocean" in E.M. Borgese & D. Krieger (Eds.), *Tides of Change* 80 (New York: Mason/Charter, 1975)

Horn, N. *Normative Problems of a New International Economic Order* 16 JWTL 338 (1982)

Hurst, C. *Whose is the Bed of the Sea?* 4 BYIL 34 (1923-24)

Hutchinson, DN. *The Seaward Limit to Continental Shelf Jurisdiction in Customary International Law* 56 BYIL 111 (1985)

Iguchi, T. "Perspectives on Proposed Revisions in Part XI" in M.H. Nordquist & J.N. Moore (Eds.), *Entry Into Force of the Law of the Sea Convention* (The Hague: Martinus Nijhoff, 1995)

International Law Response to the New International Economic Order: An Overview 9 BOSTON COLL INT & COMP L R 257 (1986)

Jaenicke, G. "The United Nations Convention on the Law of the Sea and the Agreement Relating to the Implementation of Part XI of the Convention: Treaty Law Problems in the Process of Revising the Deep Seabed Mining Regime of the Convention" in Beyerlin, U. *et al.* (Eds.), *Festschrift fur Rudolf Bernhardt* 121 (Berlin: Springer-Verlag, 1995)

Jennings, R.Y. "The Santiago Conference and the Future" in III R.R. Churchill, K.R. Simonds, & J. Welch (Eds.), *New Directions in the Law of the Sea* 12 (London: The British Institute of International and Comparative Law, 1973)

Jennings, R.Y. *The Limits of the Continental Shelf Jurisdiction: Some Possible Implications of the North Sea Case Judgement* 18 ICLQ 819 (1969)

Jesus, J.L. "Statement on the Issue of the Universality of the Convention" in R. Wolfrum (Ed.), *Law of the Sea at the Crossroads: The Continuing Search for a Universally Accepted Regime* 21 (Berlin: Duncker & Humblot, 1991)

Johnston, D.M. "UNCED: The Coastal and Ocean Challenge" in K.L. Koh, R.C. Beckman & Chia Lin Sien (Eds.), *Sustainable Development of Coastal and Ocean Areas in Southeast Asia: Post-Rio Perspectives* 1 (National University of Singapore, 1995)

Johnston, D.M. "The Foundations of Justice in International Law" in R.St.J. Macdonald, D.M. Johnston & G.L. Morris (Eds.), *The International Law and Policy of Human Welfare* 134 (The Netherlands: Sijthoff & Noordhoff, 1978)

Johnston, D.M. *Law, Technology, and the Sea* 55 CALIF L REV 449 (1967)

Joyner, C. *The United States and the New Law of the Sea* 27 ODIL 41 (1996)

Joyner, C. *The Antarctic Treaty System and the Law of the Sea - Competing Regimes in the Southern Ocean?* 10 IJMCL 301 (1995)

Joyner C.C. & Martell, E.A. *Looking Back to See Ahead: UNCLOS III and Lessons for Global Commons Law* 27 ODIL 73 (1996)

Juda, L. *World Maritime Fish Catch in the Age of Exclusive Economic Zones and Exclusive Fishing Zones* 22 ODIL 1 (1991)

Kamminga, M.T. "Principles of International Environmental Law" in P. Glasbergen & A. Blowers (Eds.), *Environmental Policy in an International Context* 111 (UK: Open University of The Netherlands, 1995)

Kay, D. *International Transfer of Marine Technology: The Transfer Process and International Organizations* 2 ODIL 351 (1974)

Kelsen, H. *The Principle of Sovereign Equality of States as a Basis for International Organization* 53 YALE L J 207 (1944)

Khan, R. "Marine Science Research: Some Thoughts on the Implications of a Free and Consent-Based Regime" in R.P. Anand (Ed.), *The Law of the Sea Caracas and Beyond* 293 (The Hague: Martinus Nijhoff, 1980)

Kimball, L. "The United Nations Convention on the Law of the Sea: A Framework for Marine Conservation" in *The Law of the Sea: Priorities and Responsibilities in Implementing the Convention* 1 (Gland: IUCN, 1995)

Kimball, L. *UNCED and the Oceans Agenda: The Process Forward* 17 MARINE POLICY 491 (1993)

Kimball, L. *International Law and Institutions: The Oceans and Beyond* 20 ODIL 147 (1989)

Kirthisingha, P.N. *The Enterprise: An Expendable Triumph* 5 MARINE POLICY 252 (1981)

Kiss, A. *The Common Heritage of Mankind: Utopia or Reality?* 60 INTL JOURNAL, No. 3, 423 (1985)

Kissinger, H. *The Law of the Sea: A Test of International Cooperation* 74 Dept of State Bulletin, 26 Sept. 1976

Kissinger, H. *Towards a New Understanding of Community*, address before the 31st UNGA 75 Dept of State Bul 497, 30 Sept. 1976

Koch, J. "Revisions in Part XI: A Necessary Compromise" in M.H. Nordquist & J.N. Moore (Eds.), *Entry Into Force of the Law of the Sea Convention* 151 (The Hague: Martinus Nijhoff, 1995)

Koh T. & Jayakumar, S. "The Negotiating Process of the Third United Nations Conference on the Law of the Sea" in Nordquist, M. (Ed.-in-chief), *United Nations Convention on the Law of the Sea 1982: A Commentary* Vol. 1, 29 (Va.: Center for Oceans Law and Policy, Univ. of Va., 1985)

Koskenniemi, M. *The Politics of International Law* 1 EJIL 4 (1990)

Kreuger, R. *The Convention on the Continental Shelf and the Need for Its Revision and Some Comments Regarding the Regime for the Lands Beyond* 1 NAT RES L, no. 3 at 1 (1968)

Kunz, J. *Continental Shelf and International Law: Confusion and Abuse* 50 AJIL 828 (1956)

Kwiatkowksa, B. *Ocean-Related Impact of Agenda 21 on International Organizations of the United Nations System in Follow-up to the Rio Summit* 1992 NILOS DOCUMENTARY YEARBOOK xiii

Kwiatkowska, B. "The Role of Regional Organizations in Development Cooperation in Marine Affairs" in A. Soons (Ed.), *Implementation of the Law of the Sea Convention Through International Institutions* 38 (Honolulu: LSI, Univ. of Hawaii, 1990)

Lachs, M. "Some Thoughts on Equality" in R.St.J. Macdonald, (Ed.), *Essays in Honour of Wang Tieya* 483 (Dordrecht: Martinus Nijhoff, 1994)

Lachs, M. "Outer Space, the Moon and Other Celestial Bodies" in M. Bedjaoui (Ed.), *International Law Achievements and Prospects* 959 (UNESCO, 1991)

Larson, D. *The Reagan Administration and the Law of the Sea* 11 ODIL 297 (1982)

Law of the Sea Forum: the 1994 Agreement on the Implementation of the Seabed Provisions of the Convention on the Law of the Sea 88 AJIL 687-714 (1994)

Laylin, J.G. "Interim Practices and Policy for the Governing of Seabed Mining Beyond the Limits of National Jurisdiction" in L. Alexander (Ed.), *The Law of the Sea: Needs and Interests of Developing Countries* 25 (RI: Law of the Sea Institute, 1973)

LeFeber, R. *The Exercise of Jurisdiction in the Antarctic Region and the Changing Structure of International Law: The International Community and Common Interests* 21 NETH YRBK INT L 81 (1990)

Luce, C. *The Development of Ocean Minerals and the Law of the Sea* 1 NAT RES L, No. 3, 29 (1968)

Macdonald, R.St.J. "The Common Heritage of Mankind" in Beyerlin, U. *et al.* (Eds.), *Festschrift fur Rudolf Bernhardt* 153 (Berlin: Springer-Verlag, 1995)

Macdonald, R.St.J. "The Principle of Solidarity in Public International Law" in C. Dominice, R. Patry & C. Reymond (Eds.), *Etudes de Droit International en L'Honneur de Pierre Lalive* 275 (Geneva: Institut de Hautes Etudes Internationales, 1993)

Macdonald, R.St.J., Johnston, D.M. & Morris, G.L. "The International Law of Human Welfare: Concepts, Experience, and Priorities" in R.St.J. Macdonald, D.M. Johnston & G.L. Morris (Eds.), *The International Law and Policy of Human Welfare* 3 (The Netherlands: Sijthoff & Noordhoff, 1978)

Magarasević, A. "The Sovereign Equality of States" in M. Sahović (Ed.), *Principles of International Law Concerning Friendly Relations and Cooperation* 171 (NY: Oceana, 1972)

Manheim, F.T. *Marine Cobalt Resources* 232 SCIENCE 600 (2 May 1986)

Manin, P. "The Viability of a Dual Approach: The French Position" in R. Krueger & S. Riesenfeld (Eds.), *The Developing Order of the Oceans* 206 (Honolulu: LSI, Univ. of Hawaii, 1985)

Mapel, D. "The Contractarian Tradition and International Ethics" in T. Nardin & D. Mapel (Eds.), *Traditions of International Ethics* 180 (Cambridge Univ. Press, 1992)

Maquieira, C. "Statement on the Implementation of Resolution III of the Third United Nations Conference on the Law of the Sea by the Preparatory Commission for the International Sea-Bed Authority" in R. Wolfrum (Ed.), *Law of the Sea at the Crossroads: The Continuing Search for a Universally Accepted Regime* 45 (Berlin: Duncker & Humblot, 1991)

Marceau, G. *Some Evidence of a New International Economic Order in Place* 22 REVUE GENERALE DE DROIT 397 (1991)

de Marffy, A. "The Pardo Declaration and the Six Years of the Sea-Bed Committee" in Dupuy & Vignes (Eds.), *A Handbook on the New Law of the Sea*, Vol. I, 141 (Martinus Nijhoff, 1991)

de Marffy, A. "Marine Scientific Research" in Dupuy & Vignes (Eds.), *A Handbook on the New Law of the Sea*, Vol. II, 1125 (Martinus Nijhoff, 1991)

de Marffy-Mantuano, A. *The Procedural Framework of the Agreement Implementing the 1982 United Nations Convention on the Law of the Sea* 89 AJIL 814(1995)

Marston, G. *The Incorporation of Continental Shelf Rights into United Kingdom Law* 45 ICLQ 13 (1996)

McConnel, M. & Gold, E. *The Modern Law of the Sea: Framework for the Protection and Preservation of the Marine Environment?* 23 CASE-WESTERN RES J INT L 83 (1991)

McDorman, T. *The Entry into Force of the 1982 LOS Convention and the Article 76 Outer Continental Shelf Regime* 10 IJMCL 165 (1996)

McNair, A.D. *Equality in International Law* 26 MICHIGAN L REV 131 (1927)

McDougal, M.S. & Reisman, W.M. "International Law in Policy-Oriented Perspective" in R.St.J. Macdonald & D.M. Johnston (Eds.), *The Structure and Process of International Law: Essays in Legal Philosophy, Doctrine, and Theory* (Dordrecht: Martinus Nihhoff, 1986)

McDougal, M. *Revision of the Geneva Conventions on the Law of the Sea. The Views of a Commentator* 1 NAT RES L, No. 2, 99 & No. 3, 19 (1968)

Mero, J. "Review of Mineral Values On and Under the Ocean Floor" in *Exploiting the Oceans: Transactions of the 2nd Annual Marine Technology Society Conference 27-29 June 1966* 61 (Washington, DC: MTS, 1966)

Micoud, A. *Du "patrimoine naturel de l'humanité" consideré comme un symptome* 30/31 DROIT ET SOCIETE 265 (1995)

Miles, E. "An Interpretation of the Negotiating Process of UNCLOS III" in R.St.J. Macdonald (Ed.), *Essays in Honour of Wang Tieya* 552 (Dordrecht: Martinus Nijhoff, 1994)

Miles, E. "The Dynamics of Global Ocean Politics" in D.M. Johnston (Ed.), *Marine Policy and the Coastal Community The Impact of the Law of the Sea* 147 (London: Croom Helm, 1976)

Miles, E. *An Interpretation of the Geneva Proceedings* 3 ODIL 187 (1975-76)

Miles, E. "Remarks" in L. Alexander (Ed.), *The Law of the Sea Needs and Interests of Developing Countries* 19 (RI: Law of the Sea Institute, 1973)

Mitlin, D. *Sustainable Development: A Guide to the Literature* 4 ENVIRONMENT AND URBANIZATION 111 (1992)

Monden, A. & Wills, G. *Art Objects as Common Heritage of Mankind* 19 REVUE BELGE DE DROIT INTERNATIONALE 327 (1986)

Monnier, J. "Right of Access to the Sea and Freedom of Transit" in R.-J. Dupuy & D. Vignes (Eds.), *A Handbook on the New Law of the Sea*, Vol. I, 501 (Dordrecht: Martinus Nijhoff, 1991)

Montgomery, N.E. "Drilling in the Sea from Floating Platforms" in *Exploiting the Oceans: Transactions of the 2nd Annual Marine Technology Society Conference 27-29 June 1966* (Washington, DC: MTS, 1966)

Moore, J.N. "The Law of the Sea: An Overview" in C.J. Joyner (Ed.), *International Law of the Sea and the Future of Deep Seabed Mining* (Proceedings of the J.B. Moore Society of International Law Symposium and the American Society of International Law Regional Meeting, Virginia, 16 Nov 1974) 25 (Va: Accent Printing, 1975)

Moore, J.N. "Renegotiating Part XI: Ensuring an Effective Seabed Mining Regime" in M.H. Nordquist (Ed.), *15th Annual Seminar of the Center for Ocean Law and Policy: Issues in Amending Part XI of the Convention* 239 (Univ. of Va.: 1991)

Moore, J.N. *The United Nations Convention on the Law of the Sea and the Rule of Law* 7 GEORGETOWN INT ENV L REV 645 (1995)

Morris, M.A. "The New International Economic Order and the New Law of the Sea" in K.P. Sauvant & H. Hasenpflug (Eds.), *The New International Economic Order: Confrontation or Cooperation between North and South?* 175 (Boulder: Westview Press, 1977)

Munier, R. "The Politics of Marine Science: Crisis and Compromise" in L. Alexander (Ed.), *The Law of the Sea Needs and Interests of Developing Countries* 219 (RI: Law of the Sea Institute, 1973)

Myrdal, A. "No Arms on the Ocean Floor" in E.M. Borgese (Ed.), *Pacem In Maribus* 322 (NY: Dodd Mead, 1972)

Najam, A. *An Environmental Negotiation Strategy for the South* 7 INTERNATIONAL ENVIRONMENTAL AFFAIRS 249 (1995)

Nandan, S. "The United Nations Convention on the Law of the Sea: Resolving the Problems of Part XI" in M.H. Nordquist (Ed.), *17th Annual Seminar of the Center for Oceans Law and Policy* 57 (Univ. of Va.: 1993)

Nandan, S. "The Exclusive Economic Zone: A Historical Perspective" in *The Law and the Sea: Essays in Memory of Jean Carroz* 171 (Rome: FAO, 1987)

Nelson, L.D.M. "The Preparatory Commission for the International Sea-Bed Authority and the International Tribunal for the Law of the Sea: An Evaluation" in R. Wolfrum (Ed.), *Law of the Sea at the Crossroads: The Continuing Search for a Universally Accepted Regime* 31 (Berlin: Duncker & Humblot, 1991)

Nelson, L.D.M. "Issues in Amending Part XI of the LOS Convention: Renewing the Dialogue" in M.H. Nordquist (Ed.), *Issues in Amending Part XI of the Convention: 15th Annual Seminar of the Center for Oceans Law and Policy* (Univ. of Va.: 1991)

Nelson, L.D.M. *The New Deep Seabed Mining Regime* 10 IJMCL 189 (1995)

NIEO discussion in 1993 ASIL Proc 459-487

Noland, G. "Ocean Frontiers: Initiatives in the 21st Century" in Seung Yong Hong, E. Miles & Choon-Ho Park (Eds.), *The Role of the Oceans in the 21st Century* 218 (Honolulu: LSI, 1995)

Oda, S. "Sharing of Ocean Resources - Unresolved Issues in the Law of the Sea" in R.-J. Dupuy (Ed.), *The Management of Humanity's Resources: The Law of the Sea* 49 (Workshop, The Hague Academy of International Law & UNU, 1982)

Oda, S. *Fisheries under the United Nations Convention on the Law of the Sea* 77 AJIL 739 (1983)

Oda, S. *The Geneva Conventions on the Law of the Sea: Some Suggestions for their Revision* 1 NAT RES L, No. 2, 103 (1968)

Oda, S. *Proposals for Revising the Continental Shelf Convention* 7 COLUMBIA J TRANS L 1 (1968)

Oda, S. "Future Regime of the Deep Ocean Floor" in *Symposium on the International Regime of the Sea-Bed Proceedings* 343 (Rome: 1970)

Okafor, O. *The Status and Effect of the Right to Development in International Law* 7 AFRICAN J INT & COMP L 865 (1995)

O'Keefe, P. & Nafziger, J. *The Draft Convention on the Protection of Underwater Cultural Heritage* 25 ODIL 391 (1994)

Oswald, J.W. "Toward a Political Theory of the Ocean" in *Exploiting the Oceans: Transactions of the 2nd Annual Marine Technology Society Conference 27-29 June 1966* 358 (Washington, DC: MTS, 1966)

Oxman, B. *The 1994 Agreement and the Convention* 88 AJIL 687-696 (1994)

Oxman, B. *The Third United Nations Conference on the Law of the Sea: The 1976 New York Session* 71 AJIL 247 (1977)

Oxman, B. "The U.S. Position" in L. Alexander (Ed.), *The Law of the Sea Needs and Interests of Developing Countries* 156 (RI: Law of the Sea Institute, 1973)

Palmer, G. *New Ways to Make International Environmental Law* 86 AJIL 259-283 (1992)

Paolillo, F. *The Institutional Arrangements for the International Seabed and their Impact on the Evolution of International Organization* 188 RECUEIL DES COURS 135 (1984 V)

Pardo, A. *The Origins of the Maltese Initiative* 9 INTERNATIONAL INSIGHTS 65 (1993)

Pardo. A. *Development of Ocean Space - An International Dilemma* 31 LOUISIANA L REV 45 (1970).

Pardo, A. *The Convention on the Law of the Sea: A Preliminary Appraisal* 20 SAN DIEGO L REV 489 (1983)

Pardo, A. & Borgese, E.M. "The Common Heritage of Mankind and the Transfer of Technology" in E.M. Borgese & P White (Eds.), *Seabed Mining: Scientific, Economic, and Political Aspects An Interdisciplinary Manual* 366 (Malta: IOI Occasional Paper No. 7.)

Pardo, A. & Christol, C. "The Common Interest: Tension Between the Whole and the Parts" in R.St.J. Macdonald & D.M. Johnston (Eds.), *The Structure and Process of International Law: Essays in Legal Philosophy, Doctrine, and Theory* 643 (Dordrecht: Martinus Nihhoff, 1986)

Participation of Mini-States in International Affairs 1968 ASIL Proc 155

Paul, J. *The United Nations and the Creation of an International Law of Development* 36 HARV INTL L J 307 (1995)

Paul, J. *The Human Right to Development: Its Meaning and Importance* 25 JOHN MARSHALL L REV 235 (1992)

Payoyo, P. *Fishing for the Common Heritage in Straddling and Highly Migratory Fish Stocks* (International Ocean Institute Training Programme Course Book, Halifax, 1994)

Pearcy, G.E. *Geographical Aspects of the Law of the Sea* 49 ANNALS ASSOC. OF AMERICAN GEOGRAPHERS 1 (March, 1959)

Pechota, V. "Equality: Political Justice in an Unequal World" in R.St.J. Macdonald & D.M. Johnston (Eds.), *The Structure and Process of International Law: Essays in Legal Philosophy, Doctrine, and Theory* 453 (Dordrecht: Martinus Nihhoff, 1986)

Petersmann, E.-U. *The Transformation of the World Trading System through the 1994 Agreement Establishing the World Trade Organization* 6 EJIL 161 (1995)

Petersmann, E.-U. "The New International Economic Order: Principles, Politics and International Law" in R.St.J. Macdonald & D.M. Johnston (Eds.), *The Structure and Process of International Law: Essays in Legal Philosophy, Doctrine, and Theory* 449 (Dordrecht: Martinus Nihhoff, 1986)

Perisić, Z. "Common Heritage of Mankind: The United Nations Convention on the Law of the Sea" in B. Vukas (Ed.), *Essays on the New Law of the Sea* (Zagreb: S. Liber, 1985)

Piel, G. "The Right to Development" in *Federico Mayor: Amicorum Liber*, Vol. II, 699 (Bruxelles: Bruylant, 1995)

Pinto, M.C.W. "Common Heritage of Mankind": From Metaphor to Myth, and the Consequences of Constructive Ambiguity" in Makarczyk, J. (Ed.), *Theory of International Law at the Threshold of the 21st Century: Essays in Honour of Krzystof Skubiszewski* 249 (The Hague: Martinus Nijhoff, 1996)

Pinto, M.C.W. "The United Nations Convention on the Law of the Sea: Sustainable Development and Institutional Implications" in P. Payoyo (Ed.), *Ocean Governance: Sustainable Development of the Seas* 3 (Tokyo: UNU Press, 1994)

Pinto, M.C.W. "The Duty to Cooperate and the United Nations Convention on the Law of the Sea" in A. Bos & H. Siblesz (Eds.), *Realism in Law Making* 153 (The Hague: TMC Asser Instituut, 1986)

Pinto, M.C.W. "The United Nations Convention on the Law of the Sea and the New International Economic Order: Interdependence and International Legislation" in A. Koers & B. Oxman (Eds.), *The 1982 Convention on the Law of the Sea* 224 (Honolulu: LSI Univ of Hawaii, 1984)

Pinto, M.C.W. "Mineral Resources" in R.-J. Dupuy (Ed.), *The Management of Humanity's Resources: The Law of the Sea* 19 (Workshop, The Hague Academy of International Law & UNU, 1982)

Pinto, M.C.W. "Scope of Operations in the Area" & "the Structure and Functions of the International Seabed Authority" in E.M. Borgese & P.

White (Eds.), *Seabed Mining: Scientific, Economic, and Political Aspects An Interdisciplinary Manual* 302, 316 (Malta: IOI Occasional Paper No. 7)

Pinto, M.C.W. "Problems of Developing States and their Effects on Decisions on the Law of the Sea" in L. Alexander (Ed.), *Needs and Interests of the Developing Countries* 4 (RI: Law of the Sea Institute, 1973)

Pontecorvo G. & Wilkerson, M. *From Cornucopia to Scarcity: The Current Status of Ocean Use* 5 ODIL 395 (1978)

Purvis, N. *Critical Legal Studies in Public International Law* 32 HARV INT L J 81 (1991)

A Quiet Revolution (NY: Department of Public Information, United Nations Secretariat, 1984)

Raleigh, C.B. *The Internationalism of Ocean Science vs. International Politics* 23 MARINE TECHNOLOGY SOCIETY JOURNAL 44 (1989)

Ratiner, L. "Reciprocating State Arrangements: A Transition or An Alternative?" in A. Koers & B. Oxman (Eds.), *The 1982 Convention on the Law of the Sea* 195 (Honolulu: LSI Univ of Hawaii, 1984)

Ratiner, L. *The Law of the Sea: A Crossroads for American Foreign Policy* 60 FOREIGN AFFAIRS 1014 (1982)

Rattray, K. "Assuring Universality: Balancing the Views of the Industrialized and Developing Worlds" in M.H. Nordquist & J.N. Moore (Eds.), *Entry Into Force of the Law of the Sea Convention* 55 (The Hague: Martinus Nijhoff, 1995)

Rest, A. *Implementation of the Rio Targets - Preliminary Efforts in State Practice* 25 EPL 312 (Nov. 1995)

Richardson, E. "Changing Circumstances Bring New Opportunities for Agreement on the Law of the Sea Convention" in M.H. Nordquist (Ed.),

17th Annual Seminar of the Center for Oceans Law and Policy 5 (Univ. of Va., 1993)

Robinson, N.A. "Problems of Definition and Scope" in J.L. Hargrove (Ed.), *Law, Institutions and the Global Environment* 44-103 (NY: Oceana, 1972)

Roling, B.V.A. "Are Grotius Ideas Obsolete in an Expanded World?" in H. Bull, B. Kingsbury, & A. Roberts (Eds.), *Hugo Grotius and International Relations* 281 (Oxford University Press, 1992).

Rona, P.A. *Mineral Deposits from Sea-Floor Hot Springs* 254 SCIENTIFIC AMERICAN 84 (January 1986)

Samuels, A. "The Continental Shelf Act of 1964" in *Developments in the Law of the Sea 1958-1964* (London: British Institute of International and Comparative Law, 1965)

Sand, P. *International Environmental Law After Rio* 4 EJIL 378 (1993)

Sand, P. *UNCED and the Development of International Environmental Law* 3 YRBK INTL ENV L 3 (1992)

Sagurian, A. "Excision of the Deep Seabed Mining Privisions from the 1982 Law of the Sea Convention: Reappraising the Principle of a Treaty's Integrity under New Realities" in J.M. van Dyke, D. Zaelke & G. Hewison (Eds.), *Freedom for the Seas in the 21st Century* 379 (Washington, DC: Island Press, 1993)

Schaar, J.H. "Some Ways of Thinking About Equality" and "Equality of Opportunity, and Beyond", both in J.H. Schaar, *Legitimacy in the Modern State* 167-209 (New Jersey: Transaction Books, 1981)

Schachte, W. "The Value of the Non-Deep Seabed Provisions: Preserving our Freedoms and Balancing Our Interests" in M.H. Nordquist (Ed.), *15th Annual Seminar of the Center for Ocean Law and Policy: Issues in Amending Part XI of the Convention* 29 (Univ. of Va.: 1991)

Schachter, O. *The Emergence of International Environmental Law* 44 J INTL AFFAIRS 457 (1991)

Schachter, O. "The Greening of International Law" in *Humanité et Droit International Mélanges René-Jean Dupuy* 272 (Paris: Pedone, 1991)

Scholz, W. "Observations on the Draft Agreement Reforming the Deep Seabed Mining Provisions of the Law of the Sea Convention" in M.H. Nordquist & J.N. Moore (Eds.), *Entry Into Force of the Law of the Sea Convention* 69 (The Hague: Martinus Nijhoff, 1995)

Scholz, W. *The Law of the Sea Convention and the Business Community: The Seabed Mining Regime and Beyond* 7 GEORGETOWN INTL ENV L REV 675 (1995)

Scholz, W. "The Consistent United States Policy for Acceptable Seabed Mining Provisions in a Universally Accepted Law of the Sea Convention" in M.H. Nordquist (Ed.), *17th Annual Seminar of the Center for Oceans Law and Policy* 51 (Univ. of Va.: 1993)

Schrijver, N. "Permanent Sovereignty Over Natural Resources Versus the Common Heritage of Mankind: Complementary or Contradictory Principles of International Economic Law?" in P. de Waart, P. Peters & E. Denters (Eds.), *International Law of Development* 87 (Dordrecht: Martinus Nijhoff, 1988)

Schwarzenberger, G. *The Fundamental Principles of International Law* RECUEIL DES COURS 195 (1955-I)

Schwarzenberger, G. "Meaning and Functions of International Development Law" in F. Snyder & P. Slinn (Eds.), *International Law of Development: Comparative Perspectives* 55 (UK: Professional Books, 1987)

Schwarzenberger, G. "The Conceptual Apparatus of International Law" in R.St.J. Macdonald & D.M. Johnston (Eds.), *The Structure and Process of International Law: Essays in Legal Philosophy, Doctrine, and Theory* 685 (Dordrecht: Martinus Nijhoff, 1986)

Schwebel, S. *Mini-States and a More Effective United Nations* 67 AJIL 108 (1973)

Shapely, D. *Oceanography: Albatross of Diplomacy Haunts Seafaring Scientist* 180 SCIENCE 1036 (1973)

Shraga, D. *The Common Heritage of Mankind: The Concept and its Application* 15 ANNALES D'ETUDES INTERNATIONALES 45 (1986)

Shue, H. "The Unavoidability of Justice" in A. Hurell and B. Kingsbury (Eds.), *The International Politics of the Environment* 373 (Oxford: Clarendon Press, 1992)

Simmonds, K.R. (Rapporteur). *The Resources of the Ocean Bed Report of a Conference at Ditchley Park, 26-29 September 1969* (England: The Ditchley Foundation, 1969)

Singer, H. "The Ethics of Foreign Aid" in M. Wright (Ed.), *Rights and Obligations in North-South Relations* 84 (NY: St. Martins Press, 1986)

Singh, N. "Sustainable Development as a Principle of International Law" in P. de Waart, P. Peters & E. Denters (Eds.), *International Law and Development* 1 (Dordrecht: Martinus Nijhoff, 1988)

Slinn, P. "Implementation of International Obligations Towards Developing States: Equality or Preferential Treatment" in W. Butler (Ed.), *Control Over Compliance With International Law* 165 (Dordrecht: Martinus Nijhoff, 1991)

Slinn, P. "Differing Approaches to the Relationship Between International Law and the Law of Development" in F. Snyder & P. Slinn (Eds.), *International Law of Development: Comparative Perspectives* (UK: Professional Books, 1987)

Sohn, L.B. *International Law Implications of the 1994 Agreement* 88 AJIL 696-705 (1994)

Springer, A. "Commentary" in W. Lang, H. Neuhold & K. Zemanek (Eds.), *Environmental Protection and International Law* 199 (Kluwer, 1991)

Statement by Expert Panel: Deep Seabed Mining and the 1982 Convention on the Law of the Sea 82 AJIL 363 (1988)

Steinhardt, R. "Outer Space" in O. Schachter & C. Joyner, *United Nations Legal Order*, Vol. II, 753 (1995)

Stephanou, C.A. "A European Perception " in C.L. Rozakis & C.A. Stephanou (Eds.), *The New Law of the Sea* 270 (NY: Elsevier: 1983)

Stevenson, J. & Oxman, B. *The Preparations for the Law of the Sea Conference* 68 AJIL 1 (1974)

Stone, J. *Non-Liquet and the Function of Law in the International Community* 39 BYIL 124 (1959)

Suganami, H. "Grotius and International Equality" in H. Bull, B. Kingsbury & A. Roberts (Eds.), *Hugo Grotius and International Relations* 221 (Oxford: Clarendon Press, 1992)

Symonides, J. "The Continental Shelf" in M. Bedjaoui (Ed.), *International Law: Achievements and Prospects* 871 (UNESCO, 1991)

Symposium on the New International Economic Order 16 VA J INT L, No. 2, 233 (1975-76)

Szell, P. "Negotiations on the Ozone Layer" in G. Sjoestedt (Ed.), *International Environmental Negotiation* 37 (Laxanberg, Austria: IIASA, 1993)

Tenebaum, E.S. *A World Park in Antarctica: The Common Heritage of Mankind* 10 VA ENV L J 109 (1990)

Thacher, P.S. "The Role of the United Nations" in A. Hurell and B. Kingsbury (Eds.), *The International Politics of the Environment* 183 (Oxford: Clarendon Press, 1992)

Thompson-Flores, S. "Remarks" in L. Alexander (Ed.), *The Law of the Sea Needs and Interests of Developing Countries* (RI: Law of the Sea Institute, 1973)

Treves, T. "Entry Into Force of the United Nations Convention on the Law of the Sea: The Road Towards Universality" in Nadjeeb Al-Nauimi & R. Meese (Eds.), *International Legal Isues Arising Under the United Nations Decade of International Law* 445 (The Hague: Martinus Nijhoff, 1995)

Tunnicliffe, V. *Hydrothermal-Vent Communities of the Deep Sea* 80 AMERICAN SCIENTIST 336 (July-Aug 1992)

Verdross, A. & Koeck, H.F. "Natural Law: The Tradition of Universal Reason and Authority" in R.St.J. Macdonald & D.M. Johnston (Eds.), *The Structure and Process of International Law: Essays in Legal Philosophy, Doctrine, and Theory* (Dordrecht: Martinus Nihhoff, 1986)

Verwey, W. *The Establishment of a New International Economic Order and the Realization of the Right to Development and Welfare - A Legal Survey* 21 INDIAN J INT L 1 (1981); see also F. Snyder & S. Sathirathai (Eds.), *Third World Attitudes Towards International Law* 825 (Dordrecht: Martinus Nijoff, 1987)

Virally, M. "Unilateral Acts of International Organizations" in M. Bedjaoui (Ed.), *International Law: Achievements and Prospects* 241 (UNESCO, 1991)

Vratusa, A. "The Convention on the Law of the Sea and the Struggle for the New International Economic Order" in B. Vukas (Ed.), *Essays on the New Law of the Sea* (Zagred, S. Liber, 1985)

Vukas, B. "Peaceful Uses of the Sea, Denuclearization and Disarmament" in R.-J. Dupuy & D. Vignes (Eds.), *A Handbook on the New Law of the Sea*, Vol. II, 1233 (Dordrecht: Martinus Nijhoff, 1991)

Warbrick, C. "The Principle of Sovereign Equality" in V. Lowe and C. Warbrick (Eds.), *The United Nations and the Principles of International Law: Essays in Memory of Michael Akehurst* 204 (London: Routledge, 1994)

Ward, B. *Rich Nations, Poor Nations* (Canada: CBC, 1961)

Ward, B. "A New Creation? Reflections on the Environmental Issue" in *Tribute to Barbara Ward* (Ottawa: World Media Institute, 1987)

Weber, A. "Our Newest Frontier: The Seabottom Some Legal Aspects of the Continental Shelf Status" in *Exploiting the Oceans: Transactions of the 2nd Annual Marine Technology Society Conference 27-29 June 1966* 405 (Washington, DC: MTS, 1966)

Weil, P. *Towards Relative Normativity in International Law?* 77 AJIL 413 (1983)

Weinschel, H. *The Docrine of Equality of States and its Recent Modification* 45 AJIL 417 (1951)

Weissberg, G. *International Law Meets the Short-Term National Interest. The Maltese Proposal on the Sea-Bed and Ocean Floor - Its Fate in Two Cities* 18 ICLQ 41 (1969)

Welling, C. & Cruickshank, M.J. "Review of Available Hardware Needed for Undersea Mining" in *Exploiting the Oceans: Transactions of the 2nd Annual Marine Technology Society Conference 27-29 June 1966* (Washington, DC: MTS, 1966)

Welling, C. "The Views of the United States Ocean Mining Licensees on Trends in the Negotiation to Make the United Nations Convention on the Law of the Sea of 1982 Universally Acceptable" in M.H. Nordquist & J.N. Moore (Eds.), *Entry Into Force of the Law of the Sea Convention* 255 (The Hague: Martinus Nijhoff, 1995)

Wenk, E. *A New National Policy for Marine Resources* 1 NAT RES L, No. 2, 3 (1968)

White, G. "The New International Economic Order: Principles and Trends" in H. Fox (Ed.), *International Economic Law and Developing States* 27 (London: British Institute of International and Comparative Law, 1992)

Whose is the Bed of the Sea? 1968 ASIL Proc 216-251

Wolfrum, R. "Law of the Sea: An Example of the Progressive Development of International Law" in C. Tomushchat (Ed.), *The United Nations at Age Fifty: A Legal Perspective* 309 (The Netherlands: Kluwer, 1995)

Wooster, W. *Ocean Research Under Foreign Jurisdiction* 212 SCIENCE 754 (1981)

Yankov, A. *A General Review of the New Convention on the Law of the Sea: Marine Science and its Application* 4 OCEAN YRBK 150 (1983)

Young, R. *The Geneva Convention on the Continental Shelf: A First Impression* 52 AJIL 733 (1958)

Zemanek, K. "State Responsibility and Liability" in W. Lang, H. Neuhold & K. Zemanek (Eds.), *Environmental Protection and International Law* 187 (Kluwer, 1991)

CASES CITED

Asylum Case (Columbia vs. *Peru)*, 1950 ICJ Rep 275

Barcelona Traction Case, 1970 ICJ Rep 32

Continental Shelf (Tunisia vs. *Libya)*, 1982 ICJ Rep 18

Continental Shelf (Libya vs. *Malta)*, 1985 ICJ Rep 4

Fisheries Jurisdiction Cases (UK and *The Federal Republic of Germany* vs. *Iceland)* 1972 ICJ Rep 11, 29; 1973 ICJ Rep 3, 49; 1974 ICJ Rep 3, 175.

North Sea Continental Shelf Cases (Denmark and *The Netherlands* vs. *The Federal Republic of Germany)* 1969 ICJ Rep 3

South-West Africa - Voting Procedure Advisory Opinion, 1955 ICJ Rep 67

SS Lotus Case (France vs. *Turkey)*, 1927 PCIJ Rep Series A. No. 10, 19

SELECTED DOCUMENTS

Agenda 21. UNCED Report, UN Doc. A/CONF.151/26 (Vols. I & II)

529

An Agenda for Development (B. Boutros-Ghali) UN Doc. A/48/935 (6 May 1994)

Agreement for the Implementation of the United Nations Convention on the Law of the Sea of 10 December 1982, relating to the Conservation and Management of Straddling and Highly Migratory Fish Stocks 34 ILM 1542-1580 (1995)

Agreement relating to the implementation of Part XI of the United Nations Convention on the Law of the Sea of 10 December 1982, UN Doc. A/RES/48/263 (17 August 1994)

Declaration of Barbados. International Conference on Small Island Developing States. UN Doc. A/Conf.167/L.4/Rev.1 (5 May 1994)

Charter of Economic Rights and Duties of States. UNGA Res. 3281 (XXIX) 12 December 1974

Charter of the United Nations and the Statute of the International Court of Justice (NY: United Nations, 1974)

Conclusions of the Sienna Forum on International Law of the Environment (April, 1990), in UN Doc. A/45/666/Annex (24 October 1990)

1958 Geneva Convention on the Continental Shelf 499 UNTS 312

Declaration on the Establishment of a New International Economic Order. UNGA Res. 3201 (S-VI), 1 May 1974

Declaration and Programme of Action of the World Summit for Social Development UN Doc. A/CONF.166/L.3/Add.1-7 (10 March 1995)

Declaration of Ministers of Foreign Affairs of the Group of 77 (5 October 1993), 1993 NILOS DOCUMENTARY YRBK 143-147

Declaration of Principles Governing the Sea-bed and the Ocean Floor and the Subsoil Thereof Beyond the Limits of National Jurisdiction UNGA Res. 2749 (17 December 1970), 25 UN GAOR, Supplement no. 28 at 24

Declaration on International Economic Cooperation, UNGA Res. 2626 (XXV), UN Doc. A/RES/S-18/3 (1 May 1990)

Declaration on Principles of International Law Concerning Friendly Relations and Co-operation among States in Accordance with the Charter of the United Nations, UNGA Res. 2625 (XXV) (24 October 1970)

"Development and Environment" Report of the panel of experts convened by the Secretary-General of the United Nations Conference on the Human Environment, Founex Switzerland, 4-12 June 1971. Text in Annex I, Doc. A/CONF.48/10 (22 December 1971)

Human Development Report (UNDP) 1996, 1994, 1993, 1992, 1991, 1990

Law of the Sea - Realization of benefits under the United Nations Convention on the Law of the Sea: Needs of States in regard to development and management of ocean resources, and approaches for further action. UN Doc. A/45/712 (16 November 1990) and UN Doc. A/46/722 (4 December 1991)

Law of the Sea: Report of the Secretary- General, UN Doc. A/46/724 (5 December 1991)

Report of the Secretary General on the Law of the Sea: Marine Scientific Research, UN Doc. A/45/563 (11 October 1990)

Report of the Secretary General to the UN General Assembly on the Item Law of the Sea, Doc. A/45/721 and Corr.1 (19 November 1990)

Law of the Sea: Report of the Secretary General, Doc. A/44/650 (1 November 1989)

The Lima Declaration, reproduced in L. Alexander (Ed.), 1971 LSI Conference Proceedings at 223-226

Malta: request for inclusion of a supplementary item in the agenda of the twenty-second session, UN Doc. A/6695 (18 August 1967), UNGA Plenary, 22nd Session, 1583rd Meeting at 18-19

531

Marine Scientific Research: Legislative History of Article 246 of the United Nations Convention on the Law of the Sea (UN DOALOS, 1994)

Note by the Secretary General, UN Doc. A/C.1/952 (31 October 1967), UN GAOR, 22nd Session, Annexes, Agenda item 92 at 4-5

Note by the Secretary-General: Long-Term and Expanded Programme of Oceanographic Research, Doc. E/1989/111 (1 June 1989)

Participation of Developing Countries in High Seas Fishing, FAO Doc. FI/HSF/ TC/92/7 (June 1992)

Platzoder, R. *The Third UN Conference on the Law of the Sea Documents* Vol. VI

Programme of Action on the Establishment of a New International Economic Order, UNGA Res. 3202 (S-VI) 1 May 1974

The Programme of Action of the [Cairo] International Conference on Population and Development, UN Doc. A/CONF.171/13 (18 October 1994).

Protection and Preservation of the Marine Environment: Report of the Secretary-General, Doc. A/44/461 (18 September 1989)

Provisional Understanding Regarding Deep Seabed Matters among Belgium, Federal Republic of Germany, France, Italy, Japan, The Netherlands, the United Kingdom, and the United States 3 August 1984 23 ILM 1354 (1984)

Report of the Ad Hoc Committee to Study the Peaceful Uses of the Seabed and Ocean Floor Beyond the Limits of National Jurisdiction UN GAOR 23rd Sess. (1968)

Reports of the UN Committee on the Peaceful Uses of the Seabed and Ocean Floor Beyond the Limits of National Jurisdiction, 1969-1973, UN GAOR 24th-28th Sess.

Report of the Secretary General: Consultations of the Secretary-General on outstanding issues relating the deep seabed mining provisions of the United

Nations Convention on the Law of the Sea LoS Bulletin 1-5 (Special Issue IV, 16 Nov 1994)

Report of the Technical Consultation on High Seas Fishing and the Papers Presented at the Technical Consultation on High Seas Fishing, A/CONF.164/INF/2 (14 May 1993)

Report of Commission for Sustainable Development, UN Docs. E/1993/25/Add.1-E/CN.17/1993/Add.1 (30 June 1993)

Specific Action Related to the Particular Needs and Problems of Land-locked Developing Countries, UNGA Res. 44/214 (28 February 1990)

Stockholm Declaration on the Human Environment 11 ILM 1416 (1972)

United Nations Convention on the Law of the Sea With Index and Final Act (UN Sales No. E.83.V.5)

UN Development Decade A Programme for International Economic Cooperation. UNGA Res. 1710 (XVI), 19 December 1961

International Development Decade Strategy for the Second United Nations Development Decade. UNGA Res. 2626 (XXV)

UNEP. *Environmental Perspective to the Year 2000 and Beyond.* UN Doc. A/42/25 (1987), UN GAOR, 42nd Session, Supp. 25, Annex 2

UN General Assembly Resolution proclaiming the UN Decade of International Law (1990-1999), UN Doc. A/RES/44/23 (17 Nov. 1989)

UN Source Documents on Seabed Mining (Wa. DC: Nautilus Press, compiled by editors of Ocean Science News)

United Nations General Assembly Official Records, First Committee, 1967-1970 (Provisional Verbatim Records)

U.K. Deep Sea Mining (Temporary Provisions) Act of 1981. Text in II E.D. Brown, *The International Law of the Sea* 349 (1994)

U.S. Deep Seabed Hard Mineral Resources Act of 1980 19 ILM 1003 (1980)

U.S. House of Representatives, Subcommittee on International Organizations and Movements, House Committee on Foreign Affairs, *The Oceans: A Challenging New Frontier. Report on the Work of the UN Ad Hoc Committee on the Seabeds*, 90th Congress, 2d Sess (Washington: 1968)

U.S. Congress, House. *Interim Report on the United Nations and the Issue of Deep Ocean Resources, together with hearings by the Subcommittee on International Organizations and Movements of the Committee on Foreign Affairs* (U.S. Government Printing Office, 1967)

U.S. Presidential Proclamation 2667 (Truman Proclamation on the Continental Shelf), in I J.N. Moore, *International and United States Documents on Oceans Law and Policy* (1986)

Washington Declaration on the Protection of the Marine Environment from Land-Based Activities, adopted 1 Nov. 1995, 26 EPL 37-51 (1996)

INDEX

A

Africa 266, 268, 327, 372, 373, 415
Archeological and historical objects 237, 392
Agenda 21 121, 125, 131
· Chapter 17 119, 120, 121, 122, 123, 124, 125, 126, 127, 128, 129, 130, 131, 132, 141, 145, 146, 147, 149, 150, 152, 154, 436, 464, 468
Amerasinghe, H.S. 179, 257, 292, 293, 297, 298, 311, 313, 357, 380, 383, 472
Antarctica 314, 470
Area, The 2, 3, 11, 50, 62, 64, 165, 167, 127, 231, 232, 235, 236, 237, 238, 239, 241, 242, 243, 244, 272, 274, 285, 294, 296, 303, 311, 314, 321, 323, 324, 326, 330, 340, 341, 347, 348, 355, 356, 357, 360, 361, 370, 376, 397, 407, 420, 434, 435, 437, 449, 453, 455, 467, 471
· Activities in 237, 238, 239, 240, 328, 332, 334, 335, 336, 337, 339, 342, 343, 344, 345, 346, 375, 387, 389, 390, 391, 392, 393, 394, 395, 396, 398, 399, 401, 410, 411, 413, 424, 430, 433, 445
· Principles governing 239, 240, 241, 243, 244, 245, 246, 266, 299, 332, 357, 407, 469
· Reservation for peaceful purposes 11, 313, 314, 316, 317, 318, 319, 344, 345, 354, 469
Assured Access 12, 376, 378, 383, 388, 394, 395, 399, 401, 402, 403, 406, 409, 410, 417, 419, 420, 422, 431, 433, 434, 444, 446, 447, 450, 454, 455, 456, 457, 458, 465
Atmosphere 7, 39, 472
Australia 86

B

Bedjaoui, M. 300, 325, 328
Belgium 371
Benefit of humanity/mankind 54, 176, 232, 323, 324, 325, 326, 327, 329, 330, 332, 344, 355, 407

Benefit-sharing 11, 320, 328, 329, 331, 332, 345, 348, 355, 356, 357, 365, 469
Biodiversity 7, 39, 127, 129, 339, 340, 348, 356, 437, 470
Biotechnology 7, 129, 436
Boat Paper 440, 441, 442, 443, 457
Borgese, Elisabeth Mann- 89, 364, 390, 411, 423, 459
Brazil 307
Brown, E.D. 365
Burke, W. 365

C

Canada 86, 93, 275, 278, 384
Capacity-building 108, 111, 119, 120, 121, 122, 124, 127, 128, 133, 136, 140, 142, 150, 154, 155, 163, 468
Chambered voting 416, 449, 450
Commission on Global Governance 8, 17, 19, 22
Commission to Study the Organization for Peace 174, 248, 251, 252, 321, 363
Committee, Seabed 60, 62, 64, 65, 66, 67, 86, 93, 223, 236, 257, 259, 267, 273, 274, 275, 277, 280, 285, 196, 300, 332, 333, 334, 336, 342, 365, 369, 370, 371, 372, 378, 383, 386, 388, 415, 452, 473
· *Ad Hoc* 61, 179, 253, 258, 264, 265, 266, 267, 268, 270, 280, 298, 299, 314, 322, 372, 373, 380

Common concern of humanity/ mankind 470
Common but differentiated responsibilities 120, 129, 132, 133, 134, 135, 137, 138, 139, 140, 142, 150, 154, 155, 162, 163, 164, 436, 464, 468, 470
Common Heritage of Mankind/ Humanity 2, 3, 4, 5, 6, 7, ,8 , 9, 10, 11, 12, 21, 25, 26, 27, 43, 44, 46, 61, 62, 94, 105, 139, 150, 155, 163, 164, 165, 166, 174, 180, 191, 204, 218, 219, 226, 227, 228, 229, 231, 232, 235, 236, 237, 238, 241, 242, 243, 244, 245, 247, 253, 265, 268, 269, 270, 271, 273, 277, 278, 279, 280, 281, 283, 284, 285, 289, 294, 295, 299, 300, 301, 302, 303, 310, 312, 317, 319, 320, 321, 322, 323, 324, 325, 331, 332, 333, 334, 337, 340, 341, 342, 343, 345, 346, 347, 348, 349, 350, 351, 352, 353, 354, 355, 356, 357, 359, 360, 361, 362, 363, 363, 364, 366, 370, 372, 373, 374, 375, 376, 377, 378, 379, 380, 381, 382, 383, 385, 386, 389, 390, 392, 393, 395, 396, 397, 398, 400, 404, 405, 406, 407, 412, 420, 421, 422, 431, 432, 434, 437, 441, 447, 452, 453, 454, 455, 456, 457, 458, 459, 466, 467, 468, 469, 470, 471, 473, 474

Consensus 65, 150, 154, 155, 402, 403, 414, 416, 419, 445, 447, 449, 453, 470
Continental Shelf 72, 79, 174, 181, 192, 200, 207, 223, 321, 350, 373
· Convention of 1958 11, 180, 181, 182, 183, 186, 188, 190, 195, 196, 198, 199, 205, 206, 209, 210, 212, 213, 215, 217, 221, 222, 225, 227, 230, 234, 247, 260, 261, 273, 274, 275, 276, 285, 286, 291, 294, 304, 308, 309, 351, 369, 407
· Extent of 182, 183, 186, 187, 190, 193, 194, 195, 196, 197, 199, 201, 202, 212, 213, 215, 216, 222, 256, 275, 284, 285, 288, 289, 290, 294, 308, 309, 353
Cooperation
· as duty 79, 83, 94, 104, 105, 107, 132, 133, 136, 139, 149, 152, 153, 154, 155, 464
· international 93, 94, 99, 100, 102, 103, 104, 105, 106, 107, 108, 109, 111, 121, 125, 126, 127, 130, 138, 141, 142, 149, 152, 155, 163, 164, 176, 179, 252, 255, 330, 345, 347, 349, 350, 436, 459, 464, 467
Culture/Cultural Heritage 7, 471

D

Declaration of Principles
Resolution 61, 62, 64, 67, 240, 246, 270, 296, 297, 298, 299, 300, 301, 302, 303, 304, 308, 309, 311, 313, 316, 318, 320, 321, 325, 333, 334, 335, 336, 341, 348, 352, 356, 359, 361, 372, 380, 381, 382, 383, 385, 386, 387, 388, 400, 408, 412, 421, 426, 454, 455, 456, 457, 458, 473
Decolonization 34, 63, 65, 66, 72, 81, 83, 113, 114, 150, 151, 153, 231, 254, 255, 281, 329, 349, 462, 463
Deep seabed and ocean floor 7, 50, 169, 180, 198, 200, 208, 211, 216, 219, 226, 248, 250, 253, 255, 269, 273, 298, 338, 349, 437, 454, 457
· International control/ internationalization 11, 12, 170, 175 171, 173, 174, 176, 177, 178, 179, 180, 202, 203, 206, 215, 217, 218, 219, 220, 222, 226, 230, 231, 248, 249, 250, 251, 258, 264, 266, 277, 280, 284, 286, 295, 296, 305, 314, 317, 318, 320, 321, 322, 323, 324, 327, 332, 350, 352, 357, 359, 361, 362, 363, 366, 370, 372, 374, 382, 389, 391, 407, 421, 444, 447, 454, 456, 469
· Institutions/Machinery 11, 248, 250, 251, 319, 342, 357, 360, 361, 362, 363, 364, 365, 366, 367, 368, 369, 370, 371, 372, 373, 374, 375, 376, 377, 378, 379, 380, 381, 382, 383, 384, 385, 386, 387, 388, 389, 390, 391, 392, 395, 396, 408, 421,

431, 444, 455 (see also International Seabed Authority)
- Mining 38, 50, 192, 193, 220, 225, 228, 237, 240, 244, 245, 247, 258, 259, 261, 306, 308, 328, 333, 334, 341, 342, 343, 353, 356, 366, 369, 392, 398, 401, 403, 411, 423, 431, 434, 436, 446, 451, 455, 456, 457, 458, 459, 465
- Regime/Status 51, 52, 61, 181, 182, 202, 204, 208, 210, 214, 222, 225, 226, 229, 276, 293, 304, 305, 306, 307, 308, 310, 311, 320, 322, 325, 329, 350, 352, 355, 359, 360, 371, 377, 382, 387, 420, 425, 429, 430, 436, 440, 465

Development (and global sharing) 15, 19, 23, 35, 46, 55, 68, 71, 82, 83, 83, 84, 86, 88, 93, 94, 101, 102, 104, 105, 106, 107, 108, 115, 116, 118, 120, 141, 143, 146, 149, 152, 175, 247, 248, 249, 250, 251, 254, 255, 256, 281, 297, 322, 327, 349, 365, 368, 381, 463, 467, 468, 473
- - gap 17, 30, 55-56, 89, 179, 257, 259, 374, 382, 462, 473
- right to 66, 117, 120, 133, 135, 138, 154, 455, 468

Disparity 9, 12, 15, 22, 23, 30, 41, 43, 45, 52, 55, 56, 73, 461, 463, 473

Dispute settlement 141, 150
Dumping 217, 333, 337, 339, 347
Dupuy, Jean-Rene 323, 324, 326

E

East-West relations 16
Ecologism 24
Ecuador 325
Egalitarianism 21, 28, 36, 41, 42, 44, 102, 323
Ely, Northcutt 192, 206, 222
Energy 7
Eighteen-Nation Disarmament Committee 314
Engo, P. 391, 444
Environment 1, 84, 85, 86, 114, 115, 116, 117, 127, 143, 144, 146, 147, 148, 149, 152, 154, 232, 332, 333, 334, 335, 337, 339, 340, 345, 467, 472
Erga omnes obligations 138
Equality, principle of 11, 15, 26, 32, 33, 34, 35, 36, 37, 38, 39, 40, 41, 42, 45, 75, 77, 80, 104, 114, 116, 117, 130, 138, 141, 150, 326, 376, 407, 410, 461, 462, 464, 468, 469, 472
Equity 22, 46, 139, 464
Evensen, J. 297, 302
Exclusive Economic Zone/EEZ 72, 73, 74, 75, 77, 78, 79, 80, 81, 82, 91, 92, 93, 100, 102, 103, 104, 105, 106, 107, 108, 109, 127, 129, 130, 132, 134, 141, 145, 151, 154, 163, 164, 241, 246, 309, 424, 436, 464, 467, 468, 469, 471
Exploitability Clause 11, 181, 182, 183, 186, 187, 188, 190, 192, 194, 196, 197, 198, 199, 200, 201, 204, 205, 212, 213, 214, 216, 218, 221, 222, 224,

225, 228, 234, 247, 260, 275, 276, 294, 304, 308, 369, 407

F
Fanon, F. 25
Fisheries 51, 59, 75, 77, 105, 129, 302, 333, 334, 340, 464, 471
· High Seas 7, 123, 124, 192
Food and Agricultural Organization 340, 347
Forests 7
France 378, 379
Freedom of the seas 37, 67, 69, 70, 74, 81, 82, 89, 102, 155, 194, 201, 203, 204, 206, 212, 214, 218, 220, 221, 222, 226, 227, 228, 229, 230, 231, 238, 242, 243, 261, 280, 305, 306, 312, 321, 350, 369, 415, 456, 463, 469
Friedmann, Wolfgang 8, 33
Frontier 52, 167, 169, 180, 218, 219, 220, 232, 249, 253, 254, 265, 280, 333, 334, 375, 407, 453
Fukuyama, F. 25
Future generations 232, 457, 472

G
GATT 38, 66
Globalization 16, 406
Global village 16
Governance 6, 8, 11, 18, 67, 124, 125, 131, 132, 142, 146, 151, 152, 159, 164, 231, 280, 324, 328, 330, 340, 345, 448, 462, 467, 468, 469, 470, 471
Grand narratives 25, 27

Group of 77 70, 72, 82, 83, 84, 85, 86, 92, 94, 151, 310, 393, 395, 397, 399, 400, 401, 408, 410, 414, 416, 417, 426, 427, 428, 433, 434, 435, 436, 437, 444, 447, 457, 458, 473

H
Hambro, Edvard 242, 281, 284, 350, 352
Handl, G. 117
Henkin, Louis 59
High Seas 129, 201, 209, 217, 223, 225, 274, 415
Holmes, Oliver Wendel 202, 260, 473
Humanism 24, 25

I
Iceland 333
Idealists 215, 230, 321, 359, 363, 365, 369
India 259
Inequality 15, 17, 21, 22, 24, 26, 28, 31, 34, 36, 42, 66, 113, 122, 224, 225, 463, 473
· Domains of 10, 11, 37, 38, 39, 40, 46, 49, 52, 53, 57, 58, 59, 64, 83, 109, 163, 219, 461, 464, 465
· North-South 10, 16, 21, 30, 37, 39, 45, 49, 52, 75, 109, 139, 224, 462, 463, 465
Integrated ocean policy 111
International community 5, 15, 28, 30, 31, 32, 35, 36, 41, 45, 46, 49, 52, 56, 61, 66, 81, 89, 97, 98, 99, 115, 130, 141, 142, 145,

160, 178, 219, 220, 227, 228, 246, 248, 255, 260, 264, 286, 288, 293, 295, 298, 300, 304, 312, 316, 319, 321, 323, 327, 328, 331, 332, 341, 351, 353, 359, 362, 363, 382, 397, 421, 425, 429, 436, 437, 438, 447, 451, 456, 457, 459, 461, 462, 463, 464, 467, 472, 473, 474

International Court of Justice 221, 328

International economic order 54, 56, 99
- New - (NIEO) 56, 96, 97, 98, 99, 107, 116, 246, 310, 420, 432, 469

International law 1, 2, 3, 6, 8, 9, 20, 21, 28, 29, 30, 31, 32, 34, 36, 38, 40, 41, 42, 43, 46, 66, 69, 103, 125, 132, 137, 138, 139, 140, 143, 144, 150, 152, 153, 162, 180, 206, 239, 277, 290, 291, 306, 328, 340, 368, 421, 447, 452, 459, 467
- Discursive approach to 30, 31
- Natural law school 30, 31
- as Positivism 30, 31, 36, 40, 41, 42, 43, 46
- of global disparities 10, 11, 40, 41, 42, 43, 44, 45, 46, 47, 52, 53, 58, 109, 140, 142, 149, 155, 162, 163, 164, 223, 331, 461, 462, 463, 464, 465, 466
- of sustainable development 10, 12, 58, 140, 146, 149, 150, 155, 162, 163, 164, 462, 463, 464, 465, 466, 467, 468, 472, 473

International Law Association 365
International Law Commission 135, 185, 199, 209, 341
International Maritime Organization 340, 347
International Ocean Institute 354
International organization/s 5, 46, 125, 127, 132, 232, 331, 340, 344, 345, 347, 363, 367, 368, 372, 379, 380, 387, 388, 398, 407, 408, 409, 410, 421, 451, 453, 454, 458
International relations 1, 9, 35, 56, 220, 226, 232, 322, 349, 367, 452, 462, 468
International responsibility/liability 135, 136, 137, 340
International Seabed Authority 11, 96, 319, 323, 330, 331, 336, 339, 342, 343, 344, 345, 346, 347, 348, 355, 356, 360, 362, 369, 391, 392, 393, 394, 395, 396, 397, 398, 401, 402, 405, 406, 408, 409, 410, 412, 417, 418, 420, 431, 433, 435, 436, 437, 443, 444, 445, 448, 451, 455, 457, 458, 466
- Assembly 388, 398, 404, 405, 408, 409, 412, 413, 414, 420, 434, 445, 447, 448
- Council 330, 388, 398, 399, 408, 409, 411, 412, 413, 414, 415, 416, 417, 418, 419, 420, 434, 445, 446, 447, 448, 449, 458
- Decision-making in the 408, 409, 410, 411, 412, 413, 414,

416, 417, 418, 419, 420, 445, 448, 449, 450, 457
· Enterprise 233, 393, 395, 398, 399, 401, 402, 403, 405, 406, 408, 409, 411, 432, 433, 434, 446
· Finance Committee 445, 448, 451
· Legal and Technical Commission 418
· Secretariat 408, 446
International society 9, 27, 28, 29, 32, 46, 139, 227, 324, 328, 351
International Tribunal for the Law of the Sea 233
· Seabed Disputes Chamber 409

J

Jamaica 287
Japan 385
Jesus, Jose Luis 360
Johnson, Lyndon 176, 252, 253, 254, 255, 256, 321, 329, 347, 349, 474
Johnston, Douglas 225, 368
Jus cogens 138, 318, 464

K

Kissinger, Henry 397, 399, 400, 401, 402, 405, 433
Kapumpa, Amb. 427
Kuhn, Thomas 159, 164, 226

L

Latin America 62, 194, 223, 274, 275, 284, 317, 372, 373
Law of the Sea 1, 10, 42, 44, 46, 47, 49, 50, 55, 58, 59, 60, 63, 64, 65, 66, 68, 73, 80, 82, 108, 114, 145, 181, 207, 280, 281, 286, 290, 298, 302, 339, 349, 352, 362, 382, 420, 452, 463, 465, 468, 469, 471

M

Malta 168, 170, 180, 217, 218, 219, 221, 226, 227, 230, 231, 242, 251, 264, 275, 285, 287, 313, 317, 349, 350, 374, 382
Manganese nodules 169, 187, 188, 190, 191, 202, 212, 213, 220, 222, 223, 230, 237, 238, 247, 321, 348, 366, 395, 406, 408, 409, 410, 411, 415, 437, 454, 455
Mare Clausum 11, 69, 71, 81, 103
Mare Liberum 11, 67, 102
Market 429, 430, 432, 433, 434, 456
Marine environment 11, 83, 85, 86, 87, 100, 144, 149
· Protection and Preservation of 82, 83, 88, 89, 93, 105, 133, 134, 149, 151, 337, 338, 339, 341, 342, 343, 348, 391, 451, 468
Marine scientific research 51, 81, 82, 83, 89, 90, 91, 92, 93, 94, 95, 100, 105, 106, 124, 127, 129, 145, 151, 240, 302, 335, 342, 343, 344, 345, 346, 347, 348, 349, 356, 375, 390, 391, 393, 394, 464, 472
Mero, John 191, 192, 193, 220, 247
Miles, Edward 74

Military activities/uses 51, 169, 195, 216, 226, 237, 240, 315, 319, 335, 339, 350, 375, 390, 392, 395
Moore, John Norton 306
Multilateralism 46, 350, 450, 451
McNair, A. 35
Moratorium Resolution 259, 260, 261, 263, 264, 291, 298, 310, 311
Morell, James 437
Myrdal, Alva 259, 279, 319

N

Navigation 51, 63, 72, 103, 451, 464
New Zealand 297
Njenga, F. 327, 402
Nixon, R. 304, 305
Non-discrimination 37
Non liquet 136, 139
North-South relations 19, 28, 40, 45, 46, 50, 51, 55, 58, 60, 62, 64, 65, 66, 70, 82, 87, 88, 90, 92, 94, 95, 101, 107, 108, 113, 114, 116, 117, 118, 124, 125, 127, 129, 130, 140, 149, 150, 151, 152, 153, 154, 155, 165, 216, 247, 257, 268, 294, 326, 361, 372, 383, 386, 387, 419, 451, 455, 458, 461, 462, 463, 464, 467, 468
· Inequality in 10, 11, 20, 27, 35, 39, 53, 55, 57, 59, 89, 100, 103, 122, 143, 178, 467, 469, 472, 473

O

Oceans 6, 10, 49, 50, 56, 60, 64, 77, 83, 103, 108, 110, 111, 112, 113, 119, 121, 122, 125, 127, 128, 131, 132, 133, 136, 142, 143, 149, 150, 154, 228, 231, 254, 280, 284, 298, 332, 436, 463, 464, 472, 474
Ocean data acquisitions systems 92, 106
Oda, Shigeru 202, 205, 206, 221, 231, 324, 363
Official Development Assistance 18, 134
Ogley, Roderick 322
Outer Space 7, 38, 265, 314, 470

P

Pacta de contrahendo 87, 95, 96, 100, 126, 152, 464
Pacta sunt servanda 37, 138, 353
Paolillo, Felipe 361
Paradigm 9, 11, 143, 159, 160, 161, 161, 163, 226, 367, 368, 369, 444, 455, 456, 457, 458, 466, 467
Parallel system 393, 394, 395, 397, 398, 399, 400, 401, 402, 404, 405, 406, 409, 432, 433, 444, 446, 455, 457
Pardo, Arvid 60, 61, 150, 170, 177, 178, 179, 180, 181, 195, 205, 214, 215, 216, 218, 219, 256, 257, 261, 266, 285, 314, 318, 321, 332, 340, 366, 370, 452, 473

Pell, Claiborne 253, 364
Peru 286, 287
Pinto, Christopher 84, 356, 386, 387, 389, 397
Polar regions 7
Pollution 84, 85, 87, 88, 100, 129, 145, 173, 217, 332, 333, 334, 335, 337, 339, 340, 375
Pound, Roscoe 353
Precautionary principle 123, 139, 343
Preparatory Commission 233, 331, 346, 360, 394, 395, 411, 421, 424, 426, 434, 473
Programmatory law 141, 231, 232, 295, 299-300, 301, 312, 313, 319, 320, 331, 342, 343, 345, 346, 352, 353, 354, 355, 357, 361, 381, 405, 453, 456

R

Realists 23, 27, 35, 215, 230, 248, 359, 363, 364, 369
Reciprocity 105, 128, 150, 153, 154, 163, 211, 289, 326, 412, 458, 462, 464
Relativism 24
Res communis 103
Residual rights 106
Review Conference 318, 319, 401, 404, 405, 406, 447, 457, 459
Rio Declaration 120, 125
Roosevelt, James 249

S

Schachter, Oscar 244
Sea-bed Treaty of 1971 313, 315, 316, 318, 319, 332, 339, 347
Social justice 366, 383, 458
Soft law 125, 131, 154
Solidarity 8, 128, 138
Sovereignty 69, 70, 73, 81, 82, 88, 91, 102, 115, 129, 130, 141, 150, 218, 226, 227, 230, 241, 242, 243, 350, 362, 369
SS Lotus case 39
States 15, 16, 21, 22, 27, 28, 32, 33, 34, 35, 36, 37, 38, 39, 40, 41, 42, 45, 46, 50, 52, 56, 59, 63, 65, 68, 69, 81, 96, 125, 128, 141, 148, 149, 172, 339, 340, 350, 367, 407, 433, 441, 442
· Archipelagic 49, 72, 122
· Broad margin 49
· Coastal State/s 49, 62, 67, 68, 70, 71, 72, 73, 74, 75, 76, 78, 80, 81, 82, 83, 84, 85, 86, 88, 89, 91, 92, 93, 94, 100, 101, 102, 104, 105, 106, 107, 108, 109, 111, 124, 151, 193, 194, 208, 211, 214, 216, 218, 221, 223, 229, 234, 241, 242, 243, 274, 333, 350, 369, 425
· Developed countries/States 10, 18, 49, 61, 66, 67, 70, 75, 77, 84, 86, 87, 89, 91, 106, 107, 115, 129, 133, 134, 136, 137, 150, 154, 258, 270, 271, 273, 278, 280, 285, 286, 299, 350, 352, 355, 362, 365, 376, 377, 378, 383, 385, 386, 387, 388, 391, 392, 393, 395, 396, 398, 399, 431, 436, 462, 464, 468, 469
· Developing countries/States 10, 16, 18, 19, 49, 54, 56, 61,

66, 67, 68, 69, 71, 73, 74, 75, 76, 77, 78, 79, 81, 82, 83, 84, 86, 87, 89, 90, 91, 92, 93, 94, 95, 98, 100, 101, 102, 103, 104, 105, 106, 107, 109, 110, 111, 113, 114, 115, 116, 117, 120, 121, 123, 124, 127, 128, 129, 133, 134, 136, 137, 140, 145, 146, 147, 150, 152, 154, 174, 193, 215, 229, 232, 236, 246, 248, 251, 252, 254, 255, 258, 261, 266, 269, 270, 271, 280, 284, 285, 286, 289, 290, 299, 310, 322, 323, 326, 327, 329, 330, 331, 345, 349, 350, 351, 354, 355, 362, 363, 370, 372, 373, 374, 375, 376, 377, 380, 383, 385, 386, 387, 388, 390, 393, 394, 395, 396, 397, 398, 401, 403, 404, 407, 411, 412, 416, 419, 421, 431, 434, 435, 436, 438, 439, 445, 447, 450, 451, 452, 453, 455, 458, 459, 462, 463, 464, 467, 468, 469, 473
· Good Samaritan 49
· Industrialized countries/States 19, 84, 223, 225, 236, 254, 257, 281, 284, 288, 308, 309, 326, 327, 328, 329, 331, 350, 351, 353, 360, 372, 380, 386, 393, 394, 395, 396, 397, 401, 403, 405, 408, 409, 414, 417, 419, 420, 424, 425, 433, 435, 436, 437, 438, 439, 445, 446, 448, 450, 451, 453, 454, 455, 456, 457, 458, 465, 466, 469, 473

· Land-locked and Geographically-disadvantaged 49, 72, 74, 75, 77, 78, 79, 80, 81, 105, 151, 322, 331, 451, 464
· Micro- 122, 123
· Research State 81, 89, 90, 92, 94, 102, 124, 127
· Small island developing - 122, 123, 127, 129, 145
· Transit State 81
Stevenson, J. 295
Sustainable Development 3, 7, 10, 12, 108, 111, 112, 113, 114, 115, 116, 118, 121, 123, 125, 126, 127, 128, 129, 130, 131, 132, 133, 134, 135, 136, 137, 138, 139, 141, 142, 143, 148, 149, 151, 153, 154, 155, 159, 160, 161, 162, 163, 164, 232, 332, 347, 354, 356, 357, 436, 437, 451, 452, 455, 456, 457, 458, 462, 464, 465, 466, 467, 468, 469, 471, 472, 473
(see also International law)
Sweden 315

T

Technology 89, 94, 100, 472
· Development and Transfer of 82, 83, 95, 96, 97, 99, 101, 141, 145, 151, 330, 345, 356, 391, 401, 405, 446
Territorial Sea 59, 63, 72, 127, 194, 206, 207, 222, 231, 302
Third World 8, 16, 58, 63-64, 66, 69, 73, 88, 109, 114, 116, 117, 146, 151, 246, 249, 255, 274, 473

Transnational corporations 97
Treaty Banning Nucear Weapons Tests 339, 341
Treves, T. 431
Trinidad & Tobago 287
Truman Proclamation 67, 193

U

Unequal treaties 34-35
Unilateral seabed mining legislation 326, 327, 360, 422
United Kingdom 378, 379, 384, 437
United Nations 5, 6, 7, 8, 15, 16, 36, 46, 170, 171, 173, 175, 176, 179, 180, 195, 215, 219, 227, 230, 248, 251, 264, 295, 297, 323, 353, 366, 416, 452, 466
- Charter 22, 36, 318, 374
- Economic and Social Council 173, 174, 249, 256, 296, 349, 370
- General Assembly 60, 61, 63, 64, 96, 97, 98, 99, 107, 109, 111, 167, 175, 177, 181, 220, 248, 251, 253, 255, 256, 257, 258, 261, 263, 264, 265, 266, 273, 275, 276, 287, 290, 291, 292, 297, 303, 308, 309, 310, 314, 315, 318, 332, 333, 342, 350, 351, 352, 360, 363, 371, 372, 374, 424, 425, 428, 429, 441, 442, 454
- Secretary General 18, 63, 109, 110, 111, 174, 250, 254, 266, 285, 287, 360, 362, 370, 372, 374, 375, 376, 377, 428, 430, 435, 437, 457
- Security Council 18
United Nations Conference on Environment and Development (UNCED) 10, 58, 89, 108, 111, 113, 114, 115, 116, 118, 119, 122, 124, 125, 126, 127, 134, 137, 141, 145, 148, 149, 153, 154, 155, 163, 436, 457, 464, 465, 467, 469, 473
United Nations Conference on the Human Environment 83, 84, 114, 117, 118
United Nations Conference on the Law of the Sea (UNCLOS)
- UNCLOS I 60, 62, 65, 185, 194, 199, 206, 209, 221, 224
- UNCLOS II 60, 62, 194
- UNCLOS III 9, 12, 28, 49, 55, 57, 58, 59, 60, 62, 64, 65, 66, 67, 70, 71, 77, 81, 82, 83, 84, 85, 89, 91, 98, 99, 105, 113, 114, 115, 122, 133, 145, 146, 151, 203, 257, 284, 287, 288, 292, 294, 295, 296, 299, 303, 304, 305, 307, 311, 312, 317, 327, 333, 341, 352, 353, 362, 369, 372, 387, 388, 389, 390, 394, 395, 397, 399, 403, 407, 408, 425, 430, 433, 435, 447, 449, 454, 455, 456, 463, 465, 466, 473
- UNCLOS III Committees 10, 58, 59, 60, 70, 71, 72, 77, 81, 82, 83, 85, 96, 100, 101, 104, 317, 320, 335, 389, 391, 392, 399, 409, 454
United Nations Conference/Agreement on Straddling and Highly

Migratory Fish Stocks 123, 129, 152, 471
United Nations Convention on Biological Diversity 129, 339, 470
United Nations Convention on the Law of the Sea 1, 9, 49, 50, 57, 66, 81, 83, 88, 91, 94, 98, 108, 110, 111, 118, 119, 120, 121, 122, 123, 125, 127, 130, 140, 141, 144, 145, 152, 154, 155, 163, 167, 225, 231, 243, 294, 312, 319, 325, 341, 353, 406, 426, 436, 440, 452, 462, 463, 464, 467, 469, 472, 473
- 1994 Agreement Relating to Implementation of Part XI 4, 5, 12, 167, 227, 233, 348, 359, 361, 395, 428, 429, 430, 438, 441, 442, 443, 444, 445, 446, 447, 448, 449, 450, 451, 452, 457, 458, 459, 466, 473
- Entry into force 3, 56, 150, 320, 331, 349, 394, 440, 441, 442, 443, 457
- ICNT 401, 402, 403, 410, 412, 414, 436
- ISNT 390, 411, 417, 436, 455
- as Package Deal 50, 65, 284, 292, 302, 303, 308, 351, 352, 360, 438
- Part XI 2, 12, 51, 52, 56, 96, 166, 219, 227, 232, 233, 235, 236, 237, 238, 239, 241, 242, 244, 245, 246, 247, 270, 293, 317, 318, 320, 323, 326, 329, 330, 331, 332, 336, 337, 342, 345, 347, 354, 355, 356, 359, 363, 389, 404, 420, 421, 422, 424, 428, 429, 430, 431, 432, 434, 435, 437, 438, 439, 440, 441, 442, 443, 444, 447, 448, 450, 456, 457, 458, 465, 466
- Preamble 53, 54, 55, 56, 57, 83, 153, 232, 240
- RSNT 391, 395, 397, 455
- Universality 6, 50, 56, 311, 426, 427, 428, 429, 435, 436, 437, 438, 439, 444, 450, 451, 452, 457, 458, 466, 473
UNCTAD 66, 97
United Nations Development Programme 18
United Nations Division of Ocean Affairs and the Law of the Sea 443
United Nations Environment Programme 347
United Nations Framework Convention on Climate Change 124, 129, 152
USSR 314, 317, 325, 384, 397
United States 175, 176, 190, 191, 192, 193, 194, 195, 196, 203, 204, 206, 212, 213, 214, 215, 220, 221, 222, 223, 224, 225, 247, 249, 253, 257, 260, 263, 264, 279, 289, 293, 294, 304, 305, 306, 307, 314, 321, 333, 359, 363, 378, 394, 397, 399, 400, 401, 402, 403, 415, 416, 420, 421, 422, 423, 425, 427, 428, 432, 433, 434, 435, 438, 446, 448, 450, 451, 473, 474
U Thant 267

V
de Visscher, Charles 368
Vitoria, Francisco 254

W
World Commission on Environment and Development 111
World Peace Through Law 174, 248, 321, 364
World Summmit for Social Development 7, 8, 16, 17

Z
Zegers Santa Cruz 433

Printed in the United States
By Bookmasters